THE COMPLETE
RHYMING
DICTIONARY
AND
POET'S CRAFT BOOK

THE COMPLETE
RHYMING
DICTIONARY

AND

POET'S CRAFT BOOK

Edited by

CLEMENT WOOD

DOUBLEDAY & COMPANY, INC.
Garden City, New York

PRINTED IN THE UNITED STATES OF AMERICA

TO GLORIA GODDARD

ACKNOWLEDGMENTS

ACKNOWLEDGMENT is gratefully made to the following publishers and poets, for the portions of their work used as illustrations herein:

Publisher	Author	Poem Source
Boni & Liveright	Samuel Hoffenstein	Poems in Praise of Practically Nothing
The Century Company	Brander Matthews	En Route
Dodd Mead & Company	Austin Dobson	July; The Ballade of Prose and Rhyme
Dodd Mead & Company	Carolyn Wells	Four Limericks
Doubleday, Doran & Company	Rudyard Kipling	The Sons of Martha
Henry Holt & Company	Walter de la Mare	The Listeners
Henry Holt & Company	Robert Frost	The Death of the Hired Man; The Black Cottage; "Out, Out—"
Henry Holt & Company	Carl Sandburg	Cahoots; Cool Tombs; Fog
Houghton, Mifflin & Company	Guy Wetmore Carryll	How the Helpmate of Bluebeard Made Free with a Door
Alfred A. Knopf, Inc.	John V. A. Weaver	Sonnet
The Macmillan Company	Edwin Arlington Robinson	Merlin; Roman Bartholow
Manas Press	Adelaide Crapsey	Triad
	Samuel Minturn Peck	"Before the Dawn"
The Poets Press	Clement Wood	Canopus; The Flight of the Eagle
Charles Scribner's Sons	Henry Cuyler Bunner	A Pitcher of Mignonette; Behold the Deeds!
Charles Scribner's Sons	William Ernest Henley	Ballade of Dead Actors
Charles Scribner's Sons	Edwin Arlington Robinson	The House on the Hill
Small, Maynard & Company	Charlotte Perkins Gilman	Homes; A Man Must Live
Frederick A. Stokes Company	Alfred Noyes	Marchaunt Adventurers

FOREWORD

THE desire to write poetry, or at least acceptable verse, is almost universal. The achievement of this desire may be gained by anyone, without excessive effort. Almost everyone, at some stage of his or her life, has yielded to the seductive siren, and has done his or her best to write poetry. An adequate craftbook on versification is a necessity, when the urge becomes unconquerable.

When the versifier's problem is narrowed down to rhyme, the need for a convenient and logically arranged rhyming dictionary soon becames self-evident. Rhyme is exclusively a matter of sound: what the scientists call phonetics. The logically arranged rhyming dictionary must be arranged scientifically by sound; arranged phonetically, to use the scientific word. The arrangement of rhyming sounds in the present volume is wholly phonetic.

The introductory study of versification is so complete, that the book will answer almost every question on technique that any would-be poet or versifier desires to have answered. Moreover, it provides models for the most intricate forms of poetry and versification that English-speaking poets use. Following a model is at best finger-exercises. But finger-exercises must precede mastery of the keyboard.

The phonetic devices in the volume are simplified from the leading standard dictionaries, by eliminating in general all phonetic signs except those placed above the accented or rhyming syllable. Once these simple phonetic devices are understood and absorbed, poets and versifiers will begin to think accurately, scientifically and phonetically about rhymes and rhyming. The technique of rhyming will become as automatic as the technique of walking: and the poetic energy will be proportionately released for the more effective creation of poetry.

CLEMENT WOOD.

Bozenkill.

CONTENTS

ix

THE POET'S CRAFT BOOK

POETRY AND VERSIFICATION

Poetry and Verse

THE word *poetry* is often used loosely to mean whatever embodies the products of imagination and fancy, the finer emotions and the sense of ideal beauty. In this lax usage, men speak of "the poetry of motion," the poetry of Rodin or Wagner, the poetry of dahlia-raising. In accurate usage, poetry is a specific fine art, defined as follows:

Poetry is the expression of thoughts which awake the higher and nobler emotions or their opposites, in words arranged according to some accepted convention.

This definition includes, for instance, Oriental forms of poetry, where the sole convention is the number of syllables to the line. Limiting it to usual Occidental poetry the following definition applies:

Occidental poetry, in its usual form, is the expression of thoughts which awake the higher and nobler emotions or their opposites, in words whose rhythm tends toward uniformity or regularity, rather than toward variety.

Both prose and poetry have rhythm. But the rhythm of prose tends toward variety; and that of poetry toward regularity. There is no definite dividing line; each poet, each reader and appreciator of poetry, must arrive at his own dividing line. To some, the borderline of poetry includes only the strict regularity of Pope or Dryden, or—

> Baby in the caldron fell,—
> See the grief on mother's brow!
> Mother loved her darling well.
> Darling's quite hard-boiled by now.
> *Baby*, Harry Graham.

No one can quarrel with this, if it is an honest boundary. To others, the magnificent wilder rhythms of Walt Whitman and

Lincoln's *Gettysburg Address* are definitely poetry. No one can quarrel with this either.

The test as to subject-matter is subjective: does the alleged poem awake in the reader the higher and nobler emotions or their opposites? Each reader, appreciator, or poet is final arbiter in this test, as in the test of technique. The expression of thoughts which fail to register emotionally with a reader as poetry is called *verse*. Thus, divided by technique, there are the two classifications, poetry and prose; divided by subject-matter and its emotional effect, there are the two classifications, poetry and verse.

Poetry in Human Affairs

Poetry preceded prose, as a persisting form of literary expression. Writing was unknown to early man; and poetry was far better adapted to be retained in the mind than its more plodding relative, prose. The conventions of poetry formed memory devices which prose lacked. In the beginning, lyric cries, folk wisdom, tales of tribal heroes, formal odes of jubilation or lamentation, religious teachings, philosophies, pseudo-sciences, histories of men, men-gods, gods and peoples, developed first in the form of poetry.

Insofar as the conventions of poetry were artificial and unnatural, poetry tended constantly to rigidify and petrify. It became artificial and unnatural, whereas prose continued natural. Man learned to write, and to preserve his writing in stone, papyrus, sheepskin, and paper. At first it was the poetry which was so preserved; at length the art patterns were broken, and humbler and more natural prose began to replace poetry. Today, we look to prose for folk wisdom, actual and fictional narratives, religious teachings, philosophies, scientific writings, and histories. Poetry, as the most concentrated and emotional expression of the soul of man, still should have its place in the lyric outbursts, the songs, of man. But poets, bound by fossilized conventions, have become a tepid social group, their words largely unimportant; and in the large prose tends today to replace poetry entirely. Many of the poets today and tomorrow seek and will to restore poetry to something of its original wide popularity, as a natural and unartificial expression of concentrated emotional speech.

Kings, rulers, statesmen, generals, philosophers, scientists, were once of necessity poets : it was their sole socially acceptable form of expression. This is so no longer. Poets were once doers; they are now at best sayers, increasingly unheard. This is one price of man's extreme specialization. The price paid may be more than the human gain, in this particular.

The Poet's Equipment

The poet, like all artists, is one of the race's sensitives : one of those more finely attuned to phrase the past and the present acceptably, and sense and phrase the future. The first necessary equipment is sincerity. This demands that commonplace phrasings must be avoided, in favor of fresh original expression of individual or group concentrated emotions. If the race recognizes these as its own, to that extent the poet will be hailed as poetically great.

Another essential is technical mastery: adeptness in the craft of poetry, skill in handling all the tools of the trade. Familiarity with all the conventions will enable you to break them and make new ones when your fresh subject-matter demands it. Technical mastery is as easy, and no easier, than learning how to raise better peas than your neighbor, or how to build better bridges and skyscrapers than anyone else. Having learned the craft, anyone with an ear for word-music can improvise flawless heroic blank verse or any other form of blank verse by the hour, or improvise elaborately rhymed sonnets with no appreciable hesitation. This is not poetry. But the familiarity with the craft makes the coming of poetry easier, in the rare hours when the poet has a concentrated word that must be said.

Poetic Greatness

One can become great poetically, either in his own sight alone or in the opinions of others, without knowledge of the craft. Homer, Sappho, Villon, Burns, made their own patterns, or poured their burning emotional beauty into ready-made patterns followed without being comprehended. The definitions of patterns were made afterwards, from a scholastic study of poetry widely recognized as great. Such greatness may be achieved by anyone today—the entirely satisfactory expression of one's soul's yearnings. But the recognition of such greatness today will ordinarily be limited to the poet and his immediate circle of admirers within or without his family.

With a complete technical mastery of the craft of poetry, any poet today can achieve complete greatness in his own sight. Whether he is hailed by others as great, and especially whether or not his name is hailed by his own and subsequent generations as great, depends largely on the extent to which his own concentrated heart-utterances express the desires of the race, in a new, fresh and original form. Given such recognition by the race, and enduring poetic greatness has been achieved. The poet can no more control this than Cnut could act as dictator over the tide.

How Poems Come

Verse upon any theme, and in treatment ranging from the most ponderously serious to the most frivolously flippant, can be manufactured at any time. Its technique is comparatively simple. Its devices, metre, rhyme, alliteration, assonance, consonance, stanza arrangement, may be mastered as easily as multiplication tables.

Poetry comes differently. It is primarily the intellect that manufactures verse; but the intellect plays only a secondary part in creating poetry. The desire that seeks expression, which it finds in the poem, springs from a deeper basic source than thinking. Man, indeed all forms of life, are compact of desires. The fulfilment of one desire causes others to spring hydra-like from its invisible corpse. Psychologists tell us that dreams are likewise expressions of desire, in the form of desires fulfilled: that is, wish-fulfilments. Much thinking is likewise wish-fulfilment; there is truth in Wordsworth's dictum, "The wish is father to the thought." There must be, also, an obstacle to the immediate fulfilment of the wish; otherwise, the poet would proceed to achieve his wish, and have no need for a poem to express it. As one poet has it:

> Singing is sweet; but be sure of this,
> Lips only sing when they cannot kiss.
> *Art,* James Thomson.

Because of the obstacle, a tremendous inner compulsion comes upon the sensitive poet to seek relief by creating his wish-fulfilment in words: and so it is that poems are born. This inner compulsion has, as one of its names, inspiration. Inspiration blows from no outer sky, but from the universe of desires within. The woman's insistent inner compulsion to deliver her child at the appointed hour is hardly more shatteringly imperative than the true poet's insistent inner commandment to write.

At times the whole poem forms itself within the mind, before the first word is written down. At times a couplet, a single line—perhaps the first, but more often the last—or even a phrase or a mood comes first, with the dominant insistence that it be given the intermittent immortality of writing. The wise procedure for the poet is to write down what comes, as it comes, even if only a single line or less is the result. As far as possible, write out the poem without delay, to prevent another visitor from Porlock's silencing part of your poem forever, as Coleridge's *Kubla Khan* was silenced forever.

When the poem or poetic fragment is written down, the critical intellect comes into play. If technical mastery has become habitual, the intellect may have no changes to suggest. The poet who fails to be a critic as well is usually his own self-slayer. More extended poems, of course, require more preparation and slower writing and criticism. In all cases the danger is rather in the overuse of the intellect, than in the use of inspiration.

Originality in Poetry

The easiest way, in poetry, is to rephrase your own emotional reactions in the words and phrases created by the favorite poets of the past: so that a thing is "white as the driven snow," or "red as a June rose." When these similes were first invented, they were creations; their repetition, unless in slightly altered form, is plagiarism or borrowing. Second-rate poets distrust their own vision, which differs in every case from that of every other person in the world; and hence sag into such uncreative repetitions. It is wisest to be true to your own differing vision, and seek to expand the boundaries of poetry by stating your own desires in your own terms.

The weakness of much verse and some poetry of the past is partly traceable to unoriginal teachers of English or versification, who advised their pupils to saturate themselves in this or that poet, and then write. Keats, saturated in Spenser, took a long time to overcome this echoey quality, and emerge into the glorious highland of his *Hyperion.* Many lesser souls never emerge. It is valuable to know the poetry of the past, and love it. But the critical brain should carefully root out every echo, every imitation—unless some alteration in phrasing or meaning makes the altered phrase your own creation.

The present double decade has splendidly altered the technique of versification in poetry, by the addition of freer rhythms, consonance, and other devices in the direction of natural speech. It has altered the themes and subjects of poetry as much, until the *Verboten* sign is unknown to the present generations of poets, as far as themes are concerned. If the speech is natural and conversational; the treatment sincere and original; the craftsmanship matured,—there is no reason in the poet's effort to withhold him from a seat among the immortals.

II

THE TECHNIQUE OF VERSIFICATION: RHYTHM

Accent and Rhythm

RHYTHM is the emphasis structure of successive sounds. It is easy to understand, and not easy to define. In prose and poetry, it means the flow of accented and unaccented syllables. It may be defined as:

The successive rise and fall of sounds, in pitch, stress, or speed; when used of words, depending on accents, pauses, or durational quantities.

In classical Greek and Latin poetry, rhythm was not based on accent, but on the conventionalized time it took to pronounce syllables. Syllables were not accented or unaccented, as in modern poetry, from a standpoint of versification; but were long or short. Since two consonants occurring together made a syllable long, and a short vowel made a syllable short when followed by one consonant, the word *honest* was scanned as short-long: the rhythmic stress occurring on the second syllable, not on the first, as with us. *Honest,* pronounced in the classical Greek or Roman way, would be ta-TUM; with us, it is pronounced rhythmically TUM-ta, the accent falling on the first syllable.

This one example will show why verse written in English according to classical rules of scansion, based upon long and short syllables instead of accent, is unnatural and only slightly pleasing to the ear. It is no more at home among modern poets writing in English than Greek clothing or the Greek language would be.

Modern poetry written in English must be in words whose rhythm, based upon accent, tends toward uniformity, rather than toward variety. Both prose and poetry have rhythm, the stream or flow of accented and unaccented syllables; in prose, the pattern constantly varies, while in poetry it approaches some sort of regularity. This is clearly poetry:

7

Music, when soft voices die,
Vibrates in the memory—
Odours, when sweet violets sicken,
Live within the sense they quicken.

Rose leaves, when the rose is dead,
Are heap'd for the beloved's bed;
And so thy thoughts, when Thou art gone,
Love itself shall slumber on.
"*Music, when Soft Voices Die,*"
Percy Bysshe Shelley.

It would be no less poetry if it were set up:

Music, when soft voices die, vibrates in the memory. Odours, when sweet violets sicken, live within the sense they quicken. Rose leaves, when the rose is dead, are heap'd for the beloved's bed.

And so thy thoughts, when Thou art gone, Love itself shall slumber on.

It did not take the line-division to make this poetry. Technically, the tendency toward regularity in the rhythm made it definitely verse, and not prose; while its emotional appeal, to most people, makes it poetry. It is equally poetic in either typographic form. Set up the opening of the first chapter of this book in the same line division:

The word poetry is often used
Loosely to mean whatever embodies
The products of imagination
And fancy, the finer emotions

And the sense of ideal beauty.
In this lax usage, men speak of
"The poetry of motion," the poetry
Of Rodin or Wagner, the poetry

This is prose. No magic worked by the line division can bring it any closer to poetry. Only a comparative regularity in the alternation of accented and unaccented syllables can make it acceptable verse; this, plus the proper emotional appeal, alone can make it poetry.

Metre and Metric Feet

Metre is a comparatively regular rhythm in verse or poetry. There are four common metric feet used in English verse. Their names are taken over from classic durational or quantity metres. In the examples below, the accented syllable is marked thus (′), and the unaccented syllables thus (˘). These feet are:

Name of Foot	Scansion	Description	Example	Example scanned	Accent pronunciation
Iamb	˘ ′	Unaccent—accent	Delight	De-líght	ta-TUM
Trochee	′ ˘	Accent—unaccent	Going	Gó-ing	TUM-ta
Anapest	˘ ˘ ′	Unaccent—unaccent—accent	Appertain	Ap-per-táin	ta-ta-TUM
Dactyl	′ ˘ ˘	Accent—unaccent—unaccent	Merrily	Mér-ri-ly	TUM-ta-ta

The first two feet listed below are occasionally encountered in English verse; the third rarely or never.

Spondee	′ ′	Accent—accent	Headlong	Héad-lóng	TUM-TUM
Amphibrach	˘ ′ ˘	Unaccent—accent—unaccent	Believing	Be-líev-ing	ta-TUM-ta
Pyrrhic	˘ ˘	Unaccent—unaccent	with a	with a	ta-ta

In practice, the spondee may be used as an iamb or as a trochee; in combination, we may have—

$$\text{In héad} \mid \text{-lóng flight}$$

in which the word is used as a trochee;

$$\text{He plúnged} \mid \text{héad-lóng}$$

in which the word is used as an iamb.

In actual verse and poetry, never forget that the actual rhythm of the words, as normally uttered in a conversational tone, differs from the artificial scansion pattern adopted. Take one of the most regular five-foot iambic lines in the language:

The curfew tolls the knell of parting day.
Elegy Written in a Country Churchyard,
Thomas Gray.

Scanned normally, as this would be spoken, we have the following natural scansion:

The cúrfĕw | tólls | thĕ knéll | ŏf pártĭng | dáy.

Here we have one iamb, two feet consisting of mere accented syllables for which we have no name, and two feet of three syllables each (unaccent—accent—unaccent, or amphibrachs). Yet this is described as an ideal iambic line, because the pattern indubitably is:

ta TUM   ta TUM   ta TUM   ta TUM   ta TUM

To make the actual line fit the planned iambic pattern, we have to divide words as follows:

The cúr- | fĕw tólls | thĕ knéll | ŏf párt- | ĭng dáy.

Absolutely natural iambic lines are rare:

Ănd dwéll | ŭpón | yŏur gráve | whĕn yóu | ăre déad.
The Comedy of Errors, William Shakespeare.

A repetition of such lines would be monotonous, unnatural and intrinsically unpoetic.

To show a still further group of variations, the opening of Hamlet's most famous soliloquy, commencing "To be or not to be," is theoretically in the same iambic five-foot pattern: three lines, each consisting theoretically of five ta-TUM's. The actual scansion brings in strange and unusual feet, or groups of unaccents with one accent; and shows that these three lines have only four actual feet apiece (a foot being, in English, normally grouped around one accent), where the pattern called for five in each line:

Tŏ bé | ŏr nót tŏ bĕ. | Thát | ĭs thĕ quéstĭŏn.
Whéthĕr | 'tĭs nóblĕr | ĭn thĕ mínd | tŏ súffĕr
Thĕ slíngs | ănd árrŏws | ŏf ŏutrágĕŏus | fórtŭne . . .
Hamlet, William Shakespeare.

Here are four feet of two syllables each (two iambs and two trochees); four of three syllables each (three amphibrachs and one anapest); one of one syllable; and three of four syllables each (two of one type, one of another). And only four natural feet to each line.

This is acceptable five-foot iambic verse, in the hands of the world's greatest master. In later plays, his variations became more extreme, until at times his rhythms were less regular than Whitman's typical free verse or polyrhythmic poetry.

What is desired, in metric poetry, is a regular pattern, with restrained freedom and variety in its use. The poet should learn to scan his poetry—that is, to mark the accented and unaccented syllables as above, and then to divide it both into the natural speech rhythm and into the artificial pattern rhythm. There is no need for pride, if the poetry is excessively regular. As a rule, that means that it is strained and unnatural in phrasing, and to that extent falls below true greatness in technique.

In reading poetry aloud or to oneself, avoid most of all an unnatural singsong. Never read the lines from Hamlet as if they had been printed:

to BE or NOT to BE that IS the QUEStion.
wheTHER 'tis NObler IN the MIND to SUFfer
the SLINGS and ARrows OF outRAgeous FORtune . . .

Instead, read this and all other poetry as naturally as if it were unpatterned prose. The pattern is there, and will make itself felt. Excellence in reading depends upon naturalness in expression.

Iambic Verse

The commonest line-pattern in English verse is based upon the iamb ($\smile$ $/$). Many more words in English are trochees than iambs. Iambic is the preferred pattern, because such trochaic words are normally introduced by a one-syllabled unaccented article, preposition, or the like. Normally lines do not open with the trochee *hoping,* but rather with such a phrase as *in hoping, for hoping, and hoping, this hoping, if hoping,* and so on.

Lines name the metric pattern; and are described by the type of foot, and the number of feet to the line. Thus a one-foot iambic line could be written:

> All hail!

A two-foot iambic line would be:

> All hail to you!

A three-foot iambic line would be:

> All hail to you, my friends!

A four-foot iambic line would be:

> All hail to you, my worthy friends!

A five-foot iambic line would be:

> All hail to you, my wholly worthy friends!

Note how naturally trochaic words like *wholly* and *worthy* fit into this iambic pattern. This line might have been:

> In hailing friendship's wholly worthy sons,

in which case four words (hailing, friendship's, wholly, worthy) are complete trochees in themselves: yet are transformed into word-split units in the iambic pattern, by the introductory unaccented word *in* and the concluding accented word *sons*. This is an entirely legitimate following of the iambic pattern, which can be most easily remembered as:

> ta TUM   ta TUM   ta TUM   ta TUM   ta TUM.

A word ending on an accented syllable is said to have a *masculine* ending; one ending on an unaccented syllable, a *feminine* ending. The iambic pattern may be used with a feminine ending: that is, with the addition of an unaccented syllable to the last foot. A stanza of five lines, successively one-, two-, three-, four-, and five-foot iambic lines with feminine endings, could be manufactured easily:

> Good morning,
> Benignant April,
> With all your rainbow blossoms,
> With birds all carolling their rapture,
> With love alive within the hearts of maidens.

The scansion for this would be:

Good morn- | ing,

Benig- | nant A- | pril,

With all | your rain- | bow blos- | soms,

With birds | all car- | olling | their rap- | ture,

With love | alive | within | the hearts | of maid- | ens.

This is often described as if the first line, for instance, were a two-foot line, with one syllable missing: and is called catalectic verse. The reality is that of an iambic foot, followed by a loose or unattached unaccented syllable.

Writing iambic verse is as easy as writing any form of verse. Get the metrical pattern firmly in mind:

ta TUM   ta TUM   ta TUM   ta TUM

and then proceed to let the words flow into this pattern.

Iambic verse may be altered into trochaic at any time, by *adding* an accented syllable to each line's beginning; or by *removing* the opening unaccented syllable. The process may be reversed as easily, thus changing trochaic verse into iambic. Start with this iambic version:

And then the little Hiawatha
Remarked unto the old Nokomis,
I know that hills are edged with valleys.

By adding an accented syllable at the beginning of each line, this becomes trochaic:

Now and then the little Hiawatha
Said aloud unto the old Nokomis,
Well I know that hills are edged with valleys.

By removing the opening unaccented syllable in each iambic line above, the lines are four-foot trochaic:

Then the little Hiawatha
Said unto the old Nokomis,
All the hills are edged with valleys.

This is the regular metre of Longfellow's *Hiawatha,* and is as easy to write as iambic verse.

Trochaic Verse

Trochaic verse is less usual in English than iambic, because the custom of the language is to introduce most remarks with an unaccented syllable or word. Based upon the trochee ($/$ ⌣), the pattern is, in the case of four-foot trochees,

TUM-ta   TUM-ta   TUM-ta   TUM-ta

Hiawatha opens upon this pattern:

> Should you ask me, whence these stories,
> Whence these legends and traditions,
> With the odours of the forest,
> With the dew and damp of meadows.
> *Hiawatha,* Henry Wadsworth Longfellow.

In natural accent, the first three of the lines quoted have only two accents apiece, and not four: so that the natural scansion, as of the third line, is

With the odours | of the forest.

Shakespeare commences a witches' incantation with the abrupt staccato natural accent:

> Round about the cauldron go;
> In the poisoned entrails throw.
> Toad, that under cold stone
> Days and nights has thirty-one
> Sweltered venom sleeping got,
> Boil thou first i' the charmed pot.
> *Macbeth,* William Shakespeare.

An interesting variation here is the use of *cold* as a dissyllable, as if it were pronounced *có-ŏld.* It may be regarded as the one-syllabled *cold,* followed by a pause consuming the length of time it would take to pronounce an unaccented syllable. In any case, it is an effective variant device.

Trochaic verse might certainly be described with propriety as iambic verse, with the introductory unaccented syllable omitted in each line. The description is unimportant; the important thing is to choose, understand, and use adequately the pattern, whatever it is called.

Again, in the sixth line quoted above from *Macbeth,* there is an extra unaccented syllable, a sort of grace-note, added: making the second foot in reality a dactyl:

Boil thou | first i' the | charmed | pot.

If preferred, though it is less usual, this could be scanned slightly differently:

Boil thou | first i' | the charmed | pot,

in which case there is an amphibrach in the third foot; or it might be scanned:

Boil thou | first i' | the char- | med pot,

regarding it as two trochees followed by two iambs. But the accepted pattern is trochaic four-foot, and the custom is to prefer the first scansion given. At any time, within reason dictated by the poet's own inner ear and sense of music, the substitution of an anapest or a dactyl for an iamb or a trochee is permitted. Or the substitution of a spondee ($//$), and any of the other feet (iamb, trochee, dactyl or spondee, as well as amphibrach etc.) may be substituted for a foot in anapestic verse. Similar substitutions may take place in dactylic verse. The best poetry contains variety within uniformity.

Notice that in the trochaic lines from *Macbeth* the last unaccented syllable is omitted in every line. This again gives an example of catalectic verse. The name is unimportant: a trochaic line may end on a masculine ending, as easily as an iambic line ends on a feminine ending. A dactylic line may end on a trochee or an accented syllable; an anapestic line may have an extra unaccented syllable, or even two of them, without losing its anapestic character. Variety in uniformity. . . .

Anapestic Verse

The anapest ($\smile \smile /$) is a foot of three syllables, the first two unaccented, the last accented. It may be described as an iamb with an extra unaccented syllable added before it. It may be indicated ta ta TUM, so that a three-foot anapestic pattern would be:

ta ta TUM   ta ta TUM   ta ta TUM.

A typical line following this pattern would be:

> To the end of the world in the dawn.

The English language has more accented syllables than many others, and a succession of two unaccented syllables is comparatively infrequent. Constantly the anapestic pattern is broken by a foot called the *amphimacer* ($/ \smile /$), accent—unaccent—accent, giving us a result such as:

> Let me go anywhere I can find,

scanned as anapestic thus:

> Lĕt mē gó | ănўwhĕre | Ĭ căn fínd,

but having a natural scansion consisting of three amphimacers:

> Lét mĕ gó | ánywhĕre | Í căn fínd.

There are so few natural anapests in the language, that this is usual and permitted. The same thing applies to dactylic verse. Even more unusual three-syllabled feet appear, each with two accents: the antibacchius, ($/ / \smile$), the bacchius, ($\smile / /$), the tribrach ($\smile \smile \smile$), the molossus ($/ / /$). In anapestic and dactylic verse, a fourth syllable, usually unaccented, again like a grace-note, may appear in any foot. So long as such variations please the inner ear, the inner sense of word music, they are aids.

The natural poet will always make his own patterns, knowing that poetry is self-created, and not devised by rigid rules.

Dactylic Verse

The dactyl ($/ \smile \smile$) is a foot of three syllables, the first accented, the next two unaccented. It may be described as a trochee with an extra unaccented syllable added after it. Here is an illustration:

> Cannon to right of them,
> Cannon to left of them,
> Cannon in front of them
>   Volleyed and thundered;
> Stormed at with shot and shell,
> Boldly they fought, and well. . . .
> *The Charge of the Light Brigade,* Alfred Tennyson.

Scanned as dactylic verse, this would appear:

Cannon to | right of them,

Cannon to | left of them,

Cannon in | front of them

Volleyed and | thundered;

Stormed at with | shot and shell,

Boldly they | fought, and well.

As a matter of fact, these last two lines would have a different natural scansion, including amphimacers:

Stormed at with | shot and shell,

Boldly they | fought, and well.

Once the technique of scansion is mastered, the poet must be his own court of last appeal upon it.

Dactylic verse is not wholly at home in English; and amphibrachic verse (using as its norm the amphibrach, $\smile\,/\,\smile$) is as much of an alien. These feet become excessively monotonous in long poems, though they may be used with advantage in brief lyrics.

Variations in Metric Verse

The use of variations in metric verse is widespread. The development of every poet of importance, whose technique did not begin and remain rigid and crystallized, has been in the direction of more and more variety. This is displayed impressively by the development of Shakespeare and of Keats. Little such development is shown in the technique of more rigid minor poets. A few examples must suffice. Shakespeare in his final peak period wrote lines whose natural scansion was as loose as:

A malady

Most in- | cident | to maids; | bold oxlips and

The crown imperial; lilies of all kinds,

The flow- | er-de-luce | being one! | O, these | I lack. . . .

The Winter's Tale, William Shakespeare.

The most unusual usage is the ending of the second line in the extraordinary foot which seems a spondee followed by a pyrrhic, (/ / ˘ ˘). The reverse foot opens a line in one of his sonnets,

Óf the wíde wórld | dréamĭng | ŏn thíngs | tŏ cóme.
Sonnet CVII, William Shakespeare.

One of the most praised lines in Keats is:

Róbs nót | one líght | séed fróm | thĕ feáth- | ĕr'd gráss.
Hyperion, John Keats.

Here two spondees introduce the rest of the line; the scansion being as if his pattern were—

TUM TUM   TUM TUM   TUM ta   ta TUM   ta TUM

Keats has at least one line, in the same pattern, consisting of five trochees:

Théǎ! | Théǎ! | Théǎ! | Where ĭs | Sátŭrn?
Hyperion, John Keats.

Robert Frost has such masterly lines as the following, in the same five foot iambic pattern:

And spread her apron to it. She put out her hand. . . .
The Death of the Hired Man, Robert Frost.
Strange how such innocence gets its own way.
The Black Cottage, Robert Frost.
And the saw snarled and rattled, snarled and rattled.
"Out, Out—", Robert Frost.
So. But the hand was gone already.
"Out, Out—", Robert Frost.

In this last line the monosyllable *So* is followed by a pause that takes the place of a foot and a half. One of Frost's most triumphant variations is:

Little—less—nothing! And that ended it.
"Out, Out—", Robert Frost.

In natural scansion, this would be:

Líttlĕ— | léss— | nóthĭng! | Ánd thăt éndĕd ĭt

A common variation is an alternation of iamb and anapest, as in this old English ballad:

> Ŏ Ăl- | ĭsŏn Gróss, | thăt líves | ĭn yŏn tówĕr.
> *Alison Gross,* Old English Ballad.

We find the reverse of this order in a Browning lyric,

> Whĕre thĕ cháf- | fĭnch síngs | ŏn thĕ ór- | chărd bóugh. . . .
> *Home-Thoughts, from Abroad,* Robert Browning.

So numerous are the variations to which the metric pattern in English can be adapted, to the greater naturalness of the poetry.

Accent Pattern Instead of Metric

Coleridge, in one poem, abandoned the formal metric foot altogether, in favor of a rediscovered old English method of letting the line pattern consist of a definite number of accents, with any number of unaccented syllables, occurring in any order. Here are the opening lines:

> 'Tĭs thĕ míd- | dlĕ ŏf níght | bў thĕ cás- | tlĕ clóck,
> Ănd thĕ ówls | hăve ăwák- | enĕd thĕ crów- | ĭng cóck.
> Tŭ- | whít! | Tŭ- | whóo!
> Ănd hárk, | ăgáin; | thĕ crów- | ĭng cóck
> Hŏw drów- | sĭlу | ĭt créw.
> *Christabel,* Samuel Taylor Coleridge.

Thomas Hood uses lines consisting of only three accented syllables,

> Stítch! | Stítch! | Stítch!
> Ĭn póv- | ĕrty, húng- | ĕr ănd dírt. . . .
> *The Song of the Shirt,* Thomas Hood.

This follows the same method of accent versification. Walter de la Mare's most famous poem is built around a pattern of three accents to the line, as the second and fourth line below indicate; he uses unaccented syllables where he pleases:

But on- | ly a host | of phantom listeners
That dwelt | in the lone | house then,
Stood lis- | tening in the qui- | et of the moonlight |
To that voice | from the world | of men.

The Listeners, Walter de la Mare.

Other modern poets have done as much, or more. Variety within uniformity. . . .

Blank Verse and Free Verse

Blank verse means simply unrhymed verse. Any line pattern, if unrhymed, is blank verse. *Heroic blank verse* is unrhymed five foot iambic poetry or verse. Most of Shakespeare is written in heroic blank verse. *Heroic couplets,* beloved of Dryden and Pope, are pairs of five foot iambic lines rhymed with each other.

Free verse may be rhymed or unrhymed, although it is usually unrhymed, since rhyming is an even more unnatural convention of poetry than metre; and the poet who has abandoned formal metre will hardly, as a rule, still use the device of rhyming. Free verse is verse without a metric pattern, but with a wider pattern than metre allows. It still tends toward regularity, rather than variety: and the final court of appeals as to whether any example should be classified as poetry or prose from a standpoint of content, or as verse or prose from a standpoint of technique, is the individual poet or reader himself. To many readers, the following are all poetry:

Lord, thou hast been our dwelling-place in all generations. Before the mountains were brought forth, or ever thou hadst formed the earth and the world, even from everlasting to everlasting, thou art God. Thou turnest man to destruction; and sayest, return, ye children of men. . . .

The Ninetieth Psalm.

But, in a larger sense, we cannot dedicate—we cannot consecrate—we cannot hallow—this ground. The brave men, living and dead, who struggled here, have consecrated it far above our poor power to add or to detract. The world will little note, nor long remember, what we say here; but it can never forget what they did here. . . .

The Gettsburg Address, Abraham Lincoln.

Out of the cradle endlessly rocking, out of the mockingbird's throat, the musical shuttle, out of the Ninth-month midnight, over the sterile sands, and the fields beyond, where the child leaving his bed wandered alone, bareheaded, barefoot, down from the showered halo, up from the mystic play of shadows twining and twisting as if they were alive. . . .

> *Out of the Cradle, Endlessly Rocking,*
> Walt Whitman.

Walt Whitman used the artificial line-division of poetry to present the third of these selections; the King James version of the Bible and Lincoln used the natural line-division so familiar in the printing of prose. Little or nothing is added by the artificial line division:

> Out of the cradle endlessly rocking,
> Out of the mocking-bird's throat, the musical shuttle,
> Out of the Ninth-month midnight,
> Over the sterile sands, and the fields beyond, where the
>   child leaving his bed wandered alone, bareheaded,
>   barefoot,
> Down from the showered halo,
> Up from the mystic play of shadows twining and
>   twisting as if they were alive. . . .

It is poetry, to many, in either form; and the first form is the more natural and readable. Scan the Whitman selection, or any of the others, and the tendency toward regularity of rhythm becomes apparent: a wider regularity, perhaps only an up-rhythm or a down-rhythm; but still inevitably there. This distinguishes free verse from prose, from the technical point of view.

At times writers of free verse let their lines reach surprising lengths, no matter how lovely the music is: thus Sandburg,

> Pocahontas' body, lovely as a poplar, sweet as a
>   red haw in November or a pawpaw in May,
> did she wonder? does she remember? in the dust,
> in the cool tombs. . . .

> *Cool Tombs,* Carl Sandburg.

Again, the lines can be extremely brief:

> It sits looking
> over harbor and city

on silent haunches
and then moves on.

Fog, Carl Sandburg.

The free verse writer devises his own line-division pattern. This form, eliminating the devices of metre and rhyme, calls on the poet to avoid the inconsequential and the trivial, and to write down only his important utterances. If rhyme is a shelter for mediocrity, as Shelley wrote in his preface to *The Revolt of Islam,* free verse is a test of the best that the poet has in him.

Line Length in Verse

Oliver Wendell Holmes, himself a doctor, advanced the theory that line length in verse marked physiologically the normal breathing of the poet. In other words, a breath should be taken at the end of each line; and the line should be no longer than the poet's ability to hold his breath. No artificial line division is used in prose, to indicate where a breath should be taken. There is no greater reason for artificial line division in poetry. It still remains true that the long Greek lines, each consisting of six feet, called for huge-breasted warrior-bards to chant them; that the norm of English verse, the five-foot iambic line, indicates a lesser chest-expansion in the typical English poet; and that the briefer modern tendency shows a further deterioration in the chest-expansion of poets.

Where poetry consists in *end-stopped* lines—lines with a natural pause at the end of each line—there is more reason for an artificial line division. Shakespeare began so; many poets never get beyond this, in the main. But when we come to poetry like—

We are such stuff
As dreams are made on, and our little life
Is rounded with a sleep,

The Tempest, William Shakespeare.

the break comes after *on,* and not after *stuff* or *life;* and the last reason for the artificial line division has vanished.

A sonnet set up in this manner appears:

O bitter moon, O cold and bitter moon, climbing your midnight hillside of bleak sky, the earth, as you, once knew a blazing noon.

Night brings the silver hour when she will die. We shall be cold as you are, and as bitter, icily circling toward a tepid fire, playing at life with our deceitful glitter, past joy, past hope, forever past desire.

Yet still the forest lifts its leafy wings to flutter for a while before the chill. And still the careless heart is gay, and sings in the green temple on the dusty hill. And the gulls tumble, and the homing ships peer for the harbor. . . .

And the sand drips.

The Flight of the Eagle, v, Clement Wood.

In an earlier volume, this had appeared with the usual line-division of poetry as ordinarily printed. Rhyme can occur of course in ordinary prose, although this usage is extremely rare. Where the rhythm of verse is used, as in the sonnet quoted, it is possible for poets to use the line and paragraph division usual to prose, if this is desired.

IMPORTANT CLASSICAL TERMS FOR POETIC DEVICES

Verses and Groups of Verses

Classical Name	*Common Name, or Explanation*
Monometer	A verse containing one metrical foot.
Dimeter	A verse containing two metrical feet.
Dipody	A measure consisting of two metrical feet; a ditrochee.
Trimeter	A verse containing three metrical feet.
Tetrameter	A verse containing four metrical feet.
Pentameter	A verse containing five metrical feet.
Hexameter	A verse containing six metrical feet.
Heptameter	A verse containing seven metrical feet.
Octometer	A verse containing eight metrical feet.
Distich	A strophic verse of two lines, usually called a couplet today.

Unusual Metric Feet

Tribrach	Three unaccented syllables	⌣ ⌣ ⌣
Molossus	Three accented syllables	╱ ╱ ╱
Amphimacer	Accent, unaccent, accent	╱ ⌣ ╱
Bacchius	Unaccent, accent, accent	⌣ ╱ ╱
Antibacchius	Accent, accent, unaccent	╱ ╱ ⌣

Ditrochee	Two trochees regarded as a compound foot	/ ˘ / ˘
Paeon	Accent, unaccent, unaccent, unaccent	/ ˘ ˘ ˘
Choriamb	Accent, unaccent, unaccent, accent	/ ˘ ˘ /
Epitrite	Three accents and one unaccent: of the 1st, 2nd, 3rd or fourth class, depending on the location of the unaccented syllable	˘ / / / / ˘ / / / / ˘ / / / / ˘

OTHER TERMS

Classical Name	*Explanation*
Acatalectic Verse	Verse not defective in the last foot; verse complete in its number of syllables.
Arsis	The lighter or unstressed part of a foot, especially in quantitative verse; later, the accented syllable of a foot.
Caesura	A break in a verse caused by the ending of a word within a foot. A *masculine caesura* follows the thesis, or stressed part of a foot. A *feminine caesura* follows the arsis or unstressed part. A *trithemimeral caesura* comes after the third half foot, which means in the second foot; a *penthemimeral caesura,* after the fifth half foot; a *hepthemimeral caesura,* after the seventh half foot; and so on. A *bucolic caesura,* in dactylic hexameter, is a caesura occurring in the fourth foot, especially in pastoral poetry.
Catalectic Verse	Verse lacking a syllable at the beginning, or terminating in an imperfect foot.
Diaeresis, Dieresis	The break caused by the coincidence of the end of a foot with the end of a word. *Bucolic diaeresis,* a diaeresis occurring in the fourth foot, especially in pastoral poetry.
Enjambement	The extension of the sentence beyond the limitations of the distich.
Ictus	Metrical stress.
Thesis	The heavier or stressed part of a foot in classical prosody, especially in quantitative verse; later, the unaccented syllable or syllables of a verse.

THE TECHNIQUE OF VERSIFICATION: RHYME

Correct and Incorrect Rhyme

RHYME is as simple to define as rhythm is difficult.

Rhyme is the identity in sound of an accented vowel in a word, usually the last one accented, and of all consonantal and vowel sounds following it; with a difference in the sound of the consonant immediately preceding the accented vowel. Rhyme deals exclusively with sounds, and has nothing to do with spelling. The rhyming dictionary terminating this book is strictly phonetic, and therefore logical and useful.

Correct rhymes may be spelled alike:

> ate, plate, mate, abate, syncopate.

They may be spelled differently:

> ate, bait, straight, freight.

In this case the spelling is immaterial.

So called "eye rhymes,"—that is, words spelt alike that look alike but are pronounced differently—are not rhymes at all; they slip into versification, if at all, as *consonance,* which will be discussed later. That is, the incorrect rhyme

> earth, hearth,

so popular among English versifiers, is no more a rhyme than the following sets of words identically spelled, but pronounced differently:

> cow, blow
> climber, timber
> finger, ginger, singer
> cough, enough, plough, though, through.

Identities do not rhyme, no matter what the spelling is; since the preceding consonantal sounds must differ. The following are identities, and not rhymes:

> bay, obey
> bare, bear, forbear
> laying, overlaying
> ability, possibility, probability.

Sounds *almost* alike, after the identical accented vowel sounds, do not rhyme. These are properly called assonance, and have not succeeded as a versification device in English. Examples are:

> main, game, reins, lamed
> hate, shape, played
> feed, sleet, creep
> sandwich, orange, lozenge
> childhood, wildwood
> Norfolk, war talk
> anguish, Flatbush
> silver, deliver

You can find examples of incorrect rhymes in poems by many accepted poets, and in a much higher percentage of popular songs and newspaper versification. Two of the above examples were taken directly out of songs nationally popular. Slovenly rhyming is one of the sure signs of mediocrity in versification. Learn correct rhyming first; then, if you wish to break the rule you understand, that is your privilege.

The language's poverty in rhyming has caused the following almost-rhymes to become widely accepted:

> given, Heaven; bosom, blossom; shadow, meadow;
> God, road; war, more; bliss, is; was, grass.

Among widely used "eye rhymes," which are not rhymes at all, but mere identities in spelling, are:

> earth, hearth; bare, are; north, forth; real, steal.

Bosom-blossom, was-grass, are combinations of consonance and assonance; *bliss-is* is assonance; the others in the first list are consonance. The first three pairs in the second set are acceptable consonance; *real, steal* is an attempt to rhyme a two-syllabled word with a one-syllabled one, and has no justification from any standpoint. Use consonance or assonance purposely, if desired; but always know that this is not correct rhyming.

If the poet is tone-deaf as to sounds, it is best to rely upon the phonetic symbols above each group of rhyming words in the rhyming dictionary that terminates this book, or upon dictionary markings. Many people can not distinguish the obvious difference in sounds between this pair of words, which do not rhyme:

north, forth.

Take away the *th* sound, and many people still hear no difference between this pair of words, which do not rhyme:

nor, fore.

Take away the *r* sound, and some people still hear no difference between this pair of words, which do not rhyme:

gnaw, foe.

Gnaw plus *r* plus *th* can not rhyme with *foe* plus *r* plus *th*. If in doubt as to such off-rhymes, follow the phonetic markings.

A third common error in rhyming comes from such mispronunciations as dropping a terminal *-g*. These do not rhyme:

martin, parting.
herding, burden.

They may be rhymed colloquially, that is, in quoted words, as follows:

martin, partin',
herdin', burden,

the latter being not quite a rhyme, at that. But unless writing colloquially, do not use such incorrect rhymes as those given first above. A similar error comes from ignoring the *r* sounds, which causes such off-rhymes as:

court (pronounced *cou't,* like *coat*), boat
Lord (pronounced *Lawd*), gaud.

Rhymes can be made of two or more words. Here are examples of perfect rhymes:

satin, flat in.
Quentin, went in.
pray tin, hate in.

Such couplings are more appropriate to light and humorous verse than to serious poetry. Rhyming must always give the effect of unobtrusive *naturalness,* or it fails of its proper effect.

Robert Browning is in a class by himself in fantastic many-word rhymings and near-rhymings, often in serious verse:

> The wolf, fox, bear and monkey
> By piping advice in one key. . . .
> *Pacchiarotto, and How He Worked*
> *in Distemper, et cetera,*
>
> Robert Browning.

This is not a rhyme, because *monkey* is, phonetically, a rhyme sound for *ŭngki*, or at best *ŭngke;* and *one key* is, phonetically, a rhyme sound for *ŭnkē:* the unguessed *g* sound in the first spoiling it as a rhyme. Again, in the same poem, he uses this fantastic coupling:

> While, treading down rose and ranunculus,
> You *Tommy-make-room-for-your-uncle-us!*

Ranunculus has as its rhyme sound *ungk'ū-lus;* the next line, *ŭngk'ŏŏl-us:* a minor difference, but enough to spoil the rhyme. Much closer is Byron's celebrated couplet:

> O ye lords of ladies inte*llectual,*
> Inform us truly, have they not hen*pecked you all?*
>
> *Don Juan,* I, xxii, Lord Byron.

The unaccented last syllable of the first line differs from the unaccented last syllable of the second with the difference of *ă* and *ô.* Barham furnishes many perfect many-worded rhymes, such as:

> Should it even set fire to one's castle and *burn it, you're*
> Amply insured for both building and *furniture.* . . .
> *Sir Rupert the Fearless,*
> Richard Harris Barham (Thomas Ingoldsby).

Samuel Hoffenstein furnishes a splendid example:

> You haven't the nerve to take b*ichloride;*
> You lie up nights till you're gaunt and *sore-eyed,*
> *Poems in Praise of Practically Nothing,*
> Samuel Hoffenstein.

In using such rhyme combinations, it is wise to put the combination with the inevitable sound first: *bichloride;* following this with the combination of words to rhyme with it. Thus W. S. Gilbert, a master rhymester, uses in this order:

> monotony, got any.
> cerebellum too, tell 'em to.

In light and humorous verse, such rhyming cleverness is a crown; in serious verse, if used sparingly, it is permitted.

Function and Types of Rhyme

In serious verse, since obvious cleverness defeats the appeal to the serious emotions, rhyming should be unobtrusive. To have your rhyme words merely conveniences demanded by your rhyming pattern is one of the chief faults of rhymed verse.

Rhyme is a potent shaper. Once you have written down a line of verse or poetry, and intend to have the next line or the next line but one rhyme with it, your choice of terminal words for the rhyming line is limited by the limited rhyming resources of the language. If a poet commences,

> October is the wildest month,

he has estopped himself from any rhyme; since *month* has no rhyme in English.

Assuming that the first line's rhyming word has certain rhyming mates, the choice of terminal rhyme words for the rhyming line is limited to these; and the direction of the poet's thought and its expression must be deflected into some natural use of one of these rhyming mate words. Rhyming is a brain-stimulant, and may even spur on the poetic imagination. The meaning of the planned poem may have been clear in the mind; but its expression, if rhyme is used, must work in limited fields, and only the master achieves in these that finality of natural utterance which is one of the charms of great poetry.

To the authentic poet, especially the living poet, there is no such thing as *poetic license:* the right to warp and twist the language out of its natural order or grammar, to suit the exigencies of rhyme. Mr. Browning continued his *Tommy-make-room-for-your-uncle-us* couplet with this:

> Quick march! for Xanthippe, my housemaid,
> If once on your pates she a souse made. . . .
> I would not for worlds be your place in,
> Recipient of slops from the basin!

What Browning meant, in the direct natural order, was:

> Quick march! for Xanthippe, my housemaid,
> If once she made a souse on your pates,
> I would not for worlds be in your place,
> Recipient of slops from the basin!

Even this is unnatural; the real order would be, "Quick march! for if once Xanthippe, my housemaid, made . . ." etc. Let us suppose that inspiration worked with him in the erratic fashion quoted above. Then would be the time for the critical sense to come in, and rigorously to eliminate all such evidences of poetic license—inversions, ungrammatical constructions, and the like. Not one has a place in poetry, more than in speech.

This is a rigid rule to lay down. It is not any individual's rule. It is the rule that Shakespeare followed, when he wrote:

> Tomorrow, and tomorrow, and tomorrow,
> Creeps in this petty pace from day to day
> To the last syllable of recorded time,
> And all our yesterdays have lighted fools
> The way to dusty death. Out, out, brief candle!
> Life's but a walking shadow, a poor player
> That struts and frets his hour upon the stage
> And then is heard no more; it is a tale
> Told by an idiot, full of sound and fury,
> Signifying nothing.
>
> *Macbeth*, William Shakespeare.

This was written some three hundred years ago. There is not an obsolete or even archaic word in it, not a strained construction, not an inversion or instance of ungrammatical poetic license. The quotation given in fragmentary form from Browning, which includes *ranunculus, homunculus, skoramis,* and countless inversions, was outdated long ago: the words of Shakespeare live. The best of Burns, of Shelley, of the Keats of *Hyperion,* of the best among the modern poets, always follows this rule: no inversions, no archaisms, no poetic license. This is the price of a chance for wide poetic greatness.

To return to the strict technique of rhyming, one-syllabled rhymes are called single or masculine rhymes. Examples are:

> we, flee, sea, apostrophe, harmony.
> disk, tamarisk, odalisque.
> fling, sing, carolling.

In the last pair of the first grouping, and the third rhymes in the others, note that only a secondary accent falls on the rhyming syllable. This is enough. A rhyme may be more smothered, if read naturally,—a modern variation in which it may be said that an accented syllable is rhymed with an unaccented one: such as *anguish, wish; ring, wedding*. Used sparingly, this is effective.

Two-syllabled rhymes are called double or feminine rhymes. Examples are:

> ocean, motion, devotion.
> traded, aided, play did.
> see us, flee us.

Three-syllabled rhymes are called triple rhymes. Examples:

> saleable, mailable.
> lyrical, miracle, empirical, satirical.
> going now, blowing now.
> rest of it, best of it, palimpsest of it.

There may be rhymes, especially in light verse, of four or even more syllables. A rhyme like the one last given shows little cleverness, since it is merely "rest, best, palimpsest" with the phrase "of it" added. The lack of cleverness makes it more suitable for serious poetry than for light verse.

End rhyme is used at the end of the lines. Here is an example, the rhyming words being italicized, and the rhyme scheme indicated by the corresponding numerals:

> Gather ye rose-buds while ye *may*,   1
>   Old Time is still *a-flying;*   2
> And this same flower that smiles *today*,   1
>   Tomorrow will be *dying*.   2
>   *Counsel to Girls,* Robert Herrick.

Rhyme 1 is a single or masculine rhyme; rhyme 2 is a double or feminine rhyme.

Internal rhyme is rhyme used within the line, to give added effectiveness by a closer repetition of the rhyming sounds.

"Each day, all day," these poor folk say,
"In the same old *year-long, drear-long* way,
We *weave* in the *mills* and *heave* in the *kilns,*
We *sieve* mine-meshes under the hills,
And *thieve* much gold from the Devil's bank tills,
To *relieve,* O God, what manner of ills?"

The Symphony, Sidney Lanier.

Here *year-long* rhymes internally with *drear-long; weave, heave, sieve, thieve* and *relieve* are further internal rhymes; and *mills* is an internal rhyme to *kilns* and the three next end rhymes.

Undesirable Rhymes

Incorrect rhymes, or rhymes constructed by straining the natural expression into inversions and grammatical perversions, excused on the outworn plea of poetic license, are always undesirable. Quite as undesirable are rhymes which are hackneyed and overworked, such as:

kiss, bliss.
yearn, burn; yearning, burning.
love, dove, above.
fire, desire.
trees, breeze.

These are unobjectionable technically. But they have been so used and overused by other poets, that the only excuse for them today is use in an entirely new manner.

It is the fact that most rhymes have been comparatively overworked that has caused the tendency toward consonance, which is such a marked feature of modern poetry, from Emily Dickinson onward.

Alliteration

Alliteration, like rhyme, is a repetition of sounds. But the sound repeated is only the initial consonant of syllables or words. This was one of the major devices of Anglo-Saxon poetry, which did not use rhyme. Langland's *Piers Plowman* opens:

In a *summer season,* when *soft* was the *sun,*
I *shope* me in *shroudes,* as I a *sheep* were.

The Vision of Piers Plowman, William Langland.

Alliteration is used effectively by later poets in connection with rhyme, as this example illustrates:

> Whether *t*empter sent, or whether *t*empest *t*ossed thee here ashore,
> *D*esolate yet all un*d*aunted, on this *d*esert land enchanted,
> In this *h*ome by *H*orror *h*aunted, tell me truly, I implore.
>
> *The Raven,* Edgar Allan Poe.

If not overused, this is highly effective. Swinburne was one of the masters of alliteration, tending to overuse it, as in—

> The *l*ilies and *l*anguors of *v*irtue
> For the *r*oses and *r*apture of *v*ice.
>
> *Dolores,* Algernon Charles Swinburne.

Where there is no sense of unnaturalness in the repetition of alliterative sounds, it may be successfully employed.

Assonance

Assonance, called also *vowel rhyme,* consists in the identity of the final accented vowel sound, with dissimilarity in the subsequent consonantal and vowel sounds. It was used in Provencal and Old French poetry, and is still used in Spanish. George Eliot tried unsuccessfully to introduce it into English, the assonances being italicized:

> Maiden crowned with glossy *blackness,*
> Lithe as panther forest-*roaming,*
> Long-armed naead, when she *dances,*
> On the stream of ether *floating,*
> Bright, O bright Fedalma!
>
> *Song of Joan,* in *The Spanish Gipsy,*
> George Eliot.

The repetition here is not sufficiently marked to make this device popular in English versification. Typical groups of assonantal masculine or single-rhymed endings are:

> grab, crack, had, tan, sham, hang, fat
> face, shade, hate, pain, claim, male
> led, wreck, hem, then, set, step
> bide, kine, fight, pipe, wise, advice

In feminine endings, we would have:

> aiming, faded, scraping, hailing, painter, lateness
> roaming, floated, coping, goader, golden
> coming, dumbness, stubborn, rustle

Unpopular so far, at any time assonance may achieve a popularity in English versification.

Consonance

Consonance, also loosely called *off rhymes, sour rhymes,* and *analyzed rhymes,* consists in an identity of all consonantal and vowel sounds after the accented vowel; and a difference in the accented vowels. An improvised model would be:

> There's a golden willow
> Underneath a hill,
> By a babbling shallow
> Brook and waterfall;
>
> And a mill-wheel turning
> Under moon and sun,
> As if gently scorning
> Time and tide and man.

There can be any combination of end and internal consonance with end or internal rhyme in the same poem, according to the best modern practice: the poet himself being the judge of what form is most pleasing to his inner sense of music, and that of his prospective readers.

Edna St. Vincent Millay, in *The Poet and His Book,* uses these pairs of words in consonance:

> worry, bury; withered, gathered; cluttered, spattered;
> quarrel, laurel; hunters, winter's; valleys, bellies.

She also twice uses assonance:

> cupboard, upward; only, homely.

Elinor Wylie uses such instances of consonance as:

> bloody, body; people, ripple; mourner, corner;
> primer, dreamer; standard, pondered; noble,
> trouble; music, physic; Circe, hearsay; Vulcan,

falcon; languish, distinguish; lost, ghost;
sword, lord; suns, bronze;

and many more. Emily Dickinson is more lavish in her use of consonance than any of these.

The reason has been hinted before: the limited field of rhymes in the language, in spite of the impressive length of any rhyming dictionary. One advantage of a phonetic rhyming dictionary is that it makes the use of precise and accurate consonance possible. Words are arranged by rhyme, and not by consonance; and yet the phonetic arrangement gives a start toward arriving at accurate consonance. If the following method is used, consonance can be achieved by little more effort than is required for rhyme.

There are five *a* sounds that occur in accented syllables; three *e*'s; two *i*'s; six *o*'s; and three *u*'s, or a total of nineteen vowel sounds appearing in accented syllables. Most of these sets are grouped together: most of the *a*'s; two of the *e*'s (omitting the *e* followed by *r*, which appears only when *er* is reached); both of the *i*'s, and so on. Thus $\bar{A}D$ is followed by $\check{A}D$ and this by $\ddot{A}D$: so that we may proceed directly from rhyming sounds like *aid* to *sad* and then to *charade*. In double rhymes, $\bar{O}'li$, $\hat{O}L'i$ and $\check{O}L'i$ follow in regular sequence; thus *holy, Macaulay,* and *folly* are near neighbors.

Suppose it is desired to locate all the consonance sounds possible for a line ending with *holy*. Turn under the *a*'s to all the phonetic symbols similar to $\bar{O}'li$—$\bar{A}'li$ (as, *daily*) $\check{A}L'i$ (as, *alley*); under *e*, to $\bar{E}'li$ (as, *freely*), $\check{E}L'i$ (as, *jelly*); under *i*, to $\bar{I}'li$ (as, *drily*) and $\check{I}L'i$ (as, *hilly*); also under *o* to $\check{O}OL'i$ (as, *woolly*), $OIL'i$ (as, *oily*); under *u*, to $\bar{U}'li$ (as, *truly*) and $\check{U}L'i$ (as, *dully*). Look up also $OUL'i$ and other possible vowel combinations, to make sure there are no rhyme sounds under them. And now the poet has an accurate test to see which words are in precise consonance with *holy*, and which are not.

Thus this most modern of all sound-repetition devices in English versification can be achieved most perfectly through the use of a phonetic rhyming dictionary. The phonetic symbols, of course, must be in precise alphabetical order. Turn, under each of the five vowels (not forgetting that the vowel sounds OI, OO and OU come alphabetically also), to the vowel followed by the identical consonant and vowel sounds following the accented vowel in the rhymed syllable you wish consonances for; and all consonances that the lists of words affords will be found.

There is small adventure in rhyming, except in the made rhymes of two or more words more common to light verse. Compilers of rhyming dictionaries have completed the adventure, long ago. There is great adventure in the use of consonance, which expands the sound-repetition resources of the language. It is possible to write a poem where not one of the consonance couplets has been used before. The adventurous will not overlook this.

Your Mental Rhyming Dictionary

At times it is inconvenient or impossible to have a rhyming dictionary available. Especially where the poet desires to write such a piece of formal verse as a ballade, requiring fourteen rhymes on one sound, no two of which could be identical, it is advisable to be able to improvise your own temporary rhyming dictionary.

The method is simple. First write down all the single, double and triple consonantal sounds you can remember. It is not necessary to write down all of them, although for your convenience the list on opposite page is approximately complete.

Having jotted down as many of these as you remember, test the rhyme sound desired against this table, and write out the results. Thus, if the rhymes to *aye*, the long *Ā* sound, are desired, the poet would get, to begin with, of the single consonantal sounds:

> aye, bay, day, fay, gay, hay, jay, kay or cay, lay, may, nay or neigh, pay, ray, say, decolleté for the *t* sound, survey for the *v* sound, way, yea.

Be careful, when a one-syllabled rhyme in such an instance is missing, to use ingenuity to find longer words with the desired rhyme, as *decolleté, survey*.

Then, for the double consonantal sound rhymes, the following could be added:

> redoublé for the *bl* sound, bray, dray, flay, fray, gray, clay, McCrae for the *cr* sound, play, pray or prey, shay, risqué

Single (Vowel)	*Double*	*Triple*	*Rare*
B	BL		BW
	BR		
	CH		
—			
D	DR		DW
F	FL		
	FR		
G	GL		GW
	GR		
H			
J			
K (C)	KL (CL)		
	KR (CR)		
L			
M			
N			
P	PL		PW
	PR		
Q (KW)			
R			
S	SH	SHR	
	SK (SC)	SKR (SCR)	
	SL		
	SM		
	SN		
	SP	SPL	
		SPR	
	SQ (SKW)		
	ST	STR	
	SV		
	SW		
T	TH		
	th	thR	
	TR		
	TW		
V			VL
W			
Y			
Z			ZH
			ZL

for the *sk* sound, slay, dismay perhaps for the *sm* sound, stay, sway, they, tray, tway.

In addition, the triple consonantal sounds would give:

splay, spray, stray.

Altogether, this has furnished thirty-nine rhymes for *aye*: and this is more than enough to satisfy the requirements of any formal verse.

Suppose only four rhymes for the purposes of the rhyming pattern are needed, and the poet decides to use *huge* as one of them. Using the above rhyming dictionary, only a group of *f* rhymes are discovered:—*febrifuge, subterfuge, vermifuge* and so on; and perhaps, if the poet is expert in pronunciation, *gamboge,* which also rhymes with it. But no fourth rhyming sound. The *huge* rhyme-sound would then have to be discarded, and some other sound tried.

Try a double rhyme, *ended.* Using this mental rhyming dictionary, the poet discovers:

ended, bended, fended or defended, Jen did, Len did, mended or amended, depended, rended, tended or attended, vended, wended;

and, using double and triple consonantal initial sounds,

blended, friended and befriended, expended for *sp,* extended for *st,* trended, then did, splendid,

and this can be supplemented with *men did* and many other two word rhymes. Here are at least eighteen rhyming mates, which can be used as the 2 rhyme in a ballade, which requires fourteen rhyming mates.

So, even if the rhyming dictionary is left behind, a mental rhyming dictionary can always be improvised, once the mechanism is learned.

IV

STANZA PATTERNS

The Couplet

A SINGLE line of poetry is called, technically, a *verse* of poetry. A series of lines arranged formally as a part of a poem is called a *stanza*. Stanza forms may be rigid, with a fixed order of sequence as to line length, metre, or rhyme; or they may be mere divisions of a poem, corresponding to the paragraphs of prose.

The simplest stanza is one of two lines, called a couplet. The word *couplet* is used to mean either a two-line poem, or a two line stanza—that is, a part of a poem: and this is equally true of triplets or tercets, quatrains, and so on. It may be rhymed:

> "Where are you going, my pretty maid?"   1
> "I'm going a milking, sir," she said.   1
> *Mother Goose's Nursery Rhymes.*

Naturally, if our stanza has only two lines, it can be rhymed in only one way: each line followed immediately by its rhyming mate. This is called rhyming in couplets, and is indicated by 1, 1. The second rhyme sound used in the poem would be designated by 2, the third by 3, and so on. Thus a series of couplet stanzas, if rhymed, would be rhymed 1, 1; 2, 2; 3, 3, and so on. This is called couplet rhyming,—a term used of any lines rhymed in this fashion, even when not divided into separate couplet stanzas.

Five-foot iambic lines rhymed couplet fashion are called *heroic couplets*. This was the favorite measure employed by Dryden and Pope, who enriched the language with many polished quotations:

> Vice is a monster of so frightful mien   1
> As, to be hated, needs but to be seen;   1
> Yet seen too oft, familiar with her face,   2
> We first endure, then pity, then embrace.   2
> *An Essay on Man,* Alexander Pope.

39

These pairs of lines are not stanzas, much less complete two-line poems. Thus *couplet* is used with the third meaning of a method of rhyming—the 1, 1; 2, 2 method.

A couplet need not be rhymed: it may be an unrhymed two line poem, or two line stanza. It may be in any rhythm or combination of rhythms.

The Triplet or Tercet

A group of three lines, whether a complete poem or a stanza, is called a triplet, or tercet. This is not as common a form as the couplet or the four-line form, the quatrain. An example is:

A still small voice spake unto me,   1
"Life is so full of misery,   1
Were it not better not to be?"   1
The Two Voices, Alfred Tennyson.

It is clear, that with three lines to work from, the lines in such a group might be rhymed 1, 1, 2, in which the third line rhymes with nothing in the triplet; or 1, 2, 2; or 1, 2, 1. In the case of groups of triplet stanzas, the rhymes may be interlocked:

Make me thy lyre, even as the forest is: 1
What if my leaves are falling like its own!   2
The tumult of thy mighty harmonies   1

Will take from both a deep autumnal tone,   2
Sweet though in sadness. Be thou, Spirit fierce,   3
My spirit! Be thou me, impetuous one!   2

Drive my dead thoughts over the universe   3
Like withered leaves to quicken a new birth!   4
And, by the incantation of this verse,   3

Scatter, as from an unextinguished hearth   4
Ashes and sparks, my words among mankind!   5
Be through my lips to unawakened earth   4

The trumpet of a prophecy! O wind,   5
If Winter comes, can Spring be far behind?   5
Ode to the West Wind, Percy Bysshe Shelley.

This interlocked rhyming, where the unrhymed middle line of one triplet becomes the rhymed first and third lines of the next, the whole ending with a thirteenth and fourteenth line rhyming with the unrhymed central line of the preceding triplet, is a special Italian verse stanza form, called *terza rima*. As Shelley used it, it might be regarded as an apt variation of the Shakespearean sonnet. It may be constituted of less or more triplets, always followed by such a concluding couplet.

Notice, in the hands of this master, the rhyming devices. *Is-harmonies* illustrates rhyming a primary accent with a secondary one: and the secondary one is an indeterminate sound, more often rhymed with *seas* than with *is*, which gives it the effect of partial consonance. *Fierce-universe* is consonance, not rhyme, as is *birth-hearth-earth*, long defended as an "eye rhyme," but admissible as consonance. The same is true of *mankind-wind-behind*. It is incorrect to pronounce the noun *wind* as if it were the verb *to wind; wind* here rhymed with *thinned*, and is in consonance with *behind*.

Triplets may be in any rhythm, including free verse or polyrhythm. And they may be unrhymed:

> I have had playmates, I have had companions,
> In my days of childhood, in my joyful school-days;
> All, all are gone, the old familiar faces.
>
> I have been laughing, I have been carousing,
> Drinking late, sitting late, with my bosom cronies;
> All, all are gone, the old familiar faces.
>   *The Old Familiar Faces*, Charles Lamb.

In this poem Lamb invented his own pattern—unrhymed six foot trochaic in the main, with seven feet in the fifth line; and with the terminal line of each triplet a refrain, repeated without alteration. Any poet may make his own pattern for any poem he wishes; and, if it finds favor, it may become a standard pattern.

The Quatrain

A quatrain is a stanza or poem of four lines. This is the most popular brief stanza in English versification, and has a variety of familiar rhyme schemes. Ordinary *ballad metre* was originally seven-foot iambic rhymed couplets:

As Robin Hood in the forest strayed, all under the greenwood tree, 1
He was aware of a brave young man, as fine as fine might be.   1
Old English Ballad.

As normally printed today, this becomes a quatrain, with the first
and third lines unrhymed, and only the second and fourth rhyming
—a rhyme scheme that may be used with other metres as well,
and with any number of feet to each line:

As Robin Hood in the forest strayed,   1
All under the greenwood tree,   2
He was aware of a brave young man,   3
As fine as fine might be.   2

Almost as popular is the quatrain rhymed on alternate lines:

A violet by a mossy stone   1
Half-hidden from the eye!   2
—Fair as a star, when only one   1
Is shining in the sky.   2
The Lost Love, William Wordsworth.

Quatrains may be rhymed couplet-wise:

Tiger, tiger, burning bright   1
In the forests of the night,   1
What immortal hand or eye   2
Framed thy fearful symmetry?   2
The Tiger, William Blake.

Note that this is not indented: that is, that line two is set directly
under line one. The purpose of *indentation* is primarily to show
the rhyme scheme: lines rhyming with each other may be normally
set beneath each other, as in the two previous examples. Indentation is used either to show identities of rhyme, or to center
briefer lines in a stanza or poem.

The *In Memoriam* stanza is built upon a four-foot iambic
pattern, rhymed as follows:

Ring out old shapes of foul disease;   1
Ring out the narrowing lust of gold;   2
Ring out the thousand wars of old,   2
Ring in the thousand years of peace.   1
In Memoriam, Alfred Tennyson.

Edward Fitzgerald's translation or recreation of the quatrains or *Rubaiyat* of Omar Khayyam has one of the most famous quatrain rhyme patterns in the language, using five-foot iambic lines:

> The Moving Finger writes; and, having writ,   1
> Moves on: nor all your Piety nor Wit   1
>   Shall lure it back to cancel half a Line   2
> Nor all your Tears wash out a Word of it.   1
>
> > *The Rubaiyat of Omar Khayyam,*
> > translated by Edward Fitzgerald.

Other possible quatrain rhyme arrangements are: 1, 1, 1, 1; 1, 1, 1, 2; 2, 2, 2, 2; 1, 2, 1, 1; 1, 2, 3, 1; 1, 1, 2, 3; 1, 2, 3, 3; 1, 2, 2, 3; and no doubt others. Hereafter, no additional rhyming patterns will be listed, since by now it should be understood that none is forbidden.

As for the number of feet to the line in these quatrains, the number for the better known patterns is as follows:

> Ballad metre, 4, 3, 4, 3. Called also Long Metre in hymns.
> *In Memoriam,* 4, 4, 4, 4.
> *Rubaiyat,* 5, 5, 5, 5.
> Short metre (in hymns), 3, 3, 4, 3.

This last was popular in the sixteenth century as *Poulter's measure.* These four are all in iambic lines. Of course, any metric foot or combination of feet may be employed. It need not be repeated again that the quatrain, as any other stanza, may be unrhymed, or may be in polyrhythm.

Stanzas of More Than Four Lines

A five-line stanza or poem is called a cinquain. Adelaide Crapsey invented one containing 1, 2, 3, 4, and 1 iambic feet respectively in the lines:

> These be
> Three silent things:
> The falling snow . . . . the hour
> Before the dawn . . . . the mouth of one
> Just dead.
>
> > *Triad,* by Adelaide Crapsey.

A rhymed cinquain is used in one of Shelley's best known odes:

Hail to thee, blithe Spirit!	1
Bird thou never wert,	2
That from heaven, or near it,	1
Pourest thy full heart	2
In profuse strains of unpremeditated art.	2

To a Skylark, by Percy Bysshe Shelley.

Notice how the indentation centers the briefer lines, as well as indicating, in the first four, rhyming mates. The number of feet here is 3, 3, 3, 3, 6. A terminal six-foot iambic line is called an *Alexandrine;* this was constantly used with iambic five-foot lines as a terminal.

Shelley uses this pattern throughout his poem *To a Skylark.* Poe, another master craftsman, altered his rhyme and metre pattern from stanza to stanza in his greatest lyrics. The familiar love song *To Helen* ("Helen, thy beauty is to me——") has, in his three cinquains or five-line stanzas, these three different rhyme arrangements: 1, 2, 1, 2, 2; 3, 4, 3, 4, 3; 5, 6, 6, 5, 6. To his inner musical ear, these changes were more musical than regularity could have been.

A six-line stanza is called a sextet or sestet. Here is an example:

Fear no more the heat o' the sun	1
Nor the furious winter's rages;	2
Thou thy worldly task hast done,	1
Home art gone and ta'en thy wages:	2
Golden lads and girls all must,	3
As chimney-sweepers, come to dust.	3

Dirge from *Cymbeline,* William Shakespeare.

The trochaic pattern here is four-foot lines. One of the favorite stanzas of Robert Burns has the iambic pattern of 4, 4, 4, 2, 4, 2; as in his *To a Field-Mouse:*

Wee, sleekit, cow'rin', tim'rous beastie,	1
O what a panic's in thy breastie!	1
Thou need na start awa sae hasty,	1
Wi' bickering brattle!	2
I wad be laith to rin and chase thee	1
Wi' murd'ring pattle!	2

To a Field-Mouse, Robert Burns.

The consonance, *beastie, breastie, hasty, chase thee* was to be expected, in the hands of a master. A popular pattern (using an unusual trochaic 4, 4, 2, 4, 4, 2 measure) was used by Whittier:

And if I should live to be	1
The last leaf upon the tree	1
In the spring,	2
Let them laugh, as I do now,	3
At the old, forsaken bough	3
Where I cling.	2

The Last Leaf, Oliver Wendell Holmes.

This may be used in longer stanzas, with a scheme such as 1, 1, 1, 2, 3, 3, 3, 2, a variant of this being popularized by Tennyson:

Willows whiten, aspens quiver,	1
Little breezes dusk and shiver	1
Through the wave that runs for ever	1
By the island in the river	1
Flowing down to Camelot.	2
Four gray walls, and four gray towers,	3
Overlook a space of flowers,	3
And the silent isle embowers	3
The Lady of Shalott.	2

The Lady of Shalott, by Alfred Tennyson.

This stanza is called *tail rhyme* stanza, and is a mere elaboration of the pattern of *The Last Leaf*.

Certain Other Stanzas

It may seem like profanation to some, to subject to the critical scalpel such a masterpiece as Keats's *Ode to a Grecian Urn*. But the poem suffers no loss from the process, for the reader returns to it to find it all uninjured in the end; and no other method will permit an understanding of the technical achievement involved in such lasting beauty. Here are five ten-line stanzas. Each opens with a 1, 2, 1, 2 sequence. Thereafter, there are differences. The first and last have the next six lines 3, 4, 5, 4, 3, 5; the fourth and fifth use instead 3, 4, 5, 3, 4, 5; while the second has 3, 4, 5, 3, 5, 4.

A famous seven-lined stanza is called *Rhyme Royal*. This was used by James I of Scotland in his *The Kinges Quhair,* and repeatedly by Chaucer and others. Here is a typical use by Chaucer:

To you, my purse, and to none other wight	1
Complain I, for ye be my lady dear.	2
I am full sorry, now that ye be light,	1
For, certes, ye now make me heavy cheer.	2
Me were as lief-y laid upon my bier	2
For which unto your mercy thus I cry,	3
Be heavy again, or elles mote I die.	3

The Complaint to His Empty Purse, Geoffrey Chaucer.

This has a terminal couplet rhyming, 3, 3, which breaks the flow of the narrative somewhat. To avoid this, the *Canopus* stanza points a way out:

The night's mysterious wings pulsed thru the dark,	1
The night's mysterious noises cracked and shivered,	2
And where their fingers met a visible spark	1
Seemed to leap forth at them, and pulsed and quivered	2
Throughout them both. Their thickened tongues were dumb,	3
The pretty words of star-lore undelivered,	2
The pretty words that found no breath would come.	3

Canopus, Clement Wood.

Note here also that the use of some feminine or double rhymes with single or masculine rhymes is effective. This is especially effective in a Shakespearean sonnet.

Ottava Rima is an Italian stanza adopted in English by many poets. It is an eight-line stanza, composed of a sestet rhymed alternately, followed by a terminal rhyming couplet. The Italians use their heroic metre, eleven syllables to the line, in it; the English prefer iambic five-foot measure. Spenser, Milton, and Keats used it, and Byron preferred it, as in his *Don Juan:*

But " why then publish?"—There are no rewards	1
Of fame or profit when the world grows weary.	2
I ask in turn,—Why do you play at cards?	1
Why drink? Why read?—To make some hour less dreary.	2
It occupies me to turn back regards	1
On what I've seen or pondered, sad or cheery;	2
And what I write I cast upon the stream	3
To sink or swim—I have had at least my dream.	3

Don Juan, Lord Byron.

Again note the use of double and single rhymes in the same stanza, quite often effective.

The *Spenserian Stanza* was invented by Edmund Spenser, and has long been used in serious dignified verse. The eight opening five-foot iambic lines are terminated by an Alexandrine, or six-foot iambic line; the pattern may be seen in this opening of Keats's poem, which uses the stanza throughout:

> St. Agnes' Eve—ah, bitter chill it was !   1
>   The owl, for all his feathers, was acold.   2
> The hare limped trembling through the frozen grass,   1
>   And silent was the flock in woolly fold.   2
>   Numb were the Beadsman's fingers while he told   2
> His rosary, and while his frosted breath   3
>   Like pious incense from a censer old,   2
> Seemed taking flight for heaven without a death,   3
> Past the sweet Virgin's picture, while his prayer he saith.   3
>
>   *The Eve of St. Agnes,* John Keats.

Terza Rima is an iambic rhythm, usually of five feet to the line. It is usually written continuously, and not in stanzas. It consists of groups of three lines, rhymed 1, 2, 1; but the rhyming sound of the middle line, 2, becomes the first and third line of the next group; and so on. The end of the canto or poem is a couplet, tieing up the rhyme sound left loose as the central line terminal sound in the preceding triplet. Thus it is a sort of chain verse, its rhyme scheme proceeding: 1, 2, 1; 2, 3, 2; 3, 4, 3; 4, 5, 4; ...... n-1, n, n-1; n, n. Shelley, in his *Ode to the West Wind,* used this in fourteen line groups, separating the triplets and concluding couplet as if they were separate stanzas.

It is advisable for the poet or versifier to spend some time in the pleasant chore of analyzing the favorite poems of the great poets—the odes of Keats, the sonnets of Shakespeare, the greater lyrics of Poe, and so on. Scansion will indicate the metre employed; and the numeral system 1, 1, 2, 2 will mark for you the rhyming pattern. Let your especial attention be directed to ingenious devices for securing variety within a formal pattern.

The sonnet, which will be reached in the study of lyric poetry, has been used often and successfully as a stanza.

In polyrhythmic or free verse, the stanza division follows the poet's inner mandate of where each group of lines should end, as if it were a paragraph in prose.

Sapphics and Other Classic Forms

Elegiac verse, according to the classical models, consists of lines alternately dactylic hexameter and dactylic pentameter; and then this difference is explained away by saying that the shorter lines have six accents, but omit the unaccented syllables in the third and sixth feet. Coleridge indicates the method:

> In the hexameter rises the fountain's all-silvery radiance;
> In the pentameter aye falling in melody back.
> *Translation from Schiller,* Samuel Taylor Coleridge.

It is significant that none of the five greatest examples of elegiac poetry—that based upon death, or reflections upon death—in the English language, use this form. These five poems are Milton's *Lycidas,* Shelley's *Adonais,* Tennyson's *In Memoriam,* Gray's famous elegy, and Whitman's *When Lilacs Last in the Dooryards Bloomed,* a tribute to Lincoln.

The Greek *dactylic hexameter,* the classic model as the iambic five-foot line is in English, is far more complicated, according to the prosodists, than it sounds. There are six feet. The first four are dactyls or spondees. The fifth must be a dactyl: otherwise, if a spondee appears here, the verse is called spondaic. The last is a spondee or a trochee. A diagram makes this clearer.

This may be written in English, with an accent basis instead of a quantity basis (that is, long and short syllables).

Hendecasyllabics were 11-syllabled lines composed of a spondee, a dactyl, and trochees. Thus:

This metre has never been successfully naturalized into English.

Alcaics, named from the lyric poet Alcaeus, a contemporary of Sappho, are of several kinds. The first variety has a five-foot line, consisting of a spondee or iamb, an iamb, a long syllable, and two dactyls. Here is the pattern:

or | ⏑ / | / | / | / ⏑ ⏑ | / ⏑ ⏑

The second variety has two dactyls and two trochees to the line:

/ ⏑ ⏑ | / ⏑ ⏑ | / ⏑ | / ⏑

And, for the third, the line is composed:

| (I)   ⏑ / / / |
| or |
| (II) / ⏑ / / |
| or |
| (III) / / ⏑ / |
| or |
| (IV) / / / ⏑ |

	/ ⏑ ⏑ /	/ ⏑ ⏑ /	⏑ / /
	(stress on	(stress on	(Stress on first
	1st or 4th	1st or 4th	long syllable)
	syllable)	syllable)	

What are the names of these feet? The first is an epitrite (first, second, third, or fourth epitrite, depending upon the location of the short syllable) ; two choriambi or choriambs as above; and a bacchius. This technique does not often produce poetry in English; more often, it produces prosody or verse.

For an *Alcaic ode,* each strophe consists of four lines. The first two are eleven-syllabled Alcaics of the first kind; the third an especial form of iambic two-foot of nine syllables, described as hypercatalectic; and the fourth a ten-syllabled Alcaic of the second kind. Tennyson tried to catch it in:

O mighty-mouthed inventor of harmonies,
O skilled to sing of time or eternity,
God-gifted organ-voice of England,
Milton, a name to resound for ages.
              Milton, Alfred Tennyson.

Sapphics are named after the poet Sappho, who is said to have used the form with high skill. A sapphic line consists of five equal beats, its central one of three syllables, and the rest of two each. The original Greek sapphic stanza consisted of three of these lines, followed by a shorter line called an *adonic,* the whole following this pattern:

| / ⏑ | or / / / ⏑ | / ⏑ ⏑ | / ⏑ | or / / / ⏑ |
| / ⏑ | or / / / ⏑ | / ⏑ ⏑ | / ⏑ | or / / / ⏑ |

Certain English poets have essayed this metre. In the examples given, the accent sign (´) means a syllable described as long; the other symbol (˘) one described as short. Here is Swinburne's use of the form:

Saw the | white im- | placable | Aphro- | dite,
Saw the | hair un- | bound and the | feet un- | sandalled
Shine as | fire of | sunset on | western | waters;
    Saw the re- | luctant

Feet, the straining plumes of the doves that drew her,
Looking, always looking with necks reverted,
  Back to Lesbos, back to the hills whereunder
      Shone Mitylene;
              Sapphics, Algernon Charles Swinburne.

and so on to the end. A *choriambic line* consists of a spondee, three choriambi, and an iamb. A *galliambic line* is composed of iambs, one of which drops its final syllable: the next foot to the last being an anapest.

Indentation

The purpose of indentation is primarily to indicate the rhyme scheme. Indenting a line means sinking it inward by an increased blank space in the left hand margin. Every paragraph in prose is indented, at its beginning. An early indentation of poetry was similar to this, and consisted in indenting only the first line of each stanza. Where the poet desires to impress the reader with his rhyme scheme, indenting of lines similarly rhymed is proper:

              Yet this inconstancy is such
                As you too shall adore:
              I could not love thee, Dear, so much,
                Loved I not Honour more.
      To Lucasta, on Going to the Wars, Richard Lovelace.

The following indentation is improper and essentially illiterate:

> That which her slender waist confined
> Shall now my joyful temples bind:
> No monarch but would give his crown
> His arms might do what this has done.
>   *On a Girdle,* Edmund Waller.

Needless to say, the poet set this up without indentation. The motive for such misindentation seems to be the following foggy thinking on the part of the versifier:

(a) Some poems by great poets are indented.
(b) Therefore I must indent my poem, to make sure it is regarded as great.

Once let the motive for indentation be learned—to show the similarity of rhyme-sounds terminating lines indented to the same point—and this error will be avoided.

A second purpose of indentation is to center short lines in the central portion of the poem, instead of leaving them dangling off to the left. One of Guy Wetmore Carryll's eight verse poems proceeds:

> A maiden from the Bosphorus,
> With eyes as bright as phosphorus,
> Once wed the wealthy bailiff
> Of the caliph
> Of Kelat.
> Though diligent and zealous, he
> Became a slave to jealousy.
> (Considering her beauty,
> 'Twas his duty
> To be that!)
> *How the Helpmate of Bluebeard Made Free with a Door,*
>   Guy Wetmore.

Here the first, third, fourth, and sixth indentations indicate rhyming changes; the second and fifth are to center briefer rhyming lines. The object is to make the poem appear as presentable as possible, considering rhyme scheme and length of line. Recall the indentation of Shelley's *To a Skylark,* already given.

As to sonnets, there are only two proper ways to present them: indenting for rhyme, and omitting indentation. The Italian and

Shakespearean form would then have the following indentation, if this is used to indicate the rhyme scheme:

Italian Sonnet	Shakespearean Sonnet
1	1
2	2
2	1
1	2
1	3
2	4
2	3
1	4
3	5
4	6
5	5
3	6
4	7
5	7

It is more usual to set up sonnets without indentation. The original method of indenting the Shakespearean sonnet consisted of twelve lines without indentation, and an indentation for the concluding couplet.

All this assumes that the poet wishes to impress on the reader the rhyming scheme, and the poet's fidelity in following it. But this is initiating the reader into the irrelevant laboratory work of the poet, and has its many disadvantages, since the reader primarily wishes to know what the poet has to say,—not the devices by which he increases his effectiveness. The modern tendency is to eliminate indentation in all poems. If poems are printed similar to prose, the indentation will be the same as prose, to indicate paragraph openings, or to inset a quotation.

V

DIVISIONS OF POETRY

Narrative Poetry

POETRY is commonly divided, from the point of view of the poet's presentation of his material, into narrative, dramatic, and lyric poetry. The distinction is simple:

> In *narrative poetry,* the poet tells a story as if he had been a spectator, but not a participant, in the events.
>
> In *dramatic poetry,* the poet lets the characters of the story speak their own words.
>
> In *lyric poetry,* the poet speaks his own moods, thoughts and aspirations.

These, like all definitions, define from the centers, not from the boundaries. A long-winded narrative in the first person, telling the poet's own adventures, might be classed with reason as any of the three: narrative poetry because it tells a story; dramatic, like a long dramatic monologue; and lyric, because the poet himself is speaking. This attitude classification is not of primary importance.

A fourth division, *didactic poetry,* that which teaches or points a moral, was once popular and is still encountered. It is regarded at best as a low flight of poetry.

Epic, Metrical Romance, Tale

An epic is——

> a long narrative poem, dealing with heroic events, usually with supernatural guidance and participation in the action.

Epics are divided into natural or folk epics, and literary epics. There is a suggested theory that folk epics are preceded by and composed of folk ballads. The earliest known epics exhibit little or no trace of any welding or amalgamating process.

The earliest literary remains in Greece are of the epic type, of three varieties. Epics of personal romance and war center around

the semi-mythical blind bard Homer, with his *Iliad*—the story of
the flight of Helen of Sparta with her Trojan lover, Paris; the
war of Greeks against Trojans to avenge this; the anger of Greek
Achilles and its effects; the defeat of Troy—and the *Odyssey*,
telling the world-wanderings of Grecian Odysseus after the sack
of Troy, and of his return to his native Ithaca. Parts of these long
poems are essentially prosy; but they have never been equalled
for long poetic flight in narrative form. Epics dealing with the
mysteries of religion center around the mythical singer Orpheus.
Epics of a didactic nature center around the name of Hesiod.
Scholars state that many lost epics in all three fields preceded the
epics now remaining.

The *Mahabharata* and the *Ramayana* in Sanskrit, the *Shah-
nameh* in Persian, the *Niebelungenlied* in Middle German, *Beo-
wulf* in Anglo-Saxon, the fragmentary *Elder Edda* from Iceland,
the *Poem of the Cid* from Spain, the *Song of Roland* in medieval
France, the *Kalevala* from Finland, are all folk epics. They
originated before the invention of writing, and were transmitted
orally, with inevitable changes and additions from time to time.
Literary epics are a later attempt to catch the charm of the ancient
epics; and as a rule they are a lower flight. Virgil's *Æneid*, Tasso's
Jerusalem Delivered, Ariosto's *Orlando Furioso*, Dante's didactic
Commedia, are the most outstanding among these. The *Lusiads*
of Camoens gave form to the Portuguese language, much as
Dante did to modern Italian, Chaucer to English, and Luther to
German. Spenser's *Faerie Queene* has lost most of its charm for
many modern English readers; even Milton's *Paradise Lost*,
which sought to express English Puritanism as Dante had sought
to express medieval Catholicism, is largely dull to modern readers.

Stories in verse preceded stories in prose. Chaucer's *Canterbury
Tales*, the narrative metrical romances and tales of Scott, Byron,
and others, preceded the novel and the short story in English. But
prose has become the popular medium, as it is the more natural
one: and the long poetic narrative today usually seems artificial.

The Ballad

The ballad, the brief story in verse, alone retains some general
popularity. The name meant first a folk song-and-dance, like the

surviving *London Bridge Is Falling Down* or *Oats, Peas, Beans and Barley Grow*. It came to mean the folksong that tells a brief story—at first to be sung, later to be said or read. The Germanic bards or scalds, the gleemen, harpers, minstrels, troubadours, minnesingers, were a distinguished lot—the oral literature (and music) of races in the pre-bookish age. The chief figures in the ballads at first were noble, since nobles were the patrons of the singers. Later on, the lower classes became vocal—the oppressed Saxons in the Robin Hood ballads, and many early ballads in which a commoner ends by marrying one of noble lineage. The technique at first was simple, often with a simple refrain that the hearers might chorus. In English, the first *ballad metre* was seven-foot iambic lines, rhymed in couplets. A variant of this is the Scottish ballad *Edward, Edward,* with a pause between the invoked names taking the place of a foot in alternate lines:

"Quhy does zour brand sae drop wi' bluid, Edward, Edward?
  Quhy does zour brand sae drop wi' bluid, and quhy sae sad
                                      gang zee, O?"
"O, I hae kill-ed my hauke sae guid, Mither, Mither,
  O, I hae kill-ed my hauke sae guid; and I had nae mair but he, O."

Like the majority of the older ballads, this is a gory thing, full of blood and stark universal passions. If modern poetry gave us more of such red meat instead of caviar canapes, it would hold a wider popularity than it now has.

The rhythm is much freer than centuries of later iambic versification. The modern versifier can learn much of the way to sprinkle anapests in an iambic pattern, and of more important devices in versification, from old English folk ballads, as from that other depository of English folk verse, *Mother Goose*. Folk ballads originate among people largely pre-bookish; certain American mountaineers and certain Negroes still commemorate thrilling events with folk ballads, like the one within our memory on *The Sinking of the Titanic*.

Literary ballads are more successful than literary epics. Ballads by Heine and Housman, Coleridge's *Rime of the Ancient Mariner,* have been taken to the heart of the race. The stanza form is almost invariably simple. Yet it is worth while to study the slight elaborations of the ballad metre that Coleridge employed—with stanzas ranging from four to nine ballad half-lines. There are many more successful literary ballads.

Dramatic Poetry

Like story-telling, drama is largely a lost field to poetry, purely because of the unnaturalness of poetic drama as usually written. There is a field for drama in natural free verse, which may yet be widely used. Classic drama was divided into *tragedy,* a play ending in death, and *comedy,* a play not ending in death. This division was unworkable, and has been abandoned today.

Thespis, reputed father of Grecian drama, never permitted more than one actor on the stage at one time, with a chorus to interpret the action to the audience. This rigid convention was shattered by Aeschylus, who added a second actor. Sophocles added a third; but classic Greek drama never permitted a fourth. The typical Shakespearean play had five acts, the climax occurring during the third act, the solution at the end. This usually meant a dragging fourth act, which only *Othello* among the great tragedies avoided. Shakespeare and most other English verse dramatists used a five-foot iambic line, most often in blank or unrhymed verse. None of these conventions are more sacred than the one actor convention of Thespis.

The *dramatic monolog* or *dramatic lyric,* sprung from the speeches of Thespis's actor and the unnatural soliloquy of classic and English drama, is the one form of drama in verse which preserves considerable popularity. Robert Browning made this field peculiarly his own, with such magnificent dramatic vignettes as *My Last Duchess, Andrea del Sarto, Caliban upon Setebos,* and so many more. His tremendous *The Ring and the Book* is, within a brief framework, ten immense dramatic monologs: the same group of facts, as seen through the eyes of ten differing personalities. Such dramatic monologs may be in any rhythm, any line length, and with or without rhyme. Success comes in proportion to the naturalness of the speech, the universality and depth of the emotion displayed, and the accuracy in character-drawing.

Lyric Poetry: Ode, Elegy, Pastoral

Perhaps the earliest, and certainly the most enduringly popular type of poetry, is the lyric. As the name indicates, it meant originally poetry to be sung to the lyre,—a dance at first accompanying this.

The *ode,* the most exalted form of lyric poetry, had strict rules in classic times. The Greek Pindaric ode had three movements: a strophe, in which the chorus moved from a given spot toward the right; the antistrophe, following the same versification pattern, and to the same tune, in which the chorus moved correspondingly to the left; and the concluding epode, different in structure, sung to a different tune, and with the chorus standing still. Efforts to revive this form in English have not succeeded. In English, the ode is a dignified lyric on some high theme, with constant progress in its stanzas toward its conclusion. Familiar odes in English include Wordsworth's:

> Our birth is but a sleep and a forgetting;
> The Soul that rises with us, our life's Star,
>> Hath elsewhere its setting
>> And cometh from afar;
> Not in entire forgetfulness,
> And not in utter nakedness,
> But trailing clouds of glory do we come
> From God, who is our home.
> Heaven lies about us in our infancy!
>> *Ode on the Intimations of Immortality from*
>> *Recollections of Early Childhood,*
>>> William Wordsworth.

and also the great odes by Shelley and Keats already referred to.

An *elegy* is a formal expression of the poet's grief at death, whether general or centered about the death of an individual. It has no more definite a pattern in English than the ode. Milton, in *Lycidas,* uses an iambic measure, with lines of differing lengths, and a fluidic rhyme scheme. Shelley, in *Adonais,* chose the Spenserian stanza. Tennyson, in *In Memoriam,* selected the quatrain pattern already encountered. Whitman, in his major Lincoln threnody, *When Lilacs Last in the Dooryard Bloomed,* wrote in magnificent polyrhythmic verse. Gray's familiar *Elegy Written in a*

Country Churchyard, alone among these a meditation upon death in general, used alternate-rhymed five-foot iambic lines. There are many familiar short elegies in the language.

The *pastoral* is a reflective lyric upon some aspect of nature, formerly concerned with shepherd life, whence its name. Milton's shapely *L'Allegro* and *Il Penseroso,* and Whittier's *Snowbound,* are examples in this genre. As city living increasingly replaces country living, some form of city lyric may supplant the pastoral, if it does not die without offspring.

The Simple Lyric: The Song

The word *song* is loosely used for any simple lyric, on the theory that it may always be set to music. It is best to reserve the word for a lyric intended to be set to music. This calls for a knowledge, on the part of the poet, of the human voice in music, and the ease or difficulty with which the various sounds are produced. Certain consonants and combinations of consonants are sinagable only with great difficulty. A line like:

The gross-sized much-touched scratch will itch

is not easily singable. The terminal consonants *m, n, l, r* are sung with ease; *s, z, ch, sh,* as terminals, with difficulty. Of the vowels, broad *a,* long *o,* long *a, ou,* are easiest to sing, though no vowel is really difficult. The words chosen should always end, and as far as possible include, only sounds which open the mouth, instead of closing it. Simple words are to be preferred to complicated ones; definite precise words to indefinite abstract ones; emotion-evoking words to intellectualized ones.

The lyric canon in English is one of the glories of its literature. After the dawn-hour lyrics before the Elizabethan age, the golden song of Campion—

> Shall I come, sweet Love, to thee,
> When the evening beams are set?
> Shall I not excluded be,
> Will you find no feigned let?
> Let me not, for pity, more
> Tell the long hours at your door;
> *Shall I Come, Sweet Love?* Thomas Campion.

the equally melodious singable lyrics of Shakespeare and his con-
temporaries, the lyrics of Shelley, Keats, Byron, Burns, Housman,
and so many more in England, and of Poe, Emily Dickinson,
Sidney Lanier, and a few later singers, together make up a body
of song that the race continues to treasure.

The themes and treatments of the lyric may vary as widely as
the desires and visions of the poets. A lyric may have any chosen
form of rhythm, with or without rhyme. It is often natural and
effective in free verse or polyrhythmic poetry, since in this form
the precise emotion-moving thoughts and images may be written
down, without the warping often demanded by such devices of
versification as rhyme, assonance, consonance, and formal metre
and stanza arrangement. Here is an example from the chief American user of the form, in a lyric called *Reconciliation:*

> Word over all, beautiful as the sky,
> Beautiful that war and all its deeds of carnage must
>   in time be utterly lost,
> That the hands of the sisters Death and Night
>   incessantly softly wash again, and ever again,
>   this soil'd world;
> For my enemy is dead, a man divine as myself is dead,
> I look where he lies white-faced and still in the
>   coffin—I draw near,
> Bend down and touch lightly with my lips the white
>   face in the coffin.
>   *Reconciliation,* Walt Whitman.

Modern users of polyrhythmic poetry as a rule use less eloquence
than Whitman, and less of the expansive cosmic note; and tend
instead toward the tense and gripping emotional appeal usual in
rhymed and metric lyrics. Much shorter line-division is also common.

The Sonnet

The sonnet is the most popular fixed form in English. It is a
lyric of fourteen iambic five-foot lines, with a defined and definite
rhyme scheme. There are two forms of it widely used in English,
the Italian or Petrarchian sonnet, and the Shakespearean sonnet.

The rhyme-scheme of the Italian sonnet appears from the
following example:

The world is too much with us; late and soon,	1
Getting and spending, we lay waste our powers:	2
Little we see in Nature that is ours;	2
We have given our hearts away, a sordid boon!	1
This sea that bares her bosom to the moon,	1
The winds that will be howling at all hours,	2
And are up-gathered now like sleeping flowers;	2
For this, for everything, we are out of tune;	1
It moves us not.—Great God! I'd rather be	3
A Pagan suckled in a creed outworn;	4
So might I, standing on this pleasant lea,	3
Have glimpses that would make me less forlorn;	4
Have sight of Proteus rising from the sea;	3
Or hear old Triton blow his wreathéd horn.	4

Sonnet, William Wordsworth.

The first eight lines of any sonnet are called the *octave*. In the Italian sonnet, the rhyme-scheme is rigid, and may not be departed from. The octave consists of two quatrains rhymed 1, 2, 2, 1, the *In Memoriam* rhyming pattern made familiar by Tennyson's use of it. The entire octave then rhymes 1, 2, 2, 1; 1, 2, 2, 1. It is not permitted to vary the rhymes in the second half of the octave, by using 1, 2, 2, 1; 3, 2, 2, 3, or a form too commonly encountered, 1, 2, 2, 1; 3, 4, 4, 3.

The concluding six lines of any sonnet are called the sestet. The two permissible rhyme-schemes for the sestet of an Italian sonnet are 3, 4, 3, 4, 3, 4, and 3, 4, 5, 3, 4, 5. It will be noted that the sonnet by Wordsworth, quoted above, uses the proper octave rhyme-scheme and the first of these two sestet arrangements.

As to treatment, the octave must be end-stopped—that is, the eighth line must mark the termination of a sentence. Even the halves of the octave should be end-stopped. The first quatrain should introduce the theme, and develop it in a certain direction; the second should continue this development in the same direction. The sestet introduces a new development in a different direction, with the first tercet carrying this new direction to a definite point; and the final tercet bringing the theme to a conclusion. The actual movement of the strict Italian sonnet may be expressed as a flow in the octave, and an ebb in the sestet—so Theodore Watts-

Dunton phrased it in his sonnet, *The Sonnet's Voice*. This does not mean, of course, that the inspiration or the emotional effect should ebb.

Wordsworth's sonnet, emotionally effective as it is, violates several of these strict rules. The octave movement does not end with the eighth line, but trespasses into the ninth. There is no break in thought between the two tercets that together comprise the sestet. We will find constantly among the masters violations of the rules, at times in the nature of experiments; none of these has as yet established its popularity in English poetry. In his sonnet *On the Extinction of the Venetian Republic,* Wordsworth's octave rhymes 1, 2, 2, 1; 1, 3, 3, 1,—another variation.

One authority examined 6,283 Italian sonnets In English, and found these variations for the terminal sestet rhymes:

3, 4, 5, 3, 4, 5	3, 3, 4, 5, 5, 4
3, 4, 3, 4, 5, 5	3, 4, 5, 5, 3, 4
3, 4, 4, 3, 5, 5	3, 4, 5, 5, 4, 3
3, 4, 5, 4, 3, 5	3, 4, 4, 5, 3, 5
3, 4, 3, 5, 4, 5	3, 4, 5, 4, 5, 3
3, 4, 5, 3, 5, 4	3, 4, 3, 5, 5, 4

Two of these have terminal couplets, the most regrettable variation of the Italian sonnet. Six others include a couplet somewhere within the sestet. In addition to the above, the following two-rhyme variants are found:

3, 4, 3, 4, 3, 4	3, 4, 3, 4, 4, 3
3, 4, 4, 3, 3, 4	3, 4, 3, 3, 4, 4
3, 4, 4, 3, 4, 3	3, 4, 3, 3, 4, 3

Only the first excludes any couplet rhyming. Shelley's poem *Ozymandias* had the rhyme scheme: 1, 2, 1, 2; 1, 3, 4, 3; 5, 4, 5, 6, 5, 6. Milton led the way in failing to separate clearly the octave and sestet, so much so that his type of sonnet is sometimes called the Miltonic—Italian in rhyme-pattern, but without the characteristic Italian flow and ebb of theme, broken after the eighth line.

The Shakespearean sonnet is simpler and more natural in rhyming, and is in wider favor among English-using poets. An example is:

When, in disgrace with fortune and men's eyes,	1
I all alone beweep my outcast state,	2
And trouble deaf heaven with my bootless cries,	1
And look upon myself and curse my fate,	2
Wishing me like to one more rich in hope,	3
Featur'd like him, like him with friends possess'd,	4
Desiring this man's art and that man's scope,	3
With what I most enjoy contented least;	4
Yet in these thoughts myself almost despising,	5
Haply I think on thee, and then my state,	6
Like to the lark at break of day arising	5
From sullen earth, sings hymns at heaven's gate;	6
For thy sweet love remember'd such wealth brings	7
That then I scorn to change my state with kings.	7

Sonnet XXIX, William Shakespeare.

This is the accepted Shakespearean indentation for this form: though it may be indented to show rhyming mates, as the Italian also may be. Both types of the sonnet at times are printed with octave and sestet separated, making a poem of two stanzas; or octave divided into two quatrains, and at times the sestet similarly divided.

The rhyming scheme of the Shakespearean sonnet is three quatrains, 1, 2, 1, 2; 3, 4, 3, 4; 5, 6, 5, 6; with a concluding couplet, 7, 7. A shrewd interspering of double or feminine rhymes aids. Many variations have been tried on this simple rhyming basis. Sir Philip Sidney repeated the rhymes of the first quatrain in the second, giving him a pattern of 1, 2, 1, 2; 1, 2, 1, 2; 3, 4, 3, 4; 5, 5. Spenser, in his hundred and twenty sonnets, used a chain-verse device of interlocking rhymes throughout each sonnet, so that his pattern was: 1, 2, 1, 2,; 2, 3, 2, 3; 3, 4, 3, 4; 5, 5. Keats, in his second sonnet on *Fame,* wedded the Shakespearean octave to the Italian sestet, with his rhyme scheme 1, 2, 1, 2; 3, 4, 3, 4; 5, 6, 5, 7, 7, 6. Rupert Brooke, in the first and fifth of his soldier sonnets, used the Shakespearean octave, and a straight Italian sestet: 5, 6, 7, 5, 6, 7. The third and fourth of the same series also wander from any strict pattern.

The sonnet was invented in Italy in the 13th century, probably by Pier delle Vigne, secretary of state in the Sicilian court of Frederick. His sonnet *Però ch' amore* is the earliest known. His rhyme form, 1, 2, 1, 2; 1, 2, 1, 2; 3, 4, 5, 3, 4, 5, has never become popular in English. The French sonnet prefers the strict Italian octave, with a sestet of three rhymes commencing with a couplet. This also has not become naturalized in English. There are occasional variations in English poetry, such as 1, 2, 1, 2; 2, 1, 2, 1; 3, 4, 3, 4, 5, 5; Italian sonnets with sestet 3, 4, 3, 4, 5, 5; and so on. Watts-Dunton points out, in his article on the sonnet in the 11th edition of *The Encyclopedia Brittanica,* that the charm of this and other fixed forms comes from familiarity in advance with the rhyme-scheme to be followed; and that this charm is dissipated, when any break in the expected rhyme-scheme occurs. We feel somewhat as if we listened to a limerick with an extra foot or an extra line: a sense of surprise, its pleasure being doubtful. In spite of this, poets continue to vary the rigid forms from time to time, and will continue to do so.

The sonnet, of either form, is used by many poets as a fourteen-line stanza. Many of the Elizabethan sonnet sequences illustrate this; and there are many more recent examples. In writing the sonnet, it will aid to write down the rhyme scheme to the right of the space where your lines are to be written, and thereafter to mark across from each numbered rhyme the initial consonantal sounds used: giving a check against repeating a rhyming sound (that is, identity), which is inexcusable false rhyming. We would then have a notebook page like:

Rhyme Sounds

		ŌLD	ĔN	IZ	ĔN
Much have I travell'd in the realms of gold	1	G			
And many goodly states and kingdoms seen;	2		S		
Round many western islands have I been	2		B		
Which bards in fealty to Apollo hold.	1	H			
Oft of one wide expanse had I been told	1	T			
That deep-browed Homer ruled as his demesne:	2		M		
Yet never did I breathe its pure serene	2		R		
Till I heard Chapman speak out loud and bold.	1	B			
—Then felt I like some watcher of the skies	3			SK	
When a new planet swims into his ken;	4				K
Or like stout Cortez—when with eagle eyes	3			Vowel	
He stared at the Pacific—and all his men	4				M
Look'd at each other with a wild surmise—	3			M	
Silent, upon a peak in Darien.	4				Vowel

On First Looking into Chapman's Homer, John Keats.

Thus, by this check, it appears that the poet used, for rhyme 1, ŌLD, these consonantal sounds: g, h, t, b; for rhyme 2, ĔN, s, b, m, r; for rhyme 3, ĪZ, sk, the unconsonanted vowel sound, and m; for rhyme 4, ĔN, k, m, and the unconsonanted vowel sound. No identities; rhyme throughout. The sonnet, from a technical rhyming standpoint, has no flaws. When this method is followed during the writing of the sonnet—the first group of columns, that containing the numerals, properly indented, being written down first—this gives a check as the writing of the sonnet proceeds, and saves much rewriting.

VI

THE FRENCH FORMS. LIGHT AND
HUMOROUS VERSE

Into Formal and Light Verse

ANY poetic form may be used either to arouse the great serious emotions, or the lighter and more frivolous ones. Nor is there any reason for holding the serious poet higher than the comic poet. Surely Aristophanes, the great Athenian comic dramatist, ranked as high, and was doubtless more popular and influential, than any of the great serious triad, Aeschylus, Sophocles and Euripides. Shakespeare the comic dramatist, the author of *Merry Wives of Windsor, Midsummer Night's Dream, The Taming of the Shrew,* is as impressive a figure as the Shakespeare who let the melancholy Dane live and die in Elsinore, the Shakespeare who was the chronicler of Othello's jealousy and Lear's senility. Cervantes, who jeered knighthood to death, is greater as a writer than any other Spaniard; Racine, Moliere, Voltaire, Anatole France, were greatest as satirists; and so the roll continues. Serious writers and poets are more popular, and are taken more seriously; but this may be because it is more civilized and difficult to laugh than to weep. Animals can suffer agonies; but they cannot chuckle. And yet the race would not willingly exchange Robert Burn's *Tam o' Shanter* and W. S. Gilbert's *The Bab Ballads* for any number of closet dramas, ponderous versified essays and odes, or a whole trainload of lyrics to spring and young love.

Fixed forms of poetry tend to become outgrown, like a child's shirt too small to close over a man's heart. They then become relegated to minor versifiers, to light verse writers, and to college and high school exercises. Prose ages more quickly than poetry: witness such masterpieces, written for adults, as the world's great fairy stories, Aesop's fables, the *Arabian Nights, Robinson Crusoe, Gulliver's Travels* in the nursery; and the essays and novels of yesterday encountered in school or college. Poetry itself ages:

Shakespeare, Milton, Virgil, Horace, are more used in the class-room than in the living room today, and so of the rest of them. In spite of constant insistence that nothing changes under the sun, the nature of man is stretched outward by his expanding environment, and coiled more tensely into molecules and atoms and complexes and other inner things: and the poetry, the concentrated heart's expression, of yesterday cannot forever be the poetry of today. Prose, in the large, must be rephrased every fifty years, or less, to be enjoyable to living men; poetry survives longer, but the hour will come when the most enduring poem of a Shakespeare or a Sappho will seem ancient, and must be restated or recreated by a living poet, to speak again for the maturing soul of man. If this is true of the poetry itself, it is truer of the patterns in which poetry has been uttered, and especially of the fixed forms.

The sonnet, an emigrant from Italy that became naturalized in English literature, still holds its own as a major method of expressing serious poetry, in the eyes of many poets and readers. Even at that, it is now regarded as puerile by the extreme advocates of free verse or polyrhythmic poetry, especially since Whitman and the Imagist movement. Numerous other alien verse forms did not fare so well, and have established themselves primarily as mediums for light and humorous verse. These include the ballade, the rondeau, the villanelle, the triolet, and so on. This may be because of their rigid rules and formal repetitions, which were not acceptable to the living poet. And yet, they started as seriously as Sapphics, heroic blank verse, or polyrhythms. . . .

Of all the forms of verse originating in medieval Provence, among those that failed to acclimatize themselves in English are the *vers, canzo, sirvente, tenso, alba, serena, pastorella, breu-doble,* and the *retroensa.* Only the most elaborate of the lot, the intricate *sestina,* has survived in English. When religious crusades wiped out this culture, the germs of formalized verse took root in northern France, especially under Charles d'Orleans and François Villon. The *ballade* appeared. Spenser used 3,848 of his nine-line Spenserian stanzas in one poem: across the Channel, Eustache Deschamps, a friend of Chaucer's, left no less than 1,175 complete ballades. Froissart the chronicler wrote many. Charles d'Orleans is hailed as the early master of the roundel, as Villon is lauded as the prince of ballade-makers. Jean Passerat gave the villanelle its present form, in the sixteenth century; Voiture, a century later, perfected the rondeau. In the seventeenth century, after the forms had been known for two hundred years in English, Patrick Carey published a series of dignified religious triolets; and the over-artificialized forms have repeatedly been revived since.

Rules of the Fixed Verse Forms

In English verse, the rules for the fixed forms are stricter than in French:

I. No syllable once used as a rhyme can be used again in the same poem as a rhyme, not even if it be spelled differently; nor if the whole word is altered by a prefix.

This bars such identities as *Ruth*, a girl's name, and *ruth*, pity; *bear*, an animal, *bear*, to support, *bare*, *forbear*, and so on; *sale* and *sail*; *claim*, *reclaim*, and *disclaim*; *facility*, *imbecility*; and, if this be taken as a single rhyme, not a triple one, it forbids the use of more than one from this group: *tea, manatee, imbecility, impossibility, lenity*, and so on.

As to the *refrain*, an important element in many of these forms:

II. The refrain must not be a meaningless repetition of sounds as in many English ballads; it must aid in the progress of the thought; come in naturally; and be repeated in all its sounds, without any change of sound.

Slipshod versifiers alter the refrain by changing the introductory word, as by using an *and* for a *but*, a *then* for an *if*. This is unforgiveable. But the requirement goes no further than the repetition of all *sounds*. Punctuation may be changed, spelling may be changed, meaning may be changed: permitting the following—

It's meet, this sale; Its meat, this sail.
Gray day; Grade aye; Grade A.

The Ballade Family

There are two standard forms of the *ballade*. The more usual one consists of three stanzas of eight lines each; followed by a concluding quatrain, known as the *envoy*. It is thus a poem of twenty-

eight lines, or twice the length of a sonnet. Each stanza, and the
envoy, terminate with a line repeated sound by sound, and called
the *refrain*. The rhyme scheme is 1, 2, 1, 2, 2, 3, 2, 3R for each
stanza, 3R being the refrain; and 2, 3, 2, 3R for the envoy. The
rules of the ballade may be stated as follows:

I. The same set of rhyme-sounds used in the first stanza, in
the same order, must be used in each stanza; and the last
half of this scheme must be used in the envoy.

II. No rhyme-sound once used as a rhyme may be used again
for that purpose anywhere in the poem.

III. Each stanza and the envoy must close with the refrain
line, repeated without any alteration of sound; though its
punctuation, meaning and spelling may be altered.

IV. The sense of the refrain must be supreme throughout the
ballade, the culminating refrain line being always brought
in without strain or effort as the natural close of the stanza
or envoy.

Formerly, the length of the refrain governed the length of the
stanza. Thus an eight-syllabled refrain dictated an eight-line
stanza, and a ten-syllabled refrain a ten-line stanza. This rule is
followed no longer.

V. The stanza should carry an unbroken sense throughout,
and not be split in meaning into two quatrains, or any other
division. The needful pauses for punctuation are allowed,
but the sense is not to be finished midway of the stanza.

VI. The envoy, as used in ballades and the chant royal, was at
first addressed to the patron of the poet. It is thus usual
to commence it with some such invocation as *Prince!
Princess! Sire!* or by some mythical or symbolic person so
introduced. This is at times omitted. The envoy is properly
both a dedication and a culmination, and should be richer
in wording and meaning and more stately in imagery than
the preceding lines.

Here is a well-wrought ballade, in four-foot iambic verse. The
rhyme-scheme is indicated by the numerals 1, 2, and 3, the refrain
line being designated 3R. To the right appear the checking col-

umns for the three rhyming sounds, to make sure that there are
no repetitions,—unforgivable, in strict formal verse of this type.

		Rhyme Sounds		
		ĀD	Ō	ŌL
Where are the passions they essayed?	1	S		
And where the tears they made to flow?	2		FL	
Where the wild humours they portrayed	1	TR		
For laughing worlds to see and know?	2		N	
Othello's wrath and Juliet's woe?	2		W	
Sir Peter's whims and Timon's gall?	3			G
And Millamant and Romeo?	2		Vowel	
Into the night go one and all.	3R			Vowel
Where are the braveries, fresh or frayed?	1	FR		
The plumes, the armours—friend and foe?	2		F	
The cloth of gold, the rare brocade,	1	K		
The mantles glittering to and fro?	2		FR	
The pomp, the pride, the royal show?	2		SH	
The cries of youth and festival?	3			V
The youth, the grace, the charm, the glow?	2		GL	
Into the night go one and all.	3R			Vowel
The curtain falls, the play is played:	1	PL		
The Beggar packs beside the Beau;	2		B	
The Monarch troops, and troops the Maid;	1	M		
The Thunder huddles with the Snow.	2		SN	
Where are the revellers high and low?	2		L	
The clashing swords? The lover's call?	3			K
The dancers gleaming row on row?	2		R	
Into the night go one and all.	3R			Vowel

Envoy.

Prince, in one common overthrow	2		THR	
The Hero tumbles with the Thrall;	3			THR
As dust that drives, as straws that blow,	2		BL	
Into the night go one and all.	3R			Vowel

Ballade of Dead Actors, William Ernest Henley.

As to the two requirements about rhyming, a ballade requires
six 1 rhymes. Here the six consonantal sounds, as the checking column establishes, are *s, tr, fr, k, pl,* and *m.*

A ballade requires fourteen 2 rhymes. Here the fourteen consonantal sounds, as the checking column establishes, are *fl, n, w,*
the unconsonanted vowel, *f, fr, sh, gl, b, sn, l, r, thr,* and *bl.*

A ballade requires five 3 rhymes, one of which reappears
three times as the refrain. The five sound used here are *g,* the

unconsonanted vowel, *v, k,* and *thr.* The rhyming is correct throughout.

The refrain line is used without any alteration of any kind throughout, satisfying the third requirement. It is used throughout as a natural climax of each stanza. Each stanza has its own climactic rise to the refrain. The envoy meets the requirements wholly.

This ballade, then may be used as a model.

The meter of a ballade need not be four-foot iambic, as in this example. Andrew Lang's *Ballade of Primitive Man* has a three-foot anapestic movement, with the refrain, " 'Twas the manner of Primitive Man." Dactyls may be used, or anapests. A recent newspaper ballade had only two trochees to the line, its refrain being "Life is gay." Another had merely one iambic foot to each line, with the refrain "I love." No doubt someone has written a ballade with only one syllable to each line.

The most famous of all ballades is François Villon's ballade *Des Dames du Temps Jadis, (Ballade of Bygone Ladies).* There are many familiar translations of this, Rossetti's with the refrain "But where are the snows of yester-year?" John Payne's with "But what is become of last year's snow?" and others. None of these are authentic recreations in living poetry; not even of the refrain *Mais ou sont les neiges d'antan?* (But where are the last year's snows?) In technique, Rossetti has entirely different rhyming sounds in each stanza, and another in the envoy. Payne is accurate, though he repeats some rhyme-sounds, and uses words as unliving as *vade* (that is, *go*), *marish, whilere, dole;* and surely "Virgin debonair" is an unfortunate mistranslation of Villon's stately *Vierge souvraine.* At least, none of this is as archaic as two words in this line of Rossetti's version:

(From love he won such dule and teen!)

Examining the Villon original, we find that he uses the terminal sound *-maine* seven times, and rhymes it with *moyne* and other apparent consonances; rhymes *lis* and *Allis;* and otherwise is as lax as French rules allow, rather than following the strict and at that time unpromulgated English rules. An acceptable version in English may take advantages of the practices in the original; although it will have to be an authentic poetic recreation.

The second standard form of the ballade consists of stanzas of ten lines, usually of ten syllables each, as in the five-foot iambic pattern; followed by an envoy of five lines. The regular rhyme scheme for each stanza is 1, 2, 1, 2, 2, 3, 3, 4, 3, 4R, 4R being the refrain line. For the envoy, the rhyme scheme is 3, 3, 4, 3, 4R. This is much rarer in English than the foregoing.

The *ballade with double refrain* uses two refrains, one occurring at the fourth line of every stanza, and one at the eighth; while, in the envoy, the refrains are the second and fourth lines respectively, the envoy being rhymed couplet-wise. The rhyme scheme for each stanza is 1, 2, 1, 2R; 2, 3, 2, 3R, 2R being the first refrain line, and 3R the second. The rhyme scheme for the envoy is 2, 2R, 3, 3R. The best technique selects two antithetical refrains, and develops each stanza upon the refrain used to close it. Here is an excellent example:

When the roads are heavy with mire and rut,	**1**
In November fogs, in December snows,	2
When the North Wind howls, and the doors are shut,	**1**
There is place and enough for the pains of prose;—	2R
But whenever a scent from the whitethorn blows,	2
And the jasmine-stars to the casement climb,	3
And a Rosalind-face at the lattic shows,	3
Then hey!—for the ripple of laughing rhyme!	3R

When the brain gets dry as an empty nut,	
When the reason stands on its squarest toes,	
When the mind (like a beard) has a "formal cut,"	
There is place and enough for the pains of prose;—	2R
But whenever the May-blood stirs and glows,	
And the young year draws to the "golden prime,"—	
And Sir Romeo sticks in his ears a rose,	
Then hey!—for the ripple of laughing rhyme!	3R

In a theme where the thoughts have a pedant strut,	
In a changing quarrel of "Ayes" and "Noes,"	
In a starched procession of "If" and "But",	
There is place and enough for the pains of prose;—	2R
But whenever a soft glance softer glows,	
And the light hours dance to the trysting-time,	
And the secret is told "that no one knows,"	
Then hey!—for the ripple of laughing rhyme!	3R

Envoy

In a work-a-day world,—for its needs and woes,   2
There is place and enough for the pains of prose;   2R
But whenever the May-bells clash and chime, . . .   3
They hey!—for the ripple of laughing rhyme!   3R
      The Ballade of Prose and Rhyme, Austin Dobson.

The position of the two refrains is indicated throughout by 2R and 3R; and the couplet rhyming of the envoy is also indicated.

The *double ballade* consists of six stanzas of eight or ten lines each, rhymed as in the ballades already given. Thus this may be six stanzas rhymed 1, 2, 1, 2, 2, 3, 2, 3R; or 1, 2, 1, 2, 2, 3, 3, 4, 3, 4R. Usually the envoy is omitted. Henley, who liked the form, always used an envoy. His *Double Ballade of the Nothingness of Things* goes beyond these schemes, and has eleven lines to each stanza, rhymed 1, 2, 1, 2, 2, 3, 3, 4, 5, 4, 5R; with an envoy rhymed 3, 3, 4, 5, 4, 5R. And he has stranger varieties. Swinburne's *Ballade of Swimming* has ten lines to the stanza, and seven anapests to each line—a long interval between rhymes.

The *chant royal* is the longest and most dignified offspring of the ballade. It has five stanzas of eleven lines each, usually rhymed 1, 2, 1, 2, 3, 3, 4, 4, 5, 4, 5R. The envoy has five lines, rhymed 4, 4, 5, 4, 5R. Sixty lines, in all. . . . Seven (5) rhymes, ten each of (1), (2), and (3), and eighteen separate rhymes for (4). . . .

Here is an amusing example:

I would that all men my hard case might know;
    How grievously I suffer for no sin;
I, Adolphe Culpepper Ferguson, for lo!
    I, of my landlady am locked in,
        For being short on this sad Saturday,
        Nor having shekels of silver wherewith to pay;
She has turned and is departed with my key;
Wherefore, not even as other boarders free,
    I sing (as prisoners to their dungeon stones
When for ten days they expiate a spree):
    Behold the deeds that are done of Mrs. Jones!

One night and one day I have wept my woe;
    Nor wot I when the morrow doth begin,
If I shall have to write to Briggs & Co.,
    To pray them to advance the requisite tin

For ransom of their salesman, that he may
Go forth as other boarders go alway—
As those I hear now flocking from their tea,
Led by the daughter of my landlady
  Piano-ward. This day, for all my moans,
Dry bread and water have been servéd me.
  Behold the deeds that are done of Mrs. Jones!

Miss Amabel Jones is musical, and so
  The heart of the young he-boardér doth win,
Playing "The Maiden's Prayer," *adagio*—
  That fetcheth him, as fetcheth the banco skin
    The innocent rustic. For my part, I pray:
    That Badarjewska maid may wait for aye
Ere she sits with a lover, as did we
Once sit together, Amabel! Can it be
  That all that arduous wooing not atones
For Saturday shortness of trade dollars three?
  Behold the deeds that are done of Mrs. Jones!

Yea! she forgets the arm was wont to go
  Around her waist. She wears a buckle whose pin
Galleth the crook of the young man's elbów;
  I forget not, for I that youth have been.
    Smith was aforetime the Lothario gay.
    Yet once, I mind me, Smith was forced to stay
Close in his room. Not calm, as I, was he:
But his noise brought no pleasaunce, verily.
  Small ease he gat of playing on the bones,
Or hammering on the stove-pipe, that I see.
  Behold the deeds that are done of Mrs. Jones!

Thou, for whose fear the figurative crow
  I eat, accursed be thou and all thy kin!
Thee will I shew up—yea, up will I shew
  Thy too thick buckwheats, and thy tea too thin.
    Ay! here I dare thee, ready for the fray!
    Thou dost *not* "keep a first-class house," I say!
It does not with the advertisements agree.
Thou lodgest a Briton with a puggaree,
  And thou hast harboured Jacobses and Cohns,
Also a Mulligan. Thus denounce I thee!
  Behold the deeds that are done of Mrs. Jones!

Envoy

Boarders; the worst I have not told to ye:
She hath stolen my trousers, that I may not flee
   Privily by the window. Hence these groans,
There is no fleeing in a *robe de nuit*.
   Behold the deeds that are done of Mrs. Jones!

> *Behold the Deeds! (Being the Plaint of Adolphe Culpepper Ferguson, Salesman of Fancy Notions, held in durance of his Landlady for a failure to connect on Saturday night,)* Henry Cuyler Bunner.

The stanza rhyme-scheme is 1, 2, 1, 2, 3, 3, 4, 4, 5, 4, 5R, 5R being the refrain; with the envoy 4, 4, 5, 3, 5R. The rhyming throughout is accurate, and the result is a perfect chant royal. The form is intricate, and the method of checking the various rhyme sounds as they are put down should be followed, to be sure that no rhyming sound is repeated. A great deal of reworking is often necessary to perfect such a form as this. In order to make the envoy the culmination of the verses, it is often necessary to shift the strongest and most vigorous rhyming sounds to it, and substitute other words in the earlier stanzas.

It is wise, for rhyme 4, which must be repeated eighteen times, and similar others repeated constantly in the fixed forms, to choose a comparatively simple rhyming sound, such as the Ē here, to prevent a lack of rhyming words.

Chain Verse

We have already noted that form of chain verse used in *terza rima,* where the triplets rhyme 1, 2, 1; 2, 3, 2; 3, 4, 3; 4, 5, 4, and so on. Any repetition of a rhyme, word, phrase, line or group of lines, to tie up a section of the poem with the succeeding section, constitutes chain verse. John Byrom lets line four of each quatrain become line one of the next:

> My spirit longeth for thee
> Within my troubled breast,
> Although I be unworthy
> Of so divine a Guest.

Of so divine a Guest
Unworthy though I be,
Yet has my heart no rest,
Unless it comes from thee.

Unless it comes from thee,
In vain I look around,
    The Desponding Soul's Wish, John Byrom.

and so on. Chain verse can rise to the elaborateness of a chain of
sonnets or more, with the final line in each repeated as the opening line of the next, or even the final word or rhyme-sound so
used.

The Kyrielle

The kyrielle, strictly described, consists of quatrains with eight
syllables to the line, each stanza terminating with the same line,—
a simple use of the refrain. Here is an example from a poem by
John Payne:

A little pain, a little pleasure,
A little heaping up of treasure,
Then no more gazing upon the sun.
All things must end that have begun.

Where is the time for hope or doubt?
A puff of the wind, and life is out;
A turn of the wheel, and the rest is won.
All things must end that have begun.

Golden morning and purple night,
Life that fails with the failing light;
Death is the only deathless one.
All things must end that have begun.
            Kyrielle, John Payne.

Here the eight-syllabled pattern is intermittently broken. There is
of course no sacredness in any pattern. Such a simple form must
compensate by climactic development from stanza to stanza, to
justify itself in poetry.

The Pantoum

Ernest Fouinet introduced the Malayan pantoum into French versification, and Victor Hugo popularized it in the *Orientales*. It is written in four-line stanzas; and the second and fourth line of each stanza become the first and third of the succeeding stanza. In the last stanza, the second and fourth lines are the third and first of the first stanza; so that the opening and closing lines of the pantoum are identical. The rhyme scheme would then be: 1, 2, 1, 2; 2, 3, 2, 3; 3, 4, 3, 4; . . . n, 1, n, 1.

Brander Matthews gives an example of one in English:

> Here we are riding the rail,
> Gliding from out of the station;
> Man though I am, I am pale,
> Certain of heat and vexation.
>
> Gliding from out of the station,
> Out from the city we thrust;
> Certain of heat and vexation,
> Sure to be covered with dust.
>
> Out from the city we thrust:
> Rattling we run o'er the bridges:
> Sure to be covered with dust,
> Stung by a thousand of midges. . . .
>
> *En Route,* Brander Matthews.

to the final stanza, ending as the verses began:

> Ears are on edge at the rattle,
> Man though I am, I am pale,
> Sounds like the noise of a battle,
> Here we are riding the rail.

The Triolet

The triolet was the first of the rondeau family to appear. The first ones known appeared in the *Cléomadés* of Adenèz-le-Roi, who wrote in the latter part of the thirteenth century. At first, with ten syllables to each line, the triolet dealt with serious subjects. Today the form is usually eight syllables to the line, or even six; and the themes have grown appreciably and constantly lighter.

It has eight lines, with only two rhymes. The first line is repeated as the fourth line; the first two lines reappear as the seventh and eighth. The rhyme scheme is 1R, 2R, 1, 1R, 1, 2, 1R, 2R, the repeated lines appearing as 1R and 2R.

Suppose you decide to write a brief triolet, opening with the couplet:

> Drink deep—the glass
> Is full—and near!

You can at once fill out your fourth, seventh and eighth lines from this, making your pattern now appear as:

> Drink deep—the glass   1R
> Is full—and near!   2R
>   1
> ————————————————
> Drink deep! The glass   1R
> ————————————————   1
> ————————————————
>   2
> Drink deep—the glass   1R
> Is full—and near!   2R

Only three lines, then, remain to be filled in. Once this is done, you have the triolet complete:

> Drink deep—the glass
> Is full—and near!
> Come, lad and lass,
> Drink deep! The glass
> Too soon will pass
> And disappear.
> Drink deep—the glass
> Is full—and near!

At times a more serious mood rules the use of the form. Thus H. C. Bunner wrote:

> A pitcher of mignonette
>   In a tenement's highest casement;
> Queer sort of a flower-pot—yet
> That pitcher of mignonette
> Is a garden of heaven set
>   To the little sick child in the basement,
> The pitcher of mignonette
>   In the tenement's highest casement.
>   *Triolet,* Henry Cuyler Bunner.

Here we have no progress in thought in the use of the reiterated refrain or repetend. Worse than that, the refrain line alters from *A pitcher* to *That pitcher* and *The pitcher,* a vital fault in the use of refrains in the French forms.

A transition to the rondeau form is furnished by this eight-line verse by Leigh Hunt:

> Jenny kissed me when we met,
>   Running to the chair I sat in.
> Time, you thief, who love to get
>   Sweets upon your list, put *that* in!
> Say I'm weary, say I'm sad,
>   Say that health and wealth have missed me;
> Say I'm growing old, but add—
>   Jenny kissed me.
>   *"Jenny Kissed Me,"* Leigh Hunt.

The opening half of line one, reappearing as the refrain in line eight, prophesies the rondeau and similar forms. This brilliant little pattern has never become accepted and named.

The Rondel, Rondeau and Roundel Family

The triolet is the seed of the rondeau family. The *rondel* (the word is an old form of the later word *rondeau*) arose in all probability in Provence, and appeared later in the fourteenth century writings of north France, in the verse of Froissart, Deschamps and others. It began as a lyric of two stanzas, each stanza having four or five lines only, and rhyming triolet-wise upon two sounds. . . . Either a triolet, or a ten-line variant of the triolet.

With Charles d'Orleans, the rondel took the distinct form now assigned to it, of fourteen lines on two rhymes. The first two lines reappear as the seventh and eighth, and as the final couplet. —A mere variation of the triolet. This double repetition of the two-lined refrain made the form unwieldy. Later French poets shortened the form to thirteen lines, omitting the second line of the original refrain at the end.

The form as Charles d'Orleans used it appears in this rondel:

Paper, inviolate, white,   1R
   Shall it be joy or pain?   2R
   Shall I of fate complain,   2
Or shall I laugh tonight?   1

Shall it be hopes that are bright?   1
   Shall it be hopes that are vain?   2
Paper, inviolate, white,   1R
   Shall it be joy or pain?   2R

A dear little hand so light,   1
   A moment in mine hath lain;   2
   Kind was its pressure again—   2
Ah, but it was so slight!   1

Paper, inviolate, white,   1R
   Shall it be joy or pain?   2R

To a Blank Sheet of Paper, Cosmo Monkhouse.

The following rondel, by Samuel Minturn Peck, is in the preferred modern pattern:

Before the dawn begins to glow,   1R
   A ghostly company I keep;   2R
   Across the silent room they creep, 2
The buried forms of friend and foe.   1
Amid the throng that come and go,   1
   There are two eyes that make me weep; 2
Before the dawn begins to glow,   1R
   A ghostly company I keep.   2R

Two dear dead eyes. I love them so!   1
   They shine like starlight on the deep, 2
   And often when I am asleep   2
They stoop and kiss me, being low,   1
Before the dawn begins to glow.   1R

"Before the Dawn," Samuel Minturn Peck.

The *rondeau* is, next to the ballade, the French form most popular in English. It is written, like triolet and rondel, on two rhymes throughout: thirteen full-length lines, and two briefer unrhymed refrains. The refrain may consist of the first half of the first line, but may consist merely of the first word. The fifteen lines are grouped in three stanzas, the first of five lines, the second of three lines and refrain, the third of five lines and refrain. The rhyme scheme then is: 1, 1, 2, 2, 1; 1, 1, 2, R; 1, 1, 2, 2, 1, R. Here is a rondeau that is a poem as well:

A man must live. We justify	1
Low shift and trick to treason high,	1
A little vote for a little gold	2
To a whole senate bought and sold	2
By that self-evident reply.	1
But is it so? Pray tell me why	1
Life at such cost you have to buy?	1
In what religion were you told	2
A man must live?	R
There are times when a man must die.	1
Imagine, for a battle-cry,	1
From soldiers, with a sword to hold,—	2
From soldiers, with the flag unrolled,	2
This coward's whine, this liar's lie,—	1
A man must live!	R

A Man Must Live, Charlotte Perkins Gilman.

The *roundel,* based upon occasional early French variants, is today associated with the name of Swinburne, because of his volume *A Century of Roundels.* As used by Swinburne, the roundel was eleven lines long, two of which were the brief refrain lines. The refrain either consisted of the opening word of line one, or of a portion or a half of that line. If it consisted of more than one word, it usually rhymed with the (2) sound rhyme. The rhyming pattern then would be 1, 2, 1, R; 2, 1, 2; 1, 2, 1, R; or 1, 2, 1, 2R; 2, 1, 2; 1, 2, 1, 2R. Here is an example:

A Roundel is wrought as a ring or a starbright sphere,
With craft of delight and with cunning of sound unsought,
That the heart of the hearer may smile if to pleasure his ear
A roundel is wrought.

Its jewel of music is carven of all or of aught—
Love, laughter, or mourning—remembrance of rapture or fear—
That fancy may fashion to hang in the ear of thought.

As a bird's quick song runs round, and the hearts in us hear—
Pause answers to pause, and again the same strain caught,
So moves the device whence, round as a pearl or tear,
    A roundel is wrought.
     The Roundel, Algernon Charles Swinburne.

The *rondelet* is a seven-line fixed form, normally of four eight-syllabled lines, and three, the refrain lines, with four syllables each. The rhyme and rhythm scheme is: 1R, 2, 1R, 1, 2, 2, 1R—1R standing for the refrain line, and 1 for the line rhyming with it. Here is an example by May Probyn:

"Which way he went?"	1R
I know not—how should I go spy	2
Which way he went?	1R
I only know him gone. "Relent?"	1
He never will—unless I die!	2
And then, what will it signify	2
Which way he went?	1R

     Rondelet, May Probyn.

The *rondeau redoublé,* a remote relative of the rondeau, is in reality a formalized Theme With Variations treatment. It starts with a quatrain as a theme. This is followed by four additional quatrains, in each of which successively lines one, two, three, and four of the theme quatrain appear as the terminal lines. A concluding stanza has four lines of regular length, and a refrain (the first half of line one of the theme) to terminate.

An example will make this clearer:

My soul is sick of nightingale and rose,	1-a
The perfume and the darkness of the grove;	2-b
I weary of the fevers and the throes,	1-c
And all the enervating dreams of love.	2-d
At morn I love to hear the lark, and rove	2
The meadows, where the simple daisy shows	1
Her guiltless bosom to the skies above—	2
My soul is sick of nightingale and rose.	1-a
The afternoon is sweet, and sweet repose,	1
But let me lie where breeze-blown branches move.	2
I hate the stillness where the sunbeams doze,	1
The perfume and the darkness of the grove.	2-b

I love to hear at eve the gentle dove   2
Contented coo the day's delightful close.   1
   She sings of love and all the calm thereof,— 2
I weary of the fevers and the throes.   1-c

I love the night, who like a mother throws   1
   Her arms round hearts that throbbed and limbs that strove, 2
As kind as Death, that puts an end to woes   1
   And all the enervating dreams of love.   2-d

   Because my soul is sick of fancies wove   2
Of fervid ecstasies and crimson glows;   1
   Because the taste of cinnamon and clove   2
Palls on my palate—let no man suppose   1
      My soul is sick.   R

Rondeau Redoublé, Cosmo Monkhouse.

As far as strict rhyming goes, *repose—suppose* and *throes—throws* are identities, and not rhymes.

The *glose,* which is superficially a freer variant of the foregoing pattern, derives apparently from a different source, and is found more often in Spanish and Portuguese verse than in French. It begins, like the rondeau redoublé, with a quatrain, here called the *texte,* which may be a quotation. This texte the glose proceeds to develop, in four stanzas of ten lines each, closing each stanza, as in the rondeau redoublé, with the successive four lines of the texte. The concluding stanza and refrain of the preceding form are omitted here. In the rhyme scheme, lines six, nine and the tenth or texte line in each stanza rhyme; the rest of the rhyme scheme differs with different users of the form.

Gleeson White, author of a definitive book on the French forms, was unable to discover at the time he wrote any example of the form in English. There are not many examples available. The texte in the following is from Graham R. Tomson's *Ballade of Asphodel.*

   "Queen Prosperpine, at whose white feet   1-a
     In life my love I may not tell,   2-b
   Wilt give me welcome when we meet   1-c
     Along the mead of Asphodel?"   2-d

Your Majesty, permit me to	3
Indite, as one would say, this bit	4
Of verse respectfully to you;	3
Of course admitting *entre nous*	3
You may not really fancy it;	4
Although it will be rather neat.	1
And yet the dedication 's fit;	4
I want assistance from your wit:	4
I should permit my heart to beat,	1
Queen Proserpine, at *whose* white feet?	1-a

Remember, Proserpine, I know	5
That quite discriminatingly	6
You made your mind up long ago;	5
You did not like your Stygian beau;	5
He smacked a bit of deviltry,—	6
And you were not designed for hell.	2
This shows you're quite a clever she;	6
Ergo, you ought to counsel me.	6
I *must* make up my mind, or,—well,	2
In life my love I may not tell.	2-b

Should I ask Venus, she would vote
    (That surely is a goddess' right)
For some dame with "a quivering throat
And bosom of desire"—I quote
    From memory the line tonight.
Minerva would choose some discreet
    Young woman, staid and erudite;
    But only she could give delight
Who would, though life's young roses sweet
Wilt, give me welcome when we meet.   1-c

Come, choose her for me! Let her be
    Stately or dumpy, brown or fair,
If only she'll agree that we
Should learn to dwell in harmony,
    Giving a gay good-bye to care,—
A beatific way to dwell!
    Come, Queen, be gracious to my prayer!
    But, no! Such maidens here are rare;
You'd scarce find such a demoiselle
Along the mead of Asphodel!   2-d

                        The Quest, Clement Wood.

Naturally, the rhyming scheme of the texte (which is 1, 2, 1, 2 here), dictates the rhyming of the sixth, ninth and tenth lines of each main stanza. In other examples, the quatrain that forms the texte may have any quatrain rhyming, and so a similar extent dictates similar rhymes in each stanza. It is permissible to use the same rhymes in each stanza, except where the rhyme-sound of the texte line ordains differently. In other words, the four stanzas might be:

1-a, 2-b, 1-c, 2-d
3, 4, 3, 3, 4, 1, 3, 3, 1, 1-a
3, 4, 3, 3, 4, 2, 3, 3, 2, 2-b
3, 4, 3, 3, 4, 1, 3, 3, 1, 1-c
3, 4, 3, 3, 4, 2, 3, 3, 2, 2-d

This is not required by the strict rules.

The Sestina

Arnaut Daniel, a Provençal troubadour, invented the sestina at the end of the thirteenth century. In France it has been slightly popular. Dante and Petrarch liked to use it. Here are the rules, as drawn up by Daniel and his followers in Italy, Spain and Portugal:

1. The sestina has six stanzas, each of six lines, of the same length; and a concluding three-line stanza.
2. The lines of the six stanzas end with the same six words, not rhyming with each other; these end words are chosen exclusively from two-syllabled nouns.
3. The arrangement of these six terminal words follows a regular law, very complex in ancient times, and altered toward simplicity later, as appears hereafter.
4. The closing three-line stanza uses the six terminal words, three at the centers of the lines, three at their ends.

Modern usage permits the variation of allowing the terminating words to rhyme, either on two rhyming sounds, as Swinburne uses it, or on three. In every case, the six terminal words must be repeated, with no change in sound or spelling, through each succeeding stanza. The order for the six terminal words in the six successive stanzas is as follows:

1st	stanza	1, 2, 3, 4, 5, 6
2nd	stanza	6, 1, 5, 2, 4, 3
3rd	stanza	3, 6, 4, 1, 2, 5
4th	stanza	5, 3, 2, 6, 1, 4
5th	stanza	4, 5, 1, 3, 6, 2
6th	stanza	2, 4, 6, 5, 3, 1

The concluding half stanza ends with 2, 4, and 6; and uses 1, 3, and 5 at the beginning—not necessarily as the first word—of the lines; or at the half-line, in rhymes that permit their introduction there.

Here is an example: The numerals refer to terminal words, and not rhyme sounds.

We are the smiling comfortable homes,	1
With happy families enthroned therein,	2
Where baby souls are brought to meet the world,	3
Where women end their duties and desires,	4
For which men labor as the goal of life,	5
That people worship now instead of God.	6
Do we not teach the child to worship God?—	6
Whose soul's young range is bounded by the homes	1
Of those he loves, and where he learns that life	5
Is all constrained to serve the wants therein,	2
Domestic needs and personal desires,—	4
These are the early limits of his world.	3
And are we not the woman's perfect world,	3
Prescribed by nature and ordained of God,	6
Beyond which she can have no right desires,	4
No need for service other than in homes?	1
For doth she not bring up her young therein?	2
And is not rearing young the end of life?	5
And man? What other need hath he in life	5
Than to go forth and labor in the world,	3
And struggle sore with other men therein?	2
Not to serve other men, nor yet his God,	6
But to maintain these comfortable homes,—	1
The end of all a normal man's desires.	4

Shall not the soul's most measureless desires	4
Learn that the very flower and fruit of life	5
Lies all attained in comfortable homes,	1
With which life's purpose is to dot the world	3
And consummate the utmost will of God,	6
By sitting down to eat and drink therein.	2
Yea, in the processes that work therein—	2
Fulfilment of our natural desires—	4
Surely man finds the proof that mighty God	6
For to maintain and reproduce his life	5
Created him and set him in the world;	3
And this high end is best attained in homes.	1
Are we not homes? And is not all therein?	1, 2
Wring dry the world to meet our wide desires!	3, 4
We crown all life! We are the aim of God!	5, 6

Homes, Charlotte Perkins Gilman.

Here the lines end on accented syllables, and by no means on two-syllabled nouns exclusively. There is no sestina in any of the collections in English which follows this convention; it may be dismissed, with the reflection that the French, Spanish and Italian languages have more double rhymes than English.

The movements of each terminal word follow a definite pattern, as a graph of the numbered terminal words will show. The order of position is successively 1, 2, 4, 5, 3, 6, 1, 2, 4, 5, 3, etc. By this means the last word of one stanza terminates the first line of the next; and meanwhile the last line of next has been shifted from third position to last, to terminate line one of the ensuing stanza.

Swinburne uses, as terminal words in one of his rhymed sestinas, *day, night, way, light, may, delight,* as 1, 2, 3, 4, 5, 6; and thereafter achieves alternate rhymes throughout, by creating his own sequence pattern, as follows: 6, 1, 4, 3, 2, 5; 5, 6, 1, 4, 3, 2; 2, 5, 6, 1, 4, 3; 3, 2, 1, 6, 5, 4; 4, 3, 2, 5, 6, 1, with the terminals of the concluding triplet *light, way, delight* (4, 3, 6), and the internal rhymes here *day, night, may* (1, 2, 5). He has worked out even more intricately his rhymed double sestina, *The Complaint of Lisa*—twelve stanzas of twelve lines each, with a concluding sestet, of one hundred and fifty lines in all. Charles W. Coleman, in his sestina *Love's Going,* used three rhyme sounds, *sing, rose, heart, thing, goes, apart;* but he retains the unrhymed sequence formula, and thus has rhyming couplets in four of his stanzas. Swinburne's variation is to be preferred to this.

Clearly, in writing the sestina, after the first stanza has been completed, the next task is to write down the terminals for all the lines of the next five stanzas, and the terminals and center words of the brief concluding stanza. Then proceed to write. . . . The form is more suitable to clever light verse, than to poetry.

The Villanelle

The villanelle lends itself to seriousness, as well as to frivolity. It consists of nineteen lines: five three-lined stanzas, concluding with a quatrain. The refrain couplet, which terminates the form, consists of lines one and three of the first triplet. Moreover, line one (the first half of the refrain) terminates stanzas two and four, and line three (the other half of the refrain) stanzas three and five. Only two rhyming sounds are used. The following villanelle follows the pattern strictly:

O Singer of Persephone!	1-a
In the dim meadows desolate,	2
Dost thou remember Sicily?	1-b
Still through the ivy flits the bee	1
Where Amaryllis lies in state,	2
O Singer of Persephone!	1-a
Simaetha calls on Hecate,	1
And hears the wild dogs at the gate;	2
Dost thou remember Sicily?	1-b
Still by the light and laughing sea	1
Poor Polypheme bemoans his fate,	2
O Singer of Persephone!	1-a
And still in boyish rivalry	1
Young Daphnis challenges his mate:	2
Dost thou remember Sicily?	1-b
Slim Lacon keeps a goat for thee;	1
For thee the jocund shepherds wait,	2
O Singer of Persephone!	1-a
Dost thou remember Sicily?	1-b

Theocritus, Oscar Wilde.

Edwin Arlington Robinson pours poetry into the form, in a villanelle concluding:

> There is ruin and decay
> In the House on the Hill:
> They are all gone away,
> There is nothing more to say.
> *The House on the Hill*, Edwin Arlington Robinson.

The Lai and the Virelai

The ancient French lai was composed of couplets of five-syllabled lines, all on the same rhyme, separated by single lines of two syllables each, which rhymed with one another. The number of lines in each stanzas was not fixed, nor the number of stanzas in the complete poem. An improvised example would be:

> Summer heat today   1
> In its torrid way,   1
> I see,   2
> With its awful ray   1
> Sears till it must slay   1
> Poor me,   2
> Tree and grass and clay.   1
> It's the bay—the spray   1
> And glee!   2

A curious old tradition connected with the form is that the indentation of the shorter lines is forbidden. This detail was called *arbre fourchu*, a forked tree, from the fancied resemblance of the poem on paper to a tree with branches projecting. Where lais have more than one stanza, the two rhymes in each stanza have no reference to the rhymes in any other.

The *virelai* or *virelai ancien* grew out of this, with a sequence of rhymes throughout. Thus, in a twelve-line stanza, the rhymes would be 1, 1, 2, 1, 1, 2, 1, 1, 2, 1, 1, 2. The next stanza would be 2, 2, 3, 2, 2, 3, 2, 2, 3, 2, 2, 3; and so on, until the last stanza appeared as n, n, 1, n, n, 1, n, n, 1, n, n, 1. Thus each rhyme sound would appear once in the longer lines, and once in the shorter. The form is too simple to need illustration.

The *virelai nouveau* is written throughout on two rhymes. Its initial rhymed couplet serves as a refrain for the later stanzas; and the two lines close each stanza alternately until the last, when they both appear together, but in inverse order. Here is an example which begins with the couplet as its first stanza,

> Good-bye to the Town!—good-bye!   1 a
> Hurrah for the sea and the sky!   1-b
> > *July,* Austin Dobson.

The second stanza is rhymed, 1, 1, 1, 2, 1, 1-a. Its third stanza is 1, 2, 1, 2, 1, 2, 2, 1, 1-b. The succeeding stanzas are as irregular, but each is confined to the two rhymed sounds, and the refrains occur in the prescribed order. And here is the concluding stanza, showing the refrain reversed:

> So Phyllis, the fawn-footed, hie   1
> For a hansom! Ere close of the day   2
> Between us a "world" must lie,—   1
> Hurrah! for the sea and the sky!   1-b
> Good-bye to the Town! GOOD-BYE!   1-a

The *Sicilian octave* at times is used as a fixed form. It consists in eight iambic five-foot lines, rhymed 1, 2, 1, 2, 1, 2, 1, 2. No difficulty will be found in writing in this pattern.

The *rispetto* is an Italian form, with inter-rhyming lines ranging from six to ten in number, though not usually exceeding eight. Used rarely in English, it is usually divided into two stanzas, rhymed 1, 2, 1, 2; 3, 3, 4, 4.

A brief American fixed form, called the *sonnette,* was originated by Sherman Ripley, and had a vogue for a time. It consisted of seven five-foot iambic lines, rhymed: 1, 2, 2, 1; 3, 2, 3. It differed only slightly from the *Canopus* stanza, already described, which also used seven five-foot iambic lines, but rhymed them 1, 2, 1, 2, 3, 2, 3. Both avoid the terminal couplet, and hence have an uninterrupted flow for narrative verse.

Another recent form is the *Douzet,* its origin unknown. It consists of twelve five-foot iambic lines, rhymed as follows: 1, 2, 2, 1; 3, 4, 4, 3; 1, 2, 3, 4. This introduces a novelty in the repetition of rhyme not encountered so far elsewhere: the concluding quatrain's rhyme-scheme amounting to a summary of the rhyme-sounds gone before.

There is no limit to the patterns that ingenuity in versification can produce. Only the rare few among these achieve enduring popularity.

The Japanese form, the *hokku,* follows Japanese poetry *(tanka or uta)* in having alternate verses of five and seven syllables. The hokku or *haikai* consists of only three lines, of 5, 7, and 5 syllables, or 17 in all. An improvised example is:

> More fleeting than the
> Flash of withered windblown leaf,
> This thing men call life.

The Japanese *tanka* ordinarily has 31 syllables, consisting of five lines, with respectively 5, 7, 5, 7, and 7 syllables. An improvised example is:

> The rippling sea-swell,
> Curling upon the gold sand,
> And, curving over,
> A bough of cherry blossoms,—
> Youth shielding eternal age.

Longer Japanese poems may be constructed in the tanka form, with the invariable alternation of 5 and 7 syllables to the line, and the addition of a terminal 7-syllabled line. The rhythm in Japanese poetry is not regarded. The only convention is the number of syllables to the line.

The Limerick

The limerick is the only fixed form indigenous to the English language. It first appeared in *Songs for the Nursery, or, Mother Goose's Melodies for Children,* published by Elizabeth Goose, (formerly Vertigoose, married to Thomas Fleet, a Boston printer,) in 1719. Moreover, in this collection it appeared in all three of its successive forms. The first stage opened and closed the five-line form with a nonsense line:

> Hickory, dickory, dock!
> The mouse ran up the clock.
> The clock struck one—
> The mouse ran down,
> Hickory, dickory, dock!
>
> *Nursery Rhymes,* Mother Goose.

The second form, the one used by Edward Lear throughout, ended the first and fifth line with a geographical name, at times these lines being identical:

> As I was going to Bonner,
> Upon my word of honor,
>   I met a pig
>   Without a wig,
> As I was going to Bonner.
>   *Nursery Rhymes,* Mother Goose.

The third and culminating form has a new rhyme sound in the fifth line—as this example:

> There was an old soldier of Bister
> Went walking one day with his sister,
>   When a cow at one poke
>   Tossed her into an oak,
> Before the old gentleman missed her.
>   *Nursery Rhymes,* Mother Goose.

A classic model to follow is the famous limerick—

> There was a young lady from Niger,
> Who smiled as she rode on a tiger.
>   They came back from the ride
>   With the lady inside,
> And the smile on the face of the tiger.
>   *More Limericks,* Cosmo Monkhouse.

The identity instead of rhyme in lines 2 and 5 cannot spoil the charm of this, although the pure pattern would avoid it. This would be—remembering that an extra unaccented syllable can be added either to the 1, 2, 5 rhyme group, or to the 3, 4 group, or to both:

> ta TUM—ta ta TUM—ta ta TUM
> ta TUM—ta ta TUM—ta ta TUM,
>   ta ta TUM—ta ta TUM
>   ta ta TUM—ta ta TUM
> ta ta TUM—ta ta TUM—ta ta TUM.

In other words, an anapestic pattern, 5, 5, 3, 3, 5 feet to the lines respectively, rhymed 1, 1, 2, 2, 1; usually with an iamb opening lines 1 and 2. Any trick rhyming device is permissible, as:

An amorous M. A.
Says that Cupid, that C. D.,
    Doesn't cast for his health,
    But is rolling in wealth—
He's the John Jaco-B. H.
                                        Anonymous.

This must be read by pronouncing *M. A.* "master of arts," and by
rhyming lines two and five properly to it,—"caster of darts" and
"Jacob Astor of hearts." Here is one of the tongue-twister variety:

A tutor who tooted the flute
Tried to teach two young tooters to toot.
    Said the two to the tutor,
    "Is it harder to toot, or
To tutor two tooters to toot?"
                          Four Limericks, Carolyn Wells.

Among other possible variations is:

There was a young lady of Diss,
Who said, "Now I think skating bliss!"
    This no more will she state,
    For a wheel off her skate
ʍɐpǝ ɥǝɹ ɟᴉuᴉsɥ dn soɯǝʇɥᴉuƃ ꞁᴉʞǝ ʇɥᴉs⸮
                                        Anonymous.

The writing of limericks at times becomes extremely popular.

Little Willies

Any form may become, almost overnight, a favorite with poets
and especially light verse writers. Some college student wrote and
published in his college paper a rhyme proceeding approximately
like this:

Tobacco is a filthy weed.
    I like it.
It satisfies no normal need.
    I like it.
It makes you thin, it makes you lean,
It takes the hair right off your bean;
It's the worst darned stuff I've ever seen.
    I like it.
                                        Anonymous.

At once this form was copied by newspaper and other light versifiers the breadth and length of the land, and is still intermittently alive.

Another form assumed wide popularity, arising from one of Col. D. Streamer's (Harry Graham's) *Ruthless Rhymes for Heartless Homes:*

> Billy, in one of his nice new sashes,
> Fell in the fire and was burned to ashes.
> Now, although the room grows chilly,
> I haven't the heart to poke poor Billy.
>
> > *Tender-Heartedness,* Harry Graham.

The quatrain here consists of two couplets, rhymed 1, 1, 2, 2. The metre combines trochees and dactyls; it might be iambs and anapests, of course, or any of the four. Somehow Billy became rechristened Willie, and at least one anonymous volume has appeared since, dealing in this or other simple quatrains with the adventures of Willie and his family. Among famous ones are:

> Willie and two other brats
> Licked up all the Rough-on-Rats.
> Father said, when mother cried,
> "Never mind, they'll die outside."
>
> > Anonymous.

> Father heard his children scream,
> So he threw them in the stream,
> Saying, as he drowned the third,
> "Children should be seen, *not* heard!"
>
> > *The Stern Parent,* Harry Graham.

> Late last night I slew my wife
> Stretched her on the parquet flooring.
> I was loath to take her life,
> But I *had* to stop her snoring.
>
> > *Necessity,* Harry Graham.

> Willie poisoned father's tea;
> Father died in agony.
> Mother looked extremely vexed:
> "Really, Will," she said, "what next?"
>
> > Anonymous.

The model for a Little Willie, with its trick last line and its sadistic content, can be taken from any of these.

Light Verse in English

Light verse, including its elegant form called *vers de société,* demand a technical dexterity greater than that of poetry; for the obviousness and cleverness of the rhyme are a charm here, where they usually interfere with the emotional effect of poetry. The student of versification will benefit by studying Tom Hood, for the use of puns in light verse; *Mother Goose,* for inspired use of rhythm; Edward Lear and Lewis Carroll, for shapely nonsense verse; Charles Stuart Calverley for mastery of every trick of rhyming, and great dexterity in stanza-devising; W. S. Gilbert, for mastery of the whole field. The long finale of his *Iolanthe* is his peak in rhyming, and almost the peak of light verse in English. Split words are a constant device: as in Carroll's—

> Who would not give all else for two p-
> Ennyworth of beautiful soup?
> > *Soup of the Evening,* Lewis Carroll.

or another surprise rhyming sung by Canning:

> Sun, moon, and thou vain world, adieu,
> > That kings and priests are plotting in;
> Here doomed to starve on water-gru-
> -El, never shall I see the U-
> > -Niversity of Gottingen,
> > -Niversity of Gottingen!
> > *Song by Rogero,* George Canning.

Humorous verse need not be clever. A poem like Ernest Lawrence Thayer's *Casey at the Bat* is a perpetual favorite because the theme invokes deep laughter, not because it is trickily versified. Dialect verse is in a class by itself. In writing dialect verse, be careful

(1) To use dialect spelling only where required.

(2) Not to overuse it, or the reader will not understand it. Such an improvised quatrain as—

> Sum niggers iz peculyer,
> I reitteratez agen,
> They mus' come f'um Atlanta
> An' not from Bummin'ham

is full of bad writing. *Sum* is the correct pronunciation of *some*, not a dialect pronunciation; the same is true of *iz, reitteratez,* and *agen.* The same is probably true of *peculyer.* And why *f'um* and *from* in the same poem? This is as inept as using *you* and *thou* (in any form) in the same poem, to refer to the same person. *F'um, mus'* and *an'* are accurate dialect speech.

Among other forms of light verse are *parody,* aping the versifying mannerisms of another; *nonsense verse; whimsical verse* of many kinds; *mosaic* or *composite verse,* each line taken from some other poet; *macaronic verse,* where two or more languages are hashed together; *shaped whimsies,* where the typography pictures the theme, as in the *Song of the Decanter,* on page 96.

Various forms of *typographical oddities* may be devised, in which certain of the lines (as the terminals of each quatrain) represent the way a person walks, sober, or intoxicated, or the way he falls down.

Acrostics are verses where the opening letters of the lines, or the closing letters, or letters arrived at by some other system, name a person, or convey a special message. Here is an example:

> *F*rom your bright sparkling Eyes I was undone;
> *R*ays, you have; more transparent than the Sun,
> *A*midst its glory in the rising Day
> *N*one can you equal in your bright array;
> *C*onstant in your calm and unspotted mind,
> *E*qual to all, but will to none Prove kind,
> *S*o knowing, seldome one so Young, you'll Find,
> *A*h! woe's me, that I should Love and conceal
> *L*ong have I wished, but never dared reveal,
> *E*ven though severely Love's Pains I feel;
> *X*erxes that great, wasn't free from Cupid's Dart,
> *A*nd all the great Heroes, felt the smart.
>   *Acrostic,* George Washington.

The words conveyed by the acrostic are revealed by reading downward the first or italicized letters of each line.

The actual writing of light verse calls upon the versifier for every resource and device within the technique of versification. The rhymes should be natural and not rhyme-induced, and the entire treatment natural and adapted to please and amuse.

> There was an old decanter
> and its mouth was gaping
> wide; the rosy wine had
> ebbed away and left
> its   crystal   side;
> and   the   wind
> went humming
> —humming up
> and   down: the
> wind it flew, and
> through the reed-
> like hollow neck the
> wildest notes it blew.
> I placed it in the window,
> where the blast was blow-
> ing free, and fancied that its
> pale mouth sang the queerest
> strains to me. "They tell me—puny
> conquerors! the Plague has slain his ten,
> and war his hundred thousand of the very
> best of men; but I"—'twas thus the Bottle spake—
> "but I have conquered more than all your famous
> conquerors, so feared and famed of yore. Then come,
> ye youths and maidens all, come drink from out my cup,
> the beverage that dulls the brain, and burns the spirits up;
> that puts to shame your conquerors that slay their scores
> below; for this has deluged millions with the lava
> tide of woe. Tho' in the path of battle darkest
> streams of blood may roll, yet while I killed the
> body, I have damned the very soul. The
> cholera, the plague, the sword such ruin
> never wrought, as I in mirth or
> malice on the innocent have
> brought. And still I breathe
> upon them, and they shrink before
> my breath, while year by year my
> thousands go my dusty way of death."

Song of the Decanter, Warfield Creath Richardson.

VII

POETRY AND TECHNIQUE

The Vocabulary of Poetry

THE vocabulary used by a poet in his poetry should be the vocabulary that he uses in his living speech. Prose uses this, or else it becomes stilted and affected. If an orator commences,

O Mississippi, Father of Waters, thou wast engendered in the hills of Minnehaha; thou hast meandered through meadows green and valleys dappled for more miles than man computeth,

his hearers feel that there is something strained and unnatural in his words. The same thought occurs, when poetry, especially modern poetry, contain words no longer in the living vocabulary of man, because they have become archaic; or else unknown to the living vocabulary, because they are artificially constructed to meet the exigencies of rhyme or metre: such words as—

Thou, thee, thy, ye, mineself.

Art (verb form), *wast, wert, dost, wilt* (verb form), *hast, hadst, wouldst, shouldst, shalt,* and all verb forms ending in *-est, -st* and the like.

'Tis, 'gainst, 'gin, 'tween, 'neath, e'er, and other contractions not in living speech; as opposed to *it's* and other contractions used in living speech.

Wroth, bethink, reft, reaving, athwart, welkin, rathe, fardel, burthen, murther, nave, chaps, gins, sooth, Norweyan, proof (for *armor*), *composition* (for *terms of peace*), *ronyon,* and all other archaic, obsolescent or obsolete words.

Except for "unless," *memorize* for "make memorable," and other outworn usages of words.

All unnatural and elliptical expressions, improper in living speech, such as *as to* for "as if to," *bethink me* for "recall," *for to that* for "for to that end," and the like.

All inversions and strained expressions improper in living speech, such as *the soldier brave, have I seen, I battles fought,* and the like. These are common, because rhyme-induced.

Poetry that speaks a dead language is dead from its birth; poetry that speaks a warped and distorted language is warped and distorted from its birth. For when real poetry from real poets is encountered, its speech is as direct, forthright and living as:

> Our revels now are ended. These our actors,
> As I foretold you, were all spirits, and
> Are melted into air, into thin air;
> And, like the baseless fabric of this vision,
> The cloud-capp'd towers, the gorgeous palaces,
> The solemn temples, the great globe itself,
> Yea, all which it *inherit,* shall dissolve,
> And, like this insubstantial pageant *faded,*
> Leave not a *rack* behind. We are such stuff
> As dreams are made *on,* and our little life
> Is rounded with a sleep.
>
> *The Tempest,* William Shakespeare.

The captious might suggest *inherits* for *inherit;* might point out that *faded* is out of place; that "made *of*" is preferable to "made *on*"; we might query the *rack.* At that, *rack* is still used in "rack and ruin," a "cloud-rack," "the rack of a storm": and *rack,* used here in the sense of a vestige, is intelligible and may be regarded as living. And this poetry was written more than three hundred years ago, by William Shakespeare, who knew too much, even then, to stud his verse with *thee's* and *thou's* and their outmoded verb forms, *welkin, athwart, amaranthine,* and so on.

The test for the phrasing of poetry is: could you have said the same thing, or its equivalent, to your maid or your butcher, and not been regarded as eccentric? If your poetry speaks your own living language, its vocabulary is acceptable. If it is marred with word-fossils no longer acceptable in living speech, to that extent it falls below its possible flight.

No word acceptable in acceptable prose is out of place in poetry. Any word may be so ineptly or awkwardly used in poetry, that it becomes a blemish. When Shakespeare wrote:

> It is a tale
> Told by an idiot, full of sound and fury,
> Signifying nothing,
>
> *Macbeth,* William Shakespeare.

he used *idiot* magnificently and poetically; when Wordsworth
wrote:

> Why bustle thus about your door?
> What means this bustle, Betty Foy?
> Why are you in this mighty fret?
> And why on horseback have you set
> Him whom you love, your Idiot Boy?
>> *The Idiot Boy*, William Wordsworth.

the word *idiot* is as unpoetic as the rest of the passage. The living
speech, the colloquial, can be magical, poetic, as in this sonnet
sestet:

> It is some lie that under a windswept tree,
>> Touching your lips, I touched my vanished youth,
> And found again a young, new ecstasy.
>> It is a lie, I say. This—this is Truth!
> Now—I shall rest. For youth and you are gone.
> Tomorrow I shall put my flannels on.
>> *Sonnet*, John V. A. Weaver.

Edwin Arlington Robinson will be remembered for lines as
colloquially magical as:

> The man who had made other men
> As ordinary as arithmetic . . .

> I'll have to tell you, Brother Bedivere,
> That crowns and orders, and high palaces, . . .
> Will not go rolling down to hell just yet
> Because a pretty woman is a fool.
>> *Merlin*, Edwin Arlington Robinson.

He will have to be forgiven for verse as bookish as:

> Born with a face
> That on a bullfrog would ensure for life
> The lucubrations of a celibate . . .

> Less to remembering an obscure monition
> Than to confessing an assured renascence—
>> *Roman Bartholow*, Edwin Arlington Robinson.

though both of these are not so much archaic as morbidly pedantic.
Frost rarely departs from living speech; he has enriched the

language by phrases immortally and colloquially true, including the familiar:

> The trial by market everything must come to.

Even slang has its place: did not Shakespeare have Hamlet say—

> So I do still, by these pickers and stealers . . .
> > *Hamlet*, William Shakespeare.

Nor is Sandburg more unpoetic, when he writes:

> Play it across the table.
> What if we steal this city blind?
> If they want anything let 'em nail it down.
> > *Cahoots*, Carl Sandburg.

John Livingston Lowes, in *Convention and Revolt in Poetry*, phrases words of gold for poets to remember:

> The very greatest effects of poetry are often produced without the use of a single word which might not be employed in ordinary speech.

Thomas Gray wrote, in one of his letters:

> The language of the age is never the language of poetry. . . . Our poetry . . . has a language peculiar to itself.

This attitude explains the common idea permitting dead speech in verse; it can not resurrect poets following it from the graves their practice of this dug. Such poets live only insofar as they violate this statement.

Wordsworth followed this, when he preluded his *The Force of Prayer* with the double archaism:

> What is good for a bootless bene?

Witty Mary Lamb flashed back, when her brother Charles read this to her, "A shoeless pea," and punned this absurd line into immortality. And there is Rossetti's phrase from his rendition of the Villon ballade,

> From Love he won such dule and teen!

Poetry does not gain by using such mummified speech.

Kipling was more successful than any previous poet so far in using the language of the machine age in poetry:

It is their care, in all the ages, to take the buffet and cushion the
    shock;
It is their care that the gear engages; it is their care that the switches
    lock;
It is their care that the wheels run truly; it is their care to embark
    and entrain,
Tally, transport, and deliver duly the sons of Mary by land and main.
                            The Sons of Martha, Rudyard Kipling.

In a memorandum dealing with the writing of *Leaves of Grass,*
Walt Whitman wrote:

> I had great trouble in leaving out the stock
> "poetical" touches, but succeeded at last.

Even this great plain-speaking master slipped back, as he aged,
into stock poeticisms such as:

> 'mid, unrecked, know I, yield we, ye valleys grand.

But in the main he avoided this blemish. And he has made the
task easier for those who followed him.

Sidney Lanier lays stress upon *phonetic syzygy,* that extension
of alliteration which includes all related consonants, as *t, d, th,* and
TH; g, k, ch, and other gutturals, and so on. Other authorities deal
extensively with *onomatopoeia,* the language device in which
words reproduce the sounds they are intended to convey, as in—

> With lisp of leaves and ripple of rain.
> *Chorus from Atalanta in Calydon,* Algernon Charles Swinburne.

With any inner sense of music, we will avoid lines as awkward,
inept and unsingable as Browning's familiar:

> Irks care the crop-full bird, frets doubt the maw-crammed beast?
>   *Rabbi Ben Ezra,* Robert Browning.

Let your poetic speech be your own living speech at its best, dictated by an innate sense of music, and the result will satisfy.

On Translating Poetry

Poetry can not be translated; it can only be recreated in the
new language. We are dealing with the ingredients of verse, not
of poetry, in this book: a study of the essence of poetry would

not deal with iambs and cinquains and sestinas, it would deal
with the stimuli that most deeply affect the human emotions. The
emotion-arousing quality in words can not be stated otherwise
even in the same language, much less in another one. There is no
translation in English for emotion-arousing words such as *home,
mother, love,* and so on; not *house* or *domicile,* not *mamma* or
maternal ancestor or *Moms* or *ma,* not *affection* or *devotion* or
lust or *rut.* How can *night* be expressed in another word, or *moon*
or *sun,* or *May,* or *December?* Each of these words—to some
extent each word in the language—has a tone-color, a history, a
personality, an effectiveness of its own. With many of the words
in the language, each person has strange and personal associations,
naturally untranslatable. There are emotions which are not translatable from country to country, but which can only be recreated
by some remote equivalent. When Noyes climaxes a poem with
the glorious invocation,

> Englande!—Englande!—Englande!—Englande!
> *Marchaunt Adventurers,* Alfred Noyes.

he utters a battle-cry that only an Englishman could thrill to. Its
word music is lost the moment it reappears as *Angleterre! Angleterre! Angleterre! Angleterre!* "Finland! Finland! Finland! Finland!" would not thrill similarly, though the rhythm and word tune
are the same. A fourfold repetition of *Switzerland,* or *Czechoslo-
vakia,* or, queerly enough, even of *United States,* would not evoke
a similar thrill. Moreover, Shelley could have used the same repetition of *England,* in a poem in the bitter mood of *The Masque of
Anarchy,* and it would have evoked utter detestation: so intangible
are the elements in sounds that uplift or break the heart, that send
a Cardigan or a Pickett with a whole brigade of men to death at
the monosyllable "Charge!," that spell heaven in a girl's whispered
"Yes," and a lifetime's dearth in her even briefer "No."

In Keats's *Ode to a Nightingale* we have two lines of peak
magic:

> Charmed magic casements, opening on the foam
> Of perilous seas, in faery lands forlorn.

These two lines can not be said differently in English, without
wrecking the magic. Accurately paraphrased, they would give:

> Enchanted supernatural windows, unclosing on the bubbles
> Of dangerous oceans, in unreal romantic countries dejected.

There is no poetry here, now. Translate it with absolute fidelity into another language, and the poetry is as dead. It must be recreated by a poet of like emotional power in the other language, if it is to survive there as poetry.

Fitzgerald did such magic, when he took a literal translation of the poetic *Rubaiyat* of Omar Khayyam, such as these two groups of lines:

> Everywhere that there has been a rose or tulip-bed,
> It has come from the redness of the blood of a king;
> Every violet shoot that grows from the earth
> Is a mole that was once on the cheek of a beauty.
>
> Quatrains, Omar Khayyam.

This is inaccurate botanically, and only whimsically effective as an idea. It is certainly not poetry. Nor is:

> Hell is a spark from my useless worries,
> Paradise is a moment of time when I am tranquil.
>
> Quatrains, Omar Khayyam.

But out of this material Fitzgerald wrought—created, recreated—what thousands hail as poetry:

> I sometimes think that never blows so red
> The Rose, as where some buried Caesar bled;
>   That every Hyacinth the Garden wears
> Dropt in her Lap from some once lovely Head. . . .

> Heav'n but the Vision of fulfilled Desire,
> And Hell the Shadow from a Soul on fire,
>   Cast on the Darkness into which Ourselves,
> So late emerged from, shall so soon expire.
>
> Rubaiyat of Omar Khayyam, Edward Fitzgerald.

This is no longer Omar Khayyam; it is far more Fitzgerald, inspired by Omar Khayyam. The reflection about the rose is acceptable now; the whimsey about the hyacinth is more pleasing to us than the more fleshly Oriental passion of the mole on the cheek of a beauty. The definitions of heaven and hell no longer resemble the original at all. Oriental impassivity and superiority to things earthly have been replaced by a viewpoint accurate enough to have come out of Freud, and acceptable as concentrated truth to many of us. All of this is expressed with the most effective devices of versification, a language in which poetry must speak, if it speak at all.

Something like this must be done, each time you seek to make a translation. A literal translation can give the idea, but never the poetry.

For a last example, here is an accurate translation of the first five verses of the first chapter of *Genesis,* by Fagnani:

> At the beginning of Elohim's forming the heavens and the earth, when darkness was upon the face of the abyss, Elohim said, "Let there be light," and there was light.
> Elohim saw that the light was excellent.
> And Elohim separated the light from the darkness and he called the light Day and the darkness he called Night.
> Evening came, and Morning came.
>> *The Beginning of History, According to the Jews,*
>> Charles Prosper Fagnani.

This is near to poetry, so magnificent is the primitive conception. But it is not mere familiarity that makes us recognize, from the hands of greater poets writing in English, the magnificent poetry of the same verses, as they appear in the King James' Bible:

> In the beginning God created the heavens and the earth.
> And the earth was without form, and void; and darkness was upon the face of the deep. And the Spirit of God moved upon the face of the waters.
> And God said, Let there be light: and there was light.
> And God saw the light, that it was good; and God divided the light from the darkness.
> And God called the light Day, and the darkness he called Night. And the evening and the morning were the first day.
>> *Genesis,* King James's Translation.

The most accurate translation of a poem is no more than rude notes for a poem to be built upon. There is always need for accurate renditions of the poetry of other lands and tongues. But, unless the English versifier re-issue the product as his own re-creation, it remains mere verse, a museum curiosity rather than impassioned song.

Exercises in Versification

To give the book its greatest value, the reader, having reached this point, should start over again, and write exercises in each poetic device treated. Practice iambic lines, each number of feet to the line, rhymed and unrhymed. The same with trochaic, anapestic, and dactylic lines. At times seek to pour poetry into these molds; at times find the relief of light verse in them.

Essay the stanzas, from the couplet up to such involved arrangements as the Spencerian stanza and *terza rima*. Work on sonnets of both kinds: aiming at technical mastery, rather than poetic excellence, at first. Get the patterns etched on your mind, and then you can write in them accurately without consciously remembering them. Try the solace of concentrated and poetic free verse. And then, if you care to, go at the fixed forms one after another, preferably in light verse, and among all these attempts you will startle yourself by achieving at times a veritable poem or gem of light verse when you merely intended finger-exercises.

And at all times, when the poetic mood comes, write what comes, from a phrase, a line, a couplet, to an epic fragment: and preserve it, on the chance that, sooner or later, the rest of the poem will come.

THE COMPLETE RHYMING DICTIONARY

What Rhyme Is

RHYME is the identity in sound of an accented vowel in a word, usually the last one accented, and of all consonantal and vowel sounds following it; with a difference in the sound of the consonant immediately preceding the accented vowel.

Rhyme thus deals exclusively with sound. Sound is indicated in all dictionaries by phonetic markings. In this rhyming dictionary, each group of words that rhyme is preceded by a heading consisting of the accented vowel, marked phonetically, and followed by all the consonantal and vowel sounds following it. The unaccented vowels are not marked phonetically, since they are relatively unimportant: except to distinguish between rhyme sounds like *pasture* (ĂS'tūr) and *faster* (ĂS'tŭr).

The one-syllabled rhymes are given first, with the rhyme-sound headings arranged alphabetically, from the first A sound to the last U sound. Then follow the two-syllabled rhymes, similarly arranged; and, last of all, the three-syllabled rhymes.

The Vowel Sounds

In this phonetic arrangement, the vowel sounds used are indicated as follows. After each is given the various ways in which the sound appears in spelling in English.

A

Ā as in ale; heard also in pain, day, break, veil, obey, gaol, gauge, eh.
Â as in care; heard also in there, pear, air, heir, prayer, e'er.
Ă as in add; heard also in plaid, bade.
Ä as in arm, father; heard also in hearth, sergeant, memoir.
Ạ as in ask. Strictly, authorities say that A should be so pronounced (midway between the A in *father* and the A in *add*) when fol-

lowed by *s, th, f,* or *m* or *n* plus a consonant. In practice, this sound is usually pronounced like the A in *add.* The rule becomes absurd, when we try to pronounce *pan* with the A sound in *add,* and *pans* with a different A sound.

E

Ē as in me; heard also in eve, feet, beam, deceive, people, key, Caesar, machine, field, quay, phoebe.

Ẹ as in here; heard also in fear, dreary, weird.

Ĕ as in end; heard also in heifer, leopard, friends, Aetna, feather, asafoetida, bury, any, Thames, said, says.

I

Ī as in ice; heard also in vie, rye, height, eye, aisle, aye meaning *yes,* sky, buy, choir.

Ĭ as in ill; heard also in sieve, English, pretty, been, breeches, women, busy, build, nymph, hymnal.

O

Ō as in old; heard also in note, oh, roam, foe, shoulder, grow, owe, sew, yeoman, beau, hautboy, brooch.

Ô as in or; heard also in all, talk, swarm, haul, caught, law, fought, broad, memoir.

Ŏ as in odd; heard also in want, wash, shone.

OI as in oil; heard also in boy.

OͦO as in foot; heard also in full, wolf, could.

OU as in out; heard also in cow, sauerkraut.

U

Ū as in use; heard also in beauty, feud, pew, queue, lieu, view, cue, suit, yule, you, do, rule, true, food, group, drew, fruit, canoe, rheum, maneuvre, blue. (The difference in sound between *dew* and *do* is that *dew* is properly dyŪ, with a consonantal *y* sound preceding the long U. This difference does not affect rhyming, except as it concerns preceding consonants. For the sake of convenience, the yŪ group ordinarily precedes the Ū group.)

Û as in urn; heard also in fern, err, heard, sir, word, journal, myrrh, colonel.

Ŭ as in up; heard also in won, one, does, flood, double.

The Consonant Sounds

The consonant sounds used in English, and in most instances spelt phonetically in the headings preceding all groups of words rhyming together, are as follows:

B   as in baby.
CH   as in chair; heard also in match, question, righteous.
D   as in did; heard also in robbed.
F   as in fill; heard also in philosophy, laugh.
G   as in go, anger; heard also in guard, plague, ghost.
GZ   as the sound represented by *x* in exist.
H   as in hat.
HW   as the sound represented by *wh* in what.
J   as in joke; heard also in gem, religion, pigeon, soldier, edge.
K   as in keep; heard also in chorus, epoch, cube, pack, conquer, pique.
KS   as the sound represented by *x* in vex.
KW   as the sound represented by *qu* in queen.
L   as in late.
M   as in man.
N   as in no.
N   The French nasal sound, not natural in English.
NG   as in sing; heard also in tongue, bank, junction, linger, canker.
P   as in papa.
R   as in red; heard also in rhombus.
S   as in so, this; heard also in cell, scene, hiss.
SH   as in she; heard also in machine, ocean, social, conscious, sure, nauseous, pension, issue, passion, nation.
T   as in time.
TH   as in then.
th   as in thin.
TU   as in nature. This sound is more accurately TY consonantal.
V   as in van.
W   as in want; heard also in persuade, choir.
Y   as in yet; heard also in union.
Z   as in zone; heard also in is, lives, Xenophon.
ZH   as the sound represented by *z* in azure; heard also in glazier, pleasure, vision, abscission, rouge, genre.

A few warnings are important.

C is not a separate sound. Words spelt with *c* appear under K or S

Q is not a separate sound. Words spelt with *qu* or *q* appear under KW.

X is not a separate sound. Words spelt with *x* appear under GZ or KS; initial *x* appears as Z.

NK, in words like *rank,* is properly NGK, and so appears. *Hankow* would appear under ĂN′kow; hanker, under ĂNGK′ur.

To form plurals and other inflections, F, K, P and T are followed by the sound S; the plain vowel, G, D, B, M, N, S, V, J, CH, L, R, KS (X) and Z are followed by the sound Z.

To form past tenses and other inflections, CH, S, F, K and P are followed by the sound T; the plain vowel, G, D, B, M, N, S, V, J, L, R and Z are followed by the sound D.

Sound Does Not Depend on Spelling

Sound does not depend on spelling. "Eye-rhymes," or words matched as rhymes only because they are spelled alike, need not be rhymes at all. For instance, here are five different sounds spelled alike, *ough:*

cough, enough, plough, though, through.

It is as logical to rhyme these together as to rhyme *earth-hearth, bare-are, north-forth, real-steal.*

Again, note that *timber* and *climber* are spelled alike; but the first rhymes with limber (ĬM′bur) and the second with rhymer (ĪM′ur). Three more words spelled alike but rhymed very differently are *ginger*(ĬNJ′ur); *singer*(ĬNG′ur); and *finger* (ĬNG′gur). Until *cow* rhymes with *blow* it is well to avoid all these words spelled alike but pronounced differently.

This Dictionary Makes Consonance Accurate

Consonance consists in the identity of all consonantal and vowel sounds after the accented vowel; and a difference in the accented vowel. This dictionary, classified according to strict phonetic pronunciation, for the first time makes consonance easy and accurate. Alphabetically arranged by the headings preceding each group of rhyme words, the following three rhyme sounds appear together: Ō′li (wholly), Ô′li (Raleigh), ŎL′i (folly). Naturally these three groups are in consonance with each other.

To get the other groups of rhyming words which may be used in consonance with these three, look up successively Ā′li, ĂL′i, Ē′li, ĔL′i, OIL′i, OŎl′i, OUL′i, Ū′li, ŬL′i; and you have all the possible sounds in consonance with the three sounds given. You may stretch a point and add ÂR′li, ĂR′li, ĒR′li and ÛR′li if you wish, and now nothing conceivable is omitted.

Consonance, always used by the best poets, is growing so increasingly in favor, that this use of the present *Complete Rhyming Dictionary* may become very important.

Why This is Called Complete

This volume contains hundreds of rhyming words omitted from former collections. Many of these omissions are inexplicable, unless by oversight. Others consist of words recently added to the vocabulary, especially in the fields of general science, pure and applied; inventions and popular applications of them, such as moving pictures, aviation, and radio; and the vivid field of recent slang words generally acceptable. The effort has been to include all words that are a proper part of the living vocabulary of man: for it is in this language that living poetry must speak.

Archaic and obsolete words, and many words used only in an artificial solemn or poetic style, have not been omitted. Instead, as a rule these have been italicized. They are still available to the seeker who wishes to use them, each in its proper niche. But this feature both includes them for convenience, and badges them with the suggestion that, since they are not a part of man's living vocabulary, they may well be avoided.

In addition to this, the present volume contains more proper names than were ever listed in a rhyming dictionary before. This includes especially:

The familiar first names of boys and girls, men and women.

The familiar and easily rhymable geographical names.

The more familiar surnames, family names or last names.

In listing proper names, the name is not repeated when it differs only from a common word by the use of a capital. Thus, since *wood* is included, *Wood* is not. Where the spelling differs, the rhyming proper name is usually added. Thus, to *main* is added

Maine. Moreover, unnecessary duplication of words is generally avoided throughout the book. A large number of words ending in *-y* is given as rhymes for the long E sound; but, at the end of this large list, the reader is referred to other words ending in *-y,* to be found in such three-syllabled rhyme groups as the words rhyming with *ability;* which is to be consulted, if the seeker desires more rhymes for long *E.* Moreover, at the end of the rhyming words listed to rhyme with 'fade,' the reader is referred to the list of words rhyming on the long A sound, to which *-ed* is to be added, to make further rhymes for 'fade'; and this is to be consulted, if the seeker desires more rhymes for 'fade.' There is as little such cross-reference as possible, and it is never perplexing.

The dictionary is not wholly complete, and probably none will ever be. Rare and unusual scientific and geographic terms and names, for instance, as a rule have been omitted. It will add to the value of your copy of the book if you add, at the appropriate place, all omitted words that you discover.

In the lists of words rhyming on the last syllable and on the syllable before the last, certain words are included, which have no rhyming mates. The monosyllables or words accented on the last syllable which appear to be rhymeless are:

aitch, H	lounge	recumb
avenge, revenge	mauve	rouge
avenged, revenged	month	sauce
bilge	morgue	scarce
bourne	mourned, bemourned,	spoilt
bourse	unmourned	swoln
bulb	mouthe	sylph
coif	of, hereof, thereof,	torsk
culm	whereof	twelfth
cusp	peart	plagued, unplagued
doth	porch	warmth
film	pork	wasp
forge	poulp	wharves
fugue	prestige	wolf
gulf, engulf	puss	wolves

In addition to these forty-three rhymeless sounds, there is a group which has no rhyme in the living vocabulary:

amongst	forth, fourth
breadth	ninth
depth	sixth
eighth	tenth
fifth	width

These can all be rhymed by using permissible contractions of archaic or obsolete forms, such as: *clung'st, shed'th, step'th, hate'th, sniff'th, pour'th, pine'th, mix'th, pen'th* and *skid'th*. There is a limited group of words which find their rhyming mates only in proper names, including:

alb (De Kalb)   hemp (Kemp)   oblige (Lije)

There are other words which have no proper rhyming mates, but have words so close in sound that they are used as rhyming mates by many poets:

blague (vague)	en masse (class)
raj (dodge)	basque (mask, masque)
wand (pond)	else (belts)
melange (blanc mange)	grilse (wilts)
swap (top)	Welsh (belch)

THE DICTIONARY
OF RHYMING WORDS

MONOSYLLABLES, AND WORDS ACCENTED ON THE LAST SYLLABLE:

MASCULINE RHYMES; SINGLE RHYMES

A

These words include the following accented vowel sounds:

Ā as in ale; heard also in pain, day, break, veil, obey, gaol, gauge, eh.

Â as in care; heard also in there, pear, air, heir, prayer, e'er.

Ă as in add; heard also in plaid, bade.

Ä as in arm, father; heard also in hearth, sergeant, memoir.

Å as in ask. In practice, this is usually pronounced like the A sound in *add*.

For the vowel sound heard in all, talk, swarm, haul, caught, law, see under Ô.

For the vowel sound heard in want and wash, see under Ŏ.

Ā	astay	belay	Bordelais
affray	astray	bepray	bouquet
agley	au fait	betray	brae
allay	auto-da-fé	*bewray*	bray
alackaday	away	birthday	bridle-way
array	aweigh	Biscay	byway
Ascension-day	*aye*	bobsleigh	cabriolet
assay	bay	bobstay	Calais
assagai	bey	Bombay	caraway

In compound words—words consisting of two or more words united—the parts of the words may be joined without a hyphen, may be joined with a hyphen, or may be written separately. In some words usage is fixed; in others it varies. No standard rule is followed; though the hyphen today is less used than formerly. In this book, the usual practice of the best prose-writers and poets is followed, modified in instances by the editor's own preference. In general, poets and versifiers make such decisions for themselves in each instance.

ōld, ôr, ŏdd, oil, fŏŏt, out; ūse, ûrn, ŭp; THis, thin

castaway	fairway	interlay	overlay
causeway	fair-play	interplay	overpay
Chevalier	fay	inveigh	overstay
Chevrolet	feather-spray	irongray	papier mâché
Christmas-day	fey	jay	passée
clay	fireclay	judgment-day	Passion-play
Cloisonné	first-day	Kay	pathway
convey	flay	lack-a-day	pay
corvée	footway	Lady-day	payday
coryphée	foray	leaden-gray	play
coupé	forelay	lay	playday
crossway	foresay	leeway	popinjay
dapple-bay	forestay	Leigh	portray
dapple-gray	forlay	Lord's-day	pray
day	fray	mainstay	prepay
dead-pay	gainsay	Malay	prey
decay	gala-day	Mandalay	protegé
defray	galloway	market-day	protegée
dejeuner	gangway	matinée	purvey
delay	gay	May	qua
dey	get-away	mid-day	quarter-day
disarray	good-day	mid-way	railway
dismay	gourmet	Milky Way	raisonné
disobey	gray	mislay	ray
display	grey	missay	relay
distingué	habitué	Monterey	repay
distrait	Haigh	Monterrey	résumé
doomsday	halfway	nay	reveillé
Doré	hay	née	ricochet
dragonné	hearsay	negligée	Roget
dray	hey	neigh	roturier
Dupré	heyday	noonday	roundelay
Easter-day	highday	nosegay	runaway
eh	highway	obey	sachet
émigré	hodden-gray	O'Day	Salomé
employé	hogmanay	Okay	San Jose
employée	holiday	O'Shay	Santa Fé
entremets	Honoré	outlay	Saturday
essay	hooray	outstay	say
estray	horseplay	outré	scray
exposé	inlay	outweigh	settling-day

seventh-day
shay
silver-gray
slay
sleigh
sley
sobriquet
soiree
soothsay
soufflé
spay
splay
spray
stageplay
stay
steerage-way
stowaway
strathspey
stray
subway
survey
sway
thereaway
they
to-day
Tokay
toupet
tourniquet
tramway
tray
trey
trysting-day
tway
underlay
underpay
underplay
undersay
unlay
unpray
unsay
uplay

upstay
virelay
visé
water-way
way
waylay
wedding-day
weekday
weigh
welladay
wellaway
wey
whey
workaday
working-day
Wray
yea
yesterday

Ä

Aceldama
ah
aha
algebra
alumina
amphibia
anathema
Andromeda
anglophobia
animalcula
Apocrypha
Aquila
automata
baa
baccarat
bacteria
bah
basilica
blah
bourgeois
camera

carnivora
chapeau bras
cholera
cinema
clepsydra
cupola
éclat
Egeria
ephemera
et cetera
fa
faux-pas
formula
genera
Golgotha
gondola
grandmamma
ha
hah
ha-ha
Hegira
holla
hurrah
huzza
hydrophobia
hypochondria
incognita
insomnia
Jah
la
ma
mamma
majolica
mandragora
nebula
opera
orchestra
pa
padishah
pah
papa

parabola
pariah
pas
pasha
peninsula
phantasma-
       goria
phenomena
plethora
prolegomena
Pthah
quadrigesima
quadrumana
quinquagesima
replica
retina
septuagesima
sexagesima
Shah
silica
spa
spatula
tarantula
tonic sol-fa
Utopia
uvula
vertebra
viola

ĀB

Abe
astrolabe
babe
cosmolabe
foster-babe

ĂB

abb
bab
Babb
baobab

ōld, ôr, ŏdd, oil. fŏŏt, out; ūse, ûrn, ŭp; THis, thin

bedab
blab
cab
Cantab
confab
crab
dab
drab
frab
gab
grab
jab
knab
lab
mab
McNabb
nab
rab
scab
shab
slab
stab
tab
taxi-cab

ĂB

squab
swab, etc.
(See blob, etc.,
  ŎB)

ĂCH

aitch
H

ĂCH

attach
batch
brach
catch
cratch

detach
dispatch
hatch
latch
match
overmatch
patch
percussion-
  match
ratch
scatch
scratch
slatch
smatch
snatch
tache
thatch
unlatch

ĂCH

watch
(see blotch,
  ŎCH)

ĂCHT

hatched
semi-detached
attached, etc.

ĀD

abrade
abraid
accolade
Ade
Adelaide
afraid
aid
alcaide
ambassade
ambuscade
arcade

bade
balustrade
barricade
bastinade
bejade
Belgrade
blade
blockade
braid
brigade
brocade
cade
camerade
camisade
cannonade
carronade
cascade
cassonade
cavalcade
centigrade
charade
co-aid
cockade
colonnade
corrade
croupade
crusade
dade
dairy-maid
Damascus-
  blade
decade
deep-laid
defilade
degrade
dissuade
dragonnade
enfilade
escalade
escapade
esplanade

estacade
estrapade
evade
fade
falcade
fanfaronade
fire-brigade
flanconnade
free-trade
fusillade
gabionnade
gallopade
gambade
gasconade
glade
glissade
grade
grass-blade
grenade
grillade
hade
handmaid
harlequinade
harquebusade
inlaid
interlaid
invade
jade
lade
laid
lancepesade
lemonade
made
maid
make the grade
marinade
marmalade
masquerade
McDade
mermaid
milkmaid

new-made	staid	*egad*	couvade
nightshade	stockade	englad	estrade
old-maid	storm-stayed	fad	façade
orangeade	*suade*	footpad	glissade
overlaid	suède	forbade	ha-ha'd
overpaid	tirade	gad	hurrahed
overstayed	trade	glad	*hussa'd*
over-persuade	unafraid	grad	lancepesade
overshade	unarrayed	had	noyade
paid	unassayed	heath-clad	pomade
palisade	unbraid	hebdomad	promenade
panade	underaid	iron-clad	psha'd
parade	underlaid	ivy-clad	roulade
pasquinade	undismayed	lad	wad
passade	unessayed	Leningrad	(see *cod*, etc.)
persuade	unlade	mad	
pervade	unlaid	moss-clad	**ĂDZ**
pesade	unmade	myriad	ads
pistolade	unmaid	Olympiad	adze
plaid	unpaid	pad	scads
plantigrade	unprayed	Petrograd	adds, etc.
pomade	unrepaid	pine-clad	
postpaid	unstaid	plaid	**ĀF**
prepaid	unweighed	*rad*	chafe
promenade	upbraid	sad	enchafe
raid	wade	scad	safe
rayed	(see Ā + ed)	shad	strafe
ready-made		superadd	unsafe
renegade	**ĂD**	tonguepad	vouchsafe
retrograde	ad	Trinidad	waif
rodomontade	add	unclad	
saccade	bad	undergrad	**ĂF**
scalade	bedad	unforbade	actinograph
sea-maid	*begad*	unsad	agraffe
self-made	bade	winter-clad	anagraph
serenade	brad	*yclad*	autograph
serving-maid	cad		behalf
shade	Chad	**ĂD**	belly-laugh
slade	chiliad	baa'd	betterhalf
spade	clad	*chamade*	calf
stade	dad	charade	calligraph

ōld, ôr, ŏdd, oil, fŏŏt, out; ūse, ûrn, ŭp; THis, thin

carafe
cenotaph
chaff
chronograph
cinematograph
cross-staff
cryptograph
diagraph
dictagraph
distaff
draff
eidograph
epigraph
epitaph
flagstaff
gaff
giraffe
graff
hagiograph
half
half-and-half
halfstaff
heliograph
holograph
ideograph
idiograph
laugh
lithograph
monograph
mooncalf
palaeograph
pantograph
paragraph
penny-gaff
phonograph
photograph
polygraph
quaff
quarter-staff
raff
riff-raff

shandy-gaff
staff
stenograph
stereograph
telegraph
tipstaff
whipstaff

ĂF

behalf
belly-laugh
betterhalf
calf
graf
haaf
half
half-and-half
laugh
mooncalf
strafe

ĂFT

abaft
aft
craft
daft
draft
draught
engraft
fellow-craft
graft
haft
handicraft
ingraft
overdraft
priestcraft
raft
river-craft
sea-craft
shaft
waft

witchcraft
chaffed, etc.

ĀG

Hague
plague
Prague
vague

ĂG

bag
battle-flag
brag
Bragg
bullyrag
cag
chew the **rag**
crag
drag
fag
fishfag
flag
gag
hag
jag
knag
lag
mag
nag
nighthag
quag
rag
ragtag
saddle-bag
sag
ᶜcallawag
scrag
shag
shrag
slag
snag

sprag
stag
swag
tag
wag
Wragg
zigzag

ĂG

blague

ĀGD

unplagued

ĂGD

betagged
bagged, etc.

ĀJ

acreage
age
alienage
anchorage
appanage
arbitrage
armitage
assuage
average
baronage
beverage
brigandage
brokerage
cage
cartilage
chaperonage
compage
concubinage
cooperage
discage
disengage
encage

āle, câre, ădd, ärm, åsk; mē, hẹre, ĕnd; īce, ĭll;

engage
enrage
equipage
espionage
flowerage
foliage
foot-page
fortilage
gage
gauge
harborage
hemorrhage
heritage
hermitage
hospitage
leverage
lineage
mage
matronage
mid-age
mucilage
outrage
page
parentage
parsonage
pastorage
pasturage
patronage
peonage
personage
pilgrimage
pilotage
plunderage
porterage
pre-engage
presage
pupilage
quarterage
rage
rampage
ramgauge

sage
saxifrage
seignorage
stage
surplusage
swage
tutelage
tutorage
uncage
unsage
vassalage
verbiage
vicarage
vicinage
villanage
villenage
wage
weather-gauge

ĂJ

badge
cadge
fadge
hadj

ÄJ

raj
(Cf. badge, ĂJ)

ĀK

ache
after-rake
aslake
awake
backache
bake
barley-brake
bellyache
betake
blacksnake
Blake

brake
break
cake
crake
day-break
drake
earache
earthquake
fake
flake
forespake
forsake
garter-snake
hake
hard-bake
heartache
heart-break
jake
johnny-cake
lake
make
mandrake
milk-snake
mistake
namesake
opaque
outbreak
overtake
partake
quake
rake
rattlesnake
robin-wake
sake
seed-cake
shake
sheik
sheldrake
slake
snake
snow-flake

spake
stake
steak
stomachache
strake
sweepstake
take
toothache
undertake
unmake
upbreak
uptake
wake
wapentake
water-break
water-crake
water-snake
wedding-cake

ĂK

aback
alack
almanac
ammoniac
attack
bac
back
bareback
bivouac
black
blackjack
bootjack
brach
bric-a-brac
cardiac
chack
clack
claque
crack
cul-de-sac
demoniac

ōld, ôr, ŏdd, oil, fŏŏt, out; ūse, ûrn, ŭp; THis, thin

dipsomaniac
Dyak
egomaniac
elegiac
Fond du Lac
good-lack
gripsack
hack
Hackensack
hackmatack
haversack
haystack
horseback
huckaback
humpback
hunchback
hypochondriac
jack
jimcrack
kayak
kleptomaniac
knack
knicknack
kodak
lac
lack
ladybrach
lakh
leather-jack
macaque
maniac
monomaniac
natterjack
pack
pickaback
plack
Pontiac
pyromaniac
quack
rack

ransack
rucksack
sac
sack
sacque
sal ammoniac
seawrack
shack
skipjack
slack
slapjack
Slovak
smack
snack
stack
stickleback
symposiac
tack
tamarack
thrack
thunder-crack
thwack
tick-tack
track
umiak
Union-jack
unpack
whack
woolpack
woolsack
wrack
yak
yashmak
yellow-jack
zodiac
zwieback

ĂK

plaque
Sarawak

ĀKS
Jakes
(see ĀK + s)

ĂKS
Analax
anticlimax
Astyanax
ax
battle-ax
flax
Halifax
income-tax
lax
parallax
pax
relax
Sachs
Saxe
slacks
tax
wax
zax
(see ĂK + s.)

ĂKT
abstract
act
attacked
attract
bract
cataract
compact
contract
counteract
detract
diffract
distract
enact
entr' acte
exact

extract
fact
impact
infract
intact
matter-of-fact
overact
pact
protract
react
redact
re-enact
refract
retract
retroact
saddle-backed
subtract
tact
tract
transact
underact
untracked
backed, etc.

ĀL
Abigail
ail
ale
all-hail
assail
avail
aventail
bail
bale
bepale
betail
bewail
blackmail
Bloomingdale
bobtail
brail

Braille
camail
canaille
cocktail
countervail
curtail
dale
dead-pale
death-pale
derail
detail
disentail
dovetail
draggle-tail
dwale
empale
engaol
engrail
enjail
enscale
entail
entrail
exhale
fail
fairy-tale
farthingale
flail
foresail, etc.
frail
Gael
Gail
gale
gaol
grail
grisaille
hail
hale
handrail
hobnail
impale
inhale

interpale
inveil
jail
kail
kale
mail
male
martingale
monorail
nail
nightingale
outsail
overveil
pail
pale
paravail
pigtail
prevail
quail
rail
regale
retail
sail
sale
scale
shale
sliding-scale
snail
spale
stale
swale
tael
tail
tale
tenaille
they'll
trail
travail
trundle-tail
unveil
vail

vale
veil
wail
wale
whale
wholesale

ĂL

aboriginal
academical
accentual
admiral
aërial
aesthetical
affectional
agricultural
Al
alchemical
alchemistical
alexipharmical
alexiterical
algebraical
alkalimetrical
allegorical
allodial
alluvial
alphabetical
amatorial
analogical
analytical
anarchical
anatomical
angelical
animal
annual
antediluvial
anthological
antiphonal
antipodal
antithetical
apochryphal

apologetical
apostolical
arboreal
arboricultural
archeological
architectural
arithmetical
arsenal
arsenical
ascetical
asthmatical
astrological
atmospherical
Babylonical
bacchanal
bacchical
bacteriological
bal
balsamical
banal
barometrical
baronial
basilical
beatifical
biblical
bibliographical
bibliomaniacal
bibliopolical
biographical
biological
boreal
botanical
Brahmanical
bureaucratical
cabal
cacophonical
Cal
Calvinistical
canal
cannibal
canonical

capital
caracal
cardinal
carnival
cartographical
casual
casuistical
categorical
catholical
cervical
chaparral
characteristical
chemical
cherubical
chimerical
chronological
circumlocu-
    tional
classical
clerical
climatical
clinical
collateral
colloquial
comical
communal
complexional
conclusional
conditional
confessional
congressional
conical
conjectural
conjugal
connubial
consanguineal
consistorial
constitutional
continual
contradictional
conventical

conventional
conventual
conversational
corporal
corral
cortical
cosmetical
cosmical
coxcombical
criminal
critical
cryptical
cubical
cyclical
cylindrical
cynical
dal
decanal
decimal
deistical
democratical
demoniacal
demonological
denominational
descensional
destinal
devotional
diabolical
diaconal
diacritical
diagonal
diagraphical
dialectical
dialogical
dialogistical
diametrical
diaphonical
dictatorial
didactical
dietetical
digital

digressional
diluvial
diplomatical
dipsomaniacal
discretional
divisional
doctrinal
dogmatical
dolorifical
dominical
dramatical
dropsical
Druidical
dynamical
eccentrical
ecclesiastical
economical
ecstatical
ecumenical
educational
effectual
egoistical
egotistical
electrical
elegiacal
elliptical
emblematical
emotional
emphatical
empirical
empyreal
encomiastical
encyclical
encyclopedical
endemical
energetical
energical
enigmatical
enthusiastical
ephemeral
epical

epidemical
epigrammati-
    cal
Episcopal
episodical
epithetical
equivocal
erotical
esoterical
ethereal
ethical
ethnical
ethnological
etymological
Eucharistical
eulogistical
euphemistical
euphonical
evangelical
eventual
evolutional
exceptional
exegetical
exoterical
exotical
expurgatorial
extemporal
extrinsical
falderal
fanatical
fantastical
farcical
federal
festival
fictional
finical
forensical
fractional
functional
funeral
funereal

āle,   câre,   ădd,   ärm,   åsk;   mē,   hĕre,   ĕnd;   īce,   ĭll;

gal
galvanical
geminal
genealogical
general
generical
genial
geographical
geological
geometrical
germinal
gradual
grammatical
graphical
habitual
Hal
harmonical
Hebraical
heliacal
hemispherical
herbal
heretical
heroical
hexagonal
hierarchical
historical
horticultural
hospital
hygienical
hymeneal
hyperbolical
hypercritical
hypochondria-
    cal
hypocritical
hysterical
identical
idiotical
illogical
imaginal
imitational

immaterial
immechanical
immemorial
imperial
impersonal
inaugural
incorporeal
individual
industrial
ineffectual
infinitesimal
infusorial
inimical
initial
inquisitorial
inspirational
institutional
instructional
insurrectional
intellectual
intentional
intercessional
interjectional
international
interval
iridal
ironical
jesuitical
jovial
juridical
lachrymal
lackadaisical
laical
lethargical
Levitical
liberal
literal
littoral
liturgical
logical
longitudinal

lyrical
madrigal
magical
magnifical
majestical
mall
maniacal
mareschal
marginal
marital
mathematical
matinal
matronal
mechanical
medical
medicinal
memorial
mercurial
meridional
metaphorical
metaphysical
methodical
Methodistical
metrical
microscopical
mineral
ministerial
misanthropical
monarchical
municipal
musical
mutual
mystical
mythical
mythological
national
natural
nautical
nectareal
nominal
nonsensical

notional
numerical
occasional
octagonal
optical
optional
oratorical
original
pal
paradisaical
parabolical
parenthetical
passional
pastoral
pathetical
pathological
patrimonial
patronal
patronymical
pedagogical
pedantical
pedestal
pedestrial
penological
pentagonal
perennial
periodical
peripheral
periphrastical
perpetual
personal
phantasma-
    gorial
Pharisaical
pharmaceutical
phenomenal
philanthropi-
    cal
philological
philosophical
photographical

ōld, ôr, ŏdd, oil, fŏŏt, out; ūse, ûrn, ŭp; THis, thin

phrenological
phthisical
physical
physiological
pictorial
pictural
pietistical
piratical
pivotal
platonical
pneumatolog-
  ical
poetical
polemical
political
pontifical
post-prandial
practical
pragmatical
precautional
preternatural
primordial
principal
probational
problematical
processional
prodigal
professional
professorial
progressional
prophetical
proportional
proverbial
provisional
psychiatrical
psychical
psychological
punctual
puritanical
purpureal
pyramidal

pyramidical
pyrotechnical
quadrennial
quadrigesimal
quadrilateral
quadrupedal
quizzical
radical
rational
recessional
reciprocal
remedial
residual
retinal
rhapsodical
rhetorical
rheumatical
rhythmical
ritual
sabbatical
sal
sartorial
satanical
satirical
scenical
skeptical
schismatical
scholastical
scriptural
sculptural
seigneurial
seigniorial
seneschal
sensational
seraphical
several
shall
sideral
sidereal
sociological
Socratical

sophistical
spasmodical
spherical
sporadical
stoical
strategical
supernatural
sybaritical
symbolical
symmetrical
synchronal
synchronical
synodical
synonymal
synonymical
synoptical
synthetical
systematical
tactical
technical
technicological
temporal
terminal
terrestrial
territorial
testimonial
theatrical
theological
theoretical
theosophical
topical
topographical
traditional
tragical
trivial
tropical
typical
typographical
tyrannical
umbilical
uncanonical

usual
uxorial
vatical
vegetal
ventriloquial
vertebral
vertical
vesperal
vicarial
victorial
viminal
virginal
virtual
visional
visual
volitional
vortical
whimsical
zodiacal
zoological

ÄL

kraal
Lasalle
morale

ÄLB

alb
De Kalb

ÅLD

bobtailed
unbewailed
unhaled
unassailed
ailed, etc.

ĂLD

caballed
corralled

āle, câre, ădd, ärm, åsk; mē, hĕre, ĕnd; īce, ĭll;

emerald	aflame	ad nauseam	Petersham
palled	aim	am	pram
	ashame	Amsterdam	ram
ĂLF	became	anagram	Rotterdam
Alf	blame	battering-ram	salaam
Ralph	came	Birmingham	Schiedam
	claim	cablegram	scram
ĂLK	counterclaim	cam	sham
catafalque	crème de la	Cham	shram
talc	crème	clam	slam
	dame	cofferdam	stereogram
ĂLKS	declaim	cram	swam
calx	defame	cryptogam	telegram
catafalques	disclaim	cryptogram	tram
	disfame	Cunningham	whim-wham
ĂLP	entame	dam	yam
alp	exclaim	damn	
palp	fame	diagram	**ĂM**
scalp	flame	diaphragm	balm
	frame	dithyramb	becalm
ĂLPS	game	drachm	calm
Alps	hame	dram	embalm
palps, etc.	inflame	epigram	Guam
	lame	flimflam	imam
ĂLT	maim	gam	impalm
shalt	Mame	gram	Islam
	melodrame	ham	ma'am
ĂLV	misname	jam	malm
bivalve	name	jamb	palm
priming-valve	nickname	lam	psalm
safety-valve	overcame	lamb	qualm
salve	proclaim	ma'am	salaam
valve	reclaim	madame	
	same	Mam	**ĂMB**
ĀLZ	self-same	marjoram	dithyramb
Marseilles	shame	McAdam	gamb
Wales	surname	monogram	
(see ĀL + s)	tame	Nizam	**ĀMD**
		Nottingham	unblamed
ĂM	**ĂM**	oriflamme	unclaimed
acclaim	Abraham	parallelogram	unframed

ōld, ôr, ŏdd, oil, fŏŏt, out· ūse, ûrn, ŭp; THis, thin

unnamed
unreclaimed
unshamed
untamed
acclaimed, etc.

ĂMP

after-damp
camp
champ
clamp
cramp
damp
Davy lamp
death-damp
decamp
encamp
enstamp
firedamp
gamp
guimpe
lamp
minedamp
ramp
revamp
safety-lamp
samp
scamp
signal-lamp
stamp
tamp
tramp
vamp

ĂMP

swamp
(see ŎMP)

ĂMPT

undamped
camped, etc.

ĀMZ

Ames
James
acclaims, etc.

ĂMZ

alms
balms, etc.

ĀN

abstain
aerophane
aeroplane
again
Aisne
allophane
amain
appertain
aquaplane
arraign
ascertain
attain
atwain
bane
battering-train
Bayne
bearing-rein
bestain
blain
boatswain
bower-thane
brain
bridle-rein
Cain
Caine
campaign
campane
cane
chain
chamberlain
champagne

champaign
Champlain
Charles's Wain
chatelaine
chicane
chilblain
chow mein
cocaine
Cockaigne
complain
constrain
contain
co-ordain
counterpane
coxswain
crane
Dane
deign
delaine
demesne
deraign
detain
detrain
diaphane
disdain
distrain
domain
drain
Duchesne
Duquesne
elecampane
enchain
engrain
entertain
entrain
explain
fain
fane
feign
fleabane
foreordain

frangipane
gain
germane
grain
henbane
humane
hurricane
hydrophane
hydroplane
immane
inane
ingrain
insane
interchain
interreign
inurbane
jain
Jane
Jayne
jean
lain
lane
legerdemain
lithophane
Lorraine
main
Maine
maintain
mane
Mayne
McLain
McLean
mediterrane
misfeign
moraine
mortmain
obtain
ordain
pain
Paine
pane

Payne
pertain
plain
plane
pleasure-train
porcelain
preordain
profane
pursuit plane
quatrain
rain
refrain
regain
reign
rein
remain
restrain
retain
sane
scatterbrain
Seine
sextain
skein
slain
soutane
Spain
sprain
stain
strain
subterrane
sugarcane
sustain
suzerain
swain
ta'en
tain
terrain
thane
thegn
train
twain

unchain
unrein
uptrain
urbane
vain
vane
vein
vervain
wain
water-crane
wane
weather-vane

ĀN

Acadian
African
alabastrian
Alcoran
Aldebaran
alderman
Alexandrian
Algerian
also ran
amatorian
Amazonian
American
amphibian
an
Anglican
Ann
Anne
antediluvian
artisan
Baconian
ban
Barbadian
barbarian
barbican
barracan
bartizan
basilican

Batavian
Bavarian
began
Bezonian
Bohemian
bran
Briarean
Bulgarian
caducean
Caledonian
Cambrian
can
Canadian
caravan
castellan
Catalan
catamaran
charlatan
Cimmerian
clan
clergyman
Columbian
comedian
Copernican
corban
Corinthian
cosmopolitan
countryman
courtesan
cran
custodian
Cyprian
Dan
Delphian
diluvian
divan
Dominican
echinidan
Englishman
equestrian
Ethiopian

fan
firman
fisherman
flan
foo young dan
foremast-man
foreran
frying-pan
fugleman
Gallican
gargantuan
gentleman
hard-pan
harridan
Hesperian
historian
husbandman
Indian
inspan
Isfahan
Isle of Man
Japan
journeyman
juryman
khan
latitudinarian
librarian
lighterman
liveryman
luggage-van
man
Marianne
Matapan
medicine-man
merchantman
meridian
merman
metropolitan
Mexican
Michigan
midshipman

ōld, ôr, ŏdd, oil, fŏŏt, out; ūse, ûrn, ŭɒ; THis, thin

Milan
minute-man
Mohammedan
Mussulman
nectarean
nobleman
octogenarian
Olympian
oppidan
orang-utan
ortolan
ottoman
outran
outspan
overman
overran
pan
Parmesan
partisan
pavane
pecan
pedestrian
pelican
pemmican
Peruvian
plan
platitudinarian
postmeridan
praetorian
predestinarian
Presbyterian
prison-van
procrustean
proletarian
Promethean
publican
puritan
quarry-man
quotidian
Ramadhan
ran

rattan
redan
Republican
Sabbatarian
Sacramenta-
   rian
sacristan
Samaritan
scan
Sedan
serving-man
shandrydan
signal-man
span
spick-and-span
Stygian
subterranean
suffragan
superman
talisman
tally-man
tan
than
Thespian
tragedian
trepan
unman
utilitarian
Utopian
valerian
valetudinarian
Valkyrian
van
Vatican
vegetarian
Vesuvian
veteran
veterinarian
vulgarian
warming-pan
waterman

wherryman
Zoroastrian

ÄN

corban
swan
wan, etc.
(see ŎN)

ÅNCH

avalanche
blanch
branch
carte-blanche
flanch
ganch
ranch
scranch
stanch

ÄNCH

Blanche
haunch
launch
manche
paunch
stanch
staunch

ÄNCHD

unstanched
launched, etc.

ÅND

bloodstained
constrained
diaphaned
disdained
feather-
   brained
hare-brained

hot-brained
interveined
maned
muddy-brained
rattle-brained
scatter-brained
self-restrained
shallow-
   brained
shatter-brained
travel-stained
unascertained
unconstrained
unplained
unprofaned
unreined
unrestrained
unstained
unstrained
unsustained
untrained
abstained, etc.

ÅND

aband
abbey-land
ampersand
and
band
bland
brand
bridle-hand
command
contraband
countermand
demand
deodand
disband
expand
fairy-land
fatherland

āle, câre, ădd, ärm, åsk : mē. hĕre, ĕnd; īce. ĭll;

firebrand
first-hand
four-in-hand
full-manned
gland
grand
hand
ill-manned
imband
land
lotus-land
manned
master-hand
minute-hand
multiplicand
overhand
overland
rand
remand
reprimand
Rio Grande
Samarcand
sand
saraband
second-hand
self-command
stand
strand
underhand
understand
unhand
unland
unmanned
unscanned
upper-hand
washstand
withstand
wonderland
(see ĂN + ed)

ĂND

wand
(see ŎND)

ĂNG

bang
bhang
boomerang
clang
fang
gang
gobang
hang
harangue
meringue
mustang
orang-outang
overhang
pang
Penang
rang
sang
sea-tang
serang
shebang
slang
slap-bang
spang
sprang
stang
swang
tang
trepang
twang
uphang
vang
whang

ĂNGD

langued

unpanged
banged, etc.

ĂNGK

bank
Blanc
blank
brank
chank
clank
crank
dank
drank
embank
enrank
flank
franc
frank
hank
lank
mountebank
outflank
outrank
plank
point-blank
prank
rank
sank
savings-bank
shank
shrank
slank
spank
stank
tank
thank
twank
water-tank
Yank

ĂNGKS

Manx
(see
ĂNGK + s)

ĂNGKT

sacrosanct
spindle-
shanked
unspanked
(see
ĂNGK + ed)

ĂNJ

arrange
change
counter-change
derange
disarrange
enrange
estrange
exchange
grange
interchange
mange
range
rearrange
seachange
strange

ĂNJ

flange
phalange

ĂNS

advance
ambulance
appurtenance
arrogance
askance

ōld, ôr, ŏdd, oil, fŏŏt, out; ūse, ûrn, ŭp; THis, thin

bechance	inconsonance	trance	taint
chance	inhabitance	utterance	'taint
circumstance	inheritance	variance	*teint*
complaisance	intemperance	vigilance	unconstraint
concomitance	intolerance	(Cf. ÁNT + s)	unsaint
consonance	irrelevance		
continuance	lance	**ÁNS**	**ÁNT or ÁNT**
conversance	luxuriance	fer-de-lance	abdicant
countenance	manse	insouciance	adamant
country-dance	mischance		adjutant
dance	Nance	**ÁNT**	adulterant
death-dance	ordinance	acquaint	agglutinant
deliverance	penetrance	ain't	*altitonant*
demi-lance	perchance	attaint	*altivolant*
discountenance	petulance	bepaint	ambulant
dissonance	prance	besaint	annuitant
dominance	precipitance	complaint	ant
elance	predominance	constraint	anticipant
elegance	preponderance	*daint*	applicant
enhance	protuberance	depaint	appurtenant
entrance	puissance	distraint	arrogant
expanse	radiance	faint	askant
extravagance	recognizance	feint	aslant
exuberance	reconnaissance	Geraint	aunt
finance	relevance	liver-complaint	brant
France	resonance	mayn't	cant
furtherance	romance	paint	can't
glance	sibilance	plaint	chant
heritance	significance	quaint	combatant
ignorance	stance	restraint	commandant
impuissance	sufferance	saint	communicant
incogitance	suppliance	self-restraint	complaisant
incognisance	tolerance	straint	concomitant

Throughout this rhyming dictionary, sounds as close alike as *ant, chant,* and *abdicant* are listed together as perfect rhymes. Strictly, these three words differ slightly in the pronunciation of the *a* sound: they are properly pronounced as

ănt   chănt   abdicănt

Similarly, words like *age* and *acreage* are listed together as perfect rhymes: for this is the immemorial practice of poets. Their strict pronunciation, as used in conversation or prose, differs: *age* rhyming with *stage,* and *acreage* with *ridge.* The poetic pronunciation might be regarded as an eye-rhyme universally accepted in versification.

āle, câre, ădd, ärm, åsk; mē, hêre, ĕnd; īce, ĭll;

confidant
confidante
congratulant
consonant
conversant
cormorant
corposant
corroborant
Corybant
courant
covenant
decant
deplant
descant
determinant
dilettant
disenchant
disputant
dissonant
dominant
elegant
elephant
emigrant
enchant
excommunicant
executant
exorbitant
extant
extravagant
exuberant
fabricant
figurant
figurante
flagellant
fulminant
gallant
gallivant
Gant
germinant
grant
gratulant

habitant
hesitant
hierophant
ignorant
illuminant
imaginant
immigrant
implant
impuissant
incogitant
incognisant
inconsonant
inhabitant
insignificant
intolerant
intoxicant
irradiant
irrelevant
irritant
itinerant
jubilant
Kant
Levant
litigant
luminant
luxuriant
mendicant
militant
miscreant
nonchalant
occupant
odorant
pant
penetrant
petulant
plant
postulant
precipitant
predominant
preponderant
procreant

Protestant
protuberant
puissant
pursuivant
quant
rant
recalcitrant
recant
recreant
recusant
refrigerant
reiterant
relevant
resonant
resuscitant
reverberant
ruminant
sacrificant
scant
scintillant
sensitive-plant
shan't
sibilant
significant
slant
stimulant
suffragant
supplant
suppliant
supplicant
sycophant
tant
termagant
tintinnabulant
tolerant
toxicant
transplant
undulant
variant
vigilant

visitant
vociferant

ĂNT

aunt
can't
debutante
shan't

ANTH

amaranth
amianth
tragacanth

ĂNTS

pants
(see ĂNT + s)

ĀNZ

Raines
Raynes
(see ĀN + s)

ĂNZ

banns
(see ĂN + s)

ĂNZH

melange

ĀP

agape
ape
cape
chape
crape
crêpe
drape
escape
fire-escape
gape

ōld, ôr, ŏdd, oil, fŏŏt, out; ūse, ûrn, ŭp; THis, thin

grape	heel-tap	Mapes	arrière
jape	Jap	traipse	aware
landscape	knap	apes, etc.	Ayr
Lape	lagniappe		*ayre*
nape	lap	**ĂPS**	backstair
pape	Lapp	apse	bare
rape	map	collapse	bear
red-tape	mayhap	craps	bêche-de-mer
scape	mishap	elapse	bedare
scrape	nap	illapse	beglare
seascape	night-cap	interlapse	beware
shape	overlap	lapse	billionaire
ship-shape	pap	perhaps	blare
tape	percussion-cap	relapse	capillaire
transshape	rap	schnapps	care
trape	rattle-trap	after-claps, etc.	chair
uncape	sap		chare
unshape	scrap	**ĀPT**	chargé
	shoulder-strap	aped	d'affaires
ĂP	slap	(see ĀP + ed)	claire
after-clap	snap		*clare*
agape	stopgap	**ĂPT**	*cockle-stair*
bestrap	strap	adapt	commissionaire
cap	tap	apt	compare
chap	thunder-clap	enrapt	concessionnaire
clap	trap	inapt	dare
claptrap	unlap	moss-capped	debonair
dap	unwrap	rapt	declare
entrap	wapp	snow-capped	Delaware
enwrap	water-tap	wrapt	despair
flap	wishing-cap	bestrapped,	devil-may-care
flip-flap	wrap	etc.	disrepair
foolscap	yap		doctrinaire
forage-cap		**ĀR**	earthenware
frap	**ĀP**	Adair	eclair
gap	gape	affair	e'er
gape	swap	affaire	elsewhere
genapp	(see ŎP)	air	ensnare
genappe		aire	ere
handicap	**ĀPS**	anywhere	etagère
hap	jackanapes	armchair	everywhere

eyre	prayer	vin-ordinaire	debar
fair	prepare	vivandière	deodar
fare	prickly-pear	ware	disbar
flair	proletaire	wear	dissimilar
flare	*quair*	whate'er	embar
forbear	rare	whatsoe'er	evening-star
forswear	repair	whene'er	Excalibar
gare	scare	where	falling-star
glair	sedan-chair	where'er	far
glare	share	wheresoe'er	Farr
Gruyère	Sinclair	yare	feldspar
hair	snare		funicular
hare	solitaire	**ÄR**	gar
heir	somewhere	afar	globular
howe'er	spare	ajar	gnar
impair	square	angular	guitar
jardinière	stair	animalcular	hospodar
lair	stare	annular	hussar
laissez-faire	stere	are	instar
maidenhair	*sware*	avatar	insular
mal de mer	swear	axle-bar	irregular
mare	tare	bar	jaguar
McNair	tear	bazaar	jar
McNare	their	binocular	jaunting-car
mid-air	there	bizarre	jemadar
millionaire	thoroughfare	boulevard	jocular
misfare	threadbare	calendar	jugular
mohair	trouvère	canard	knar
ne'er	tuyère	car	Lascar
otherwhere	unaware	catarrh	lodestar
outdare	*unbeware*	caviar	Loire
outstare	underbear	char	Malabar
outswear	underwear	cigar	mar
outwear	unfair	cinnabar	modular
overbear	unswear	circular	molecular
pair	*unware*	consular	morning-star
pare	upbear	crepuscular	night-jar
parterre	upstare	cymar	north-star
pear	uptear	czar	ocular
Pierre	vair	dar	par
portiere	vare	daystar	parr

ōld, ôr, ŏdd, oil, fŏŏt, out; ūse, ûrn, ŭp; THis, thin

particular	versicular	Bernard	**ÄRF**
peninsular	vinegar	blackguard	'arf and 'arf
perpendicular	Zanzibar	body-guard	larf
pilot-star	zamindar	bombard	scarf
popular		boulevard	
quadrangular	**ÄRB**	camelopard	**ÄRJ**
registrar	barb	canard	barge
regular	garb	card	charge
saddle-bar	yarb	chard	discharge
scapular		closebarred	*embarge*
scar	**ÄRCH**	discard	*encharge*
scimitar	arch	disregard	enlarge
sea-star	countermarch	dynamitard	Farge
secular	dead march	enguard	La Farge
shackle-bar	inarch	evil-starred	large
shooting-star	larch	*fard*	litharge
similar	march	foulard	marge
singular	outmarch	Girard	overcharge
somnambular	overarch	guard	sea-marge
spar	overmarch	hard	sparge
spectacular	parch	interlard	surcharge
star	starch	lard	targe
stellular		life-guard	uncharge
subahdar	**ÄRD**	milliard	undercharge
tabernacular	Baird	nard	
tabular	golden-haired	pard	**ÄRJD**
tar	laird	petard	undischarged
tintamarre	silver-haired	placard	barged, etc.
tintinnabular	uncared	poultry-yard	
titular	unheired	regard	**ÄRK**
triangular	unimpaired	retard	aardvark
tsar	unpaired	sard	arc
tutelar	unprepared	shard	ark
unbar	unshared	spikenard	Asiarch
unspar	unspared	starred	bark
upbar	aired, etc.	under-sparred	barque
uvular		unguard	bedark
valvular	**ÄRD**	unmarred	cark
vehicular	after-guard	wedding-card	Clark
vermicular	avant-garde	yard	Clarke
vernacular	bard	(see ÄR + ed)	clerk

dark
debark
disembark
dispark
easy mark
ecclesiarch
embark
endark
flood-mark
foot-mark
hark
hierarch
impark
iremarch
knark
lark
marc
mark
marque
meadow-lark
oligarch
park
patriarch
remark
sark
sea-lark
shark
sky-lark
snark
spark
stark
Starke
water-mark

ÄRKS

Marx
(see ÄRK + s)

ÄRKT

unmarked
barked, etc.

ÄRL

Albemarle
carl
ensnarl
gnarl
harl
imparl
jarl
Karl
marl
snarl

ÄRLZ

Charles
(see ÄRL + s)

ÄRM

alarm
arm
axle-arm
barm
becharm
charm
counter-charm
decharm
disarm
disencharm
farm
fire-alarm
firearm
forearm
gendarme
harm
love-charm
unarm
uncharm
unharm

ÄRMD

forearmed

unalarmed
alarmed, etc.

ÄRMZ

Armes
assault-at-arms
gentleman-at-arms
king-at-arms
man-at-arms
alarms, etc.

ARN

bairn
cairn
tairn

ÄRN

barn
darn
imbarn
incarn
Marne
tarn
yarn

ÄRNZ

Barnes
(see ÄRN + s)

ÄRP

carp
epicarp
escarp
harp
monocarp
pericarp
scarp
sharp

ARS

scarce

ÄRS

farce
parse
sarse
sparse

ÄRSH

harsh
marsh

ÄRT

apart
art
cart
carte
chart
counterpart
dart
depart
dispart
flint-heart
hart
heart
impart
indart
lion-heart
mart
part
quarte
sart
smart
start
sweetheart
tart
uncart
unheart
upstart
water-cart

ÄRTH

Applegarth

garth
hearth
swarth

ÄRV

carve
larve
starve

ÄRTS

Harz
(see ÄRT + s)

ÄRZ

backstairs
stairs
theirs
unawares
unbewares
unwares
airs, etc.

ÄRZ

Mars
(see ÄR + s)

ÄS

abase
ace
aface
anelace
apace
base
bass
begrace
belace
birthplace
boniface
brace
breathing-
 space

carapace
case
chariot-race
chase
commonplace
dace
debase
deface
disgrace
displace
efface
embrace
encase
enchase
enlace
erase
face
footpace
footrace
grace
grimace
hiding-place
horse-race
idocrase
interlace
interspace
lace
mace
misplace
outface
outpace
pace
place
plaice
populace
race
replace
resting-place
retrace
scapegrace
space

steeple-chase
thorough-bass
Thrace
trace
trysting-place
ukase
unbrace
uncase
underbrace
unlace
vase

AS

after-grass
alas
All-hallowmas
amass
ass
bass
bonnilass
brass
Candlemas
class
crass
crevasse
cuirass
declass
demi-tasse
en masse
first-class
flint-glass
galloglass
gas
glass
grass
Hallowmas
hippocras
hour-glass
isinglass
kavass
Khyber Pass

kvass
lass
looking-glass
mass
Michaelmas
middle-class
minute-glass
morass
object-glass
overpass
paillasse
pass
paterfamilias
rubasse
sassafras
sparrow-grass
strass
surpass
tarantass
tass
weather-glass
working-class

ÄS

en masse

ÄSH

crèche

ÄSH

abash
ash
balderdash
bash
bedash
brache
brash
cache
calabash
calash
calipash

āle, câre, ădd, ärm, ȧsk; mē, hĕre, ĕnd; īce, ĭll;

cash
clash
crash
dash
fash
flash
gash
gnash
hash
interdash
lâche
lash
mash
mountain-ash
moustache
Nash
pash
patache
plash
rash
rehash
sabretache
sash
slap-dash
slash
smash
splash
splatter-dash
squabash
thrash
trash
unlash
weeping-ash

ĂSH

quash
wash, etc.
(see ŎSH)

ĂSHT

undashed

unlashed
unthrashed
abashed, etc.

ASK

antimask
ask
bask
basque
bemask
Bergamask
cask
casque
flask
immask
mask
masque
overtask
Pasch
powder-flask
task
unmask
water-cask

ASKT

unasked
unmasked
basked, etc.

ĂSP

asp
clasp
enclasp
engrasp
gasp
grasp
hasp
rasp
unclasp

ĂSP

wasp

ĀST

after-taste
apple-faced
barefaced
baste
brazen-faced
chaste
distaste
double-faced
dough-faced
fair-faced
foretaste
freckle-faced
furrow-faced
hard-faced
haste
hatchet-faced
horse-faced
impaste
Janus-faced
laced
lambaste
leaden-paced
lean-faced
lily-faced
mottle-faced
pale-faced
paper-faced
paste
pippin-faced
platter-faced
plump-faced
poste-haste
pudding-faced
pug-faced
retraced
sad-faced
self-abased
shame-faced
sheep-faced
slow-paced

smock-faced
smooth-faced
smug-faced
snail-paced
strait-laced
tallow-faced
taste
thorough-
  paced
two-faced
traced
unbraced
unchaste
undefaced
undisgraced
ungraced
unshamefaced
untraced
waist
waste
weasel-faced
well-graced
whey-faced
wizen-faced
abased, etc.

ĂST

aghast
avast
bast
blast
bombast
cast
caste
contrast
devast
downcast
ecclesiast
elegiast
ember-fast
encomiast

enthusiast	abominate	annihilate	bimaculate
fast	abrogate	annotate	binoculate
flabbergast	absinthiate	annulate	cachinnate
forecast	absquatulate	*annumerate*	calculate
ghast	accelerate	annunciate	caliphate
handfast	accentuate	antedate	calumniate
hast	*acclamate*	antepenulti-	campanulate
high-caste	acclimate	mate	camphorate
iconoclast	accommodate	anticipate	cancellate
idoloclast	accumulate	antiquate	candidate
jury-mast	accurate	apostolate	capacitate
last	acidulate	applicate	capitate
mast	actuate	appreciate	capitulate
metaphrast	acuminate	approbate	captivate
metaplast	adequate	appropriate	carbonate
outlast	adjudicate	approximate	cardinalate
overcast	adulate	arbitrate	casemate
paraphrast	adulterate	armour-plate	castigate
past	advocate	arrogate	cate
protoplast	aërate	articulate	celebrate
recast	affectionate	asphyxiate	celibate
repast	affiliate	aspirate	certificate
scholiast	affreight	assassinate	chalybeate
steadfast	agglomerate	asseverate	checkmate
storm-blast	agglutinate	assimilate	chocolate
symposiast	aggravate	*assimulate*	circulate
unfast	aggregate	associate	circumstantiate
unsurpassed	agitate	ate	classmate
vast	alienate	attenuate	coagulate
amassed, etc.	alleviate	*augurate*	cogitate
wast	allocate	aureate	collaborate
	altercate	auspicate	collate
AT	alternate	authenticate	collegiate
	alveolate	aviate	collocate
abalienate	amalgamate	await	commemorate
abate	ambulate	baccalaureate	commensurate
abacinate	ameliorate	bait	comminate
abbreviate	ampliate	bate	commiserate
abdicate	amputate	belate	communicate
ablocate	angulate	berate	compassionate
abnegate	animate	Billingsgate	compensate
abnodate			

āle, câre, ădd, ärm, åsk; mē, hẹre, ĕnd; īce, ĭll;

complicate
concatenate
concentrate
conciliate
conditionate
confabulate
confederate
confiscate
conflate
conglomerate
congratulate
congregate
conjugate
consecrate
considerate
consolidate
constipate
consulate
consummate
contaminate
contemplate
co-operate
co-ordinate
copper-plate
copulate
coronate
corporate
correlate
corroborate
corrugate
crate
create
cremate
crenellate
crepitate
criminate
culminate
cultivate
date
dead-weight
death-rate

debate
debilitate
decapitate
decimate
decolorate
decorate
dedicate
degenerate
delate
delegate
deliberate
delicate
delineate
demonstrate
denominate
denunciate
deodate
depopulate
deprecate
depreciate
depredate
depucelate
derivate
derogate
desecrate
desiderate
designate
desolate
desperate
deteriorate
determinate
detonate
devastate
deviate
devirginate
diaconate
diagnosticate
dial-plate
dictate
differentiate
digitate

dilapidate
dilate
directorate
disconsolate
discriminate
disintegrate
dislocate
disseminate
dissimulate
dissipate
dissociate
doctorate
domesticate
dominate
donate
dunder-pate
duplicate
educate
effectuate
effeminate
efflate
eight
ejaculate
elaborate
elate
electorate
electro-plate
elevate
eliminate
elucidate
emaciate
emanate
emancipate
emasculate
emigrate
emolliate
emulate
enervate
enumerate
enunciate
episcopate

equate
equivocate
eradicate
estate
estimate
estivate
etiolate
evacuate
evaluate
evaporate
eventuate
exacerbate
exacinate
exaggerate
exasperate
excavate
excogitate
excommunicate
excoriate
excruciate
exculpate
execrate
exhilarate
exonerate
exorbitate
expatiate
expatriate
expectorate
expiate
expostulate
extenuate
exterminate
extirpate
extortionate
extravagate
extricate
fabricate
facilitate
fascinate
fate
feather-weight

federate	illuminate	indeterminate	invalidate
felicitate	illustrate	indevirginate	investigate
fête	imitate	indicate	invertebrate
first-mate	immaculate	indiscriminate	inveterate
first-rate	immarginate	individuate	invigorate
flagellate	*immateriate*	indoctrinate	inviolate
floodgate	immediate	indurate	invocate
fluctuate	*immensurate*	inebriate	irate
foliolate	immigrate	infatuate	irradiate
foreordinate	immoderate	inflate	irrigate
formulate	immolate	infuriate	irritate
fortunate	impassionate	ingerminate	isolate
freight	impersonate	*ingrate*	iterate
fructuate	impetrate	ingratiate	itinerate
frustrate	implicate	ingurgitate	Kate
fulminate	importunate	initiate	lacerate
fumigate	imprecate	innate	lanceolate
funambulate	impropriate	innovate	late
gait	improvisate	inoculate	laureate
gate	inaccurate	inordinate	legislate
gelatinate	inadequate	insatiate	legitimate
generate	inanimate	inseminate	levigate
germinate	inappropriate	insinuate	levirate
gesticulate	inarticulate	instate	liberate
glaciate	inaugurate	instigate	licentiate
graduate	incapacitate	insubordinate	liquidate
granulate	incarcerate	insulate	literate
grate	*incastellate*	integrate	litigate
gratulate	inchoate	intenerate	lixiviate
gravitate	incinerate	intemperate	locate
great	incommensur-	*intercessionate*	lubricate
habilitate	ate	intermediate	lucubrate
habituate	incompassion-	interminate	luxuriate
hate	ate	interpolate	macerate
heavy-weight	inconsiderate	interrogate	machinate
helpmate	incorporate	intimate	magistrate
hesitate	increate	intimidate	magnate
hibernate	incriminate	intonate	manipulate
humiliate	incubate	intoxicate	marinate
hypothecate	inculcate	intricate	marquisate
illiterate	indelicate	inundate	masticate

āle,   câre,   ădd,   ārm,   åsk;   mē,   hęre,   ĕnd;   īce,   ĭll;

mate	participate	promulgate	reprobate
matriculate	passionate	propagate	repudiate
mediate	pastorate	propitiate	restate
meditate	pate	proportionate	resuscitate
mess-mate	patronate	pro-rate	retaliate
migrate	peculate	prostrate	reticulate
militate	penetrate	protectorate	reverberate
mitigate	peninsulate	protuberate	roseate
moderate	pennyweight	provinciate	rotate
modulate	perambulate	proximate	ruminate
motivate	percolate	pulsate	runagate
mutilate	peregrinate	punctuate	rusticate
narrate	perforate	quadruplicate	salivate
Nate	permeate	radiate	sanitate
navigate	perorate	rate	sate
necessitate	perpetrate	ratiocinate	satiate
negociate	perpetuate	rattle-pate	saturate
nickle-plate	personate	rebate	scintillate
nominate	placate	recalcitrate	Sea Gate
novitiate	plait	recapitulate	second-rate
obdurate	plate	reciprocate	secretariate
obligate	playmate	recreate	sedate
obliterate	poet-laureate	recriminate	segregate
obstinate	pontificate	rectorate	separate
obviate	populate	recuperate	shipmate
officiate	postulate	refrigerate	sibilate
operate	potentate	regenerate	silicate
opiate	prate	regrate	silver-plate
orate	precipitate	regulate	simulate
orchestrate	predate	regurgitate	situate
originate	predestinate	rehabilitate	skate
ornate	predicate	reinstate	slate
oscillate	predominate	reiterate	somnambulate
osculate	premeditate	rejuvenate	sophisticate
over-rate	preponderate	relate	spate
overstate	prevaricate	relegate	speculate
overweight	procrastinate	remediate	spifflicate
oxygenate	procreate	remonstrate	spoliate
palliate	professoriate	remunerate	stalemate
palpitate	profligate	renovate	state
paper-weight	prognosticate	repatriate	stearate

stellulate
stimulate
stipulate
straight
strait
stridulate
stylobate
subjugate
sublimate
subordinate
subrogate
substantiate
sufflate
suffocate
superannuate
supererogate
supplicate
suppurate
syncopate
syndicate
tabulate
Tait
temperate
tergiversate
terminate
tête-à-tête
third-rate
titillate
titivate
tolerate
trait
translate
transliterate
transubstan-
   tiate
triangulate
triturate
triumvirate
ulcerate
ultimate
ululate

uncreate
underrate
understate
underweight
undulate
unfortunate
unstate
vacate
vaccinate
vacillate
validate
variate
variegate
vassalate
vaticinate
vegetate
venerate
ventilate
verberate
vermiculate
vertebrate
vertiginate
vicariate
vindicate
violate
vitiate
vituperate
vizierate
vociferate
wait
water-rate
weight

ĂT

acrobat
aflat
Ararat
aristocrat
assignat
at
autocrat

automat
bat
bepat
brat
brickbat
cat
caveat
chat
civet-cat
commissariat
cravat
dandiprat
democrat
diplomat
drat
fallow-chat
fat
flat
frat
forgat
gat
gnat
habitat
hat
heliostat
hellcat
hereat
high-hat
hydrostat
kittycat
lariat
Magnificat
marrow-fat
mat
matte
monocrat
pat
pitapat
plat
Platt
Platte

proletariat
plutocrat
polecat
rat
requiescat
rheostat
sat
scat
secretariat
slat
spat
sprat
Surat
tabby-cat
tat
that
theocrat
thereat
thermostat
unhat
vampire-bat
vat
water-rat
whereat

ĂT

Kalat
Khelat
squat
what, etc.
yacht
(see ŎT)

ĀTH

bathe
lathe
scathe
snathe
spathe
swathe
unswathe

āle, câre, ădd, ärm, ăsk; mē, hĕre, ĕnd; īce, ĭll;

Āth
faith
i'faith
misfaith
rathe
Snaith
unfaith
water-wraith
wraith

ĀTth
eighth
hate'th, etc.

ĀTH
aftermath
allopath
Gath
hath
homeopath
math
osteopath
philomath
physiopath
psychopath
snath

ATH
bath
bridle-path
footpath
lath
path
rath
wrath

ATS
Bates
Cates
Yates
Yeats
(see Ā T + s)

ĀV
angusticlave
architrave
behave
belave
beslave
brave
cave
concave
crave
Dave
deprave
drave
élève
encave
enclave
engrave
enslave
forgave
galley-slave
gave
glaive
grave
impave
knave
lave
misbehave
misgave
nave
outbrave
pave
rave
save
shave
slave
stave
suave
they've
thrave
trave
ungrave
waive
wave

ĂV
have
Slav

ÄV
calve
enclave
halve
salve
Slav
suave
zouave

ĀZ
ablaze
adaze
amaze
appraise
baize
Blaise
beacon-blaze
bepraise
blaze
braise
braze
chaise
chrysoprase
craze
daze
dispraise
emblaze
faze
fraise
gaze
glaze
graze
Haas
Hayes
haze
laze
maize
malaise
Marseillaise
Mays
Mayes
mayonnaise
maze
metaphrase
naze
nowadays
outblaze
outgaze
paraphrase
phase
phrase
polonaise
praise
raise
rase
raze
self-praise
then-a-days
underpraise
unpraise
upblaze
upgaze
upraise
vase
wonder-maze
(see Ā + s)

ĂZ
as
has
jazz
razz
whereas

ÄZ	ÄZD	entourage	ectoplasm
Shiraz	jazzed	garage	enthusiasm
vase	razzed	menage	iconoclasm
(see Ä + s)		mirage	metaplasm
	ÄZH	persiflage	miasm
ÄZD	cortegé		phantasm
adazed		**ÄZM**	*phasm*
bemazed	**ÄZH**	bioplasm	plasm
unamazed	badinage	cataplasm	pleonasm
unpraised	barrage	chasm	protoplasm
amazed, etc.	camouflage	demoniasm	sarcasm
			spasm

E

These words include the following accented vowel sounds:

Ē as in me; heard also in eve, feet, beam, deceive, people, key, Caesar, machine, field, quay, phoebe.

Ḝ as in here; heard also in fear, dreary, weird.

Ĕ as in end; heard also in heifer, leopard, friend, Aetna, feather, asafoetida, bury, any, Thames, said, says.

Ē	appellee	bohea	chickadee
A.B.	appointee	bonhomie	chickeree
abandonee	assignee	bootee	chimpanzee
absentee	avowee	bouilli	Chinee
addressee	axle-tree	bourgeoisie	Christmas-tree
advowee	bailee	bumblebee	coatee
agape	bain-marie	burgee	consignee
Agapemone	banshee	B.V.D.	corroboree
agree	bargee	C.O.D.	coryphee
aknee	bawbee	calipee	Cybele
alee	be	Calliope	D.D.
allottee	bee	calorie	debauchee
anemone	belee	cap-a-pie	debris
Anglice	bel-esprit	catastrophe	decree
antistrophe	Benedicite	Chaldee	dedicatee
apogee	biographee	chariotee	Dee
apostraphe	*blea*	Cherokee	degree

āle,   câre,   ădd,   ärm,   åsk;   mē,   hḝre,   ĕnd;   īce,   ĭll;

devisee	garnishee	McFee	pugaree
devotee	gee	McGee	Q.T.
diablerie	geegee	McKee	quay
disagree	Gethsemane	me	raki
divorcee	ghee	Melpomene	rani
dominie	glee	mestee	rapparee
donee	goatee	mortgagee	rappee
drawee	grandee	mustee	razee
dree	grantee	N.G.	recipe
Dundee	guarantee	nebulae	referee
dungaree	he	Niobe	refugee
Dupree	heart-free	nominee	releasee
eau de vie	honey-bee	O.G.	remittee
employee	humblebee	obligee	repartee
endorsee	hyperbole	ogee	rhe
enfree	interrogatee	on dit	Rosalie
ennui	jamboree	oversea	rupee
epopee	Japanee	oversee	Sadducee
esprit	jeu d'esprit	Ph.D.	sangaree
etui	jinnee	Parsee	Sault St. Marie
Eugenie	jubilee	passaree	scarabee
Eulalie	key	patentee	scree
examinee	killdee	Pawnee	sea
extempore	knee	payee	see
facetiae	langue d'oui	pea	selvagee
facsimile	lea	pedigree	sesame
fäerie	lee	Penelope	settee
fancy-free	legatee	perigee	she
fee	lessee	permittee	si
felo de se	levee	petitionee	simile
fiddle-de-dee	ley	Pharisee	skilligalee
filigree	li	picotee	snee
flea	licensee	plea	snickersnee
flee	litchi	pledgee	spree
fleur-de-lis	M.D.	point-d'appui	stingaree
foresee	manatee	poison-tree	suttee
free	Manichee	pongee	sycee
fricassee	Marie	pontee	synecdoche
fusee	marquee	pot-pourri	systole
Galilee	Marshalsea	presentee	tea
gallows-tree	master-key	promisee	tee

tehee	adversity	ascendancy	Calvary
Tennessee	advisability	asperity	canopy
Terpsichore	affability	assiduity	capability
the	affinity	astrology	capacity
thee	agency	astronomy	captivity
third degree	agility	atrocity	casualty
three	agony	atrophy	catholicity
topee	alacrity	audacity	causticity
toupee	alchemy	augury	cavalry
transferee	allopathy	austerity	cavity
tree	ambiguity	authenticity	celebrity
trustee	amenability	authority	celerity
Tweedledee	amenity	autonomy	century
unforesee	amicability	avidity	certainty
unfree	amity	bakery	changeability
vendee	amnesty	balcony	chancery
vertebrae	analogy	barbarity	charity
vis-a-vis	anarchy	barony	chastity
vouchee	anatomy	barratry	chivalry
warrantee	ancestry	bastardy	Christianity
we	animosity	battery	chronology
wee	anniversary	beggary	civility
weeping-tree	annuity	benignity	clemency
whiffletree	anomaly	bigamy	cogency
whippletree	anonymity	bigotry	colloquy
ye	antipathy	billowy	colony
	antiphony	biography	combustibility
Zuyder Zee	antiquity	biology	comedy
abbacy	anxiety	blasphemy	comity
ability	apathy	blossomy	commodity
absurdity	apology	botany	community
academy	apostasy	bravery	company
acclivity	applicability	brevity	compatability
accompany	archery	bribery	complacency
acerbity	argosy	brilliancy	complexity
acidity	aridity	brutality	complicity
acridity	aristocracy	bryony	complimentary
activity	armory	burglary	comprehensi-
actuality	arrowy	cadency	bility
adaptability	artillery	calamity	compulsory
adultery	artistry	calumny	conformity

connubiality	dexterity	enginery	flattery
consanguinity	diary	enmity	flippancy
consistency	dignity	enormity	fluency
conspiracy	dimity	entity	flummery
constancy	diplomacy	Epiphany	foppery
contiguity	directory	epitome	forestry
contingency	discordancy	equality	forgery
contradictory	discourtesy	equanimity	formality
contrariety	discovery	equity	fortuity
conveniency	discrepancy	errantry	fragility
convention-	dishonesty	eternity	fragrancy
ality	disparity	eulogy	fraternity
convexity	dissatisfactory	euphony	frequency
coquetry	dissimilarity	expectancy	frigidity
courtesy	dissuasory	expediency	frivolity
Coventry	diversity	extremity	frugality
credulity	divinity	facility	futility
criminality	docility	factory	futurity
crotchety	domesticity	faculty	gaiety
crudity	doxology	fallacy	galaxy
cruelty	drapery	falsity	gallantry
cupidity	drudgery	familiarity	gallery
curacy	dubiety	family	garrulity
curiosity	duplicity	fantasy	genealogy
custody	dynasty	fatality	generosity
debauchery	ebony	fatuity	geniality
debility	eccentricity	feathery	gentility
decency	economy	fecundity	geography
declivity	ecstasy	felicity	geology
deformity	efficiency	felony	geometry
deity	effigy	fernery	Germany
delivery	effrontery	ferocity	gluttony
democracy	elasticity	fertility	gratuity
demonry	electricity	fervency	gravity
density	elegy	festivity	harmony
dependency	elementary	fidelity	harvestry
depravity	elusory	fidgety	heathery
deputy	embassy	fiery	heraldry
destiny	emergency	finery	heredity
devilry	enemy	fixity	heresy
deviltry	energy	flagrancy	hilarity

ōld, ôr, ŏdd, oil, fŏŏt, out; ūse, ûrn, ŭp; THis, thin

history	incongruity	jugglery	mediocrity
homeopathy	inconsistency	juvenility	melody
homily	inconstancy	knavery	memory
honesty	incredulity	knight-errantry	mendacity
hospitality	indignity	laity	mendicity
hostelry	individuality	larceny	merchantry
hostility	industry	laxity	mercury
humanity	inebriety	legacy	mimicry
humility	infallibility	legality	ministry
husbandry	infamy	leniency	minority
hypocrisy	infancy	lenity	misanthropy
identity	infantry	lethargy	misery
idiocy	infelicity	levity	mobility
idiosyncrasy	inferiority	liberality	mockery
idolatry	infertility	liberty	modesty
illiteracy	infidelity	limpidity	monarchy
illusory	infinity	litany	monody
imagery	infirmary	liturgy	monopoly
imbecility	infirmity	livery	monotony
immaturity	ingenuity	Lombardy	monstrosity
immensity	inhumanity	longevity	morality
immodesty	iniquity	loquacity	mortality
immorality	injury	lottery	multiplicity
immortality	insincerity	loyalty	mummery
immunity	insipidity	lubricity	municipality
imparity	insufficiency	lucidity	mutability
impassivity	insularity	lunacy	mutiny
impecuniosity	insurgency	luxuriancy	mystery
impetuosity	integrity	luxury	mythology
impiety	intensity	machinery	nationality
importunity	intestacy	magnanimity	nativity
impropriety	intrepidity	mahogany	necessity
impunity	irony	majesty	neutrality
impurity	Italy	majority	nobility
inability	ivory	malady	non-conformity
inadvertency	jealousy	malignancy	normalcy
incapacity	jeopardy	malignity	Normandy
inclemency	jewelry	masonry	notary
incompatibility	jocundity	mastery	notoriety
incomprehen-	jollity	maternity	novelty
sibility	joviality	maturity	nudity

nullity
nursery
obeisancy
obesity
obliquity
obloquy
obscurity
oddity
Odyssey
opportunity
originality
pageantry
palmary
panoply
papacy
parity
parliamentary
parody
partiality
particularity
paternity
peculiarity
pedantry
penalty
penury
peppery
perfidy
perfumery
perfunctory
perjury
perpetuity
perplexity
personality
perspicuity
pertinacity
perversity
philanthropy
philosophy
phylactery
physiognomy
Picardy

piety
pillory
pillowy
piracy
pleasantry
pliancy
poesy
poetry
poignancy
policy
polity
polygamy
pomposity
ponderosity
popery
popularity
pornography
posterity
potency
poverty
precocity
precursory
prelacy
priority
priory
privacy
privity
probity
proclivity
prodigality
prodigy
profanity
professory
proficiency
profundity
progeny
prolixity
promiscuity
propensity
property
prophecy

propinquity
propriety
prosperity
provinciality
proximity
prudery
psalmistry
psalmody
psychiatry
publicity
puerility
pugnacity
punctuality
pungency
purity
pusillanimity
putridity
quackery
quality
quandary
quantity
quiescency
raillery
rapacity
rapidity
rarity
rascality
reality
reciprocity
recovery
rectory
refractory
regency
regeneracy
remedy
revelry
rhapsody
ribaldry
rickety
rigidity
rivalry

robbery
rockery
roguery
Romany
rosary
rosemary
rotundity
royalty
rubicundity
rudimentary
rusticity
sagacity
salary
salinity
salubrity
sanctity
sanity
satiety
satisfactory
savagery
scarcity
scenery
scrutiny
secrecy
security
seigniory
senility
sensibility
sensuality
sentimentality
serenity
servility
severity
shadowy
shivery
silvery
similarity
simony
simplicity
sincerity
sinewy

ōld, ôr, ŏdd, oil, fŏŏt, out; ūse, ûrn, ŭp; THis, thin

singularity | tenantry | vagrancy | words ending
slavery | tendency | valedictory | in "y")
slippery | tenuity | valiancy | absorbingly
snuggery | testamentary | validity | abusively
sobriety | theocracy | vanity | accordingly
society | theology | vapidity | accurately
solemnity | theory | vapoury | acidly
solidity | theosophy | variety | affectedly
soliloquy | thievery | velocity | aimlessly
solvency | threnody | velvety | airily
sophistry | thundery | venality | alluringly
sorcery | timidity | verbosity | allusively
spontaneity | tonicity | verdancy | ambitiously
stability | topography | verity | amusingly
stagnancy | torpidity | versatility | anciently
sterility | totality | vicinity | appealingly
stolidity | tracery | victory | ardently
strategy | tragedy | villainy | assertively
stupidity | tranquillity | virginity | atrociously
suavity | travesty | viridity | auspiciously
subjectivity | treachery | virility | awfully
sublimity | treasury | virtuality | banefully
subsidy | trickery | virtuosity | becomingly
subtlety | trilogy | viscidity | befittingly
sufficiency | trinity | viscosity | beggarly
sugary | triviality | vivacity | bespottedly
summary | truancy | volatility | bewailingly
superficiality | trumpery | voracity | bitterly
superfluity | tyranny | votary | bloodlessly
superiority | ubiquity | vulgarity | bloomingly
supremacy | unanimity | waggery | bloomlessly
symmetry | uniformity | watery | blushingly
sympathy | unity | whimsicality | blushlessly
symphony | university | willowy | bodily
taciturnity | unsavoury | wintery | bootlessly
tapestry | urbanity | witchery | boundlessly
technicality | urgency | yeomanry | boyishly
telegraphy | usury | zoology | brainlessly
temerity | utility | (see ability, etc., | breathlessly
tenacity | vacancy | part iii, for | broodingly
tenancy | vacuity | many more | brotherly

āle, câre, ădd, ärm, åsk; mē, hĕre, ĕnd; īce, ĭll;

brutally	divergently	fruitlessly	insensately
bumptiously	divertingly	fulsomely	instantly
carefully	doggedly	giddily	instructively
carelessly	dolefully	girlishly	insultingly
changelessly	doubtfully	gloomily	intermittently
chirpingly	doubtingly	gloriously	inwardly
chokingly	dreamingly	gorgeously	irksomely
churlishly	dreamlessly	gropingly	iridescently
civilly	drippingly	groundlessly	jokingly
clownishly	droopingly	grudgingly	joyfully
complainingly	dustily	gruesomely	joyously
concludingly	easterly	grumblingly	judiciously
condescend-	elusively	grumpily	juicily
ingly	enduringly	guiltily	laughingly
conducively	engagingly	guiltlessly	lavishly
confoundedly	engrossingly	gushingly	legendarily
confusedly	eternally	gustily	lightfootedly
consummately	exclusively	happily	loathingly
convivially	expansively	harmfully	locally
countlessly	exultantly	harmlessly	lonesomely
cousinly	exultingly	heartbrokenly	loungingly
cowardly	fadelessly	heart-rending-	lovelessly
cravingly	fairly	ly	loverly
crouchingly	faithlessly	heavenly	lovingly
crownlessly	fatherly	hereditarily	loyally
cruelly	feelingly	homelessly	lucidly
crushingly	ferociously	hopefully	luckily
cumbrously	fervidly	hopelessly	lucklessly
dastardly	feudally	horridly	luridly
daughterly	flippantly	humanly	luringly
decorously	floridly	hungrily	lustrously
deductively	flurriedly	hurriedly	maidenly
defencelessly	flushingly	illusively	maliciously
deliciously	foolishly	immorally	mannerly
delusively	foppishly	immortally	masterly
devotedly	forebodingly	imploringly	maternally
disapprovingly	foreknowingly	inclusively	matronly
discerningly	forgivingly	indignantly	meltingly
disorderly	formerly	indulgently	merrily
distastefully	forsakenly	infernally	misgivingly
distrustfully	fruitfully	inhumanly	mistrustingly

modestly	pluckily	scowlingly	stolenly
morally	poetically	secretively	stormfully
morbidly	portentously	secretly	stormily
mortally	prayerfully	seducively	stormlessly
motherly	precociously	seductively	straightfor-
mournfully	prepossess-	seemingly	wardly
mournsomely	ingly	self-accusingly	stubbornly
musingly	pretendingly	self-consciously	studiedly
nakedly	productively	shamefully	stupendously
namelessly	properly	shamelessly	stupidly
necessarily	propitiously	shapelessly	sturdily
neighbourly	provokingly	sharp-wittedly	stylishly
niggardly	publicly	shiftlessly	suddenly
noiselessly	pungently	shrewishly	sultrily
normally	pursuantly	silently	sunnily
northerly	quarterly	sisterly	superhumanly
northwardly	quiescently	sleepily	superstitiously
obnoxiously	rapidly	sleeplessly	surefootedly
obstructively	readily	slouchingly	suspiciously
obtrusively	ready-wittedly	slovenly	swimmingly
officiously	recklessly	sluggishly	swollenly
onwardly	recurrently	smilingly	sylvanly
opposingly	refulgently	smokily	tauntingly
oppressively	rejoicingly	soakingly	tediously
orderly	relentlessly	soberly	thanklessly
outrageously	reluctantly	solemnly	thornily
overtoppingly	remorsefully	solidly	thoroughly
owlishly	remorselessly	sombrely	thumpingly
painfully	responsively	sordidly	tonelessly
painlessly	revengefully	sorrily	tranquilly
pallidly	rippingly	sorrowfully	tremendously
pathetically	ripplingly	soulfully	trippingly
peculiarly	roaringly	soullessly	triumphally
peerlessly	rovingly	soundlessly	triumphantly
peevishly	royally	spirally	troublously
pellucidly	ruefully	splendidly	trustfully
pervertedly	ruffianly	spoonily	trustily
piquantly	ruggedly	sportfully	trustingly
plaintfully	savagely	sportively	truthfully
plaintlessly	scholarly	spotlessly	truthlessly
playfully	scornfully	stirringly	tunefully

tunelessly
unbecomingly
unbendingly
unbiddenly
unblushingly
unboundedly
unceasingly
unchangingly
uncloudedly
unerringly
unfailingly
unfeelingly
unfeignedly
unflaggingly
unguardedly
unknowingly
unlovingly
unmaidenly
unmannerly
unmotherly
unneighborly
unresistingly
unswervingly
unweariedly
unwittingly
unwontedly
unyieldingly
urgently
usurpingly
utterly
verily
vividly
voluntarily
wantonly
warningly
wastefully
waywardly
wearily
wholesomely
wittingly
wontedly

worthily
worthlessly
yearningly
yeomanly

ĔB

glebe
grebe

ĔB

cobweb
deb
ebb
keb
neb
Seb
web
Webb

ĔBD

ebbed
webbed

ĒBZ

Thebes
(see ĒB + s)

ĔBZ

Debs
ebbs
plebs
webs, etc.

ĒCH

beach
beseech
beech
bleach
breach
breech
each
forereach

forespeech
foreteach
impeach
keech
leach
leech
overreach
peach
preach
queach
reach
screech
sea-reach
sleech
speech
teach
unbreech
unpreach

ĔCH

etch
fetch
fletch
Jack-Ketch
ketch
letch
out-stretch
retch
sketch
stretch
vetch
wretch

ĔCHD

unbleached
unimpeached
beached, etc.

ĔCHD

far-fetched
etched, etc.

ĒD

accede
antecede
bead
bleed
brede
breed
cede
centipede
concede
creed
deed
dispeed
Ead
exceed
feed
Ganymede
glede
gleed
god-speed
greed
heed
impede
implead
inbreed
indeed
interbreed
intercede
interplead
invalid
jereed
knead
knock-kneed
lead
mead
Meade
Mede
meed
millipede
misdeed

õld, ôr, ŏdd, oil, fŏŏt, out: ū͜se, ûrn, ŭp; THis, thin

	ĔD		
mislead	abed	inbred	trundle-bed
misread	*adread*	instead	trundle-head
need	ahead	jolter-head	underbred
off his feed	arrow-head	lead	unhead
outspeed	bed	led	unread
overfeed	bedspread	loggerhead	unsaid
plead	bedstead	*lowlihead*	unsped
precede	behead	maidenhead	unthread
proceed	bespread	mast-head	unwed
read	bestead	misled	watershed
Reade	billet-head	Ned	wed
recede	bled	negro-head	well-sped
rede	blunder-head	niggerhead	Winifred
reed	bread	outspread	woolly-head
Reid	breviped	overfed	zed
retrocede	chuckle-head	overhead	*accustomed*
Runnymede	co-ed	overspread	*anchored*
screed	copper-head	pilot-bread	*answered*
sea-weed	dead	pled	*astonished*
secede	dead-head	poppy-head	attributed
seed	death-bed	quadruped	*balanced*
speed	death's-head	read	*banished*
stampede	dread	red	barren-spirited
steed	dunderhead	redd	base-spirited
succeed	Ed	said	bediamonded
supersede	embed	shed	*bewildered*
swede	feather-head	shewbread	bigoted
teed	fed	shred	*blemished*
treed	figure-head	sled	*blistered*
Tweed	fissiped	sped	bold-spirited
undecreed	fled	spread	bonneted
unfeed	foresaid	stead	*brandished*
unpedigreed	fountain-head	surbed	breakfasted
upbreed	Fred	ted	*burnished*
uplead	full-fed	thorough-bred	carpeted
velocipede	ginger-bread	thread	*clustered*
weed	go-ahead	thunder-head	*conquered*
we'd	head	timber-head	*continued*
(see Ē + d)	highbred	tread	contributed
	homebred	truckle-bed	*covered*
		truebred	coveted

crescented	*measured*	unprofited	fief
diamonded	merited	unrespited	grief
diminished	*murmured*	untenanted	interleaf
discomforted	*overpowered*	visited	leaf
discredited	*overtowered*	*wandered*	lief
dispirited	*pardoned*	weak-spirited	reef
disquieted	patented	*wearied*	relief
distributed	*perjured*	*winnowed*	sheaf
dowered	pirated	*witnessed*	shereef
embarrassed	poor-spirited	*wondered*	thief
emblazoned	prohibited	*worshipped*	unbelief
enamored	public-spirited		
exhibited	*punished*	**ĔDST**	**ĔF**
faceted	quieted	*bespread'st*	F
famished	ravaged	dread'st	chef
fine-spirited	*recovered*	fed'st	clef
flowered	*relinquished*	fled'st	deaf
forfeited	*remembered*	led'st	enfeoff
furnished	ringleted	*overspread'st*	feoff
garlanded	*rivalled*	said'st	
gathered	sanctioned	thread'st	**ĔFT**
gay-spirited	shepherded	tread'st	aleft
glimmered	*shimmered*	wed'st	bereft
glistened	*showered*		cleft
hearkened	*shuddered*	**ĔDTH**	deft
helmeted	signeted	breadth	eft
heralded	*slumbered*	hairbreadth	enfeoffed
high-spirited	soft-spirited	*bespread'th*, etc.	heft
hungered	*sorrowed*		left
imprisoned	spirited	**ĔDZ**	reft
inhabited	*suffered*	Eades	theft
inherited	talented	Leeds	unbereft
inspirited	*tempered*	(see ĒD + s)	weft
jeoparded	tenanted		wheft
languished	*thundered*	**ĒF**	
light-spirited	turreted	bas-relief	**ĒG**
limited	unballasted	beef	
lingered	unbonneted	belief	colleague
low-spirited	uninhabited	brief	enleague
marvelled	unlimited	chief	fatigue
mean-spirited	unmerited	disbelief	intrigue

ōld, ôr, ŏdd, oil, foŏt, out; ūse, ûrn, ŭp; THis, thin

league	dredge	chic	upseek
renege	edge	cleek	weak
	enhedge	clinique	week
ĔG	fledge	clique	wreak
beg	hedge	comique	
beglerbeg	impledge	creak	**ĔK**
egg	interpledge	creek	beck
goose-egg	kedge	critique	bedeck
keg	ledge	eke	bewreck
leg	pledge	forepeak	breakneck
Meg	privilege	forespeak	by heck
peg	sacrilege	freak	check
philabeg	sedge	gleek	cheque
skeg	sledge	Greek	Czech
teg	tedge	hide-and-seek	deck
unpeg	unedge	leak	fleck
Winnipeg	wedge	leek	henpeck
yegg		Martinique	Kennebec
	ĔJD	meak	leatherneck
ĔGD	double-edged	meek	neck
overfatigued	sedged	Mozambique	neck-and-neck
fatigued, etc.	two-edged	oblique	peck
	unhedged	Passion-week	quarter-deck
ĔGD	dredged, etc.	peak	Quebec
spindle-legged		physique	reck
begged, etc.	**ĔK**	pique	rubberneck
	after-peak	reek	shipwreck
ĔGZ	aleak	relique	spec
dregs	antique	seek	speck
Meggs	apeak	sheik	trek
sea-legs	areek	shriek	undeck
begs, etc.	beak	Sikh	wreck
	bespeak	sleek	
ĔJ	bezique	sneak	**ĔKS**
besiege	bleak	speak	breeks
liege	bubble and	squeak	sneaks
siege	squeak	streak	beaks, etc.
	cacique	teak	
ĔJ	caique	tweak	**ĔKS**
allege	cheek	unique	annex
cledge	Chesapeake	unspeak	becks

āle, câre, ădd, ärm, åsk; mē, hēre, ĕnd; īce, ĭll;

bedecks	**ĔKT**	intersect	Camille
Celotex	abject	introspect	Castile
circumflex	adject	misdirect	chenille
complex	affect	neglect	cochineal
convex	analect	non-elect	commonweal
ex	*annect*	object	conceal
Exe	architect	perfect	congeal
flex	*arrect*	porrect	creel
inflex	bisect	*prefect*	deal
kex	circumspect	prelect	deil
lex	collect	project	deshabille
Middlesex	confect	prospect	dial-wheel
multiplex	conject	protect	difficile
perplex	connect	recollect	driving-wheel
prex	correct	*refect*	eel
reflex	defect	reflect	enseal
rex	deflect	reject	feel
sex	deject	respect	fly-wheel
unsex	detect	resurrect	forefeel
vex	dialect	retrospect	genteel
(see ĔK + s)	direct	sect	heal
	disaffect	select	heel
ĔKST	disconnect	self-respect	he'll
next	disinfect	subject	imbecile
pretext	disrespect	suspect	infantile
sexed	dissect	traject	*interdeal*
sext	effect	trisect	keel
text	eject	unchecked	Kiel
unperplexed	elect	undecked	kneel
unsexed	erect	unsuspect	leal
unvexed	expect	bedecked, etc.	Lille
annexed, etc.	exsect		Lucille
	genuflect	**ĒL**	meal
ĔKT	incorrect	alguazil	misdeal
cherry-cheeked	indirect	all heal	Neal
peaked	infect	anneal	Neil
rosy-cheeked	inflect	appeal	Neill
unwreaked	inject	automobile	ne'er-do-weel
beaked, etc.	inspect	balance-wheel	O'Neal
	intellect	barleymeal	O'Neill
	interject	bastille	O'Sheel

paddle-wheel	bel	fricandel	Philomel
pastille	bell	gabelle	pimpernel
peal	belle	gazelle	propel
peel	*bonnibel*	harebell	*pucelle*
privy-seal	brocatel	heather-bell	Purnell
reel	Canterbury bell	hell	*quadrelle*
repeal	caramel	hotel	quell
reveal	caravel	hydromel	rebel
seal	carrousel	Immanuel	*refel*
seel	cell	immortelle	repel
shabby-genteel	chanterelle	impel	rondelle
sheal	Chaumontel	infidel	sacring-bell
she'll	citadel	inshell	sanctus-bell
speel	clientele	*intermell*	sea-shell
spiel	claribel	Isabel	sell
squeal	cockerel	jargonelle	sentinel
steal	cockle-shell	jell	shell
steel	compel	Jezebel	smell
sweal	cordelle	kell	snell
teal	*coronel*	knell	spell
thunder-peal	Crannell	lapel	swell
tweel	crenel	Lionel	tell
uncongeal	*damoiselle*	love-spell	*tourelle*
unseal	*damoselle*	mackerel	undersell
unseel	deathbell	mademoiselle	unshell
vakil	dell	mangonel	unspell
veal	demoiselle	minute-bell	upswell
weal	dentelle	Moselle	vesper-bell
we'll	dinner-bell	muscatel	vielle
wheal	dispel	Nell	villanelle
wheel	diving-bell	nonpareil	well
zeal	doggerel	pallmall	yell
	dwell	parallel	zel
ĔL	El	Parnell	Zell
Abarbanel	ell	passing-bell	
asphodel	Emmanuel	pell	**ĔLCH**
Astrophel	excel	pell-mell	belch
A.W.O.L.	expel	pennoncelle	squelch
bagatelle	farewell	personnel	Welch
bechamel	fell	petronel	Welsh
befell	foretell	petronel	

āle, câre, ădd, ärm, åsk; mē, hĕre, ĕnd; īce, ĭll:

ĔLD
afield
battlefield
Chesterfield
Dangerfield
Delafield
enshield
field
harvest-field
shield
unaneled
unrepealed
weald
wield
yield
annealed, etc.

ĔLD
beheld
eld
geld
held
meld
seld
unbeheld
unknelled
unparalleled
unquelled
upheld
weld
withheld
belled, etc.

ĔLF
delf
elf
Guelph
herself
himself
itself
mantel-shelf

myself
oneself
ourself
pelf
self
shelf
thyself
yourself

ĔLFT
delft

ĔLFTH
twelfth

ĔLK
elk
whelk
yelk

ĔLM
dishelm
elm
helm
overwhelm
realm
unhelm
weather-helm
whelm

ĔLP
help
kelp
self-help
skelp
swelp
whelp
yelp

ĔLPS
Phelps
(see ĔLP + s)

ĔLS
else
(cf. belts, etc.)

ĔLSH
Welsh
(see—leh)

ĔLT
belt
celt
dealt
dwelt
felt
gelt
heart-felt
kelt
knelt
melt
misspelt
pelt
smelt
spelt
svelte
swelt
unbelt
unfelt
veldt
welt

ĔLTH
commonwealth
stealth
health
wealth
dwell'th, etc.

ĔLV
delve
helve

shelve
twelve

ĔLVZ
elves
ourselves
selves
themselves
yourselves
delves, etc.

ĔLZ
Dardanelles
Elles
Lascelles
Seychelles
Welles
Wells
(see ĔL + s)

ĒM
abeam
academe
anatheme
beam
beseem
blaspheme
bream
centime
cream
daydream
deem
disesteem
distream
dream
embeam
enseam
esteem
extreme
fleam
gleam

ice-cream
leam
misdeem
moon-beam
ream
redeem
reem
regime
riem
scheme
scream
seam
seem
self-esteem
steam
stream
supreme
team
teem
theme
unbeseem
unseam
unteam
weather-gleam

ĔM

ad hominem
ahem
anadem
apothegm
bediadem
begem
Bethlehem
Brummagem
clem
condemn
contemn
diadem
em
'em

gem
hem
mem
phlegm
pro tem
requiem
stem
stratagem
them
theorem

ĒMD

undreamed
unredeemed
beamed, etc.

ĔMD

uncondemned
undiademed
begemmed, etc.

ĔMP

hemp
Kemp

ĔMS

temse

ĔMT

adreamt
attempt
contempt
dreamt
exempt
kempt
pre-empt
self-contempt
tempt
undreamt
unkempt

ĒMZ

meseems
beams, etc.

ĔMZ

temse
Thames
gems, etc.

ĒN

advene
Algerine
almandine
alpigene
aniline
anserine
aquamarine
argentine
atropine
atween
Augustine
baleen
bandoline
barkentine
bean
been
Beguine
benzene
benzine
bescreen
between
bombazine
bottine
bowling-green
brigantine
caffeine
canteen
Capuchin
careen
carotene
carrageen

chagrin
chorine
clean
codeine
colleen
come clean
Constantine
contravene
convene
crinoline
cuisine
damascene
dean
demean
demesne
dene
dudeen
duvetyn
ean
e'en
eighteen
Eocene
epicene
Ernestine
Eugene
Evangeline
evergreen
fairy-queen
fascine
fellahin
fifteen
fillipeen
Florentine
foreseen
fourteen
gabardine
galantine
gasoline
gazogene
gelatine
Geraldine

Ghibelline	misdemean	sea-green	wolverine
glean	moreen	seen	yean
gleen	nankeen	seine	*yestreen*
go-between	naphthalene	seltzogene	
good-e'en	Nazarene	serene	**ĔN**
gradine	nectarine	serpentine	again
grass-green	Nicene	seventeen	aldermen
green	nicotine	shagreen	amen
guillotine	nineteen	Shean	ben
Hallow-e'en	obscene	shebeen	brevipen
harvest-queen	oleomargarine	sheen	cayenne
heterogene	opaline	sixteen	Cheyenne
impregn	overseen	spalpeen	citizen
incarnadine	overween	spleen	cyclamen
indigene	palanquin	stein	Darien
intervene	Palmyrene	submarine	den
Irene	Pauline	subterrene	denizen
Jean	pean	subvene	equestrienne
Josephine	peen	superterrene	fen
keen	Peregrine	supervene	fountain-pen
kerosene	pistareen	tambourine	glen
lateen	Pleistocene	teen	halogen
lean	Pliocene	terrene	hen
lene	poteen	thirteen	hydrogen
libertine	praying-	tourmaline	impen
lien	machine	trephine	ken
long green	preen	tureen	Magdalen
machine	putting-green	'tween	men
magazine	*quadragene*	ultramarine	nitrogen
Magdalene	quarantine	umfteen	oxygen
margarine	quean	unclean	Parisienne
margravine	queen	unforeseen	pen
marine	quinine	unqueen	prairie-hen
May-queen	ravine	unseen	regimen
mazarine	routine	uplean	Saracen
meadow-queen	St. Augustine	vaseline	sen
mean	sardine	velveteen	sen-sen
mesne	sateen	visne	specimen
mezzanine	scalene	wean	ten
mien	scene	*ween*	then
Miocene	screen	winter-green	tragedienne

ōld, ôr, ŏdd, oil, fŏŏt, out; ūse, ûrn, ŭp; THis, thin

unpen
Valenciennes
varsovienne
water-hen
wen
when
wren
yen

ĔNCH

bedrench
bench
blench
clench
drench
flench
French
intrench
monkey-
  wrench
quench
retrench
squench
stench
tench
trench
unclench
wench
wrench

ĔNCHD

unblenched
bedrenched,
  etc.

ĔND

fiend
piend
teind
advened, etc.
cleaned, etc.

ĔND

amend
an-end
append
apprehend
ascend
attend
befriend
bend
blend
commend
comprehend
condescend
contend
defend
depend
descend
distend
dividend
emend
end
expend
extend
fend
forefend
forfend
friend
gable-end
godsend
hornblende
impend
intend
interblend
kenned
lend
mend
minuend
misapprehend
misspend
obtend
offend

Ostend
penned
perpend
pitch-blende
portend
prepend
pretend
recommend
rend
repetend
reprehend
reverend
send
South Bend
spend
subtend
subtrahend
superintend
suspend
tend
transcend
trend
unbend
unfriend
unkenned
unpenned
upend
upsend
vend
vilipend
weather-fend
wend
Zend

ĔNDZ

amends
ascends, etc.

ĔNGK

Schenck

ĔNGKS

Jenkes
Jenks

ĔNGTH

full-length
length
strength

ĔNJ

avenge
revenge
Stonehenge

ĔNJD

unavenged

ĔNS

abstinence
accidence
affluence
beneficence
benevolence
blandiloquence
breviloquence
circumference
coincidence
commence
commonsense
competence
concupiscence
condense
conference
confidence
confluence
consequence
continence
convenience
corpulence
defence
deference

dense	indifference	*propense*	experienced
difference	indigence	providence	fenced
diffidence	indolence	prurience	fornenst
diligence	inexpedience	quantivalence	'gainst
disobedience	inexperience	recompense	incensed
dispense	inference	redolence	inexperienced
dissidence	influence	reference	influenced
eloquence	innocence	residence	reverenced
eminence	insipience	resilience	sensed
equivalence	insolence	reticence	
evidence	intelligence	reverence	**ĔNT**
excellence	intense	salience	abandonment
exigence	irreverence	sapience	abolishment
expedience	magnificence	self-confidence	absent
expense	magniloquence	self-defence	abstinent
experience	maleficence	sense	accent
fence	malevolence	somnolence	accident
flatulence	mellifluence	spence	accipient
flocculence	munificence	subservience	accompaniment
frankincense	negligence	subsidence	accomplish-
fraudulence	nescience	subtense	ment
grandiloquence	non-residence	succulence	accoutrement
hence	obedience	supereminence	acknowledg-
immanence	offence	suspense	ment
immense	omnipotence	tense	admeasurement
imminence	omniscience	thence	admonishment
impenitence	opulence	truculence	advertisement
impertinence	pence	turbulence	*affamishment*
impotence	penitence	vehemence	affluent
imprevalence	percipience	violence	affranchise-
improvidence	permanence	virulence	ment
impudence	pertinence	whence	aggrandize-
incense	pestilence	(Cf. ĔNTS)	ment
incidence	plenipotence		aliment
incipience	pre-eminence	**ĔNST**	ambient
incoincidence	preference	against	anent
incompetence	prepense	anenst	aperient
incongruence	prescience	commenced	apportionment
inconsequence	pretence	condensed	*acquent*
incontinence	prevalence	dispensed	arbitrament
inconvenience	prominence	evidenced	argument

ōld, ôr, ŏdd, oil, fŏŏt, out; ūse, ûrn, ŭp; THis, thin

armament	consent	document	extinguishment
ascent	consequent	element	famishment
assent	constituent	eloquent	fent
astonishment	content	embarrassment	ferment
attent	continent	embattlement	filament
augment	convenient	embellishment	firmament
babblement	corpulent	embezzlement	flocculent
banishment	dazzlement	embitterment	foment
battlement	decipherment	emblazonment	foremeant
bedevilment	decrement	embodiment	*forespent*
bedizenment	deferent	eminent	fornent
belligerent	dement	emollient	fosterment
beneficent	demolishment	emolument	franchisement
benevolent	dent	empannelment	fraudulent
bent	descent	enablement	frequent
besprent	detent	encompassment	garnishment
betterment	detriment	encouragement	gent
bewilderment	development	endangerment	Ghent
blandishment	devilment	*endeavorment*	government
blazonment	different	enfeeblement	*gracilent*
blemishment	diffident	enfranchise-	gradient
blent	diffluent	ment	grandiloquent
botherment	diligent	enlightenment	habiliment
brabblement	diminishment	ennoblement	harassment
brent	dimplement	enravishment	hereditament
cement	disablement	entanglement	ignipotent
cent	disarmament	envelopment	ill-content
chastisement	discontent	environment	immanent
cherishment	discourage-	envisagement	imminent
circumambient	ment	equivalent	impediment
circumfluent	disfigurement	esculent	impenitent
circumvent	disfranchise-	establishment	imperilment
coincident	ment	esurient	impertinent
comment	disobedient	event	implement
competent	disparagement	evident	impotent
complement	dispiritment	excellent	impoverish-
compliment	dissent	excrement	ment
condiment	dissident	exigent	imprisonment
confident	distinguish-	expedient	improvident
confluent	ment	experiment	impudent
congruent	divertisement	extent	incident

incipient
incoincident
incompetent
incongruent
inconsequent
incontinent
inconvenient
increment
indent
indifferent
indigent
indolent
inexpedient
influent
ingredient
innocent
insentient
insipient
insolent
instrument
integument
intelligent
intent
inveiglement
invent
irreverent
Kent
lament
languishment
lavishment
leant
lenient
lent
ligament
lineament
liniment
luculent
magnificent
magniloquent
malcontent
maleficent

malevolent
management
meant
measurement
medicament
mellifluent
merriment
miscontent
misrepresent
misspent
monument
munificent
muniment
negligent
nourishment
nutriment
obedient
occident
omnipotent
opulent
orient
ornament
ostent
overspent
parliament
pediment
penitent
pent
percipient
permanent
pertinent
pesterment
pestilent
plenipotent
portent
prattlement
precedent
predicament
pre-eminent
premonishment
prescient

present
presentiment
president
prevalent
prevent
prominent
provident
prurient
punishment
ravishment
recipient
redolent
refluent
regiment
relent
relinquishment
rent
repent
replenishment
represent
resent
resident
resilient
reticent
reverent
rudiment
sacrament
salient
sapient
scent
sediment
self-confident
sent
sentient
sentiment
settlement
somnolent
spent
sprent
stent
subsequent

subservient
succulent
supereminent
supplement
temperament
tenement
tent
testament
thereanent
torment
tournament
tremblement
Trent
truculent
turbulent
unbent
underwent
unkent
unmeant
unsent
unspent
untent
vanishment
vanquishment
vehement
vent
vinolent
violent
virulent
wanderment
well-content
well-meant
well-spent
went
wilderment
wonderment
worriment

ÉNTH

greenth
thirteenth

ōld, ôr, ŏdd, oil, fŏŏt, out; ūse, ûrn, ŭp; THis, thin

fourteenth, etc.
lean'th, etc.

ĒNTH

tenth
pen'th, etc.

ĔNTS

accoutrements
contents
cents, etc.
(Cf. ĔNS)

ĒNZ

Essenes
greens
smithereens
teens
advenes, etc.

ĔNZ

cleanse
ens
flense
gens
lens
Valenciennes
Vincennes
(see ĔN + s)

ĒP

adeep
aheap
asleep
beauty-sleep
beweep
bo-peep
cheap
cheep
clepe
chimney-sweep
chepe

creep
deep
ensweep
estrepe
forweep
heap
keep
leap
neap
outleap
outsleep
outweep
overleap
oversleep
peep
reap
seep
sheep
sleep
steep
sweep
swepe
threap
under-peep
upkeep
weep

ĔP

demi-rep
footstep
hep
overstep
pep
rep
skep
step
steppe

ĒPS

creeps
cheeps, etc.

ĒPS

steps, etc.

ĒPT

beneaped
neaped
unsteeped
upheaped
heaped, etc.

ĔPT

accept
adept
crept
except
inept
intercept
kept
leapt
outslept
overslept
overstepped
pepped
sept
slept
stepped
swept
unkept
unswept
unwept
wept
yclept

EPTH

depth
stepp'th, etc.

ĒR

adhere
äerosphere
affeer

amir
anear
appear
arrear
asmear
atmosphere
auctioneer
austere
bandoleer
bayadere
beer
belvedere
besmear
bevel-gear
bier
blear
bombardier
brevier
brigadier
buccaneer
canceleer
cannoneer
caravaneer
carbineer
career
cashier
cavalier
cere
chandelier
chanticleer
charioteer
cheer
chevalier
chiffonier
chimere
circuiteer
clear
cohere
commandeer
compeer
congé d'élire

crotcheteer	insphere	sheer	adhered, etc.
cuirassier	interfere	sincere	feared, etc.
dear	jeer	skeer	
deer	killdeer	smear	**ẸRS**
disappear	lear	sneer	fierce
domineer	leer	sonneteer	pierce
drear	madrier	souvenir	tierce
ear	meer	spear	transpierce
electioneer	mere	specksioneer	
emir	mir	sphere	**ẸRT**
endear	mountaineer	steer	peart
engineer	muffineer	tabasheer	
ensear	muleteer	targeteer	**ẸRZ**
ensphere	musketeer	tear	Algiers
fakir	mutineer	teer	shears
fallow-deer	near	tier	sheers
fear	overhear	*timberstere*	adheres, etc.
financier	overseer	timoneer	
fineer	pamphleteer	Tyr	**ẸS**
fleer	peer	undersphere	afterpiece
friction-gear	persevere	ungear	ambergris
frontier	petardeer	*unnear*	apiece
fusileer	pier	unsphere	battlepiece
garreteer	pioneer	upcheer	Berenice
gaselier	pistoleer	uprear	Bernice
gazeteer	planisphere	veer	cantatrice
gear	privateer	veneer	caprice
ginger-beer	pulpiteer	vizier	cease
gondolier	queer	volunteer	cerise
gonfalonier	racketeer	weir	chimney-piece
grand-vizier	reappear	year	Clarice
grenadier	rear		coulisse
halberdier	reindeer	**ẸRD**	crease
hear	revere	beard	creese
Heer	scrutineer	flap-eared	decease
hemisphere	sear	lop-eared	decrease
here	seer	*uneared*	esquisse
indear	sere	unfeared	Felice
Indianeer	sermoneer	unpeered	fleece
inhere	severe	weird	fowling-piece
insincere	shear		frontispiece

ōld, ôr, ŏdd, oil, fŏŏt, cut; ūse, ûrn, ŭp; THis, thin

geese
grease
grece
Greece
increase
lease
Lucrece
mantel-piece
master-piece
Maurice
Nice
niece
obese
peace
pelisse
piece
pocket-piece
police
popping-crease
predecease
Reese
release
semese
surcease
Therese
valise
verdigris

ĔS

accresce
acquiesce
address
aggress
ambassadress
ancestress
archeress
assess
baroness
Bess
blemishless
bless

bodiless
bottomless
canoness
caress
cess
chess
coalesce
color!ess
comfortless
comfortress
compress
confess
conqueress
conscienceless
convalesce
cress
cultureless
cumberless
dauphiness
deaconess
deliquesce
demoness
depress
digress
dinnerless
dispossess
distress
diving-dress
dress
duress
editress
effervesce
effloresce
effortless
egress
evanesce
excess
executress
express
fanciless
fatherless

fathomless
favorless
featureless
fess
fetterless
finesse
flavorless
flowerless
foreguess
fortuneless
frondesce
full-dress
gala-dress
gentilesse
giantess
governess
guess
harborless
head-dress
idolatress
impress
ingress
inheritress
intumesce
jess
Kress
less
limitless
marchioness
masterless
mayoress
meaningless
measureless
merciless
mess
ministress
moneyless
monitress
motherless
motionless
motiveless

nevertheless
noblesse
numberless
obsess
obsolesce
odorless
opalesce
oppress
overdress
pantheress
patroness
penniless
phosophoresce
pitiless
pleasureless
poetess
politesse
possess
powerless
power-press
prepossess
press
prioress
procuress
profess
progress
prophetess
proprietress
purposeless
pythoness
Quakeress
quiesce
ransomless
recess
redress
regress
repossess
repress
respiteless
retrogress
rudderless

S.O.S.
shadowless
shelterless
shepherdess
silverless
slumberless
sorceress
spiritless
stewardess
stress
success
sultaness
suppress
tailoress
temptationless
Tess
Titaness
transgress
tress
turgesce
unbless
underdress
undress
unless
valueless
virtueless
votaress
water-cress
weaponless
yes
abjectedness
abstractedness
abusiveness
accidentalness
adaptiveness
addictedness
adhesiveness
advantageous-
  ness
affectedness
affrontiveness

agedness
aggressiveness
agileness
agreeableness
airiness
alimentiveness
alliterativeness
allusiveness
almightiness
amazedness
ambitiousness
amiableness
amicableness
ampleness
ancientness
angelicalness
angriness
anonymousness
anticness
anxiousness
apishness
apparentness
appeasableness
appositeness
apprehensive-
  ness
approachable-
  ness
arbitrariness
ardentness
arduousness
aridness
artfulness
articulateness
artificialness
artlessness
assiduousness
atrociousness
attentiveness
attractiveness
auspiciousness

avariciousness
awfulness
awkwardness
backhanded-
  ness
backwardness
balefulness
banefulness
bareheadedness
barrenness
bashfulness
beastliness
beeriness
beseechingness
besottedness
bitterness
blamelessness
blessedness
blissfulness
blithesomeness
bloatedness
blockishness
blood-guiltiness
bloodiness
bloodthirsti-
  ness
bloomingness
bluntishness
boastfulness
boisterousness
bonniness
bookishness
boorishness
bootlessness
boundlessness
bounteousness
boyishness
brackishness
brassiness
brawniness
brazenness

breathlessness
brilliantness
brittleness
brokenness
brotherliness
brushiness
brutishness
bulkiness
bumptiousness
bunchiness
burliness
bushiness
buxomness
candidness
capaciousness
capriciousness
captiousness
carefulness
carelessness
cautiousness
ceaselessness
chalkiness
changefulness
chariness
charmingness
chattiness
cheerfulness
cheeriness
cheerlessness
childishness
childlessness
chilliness
chubbiness
churlishness
clandestine-
  ness
clannishness
cleanliness
clearsighted-
  ness
cleverness

ōld, ôr, ŏdd, oil, fŏŏt, out; ūse, ûrn, ŭp; THis, thin

cliquishness
cloddishness
cloudiness
clownishness
clumsiness
coldhearted-
    ness
collectedness
collusiveness
comeliness
commonness
composedness
comprehen-
    siveness
compulsiveness
conceitedness
conclusiveness
conduciveness
confusedness
conjunctive-
    ness
conscientious-
    ness
consciousness
consecutive-
    ness
conspicuous-
    ness
constructive-
    ness
contentedness
contentious-
    ness
contradictious-
    ness
contrariness
contumacious-
    ness
copiousness
cordialness
corrosiveness

costliness
courageousness
courtliness
covertness
covetousness
crabbedness
craftiness
craggedness
cragginess
cravingness
craziness
creaminess
credulousness
crookedness
cruelness
crustiness
cumbrousness
curiousness
curliness
customariness
daintiness
dampishness
daringness
dauntlessness
deadliness
deathfulness
deathiness
debauchedness
deceitfulness
deceptiveness
decisiveness
decorativeness
defectiveness
defenceless-
    ness
defiantness
definiteness
deformedness
degenerateness
dejectedness
deliciousness

delightfulness
delightsome-
    ness
deliriousness
delusiveness
dementedness
depressiveness
derisiveness
desirousness
despitefulness
destructiveness
desultoriness
detersiveness
detractiveness
devotedness
dewiness
diffusedness
diffusiveness
dilatoriness
dilutedness
dinginess
direfulness
disastrousness
discontented-
    ness
discursiveness
disdainfulness
disinterested-
    ness
dismalness
disposedness
disputatious-
    ness
distastefulness
distinctiveness
dizziness
doggedness
dolefulness
doubtfulness
doughtiness
downiness

dreadfulness
dreaminess
dreariness
droughtiness
drowsiness
drunkenness
dumpishness
duskiness
dustiness
dwarfishness
eagerness
earliness
earnestness
earthiness
earthliness
earthly-
    mindedness
easefulness
easiness
eeriness
effectiveness
efficaciousness
effusiveness
egregiousness
elatedness
emotiveness
emptiness
endearedness
endlessness
enduringness
engagingness
enormousness
entertaining-
    ness
equalness
essentialness
estrangedness
evasiveness
everlastingness
exaltedness
exceptiousness

excessiveness
exclusiveness
excursiveness
expansiveness
expeditiousness
expensiveness
explicitness
expressiveness
exquisiteness
extensiveness
facetiousness
factiousness
faithfulness
faithlessness
fallaciousness
false-hearted-
  ness
far-sightedness
fastidiousness
fatefulness
fatherliness
faultlessness
favoredness
fearfulness
fearlessness
feeble-
  mindedness
feebleness
feignedness
ferociousness
fervidness
fickleness
fictiousness
fiendishness
fieriness
filminess
fishiness
fitfulness
fixedness
flabbiness
flaccidness

flakiness
flashiness
fleshiness
fleshliness
flexibleness
flightiness
flimsiness
flippantness
floridness
floweriness
fluentness
fogginess
foolhardiness
foolishness
foppishness
forcedness
foreignness
forgetfulness
formlessness
forwardness
fractiousness
fragileness
frankhearted-
  ness
francticness
fraudlessness
freakishness
freckledness
freehearted-
  ness
fretfulness
friendlessness
friendliness
frightfulness
frigidness
friskiness
frivolousness
frostiness
frothiness
frowardness
frozenness

frugalness
fruitfulness
fruitlessness
frumpishness
fugaciousness
fulsomeness
fumishness
fundamental-
  ness
furiousness
fussiness
fustiness
gaddishness
gallantness
gamesomeness
garishness
garrulousness
gashliness
gaudiness
generousness
genialness
gentleness
ghastliness
ghostliness
giddiness
giftedness
girlishness
gladfulness
gladsomeness
glariness
glassiness
gloominess
gloriousness
glossiness
godlessness
godliness
goodliness
gorgeousness
gracefulness
gracelessness
graciousness

graphicness
grassiness
gratefulness
greasiness
greediness
greenishness
grievousness
griminess
grittiness
grogginess
groundlessness
guardedness
guidelessness
guilefulness
guiltiness
guiltlessness
gustfulness
hairiness
handiness
handsomeness
haplessness
happiness
hard-hearted-
  ness
hardiness
harmfulness
harmlessness
harmonious-
  ness
hastiness
hatefulness
haughtiness
haziness
headiness
healthfulness
healthiness
healthlessness
heartedness
heartiness
heartlessness
heathenness

ōld, ôr, ŏdd, oil, fŏŏt, out; ūse, ûrn, ŭp; THis, thin

heavenliness
heavenly-
    mindedness
heaviness
heedfulness
heedlessness
heinousness
hellishness
helpfulness
helplessness
heterogeneous-
    ness
hiddenness
hideousness
highminded-
    ness
hilliness
hoariness
hoggishness
holiness
hollowness
homelessness
homeliness
hopefulness
hopelessness
horridness
huffishness
humbleness
humidness
humorousness
hurtfulness
huskiness
iciness
idleness
ignobleness
illicitness
illiterateness
ill-naturedness
illusiveness
illustriousness

imaginative-
    ness
imitativeness
immaculate-
    ness
impartialness
impassiveness
imperfectness
imperiousness
imperviousness
impetuousness
impiousness
implicitness
imponderous-
    ness
imposingness
impressiveness
impulsiveness
inattentiveness
inauspicious-
    ness
incapaciousness
incautiousness
incidentalness
incoherentness
incomprehen-
    siveness
inconclusive-
    ness
incongruous-
    ness
inconsistent-
    ness
inconspicuous-
    ness
indebtedness
indecisiveness
indecorous-
    ness
inefficacious-
    ness

infectiousness
ingeniousness
ingenuousness
injuriousness
inkiness
innoxiousness
inobtrusive-
    ness
inoffensiveness
insidiousness
insipidness
instructiveness
intensiveness
intrusiveness
inventiveness
invidiousness
invincibleness
involuntariness
inwardness
irefulness
irksomeness
jaggedness
jauntiness
jealousness
jettiness
Jewishness
jolliness
jovialness
joyfulness
joylessness
joyousness
judiciousness
juiciness
jumpiness
kind-hearted-
    ness
kindliness
kingliness
knavishness
knightliness
knottiness

languidness
large-hearted-
    ness
lasciviousness
lawfulness
lawlessness
laziness
leafiness
leaflessness
leaviness
lengthiness
licentiousness
lifelessness
light-hearted-
    ness
lightsomeness
likeableness
likeliness
limberness
limpidness
liquidness
lissomeness
listlessness
literalness
litigiousness
littleness
liveliness
lividness
livingness
loathliness
loathsomeness
loftiness
loneliness
lonesomeness
longsomeness
loquaciousness
lordliness
loutishness
love-in-idleness
loveliness
lovingness

---

lowliness
loyalness
lucidness
luckiness
lugubriousness
luminousness
lumpishness
lusciousness
lustfulness
lustiness
maidenliness
maliciousness
manfulness
manliness
mannerliness
mannishness
many-sidedness
marshiness
massiness
massiveness
matchlessness
mawkishness
maziness
meagreness
mealiness
meatiness
meditativeness
mellowness
meltingness
meretorious-
  ness
meretricious-
  ness
merriness
mightiness
milkiness
mindfulness
miraculousness
miriness
mirthfulness
mirthlessness

miscellaneous-
  ness
mischievous-
  ness
misshapenness
missishness
mistiness
modernness
modishness
momentous-
  ness
monkishness
monotonous-
  ness
monstrousness
moodiness
mopishness
morbidness
mortalness
mossiness
motherliness
mouldiness
mournfulness
mulishness
multifarious-
  ness
mumpishness
murkiness
muskiness
mustiness
mutinousness
mysteriousness
mysticalness
nakedness
namelessness
narrow-mind-
  edness
narrowness
nastiness
nationalness
nativeness

nattiness
naturalness
naughtiness
near-sighted-
  ness
nebulousness
necessariness
necessitious-
  ness
nectareousness
needfulness
neediness
needlessness
nefariousne˜s
neglectedness
neglectfulness
neighborliness
nervousness
niggardliness
nimbleness
nobleness
noiselessness
noisiness
noisomeness
notableness
notedness
notelessness
nothingness
notoriousness
noxiousness
numerousness
nutritiousness
objectiveness
obligatoriness
obligingness
obliviousness
obsequiousness
observableness
obstreperous-
  ness
obtrusiveness

obviousness
odiousness
odoriferous-
  ness
odorousness
offensiveness
officiousness
oiliness
oleaginousness
openhanded-
  ness
openhearted-
  ness
openness
oppressiveness
opprobrious-
  ness
orderliness
ostentatious-
  ness
outlandishness
outrageousness
outwardness
painfulness
painlessness
pallidness
paltriness
parlousness
parsimonious-
  ness
passiveness
pawkiness
peaceableness
peacefulness
pearliness
peerlessness
peevishness
pellucidness
penetrative-
  ness
pennilessness

ōld. ôr, ŏdd, oil, fŏŏt, out; ūse, ûrn, ŭp; THis, thin

pensileness
pensiveness
penuriousness
peremptoriness
perfectness
perfidiousness
perfunctoriness
perilousness
perniciousness
perplexedness
perplexiveness
perspicacious-
    ness
perspicuous-
    ness
persuasiveness
pertinacious-
    ness
pervicacious-
    ness
perviousness
pestilential-
    ness
pettiness
pettishness
piercingness
pig-headedness
pitchiness
piteousness
pithiness
pitiableness
pitilessness
placableness
placidness
plaintiveness
playfulness
playsomeness
pleasantness
pleasingness
plenteousness
pliantness

poachiness
pointedness
pompousness
ponderous-
    ness
poorliness
porousness
portliness
positiveness
powerfulness
powerlessness
practicalness
praiseworthi-
    ness
prayerfulness
prayerlessness
precariousness
preciousness
precipitous-
    ness
precociousness
prejudicialness
preposterous-
    ness
presumptu-
    ousness
pretentious-
    ness
prettiness
previousness
prickliness
pridefulness
priestliness
priggishness
primitiveness
princeliness
prodigiousness
productive-
    ness
progressive-
    ness

properness
propitiousness
prosiness
prospective-
    ness
protectiveness
prudishness
public-minded-
    ness
puffiness
pugnacious-
    ness
pulpiness
pulpousness
pulselessness
punctiliousness
puniness
pursiness
pusillanimous-
    ness
putridness
quakiness
qualmishness
queasiness
queenliness
quenchlessness
querulousness
quick-sighted-
    ness
quick-witted-
    ness
quietness
rabidness
raciness
raggedness
raininess
rakishness
rancidness
rapaciousness
rapidness
ravenousness

readiness
rebelliousness
recentness
receptiveness
recklessness
reddishness
reflectiveness
refractiveness
refractoriness
regardlessness
relativeness
relentlessness
remorsefulness
remorseless-
    ness
reproachful-
    ness
repulsiveness
resistlessness
resoluteness
respectfulness
responsiveness
restfulness
restiveness
restlessness
restrictiveness
retentiveness
revengefulness
rightfulness
right-handed-
    ness
right-minded-
    ness
rigidness
rigorousness
riotousness
robustiousness
rockiness
roguishness
rompishness
roominess

āle, câre, ădd, ärm, åsk; mē, hĕre, ĕnd; īce, ĭll;

ropiness	self-conceited-	simplemind-	sorriness
rosiness	ness	edness	sorrowfulness
rottenness	self-conscious-	simpleness	sottishness
ruddiness	ness	simultaneous-	spaciousness
ruefulness	selfishness	ness	sparklingness
ruggedness	self-righteous-	sinfulness	speciousness
ruthlessness	ness	singleness	speckledness
sacredness	senselessness	sinlessness	speculativeness
sacrilegious-	sensitiveness	sketchiness	speechlessness
ness	sensuousness	skilfulness	speediness
sagaciousness	sententious-	skittishness	spiciness
saintliness	ness	slabbiness	spitefulness
salaciousness	seriousness	slatiness	splendidness
sallowness	shabbiness	slavishness	sponginess
salutariness	shadiness	sleaziness	spontaneous-
sanctimonious-	shadowiness	sleepiness	ness
ness	shagginess	sleeplessness	sportiveness
sandiness	shakiness	sleetiness	spotlessness
sanguineness	shallowness	slenderness	spottedness
sappiness	shamefulness	sliminess	spottiness
satisfactoriness	shamelessness	slipperiness	springiness
sauciness	shapelessness	slothfulness	spriteliness
savageness	shapeliness	sluggishness	spuminess
savingness	sheepishness	smilingness	spuriousness
savoriness	shieldlessness	smokiness	squeamishness
scaliness	shiftiness	snappishness	starchiness
scantiness	shiftlessness	sneakiness	starriness
scorchingness	shiningness	snobbishness	stateliness
scornfulness	shoaliness	sober-minded-	steadfastness
scragginess	short-sighted-	ness	steadiness
scurviness	ness	soberness	stealthfulness
sea-worthiness	showeriness	sociableness	stealthiness
secondariness	showiness	soft-hearted-	steeliness
secretiveness	shrewishness	ness	*steepiness*
secretness	shrubbiness	solidness	stickiness
sedentariness	sickliness	solitariness	stinginess
seditiousness	sightlessness	solubleness	stintedness
seediness	silentness	sombreness	stolidness
seemingness	silkiness	sombrousness	stoniness
seemliness	silliness	sonorousness	storminess
seldomness		sordidness	

ōld, ôr, ŏdd, oil, fŏŏt, out; ūse, ûrn, ŭp; THis, thin

straightfor-
wardness
strenuousness
stringentness
stringiness
stubbiness
stubbornness
studiousness
stuffiness
stuntedness
stupendousness
stupidness
sturdiness
stylishness
subjectiveness
submissiveness
subordinate-
ness
substantialness
subtleness
successfulness
suddenness
sugariness
suggestiveness
suitableness
sulkiness
sulleness
sultriness
sumptuousness
sunniness
supercilious-
ness
superstitious-
ness
suppleness
suppliantness
surliness
surprisingness
susceptiveness
suspectedness
suspiciousness

swarthiness
sweatiness
sweetishness
talkativeness
tamelessness
tardiness
tastefulness
tastelessness
tawdriness
tawniness
tediousness
tempestuous-
ness
temporariness
temptingness
tenaciousness
tender-hearted-
ness
tepidness
testiness
thankfulness
thievishness
thirstiness
thoroughness
thoughtfulness
thoughtless-
ness
threadiness
thriftiness
thriftlessness
thrivingness
ticklishness
tidiness
timeliness
timidness
timorousness
tipsiness
tiresomeness
toilsomeness
toothsomeness
torpidness

torridness
tortuousness
totalness
touchiness
toyishness
tracklessness
traitorousness
tranquilness
transcendent-
ness
transientness
transitiveness
transitoriness
transparent-
ness
trashiness
treacherous-
ness
tremendous-
ness
tremulousness
tributariness
trickiness
trickishness
tricksiness
true-hearted-
ness
trustfulness
trustiness
trustlessness
trustworthi-
ness
truthfulness
truthlessness
tunefulness
turfiness
turgidness
ugliness
umbrageous-
ness

unanimous-
ness
unbendingness
unblessedness
unbounded-
ness
uncleanliness
uncloudedness
uncourtliness
undauntedness
uneasiness
unexpected-
ness
unfeignedness
unfriendliness
ungainliness
ungentleness
ungodliness
ungrounded-
ness
unholiness
universalness
unkindliness
unlikeliness
unloveliness
unmanliness
unprepared-
ness
unquietness
unreadiness
unrighteous-
ness
unruliness
unseaworthi-
ness
unseemliness
unsightliness
unstableness
untowardness
untrustiness
unwieldiness

āle, câre, ădd, ärm, åsk; mē, hĕre, ĕnd; īce, ĭll;

unwillingness
unwontedness
unworldliness
unworthiness
uppishness
usefulness
uselessness
uxoriousness
vacuousness
vagrantness
valetudinari-
   ness
valiantness
validness
vapidness
vexatiousness
viciousness
victoriousness
vigorousness
vindictiveness
viridness
virtuousness
viscousness
visionariness
vitreousness
vivaciousness
vividness
vociferousness
voluminous-
   ness
voluntariness
voluptuousness
voraciousness
vulgarness
waggishness
wakefulness
wantonness
warefulness
wariness
warm-hearted-
   ness

washiness
waspishness
wastefulness
watchfulness
waveringness
waviness
waxiness
waywardness
wealthiness
weariness
wearisomeness
weightiness
welcomeness
whimsicalness
whitishness
wholesome-
   ness
wickedness
wilderness
wilfulness
wiliness
willingness
winsomeness
wiriness
wishfulness
wistfulness
witheredness
witlessness
wittiness
woefulness
womanliness
wondrousness
wontedness
woodiness
woolliness
wordiness
wordishness
worldliness
worldy-mind-
   edness
worshipfulness

worthiness
worthlessness
wrathfulness
wretchedness
wretchlessness
wrongfulness
wrongheaded-
   ness
yeastiness
yellowishness
yellowness
yieldingness
youthfulness
zealousness

ĒSH

affiche
leash
McLeish
McNeish
schottische
unleash

ĔSH

afresh
crèche
enmesh
flesh
fresh
mesh
nesh
refresh
secesh
thresh

ĔSK

arabesque
barbaresque
burlesque
chivalresque
Dantesque

desk
gardensque
gigantesque
grotesque
Moresque
naturalesque
picaresque
picturesque
plateresque
reading-desk
Romanesque
sculpturesque
soldatesque
statuesque

ĒST

archpriest
artiste
batiste
beast
deceased
east
feast
harvest-feast
least
modiste
priest
queest
triste
underpoliced
unpriest
wedding-feast
yeast
pieced, etc.
ceased, etc.
fleeced, etc.

ĔST

abreast
acquest
alkahest

ōld, ôr, ŏdd, oil, fŏŏt, out; ūse, ûrn, ŭp; THis, thin

anapest	molest	*attributest*	dreamiest
arrest	nest	*banishest*	dreariest
attest	north-west	beamiest	drowsiest
behest	obsessed	beguilingest	dustiest
bequest	obtest	bleariest	earliest
best	over-dressed	blestfullest	easiest
blest	palimpsest	blithefulest	eeriest
breast	pest	blithefulest	effectedest
Brest	predigest	blithesomest	*emblazonest*
Bucharest	protest	*blunderest*	emptiest
Budapest	quest	breeziest	*enviest*
cest	recessed	brilliantest	evenest
chest	request	briniest	*exhibitest*
congest	rest	burliest	filmiest
contest	second-best	cheerfullest	filthiest
crest	self-possessed	cheeriest	fleeciest
depressed	suggest	cheerliest	flimsiest
detest	test	chilliest	flightiest
devest	tressed	chokiest	flintiest
digest	Trieste	cleanliest	*flowerest*
distressed	unblest	*clusterest*	foamiest
divest	unbreast	*conquerest*	forcefullest
dressed	under-crest	*continuest*	*forfeitest*
Everest	underdressed	cosiest	*freshenest*
funest	undressed	costliest	friendliest
gest	unexpressed	courtliest	funniest
golden-tressed	unguessed	*coverest*	fussiest
guest	unprepossessed	creamiest	*gatherest*
hard-pressed	unpressed	creepiest	genialest
hest	unredressed	cruellest	giddiest
imprest	unrest	crustiest	*glimmerest*
increst	untressed	curliest	*glistenest*
infest	vest	daintiest	gloomiest
ingest	west	decisivest	glossiest
interest	wrest	derisivest	*glowerest*
invest	yessed	*determinest*	goutiest
jessed	zest	dingiest	grimiest
jest	(see ĔS + ed)	dizziest	guilefullest
Key West	*answerest*	doughtiest	guiltiest
lest	*astonishest*	dowdiest	gustiest
manifest	attentivest	*dowerest*	happiest

haughtiest	mellowest	ruggedest	*sufferest*
healthiest	*meritest*	rustiest	*sunderest*
hearkenest	merriest	sacredest	sunniest
heartiest	mightiest	sedgiest	surliest
heaviest	moistiest	seemliest	tearfullest
holiest	morbidest	*severest*	*temperest*
homeliest	mossiest	*shimmerest*	thirstiest
hopefullest	mouldiest	shiniest	thriftiest
horridest	mournfullest	shoddiest	*thunderest*
huffiest	*murmurest*	showiest	timidest
hungerest	muskiest	*shudderest*	trustiest
hungriest	mustiest	sightliest	ugliest
huskiest	*narrowest*	silentest	unholiest
iciest	noisiest	silliest	unreadiest
incumberest	*nourishest*	sketchiest	veriest
inheritest	*offerest*	skilfullest	vindictivest
inkiest	*pardonest*	skinniest	vulgarest
inliest	patentest	sleepiest	*wanderest*
inspiritest	pearliest	slimiest	wealthiest
jolliest	pensivest	*slumberest*	weariest
juiciest	pleasantest	smokiest	wheeziest
kindliest	*pleasurest*	snuffiest	windiest
kingliest	portliest	soapiest	wilfulest
knightliest	preciousest	solidest	*winnowest*
labourest	*predestinest*	*sorrowest*	winsomest
languishest	princeliest	spiciest	wintriest
libellest	prosiest	spikiest	*witnessest*
likeliest	*punishest*	*spiritest*	*wonderest*
lingerest	*quarrellest*	splendidest	*worriest*
lissomest	*questionest*	spongiest	yeastiest
listenest	quietest	spooniest	
lithesomest	*recoverest*	springiest	**ĒT**
liveliest	*relinquishest*	spriteliest	accrete
livenest	*rememberest*	steadiest	afreet
loftiest	*rescuest*	stealthiest	athlete
loneliest	restfulest	stilliest	balance-sheet
loveliest	rightfulest	stingiest	beat
lowerest	*rivallest*	stormiest	beet
lowliest	rosiest	stuffiest	bitter-sweet
loyalest	rowdiest	stupidest	bleat
marvellest	royalest	sturdiest	carte-de-visite

ōld, ôr, ŏdd, oil, fŏŏt, out; ūse, ûrn, ŭp; THis, thin

cheat

cheet

cleat

cleet

compete

complete

conceit

concrete

country-seat

county-seat

Crete

dead-beat

dead-heat

dead-meat

deceit

defeat

delete

deplete

discreet

Dutch treat

eat

effete

elite

entreat

escheat

estreat

facete

feat

feet

fleet

geat

greet

heat

help-meet

honey-sweet

ill-treat

incomplete

indiscreet

judgment-seat

Lafitte

leat

leet

lorikeet

maltreat

marguerite

meadow-sweet

meat

meet

mercy-seat

mete

neat

obsolete

overeat

parrakeet

peat

pleat

preconceit

receipt

repeat

replete

retreat

sea-beat

seat

secrete

self-conceit

self-deceit

sheet

skeet

sleet

street

suite

sunny-sweet

sweet

teat

terete

treat

unmeet

unseat

unsweet

vegete

weet

wheat

winding-sheet

ĔT

abet

aigrette

ailette

alette

allumette

all wet

alphabet

amourette

amulet

anchoret

angelet

anisette

Annette

Antoinette

backset

baguette

banneret

banquette

barbette

Barnett

baronet

bassinet

bayonet

beget

benet

beset

bet

bewet

blanquette

bobbinet

Brett

brevet

brochette

brunette

Burnett

cabinet

cadet

calumet

canzonet

carcanet

cassolette

castanet

cellaret

chansonette

chemisette

cigarette

clarinet

coquette

coronet

corvette

coverlet

croquette

crossette

crystal set

curvet

dancette

dead-set

debt

duet

epaulet

epithet

estafette

etiquette

facette

falconet

farmerette

flageolet

flet

floweret

forget

formeret

fossette

fourchette

fret

frett

fumette

gazette

genet

get
Gillette
globulet
grisette
Harriet
historiette
illset
inset
interset
jet
Jeanette
Joliet
judgment-debt
Juliet
Juliette
landaulet
leaderette
let
Lett
leveret
lorgnette
Lucette
luncheonette
lunette
Margaret
marionette
marmoset
martinet
medalet
met
mignonette
minaret
minionette
minuet
misbeget
motet
musette
Nanette
net
noisette
novelette

octet
off-set
Olivet
omelet
oubliette
overset
parapet
parroket
parquet
pet
pianette
pillaret
pipette
piquet
piquette
pirouette
planchette
poussette
quartet
quintet
regret
ret
revet
ricochet
rivulet
rosette
roulette
sarcenet
septet
serviette
sestet
set
sett
sextet
sharp-set
silhouette
somerset
soubrette
statuette
stet
suffragette

sunset
sweat
tabaret
tabinet
taboret
Thibet
thickset
threat
Tibet
toilette
tournette
tourniquet
tret
underset
unfret
unget
upset
vedette
vet
vignette
villanette
vinaigrette
violet
wagonette
well-met
wet
whet
yet
zonulet

ĒTH

bequeath
breathe
ensheath
enwreathe
inbreathe
insheathe
interwreathe
inwreathe
seethe
sheathe

sneathe
teethe
unsheathe
unwreathe
upbreathe
wreathe

Ēth

beneath
heath
Keith
Leith
'neath
sheath
sneath
teeth
underneath
wreath

Ĕth

Ashtoreth
breath
death
Elizabeth
Macbeth
saith
'sdeath
Seth
shibboleth
twentieth
thirtieth, etc.
answereth
astonisheth
attributeth
banisheth
blemisheth
blistereth
blundereth
busieth
clustereth
conquereth

ōld, ôr, ŏdd, oil, fŏŏt, out; ūse, ûrn, ŭp; THis, thin

continueth	relinquisheth	aggrieve	shire-reeve
covereth	remembereth	beeve	shrieve
determineth	rescueth	believe	sleave
dowereth	rivalleth	bereave	sleeve
emblazoneth	severeth	breve	steeve
enspiriteth	shimmereth	Christmas-eve	Steve
envieth	showereth	cleave	thieve
exhibiteth	shuddereth	conceive	undeceive
flowereth	silvereth	deceive	unreave
forfeiteth	slumbereth	deev	unreeve
gathereth	sorroweth	disbelieve	unweave
glisteneth	spiriteth	eave	upheave
glowereth	suffereth	engrieve	vive
hearkeneth	sundereth	eve	weave
hungereth	tempereth	greave	we've
incumbereth	thundereth	grieve	yester-eve
inheriteth	ventureth	heave	
inspiriteth	wandereth	interleave	ĒVD
laboureth	wearieth	interweave	self-deceived
languisheth	whispereth	inweave	unbelieved
libelleth	winnoweth	keeve	unperceived
lingereth	witnesseth	khedive	unrelieved
listeneth	wondereth	leave	achieved, etc.
liveneth	worrieth	lieve	
lowereth	worshippeth	make-believe	ĒVZ
marvelleth		misconceive	eaves
measureth	ĒTHD	naive	achieves, etc.
meriteth	unbreathed	New Year's	
murmureth	bequeathed,	eve	Ēz
nourisheth	etc.	perceive	aborigines
offereth		preconceive	analyses
overpowereth	ĒTZ	qui vive	Annamese
overtowereth	Keats	reave	antipodes
pardoneth	beats, etc.	receive	antitheses
pleasureth		recitative	appease
predestineth	ĔTZ	reeve	Arakanese
punisheth	Metz	relieve	Aragonese
quarrelleth	bets, etc.	reprieve	Assamese
questioneth		retrieve	bee's knees
quieteth	ĒV	seave	Belize
recovereth	achieve	sheave	Bengalese

bise	frieze	obsequies	Tyrolese
Bolognese	Genevese	parentheses	unease
breeze	grease	pease	unfreeze
Burmese	Havanese	periphrases	valise
B.V.D.s	heart's-ease	Pierides	Veronese
Carlylese	heeze	please	Viennese
Caryatides	Hesperides	Pleiades	vortices
cerise	hypotheses	*Polonese*	wheeze
Ceylonese	imprese	Portuguese	(see Ē + s)
cheese	indices	Pyrenees	
chemise	isosceles	rabies	**ĔZ**
chersonese	Japanese	remise	
cheval-de-frise	Javanese	sea-breeze	cortez
Chinese	Johnsonese	seize	fez
congeries	journalese	Siamese	says
D.T.'s	lees	Singhalese	**ĒZH**
Diogenes	Leonese	sneeze	prestige
disease	Louise	squeeze	tige
displease	Maltese	syntheses	
ease	Milanese	tease	**ĔZH**
enfreeze	mease	these	barège
Eumenides	Navarrese	trapeze	cortège
feaze	Nepaulese	tweeze	manège
freeze			

I

These words include the following accented vowel sounds :

Ī as in ice; heard also in vie, rye, height, eye, aisle, aye meaning *yes,* sky, buy, choir.

Ĭ as in ill; heard also in sieve, English, pretty, been, breeches, women, busy, build, nymph, hymnal.

Ī	alkalify	apply	bedye
acidify	ally	awry	belie
adry	amplify	ay	bespy
alacrify	angelify	aye	black eye
alibi	Anglify	beatify	brutify
alkali	apple-pie	beautify	butterfly

buy	falsify	lye	rye
by	fie	magnify	saccharify
bye	firefly	magpie	sanctify
bye-bye	fly	modify	satisfy
by-and-by	forby	mollify	scarify
by the by	fortify	mortify	scorify
candify	fossilify	multiply	scye
certify	Frenchify	my	sea-pie
clarify	fructify	my eye	sheep's-eye
classify	fry	mystify	shy
cockneyfy	gasify	nigh	sigh
codify	genii	notify	signify
comply	glorify	nullify	simplify
countrify	go-by	nye	sky
crucify	good-bye	occupy	Skye
cry	gratify	ossify	sky-high
damnify	gri	outcry	sly
dandify	guy	outfly	sny
decry	heigh	outvie	solidify
defy	hereby	pacify	specify
deify	hie	passer-by	spry
demi	high	personify	spy
demy	horrify	petrify	stander-by
deny	humanify	pi	stellify
descry	humble-pie	pie	stultify
die	hushaby	ply	stupefy
dignify	identify	preachify	sty
disqualify	imply	preoccupy	supply
dissatisfy	incubi	prophesy	tabefy
diversify	indemnify	pry	termini
dragon-fly	ineye	purify	terrify
dry	intensify	putrefy	testify
dye	July	qualify	thereby
edify	justify	quantify	thigh
electrify	labefy	ramify	thy
emulsify	lazuli	rarefy	tie
ensky	lenify	ratify	torpify
espy	lie	rectify	torrefy
eternify	lignify	rely	transmogrify
exemplify	liquefy	reply	try
eye	lullaby	revivify	typify

umble-pie
under-buy
underlie
unify
unshy
untie
verbify
verify
versify
vie
vilify
vitrify
vivify
weather-eye
weather-spy
well-nigh
whereby
why
wry
wye

ĪB

ascribe
bribe
circumscribe
describe
diatribe
gibe
imbibe
inscribe
interscribe
jibe
kibe
prescribe
proscribe
scribe
subscribe
superscribe
transcribe
tribe

ĬB

ad lib
bib
Bibb
crib
dib
drib
fib
gib
Gibb
glib
jib
nib
quib
rib
sib
squib

ĪBD

uninscribed
ascribed, etc.

ĬBD

rock-ribbed
cribbed, etc.

ĬBZ

dibs
Gibbs
his nibs
cribs, etc.

ĬCH

bewitch
bitch
Cesarewitch
chich
czarevitch
ditch
enrich
fitch
flitch
Gabrilowitsch
hitch
itch
lich
miche
niche
pitch
quitch
rich
scritch
stitch
switch
twitch
which
witch

ĬCHT

unbewitched
unhitched
unwitched
bewitched, etc.

ĪD

abide
Allhallow-tide
alongside
Argus-eyed
aside
astride
backslide
barmecide
Bartholomew-
      tide
bedside
beside
bestride
betide
bide
bonafide
bride

broadside
bromide
chide
Christmas-tide
Clyde
cockeyed
coincide
collide
confide
countrified
countryside
decide
deicide
deride
dignified
dissatisfied
diversified
divide
double-dyed
dove-eyed
dull-eyed
eagle-eyed
Eastertide
ebb-tide
elide
Ember-tide
eventide
evil-eyed
excide
fireside
flood-tide
foreside
fortified
fratricide
full-eyed
glide
goggle-eyed
green-eyed
gride
guide
Hallowtide

hawk-eyed	pop-eyed	unsanctified	pyramid
herpicide	preside	unsatisfied	quid
hide	pride	unspied	rid
high-tide	provide	untried	skid
hillside	purified	uxoricide	slid
homicide	qualified	vaticide	squid
Hyde	regicide	vermicide	thrid
I'd	reside	vitrified	unbid
infanticide	ride	vulpicide	underbid
insecticide	riverside	wall-eyed	undid
inside	sea-side	water-side	unforbid
iodide	self-pride	wayside	
justified	self-satisfied	weather-side	**ĪDST**
Lammas-tide	Shrove-tide	weather-tide	amidst
landslide	side	Whitsuntide	*bid'st*
lapicide	slide	wide	*chid'st*
lee-tide	snide	Yule-tide	*did'st*
liberticide	soft-eyed	(see Ī + ed)	*forbid'st*
lynx-eyed	sororicide		*hid'st*
matricide	spring-tide	**ĬD**	*kid'st*
meek-eyed	squint-eyed	amid	midst
misallied	state-wide	bid	*rid'st*
misguide	stillicide	*chid*	*slid'st*
morning-tide	stride	Cid	
nation-wide	subdivide	did	**ĬDTH**
nide	subside	fid	width
noontide	suicide	forbid	*bid'th*, etc.
open-eyed	sulphide	*fordid*	
outride	tide	gid	**ĪDZ**
outside	tyrannicide	grid	besides
outstride	unapplied	hid	ides
override	unbetide	invalid	abides, etc.
owl-eyed	underside	katydid	
ox-eyed	undertide	kid	**ĪF**
pale-eyed	undescried	lid	after-life
parenticide	undignified	Madrid	bowie-knife
parricide	undried	mid	fife
Passion-tide	unespied	outbid	fishwife
patricide	ungratified	outdid	goodwife
pied	unpurified	overbid	housewife
pie-eyed	unqualified	overdid	knife

life
rife
still-life
strife
wife

ĬF

biff
cliff
diff
glyph
griff
handkerchief
hieroglyph
hippogriff
if
jiff
miff
neckerchief
skiff
sniff
stiff
Tenerife
Teneriffe
tiff
undercliff
whiff
wiff

ĬFT

adrift
drift
forelift
gift
lift
rift
shift
shrift
sift
snow-drift
spendthrift

spiffed
spindrift
swift
thrift
tift
topping-lift
unthrift
uplift
miffed, etc.

ĬFTH

fifth
miff'th, etc.

ĬG

big
brig
cig
dig
fig
gig
grig
guinea-pig
infra-dig
jig
nig
periwig
pig
prig
renege
rig
snig
sprig
swig
thimblerig
thingumajig
trig
twig
unrig
Whig

whirligig
wig

ĬGD

bewigged
full-rigged
jury-rigged
square-rigged
digged, etc.

ĬGZ

Biggs
Briggs
Higgs
Riggs
(see ĬG + s)

ĪJ

Lije
oblige

ĬJ

abridge
bridge
enridge
midge
nidge
ridge
upridge
(see also ĂJ)

ĬJD

unabridged
unbridged
abridged, etc.

ĪK

Alibi Ike
alike
assassin-like
belike

bike
boarding-pike
brotherlike
dislike
dyke
fairy-like
fyke
ghostlike
hike
kike
like
maidenlike
manlike
marlinspike
mike
mislike
oblique
peasantlike
pike
shrike
spike
starlike
strike
tyke
unlike
Vandyck
Vandyke
Van Wyck
womanlike
workmanlike
Wyke

ĬK

arithmetic
arsenic
bailiwick
Benedick
bestick
bishopric
brick
candlestick

ōld, ôr, ŏdd, oil, fŏŏt, out; ūse, ûrn, ŭp; THis, thin

candlewick
Catholic
chick
chivalric
choleric
click
crick
Dick
double-quick
fiddle-stick
flick
heart-sick
heretic
hick
impolitic
kick
kinnikinnick
lick
limerick
love-sick
lunatic
maverick
mick
nick
pick
plethoric
pogo-stick
politic
prick
quick
rhetoric
rick
sic
sick
single-stick
slick
snick
stich
stick
thick
tic

tick
trick
turmeric
walking stick
wick

ĬKS
Dykes
Rikes
Sykes
(see ĬK + s)

ĬKS
admix
affix
Beatrix
cicatrix
commix
crucifix
Dix
executrix
fiddlesticks
fix
Hicks
Hix
immix
inheritrix
intermix
mix
nix
Pnyx
politics
prefix
prolix
pyx
Ricks
Rix
six
Styx
transfix

Trix
(see ĬK + s)

ĬKST
atwixt
betwixt
click'st
kick'st
lick'st
pick'st
prick'st
stick'st
trick'st
'twixt
unfixed
unmixed
admixed, etc.

ĬKSTH
sixth
mix'th, etc.

ĬKT
addict
afflict
astrict
benedict
conflict
constrict
contradict
convict
delict
depict
derelict
evict
inflict
interdict
Pict
predict
relict
restrict

strict
unlicked
unpicked
bricked, etc.

ĪL
aisle
Anglophile
awhile
beguile
bibliophile
bile
camomile
chyle
compile
crocodile
defile
diastyle
enisle
ensile
erewhile
erstwhile
file
Francophile,
    etc.
guile
infantile
isle
juvenile
Kabyle
lisle
Lyle
meanwhile
mercantile
mile
Nile
otherwhile
paper-file
pentastyle
peristyle
pile

āle, câre, ădd, ärm, åsk; mē, hĕre, ĕnd; īce, ĭll;

puerile	*enthrill*	squill	Wilde
reconcile	Evansville	still	beguiled, etc.
resile	espadrille	stock-still	aisled
revile	fill	swill	
rile	Francophile,	thill	**ĪLD**
smile	etc.	thrill	befrilled
somewhile	freewill	till	begild
spile	frill	trill	build
stile	fulfil	twill	gild
style	gill	'twill	guild
therewhile	good-will	until	rebuild
tile	grill	unwill	self-willed
up-pile	grille	uphill	unbuild
versatile	hill	versatile	unchilled
vibratile	ill	vibratile	unfulfilled
vile	ill-will	vill	unskilled
voltaic pile	imbecile	volatile	untilled
while	infantile	water-mill	unwilled
wile	instil	whip-poor-will	chilled, etc.
	jill	will	
ĪL	juvenile		**ĪLF**
Amityville	kill	**ĪLCH**	sylph
Anglophile	kiln	filch	**ĪLJ**
befrill	Louisville	milch	bilge
bestill	mercantile	pilch	
bibliophile	mill	Zilch	**ĪLK**
bill	nil		bilk
Bozenkill	pill	**ĪLD**	ilk
Brazil	powder-mill	child	milk
brill	prill	childe	silk
chill	puerile	enfiled	spun-silk
chlorophyle	quadrille	foster-child	
chrysophyll	quill	love-child	**ĪLKS**
Cobleskill	rill	mild	Wilkes
codicil	self-will	self-styled	(see ĪLK + s)
daffodil	Seville	unbeguiled	
dill	shrill	unchild	**ĪLM**
distil	sill	unmild	film
domicile	skill	unreconciled	**ĪLN**
downhill	spadille	unwild	kiln
drill	spill	wild	Milne

ĪLS
grilse
(cf.—lts)

ĪLST
beguil'st
defil'st
whilst
whils't, etc.

ĬLT
atilt
basket-hilt
begilt
built
clinker-built
clipper-built
frigate-built
gilt
guilt
hilt
jilt
kilt
lilt
milt
quilt
rebuilt
silt
spilt
stilt
tilt
unbuilt
ungilt
Vanderbilt
wilt

ĬLTH
filth
spilth
tilth
till'th, etc.

ĬLTS
kilts
[cf. grilse]
basket-hilts,
etc.

ĬLZ
Giles
Miles
otherwhiles
whiles
wiles
beguiles, etc.

ĪM
aftertime
bedtime
begrime
belime
berhyme
beslime
birdlime
breathing-time
chime
chyme
climb
clime
crime
daytime
dime
eaning-time
grime
Guggenheim
haying-time
I'm
lifetime
lime
Lyme
maritime
meantime
mime

overtime
pairing-time
pantomime
prime
quicklime
rhyme
Rosenheim
rime
seed-time
slime
sometime
spring-time
sublime
summer-time
thyme
time
upclimb

ĬM
antonym
bedim
betrim
brim
cherubim
dim
enlimn
gim
glim
grim
gym
him
hymn
interim
Jim
Kĭm
Klim
limb
limn
maritime
Nym
prelim

prim
pseudonym
rim
Sanhedrim
seraphim
shim
skim
slim
swim
synonym
Tim
trim
vim
whim
zimb

ĪMD
well-timed
begrimed, etc.

ĬMD
brimmed
untrimmed
bedimmed, etc.

ĬMF
lymph
nymph
sea-nymph

ĬMP
blimp
crimp
gimp
imp
jimp
limp
pimp
primp
scrimp
shrimp

simp	brine	Evangeline	pine
skimp	Byzantine	*eyne*	porcupine
tymp	caballine	Fescennine	powder-mine
	caffeine	fine	Proserpine
ÌMPS	calcine	Florentine	recline
glimpse	canine	Ghibelline	refine
crimps, etc.	Capitoline	Goldstein	repine
	carabine	Hoffenstein	resign
ÌMZ	Caroline	hyaline	resupine
betimes	celandine	incarnadine	Rhine
oftentimes	Celestine	incline	Rubinstein
ofttimes	chine	infantine	saline
sometimes	Clementine	interline	sapphirine
begrimes, etc.	Clyne	intermine	saturnine
	columbine	intertwine	serpentine
ÌMZ	combine	Jacqueline	shine
Simms	concubine	kine	shrine
(see ÌM + s)	condign	Klein	sibylline
	confine	Kline	sign
ÌN	consign	*langsyne*	sine
Adaline	Constantine	leonine	snow-line
Adeline	coraline	libertine	spine
adulterine	countermine	Liechtenstein	spline
agatine	countersign	life-line	star-shine
align	crystalline	line	stein
alkaline	decline	load-line	subdivine
aniline	define	Madeline	*subsign*
anodyne	design	malign	sunshine
anserine	dine	matutine	superfine
Apennine	disincline	mine	supine
apple-wine	divine	moonshine	swine
aquiline	dyne	nine	sycamine
argentine	eglantine	opaline	*syne*
ashine	Esquiline	opine	*thine*
asinine	enshrine	outshine	tine
assign	ensign	overtwine	trephine
Beckstein	entwine	Palatine	trine
benign	Epstein	pavonine	Turn Verein
beshine	Esenwein	peregrine	turpentine
bine	Esquiline	petaline	twine
brigantine	Evaline	Philistine	Tyne

ōld, ôr, ŏdd, oil, fŏŏt, out; ūse, ûrn, ŭp; THis, thin

unbenign
underline
undermine
undersign
unline
untwine
Ursuline
valentine
vespertine
vine
viperine
vulturine
water-line
Weinstein
whine
wine
wolverine
woodbine
Zollverein

IN

adulterine
agatine
agrin
akin
alizarin
alkaline
all in
almandine
aniline
anserine
aquiline
argentine
aspirin
atropine
baldachin
bandoline
bearskin
been
begin
belaying-pin

Berlin
bin
Boleyn
bulletin
Byzantine
caballine
caffeine
cannikin
Capuchin
carabine
carotin
Catherine
Celestine
chagrin
chin
chinquapin
clavecin
codeine
coraline
crinoline
crystalline
culverin
din
discipline
Evangeline
feminine
Fescennine
fin
finikin
Finn
Florentine
francolin
gelatin
genuine
Ghibelline
gin
Glyn
Glynn
grin
gyn
harlequin

herein
heroine
hyaline
in
incarnadine
infantine
inn
Jacobin
javelin
jessamine
jinn
Katherine
kilderkin
kin
libertine
lin
Lynn
mandarin
mandolin
manikin
masculine
mezzanine
minikin
moccasin
nectarine
nicotine
opaline
origin
paladin
pavonine
peregrine
petaline
Philistine
pin
Quinn
saccharine
sapphirine
seal-skin
shin
sibylline
side-spin

sin
skin
spin
sycamine
take-in
tambourin
therein
thick-and-thin
thin
tigerkin
tiger-skin
tin
tourmaline
twin
underpin
Ursuline
unpin
unsin
vaseline
vespertine
violin
viperine
vulturine
wherein
whin
whipper-in
win
within
Zeppelin

INCH

bepinch
cinch
chinch
clinch
fallow-finch
finch
flinch
inch
linch
lynch

pinch	upbind	fling	altering
unclinch	upwind	full-swing	angering
winch	vined	heart-string	answering
	wind	king	apparelling
ĬND	womankind	lifespring	arguing
behind	combined, etc.	ling	armouring
bind		Ming	astonishing
blind	**ĬND**	outwing	attributing
color-blind	abscind	ping	auctioning
crined	disciplined	ring	auditing
disinclined	exscind	sea-king	auguring
find	lind	seal-ring	awakening
gavelkind	Lynd	sea-wing	badgering
grind	rescind	shuffle-wing	balancing
hind	Rosalind	signet-ring	ballasting
humankind	storm-wind	sing	bandying
inbind	tamarind	sling	banishing
interwind	thick-skinned	spring	bantering
intertwined	thin-skinned	starveling	barbering
kind	undisciplined	sting	bargaining
mankind	wind	string	barracking
master-mind	grinned, etc.	swing	barrelling
mind		Synge	bartering
overtwined	**ĬNG**	thing	battering
purblind	anything	ting	bedeviling
remind	atheling	underling	beflattering
rind	besing	underwing	beggaring
rynd	bewing	unking	belaboring
snow-blind	bing	unsling	beleaguering
storm-wind	bring	unstring	belecturing
unbind	chitterling	wedding-ring	bellowing
unblind	cling	weeping-spring	bepattering
unconfined	daughterling	wing	bepowdering
undefined	dayspring	wring	bepummelling
underbind	ding	abandoning	bescattering
undersigned	driving-spring	accomplishing	beslabbering
undesigned	easterling	accrediting	bespattering
unkind	enring	accustoming	betokening
unrefined	evening	actioning	bevelling
unshrined	everything	admonishing	bewildering
unwind	fairy-king	afforesting	bickering

blackening	chastening	dishonoring	filtering
blandishing	chattering	disparaging	fingering
blanketing	chiselling	dispiriting	finicking
blarneying	christening	displeasuring	finishing
blathering	Christmasing	disquieting	flattering
blazoning	ciphering	dissevering	flavoring
blemishing	clambering	distinguishing	flickering
blistering	clamoring	distributing	flittering
blossoming	clattering	dowering	flourishing
blubbering	clustering	drivelling	flowering
blundering	cockering	duelling	flurrying
blustering	coloring	embarrassing	flustering
bolstering	compassioning	embellishing	fluttering
bonneting	conjecturing	emblazoning	focussing
brandishing	conquering	embodying	following
breakfasting	considering	emboldening	foregathering
broadening	continuing	embosoming	foreshadowing
buffeting	contributing	empitying	foretokening
bullying	conveyancing	enameling	forfeiting
burdening	covering	enamoring	forwarding
burnishing	coveting	encouraging	freshening
burying	cowering	encumbering	furnishing
busying	crediting	enharboring	furthering
butchering	cudgelling	enheartening	galloping
buttressing	cumbering	enravishing	gambolling
cancelling	dallying	entering	gammoning
candying	damaging	entrammelling	gardening
cankering	darkening	envisaging	garlanding
cannoning	deadening	envying	garnishing
cantering	deciphering	establishing	gathering
canvassing	destining	examining	gesturing
capering	determining	exhibiting	gladdening
capturing	devilling	faltering	glimmering
carolling	dickering	famishing	glittering
carpeting	dieting	fancying	glowering
carrying	diminishing	farrowing	gravelling
cautioning	discouraging	fashioning	grovelling
cavilling	discrediting	fathoming	hallowing
challenging	disestablishing	favoring	hammering
channelling	disfavoring	feathering	hampering
chartering	dishallowing	festering	hankering

āle, câre, ădd, ärm, ăsk; mē, hĕre, ĕnd; īce, ĭll;

happening	littering	overmastering	pilfering
harassing	livening	overpowering	pillaging
harboring	lobbying	overshadowing	placarding
hardening	long-suffering	overtowering	plastering
harrowing	lowering	paltering	pleasuring
harrying	lumbering	pampering	plundering
harvesting	maddening	polishing	racketing
hastening	managing	pommelling	rallying
hazarding	manufacturing	pondering	ransoming
hearkening	marketing	pottering	rapturing
heartening	marrying	powdering	ravaging
heralding	marshalling	practising	ravening
hovering	martyring	predestining	ravishing
humoring	marvelling	prohibiting	reasoning
hungering	meandering	promising	reckoning
imagining	measuring	prospering	recovering
imprisoning	menacing	publishing	remembering
incumbering	mentioning	punishing	rendering
indenturing	meriting	purposing	rescuing
inhabiting	mirroring	quarrelling	revelling
inheriting	modelling	quarrying	rivalling
inspiriting	monkeying	quartering	riveting
issuing	mothering	quavering	roystering
jabbering	motoring	querying	rubbering
jeoparding	murdering	questioning	rubbishing
jollying	murmuring	quieting	saddening
junketing	mustering	quivering	sallying
labelling	muttering	pandering	sanctioning
laboring	narrowing	panelling	sauntering
lacquering	neighboring	pardoning	savaging
languishing	nourishing	parrying	savoring
lathering	numbering	passioning	scaffolding
lavishing	offering	patenting	scampering
lazying	omening	pattering	scattering
lecturing	opening	pedalling	scavenging
lessening	ordering	pencilling	seasoning
levelling	outbalancing	pensioning	severing
libelling	outnumbering	peppering	shadowing
limiting	outrivalling	perishing	shattering
lingering	overbalancing	perjuring	shepherding
listening	overburdening	pestering	shimmering

ōld, ôr, ŏdd, oil, fŏŏt, out; ūse, ûrn, ŭp; THis, thin

shivering
shouldering
showering
shuddering
sickening
silvering
simmering
simpering
sistering
slackening
slandering
slaughtering
slobbering
slumbering
smartening
smattering
smouldering
snivelling
sorrowing
spattering
spiralling
spiriting
spluttering
stammering
stationing
stencilling
stuttering
suffering
sugaring
summering
sundering
sweetening
tallying
tampering
tapering
tarnishing
tarrying
tasselling
tempering
thundering
tinselling

tittering
toadying
tottering
towelling
towering
trafficing
travelling
tunnelling
undervaluing
unfaltering
unflattering
unmeriting
unmurmuring
unperishing
unpitying
unpromising
unravelling
unreasoning
unremember-
   ing
unslumbering
unwandering
unwavering
upholstering
uttering
valuing
vanishing
vanquishing
vaporing
varnishing
velveting
venturing
visioning
visiting
volleying
voyaging
wakening
walloping
wandering
wantoning
wassailling

watering
wavering
weakening
wearying
weathering
westering
whimpering
whinneying
whispering
winnowing
wintering
witnessing
wondering
worrying
worshipping

INGD

bewinged
dinged
eagle-winged
ringed
stringed
winged, etc.

INGK

bethink
blink
bobolink
brink
chink
cinque
clink
counter-sink
drink
enlink
Finck
Fink
forethink
gink
hoodwink
Humperdinck

ink
interlink
jink
kink
link
meadow-pink
mink
pink
prink
rink
shrink
sink
skink
slink
snow-blink
stink
think
tiddlywink
tink
trink
twink
unlink
unthink
wink
zinc

INGKS

jinx
lynx
methinks
minx
sphinx
tiddledywinks
tiddlywinks
clinks, etc.

INGKT

blinked
distinct
extinct
indistinct

āle, câre, ădd, ärm, ȧsk; mē, hẹre, ĕnd; īce, ĭll;

instinct
procinct
succinct
tinct
clinked, etc.

INGZ

awakenings
leading-strings
besings, etc.

INJ

befringe
binge
constringe
cringe
dinge
fringe
hinge
impinge
infringe
perstringe
scringe
singe
springe
swinge
tinge
twinge
unhinge

INJD

unhinged
unsinged
befringed, etc.

INS

convince
evince
merchant-
   prince
mince

prince
quince
rinse
since
unprince
Vince
wince
(cf. flints,
   chintz)

INSK

Dvinsk
Minsk
Pinsk

INT

ahint
behint
pint

INT

asquint
calamint
dint
flint
footprint
glint
hint
imprint
lint
mezzotint
mint
misprint
peppermint
print
quint
reprint
septuagint
sodamint
spearmint
splint

sprint
squint
stint
tint
vint

INTH

ninth
pine'th, etc.

INTH

colocynth
hyacinth
labyrinth
plinth
terebinth

INTS

Heintz
pints

INTS

aquatints
chintz
flints, etc.
(cf. convince,
   etc.)

INZ

Appenines
Tynes
dines, etc.

INZ

ods-bodikins
winze
withershins
(see IN + s)

IP

antitype
archetype

autotype
bagpipe
blowpipe
daguerreotype
dead-ripe
electrotype
graphotype
gripe
gutter-snipe
heliotype
hornpipe
hype
kipe
linotype
logotype
monotype
overripe
pipe
pitchpipe
prototype
ripe
snipe
stereotype
stipe
stripe
swipe
teletype
tintype
tripe
type
unripe
windpipe
wipe

IP

apple-pip
atrip
battleship
chip
clip
dip

drip
equip
flip
grip
grippe
gyp
hip
horsewhip
hyp
kip
landslip
lip
nip
outstrip
overtrip
pip
pleasure-trip
quip
rip
scrip
ship
sip
skip
slip
snip
strip
tip
training-ship
tranship
trip
underlip
unrip
unship
warship
weather-strip
whip
zip
acquaintance-
  ship
administra-
  torship

agentship
aldemanship
apprentice-
  ship
archonship
babyship
bachelorship
cardinalsip
censorship
chairmanship
championship
chancellorship
chaplainship
chieftainship
churchman-
  ship
churchmem-
  bership
citizenship
collectorship
commander-
  ship
companion-
  ship
consortship
consulship
controllership
co-partner-
  ship
cousinship
craftsmanship
creatorship
deaconship
demonship
draughtsman-
  ship
eldership
electorship
emperorship
ensignship
farmership

fathership
fellowship
generalship
good-fellow-
  ship
governorship
guardianship
horsemanship
huntsmanship
impostorship
inspectorship
jockeyship
justiceship
leadership
lectureship
legislatorship
librarianship
lordship
marksmanship
marshalship
mastership
membership
Messiahship
neighborship
noviceship
ownership
paintership
partnership
pastorship
penmanship
praetorship
preachership
prelateship
probationship
professorship
proprietorship
questorship
rajahship
rangership
readership
recordership

rectorship
regentship
relationship
scholarship
seamanship
secretaryship
senatorship
sextonship
sheriffship
sizarship
speakership
spectatorship
sponsorship
sportsmanship
statesmanship
stewardship
studentship
sultanship
suretyship
survivorship
swordsman-
  ship
treasurership
umpireship
viceroyship
virtuosoship
wardenship
workmanship
wranglership

ĬPS
pipes, etc.

ĪPS
Apocalypse
chips
eclipse
ellipse
Phipps
apple-pips

---

acquaintance- ships, etc.	afire	spire	price
	aspire	suspire	rice
	attire	*swire*	sacrifice
ĪPST	beacon-fire	tire	self-sacrifice
chip'st	bemire	transpire	sice
clip'st	byre	Tyre	slice
dip'st	choir	unsquire	spice
eclipsed	conspire	Untermyer	splice
equip'st	death-fire	vire	suffice
grip'st	desire	wildfire	syce
rip'st	dire	wire	thrice
ship'st	enquire	(cf. crier, high-	trice
sip'st	entire	er, prior, fri-	twice
skip'st	esquire	ar, etc.)	vice
slip'st	expire		vise
strip'st	fire	**ĪRD**	vise
tip'st	flat tire	overtired	Weiss
trip'st	galley-fire	spired	Zeiss
uneclipsed	grandsire	unacquired	
whip'st	gyre	undesired	**ĬS**
	hell-fire	unexpired	abiogenesis
ĪPT	hire	uninspired	abyss
hunger-griped	inquire	acquired, etc.	acropolis
prison-striped	inspire		ambergris
griped, etc.	ire	**ĪS**	amiss
	lyre	advice	anabasis
ĬPT	McIntyre	bespice	analysis
apocalypt	Meyer	bice	antithesis
crypt	mire	concise	apheresis
frost-nipped	Molly Maguire	device	aphesis
hipped	perspire	dice	armistice
manuscript	pyre	entice	artifice
script	quire	gneiss	avarice
subscript	require	grice	Beatrice
superscript	respire	ice	benefice
tipt	retire	lice	biogenesis
chipped, etc.	shire	mice	bis
	signal-fire	nice	bliss
ĪR	sire	overnice	chrysalis
acquire	spitfire	Paradise	cicatrice
admire	squire	precise	clematis
			cockatrice

ōld, ôr, ŏdd, oil, fŏŏt, out; ūse, ûrn, ŭp; THis, thin

cowardice	Swiss	waterish	bekissed
cuisse	synthesis	willowish	bemist
dehisce	this	womanish	beneficed
dentifrice	verdigris	yellowish, etc.	cist
diæresis	vis		coexist
dialysis	*wis*	ĬSK	consist
diathesis	*y-wis*	asterisk	cyst
Dis		basilisk	desist
dismiss	ĬSH	bisque	dismissed
edifice	cnish	brisk	enlist
ectogenesis	dish	disc	entwist
elephantiasis	fish	disk	exist
emphasis	gibberish	fisc	fist
fortalice	impoverish	Fiske	*frist*
genesis	McNish	frisk	gist
hiss	pilot-fish	obelisk	*glist*
hypostasis	pish	odalisque	grist
hypothesis	*slish*	risk	hissed
kiss	squish	tamarisk	hist
liquorice	swish	whisk	insist
Liss	Tish		intertwist
metabasis	unwish	ĬSP	kissed
metamorphosis	wish	crisp	list
metastasis	babyish	*encrisp*	missed
metathesis	bitterish	lisp	mist
metropolis	cleverish	whisp	persist
miss	Cockneyish	wisp	pre-exist
M'liss	devilish		prejudiced
necropolis	dowdyish	ĬST	resist
nemesis	feverish	antichrist	schist
orifice	heathenish	Christ	sissed
paralysis	kittenish	emparadised	sist
parenthesis	lickerish	enticed	subsist
periphrasis	mammonish	tryst	*trist*
precipice	ogreish	bespiced, etc.	tryst
prejudice	quakerish		twist
remiss	tigerish	ĬST	unkissed
Salamis	vaporish	agist	unmissed
sis	viperish	amethyst	untwist
siss	vixenish	assist	*unwist*
sui generis	vulturish	atwist	whist

---

wist	augurist	constructionist	equilibrist
wrist	balladist	contortionist	essayist
xyst	biblicist	controversialist	eternalist
abolitionist	bibliophilist	conversationist	ethicist
absolutist	bibliopolist	corruptionist	etymologist
academist	bicyclist	cremationist	Eucharist
accompanist	bigamist	culturist	eudemonist
aerologist	bimetallist	dactylist	eulogist
agamist	biologist	Darwinist	euphuist
agonist	Bolshevist	degenerationist	evangelist
agricolist	botanist	demonist	evolutionist
agriculturalist	Bourbonist	demonologist	excursionist
agriculturist	Brahmanist	despotist	exorcist
alchemist	cabalist	destinist	experimental-
allegorist	Calvinist	destructionist	ist
allopathist	campanologist	deuterogamist	externalist
amorist	canonist	devotionalist	fabulist
anagrammatist	capitalist	devotionist	fatalist
analogist	casuist	dialist	federalist
analyst	catechist	dialogist	feudalist
anarchist	centralist	diplomatist	fictionist
anatomist	chirographist	dogmatist	financialist
animalculist	chiropodist	dramatist	floriculturist
animist	choralist	dualist	formalist
annalist	chronologist	duellist	fossilist
annualist	circumlocu-	ecclesiologist	fossilogist
antagonist	tionist	economist	funambulist
anthropologist	classicalist	educationalist	futilist
antinomist	classicist	educationist	galvanist
antipathist	coalitionist	egoist	genealogist
apathist	colloquist	egotist	geologist
aphorist	colonist	electro-	glacialist
apiarist	colorist	biologist	gymnosophist
apologist	communist	elegist	harmonist
Arabist	conchologist	elocutionist	Hebraist
arboriculturist	Confucionist	empiricist	hedonist
arborist	congregation-	enamelist	Hellenist
archaeologist	alist	enigmatist	herbalist
artillerist	constitutional-	entomologist	horticulturist
atheist	ist	epigrammatist	humanist
atomist	constitutionist	epitomist	humorist

---

hyperbolist	misanthropist	philologist	revivalist
hypnotist	miscellanist	philosophist	revolutionist
idealist	misogamist	phlebotomist	rhapodist
illusionist	misogynist	photographist	rigorist
imitationist	modernist	phrenologist	ritualist
immaterialist	monogamist	philatelist	Romanist
immersionist	monopolist	physicist	romanticist
immortalist	moralist	physiognomist	royalist
imperialist	motorist	physiologist	ruralist
inspirationist	mythologist	pianist	satanist
instrumentalist	Napoleonist	pietist	satirist
insurrectionist	nationalist	plagiarist	schematist
intellectualist	naturalist	platonist	scientist
internationalist	necrologist	pleasurist	sciolist
journalist	neologist	pluralist	scripturalist
Judaist	Neoplatonist	pneumatologist	scripturist
Latinist	nepotist	polygamist	secessionist
legitimist	nihilist	positivist	secularist
liberalist	nominalist	posturist	seismologist
literalist	novelist	pragmatist	sensationalist
lithologist	obstructionist	precisianist	sensualist
lobbyist	oculist	prelatist	sentimentalist
loyalist	ontologist	progressionist	sexualist
magnetist	opinionist	prohibitionist	sibyllist
malthusianist	oppositionist	protagonist	socialist
mammonist	optimist	protectionist	sociologist
mannerist	organist	proverbialist	soloist
martyrologist	Orientalist	provincialist	somnambulist
materialist	ornithologist	psalmodist	Sorbonist
mechanist	pacifist	psychologist	specialist
medallist	passionist	publicist	spiritualist
melodist	pathologist	pugilist	steganograph-
melodramatist	penologist	pythonist	ist
memorialist	perfectionist	quietist	stenographist
Menshevist	pessimist	rabbinist	strategist
mesmerist	petrologist	rapturist	subjectivist
metalist	pharmacist	rationalist	suffragist
meteorologist	pharmacologist	realist	symbolist
methodist	phenomenist	religionist	sympathist
mineralogist	philanthropist	repudiationist	syncopist
ministerialist	Philhellenist	resurrectionist	syncretist

synodist	zoophilist	cosmopolite	indite
synonymist	zootomist	crystallite	invite
synthesist		daylight	Ishmaelite
tautologist	**IT**	dead-light	Islamite
technicist	Aaronite	delight	Israelite
technologist	acolyte	despite	Jacobite
telegraphist	aconite	*dight*	kite
teleologist	actinolite	disunite	knight
telephonist	Adamite	dolomite	light
terrorist	Adullamite	downright	malachite
textualist	aerolite	dynamite	mammonite
theologist	affright	Ebionite	Maronite
theophilan-	alight	ebonite	McKnight
thropist	aluminite	Elamite	meteorite
theorist	Ammonite	electrolyte	midnight
theosophist	anchorite	entomolite	midshipmite
threnodist	*anight*	enwrite	might
tobacconist	anthracite	eremite	mite
topographist	appetite	erudite	Moabite
toxicologist	aright	excite	moonlight
trades-unionist	Baalite	expedite	Mormonite
traditionalist	Babylonite	Fahrenheit	Muscovite
traditionist	*bedight*	fight	Nazarite
transcenden-	bedlamite	Fite	neophyte
talist	*behight*	flight	night
unionist	beknight	foresight	outright
universalist	belemnite	forthright	*overdight*
vaccinist	benight	fright	overnight
vacuist	Bethlehemite	good-night	oversight
vaticanist	bight	Gothamite	parasite
ventriloquist	bipartite	grapholite	plebiscite
verbalist	bite	harbor-light	plight
violist	blatherskite	headlight	polite
visionist	blight	height	pre-Adamite
vitalist	bright	heteroclite	pre-Raphaelite
vocabulist	Canaanite	*hight*	proselyte
vocalist	Carmelite	ichnolite	Puseyite
volumist	chrysolite	ignite	quite
votarist	cite	impolite	recite
zealotist	contrite	incite	recondite
zoologist	copyright	indict	requite

reunite	wright	kit	twit
right	write	knit	unbit
rite	*yesternight*	lit	unfit
satellite	zoolite	manumit	unknit
sea-fight	zoophyte	McNitt	*unwit*
sea-light		misfit	whit
second-sight	**ĬT**	mitt	wit
siderolite		moon-lit	Witt
sight	acquit	mother-wit	writ
signal-light	admit	nit	
site	after-wit	omit	**ĬTH**
sleight	apposite	opposite	blithe
slight	befit	outfit	lithe
smite	beknit	outsit	scythe
snow-white	benefit	outwit	Smythe
spite	bit	permit	tithe
sprite	bitt	perquisite	withe
starlight	chit	pit	writhe
sunlight	cit	Pitt	
sybarite	commit	plebiscite	**Ĭth**
theodolite	counterfeit	pretermit	myth
tight	definite	preterite	stythe
to-night	demit	prerequisite	
toxophilite	DeWitt	quit	**ĬTH**
tripartite	emit	recommit	forthwith
trite	exquisite	refit	herewith
troglodyte	favorite	remit	therewith
troth-plight	fit	requisite	wherewith
twilight	flit	rifle-pit	with
underwrite	frit	Schmidt	withe
undight	grit	sit	
unite	hit	slit	**Ĭth**
unright	hypocrite	smit	blithe
unsight	immit	spit	acrolith
unwrite	indefinite	split	aerolith
upright	infinite	sprit	Arrowsmith
vulcanite	*inknit*	submit	frith
water-sprite	interknit	tit	kith
water-tight	intermit	tom-tit	Ladysmith
white	intromit	to-wit	lith
wight	it	transmit	monolith
	Jesuit		myth

palaeolith	rive	compulsative	laudative
pith	shive	confirmative	lenitive
sith	shrive	consecutive	lucrative
smith	skive	conservative	nominative
withe	stive	contemplative	nutritive
forthwith	strive	contributive	premonitive
herewith	survive	correlative	preparative
therewith	thrive	curative	prerogative
wherewith	unhive	declarative	preservative
with	wive	definitive	primitive
		demonstrative	prohibitive
ĬTS	**ĪV**	derivative	provocative
anights	forgive	derogative	pulsative
footlights	fugitive	desiccative	punitive
tights	give	diminutive	putative
acolytes, etc.	live	dispensative	quantitive
	misgive	disputative	recitative
ĬTS	narrative	distributive	reformative
Fritz	negative	evocative	reparative
quits	outlive	exclamative	representative
Schlitz	overlive	executive	restorative
acquits, etc.	positive	expletive	retributive
	relative	figurative	sanative
ĪV	sieve	formative	sedative
alive	ablative	fugitive	semblative
arrive	accusative	genitive	sensitive
chive	acquisitive	illustrative	siccative
Clive	admonitive	impeditive	substantive
connive	affirmative	imperative	superlative
contrive	alternative	imputative	talkative
deprive	amative	incarnative	tentative
derive	argumentative	inchoative	transitive
dive	causative	incrassative	vibrative
drive	coercitive	indicative	vocative
five	combative	infinitive	
gyve	comparative	informative	**ĪVD**
hive	compellative	inquisitive	long-lived
I've	compensative	insensitive	short-lived
live	competitive	intensative	unshrived
power dive	complimenta-	interrogative	unwived
revive	tive	intuitive	arrived, etc.

ĬVD

long-lived
negatived
outlived
short-lived
unlived

ĬVZ

fives
knives
lives
arrives, etc.

ĪZ

acclimatize
achromatize
actualize
adonize
advertise
advise
Africanize
after-wise
agatize
aggrandize
agonize
agrarianize
albumenize
alchemize
alcoholize
alkalize
allegorize
alphabetize
amalgamize
ambrosialize
Americanize
analyze
anathematize
anatomize
angelize
Anglicize
animalize

annalize
antagonize
anywise
aphorize
apologize
apostatize
apostrophize
apotheosize
appetize
apprise
arise
aromatize
artificialize
assize
astrologize
astronomize
atheize
atomize
atticize
attitudinize
augurize
authorize
balladize
baptize
barbarize
battologize
botanize
bowdlerize
brutalize
canonize
capitalize
capsize
catechize
cauterize
centralize
characterize
chastise
chimerize
Christianize
circularize
civilize

climatize
cognize
colonize
comprize
compromise
constitution-
    alize
contrariwise
conventionalize
corner-wise
crescent-wise
criticise
crystallize
dandyize
dastardize
decimalize
decolorize
dehumanize
demagnetize
demise
democratize
demonetize
demoralize
denarcotize
denaturalize
deodorize
deputize
despise
detonize
devilize
devise
devitalize
diabolize
dialogize
dialyze
disguise
disillusionize
disorganize
dogmatize
doxologize
dramatize

ebonize
economize
ecstasize
Edenize
effeminize
electrolyze
emblematicize
emblematize
emblemize
emphasize
emprize
energize
enigmatize
enterprise
epigrammatize
epitomize
equalize
eternalize
etherealize
etherize
etymologize
eulogize
euphemize
euphonize
euphuize
Europeanize
evangelize
excise
excursionize
exercise
exorcise
experimental-
    ize
extemporize
fabulize
familiarize
fanaticize
federalize
fertilize
feudalize
fluidize

āle, câre, ădd, ärm, åsk; mē, hęre, ĕnd; īce, ĭll;

focalize	italicize	Mohammedan-	Platonize
formalize	jeopardize	ize	plebeianize
formulize	journalize	monetize	pluralize
fossilize	Judaize	monopolize	poetize
fraternize	Latinize	moonrise	polarize
galvanize	legalize	moralize	pollenize
gelatinize	legitimatize	mythologize	polygamize
genealogize	lethargize	narcotize	popularize
generalize	liberalize	nasalize	prelatize
gentilize	likewise	nationalize	remise
geologize	lionize	naturalize	revise
geometrize	liquidize	neutralize	prize
gluttonize	literalize	novelize	proselytize
gorgonize	Lize	organize	Protestantize
gormandize	localize	ostracize	proverbialize
gospelize	Londonize	*otherguise*	provincialize
guise	macadamize	otherwise	psalmodize
gutteralize	magnetize	overwise	pulverize
harmonize	Mahomedanize	oxidize	Puritanize
heathenize	mammonize	oxygenize	rapturize
Hebraicize	manumize	paganize	rationalize
Hebraize	martialize	panegyrize	realize
Hellenize	martyrize	parallelize	recognize
Hibernicize	materialize	paralyze	rejuvenize
histrionize	matronize	particularize	remise
humanize	mechanize	patronize	remonetise
hyperbolize	mediatize	pauperize	reprise
hypnotize	memorialize	pavonize	republicanize
hypothesize	memorize	peculiarize	resurrectionize
idealize	mercerize	pedestrianize	revise
idiotize	merchandise	penalize	revolutionize
idolatrize	mesmerize	penny-wise	rhapsodize
idolize	methodize	personalize	rhetorize
immortalize	mineralize	personize	rise
impatronize	minimize	pessimize	Romanize
imperialize	misanthropize	philologize	royalize
improvise	misprize	philosophize	ruralize
incise	mobilize	physiognomize	saccharize
individualize	modelize	pilgrimize	sacrifice
internationalize	modernize	plagiarize	satirize
Italianize		platitudinize	scandalize

ōld, ôr, ŏdd, oil, fŏŏt, out; ūse, ûrn, ŭp; THis, thin

		ĬZ	actinism
scepticize	synchronize	Ariz.	aestheticism
schismatize	syncopize	befriz	Africanism
Scotticize	synonymize	biz	agnosticism
scrupulize	synthesize	Cadiz	agonism
scrutinize	synthetize	fizz	agrarianism
sectarianize	systematize	friz	agriculturism
secularize	systemize	his	alcoholism
seigniorize	tabularize	is	alienism
seniorize	tantalize	Liz	altruism
sensualize	tautologize	phiz	Americanism
sentimentalize	temporize	quiz	anachronism
sepulchralize	terrorize	riz	anarchism
sermonize	Teutonize	sizz	anathematism
sexualize	theologize	'tis	anatomism
sice	theorize	viz	aneurism
signalize	theosophize	whiz	Anglicanism
silverize	timonize		Anglicism
singularize	totalize	ĬZD	Anglo-
size	tranquillize	ill-advised	Saxonism
soberize	tyrannize	unadvised	animalism
socialize	underprize	unapprised	animism
Socinianize	universalize	unauthorized	anomalism
solarize	unwise	unbaptized	antagonism
solemnize	uprise	uncanonized	antiquarianism
soliloquize	utilize	uncivilized	anti-Semitism
sonnetize	vagabondize	undersized	aphorism
specialize	vaporize	undespised	archaism
spiritualize	ventriloquize	undisguised	asceticism
sterilize	verbalize	unprized	Asiaticism
stigmatize	victimize	unsurmised	asteism
subsidize	villianize	acclimatized,	asterism
subtilize	visualize	etc.	astigmatism
summarize	vitalize		atavism
sunrise	vocalize	ĬZM	atheism
supervise	volatilize	abolitionism	atomism
surmise	vulcanize	absolutism	Baalism
surprise	vulgarize	abysm	babyism
syllogize	wantonize	academism	bacchanalian-
symbolize	weather-wise	accidentalism	ism
sympathize	wise	achromatism	bachelorism
symphonize	(see Ī + s)		

barbarism
behaviorism
biblicism
bibliophilism
bibliopolism
bi-metallism
bloomerism
bluestocking-
   ism
bogeyism
Bohemianism
Bolshevism
boobyism
Bourbonism
braggardism
Brahmanism
brutalism
Buchmanism
cabalism
Calvinism
cataclysm
catechism
Catholicism
centralism
characterism
Chauvinism
chloralism
chrism
classicalism
classicism
clericalism
Cockneyism
colloquialism
colonialism
communalism
communism
Confucianism
congregational-
   ism
conservatism

constitutional-
   ism
cosmopolitan-
   ism
cretinism
criticism
cynicism
dandyism
Darwinism
demoniacism
demonianism
demonism
denomina-
   tionalism
despotism
determinism
devilism
diabolism
dialogism
diamagnetism
diplomatism
dogmatism
dualism
ecclesiasticism
eclecticism
egoism
egotism
electicism
embolism
emotionalism
empiricism
epicureanism
equestrianism
Erastianism
esotericism
etherealism
etherism
eudemonism
euphemism
euphonism
euphuism

evangelism
exorcism
exoticism
exquisitism
fairyism
fanaticism
fantasticism
fatalism
federalism
Fenianism
fetishism
feudalism
flunkeyism
fogeyism
foreignism
formalism
fossilism
Fourierism
frivolism
Gallicism
galvanism
gentilism
Germanism
Ghandiism
heathenism
Hebraism
hedonism
Hellenism
heroism
Hibernianism
Hibernicism
Hinduism
histrionicism
histrionism
Hitlerism
humanism
hyperbolism
hypercriticism
hypnotism
hypochondriac-
   ism

Ibsenism
idealism
ism
idiotism
immaterialism
imperialism
individualism
industrialism
intellectualism
international-
   ism
Irishism
Islamism
Italianism
Italicism
Jesuitism
jockeyism
journalism
Judaism
laconicism
laconism
ladyism
Latinism
latitudinarian-
   ism
legitimism
Leninism
liberalism
libertinism
literalism
localism
Lollardism
Londonism
loyalism
lyricism
magnetism
Mahometan-
   ism
mammonism
mannerism
materialism

mechanism
mediaevalism
Menshevism
mesmerism
metacism
methodism
modernism
Mohammedan-
ism
monarchism
monasticism
monkeyism
Montanism
moralism
Mormonism
mysticism
nativism
naturalism
necessarianism
neologism
Neoplatonism
nepotism
nihilism
nominalism
occultism
ogreism
optimism
organism
orientalism
ostracism
pacifism
paganism
pantheism
parallelism
paroxysm
patricianism
patriotism
pauperism
peanism
pedantism
pedestrianism

peonism
peripateticism
personalism
pessimism
phalansterism
phenomenalism
phenomenism
philanthropic-
ism
Philhellenism
Philistinism
philosophism
physicism
pietism
plagiarism
Platonism
plebeianism
pluralism
positivism
pragmatism
precisianism
predestinarian-
ism
prelatism
pre-Raphaelism
Presbyterian-
ism
prism
proletarianism
protectionism
Protestantism
proverbialism
provincialism
pugilism
puppyism
Puritanism
Puseyism
pythonism
Quakerism
quietism
Quixotism

rabbinism
radicalism
realism
religionism
Republicanism
rationalism
revivalism
rheumatism
rigorism
ritualism
Romanism
romanticism
royalism
ruffianism
ruralism
sabbatarianism
sacerdotalism
satanism
savagism
Saxonism
scepticism
schism
scholasticism
sciolism
Scotticism
scoundrelism
scripturalism
secessionism
sectarianism
secularism
Semitism
sensationalism
sensualism
sentimentalism
shamanism
Shavianism
Shintoism
socialism
Socinianism
solecism

somnambulism
somnolism
sovietism
Stalinism
stoicism
subjectivism
subtilism
supernatural-
ism
syllogism
symbolism
synchronism
syncretism
Syrianism
terrorism
Teutonicism
theosophism
tigerism
Toryism
totemism
trades-union-
ism
traditionalism
transcendental-
ism
tribalism
unionism
Unitarianism
universalism
utilitarianism
Utopianism
valetudinarian-
ism
vampirism
vandalism
Vaticanism
vegetarianism
ventriloquism
verbalism
vitalism

| vocalism | vulpinism | Wesleyanism | Yankeeism |
| vulgarism | vulturism | witticism | zanyism |

O

These words include the following accented vowel sounds:

Ō   as in old; heard also in note, oh, roam, foe, shoulder, grow, owe, sew, yeoman, beau, hautboy, brooch.

Ô   as in or; heard also in all, talk, swarm, haul, caught, law, fought, broad, memoir.

Ŏ   as in odd; heard also in want, wash, shone.

OI   as in oil; heard also in boy.

OŎ   as in foot; heard also in full, wolf, could.

OU   as in out; heard also in cow, sauerkraut.

For the vowel sound heard in *do*, see under Ū.

For the vowel sound heard in *one, flood,* see under Ŭ

Ō	bravissimo	domino	furbelow
adagio	buffalo	dough	gazabo
aglow	bummalo	duodecimo	generalissimo
ago	bungalow	eau	gigolo
alow	bureau	*embow*	glow
although	cachalot	embroglio	go
apropos	calico	embryo	grow
archipelago	cameo	entrepot	half-a-mo
arow	chapeau	escrow	haricot
banjo	chateau	Eskimo	heigh-ho
bateau	Co.	ex-officio	ho
beau	comme il faut	Flo	hoe
below	crow	floe	how-so
besnow	curaçoa	flow	hullo
bestow	death-blow	foe	ice-flow
blow	death-throe	folio	imbroglio
bo	depot	forego	impresario
bon-mot	de trop	foreknow	incognito
Bordeaux	Diderot	foreshow	indigo
bow	do	fortissimo	inflow
braggadocio	doe	fro	in statu quo

ōld, ôr, ŏdd, oil, foŏt, out; ūse, ûrn, ŭp; THis, thin

intaglio	Poe	toe	jackdaw
jabot	portfolio	Tokio	jaw
Jo	portico	touch-and-go	landau
Joe	portmanteau	tow	law
know	pro	tremolo	macaw
little-go	proximo	trousseau	maw
lo	punctilio	trow	McGraw
long-ago	quid-pro-quo	ultimo	mother-in-law
long-bow	rainbow	undergo	overawe
Lothario	raree-show	under-tow	overdraw
low	ratio	unknow	oversaw
Lowe	roe	upgrow	papaw
magnifico	rondeau	upthrow	paw
malapropos	rouleau	vertigo	pilau
manito	Rousseau	Westward ho	pshaw
Mexico	row	woe	raw
mistletoe	Rowe		saw
morceau	sabot	Ô	scaw
mot	saddle-bow	Arkansas	see-saw
mow	seraglio	awe	Shaw
mustachio	sew	begnaw	sister-in-law
no	shew	braw	slaw
nuncio	show	brother-in-law	son-in-law
O	sloe	caw	spa
oboe	slow	chaw	squaw
oh	snow	claw	straw
olio	so	craw	tau
oratorio	so-and-so	daughter-in-	taw
outflow	soho	law	thaw
outgo	sow	dauw	thraw
outgrow	stow	daw	underjaw
overcrow	strow	dawe	undraw
overflow	studio	draw	unlaw
overgrow	tableau	father-in-law	usquebaugh
overthrow	tally ho	faugh	withdraw
owe	though	flaw	yaw
Papilio	throe	foresaw	
pianissimo	throw	gnaw	ŌB
pistachio	timber-toe	guffaw	conglobe
plateau	tiptoe	haw	disrobe
Po	to-and-fro	heehaw	enrobe

āle, câre, ădd, ärm, åsk; mē, hĕre, ĕnd; īce, ĭll;

globe	ŎBZ	notch	rode
Job	Dobbs	outwatch	spode
lobe	Hobbes	Scotch	strode
Loeb	Hobbs	splotch	toad
probe	ods-bobs	swatch	unbestowed
robe	scobs	watch	unload
unrobe	blobs, etc.		unowed
		ŎCHD	woad
ŎB	**ŎCH**	unapproached	(see Ŏ + ed)
bedaub	abroach	unbroached	
daub	approach	approached,	**ŎD**
nawab	broach	etc.	abroad
	brooch		applaud
ŎB	coach	**ŎD**	bawd
athrob	cockroach	abode	belaud
blob	croche	a la mode	broad
bob	encoach	antipode	Claude
cabob	encroach	*arrode*	defraud
cob	loach	bestrode	fraud
Cobb	poach	bode	gaud
corncob	reproach	bridle-road	lantern-jawed
fob	roach	Clode	laud
gob	self-reproach	code	maraud
hob	slowcoach	commode	maud
hob-and-nob		corrode	overawed
hobnob	**ŎCH**	discommode	unawed
job	debauch	episode	whopper-jawed
knob	nautch	erode	awed, etc.
lob		explode	
mob	**ŎCH**	forebode	**ŎD**
nob	anchor-watch	goad	Aaron's-rod
quab	blotch	incommode	*begod*
rob	botch	load	clod
slob	crotch	lode	cod
snob	death-watch	lycopode	Codd
sob	gotch	mode	demi-god
squab	harbour-watch	node	divining-rod
stob	hotch	ode	Dodd
swab	hopscotch	overload	dry-shod
thingumbob	hotch-potch	pigeon-toed	Eisteddfod
throb	larboard-watch	road	God

ōld, ôr, ŏdd, oil, fŏŏt, out; ūse, ûrn, ŭp; THis, thin

golden-rod	oaf	rogue	philologue
hod	quartern-loaf	togue	Pokogue
lycopod		trogue	polliwog
nod	**ŎF**	vogue	prairie-dog
od	cloff		prog
odd	cough	**ŎG**	Quogue
piston-rod	doff	agog	scrog
platypod	golf	analogue	shog
plod	koff	apologue	slog
pod	long-field-off	befog	synagogue
prod	off	bog	theologue
quad	pairing-off	bulldog	travelog
quod	philosophe	catalogue	unclog
river-god	prof	clog	
rod	scoff	cog	**ŎGD**
rough-shod	shroff	Dannebrog	frogged
sea-god	sign off	decalogue	water-logged
shod	soph	demagogue	befogged, etc.
slipshod	toff	dialogue	
sod	toph	dog	**ŎGZ**
squad	trough	egg-nog	togs
tod		embog	befogs, etc.
trod	**ŎFT**	epilogue	
ungod	aloft	flog	**OI**
unshod	croft	fog	ahoy
untrod	loft	frog	alloy
wad	oft	Gog	annoy
	soft	grog	boy
ŎDZ	toft	hedgehog	buoy
Rhoades	undercroft	Herzog	charity-boy
Rhodes	doffed, etc.	hog	cloy
(see ŎD + s)		hot dog	convoy
	ŌG	incog	corduroy
ŎDZ	apologue	jog	coy
emerods	astrologue	log	decoy
odds	brogue	monologue	deploy
clods, etc.	collogue	mystagogue	destroy
	embogue	nog	employ
ŌF	Hogue	Patchogue	enjoy
goaf	pirogue	pedagogue	foy
loaf	prorogue	pettifog	goy

āle,   câre,   ădd,   ärm,   åsk;   mē,   hęre,   ĕnd;   īce,   ĭll;

hobbledehoy
hoy
Illinois
joy
loblolly-boy
Loy
overjoy
paduasoy
Pomeroy
saveloy
Savoy
sepoy
soy
teapoy
toy
troy
viceroy
yellow-boy

OID

actinoid
albuminoid
alkaloid
aneroid
anthropoid
asteroid
avoid
"boid"
celluloid
coralloid
crystalloid
deltoid
dendroid
devoid
helicoid
hyaloid
metalloid
mongoloid
negroid
overjoyed
ovoid

pachyderma-
    toid
paraboloid
petaloid
pyramidoid
tabloid
trapezoid
unalloyed
unbuoyed
unemployed
varioloid
void
alloyed, etc.

OIDZ

Lloyd's
avoids, etc.

OIF

coif

OIL

aboil
assoil
boil
Boyle
broil
coil
counterfoil
Coyle
despoil
disembroil
Doyle
embroil
entoil
estoile
foil
langue d'oil
moil
noil
oil

overtoil
parboil
quatrefoil
recoil
roil
soil
spoil
toil
turmoil
uncoil
upcoil

OILD

hard boiled
unsoiled
unspoiled
boiled, etc.

OILT

spoilt

OILZ

noils
boils, etc.

OIN

adjoin
almoign
Boyne
coign
coin
conjoin
Des Moines
disjoin
eloign
enjoin
foin
frankalmoigne
groin
interjoin
join

loin
purloin
quoin
rejoin
sejoin
sirloin
subjoin
tenderloin

OIND

dead point
point
uncoined
adjoined, etc.

OINT

adjoint
anoint
appoint
aroint
conjoint
counterpoint
coverpoint
disappoint
disjoint
dowel-joint
dry-point
joint
point
reappoint
repoint

OIS

Boyce
choice
invoice
Joyce
outvoice
rejoice
voice

ōld, ôr, ŏdd, oil, fŏŏt, out; ūse, ûrn, ŭp; THis, this

OIST
foist
hoist
joist
loud-voiced
moist
shrill-voiced
unrejoiced
unvoiced
voiced, etc.

OIT
adroit
dacoit
Detroit
doit
droit
exploit
maladroit
quoit
Voight

OIZ
avoirdupois
counterpoise
equipoise
erminois
froise
noise
Noyes
poise
(see OI + s)

ŌJ
doge
gamboge
horologe

ŎJ
dislodge
dodge

hodge
hodge-podge
horologe
lodge
splodge
stodge
unlodge

ŌK
artichoke
asoak
awoke
baroque
besmoke
bespoke
bloke
broke
choke
cloak
coak
coke
convoke
counterstroke
croak
death-stroke
equivoque
evoke
folk
forespoke
forspoke
gentlefolk
invoke
joke
Larocque
loke
master-stroke
moke
oak
outbroke
poke
provoke

revoke
scrub-oak
sloke
smoke
soak
spoke
stoke
stroke
thunder-stroke
toke
toque
unbroke
uncloak
understroke
unyoke
up-broke
woke
yoke
yolk

ŎK
auk
awk
balk
cakewalk
calk
chalk
dawk
Falk
gawk
hawk
mawk
Mohawk
outwalk
pawk
sidewalk
sparrow-hawk
squawk
stalk
talk

tomahawk
walk

ŎK
acock
alpenstock
amok
Antioch
Bach
Bankok
baroque
bedrock
belock
bemock
billycock
Bloch
block
bock
brock
chock
chockablock
clock
cock
crock
dead-lock
dock
fetlock
firelock
flintlock
flock
forelock
frock
half-cock
havelock
hoc
hock
hollyhock
interlock
jock
knock
lady's-smock

āle, câre, ădd, ärm, ȧsk; mē, hẹre, ĕnd; īce, ĭll;

langue d'oc	**ŎKS**	**ŎKT**	feme-sole
laughing-	coax	concoct	foal
stock	hoax	decoct	foliole
Little Rock	Nokes	recoct	fumarole
loch	Oakes	unfrocked	furole
lock	Stokes	blocked, etc.	fusarole
love-lock	Vokes		girandole
Medoc	artichokes,	**ŌL**	girasole
mock	etc.	augur-hole	gloriole
Mohock		aureole	gloryhole
padlock	**ŎKS**	banderole	goal
Painted Rock	ballot-box	barcarolle	heart-whole
peacock	bandbox	bibliopole	hole
penstock	box	blowhole	inscroll
percussion-	chickenpox	bole	jowl
lock	Christmas-	boll	knoll
plock	box	borecole	kohl
pock	Cox	bowl	log-roll
poppycock	equinox	bunghole	loophole
Ragnarock	fox	buttonhole	Maypole
roc	hatbox	cajole	mole
rock	heterodox	camisole	oriole
shock	mailbox	capriole	parole
shuttle-cock	orthodox	caracole	patrol
smock	ox	carambole	peephole
soc	paddlebox	cariole	petiole
sock	paradox	carmagnole	pigeon-hole
spatch-cock	phlox	casserole	pinhole
stock	pillar-box	coal	pinole
stumbling-	powder-box	cole	pistole
block	signal-box	comptrol	pole
turkey-cock	smallpox	condole	poll
turncock	vox	console	porthole
understock	alpenstocks,	control	rantipole
undock	etc.	curtainpole	rigmarole
unfrock		dhole	role
unlock	**ŌKT**	dole	roll
weathercock	unprovoked	droll	scroll
weepingrock	water-soaked	enbowl	scupper-hole
woodcock	evoked, etc.	enroll	segol
		extoll	self-control

Seminole	caterwaul	spall	**ŌLD**
shoal	caul	spawl	acold
shole	crawl	sprawl	afterhold
sole	disenthrall	spurgall	ahold
soul	drawl	squall	anchor-hold
stole	dwal	stall	behold
stroll	enthrall	tall	blindfold
tadpole	evenfall	therewithal	bold
thole	fall	thrall	bullet-mould
toll	fireball	trawl	clay-cold
tophole	football	trumpet-call	coaled
troll	footfall	wall	cold
unroll	forestall	waterfall	copyhold
unsoul	gall	wherewithal	enfold
unwhole	Gaul	windfall	fold
uproll	hall	withal	foothold
vacuole	haul	yawl	foretold
variole	install		fourfold
virole	judgment-hall	**ŎL**	freehold
vole	kraal	alcohol	gold
wassail-bowl	landfall	atoll	half-soled
whole	mall	baby doll	high-souled
	maul	capitol	hold
ŎL	McCall	consol	household
all	miscall	doll	ice-cold
all-in-all	nightfall	entresol	infold
appal	overfall	extol	interfold
awl	overhaul	folderol	leaf-mold
ball	pall	girasol	leasehold
banquet-hall	Paul	gun moll	Leopold
baseball	pawl	loll	manifold
basketball	pitfall	moll	marigold
bawl	rainfall	parasol	mold
befall	recall	poll	multifold
bemawl	Saul	protocol	old
Bengal	scall	Sol	overbold
bethrall	scrawl	vitriol	refold
blackball	sea-wall		retold
boxstall	shawl	**ŎLCH**	sable-stoled
brawl	small	Balch	scold
call	snowball	Walch	sold

spun-gold
stone-cold
stronghold
thousandfold
told
twice-told
twofold, etc.
uncontrolled
unfold
unsold
untold
uphold
withhold
wold
cajoled, etc.

ŎLD

Archibald
auld
blackballed
bald
scald
so called
unappalled
uncalled
unenthralled
ungalled
unrecalled
appalled, etc.

ŌLN

swoln

ŎLSH

Walsh

ŌLT

bolt
colt
demi-volt
dolt

holt
jolt
lavolt
molt
poult
revolt
shackle-bolt
smolt
thunderbolt
unbolt
volt

ŎLT

assault
basalt
cobalt
default
envault
exalt
fault
gault
halt
malt
salt
seasalt
smalt
somersault
spalt
vault

ŎLTS

false
salts
valse
waltz
assaults, etc.

ŎLV

absolve
circumvolve
convolve

devolve
dissolve
evolve
exolve
intervolve
involve
resolve
revolve
solve

ŎLVD

undissolved
unresolved
unsolved
absolved, etc.

ŌM

aerodrome
afoam
befoam
brome
catacomb
chrome
chromosome
clomb
comb
currycomb
dome
endome
foam
Frome
gastronome
gloam
gnome
harvest-home
heliochrome
hippodrome
holm
home
honey-comb

Jerome
loam
metallochrome
metronome
microsome
monochrome
nobody home
no'm
Nome
ohm
palindrome
polychrome
pome
roam
Rome
Salome
sea-foam
sea-holm
sloam
tome

ÔM

haum
imaum
maum
shawm

ŎM

aplomb
axiom
bomb
dom
from
hecatomb
om
pogrom
pompom
rhomb
swom
therefrom

ōld, ôr, ŏdd, oil, fŏŏt, out; ūse, ûrn, ŭp; THis, thin

ŎMP

comp
pomp
romp
swamp
trompe

ŎMPT

imprompt
prompt
romped, etc.

ŎMZ

Holmes
(see ŎM + s)

ŎN

alone
antiphone
Athlone
atone
audiphone
backbone
baritone
begroan
bemoan
bestrown
blown
bone
Boulogne
brimstone
chaperone
cicerone
clingstone
Cologne
condone
cone
corner-stone
crone
curbstone
depone

dethrone
dictaphone
disown
dispone
Dordogne
drone
eau-de-cologne
electrophone
enthrone
enzone
flagstone
flown
foreknown
foreshown
foundation-
   stone
fresh-blown
full-blown
full-grown
gramophone
graphophone
grass-grown
grindlestone
grindstone
groan
grown
hailstone
headstone
hearthstone
high-flown
holy stone
hone
impone
imposing-stone
interpone
intone
Joan
keystone
known
knucklebone
ladrone

limestone
loadstone
loan
lone
macrotone
marrow-bone
megaphone
microphone
milestone
millstone
moan
monotone
moonstone
moss-grown
mown
ochone
outblown
overgrown
overthrown
own
phone
pone
postpone
prone
propone
radiophone
Rhone
roan
saxophone
semitone
sewn
shewn
shown
soapstone
sown
stone
strown
telephone
throne
thrown
tone

trombone
unbeknown
unblown
undertone
unforeknown
ungrown
unknown
unsewn
unsown
unthrone
vitaphone
weather-blown
whalebone
whetstone
xylophone
zone

ŎN

awn
"bawn"
brawn
"cawn"
dawn
drawn
faun
fawn
impawn
indrawn
lawn
pawn
prawn
sawn
spawn
undrawn
withdrawn
yawn

ŎN

agone
amazon
anon

antiphon	mastodon	haunch	**ŎNG**
automaton	Micklejohn	launch	all-along
Babylon	myrmidon	paunch	along
begone	Oberon		battlesong
Bellerophon	octagon	**ŎND**	belong
benison	on	high-toned	daylong
bonbon	Oregon	unatoned	ding dong
bonne	outshone	unmoaned	drinking-song
celadon	pantechnicon	unowned	dugong
Ceylon	paragon	unzoned	erelong
chiffon	Parthenon	zoned	evensong
colophon	pentagon	atoned, etc.	flong
con	phaeton		gong
cretonne	phenomenon	**ŎND**	headlong
decagon	polygon	beau monde	headstrong
demijohn	prolegomenon	demi-monde	Hong Kong
dies non	put upon	Fronde	lifelong
don	Rubicon	Gironde	livelong
Donne	Saskatchewan	monde	long
echelon	shone		mah-jongg
encephalon	silicon	**ŎND**	night-long
enchiridion	sine quâ non	abscond	overlong
encomion	stereopticon	beau monde	pingpong
Euroclydon	swan	beyond	prolong
glyptodon	tarragon	blond	prong
gone	thereon	bond	scuppernong
gonfalon	thereupon	correspond	sing-song
hanger-on	undergone	demi-monde	song
Helicon	upon	despond	souchong
hereon	wan	fond	strong
hereupon	whereon	frond	thong
hexagon	whereupon	overfond	throng
hoot mon	woebegone	plafond	tong
Hyperion	*yon*	monde	undersong
iguanodon	(cf. accordion,	pond	wong
irenicon	etc., under	respond	wrong
Jeanne	ŬN)	unparagoned	
John	Yvonne	vagabond	**ŎNGD**
lexicon		wand	unwronged
long-field-on	**ŎNCH**	*yond*	belonged, etc.
Luzon	craunch	donned, etc.	

ōld,   ôr,   ŏdd,   oil,   fŏŏt,   out;   ūse,   ûrn,   ŭp;   THis,   thin

ŎNGK

conch
conk
honk
honky-tonk

ŎNGKS

Bronx
conchs, etc.

ŎNGST

alongst
belong'st
long'st
prolong'st
throng'st
wrong'st

ŎNGZ

tongs
belongs, etc.

ŎNS

ensconce
nonce
response
sconce

ŎNT

don't
won't

ÔNT

aflaunt
a-taunt
avaunt
daunt
flaunt
gaunt
haunt
jaunt

romaunt
taunt
vaunt
want

ÔNT

Dupont
font
Hellespont
want

ÔNTS

fonts
wants
(cf. nonce)

ŎNZ

Davy Jones
Jones
nones
atones, etc.

ŎNZ

bonze
bronze
by-gones
Johns
pons
(see ŎN+s)

ŎOD

could
dead-wood
firewood
good
hood
misunderstood
plastic wood
purple-wood
sandal-wood
should

stood
understood
Underwood
unhood
wildwood
withstood
wood
would
angelhood
babyhood
brotherhood
deaconhood
fatherhood
foolhardihood
gentlemanhood
hardihood
kinglihood
kittenhood
ladyhood
likelihood
livelihood
lustihood
maidenhood
manhood
matronhood
monk's-hood
motherhood
neighbourhood
orphanhood
parenthood
sisterhood
spinsterhood
unlikelihood
widowerhood
widowhood
womanhood

ŎOK

betook
book
brook

Chinook
cook
crook
forsook
hook
ingle-nook
look
minute-book
mistook
nook
outlook
overlook
overtook
partook
pastry-cook
pocket-book
rook
shook
took
unhook
undertook
uplook

ŎOKS

Crookes
snooks
tenterhooks
crooks, etc.

ŎOL

abb-wool
bull
cock-and-bull
full
lamb's-wool
pull
wool
beautiful
bountiful
dutiful
fanciful

masterful	illegible	insensible	ratable
merciful	immovable	insoluble	redeemable
pitiful	immutable	insupportable	reliable
plentiful	impalpable	insupposable	reprehensible
powerful	impassable	insuppressible	respectable
sorrowful	impeccable	insurmountable	responsible
thimbleful	imperturbable	intangible	sensible
unmerciful	implacable	intelligible	susceptible
weariful	impossible	interchange-	syllable
wonderful	impregnable	able	tangible
worshipful	improbable	intractible	tenable
acceptable	improvable	invaluable	terrible
accessible	inaccessible	invincible	tractable
accountable	inadmissible	irascible	unimpeachable
adorable	inaudible	irrepressible	unmatchable
affable	incapable	irreproachable	unquenchable
amenable	incomparable	irresistible	visible
amiable	incompatible	irresponsible	voluble
attainable	incomprehen-	irretrievable	
audible	sible	justifiable	OͦOLF
available	inconceivable	laudable	wolf
avoidable	incontestable	legible	
believable	incontrovert-	Mehitable	OͦOLVZ
capable	ible	mutable	wolves
changeable	incorruptible	notable	
combustible	incredible	ostensible	OͦOS
commendable	incurable	palpable	puss
compatible	indelible	passable	
constable	indescribable	perceptible	OͦOSH
contemptible	indestructible	permissible	bramble-bush
corruptible	indispensable	placable	bush
crucible	ineffable	plausible	push
culpable	ineffaceable	portable	
damnable	inexcusable	possible	OͦOSK
delectable	inexhaustible	praisable	brusque
deplorable	inexpressible	presentable	
desirable	infallible	principle	OͦOT
detestable	inflammable	probable	afoot
flexible	inflexible	procurable	foot
forcible	infrangible	producible	forefoot
horrible	inscrutable	pronounceable	pussyfoot

ōld, ôr, ŏdd, oil, fŏŏt, out; ūse, ûrn, ŭp; THis, thin

put
underfoot

ŌP

agrope
antelope
anti-pope
aslope
astroscope
baroscope
bioscope
cantaloupe
Cape of Good
  Hope
cope
dispope
dope
electroscope
elope
envelope
foot-rope
galvanoscope
grope
gyroscope
helioscope
heliotrope
hope
horoscope
hydroscope
interlope
kaleidoscope
lope
microscope
misanthrope
mope
ope
polariscope
pope
rope
scope
seismoscope

slope
soap
spectroscope
stereoscope
stethoscope
stope
telescope
thermoscope
tope
trope
unpope

ŎP

gaup
scaup
whaup
yawp

ŎP

after-crop
atop
bedrop
chop
co-op
cop
crop
drop
eavesdrop
estop
flipflop
flippity-flop
flop
fop
foretop
galop
ginger-pop
hop
knop
lollipop
lop

overtop
mizzen top
mop
overtop
plop
pop
prop
shop
slop
snowdrop
soda pop
sop
stop
strop
swap
tiptop
top
underprop
unstop
whop
wop
workshop

ŎPS

copse
drops, etc.

ŌPT

unhoped
unsoaped
eloped, etc.

ŎPT

adopt
copped
Copt
outcropped
uncropped
unstopped
dropped, etc.

ŌR

adore
afore
albacore
ashore
back-door
Baltimore
battledore
before
boar
Boer
bore
chore
commodore
core
corps
crore
death's-door
deplore
door
encore
evermore
explore
first-floor
floor
folklore
foot-sore
forbore
fore
foreshore
forswore
four
fourscore
frore
furthermore
galore
gore
heartsore
heretofore
hoar
ignore

āle, câre, ădd, ärm, ăsk; mē, hĕre, ĕnd; īce, ĭll;

implore
inshore
Lahore
lore
matador
mirador
more
nevermore
oar
o'er
ore
outpour
outroar
outsoar
Parramore
picador
pinafore
pore
pour
restore
roar
sagamore
score
sea-shore
semaphore
shore
Singapore
snore
soar
sophomore
sore
spore
stevedore
store
swore
sycamore
Theodore
tore
troubadour
underscore
uproar

upsoar
weather-shore
whore
wore
yore

ŌR

abhor
ambassador
ancestor
anterior
apparitor
assignor
auditor
bachelor
chancellor
competitor
compositor
conqueror
conspirator
contributor
corridor
councillor
counsellor
creditor
depositor
dinosaur
dor
Dukhobor
Ecuador
editor
emperor
excelsior
executor
expositor
exterior
for
governor
guarantor
ichthyosaur
inferior

inheritor
inquisitor
interior
interlocutor
janitor
Labrador
legator
lessor
lor
louis d'or
man-of-war
matador
metaphor
meteor
minotaur
mirador
monitor
mortgagor
nominor
nor
or
orator
posterior
primogenitor
progenitor
proprietor
Salvador
scaur
senator
senor
servitor
solicitor
superior
therefor
Thor
tor
toreador
troubadour
ulterior
verderor
vice-chancellor

visitor
war

ŌRB

absorb
corb
orb
reabsorb
resorb

ŌRBD

full-orbed
absorbed, etc.

ŌRCH

porch

ŌRCH

bortsch
scorch
torch

ŌRD

aboard
afford
beaverboard
board
broadsword
ford
gourd
hoard
horde
ironing-board
oared
seaboard
shuffle-board
surfboard
sword
undeplored
unexplored
ungored

ōld, ôr, ŏdd, oil, fōŏt, out; ūse, ûrn, ŭp; THis, thin

unhoard
unimplored
unrestored
weather-board
adored, etc.

ŌRD

accord
award
belord
bord
chord
concord
cord
disaccord
fiord
fjord
harpsichord
landlord
lord
lyrichord
master-chord
McCord
misericord
Orde
overlord
polychord
record
reward
sward
unlord
ward
abhorred, etc.

ŌRF

corf
dwarf
wharf

ŌRG

morgue

ŌRJ

forge

ŌRJ

disgorge
engorge
George
gorge
regorge

ŌRK

pork

ŌRK

cork
fork
New York
"orch"
stork
torque
uncork
weeding-fork
York

ŌRKD

storked
corked, etc.

ŌRL

orle
schorl
whorl

ŌRM

aeriform
aquiform
bestorm
chloroform
conform
cruciform
cuneiform
deform

deiform
dendriform
diversiform
floriform
form
inform
misform
misinform
multiform
norm
perform
reform
snow-storm
stelliform
storm
sunny-warm
swarm
thunder-storm
transform
uniform
unwarm
upswarm
vermiform
warm

ŌRMD

unformed
uninformed
unperformed
unreformed
unstormed
well-informed
bestormed, etc.

ŌRMTH

warmth
storm'th, etc.

ŌRN

bemourn
betorn

borne
bourn
foot-worn
forborne
forsworn
mourn
outworn
overborne
sea-worn
shorn
sworn
toil-worn
torn
unshorn
unsworn
water-worn
wave-worn
way-worn
weather-worn
worn
(cf. adorn, etc.)

ŌRN

adorn
alpen-horn
barleycorn
bescorn
blackthorn
born
buckthorn
Cape Horn
Capricorn
cloudborn
corn
disadorn
dishorn
drinking-horn
first-born
fog-horn
forewarn
forlorn

French-horn	**ÔRND**	remorse	**ÔRT**
greenhorn	unadorned	retrorse	abort
hawthorn	unforewarned	sea-horse	amort
heaven-born	adorned, etc.	stalking-horse	assort
high-born		torse	athwart
horn	**ÔRP**	unhorse	bort
Horne	dorp		cavort
hunting-horn	thorp	**ÔRSK**	consort
inborn	warp	torsk	contort
Langhorne			*detort*
longicorn	**ÔRPS**	**ÔRST**	distort
lorn	corpse	addorsed	escort
love-lorn	warps, etc.	endorsed	exhort
Matterhorn		horsed	extort
morn	**ÔRS**	Horst	mort
night-born	coarse	unhorsed	*ort*
Norn	course		quart
peppercorn	discourse	**ÔRT**	resort
popcorn	divorce	comport	retort
powder-horn	enforce	county court	short
priming-horn	force	court	snort
readorn	hoarse	davenport	sort
scorn	intercourse	*decourt*	*swart*
sea-born	perforce	deport	thwart
self-scorn	recourse	disport	tort
sky-born	reinforce	export	wart
still-born	resource	fort	(cf. court, etc.)
suborn	source	forte	
thorn	water-course	import	**ÔRTH**
tricorn		misreport	forth
trueborn	**ÔRS**	passport	fourth
unborn	corse	port	henceforth
unicorn	deadhorse	Porte	setter-forth
warn	dextrorse	rapport	thenceforth
yestermorn	*dorse*	report	*pour'th,* etc.
	endorse	sally-port	
	gorse	seaport	**ÔRTH**
ÔRND	hobby-horse	sport	north
bemourned	horse	support	Orth
mourned	Morse	transport	swarth
unmourned	Norse	(cf. ÔRT)	*abhorr'th,* etc.

ōld, ôr, ŏdd, oil, fŏŏt, out; ūse, ûrn, ŭp; THis, thin

ŎRTS
quartz
Schwartz
shorts
Swarz
aborts, etc.

ŎRVZ
wharves

ŎRZ
all-fours
Azores
indoors
outdoors
adores, etc.

ŎRZ
Louis-
  Quatorze
quatorze
(see ŎR + s)

ŌS
actuose
adipose
aggerose
albuminose
animose
annulose
bellicose
cellulose
close
comatose
cose
diagnose
dose
engross
floccose
foliose
gibbose

globose
glucose
grandiose
gross
jocose
metempsy-
  chose
morose
nodose
otiose
overdose
underdose
verbose

ŎS
applesauce
sauce

ŎS
across
albatross
Bos
boss
coloss
cross
doss
double cross
dross
emboss
fiery-cross
floss
fosse
gloss
joss
lacrosse
loss
moss
recross
rhinoceros
rosy-cross
sea-moss

Setebos
toss
weeping-cross

ŎSH
Foch
gauche
guilloche

ŎSH
awash
bellywash
bewash
bosch
bosh
debosh
frosh
galosh
gosh
hogwash
kibosh
josh
mackintosh
McIntosh
musquash
quash
slosh
squash
swash
splosh
tosh
wash

ŎSHT
caboshed
great unwashed
unwashed
squashed, etc.

ŎSK
bosk

imbosk
kiosk
mosque

ŎSP
wasp

ŌST
aftermost
bettermost
boast
bottommost
coast
dosed
engrossed
finger-post
foremost
furthermost
ghost
hindermost
hithermost
host
innermost
lowermost
most
nethermost
northernmost
oast
outermost
post
riposte
roast
sea-coast
southernmost
toast
undermost
uppermost
uttermost
westernmost
whipping-post

āle, câre, ădd, ārm, ȧsk; mē, hȩre, ĕnd; īce, ĭll;

ÔST

exhaust
holocaust

ŎST

accost
adossed
betossed
cabossed
cost
double crossed
embossed
enmossed
frost
geognost
hoar-frost
Lacoste
lost
Pentecost
sea-tossed
tempest-tost
uncrossed
unlost
wast
crossed, etc.

ŌT

afloat
anecdote
antidote
asymptote
bedote
bequote
bloat
boat
capote
coat
commote
connote
cote
creosote

denote
devote
dote
float
folkmote
footnote
garrote
gloat
goat
groat
life-boat
lote
misquote
moat
mote
note
oat
outvote
overcoat
petticoat
pilot-boat
promote
quote
redevote
redingote
remote
river-boat
rote
scote
sea-boat
shote
slote
smote
stoat
table d'hote
telephote
throat
tote
troat
underwrote
unsmote

vote
wrote
Witenagemot
wrote

ŌT

aeronaut
after-thought
argonaut
astraught
aught
besought
bestraught
bethought
bewrought
bought
brought
caught
dear-bought
distraught
dreadnought
forethought
fought
fraught
freethought
ghât
hard-fought
inwrought
Juggernaut
maut
merry-thought
methought
naught
nought
onslaught
ought
overwrought
selftaught
sought
taught
taut

thought
unbesought
unbought
unfraught
unfought
untaught
unthought
unwrought
upbrought
upcaught
wrought

ŎT

aliquot
allot
apricot
asquat
beauty-spot
begot
bergamot
besot
blot
bott
cachalot
calotte
Camelot
capot
clot
compatriot
cocotte
cot
counterplot
dogtrot
dot
dry-rot
eschalot
fiery-hot
first-begot
forget-me-not
forgot
gallipot

garrote
gavotte
got
grape-shot
grass-plot
grot
hard-got
hot
Hottentot
Huguenot
ill-got
ink-pot
jogtrot
jot
knot
kumquat
lot
love-knot
misbegot
not
overshot
patriot
plague-spot
plot
polyglot
pot
quot
rot
sans-culotte
Scot
Scott
shallot
shot
shoulder-knot
sighting-shot
slot
somewhat
sot
spot
squat
Stott

swat
tot
tommyrot
trot
unbegot
underplot
undershot
unforgot
ungot
unknot
wat
watt
what
witenagemot
wot
yacht

ŌTH

clothe
loathe

Ŏth

aftergrowth
behemoth
betroth
both
growth
loath
oath
overgrowth
quoth
sloth
Thoth
troth
undergrowth

Ŏth

swath
wrath
wroth

Ŏth

Ashtaroth
barley-broth
behemoth
broadcloth
broth
cloth
Coth
froth
Goth
moth
Ostrogoth
pilot-cloth
saddle-cloth
troth
Visigoth
wroth

ŌTS

Coates
Oates
boats, etc.

ŎTS

Potts
(see ŎT + s)

OU

allow
anyhow
avow
bough
bow
bow-wow
brow
chow
cow
dhow
disallow
disavow
endow

enow
Foochow
frau
frow
Hankow
hoosegow
how
Howe
kow-tow
Kwangchow
landau
mow
now
overbrow
plough
plow
powwow
prow
row
scow
slough
snow-plough
somehow
Soochow
sow
Swatow
thou
upplow
vow
Wenchow
wow

OUCH

avouch
couch
crouch
grouch
ouch
pouch
scaramouch

āle, câre, ădd, ärm, ăsk; mē, hēre, ĕnd; īce, ĭll;

slouch
vouch

OUD

aloud
becloud
beetle-browed
beshroud
cloud
crowd
disendowed
disenshroud
encloud
enshroud
intercloud
loud
overcloud
overcrowd
proud
shroud
thunder-cloud
unbowed
uncloud
unshroud
allowed, etc.

OUJ

gouge
scrouge

OUL

afoul
befoul
behowl
cowl
dowl
foul
fowl
growl
guinea-fowl

howl
jowl
owl
peafowl
prowl
scowl
screech-owl
sea-fowl
water-fowl

OULD

uncowled
befouled, etc.

OUN

adown
brown
clown
crown
decrown
discrown
down
downtown
drown
eider-down
embrown
frown
godown
gown
hand-me-down
noun
nut-brown
reach-me-down
renown
town
tumble-down
uncrown
ungown
upside-down
uptown

OUND

abound
aground
around
astound
back-ground
bloodhound
bound
boozehound
compound
confound
dumfound
expound
flower-crowned
found
ground
hell bound
hidebound
home-bound
hound
icebound
impound
inbound
iron-bound
Mahound
merry-go-round
middle-ground
mound
outbound
outward-bound
pine-crowned
pleasure-
    ground
pound
profound
propound
rebound
redound
renowned
resound
round

smuthound
sound
spell-bound
superabound
surround
triple-crowned
unbound
underground
unground
unsound
vantage-ground
wound
browned, etc.

OUNDZ

zounds
abounds, etc.

OUNJ

lounge

OUNS

announce
bounce
denounce
enounce
flounce
frounce
ounce
pounce
pronounce
renounce
rounce
trounce
(cf. accounts,
    etc.)

OUNT

account
amount
catamount

õld, ôr, ŏdd, oil, fŏŏt, out; ūse, ûrn, ŭp; THis, thin

count
discount
dismount
fount
miscount
mount
paramount
recount
remount
surmount
tantamount

OUNTS

accounts, etc.
(cf. announce,
   etc.)

OUR

bescour
besour
deflour
devour
flour
hour
our
scour
sour
sustaining hour
(cf. OU'ur.)

OURD

unsoured
bescoured, etc.

OUS

backhouse
blouse
chapterhouse
charnelhouse
charterhouse
chouse

customhouse
doghouse
douse
flindermouse
flittermouse
Gnauss
grouse
house
Kraus
louse
madhouse
Mickey Mouse
mouse
nous
outhouse
penthouse
pleasure-house
poorhouse
prison-house
public-house
slaughterhouse
souse
storehouse
warehouse
whorehouse
workhouse

OUST

browst
oust
roust
unhoused
choused, etc.

OUT

about
beshout
bespout
bout
clout
devout

diner-out
doubt
drinking-bout
drought
flout
gadabout
gout
grout
hereabout
hereout
holing-out
knockabout
knockout
knout
kraut
look-out
lout
mahout
out
out-and-out
pout
redoubt
right-about
roundabout
roustabout
rout
sauerkraut
scout
shout
snout
spout
sprout
stirabout
stout
thereabout
thereout
throughout
tout
trout
water-spout
whereabout

whereout
without

OUTH

mouthe

OUth

bemouth
drouth
mouth
south
allow'th, etc.

OUTS

hereabouts
outs
thereabouts
whereabouts
bouts, etc.

OUZ

arouse
blouse
blowze
bouse
browse
carouse
drowse
espouse
house
rouse
souse
spouse
touse
unhouse
uprouse
(see OU + s)

ŌV

clove
cove

---

dove	close	presuppose	taws
drove	clothes	propose	vase
grove	compose	prose	yaws
hove	couleur-de-rose	recompose	(see Ō + s)
interwove	damask-rose	repose	
inwove	decompose	rose	**ŎZ**
Jove	depose	superpose	Boz
mauve	disclose	suppose	Oz
rove	discompose	those	was
shrove	dispose	transpose	
stove	doze	tuberose	**ŎZD**
strove	enclose	unclose	dozed
throve	expose	unfroze	ill-disposed
treasure-trove	foreclose	(see Ō + s)	indisposed
wove	froze		juxtaposed
	gloze	**ÔZ**	predisposed
ŎV	hose	applause	unopposed
hereof	impose	because	well-disposed
of	inclose	cause	closed, etc.
thereof	indispose	clause	
whereof	*interclose*	Dawes	**ŎZH**
	interpose	gauze	eloge
ŌZ	moss-rose	Hawes	loge
arose	nose	hawse	
bramble-rose	oppose	lantern-jaws	**ŎZM**
brose	pose	menopause	macrocosm
chose	predispose	pause	microcosm

ōld, ôr ŏdd, oil, fŏŏt, out; ūse, ûrn, ŭp; THis, thin

U

These words include the following accented vowels sounds:

Ū as in use; heard also in beauty, feud, pew, queue, lieu, view, cue, suit, yule, you, do, rule, true, food, group, drew, fruit, canoe, rheum, maneuvre, blue. The difference between *dew* and *do* is that *dew* is properly dyŪ, with a consonantal *y* sound preceding the long U; while *do* is merely dŪ.

Û as in urn; heard also in fern, err, heard, sir, word, journal, myrrh, colonel.

Ŭ as in up; heard also in won, one, does, flood, double.

For the vowel sound in *full,* see under ŎŎ.

Ū			
	brew	derring-do	Gentoo
acajou	bugaboo	dew	glue
accrue	cachou	do	gillaroo
adieu	canoe	drew	gnu
ado	caribou	due	googoo
anew	cashew	Elihu	grew
aperçu	catechu	emu	halloo
askew	chandoo	endew	haut-gout
avenue	chew	endue	hereinto
baboo	clew	ensue	hereto
ballyhoo	clue	entre nous	hereunto
bamboo	cockatoo	eschew	hew
barbecue	construe	ewe	Hindu
barley-broo	coo	feu	hitherto
battue	corkscrew	feverfew	honeydew
bayou	coup	few	hoodoo
bedew	crew	fichu	hue
beshrew	cuckoo	firenew	Hugh
bestrew	cue	Fitzhugh	hullabaloo
billet-doux	curlew	flew	igloo
blew	Daibutsu	flu	imbrue
blue	Daikoku	flue	imbue
boo	debut	*fordo*	immew
boohoo	Depew	foreknew	impromptu

---

indue	pursue	tew	yahoo
ingenue	queue	thereinto	yew
interview	ragout	thereto	yoohoo
in transitu	rendezvous	thereunto	you
I.O.U	renew	thew	zoo
Jew	residue	thitherto	Zulu
Kalamazoo	retinue	threw	
kangaroo	revenue	through	**ŬB**
karroo	review	Timbuktu	boob
Kew	rough hew	to	cube
kinkajou	roux	to-do	Rube
knew	rue	too	tube
lieu	screw	toodle-oo	
loo	sea-mew	to-whit-towhoo	**ŬB**
Manitou	set-to	true	battle-club
meadow-rue	shampoo	trueblue	Beelzebub
mew	shoe	two	blub
misconstrue	shoo	unclew	bub
misdo	shrew	underdo	chub
moo	Sioux	undo	Chubb
mountain-dew	skew	undue	club
napoo	skidoo	unglue	Clubb
new	sky-blue	unmew	cub
night-dew	slew	unscrew	drub
outdo	sloo	untrue	dub
overdo	slough	view	fub
overdue	slue	view-halloo	grub
overstrew	smew	virtu	hub
overthrew	sou	voodoo	hubbub
parvenu	spew	wahoo	nub
passe-partout	sprue	wallaroo	pub
peekaboo	stew	wanderoo	rub
perdu	strew	well-to-do	rub-a-dub
Peru	subdue	whew	scrub
pew	sue	whereinto	shrub
phew	sundew	whereto	sillabub
pooh	surtout	whereunto	slub
preview	*surview*	who	snub
prie-dieu	taboo	withdrew	stub
Pugh	tattoo	woo	sub
Purdue			tub

ōld, ôr, ŏdd, oil, fŏŏt, out; ūse, ûrn, ŭp; THis, thin

ŪCH

brooch
cooch
hooch
hoochy-cooch
mooch
pooch

ŬCH

clutch
crutch
cutch
Dutch
for-as-much
hutch
in-as-much
in-so-much
master-touch
much
mutch
overmuch
retouch
scutch
smutch
such
touch

ŬCHD

untouched
clutched, etc.

ŪD

abrood
abstrude
acerbitude
acritude
allude
altitude
amaritude
amplitude

aptitude
assuetude
attitude
beatitude
brood
certitude
claritude
collude
conclude
consuetude
crassitude
crude
decrepitude
definitude
delude
denude
desuetude
detrude
disquietude
dude
elude
exactitude
exclude
extrude
exude
feud
finitude
food
fortitude
gratitude
habitude
hebetude
home-brewed
illude
inaptitude
incertitude
include
ineptitude
infinitude
ingratitude

inquietude
insuetude
interclude
interlude
intrude
Jude
lassitude
latitude
lenitude
lewd
longitude
magnitude
mansuetude
mollitude
mood
multitude
necessitude
nude
obtrude
occlude
parvitude
platitude
plenitude
pood
preclude
prelude
promptitude
protrude
prude
pulchritude
quietude
rainbow-hued
reclude
rectitude
retrude
rood
rude
seclude
senectitude
serenitude

servitude
shrewd
similitude
slewed
snood
solicitude
solitude
stude
subnude
subtrude
thewed
torpitude
transude
turpitude
unglued
unpursued
unrenewed
unrude
unrued
unstrewed
unsubdued
unwooed
(see Ū+ed)
vastitude
verisimilitude
vicissitude
you'd

ŬD

bestud
blood
bud
Budd
cud
dud
flood
fud
Judd
life-blood
lud
mud

rudd | breadstuff | bepuffed, etc. | subterfuge
'sblood | buff | (cf. scuft) | vermifuge
scud | chough | |
spud | chuff | **ŪG** | **ŬJ**
stud | clough | fugue | adjudge
thud | counterbuff | | begrudge
| cuff | **ŬG** | budge
ŬDZ | duff | bug | drudge
duds | enough | bunnyhug | forejudge
suds | fluff | doodlebug | fudge
buds, etc. | garden-stuff | drug | grudge
| gruff | dug | judge
ŪF | huff | fug | misjudge
aloof | luff | hug | nudge
behoof | muff | jug | prejudge
bullet-proof | powder-puff | lug | rejudge
disproof | puff | mug | Rudge
fire-proof | rebuff | plug | sludge
foolproof | rough | pug | smudge
gable-roof | ruff | rug | trudge
goof | scruff | shrug |
hoof | scuff | slug | **ŬJD**
loof | slough | smug | ill-judged
opera-bouffe | snuff | snug | unjudged
proof | sough | thug | adjudged, etc.
reproof | stuff | trug |
roof | tough | tug | **ŪK**
shadoof | tuff | | archduke
spoof | | **ŬGZ** | bashi-bazouk
Tartuffe | **ŬFS** | go bugs | beduke
unroof | fisticuffs | drugs, etc. | chibouk
virtue-proof | bepuffs, etc. | | Chinook
waterproof | | **ŪJ** | duke
weather-proof | **ŪFT** | demonifuge | fluke
woof | clovenhoofed | febrifuge | Heptateuch
| hoofed | gamboge | Hexateuch
ŬF | roofed, etc. | huge | juke
bepuff | | insectifuge | Luke
besnuff | **ŬFT** | Scrooge | mameluke
blindman's-buff | candytuft | scrouge | Marmaduke
bluff | tuft | stooge | Pentateuch

ōld, ôr, ŏdd, oil, fŏŏt, out; ūse, ûrn, ŭp; THis, thin

peruke
puke
rebuke
snook
spook
stook

ŬK

amuck
awestruck
beduck
buck
Canuck
chuck
cluck
Donald Duck
duck
horror-struck
ill-luck
Kalmuck
lame duck
laverock
luck
misluck
muck
pluck
pot-luck
puck
roebuck
ruck
rukh
shuck
struck
stuck
suck
terror-struck
thunder-struck
truck
tuck
waterbuck

woodchuck
wonderstruck

ŬKS

crux
dux
flux
lux
shucks
(see ŬK + s)

ŬKT

abduct
aqueduct
conduct
construct
deduct
duct
educt
eruct
good-plucked
induct
instruct
misconduct
misconstruct
obstruct
oviduct
product
reduct
reluct
subduct
substruct
superstruct
unplucked
usufruct
viaduct
beducked, etc.

ŬL

April-fool
befool

buhl
charity-school
cool
drool
ducking-stool
fool
footstool
ghoul
Istambul
Liverpool
mewl
misrule
molecule
mule
O'Toole
overrule
pool
pule
reticule
ridicule
rule
school
spool
stool
Sunday School
toadstool
tool
Toole
tulle
vermicule
vestibule
whirlpool
who'll
you'll
Yule

ŬL

ahull
annul
barnacle

chronicle
cull
disannul
dull
gull
hull
lull
miracle
Mogul
monocle
mull
null
numskull
obstacle
pinnacle
scull
sea-gull
skull
spectacle
stull
trull
vehicle
versicle

ŬLB

bulb

ŬLCH

gulch
mulch

ŬLD

unruled
unschooled
(see UL + d)

ŬLD

mulled
thick-skulled
annulled, etc.

ŬLF	pulse	diningroom	unplume
engulf	repulse	drawing-room	tomb
gulf	(cf. adult + s)	dressing-room	untomb
		elbow-room	whom
ŬLJ	**ŬLT**	embloom	womb
bulge	adult	engloom	**ŬM**
divulge	catapult	entomb	
effulge	consult	enwomb	ad libitum
indulge	cult	exhume	adventuresome
promulge	difficult	flume	adytum
	exult	foredoom	aquarium
ŬLK	incult	fume	auditorium
bulk	indult	gloom	become
hulk	insult	groom	benumb
skulk	occult	grume	bum
sulk	result	heirloom	Bumbledom
		illume	burdensome
ŬLKT	**ŬLZ**	inhume	cardamom
bulked	gules	jibboom	Christendom
mulct	(see ŪL + s)	Khartoum	chrysanthe-
hulked, etc.		legume	mum
	ŪM	livingroom	chum
ŬLM	abloom	loom	Cockneydom
culm	*addoom*	lumber-room	come
	anteroom	perfume	compendium
ŪLP	assume	plume	cranium
poulp	begloom	power-loom	crematorium
	beplume	predoom	crum
ŬLP	bloom	presume	crumb
gulp	boom	reading-room	cumbersome
pulp	bridegroom	reassume	curriculum
sculp	broom	relume	delirium
	brougham	resume	drearisome
ŬLS	brume	rheum	drum
appulse	consume	room	dumb
bulse	coom	sea-room	emporium
convulse	coomb	simoom	encomium
dulse	costume	spoom	epithalamium
expulse	disentomb	spume	equilibrium
impulse	displume	subsume	exordium
mulse	doom		fee-fi-fo-fum

---

flunkeydom	platinum	wearisome	tump
frolicsome	plum	worrisome	ump
geranium	plumb	wranglesome	
glum	premium		**ŬMPS**
grum	prud'homme	**ŬMD**	mumps
gum	quarrelsome	assumed, etc.	bethumps, etc.
gymnasium	quietsome	full-bloomed	
halidom	radium	implumed	**ŬN**
heathendom	rascaldom	unfumed	afternoon
hum	rebeldom	ungloomed	aswoon
humdrum	*recumb*	unillumed	attune
humorsome	residuum	*addoomed*, etc.	baboon
intermeddle-	rhumb		balloon
some	rum	**ŬMD**	barracoon
kettle-drum	sanatorium	begummed	bassoon
laudanum	Saxondom	bethumbed	*batoon*
Lum	scrum	unplumbed	bestrewn
martyrdom	scum	benumbed, etc.	boon
maximum	sensorium		bridoon
meddlesome	slum	**ŬMP**	Broun
medium	some	bethump	buffoon
mettlesome	speculum	bump	Calhoun
millennium	strum	chump	cartoon
minimum	stum	clump	cocoon
misbecome	succumb	crump	Colquoun
modicum	sugar-plum	dump	commune
moratorium	sum	frump	coon
mum	swum	hump	croon
natatorium	symposium	jump	Doon
numb	tedium	lump	doubloon
odium	thrum	mugwump	dragoon
opium	thumb	mump	dune
opprobrium	troublesome	plump	*eftsoon*
overcome	tum	pump	entune
pabulum	tum-tum	rump	*excommune*
palladium	tweedledum	slump	*expugn*
pandemonium	tympanum	stump	festoon
pelargonium	unplumb	sump	forenoon
pendulum	vacuum	thump	frigatoon
pericardium	venturesome	trump	gadroon
petroleum	viaticum		galloon

āle, câre, ădd, ärm, åsk; mē, hẹre, ĕnd; īce, ĭll;

gambroon	quintroon	Chesterton	Parthenon
gazon	racoon	done	pentagon
gossoon	Rangoon	dun	percussion-gun
harpoon	ratoon	Dunn	phenomenon
harvest-moon	rigadoon	foredone	polygon
hewn	rough-hewn	forerun	prolegomenon
honey-moon	rune	foster-son	pun
immune	saloon	fun	quaternion
inopportune	Schroon	galleon	run
importune	seroon	Galveston	sally lunn
impugn	shalloon	ganglion	shun
intercommune	*shoon*	garrison	simpleton
jejune	simoon	gonfalon	singleton
June	soon	gun	skeleton
lacune	spadroon	halcyon	son
lagoon	spittoon	hard-run	spun
lampoon	spontoon	hard-won	stun
loon	spoon	Helicon	sun
lune	strewn	homespun	sunn
macaroon	swoon	hon	ton
Mahoun	tune	Hun	tun
maroon	Tycoon	jettison	unbegun
mid-noon	typhoon	Middleton	underrun
monsoon	untune	minute-gun	undone
moon	walloon	mon	unison
musketoon		myrmidon	unnun
noon	**ŬN**	none	venison
octoroon	A 1	nun	Whitsun
opportune	accordion	Number one	won
oppugn	Albion	Oberon	
oversoon	amazon	oblivion	**ŬNCH**
overstrewn	begun	octagon	brunch
pantaloon	benison	one	bunch
patroon	bun	orison	clunch
picaroon	Bunn	outdone	crunch
picayune	cardamon	outrun	hunch
platoon	caparison	orison	lunch
poltroon	cinnamon	overdone	munch
pontoon	colophon	overrun	punch
prune	comparison	pantechnicon	scrunch
quadroon		paragon	

ōld, ôr, ŏdd, oil, fŏŏt, out; ūse, ûrn, ŭp; THis, thin

ŬND

disattuned
unattuned
untuned
wound
attuned, etc.
crooned, etc.

ŬND

bund
cummerbund
dunned
fund
immund
moribund
obrotund
orotund
punned
refund
retund
Rosamond
rotund
rubicund
shunned
stunned
unparagoned
unsunned
verecund
(cf. ŬN+ed)

ŬNG

among
behung
betongue
bung
clung
dung
flung
high-strung
hung
lung

mother-tongue
overhung
pung
rung
slung
sprung
strung
stung
sung
swung
tongue
underhung
Ung
unhung
unstrung
unsung
unwrung
upsprung
wither-wrung
wrung
young

ŬNGD

bunged
double-tongued
honey-tongued
leather-lunged
loud-lunged
pleasant-
    tongued
shrill-tongued
silver-tongued
tongued
trumpet-
    tongued

ŬNGK

bunk
chunk
drunk

flunk
funk
hunk
junk
monk
plunk
punk
quidnunc
shrunk
skunk
slunk
spunk
stunk
sunk
trunk
unk
wunk

ŬNGKT

bunked
compunct
conjunct
defunct
disjunct
funked
trunked

ŬNGST

amongst
clung'st, etc.

ŬNJ

allonge
blunge
dispunge
expunge
lunge
muskellunge
plunge
sponge

ŬNS

dunce
once
(cf. affront+s)

ŬNT

affront
afront
blunt
brunt
bunt
confront
exeunt
forefront
front
grunt
hunt
Lunt
punt
runt
shunt
sprunt
stunt
wont

ŬNTH

month
run'th, etc.

ŬNZ

Cameroons
eftsoons
croons, etc.

ŬP

adroop
aggroup
apple-scoop
cantaloupe

āle, câre, ădd, ärm, åsk; mē, hĕre, ĕnd; īce, ĭll;

cock-a-hoop
coop
croup
droop
drupe
dupe
Guadeloupe
group
hoop
jupe
liripoop
loop
nincompoop
poop
recoup
roup
scoop
scroop
sloop
soup
stoop
stoup
supe
swoop
troop
troupe
unhoop
whoop

ŪP

blowing-up
buttercup
crup
cup
fed up
grace-cup
gup
hard-up
keyed-up
loving-cup
make-up

pup
scup
setter-up
slap-up
stirrup-cup
sup
tup
up
up-and-up
wassail-cup

ŪPT

abrupt
corrupt
cupped
disrupt
erupt
incorrupt
interrupt
supped

ŪR

abature
abbreviature
abjure
adjure
allure
amateur
amour
aperture
armature
assure
blackamoor
boor
breviature
brochure
calenture
candidature
caricature
cocksure
colure

comfiture
conjure
connoisseur
contour
coverture
cure
curvature
cynosure
demure
detour
discomfiture
divestiture
dure
endure
ensure
entablature
epicure
expenditure
forfeiture
furniture
garmenture
garniture
guipure
immature
immure
impure
insecure
insure
intermure
inure
investiture
judicature
Kohinoor
ligature
liqueur
literature
lure
manicure
manure
mature
miniature

moor
obscure
Ostermoor
overture
paramour
pedicure
perdure
perendure
poor
portraiture
premature
primogeniture
procure
pure
quadrature
reassure
reinsure
secure
sepulture
signature
sinecure
spoor
sure
tablature
temperature
tour
troubadour
unmoor
unsure
vestiture
water-cure
your
you're
(cf. Ū+er)

ŪR

aberr
astir
aver
befur

bestir	coeur	batterer	demolisher
blur	colporteur	bibliographer	determiner
burr	connoisseur	bickerer	diameter
chirr	farceur	biographer	diaper
concur	franc-tireur	blandisher	discoverer
confer	friseur	blazoner	disparager
cur	frondeur	blunderer	distributer
defer	hauteur	blusterer	dowager
demur	litterateur	borrower	driveller
deter	mitrailleur	botherer	embellisher
disinter	persifleur	brandisher	emblazoner
err	restaurateur	broiderer	enameler
fir	trouveur	burdener	encourager
fur	voltigeur	burnisher	endeavourer
her	voyageur	calender	engenderer
incur		caliper	enlightener
infer	administer	canister	enlivener
inter	admonisher	carpenter	establisher
Kerr	adulterer	caterer	examiner
knur	adventurer	cellarer	Excalibur
liqueur	affiancer	chafferer	executioner
myrrh	almoner	challenger	fashioner
occur	amphitheatre	character	favorer
per	answerer	chatterer	flatterer
prefer	arbiter	cherisher	flutterer
purr	archiater	chorister	forager
recur	armiger	chronicler	foreigner
refer	armourer	cofferer	forester
shirr	artificer	comforter	forfeiter
sir	astrologer	commissioner	furtherer
slur	astronomer	commoner	galloper
spur	autobiographer	confectioner	gardener
stir	baluster	conjurer	gatherer
transfer	banisher	coroner	gossamer
were	banister	cottager	gossiper
whir	banqueter	coverer	harbinger
	banterer	cricketer	harborer
accoucheur	bargainer	customer	harvester
amateur	barometer	cylinder	hexameter
chasseur	barrister	decipherer	idolater
chauffeur	barterer	deliverer	imprisoner

āle, câre, ădd, ärm, ăsk; mē, hẹre, ĕnd; īce, ĭll;

interpreter	pepperer	saunterer	victualer
islander	perjurer	scavenger	villager
jabberer	pesterer	scimiter	vintager
juniper	petitioner	sepulchre	visiter
Jupiter	pewterer	sinister	voyager
languisher	philologer	skirmisher	wagerer
lavender	philosopher	slanderer	wagoner
lavisher	phonographer	slaughterer	wanderer
lecturer	photographer	slumberer	wassailer
leveller	pilferer	smatterer	waverer
libeller	pillager	sophister	whimperer
lingerer	pitier	sorcerer	whisperer
lithographer	plasterer	splutterer	widower
loiterer	plunderer	squanderer	wonderer
Londoner	polisher	stenographer	worshipper
Lowlander	porringer	stutterer	
lucifer	posturer	succorer	blearier
malingerer	poulterer	sufferer	breezier
manager	practitioner	swaggerer	brinier
manufacturer	presbyter	tamperer	burlier
mariner	prisoner	terrier	cheerfuller
marshaller	probationer	tetrameter, etc.	cheerier
massacre	profferer	theatre	cheerlier
measurer	provender	thermometer	chillier
messenger	publisher	thunderer	cleanlier
milliner	punisher	topographer	cosier
minister	purchaser	torturer	costlier
miniver	quarreller	totterer	creamier
modeller	quaverer	traveller	creepier
murderer	questioner	treasurer	crueller
murmurer	ransomer	trespasser	curlier
mutterer	ravager	trumpeter	dingier
nourisher	ravisher	typographer	dizzier
officer	reasoner	upholsterer	doughtier
palaverer	register	usurer	dowdier
parishioner	relinquisher	utterer	drearier
passenger	reveller	valuer	drowsier
pasturer	reversioner	vanquisher	dustier
patterer	rioter	vaporer	earlier
pensioner	riveter	venturer	easier
pentameter	roisterer	verderer	eerier

emptier
evener
filmier
filthier
fleecier
flightier
flimsier
foamier
friendlier
funnier
fussier
giddier
gloomier
glossier
goutier
grimier
guiltier
happier
healthier
heavier
hillier
holier
homelier
horrider
huffier
hungrier
huskier
icier
inkier
jollier
juicier
kindlier
kinglier
knightlier
likelier
lissomer
lithesomer
livelier
loftier
lonelier
lonesomer

lovelier
lowlier
loyaler
merrier
mightier
moldier
mossier
mournfuller
muskier
mustier
narrower
noisier
pearlier
pleasanter
portlier
princelier
prosier
rosier
rowdier
ruggeder
seemlier
shinier
shoddier
showier
sightlier
silenter
sillier
skilfuller
skinnier
sleepier
slimier
soapier
solider
spicier
spikier
spongier
spoonier
springier
spritelier
steadier
stealthier

stingier
stormier
stuffier
stupider
sturdier
sunnier
surlier
thirstier
thriftier
timider
trustier
vivider
wealthier
wearier
wheezier
windier
winsomer
wintrier
(cf. ambassador
and other ŎR
words)

ŬRB

acerb
blurb
curb
disturb
gerb
herb
perturb
Serb
suburb
superb
verb

ŬRBD

imperturbed
uncurbed
undisturbed
unperturbed
curbed, etc.

ŬRCH

besmirch
birch
church
lurch
perch
research
search
smirch
weeping-birch

ŬRCHT

unsmirched
birched, etc.

ŪRD

gourd
reassured
self-assured
unassured
uninsured
unmatured
abjured, etc.
ensured, etc.

ŬRD

absurd
begird
bird
Cape Verde
curd
engird
frigate-bird
gallows-bird
gird
heard
hedge-bird
herd
humming-bird
Kurd

lady-bird
lovebird
mocking-bird
night-bird
overheard
pilot-bird
sea-bird
sherd
shirred
snow-bird
song-bird
storm-bird
surd
third
undergird
ungird
unsepulchred
verd
word
(see ŬR + ed)

ŬRF

scurf
serf
surf
turf

ŬRG

berg
burg
exergue
Goldberg
Heidelberg
iceberg

ŬRJ

converge
demiurge
deterge
dirge
diverge

dramaturge
emerge
gurge
immerge
merge
purge
scourge
serge
splurge
Spurge
submerge
surge
thaumaturge
urge
verge

ŬRJD

unurged
converged, etc.

ŬRK

O'Rourke

ŬRK

Burke
cirque
clerk
dirk
fancy-work
frostwork
handiwork
irk
jerk
jerque
kirk
lurk
master-work
murk
perk
quirk
shirk

smirk
stirk
Turk
underwork
water-work
wonderwork
work
yerk

ŬRKT

overworked
irked, etc.

ŬRL

becurl
bepearl
burl
charity-girl
churl
curl
earl
furl
girl
hurl
impearl
knurl
merle
mother-of-pearl
pearl
pirl
purl
querl
seed-pearl
skirl
swirl
thurl
twirl
uncurl
unfurl
upcurl
upwhirl

whirl
whorl

ŬRLD

impearled
new-world
old-world
pearled
uncurled
underworld
world
becurled, etc.

ŬRM

affirm
berm
confirm
derm
disaffirm
firm
germ
infirm
isotherm
misterm
pachyderm
reaffirm
sperm
squirm
term
worm

ŬRMD

unconfirmed
affirmed, etc.

ŬRN

bourn

ŬRN

adjourn
astern

		ŪRS	verse
attorn	urn	accurse	worse
Berne	yearn	adverse	
burn		amerce	
Byrne	**ŪRND**	asperse	**ŪRST**
churn	hard-earned	averse	accurst
concern	unconcerned	becurse	athirst
Dern	undiscerned	birse	becurst
durn	unlearned	burse	burst
discern	unturned	coerce	curst
earn	adjourned, etc.	converse	double-first
erne		curse	durst
eterne	**ŪRNT**	cutpurse	*erst*
externe	burnt	disburse	first
fern	earnt	disperse	Hearst
Hearn	learnt	diverse	Hurst
Hearne	unburnt	Erse	outburst
hern	unlearnt	excurse	thirst
intern	weren't	foster-nurse	uncursed
interne		hearse	unversed
inurn	**ŪRNZ**	herse	versed
kern	Burns	imburse	verst
learn	Kearns	immerse	worst
lucern	(see ŪRN + s)	inhearse	accursed, etc.
lucerne		intersperse	
O'Byrne	**ŪRP**	inverse	**ŪRT**
overturn	blurp	nurse	Adelbert
pirn	burp	perverse	advert
quern	chirp	precurse	alert
return	discerp	purse	animadvert
secern	*extirp*	rehearse	assert
sojourn	twirp	reimburse	avert
spurn	usurp	reverse	begirt
stern		sesterce	Bert
subaltern	**ŪRPT**	submerse	blurt
taciturn	chirped	subverse	cert
tern	excerpt	terce	chert
turn	usurped	terse	concert
unconcern		transverse	controvert
unlearn	**ŪRS**	traverse	convert
upturn	bourse	universe	curt
			desert

āle, câre, ădd, ärm, åsk; mē, hęre, ĕnd; īce, ĭll;

dessert
dirt
disconcert
divert
engirt
Englebert
Ethelbert
evert
exert
expert
exsert
extrovert
flirt
girt
gurt
hurt
indesert
inert
inexpert
insert
intersert
intervert
introvert
invert
liverwort
malapert
obvert
pert
pervert
preconcert
retrovert
revert
sea-girt
shirt
skirt
spirt
spurt
squirt
subvert
syrt
transvert

ungirt
unhurt
vert
wert
Wirt
wort

ÛRTH

berth
birth
dearth
earth
firth
fuller's-earth
girth
inearth
mirth
penny-worth
Perth
unearth
unworth
worth

ÛRTZ

Wurtz
(see ÛRT + s)

ÛRV

conserve
curve
deserve
disserve
incurve
nerve
observe
outcurve
preserve
reserve
serve
subserve
swerve

unnerve
verve

ÛRVD

ill-deserved
undeserved
well-preserved
conserved, etc.

ÛRVZ

turves
conserves, etc.

ŪRZ

Tours
yours
amours, etc.

ÛRZ

furze
(see ÛR + s)

ŪS

abstruse
abuse
adduce
Bruce
burnoose
caboose
calaboose
Charlotte-russe
conduce
cruse
deduce
deuce
diffuse
disuse
douce
Druce
educe

excuse
flower-de-luce
goose
hypotenuse
induce
introduce
juice
loose
luce
misuse
moose
noose
nous
pappoose
obtuse
occluse
pertuse
produce
profuse
puce
recluse
reduce
reproduce
retuse
Roos
Russ
seduce
sluice
spruce
superinduce
Syracuse
Toulouse
traduce
transluce
truce
unloose
unsluice
use
vamoose
Zeus

ŬS

abaculus	platypus	amphibious	cautelous
abacus	plus	analogous	cavernous
acephalus	polypus	androgenous	censorious
angelus	pus	androphagous	ceremonious
animus	radius	anemophilous	chivalrous
blunderbuss	ranunculus	anfractuous	cinereous
bus	repercuss	angulous	circuitous
buss	rhus	anomalous	clamorous
caduceus	Russ	anonymous	commodious
Cerberus	sarcophagus	anserous	congruous
convolvulus	Sirius	antipathous	compendious
cumulus	stimulus	aqueous	consanguin-
cuss	succubus	arborous	eous
denarius	syllabus	arduous	conspicuous
discuss	tantalus	armigerous	contempora-
Erebus	Tartarus	assiduous	neous
esophagus	terminus	augurous	contemptuous
excuss	thus	balsamiferous	conterminous
fuss	truss	barbarous	contiguous
harquebus	untruss	beauteous	continuous
Hesperus	us	bibulous	contrarious
hippopotamus		bicephalous	contumelious
humerus	abstemious	bigamous	copious
hydrocephalus	acclivitous	bipetalous	courteous
ignis fatuus	acephalous	bituminous	covetous
impetus	acidulous	blasphemous	crapulous
incubus	adulterous	blusterous	credulous
incuss	adventurous	boisterous	crepusculous
Leviticus	agricolous	bounteous	Cretaceous
minimus	albuminous	bulbiferous	criminous
muss	aliferous	*burdenous*	curious
nautilus	aligerous	burglarious	dangerous
nonplus	alimonious	cadaverous	deciduous
nucleus	alkalous	calamitous	deleterious
octopus	alluvious	calcareous	delirious
omnibus	aluminous	calumnious	devious
overplus	amatorious	cancerous	dexterous
Pegasus	Americus	cankerous	diaphanous
percuss	amorous	cantankerous	diatomous
phosphorus	ambiguous	carboniferous	discourteous
	amphibolous	carnivorous	disingenuous

doloriferous	gratuitous	inharmonious	multivious
dolorous	gregarious	iniquitous	murderous
dubious	harmonious	injurious	murmurous
dulcifluous	hazardous	innocuous	mutinous
duteous	herbaceous	inodorous	mysterious
emulous	heterogeneous	inquisitorious	nauseous
endogenous	hideous	insensuous	nebulous
envious	hilarious	insidious	necessitous
eponymous	homogeneous	instantaneous	nectareous
equilibrious	homologous	invidious	nefarious
erroneous	humorous	jeopardous	notorious
ethereous	idolatrous	laborious	numerous
exiduous	igneous	languorous	oblivious
expurgatorious	ignominious	lascivious	obsequious
extempora-	illustrious	lecherous	obstreperous
neous	*imaginous*	leguminous	obvious
extraneous	*immeritous*	libellous	odious
fabulous	impecunious	libidinous	odoriferous
farinaceous	imperious	ligneous	odorous
fastidious	impervious	litigious	oleaginous
fatuitous	impetuous	ludicrous	ominous
fatuous	impious	lugubrious	omnivorous
felicitous	imponderous	luminous	onerous
felonious	imposturous	luxurious	opprobrious
ferruginous	incendious	magnanimous	oviparous
fluminous	incestuous	marvelous	pachyderma-
fortitudinous	incommodious	mellifluous	tous
fortuitous	incongruous	melodious	parsimonious
fossiliferous	inconspicuous	membranous	pendulous
frivolous	incredulous	meretorious	penurious
fuliginous	incurious	metalliferous	perfidious
furious	indecorous	meticulous	periculous
garrulous	indigenous	miraculous	perilous
gelatinous	indubious	miscellaneous	perjurous
generous	industrious	mischievous	perspicuous
globulous	inebrious	monogamous	pervious
glorious	infamous	monotonous	pesterous
glutenous	infelicitous	mountainous	pestiferous
glutinous	ingenious	mucilaginous	petalous
gluttonous	ingenuous	multifarious	piteous
graminivorous	inglorious	multitudinous	platinous

platitudinous
plenteous
poisonous
polygamous
ponderous
populous
posthumous
precarious
precipitous
predaceous
preposterous
presumptuous
previous
promiscuous
prosperous
pseudony-
mous
punctilious
pusillanimous
quarrelous
querulous
rancorous
rapturous
ravenous
rebellious
resinous
ridiculous
rigorous
riotous
roisterous
ruinous
sacchariferous
salacious
salubrious
sanctimonious
sanguineous
saponaceous
savorous
scandalous
scintillous
scrofulous

scrupulous
scrutinous
scurrilous
sedulous
sensuous
serious
setaceous
sibilous
simultaneous
sinuous
slanderous
slumberous
solicitous
somniferous
spontaneous
spurious
stentorious
strenuous
stridulous
studious
subterraneous
sulphurous
sumptuous
supercilious
superfluous
synchronous
synonymous
tautologous
tedious
temerarious
tempestuous
tenebrous
tenuous
thunderous
timidous
timorous
tintinnabulous
tortuous
torturous
traitorous
treacherous

treasonous
tremulous
tuberculous
tumultuous
tyrannous
ubiquitous
unanimous
unchivalrous
undulous
unscrupulous
uproarious
ungenerous
usurious
uxorious
vacuous
vagarious
vainglorious
valetudinarious
valetudinous
valorous
vaporous
various
vegetous
velutinous
venomous
ventriculous
venturous
verdurous
verisimilous
verminous
vernaculous
vertiginous
vicarious
vicissitudinous
victorious
vigorous
villainous
viperous
virtuous
vitreous
viviparous

vociferous
voluminous
voluptuous
voraginous
vortiginous
vulturous
zoophagous

ŬSH

barouche
bonne-bouche
bouche
cartouche
debouch
douche
gobemouche
Hindu Kush
Joosh
mouche
ruche
Scaramouch

ŬSH

blush
brush
crush
flush
gush
hush
lush
missel-thrush
mush
outblush
outrush
plush
rush
slush
thrush
tush
underbrush
uprush

āle, câre, ădd, ärm, ȧsk; mē, hęre, ĕnd; īce, ĭll;

ŬSK

adusk
brusque
busk
dehusk
dusk
fusc
husk
Lusk
musk
rusk
subfusk
tusk

ŬSP

cusp

ŪST

adduced
unproduced
deduced, etc.

boost
browst
joust
loosed
noosed
roost
spruced
unloosed
roust
vamoosed

ŬST

adjust
adust
angust
august
bedust
betrust
bust

coadjust
combust
crust
disgust
distrust
dost
dust
encrust
entrust
fust
gust
just
lust
mistrust
must
non-plussed
robust
rust
self-distrust
stardust
thrust
trust
unjust
untrussed
(see ŬS + ed)

ŪT

absolute
acute
argute
arrowroot
astute
attribute
baldicoot
beaut
birthday suit
boot
bruit
brute
Butte
cahoot

cheroot
chute
comminute
commute
compute
confute
constitute
coot
cornute
cute
deaf-mute
depute
destitute
dilute
dispute
disrepute
dissolute
electrocute
emeute
enroot
en route
execute
first-fruit
flute
forbidden-fruit
fruit
galoot
hirsute
hoot
imbrute
immute
impute
institute
involute
irresolute
jute
loot
lute
marabout
meute
minute

moot
mute
newt
outshoot
overshoot
parachute
permute
persecute
Piute
pollute
prosecute
prostitute
pursuit
Rajput
recruit
refute
repute
resolute
root
route
salute
scoot
scute
shoot
snoot
solute
soot
subacute
substitute
suit
suppute
toot
transmute
unboot
unroot
uproot
upshoot
Ute
versute
volute

ōld, ôr, ŏdd, oil, fŏŏt, out; ūse, ûrn, ŭp; THis, thin

ŬT

abut
astrut
besmut
betel-nut
but
butt
catgut
clear-cut
coconut
crut
cut
glut
gut
halibut
hut
jut
Lilliput
McNutt
mutt
nut
occiput
outshut
peanut
putt
rebut
rut
scut
scuttle-butt
shut
slut
smut
strut
surrebut
tut
uncut
waterbutt
woodcut

ŪTH

besmooth

booth
polling-booth
smooth
soothe

Ūth

booth
Duluth
forsooth
insooth
ruth
sleuth
sooth
tooth
truth
uncouth
untooth
untruth
youth

Ŭth

doth

ŪTHD

unsoothed
smoothed, etc.

ŪTS

cahoots
boots, etc.

ŬTS

smuts
(see ŬT + s)

ŪV

amove
approve
behoove
disapprove
disprove

groove
improve
ingroove
move
prove
remove
reprove
you've

ŬV

above
belove
dove
foxglove
glove
lady-love
light-o'-love
love
mourning-dove
self-love
shove
true-love
turtle-dove
unglove

ŪVD

unimproved
unmoved
unproved
unreproved
approved, etc.

ŬVD

unbeloved
unloved
beloved, etc.

ŪZ

abuse
accuse
amuse

bemuse
Betelgeuse
blues
booze
bruise
choose
circumfuse
confuse
contuse
cruise
cruse
diffuse
disabuse
disuse
effuse
enthuse
excuse
fuse
guze
Hughes
incuse
infuse
interfuse
lose
mews
misuse
muse
news
noose
ooze
percussion-fuse
perfuse
peruse
refuse
ruse
Santa Cruz
sea-ooze
snooze
suffuse
superinfuse

āle, câre, ădd, ärm, ăsk; mē, hęre, ĕnd; īce, ĭll;

the blues	**ŪZ**	does	ill-used
transfuse	Chartreuse	doz.	misused
trews		fuzz	self-accused
use	**ŬZ**	Luz	abused, etc.
Vera Cruz		Uz	
who's	abuzz		**ŪZH**
whose	buzz	**ŪZD**	rouge
(see Ū + s)	coz	fused	Bruges

ōld, ôr, ŏdd, oil, fŏŏt, out; ūse, ûrn, ŭp; THis, thin

Section II

WORDS ACCENTED ON THE SYLLABLE BEFORE THE LAST: PENULTS; FEMININE RHYMES; DOUBLE RHYMES

A

For a discussion of words included under the accented vowels following, see the beginning of A rhymes in Section I.

Ā'ad
naiad

Ā'al
Baal
betrayal
defrayal
portrayal
surveyal

Ā'an
Biscayan

Ā'ans
abeyance
conveyance
purveyance
surveyance

Ā'ant
abeyant

Ā'ba
copaiba
Faba

Ä'ba
Kaaba

Ā'ban
Laban

ĂB'ard
(see ĂB'urd)

ĂB'as
Barabbas

ĂB'ath
Sabbath

Ä'be
Rabe

ĂB'er etc.
(see ĂB'ur, etc.)

ĂB'es
abbess

ĂB'est
blabbest
dabbest
drabbest
gabbest
grabbest

jabbest
stabbest

ĂB'eth
blabbeth
dabbeth
gabbeth
grabbeth
jabbeth
stabbeth

Ā'bez
Jabez
tabes
(cf. Ā'bi + s)

Ā'bi
Abey
baby
maybe

ĂB'i
abbey
Abbie
babby
cabby
crabby
dabby

drabby
flabby
gabby
grabby
rabbi
scabby
shabby
slabby
tabby

Ä'bi
kohl-rabi
tabi
Wahabi

ĂB'id
rabid
tabid

ĂB'ij
cabbage

ĂB'ik
decasyllabic
dissyllabic
hendecasylla-
bic
imparisyllabic

āle, câre, ădd, ärm, àsk; mē, hĕre, ĕnd; īce, ĭll;

monosyllabic
multisyllabic
octosyllabic
parisyllabic
polysyllabic
quadrisyllabic
syllabic
trisyllabic

ĂB'il

labile
(cf. ĂB'l)

Ā'bin

Sabine

ĂB'ing

blabbing
cabbing
confabbing
dabbing
gabbing
jabbing
nabbing
slabbing
stabbing
taxicabbing

ĂB'it

cohabit
grab it
habit
inhabit
rabbet
rabbit
riding-habit

ĂB'jekt

abject

Ā'b'l

Abel

able
Abe'll
Babel
cable
disable
enable
fable
flabel
gable
label
Mabel
sable
stable
table
unable
unstable

ĂB''l

babble
bedabble
bedrabble
brabble
cabble
dabble
drabble
gabble
gibble-gabble
grabble
rabble
ribble-rabble
scabble
scrabble

Ā'blest

ablest
cablest, etc.

ĂB'lest

babblest
bedabblest
brabblest

dabblest
drabblest
gabblest
scrabblest

ĂB'let

tablet

ĂB'leth

cableth, etc.

ĂB'leth

babbleth
bedabbleth
brabbleth
dabbleth
drabbleth
gabbleth
grabbeth
scrabbleth

ĂB'li

babbly
dabbly
drably

ĂB'ling

babbling
bedabbling
bedrabbling
brabbling
cabbling
dabbling
drabbling
gabbling
grabbling
scrabbling

ĂB'lish

disestablish
establish

re-establish
stablish

Ā'blur

abler
disabler
enabler
fabler
stabler
tabler

ĂB'lur

babbler
bedrabbler
brabbler
cabbler
dabbler
drabbler
gabbler
grabbler
scabbler
scrabbler

Ā'bob

nabob

ĂB'ot

abbot
Abbott
Cabot
sabot

Ā'bra

candelabra

Ā'brak

day-break

ĂB'sens

absence

ĂB'sent

absent

ōld, ôr, ŏdd, oil, fŏŏt, out; ūse, ûrn, ŭp; THis, thin

Ā'bur	**ĂCH'est**	hatches	hatchment
beggar-my-	*attachest*	latches	*ratchment*
neighbor	*catchest*	matches	
belabor	*detachest*	Natchez	**ĂCH'up**
caber	*dispatchest*	patches	catchup
Gheber	*hatchest*	scratches	
labor	*latchest*	snatches	**ĂCH'ur**
neighbor	*matchest*	thatches	attacher
saber	*patchest*	unlatches	back-scratcher
tabor	*scratchest*		body-snatcher
	snatchest	**ĂCH'i**	catcher
ĂB'ur	*thatchest*	catchy	cony-catcher
beslabber	*unlatchest*	patchy	detacher
blabber		snatchy	dispatcher
bonny-clabber	**ĂCH'et**		fly-catcher
dabber	Bob Cratchet	**ĂCH'ing**	hatcher
grabber	hatchet	attaching	matcher
jabber	latchet	batching	patcher
knabber	ratchet	catching	scratcher
nabber		detaching	snatcher
slabber	**ĂCH'eth**	dispatching	Thacher
stabber	*attacheth*	hatching	thatcher
	batcheth	latching	unlatcher
ĂB'urd	*catcheth*	matching	
unlabored	*detacheth*	patching	**ĂCH'wa**
belabored, etc.	*dispatcheth*	scratching	hatchway
	hatcheth	snatching	
ĂB'urd	*latcheth*	thatching	**ĂCH'wurk**
beslabbered	*matcheth*	unlatching	catchwork
jabbered	*patcheth*		patchwork
scabbard	*scratcheth*	**ĂCH'les**	
slabbered	*snatcheth*	matchless	**Ā'dä**
tabard	*thatcheth*	patchless	hey-day
	unlatched	scratchless	lay-day
ĂCH'el		thatchless	May-day
Rachel	**ĂCH'ez**		pay-day
Vachel	attaches	**ĂCH'ment**	play-day
	batches	attachment	
ĂCH'el	catches	catchment	**Ā'dä**
hatchel	detaches	detachment	Ada
satchel	dispatches	dispatchment	armada

cicada	aided	heavy-laden	*madest*
Grenada	ambuscaded	laden	*over-persuadest*
Maida	barricaded	maiden	*persuadest*
Veda	bejaded	menhaden	*pervadest*
Zayda	blockaded	mermaiden	staidest
	braided	milkmaiden	*tradest*
ĂD'a	brocaded	overladen	*upbraidest*
dada	cannonaded	sea-maiden	*wadest*
	degraded	serving-maiden	
ĂD'a	dissuaded	underladen	**ĂD'est**
armada	evaded	unladen	*addest*
cicada	faded		baddest
Dada	graded	**ĂD'en**	*gaddest*
Granada	invaded	engladden	gladdest
Grenada	jaded	gladden	maddest
haggada	masqueraded	McFadden	*paddest*
Nevada	persuaded	madden	saddest
posada	pervaded	Macfadden	
Sierra Nevada	raided	sadden	**ĂD'eth**
	serenaded		*aideth*
	shaded	**ĂD'en**	*bejadeth*
ĂD'am	traded	Aden	*braideth*
Adam	unaided		*degradeth*
madam	unbraided	**ĂD'ens**	*dissuadeth*
McAdam	unfaded	cadence	*evadeth*
	unshaded	(see ĂD'ans)	*fadeth*
ĂD'ans, ĂD'ens	upbraided		*invadeth*
aidance	waded	**ĂD'ent**	*madeth*
cadence		cadent	*over-per-*
decadence	**ĂD'ed**	(see ĂD'ant)	*suadeth*
	added		*persuadeth*
ĂD'ant, ĂD'ent	padded	**ĂD'est**	*pervadeth*
abradant	plaided	*abradest*	*raideth*
aidant	superadded	*aidest*	*serenadeth*
cadent		*bejadest*	*spadeth*
decadent	**ĂD'en**	*braidest*	*tradeth*
	Aden	*degradest*	*upbraideth*
ĂD'kap	Aidenn	*dissuadest*	*wadeth*
madcap	bower-maiden	*evadest*	
	dairy-maiden	*fadest*	**ĂD'eth**
ĀD'ed	handmaiden	*invadest*	*addeth*
abraded			

ōld, ôr, ŏdd, oil, foŏt, out; ūse, ûrn, ŭp; THis, thin

gladdeth
paddeth

ĂD'ez
Hades
(cf. ĂD'its)

ĂD'ful
gladful
madful
sadful, etc.

Ā'di
belady
Brady
braidy
cadi
cascady
fady
glady
Grady
lady
landlady
Maidie
O'Grady
shady

ĂD'ĭ
caddie
caddy
daddy
faddy
finnan haddie
laddie
paddy
plaidie
sugar daddy

Ä'di
cadi
irade

Mahdi
wadi

ĂD'ij
adage

ĂD'ik
decadic
dyadic
faradic
haggadic
monadic
nomadic
Sotadic
sporadic
tetradic
triadic
vanadic

ĂD'ing
abrading
aiding
ambuscading
barricading
bejading
blockading
braiding
brocading
cascading
co-aiding
crusading
degrading
dissuading
enfilading
evading
fading
free-trading
gasconading
grading
invading
jading

lading
masquerading
overlading
over-persuad-
   ing
parading
persuading
pervading
raiding
retrograding
serenading
shading
spading
trading
unbraiding
underaiding
unlading
upbraiding
wading

ĂD'ing
adding
gadding
gladding
madding
padding
superadding

ĂD'is
Addis
caddis

ĂD'ish
maidish
mermaidish
oldmaidish
staidish

ĂD'ish
baddish
caddish

faddish
gladdish
maddish
radish
saddish

ĂD'it
adit

ĂD'iz
ladies, etc.

ĂD'iz
caddies, etc.

ĂD'jet
gadget
Padgett

ĂD''l
cradle
encradle
ladle

ĂD''l
addle
astraddle
bestraddle
daddle
faddle
fiddle-faddle
paddle
raddle
saddle
skedaddle
spraddle
staddle
straddle
unsaddle

ĂD'les
aidless

āle, câre, ădd, ärm, åsk; mē, hėre, ĕnd; īce, ĭll;

barricadeless
bladeless
braidless
brigadeless
brocadeless
fadeless
gradeless
maidless
paradeless
serenadeless
shadeless
spadeless
tradeless

ĂD'li

gradely
retrogradely
staidly

ĂD'li

badly
Bradley
gladly
madly
sadly

ĂD'ling

cradling
encradling
ladling

ĂD'ling

addling
daddling
faddling
fiddle-faddling
paddling
raddling
saddling
skedaddling
straddling

spraddling
unsaddling

ĂD'lok

padlock

ĂD'lur

addler
daddler
faddler
fiddle-faddler
paddler
raddler
saddler
skedaddler
straddler

ĂD'man

Cadman

ĂD'mus

Cadmus

ĂD'ne

Ariadne

ĂD'nes

staidness
unstaidness

ĂD'nes

badness
gladness
madness
plaidness
sadness

Ā'do

ambuscado
barricado
bastinado

camisado
carbonado
crusado
dado
desperado
fumado
gambado
grenado
muscovado
renegado
scalado
stoccado
strappado
tornado

ĂD'o

foreshadow
overshadow
shadow

Ă'do

amontillado
amorado
avocado
bravado
Colorado
dado
desperado
El Dorado
imbrocado
Mikado
passado
pintado
stoccado
strappado
travado

ĂD'od

foreshadowed
overshadowed

shadowed
unshadowed

ĂD'ok

haddock
paddock
raddocke
shaddock

ĂD'on

Abaddon

ĂD'os

extrados
intrados

ĂD'pol

tadpole

ĂD'som

gladsome
madsome

ĂD'ur

aider
barricader
blockader
braider
crusader
degrader
dissuader
evader
free-trader
gasconader
grader
harquebusader
invader
nadir
over-persuader
parader
persuader

promenader	*delayest*	*betrayeth*	Ā'far
raider	*dismayest*	*bewrayeth*	Mayfair
serenader	*disobeyest*	*brayeth*	Playfair
trader	*displayest*	*conveyeth*	
unbraider	*essayest*	*decayeth*	Ā'feld
upbraider	*flayest*	*defrayeth*	Mayfield
wader	*frayest*	*delayeth*	Rayfield
	gainsayest	*dismayeth*	
ĂD'ur	*gayest*	*disobeyeth*	ĂF'est
adder	*grayest*	*displayeth*	*chafest*
bladder	*greyest*	*essayeth*	safest
gadder	*inlayest*	*frayeth*	*vouchafest*
gladder	*inveighest*	*gainsayeth*	
ladder	*layest*	*inlayeth*	ĂF'eth
madder	*mislayest*	*inveigheth*	*chafeth*
padder	*missayest*	*layeth*	Japheth
sadder	*obeyest*	*mislayeth*	*vouchsafeth*
step-ladder	*overpayest*	*missayeth*	
	overstayest	*obeyeth*	ĂF'gan
Ă'dur	*payest*	*overpayeth*	Afghan
cadre	*playest*	*overstayeth*	
	portrayest	*payeth*	ĂF'i
ĂD'us	*prayest*	*playeth*	baffy
gradus	*preyest*	*portrayeth*	chaffy
	purveyest	*prayeth*	daffy
ĂD'vent	*repayest*	*preyeth*	draffy
advent	*sayest*	*purveyeth*	taffy
	slayest	*repayeth*	
ĂD'vurb	*sprayest*	*sayeth*	ĂF'ik
adverb	*stayest*	*slayeth*	anaglypto-
	surveyest	*stayeth*	graphic
Ā'est	*swayest*	*strayeth*	autobiographic
allayest	*underpayest*	*surveyeth*	autographic
arrayest	*uplayest*	*swayeth*	bibliographic
assayest	*waylayest*	*underpayeth*	biographic
bayest	*weighest*	*uplayeth*	cacographic
betrayest		*waylayeth*	calligraphic
bewrayest	Ā'eth	*weigheth*	cartographic
brayest	*allayeth*		cinemato-
conveyest	*arrayeth*	ĂF'a	graphic
defrayest	*assayeth*	café	chirographic

choregraphic
chorographic
clinographic
cosmographic
cryptographic
crystallo-
  graphic
diagraphic
epigraphic
epitaphic
ethnographic
galvanographic
geographic
glyptographic
graphic
heliographic
heterographic
hierographic
historiographic
holographic
homolographic
horologio-
  graphic
hydrographic
hyetographic
ichnographic
ideographic
idiographic
lexicographic
lexigraphic
lichenographic
lithographic
logographic
maffick
monographic
orographic
orthographic
paleographic
pantographic
paragraphic
pasigraphic

petrographic
phonographic
photographic
polygraphic
pornographic
Sapphic
scenographic
sciagraphic
seismographic
selenographic
seraphic
siderographic
sphenographic
stenographic
stereographic
stratigraphic
stratographic
stylographic
tachygraphic
telegraphic
topographic
traffic
uranographic
xylographic
zincographic
zoographic

ÅF'ing

chafing
enchafing
vouchsafing

ÅF'ing

chaffing
gaffing
graffing
heliographing
lithographing
paragraphing
photographing

stenographing
telegraphing

ÅF'ing

laughing
quaffing
strafing

ÅF'ir

sapphire

ÅF'ish

raffish

ÅF''l

baffle
gaffle
haffle
raffle
scraffle
snaffle
yaffle

ÅF'li

safely
unsafely

ÅF'ling

baffling
haffling
raffling
scraffling
snaffling

ÅF'lur

baffler
haffler
raffler
scraffler

ÅF'ne

Daphne

ÅF'old

Saffold
scaffold
(cf. baffled,
  etc.)

ÅF'ral

taffrail

ÅF'rik

Afric

ÅF'ron

saffron

ÅF'som

laughsome

ÅF'ted

upwafted
wafted

ÅF'ted

drafted
engrafted
grafted
ingrafted
rafted
shafted
wafted

ÅF'test

daftest
draughtest
graftest
waftest

ÅF'teth

draughteth
grafteth
wafteth

ōld, ôr, ŏdd, oil, fŏŏt, out; ūse, ûrn, ŭp; THis, thin

ĂFT'hors	**ĂF'tŭr**	**ĂG'a**	jagged
draft-horse	wafture	plaga	ragged
shaft-horse		rutabaga	scragged
	ĂF'tŭr	saga	
ĂF'ti	after		**ĂG'end**
safety	dafter	**ĂG'a**	fag-end
	drafter	aga	lagend
ĂF'ti	grafter	quagga	
crafty	hafter		**ĂG'est**
drafty	hereafter	**Ā'ga**	*plaguest*
grafty	hereinafter	aga	vaguest
	laughter	saga	
ĂF'tij	rafter		**ĂG'est**
waftage	thereafter	**ĂG'al**	*braggest*
	wafter	plagal	*draggest*
ĂF'ting		vagal	*faggest*
engrafting	**Ā'ful**		*flaggest*
drafting	playful	**ĂG'an**	*gaggest*
grafting	trayful	Hagan	*laggest*
hafting		pagan	*naggest*
rafting	**Ā'fur**	O'Hagan	*waggest*
shafting	chafer	Regan	
wafting	cockchafer		**ĂG'eth**
	safer	**ĂG'ard**	*braggeth*
ĂFT'les	wafer	haggard	*draggeth*
craftless		laggard	*faggeth*
draftless	**ĂF'ur**	staggard	*flaggeth*
graftless	Kaffir	staggered	*gaggeth*
raftless	zaffer	swaggered	*laggeth*
shaftless			*naggeth*
	ĂF'ur	**ĂG'art**	*raggeth*
ĂF'ton	chaffer	braggart	*waggeth*
Afton	gaffer	Taggart	
Grafton	*graffer*		**ĂG'i**
	laugher	**ĂG'at**	Aggie
ĂFTS'man	quaffer	agate	baggy
craftsman		moss-agate	braggy
draftsman	**ĂF'urd**	(cf. faggot,	craggy
handicraftsman	Safford	etc.)	faggy
raftsman	Stafford	**ĂG'ed**	flaggy
	Trafford	cragged	gaggy

jaggy	naggish	flagman	Ā'go
knaggy	waggish	ragman	farrago
laggy			Chicago
Maggie	**ĂG'l**	**ĂG'ment**	Santiago
naggy	*bedaggle*	fragment	
quaggy	bedraggle		**ĂG'on**
raggy	daggle	**ĂG'mir**	dragon
saggy	draggle	quagmire	flagon
scraggy	gaggle		pendragon
shaggy	haggle	**ĂG'mit**	snap-dragon
slaggy	raggle	stalagmite	wagon
snaggy	raggle-taggle		
swaggy	straggle	**ĂG'nant**	**ĂG'ot**
taggy	waggel	stagnant	fagot
waggy	waggle		maggot
		ĂG'nat	magot
ĂG'ij	**ĂG'ling**	agnate	(cf. agate)
baggage	*bedaggling*	magnate	
	bedraggling	stagnate	**ĂG'pi**
ĂG'ing	daggling		magpie
bagging	draggling	**ĂG'nes**	
bragging	gaggling	Agnes	**ĂG'pip**
dragging	haggling		bagpipe
fagging	raggling	**ĂG'net**	
flagging	straggling	magnet	**ĂG'rans**
gagging	waggling		flagrance
lagging		**ĂG'num**	fragrance
magging	**ĂG'lur**	magnum	(cf. vagrants)
nagging	bedraggler		
ragging	daggler	**Ā'go**	**ĂG'rant**
sagging	draggler	farrago	flagrant
tagging	haggler	imago	fragrant
unflagging	straggler	lumbago	infragrant
wagging	waggler	plumbago	vagrant
		sago	
ĂG'is	**ĂG'mag**	San Diego	**ĂG'rik**
haggis	cagmag	Terra del	chiragric
		Fuego	podagric
ĂG'ish	**ĂG'man**	Tobago	
haggish	bagman	virago	**Ā'gu**
laggish	dragman	vorago	ague

ĀG′ur

maigre
plaguer
vaguer

ĀG′ur

bagger
bragger
carpet-bagger
dagger
dragger
fagger
flagger
four-bagger
gagger
jagger
lagger
magger
nagger
one-bagger
ragger
sagger
stagger
swagger
tagger
three-bagger
two-bagger
wagger

Ā′gus

archimagus
choragus
magus

ĀGZ′man

cragsman
dragsman

Ä′hoo

wahoo
yahoo

Ā′i

clayey
sprayey
wheyey

Ä′ib

sahib

Ā′ij

drayage
weighage

Ā′ik

alcaic
algebraic
alhambraic
altaic
ante-Mosaic
Aramaic
archaic
Brahmaic
Chaldaic
Cyrenaic
deltaic
Eddaic
Hebraic
Jagataic
Judaic
laic
mosaic
paradisaic
pharisaic
prosaic
Ptolemaic
Passaic
Romaic
saddusaic
Sinaic
sodaic
spondaic
stanzaic

tesseraic
trochaic
voltaic

Ā′ing

allaying
amaying
arraying
assaying
baying
belaying
betraying
bewraying
braying
claying
conveying
decaying
defraying
delaying
disarraying
dismaying
disobeying
displaying
essaying
flaying
foresaying
fraying
gainsaying
haying
horseplaying
hurraying
inlaying
interlaying
interplaying
inveighing
laying
maying
mislaying
missaying
neighing
obeying

outlaying
outstaying
outweighing
overlaying
overpaying
overstaying
paying
playing
portraying
praying
prepaying
preying
purveying
relaying
repaying
saying
slaying
soothsaying
spraying
staying
surveying
swaying
undecaying
underpaying
underplaying
unsaying
unweighing
waylaying
weighing

Ā′is

dais
Lais

Ā′ish

clayish
gayish
grayish
greyish
silver-grayish

Ā'ist	ĂJ'eth	hadji	cageless
algebraist	*ageth*	howadji	gageless
archaist	*assuageth*		gaugeless
prosaist	*engageth*	ĂJ'ik	pageless
Ptolemaist	*enrageth*	archipelagic	rageless
	gageth	ellagic	sageless
Ā'izm	*gaugeth*	hemorrhagic	stageless
Chaldaism	*outrageth*	magic	wageless
Laism	*presageth*	omophagic	
Mosaism	*rageth*	pelagic	ĂJ'li
prosaism	*wageth*	tragic	sagely
Ă'ja	ĂJ'ez	ĂJ'il	ĂJ'ling
maharajah	ages	agile	cageling
rajah	assuages	fragile	
	cages		ĂJ'ment
ĂJ'ant	disengages	ĂJ'in	assuagement
pageant	encages	imagine	encagement
	engages		engagement
ĂJ'ed	enrages	ĂJ'ind	enragement
aged	gages	imagined	pre-engagement
	gauges	unimagined	presagement
Ā'jent	greengages		
agent	outrages	ĂJ'ing	ĂJ'nes
reagent	pages	aging	sageness
	pre-engages	assuaging	
ĂJ'est	presages	caging	ĂJ'ur
agest	rages	engaging	assuager
assuagest	sages	enraging	cager
engagest	stages	gaging	disengager
enragest	wages	gauging	engager
gagest	weather-gages	paging	enrager
gaugest		presaging	gager
outragest	Ā'ji	raging	gauger
presagest	cagey	staging	major
ragest	ragy		old-stager
sagest	sagy	ĂJ'ing	pager
stagest	stagy	badging	presager
swagest		cadging	sager
wagest	ĂJ'i	ĂJ'les	stager
	cadgy	ageless	

trumpet-major
wager

ĂJ'ur
agger
badger
cadger

ĂJ'us
advantageous
ambagious
contagious
courageous
disadvanta-
  geous
oragious
outrageous
rampageous
umbrageous

Ă'ka
raca
Jamaica

ĂK'a
alpaca
Malacca
polacca

Ă'ka
jararaca

ĂK'al
jackal
pack-all

ĂK'ard
placard

ĂK'at
baccate

placate
saccate

ĂK'brand
crack-brained
slack-brained

ĂK'but
hackbut
sackbut

ĂK'daw
jackdaw

ĂK'doun
breakdown
shakedown

ĂK'ed
naked
(see ĂK + ed)

ĂK'en
awaken
bacon
forsaken
Jamaican
kraken
mistaken
overtaken
shaken
taken
undertaken
uptaken
waken
wind-shaken

ĂK'en
blacken
bracken
slacken

Ă'ken
kraken

ĂK'end
unawakened
awakened, etc.

ĂK'est
achest
awakest
bakest
betakest
breakest
fakest
forsakest
makest
mistakest
opaquest
overtakest
partakest
quakest
rakest
shakest
spakest
stakest
takest
undertakest
wakest

ĂK'est
attackest
backest
blackest
clackest
crackest
hackest
lackest
packest
quackest
rackest
ransackest

sackest
slackest
smackest
tackest
trackest
unpackest
whackest

ĂK'et
bracket
flacket
Hackett
jacket
packet
placket
racket
tacket

ĂK'eth
acheth
awaketh
baketh
betaketh
breaketh
faketh
forsaketh
maketh
mistaketh
overtaketh
partaketh
quaketh
raketh
shaketh
staketh
taketh
undertaketh
waketh

ĂK'eth
attacketh
backeth

blacketh
clacketh
cracketh
hacketh
lacketh
packeth
quacketh
racketh
ransacketh
sacketh
slacketh
smacketh
tacketh
tracketh
unpacketh
whacketh

ĂK'ful
wakeful

ĂK'i
achey
braky
caky
faky
flaky
quaky
shaky
snaky

ĂK'i
blackey
cracky
knacky
lackey

Ä'ki, Ā'ki
sake
saki

ĂK'ij
breakage

ĂK'ij
package
sackage
stackage
trackage
wrackage

ĂK'ik
bacchic
stomachic

ĂK'sen
vaccine

ĂK'ing
aching
awaking
baking
betaking
braking
breaking
caking
faking
flaking
forsaking
heartbreaking
making
mistaking
overtaking
partaking
quaking
raking
shaking
slaking
spaking
staking
taking
undertaking
unmaking
upbreaking

uptaking
waking

ĂK'ing
attacking
backing
bivouacing
blacking
clacking
cracking
hacking
knacking
lacking
packing
quacking
racking
ransacking
sacking
slacking
smacking
tacking
thwacking
tracking
unpacking

ĂK'ish
rakish
snakish

ĂK'ish
blackish
brackish
knackish
quackish

ĂK'kloth
packcloth
sackcloth

ĂK'l
cackle

crackle
grackle
hackle
macle
quackle
ramshackle
shackle
tackle

ĂK"ld
unshackled
cackled, etc.

ĂK'les
knackless
sackless
trackless

ĂK'let
lakelet

ĂK'li
blackly
cackly
crackly
shackly
tackly

ĂK'ling
cackling
crackling
hackling
shackling
tackling

ĂK'log
backlog
hacklog

ĂK'lur
cackler

crackler	Ā'kob	arefaction	subtraction
hackler	Jacob	*assuefaction*	tabefaction
shackler		attraction	taction
tackler	ĂK'on	benefaction	tepefaction
	bacon	calefaction	torrefaction
ĂK'man	Lacon	coaction	traction
blackman	Macon	compaction	transaction
jackman	(see ĀK'en)	contaction	tumefaction
packman		contraction	
	Ā'korn	counteraction	ĂK'shus
ĂK'me	acorn	counter-	factious
acme		attraction	fractious
	ĀP'pot	detraction	
ĂK'nes	crackpot	dissatisfaction	ĂK'sez
blackness	jackpot	distraction	axes
slackness		exaction	battle-axes
	ĂK'red	extraction	relaxes
ĂK'ne	sacred	faction	taxes
acne		fraction	waxes
hackney	ĂK'rid	inaction	Maxie's
	acrid	infraction	
ĀK'ning		interaction	ĂK'si
wakening	ĂK'ring	labefaction	biotaxy
	sacring	liquefaction	braxy
Ā'ko		lubrifaction	Cotopaxi
Saco	ĂK'rist	madefaction	flaxy
Waco	sacrist	malefaction	heterotaxy
		paction	homotaxy
ĂK'o	ĂK'rum	petrifaction	taxi
goracco	sacrum	protraction	waxy
shako	simulacrum	putrefaction	
Sacco		rarefaction	
tobacco	ĂK'sent	reaction	ĂK'sid
	accent	redaction	flaccid
Ă'ko		refraction	
guaco	ĂK'ses	retraction	ĂK'sim
guanaco	access	retroaction	maxim
Gran Chaco		rubefaction	
	ĂK'shun	satisfaction	ĂK'sis
ĂK'of	abstraction	stupefaction	axis
take-off	action	subaction	praxis

āle, câre, ădd, ārm, ȧsk; mē, hẽre, ĕnd; īce, ĭll;

synaxis	contracted	*distracteth*	retractile
taxis	counteracted	*enacteth*	tactile
	detracted	*exacteth*	tractile
ĂK"sl	distracted	*extracteth*	
axle	enacted	*protracteth*	ĂK'ting
	exacted	*reacteth*	abstracting
ĂK'sman	extracted	*retracteth*	acting
cracksman	overacted	*subtracteth*	attracting
tacksman	protracted	*transacteth*	contracting
	reacted		counteracting
ĂK'son	refracted	ĂKT'ful	detracting
Anglo-Saxon	retracted	tactful	distracting
caxon	subtracted		double-acting
flaxen	transacted	ĂK'tik	enacting
Jackson	unacted	catallactic	exacting
klaxon	underacted	didactic	infracting
Saxon		emphractic	overacting
waxen	ĂK'test	eupractic	protracting
	abstractest	galactic	reacting
ĂK'sta	*actest*	lactic	refracting
backstay	*attractest*	parallactic	retracting
jack-stay	*contractest*	prophylactic	retroacting
	counteractest	protactic	self-acting
ĂK'ston	*detractest*	stalactic	subtracting
Braxton	*distractest*	syntactic	transacting
Caxton	*enactest*	tactic	underacting
Claxton	exactest		
	extractest	ĂK'tiks	ĂK'tis
ĂK'swell	*protractest*	catallactics	practice
Maxwell	*reactest*	tactics	
	retractest		ĂK'tit
ĂK'tat	*subtractest*	ĂK'til	stalactite
ablactate	*transactest*	attractile	
lactate		contractile	ĂK'tiv
tractate	ĂK'teth	dactyl	abstractive
	abstracteth	didactyl	active
ĂK'ted	*acteth*	heterodactyl	attractive
abstracted	*attracteth*	leptodactyl	calefactive
acted	*contracteth*	pachydactyl	coactive
attracted	*counteracteth*	protractile	contractive
compacted	*detracteth*	pterodactyl	counteractive

ōld, ôr, ŏdd, oil, fŏŏt, out; ūse, ûrn, ŭp; THis, thin

counter-
  attractive
detractive
diffractive
distractive
enactive
extractive
inactive
liquefactive
olfactive
petrifactive
protractive
putrefactive
radioactive
rarefactive
reactive
refractive
retractive
retroactive
satisfactive
stupefactive
subtractive
tractive

ĂKT'les

actless
bractless
factless
tactless
tractless

ĂKT'li

compactly
exactly
matter-of-factly

ĂKT'ment

enactment
extractment
reenactment

ĂKT'nes

compactness
exactness
intactness

ĂK'to

de facto
ex post facto

ĂK'tres

actress
benefactress
contractress
detractress
exactress
factress
malefactress

ĂK'tūr

facture
fracture
manufacture
vitrifacture

ĂK'tūr

abstracter
actor
attracter
benefactor
climacter
compacter
contractor
detractor
distracter
enactor
exacter
extractor
factor
infractor
malefactor
olfactor

phylacter
protractor
refractor
retractor
subtracter
tractor
transactor

ĂK'tus

cactus

ĂK'up

break-up
make-up
wake-up

ĀK'ur

acre
awaker
baker
ballad-maker
bookmaker
breaker
dressmaker
faker
fakir
forsaker
God's-acre
heart-breaker
image-breaker
maker
match-maker
mischief-maker
mistaker
nacre
painstaker
partəker
peacemaker
Quaker
raker

Sabbath-
  breaker
shaker
taker
truce-breaker
undertaker
watchmaker

ĂK'ur

attacker
backer
blacker
bushwhacker
clacker
cracker
hacker
hijacker
knacker
lacker
lacquer
nut-cracker
packer
racker
ransacker
sacker
slacker
smacker
tacker
tracker
unpacker
whacker

ĀK'urz

breakers
awakers, etc.

ĂK'us

Bacchus
Flaccus
jacchus

ĂK'wa
backway
pack-way
trackway

Ā'kwen
fay-queen
May-queen

ĂK'woodz
backwoods

Ā'la
gala
shillalah

ĂL'a
Allah
calla
galla
mashallah
Valhalla

Ă'la
gala

ĂL'ad
ballad
salad

ĂL'ans
balance
counter-
  balance
outbalance
overbalance
valance

ĂL'anst
balanced
outbalanced

overbalanced
unbalanced

ĂL'ant
assailant
exhalent
inhalent
intranscalent
transcalent

Ā'lanks
phalanx

ĂL'ard
Allard
Ballard
Callard
mallard

ĂL'as
balas
Dallas
palace
Pallas
(cf. chalice)

ĂL'ast
ballast

ĂL'bum
album

ĂL'burd
jailbird

ĂL'burt
Albert

ĂL'dik
heraldic

ĂL'din
Aldine

Ă'le
finale
kali
pastorale

Ā'leb
Caleb

ĂL'ek
Aleck
Halleck
smart Aleck
Talleck

ĂL'en
Alan
Allen

ĂL'enj
challenge

ĂL'enjd
challenged
unchallenged

ĂL'ens
valence

ĂL'ent
gallant
talent
ungallant

Ā'les
clayless
dayless
hayless
payless

playless
preyless
rayless
sprayless
wayless

ĂL'est
ailest
assailest
availest
bailest
balest
bewailest
curtailest
derailest
detailest
engaolest
entailest
exhalest
failest
frailest
hailest
halest
impalest
inhalest
mailest
nailest
outsailest
palest
prevailest
quailest
railest
regalest
retailest
sailest
scalest
trailest
unveilest
wailest

ĂL'et	**Ā'lez** or **Ā'lez**	Aunt Sally	**ĂL'ik**
gallet	or **Ä'lez**	bally	Gaelic
mallet	Gonzales	dally	malic
palate		dilly-dally	Salic
palette	**ĂL'fa**	galley	
pallet	alfalfa	Hallie	**ĂL'ik**
sallet	alpha	kali	acrocephalic
valet		Lallie	bimetallic
	ĂL'fred	O'Malley	brachisto-
ĂL'eth	Alfred	rally	cephalic
aileth		Sallie	brachycephalic
assaileth	**ĂL'ful**	sally	cephalic
availeth	baleful	shilly-shally	dolichocephalic
baileth	pailful	tally	encephalic
baleth	wailful	tomalley	eurycephalic
bewaileth		valley	Gallic
curtaileth	**ĂL'gam**	(see estatically,	grallic
deraileth	amalgam	and all other	italic
detaileth		-ally adjec-	macrencephalic
engaoleth	**Ā'li**	tives, ĂL +	macrocephalic
entaileth	Bailey	i)	malic
exhaleth	bailie		medallic
haileth	Braley	**ĂL'id**	mesocephalic
impaleth	capercaillie	dallied	metallic
inhaleth	daily	dilly-dallied	microcephalic
naileth	Daly	impallid	monometallic
outsaileth	gaily	invalid	oxalic
paleth	Haley	pallid	phallic
prevaileth	kali	rallied	platycephalic
quaileth	Mailly	sallied	salic
raileth	Maley	shilly-shallied	thallic
regaleth	rationale	tallied	Uralic
retaileth	shaly	valid	Vandalic
saileth	shillaly		vocalic
scaleth	ukelele	**ĂL'if**	
traileth	vale	bailiff	**ĂL'ik**
unveileth	(cf. palely,	Caliph	pashalik
veileth	etc.)		
waileth		**ĂL'ij**	**ĂL'iks**
	ĂL'i	bailage	calyx
	alley	curtailage	Salix
	Allie	retailage	

āle, câre, ădd, ärm, ăsk; mē, hęre, ĕnd; īce, ĭll;

ĂL'in or ÄL'in
Stalin

ĂL'ing
ailing
assailing
availing
bailing
baling
bewailing
blackmailing
countervailing
curtailing
derailing
detailing
empaling
entailing
exhaling
grayling
Greyling
hailing
haling
impaling
inhaling
jailing
mailing
nailing
outsailing
paling
prevailing
quailing
railing
regaling
retailing
sailing
scaling
Schmeling
tailing
trailing
unveiling

veiling
wailing
whaling
wholesaling

ĂL'ing
caballing
palling

ĂL'is
Alice
allice
chalice
Challis
malice
(cf. palace)

ĂL'is
Cornwallis

ĂL'ish
palish
shalish
stalish

ĂL'ji
cephalalgy
neuralgy
nostalgy
odontalgy

ĂL'jik
antalgic
cephalalgic
neuralgic
nostalgic
odontalgic

ĂL'kar
mailcar
railcar

ĂL'kat
defalcate
falcate

ĂL'kin
grimalkin

ĂL'ker
valkyr

ĂL'li
frailly
halely
palely
stalely
(cf. ĂL'i)

ĂL'ma
Alma
Thalma

ĂL'mat
palmate

ĂL'ment
ailment
assailment
availment
bailment
bewailment
curtailment
derailment
entailment
impalement
inhalement
prevailment
regalement
retailment

ĂL'mud
Talmud

ĂL'muk
Kalmuck

ĂL'nes
frailness
haleness
paleness
staleness

Ā'lo
halo

ĂL'o
All-hallow
aloe
callow
dishallow
fallow
hallow
mallow
marshmallow
sallow
shallow
summer-fallow
tallow
unhallow

ĂL'o
swallow
wallow
(see Ŏ'lo)

ĂL'on
gallon
talon

ĂL'on
salon

ĂL'op
gallop

ōld, ôr ŏdd, oil, fŏŏt, out; ūse, ûrᶇ, ŭp; THis, thin

jalap
scallop
shallop

ĂL'ot
ballot

ĂL'oz
gallows
hallows, etc.

ĂL'pin
Alpine
cisalpine
transalpine

ĂL'ping
scalping

ĂL'spin
tailspin

ĂL'ti
frailty

ĂL'to
alto
contralto

ĂL'to
rialto

ĂL'u
undervalue
value

ĂL'um
alum

ĂL'ūr
failure

ĂL'ŭr
assailer
bailer
baler
bewailer
curtailer
derailer
detailer
entailer
failer
frailer
gaoler
haler
impaler
inhaler
jailer
nailer
paler
prevailer
quailer
railer
regaler
retailer
sailer
sailor
Sayler
scaler
squalor
staler
tailor
Taylor
trailer
unveiler
wailer
whaler

ĂL'ur
caballer
pallor
valor

ĂL'us
callous
gallus

ĂL'va
Alva
Alvah
Halveh

ĂL'vij
salvage

ĂL'vin
Alvin
Calvin

ĂL'vo
salvo

ĂL'vur
quack-salver
salver
salvor

ĂL'vurt
Calvert

ĂL'win
Alwin

ĂL'ya
Bacchanalia
castalia
dahlia
mammalia
marginalia
paraphernalia
penetralia
regalia
saturnalia

terminalia
(cf. azalea)

ĂL'ya
dahlia

ĂL'ya
dahlia

ĂL'yan
alien
Australian
bacchanalian
Dædalian
episcopalian
Idalian
mammalian
marsupialian
Messalian
paralian
phantasmalian
Phigalian
Pygmalion
regalian
saturnalian
sesquipedalian
tenaillon
tobaccanalian
universalian

ĂL'yant
valiant

ĂL'yard
gaolyard
kailyard

ĂL'yo
intaglio
seraglio

ĂL'yon
battalion
Italian
medallion
rapscallion
rascallion
scallion
stallion

ĀLZ'man
dalesman
salesman
talesman
whalesman

ĂM'a
Bahama
krama

ĂM'a
Alabama
digamma
mamma

ĂM'a
Bahama
Brahma
cyclorama
cosmorama
Dalai Lama
diorama
drama
Fujiyama
georama
kaama
Kama
lama
llama
mamma
melodrama
neorama

panorama
pajama
pyjama
Rama
Teshu Lama
Yama
Yokohama

Ā'man
cayman
dayman
drayman
highwayman
layman

ĂM'ant
claimant
(cf. raiment,
    etc.)

ĂM'ant
clamant

ĂM'as
Lammas

ĂM'ask
damask

Ā'mat
day-mate
desquamate
hamate
playmate

ĂM'az
cat's pajamas
Brahmas, etc.

ĂM'ba
gamba

ĂM'bent
lambent

ĂM'bi
namby-pamby

ĂM'bik
choliambic
choriambic
dithyrambic
elegiambic
galliambic
iambic

ĂM'bist
cambist
gambist

ĂM'bit
ambit
gambit

ĂM'kin
lambkin

ĂM'b'l
amble
bramble
gamble
preamble
ramble
scamble
scramble
shamble
skimble-
    skamble

ĂM'blest
amblest
gamblest
ramblest

scramblest
shamblest

ĂM'bleth
ambleth
gambleth
rambleth
scrambleth
shambleth

ĂM'b'lz
ambles
gambles
rambles
scrambles
shambles

ĂM'bling
ambling
brambling
gambling
rambling
scambling
scrambling
shambling

ĂM'blur
ambler
gambler
rambler
scambler
scrambler
shambler

ĂM'bo
ambo
crambo
flambeau
sambo
zambo

ĂM'bol
gambol

ĂM'brik
cambric

ĂM'bur
ante-chamber
chamber

ĂM'būr
tambour

ĂM'bur
amber
camber
clamber

ĂM'bus
dithyrambus
iambus

ĂM'bush
ambush

ĂM'el
camel
Campbell
enamel
entrammel
Hamal
mammal
trammel

ĂM'eld
enamelled
untrammelled

Ā'men
amen
Bremen

examen
flamen
foramen
gravamen
Haman
Lehmann
stamen

Ä'men
amen

Ā'ment
allayment
betrayment
defrayment
payment
prepayment
raiment
(cf. claimant)

ĀM'est
acclaimest
aimest
blamest
claimest
declaimest
defamest
disclaimest
exclaimest
flamest
framest
gamest
inflamest
lamest
maimest
namest
proclaimest
reclaimest
shamest
tamest

ĂM'est
crammest
dammest
damnest
rammest
shammest
slammest

ĂM'est
calmest
embalmest
salaamest

ĀM'eth
acclaimeth
aimeth
blameth
claimeth
declaimeth
defameth
disclaimeth
exclaimeth
flameth
foreshameth
frameth
inflameth
lameth
maimeth
nameth
overcameth
proclaimeth
reclaimeth
shameth
tameth

ĂM'eth
crammeth
dammeth
damneth
rammeth

shammeth
slammeth

ĂM'eth
calmeth
embalmeth
salaameth

ĂM'fir
samphire

ĂM'flet
pamphlet

ĂM'for
camphor

ĂM'ful
blameful
flameful
shameful

ĀM'ĭ
Amy
gamy
flamy
Mamie

ĀM'ĭ
chamois
clammy
gammy
mammy
rammy
shammy
tammy

ĂM'ĭ
balmy
calmy
Miami

palmy
pastrami
qualmy
salmi
swami

ÄM'ij
damage

ÄM'ik
Abrahamic
Adamic
adynamic
agamic
autodynamic
balsamic
biodynamic
ceramic
cinnamic
cosmoramic
cryptogamic
cycloramic
dioramic
dynamic
electro-
  dynamic
epithalamic
gamic
hydrodynamic
hyperdynamic
Islamic
isodynamic
keramic
monogamic
monogrammic
panoramic
parallelogram-
  mic
phanerogamic
polygamic
potamic

preadamic
telegrammic
trigrammic

ÄM'il
amyl
Tamil

ÄM'in
examine
famine
gamin

ÄM'ing
acclaiming
aiming
blaming
claiming
declaiming
defaming
disclaiming
exclaiming
flaming
framing
gaming
inflaming
laming
maiming
misnaming
naming
nicknaming
proclaiming
reclaiming
shaming
surnaming
taming

ÄM'ing
cramming
damming
damning

lambing
lamming
ramming
shamming
slamming
tramming

ÄM'ing
becalming
calming
embalming
qualming
salaaming

ÄM'is
amice
chlamys
tamis

ÄM'ish
lamish
tamish

ÄM'ish
affamish
enfamish
famish
Hamish
rammish

ÄM'ish
calmish
qualmish

ÄM'ist
embalmist
palmist
psalmist

ÄM'it
samite

ĀM'les
aimless
blameless
claimless
fameless
flameless
frameless
gameless
nameless
shameless
tameless

ÄM'les
balmless
palmless
psalmless
qualmless

ÄM'let
camlet
hamlet
samlet

ĀM'li
gamely
lamely
namely
tamely

ÄM'li
calmly

ÄM'ling
lambling

ÄM'ment
becalmment
embalmment

ĀM'nes
gameness

ōld, ôr, ŏdd, oil, fŏŏt, out; ūse, ûrn, ŭp; THis, thin

lameness	**ĂM'paz**	decamping	**AMP'ment**
sameness	pampas	encamping	decampment
tameness		lamping	encampment
	ĂM'pen	ramping	
ĂM'nes	dampen	scamping	**AMP'nes**
calmness		stamping	dampness
	ĂM'per	tamping	
ĂM'ok	ampere	tramping	**ĂM'pri**
hammock		vamping	lamprey
mammock	**ĂM'pest**		
	campest	**ĂM'pir**	**AMP'son**
ĂM'on	*crampest*	vampire	Lampson
Ammon	*dampest*		Sampson
backgammon	*decampest*	**ĂM'pish**	(cf. Samson)
daman	*encampest*	dampish	**AMP'ton**
gammon	*rampest*	scampish	Crampton
mammon	*scampest*		Hampton
salmon	*stampest*	**ĂM'p'l**	
shaman	*trampest*	ample	**ĂM'pur**
	vampest	*ensample*	camper
Ā'mond		example	champer
Raymond	**ĂM'peth**	sample	clamper
	campeth	trample	cramper
ĂM'ond	*crampeth*		damper
Hammond	*dampeth*	**ĂM'p'ld**	hamper
	decampeth	untrampled	pamper
Ā'mos	*encampeth*	sampled, etc.	scamper
Amos	*rampeth*		stamper
Shaemas	*scampeth*	**AMP'li**	tamper
	stampeth	damply	tramper
ĂM'oth	*trampeth*		vamper
mammoth	*vampeth*	**AMP'ling**	
		ensampling	**ĂM'purd**
ĂM'pan	**ĂM'pi**	sampling	hampered
jampan	crampy	trampling	pampered
sampan			tampered
tampan	**ĂM'ping**	**AMP'lur**	unhampered
	camping	ampler	
ĂM'part	clamping	exampler	**ĂM'pus**
rampart	cramping	sampler	campus
	damping	trampler	grampus

ĂM'rod	dammer	ĂM'zon	Susanna
ramrod	damner	damson	Susquehanna
	enamor		sultana
ĂM'rok	gammer	Ā'na	Texarkana
shamrock	glamor	Americana, etc	Tia Juana
	grammar	ana	Urbana
ĂM'stur	hammer	anana	
gamester	ninnyhammer	arcana	Ăn'a
	rammer	campana	Americana, etc.
ĂM'ond	shammer	Cartagena	acqua tofana
almond	slammer	Curtana	anana
bitter-almond	sledge-hammer	fistiana	banana
	stammer	Nicotiana	Curtana
ĀM'ur	yammer	poinciana	Fata Morgana
acclaimer	yellow-hammer	scena	fistiana
aimer		vox-humana	Guiana
blamer	ĂM'ur		iguana
claimer	Balmer	ĂN'a	kerana
declaimer	calmer	Americana, etc.	liana
defamer	embalmer	anna	Messana
disclaimer	palmer	bandana	Nirvana
disfamer		Christiana	purana
exclaimer	ĂM'wa	Diana	sultana
framer	tramway	fistiana	thana
gamer		Georgiana	zenana
inflamer	ĂM'us	Hanna	
Kramer	biramous	Hannah	Ā'nal
lamer	famous	Havana	anal
maimer	hamous	hosanna	
misnamer	ignoramus	Indiana	ĂN'al
namer	mandamus	ipecacuanha	annal
nicknamer	squamous	Joanna	cannel
proclaimer		Juliana	channel
reclaimer	ĂM'ut	Louisiana	empanel
shamer	gamut	manna	flannel
tamer		Montana	impanel
testamur	ĂM'zel	Pollyanna	panel
	amsel	Roxana	pannel
ĂM'ur	damsel	savanna	scrannel
clamor		Savannah	stannel
crammer	ĂM'zi	Stephana	unpanel
	Malmsey		

ĂN′alz
annals
flannels, etc.

ĂN′ant
complainant

ĂN′at
impanate
lanate

ĂN′at
khanate
pomegranate
tannate

ĂN′at
khanate

ĂN′bo
rainbow

ĂN′chest
launchest
stanchest

ĂN′chest
blanchest
scranchest

ĂN′chet
manchet
planchet

ĂN′cheth
launcheth
stancheth

ĂN′cheth
blancheth
scrancheth

ĂN′chez
launches
paunches
stanches

ĂN′chez
avalanches
blanches
branches
ranches

ĂN′chĭ
paunchy

ĂN′chĭ
branchy

ĂN′ching
launching
stanching

ĂN′ching
blanching
branching
ranching

ĂN′chĭz
affranchise
disfranchise
enfranchise
franchise

ĂNCH′les
launchless
paunchless

ANCH′les
branchless
ranchless
stanchless

ĂN′chur
launcher
stancher

ĂN′chur
brancher
rancher

ĂN′da
Amanda
jacaranda
Miranda
memoranda
propaganda
veranda

ĂN′ dal
Randall
(cf. Randle)

ĂN′dant
commandant
demandant
mandant

ĂN′dat
mandate

AND′bag
handbag
sand-bag

AND′bal
hand-ball
sand-ball

AND′boi
band-boy
sand-boy

AND′boks
bandbox
sand-box

AND′child
grand-child

ĂN′de
Rio Grande

ĂN′ded or
ĂN′ded
backhanded
banded
blackhanded
branded
candid
clean-handed
close-handed
commanded
contrabanded
countermanded
demanded
deodanded
disbanded
empty-handed
even-handed
expanded
first-handed
forehanded
fourhanded
freehanded
full-handed
handed
hard-handed
heavy-handed
high-handed
landed
left-handed
light-handed
lily-handed
neat-handed
open-handed
over-handed
red-handed

āle,   câre,   ădd,   arm,   ăsk;   mē,   hęre,   ĕnd;   īce,   ĭll;

remanded	*disbandeth*	**AN'dij**	**AN'd'l**
reprimanded	*expandeth*	bandage	candle
right-handed	*handeth*	glandage	dandle
short-handed	*landeth*	standage	handle
single-handed	*remandeth*		sandal
stranded	*reprimandeth*	**AN'ding** or	scandal
swift-handed	*standeth*	**AN'ding**	vandal
two-handed	*withstandeth*	ampersanding	
unbranded		banding	**AND'les** or
underhanded	**AN'dez**	branding	**AND'les**
unhanded	Andes	commanding	bandless
unlanded	Hernandez	countermand-	brandless
		ing	commandless
AN'dent	**AND'fast**	demanding	glandless
candent	handfast	disbanding	handless
scandent		expanding	landless
	AN'di	handing	sandless
AN'der	Andy	landing	strandless
reindeer	bandy	notwithstand-	
	brandy	ing	**AND'ling**
AN'dest or	candy	outstanding	brandling
AN'dest	dandy	remanding	handling
bandest	handy	reprimanding	
brandest	jaborandi	sanding	**AND'lur**
commandest	jackadandy	standing	Candler
demandest	Jim Dandy	stranding	chandler
disbandest	Mandy	understanding	dandler
expandest	pandy	withstanding	handler
grandest	randy		tallow-chandler
handest	Rio Grande	**AN'dish**	
landest	sandy	blandish	**AND'lord**
remandest	sugar-candy	brandish	landlord
reprimandest	unhandy	grandish	
standest		outlandish	**AND'li**
withstandest	**AN'did**		blandly
	bandied	**AN'dist**	grandly
AN'deth or	brandied	contrabandist	
AN'deth	candid	propagandist	**AND'mad**
bandeth	candied		hand-made
brandeth	uncandid	**AN'dit**	handmaid
commandeth	(cf. banded,	bandit	
demandeth	p. 328)		

ōld, ôr, ŏdd, oil, fŏŏt, out; ūse, ûrn, ŭp; THis, thin

ĂND'mark
landmark

ĂND'ment or
  ĂND'ment
commandment
disbandment
remandment

ĂND'nes
blandness
grandness

ĂN'do or
  ĂN'do
commando
Ferdinando
Fernando
grando
Hernando
lentando
Orlando

ĂN'don
abandon
Landon
Shandon

ĂND'out
handout

ĂN'dra or
  ĂN'dra
Alessandra
Alexandra
Cassandra

ĂN'drel
spandrel

ĂN'dres
pandress

ĂN'dres
laundress

ĂN'drik
polyandric
theandric

ĂN'dril
mandril

ĂN'drin
Alexandrine
salamandrine

ĂN'dri or
  ĂN'dri
chandry
commandry
meandry
polyandry
shandry

ĂN'dri
laundry

ĂN'drus
meandrous
polyandrous

ĂND'sir
grandsire

ĂND'skap
landscape

ĂND'son
grandson

ĂND'stand
band-stand
grand-stand

ĂN'dum
ad captandum
avizandum
mandom
memorandum
random
tandem

ĂN'dur
attainder
remainder

ĂN'dūr
grandeur

ĂN'dur or
  ĂN'dur
Africander
Alexander
back-hander
blander
bystander
brander
candor
commander
coriander
dander
demander
disbander
dittander
expander
gander
gerrymander
glander
goosey-gander
grander
hander
lander
Leander
meander
Menander

oleander
pander
philander
Pomander
remander
reprimander
right-hander
salamander
sander
slander
stander
understander
withstander

ĂN'dur
launder

ĂN'durd or
  ĂN'durd
meandered
pandered
philandered
slandered
standard

ĂN'durz
Sanders
Saunders

ĂNDZ'man
bandsman
landsman

Ā'nes
gayness
greyness

ĂN'est
abstainest
appertainest

arraignest

ĂN'est

ascertainest
attainest
canest
chainest
complainest
constrainest
containest
cranest
deignest
detainest
disdainest
enchainest
entertainest
explainest
feignest
humanest
inanest
maintainest
obtainest
ordainest
painest
plainest
profanest
rainest
refrainest
regainest
reignest
remainest
restrainest
retainest
sanest
stainest
strainest
sustainest
trainest
unchainest
urbanest
vainest
wanest

bannest
fannest
mannest
plannest
scannest
spannest
tannest

ĂN'et

gannet
granite
Janet
planet
quannet
(cf. pomegran-
ate)

ĂN'eth

abstaineth
appertaineth
arraigneth
ascertaineth
attaineth
caneth
chaineth
complaineth
constraineth
containeth
craneth
deigneth
detaineth
disdaineth
draineth
enchaineth
entertaineth
explaineth
feigneth
foreordaineth
gaineth
maintaineth

obtaineth
ordaineth
paineth
profaneth
raineth
refraineth
regaineth
reigneth
remaineth
restraineth
retaineth
staineth
straineth
sustaineth
traineth
unchaineth
waneth

ĂN'eth

banneth
fanneth
manneth
planneth
scanneth
spanneth
tanneth

ĂN'far

fanfare

ĂN'feld

Canfield

ĂN'ful

baneful
complainful
disdainful
painful

ĂN'gang

chain-gang
train-gang

ĂNG'gar

hangar

ĂNG'gor

languor

ĂNG'gur

anger
angor
clangor

ĂNG'gwid

languid

ĂNG'gwij

language

ĂNG'gwin

anguine
ensanguine
sanguine

ĂNG'gwish

anguish
languish

ĂNG'i

clangy
fangy
slangy

ĂNG'ing

banging
clanging
hanging
haranguing
overhanging
paper-hanging
slanging
slangwhanging
twanging

ōld, ôr, ŏdd, oil, fŏŏt, out; ūse, ûrn, ŭp; THis, thin

ĂNG′kest	ĂNG′king	ĂNGK′li	ĂNGK′wish
blankest	banking	blankly	vanquish
clankest	clanking	dankly	
dankest	embanking	frankly	**ĂNG′kur**
embankest	flanking	lankly	anchor
flankest	franking	rankly	banker
frankest	outflanking		blanker
lankest	outranking	**ĂNGK′ling**	canker
outflankest	planking	hankling	clanker
rankest	ranking	rankling	danker
thankest	spanking		encanker
sankest	thanking	**ĂNGK′ment**	flanker
spankest	yanking	bankment	franker
		embankment	hanker
ĂNG′ket	**ĂNG′kish**	outflankment	outflanker
banket	dankish		planker
blanket	frankish	**ĂNGK′nes**	pranker
	lankish	blankness	rancor
ĂNG′keth	prankish	crankness	ranker
clanketh		dankness	sheet-anchor
embanketh	**ĂNGK″l**	frankness	spanker
flanketh	ankle	lankness	tanker
franketh	crankle	rankness	thanker
outflanketh	hankle		unanchor
ranketh	rankle	**ĂNG′ko**	
sanketh		banco	**ĂNG′kurd**
thanketh	**ĂNGK′les**	calamanco	brancard
	bankless		cankered
ĂNGK′ful	clankless	**ĂNGK′shun**	tankard
prankful	crankless	sanction	unanchored
thankful	flankless		anchored, etc.
	plankless	**ĂNGK′shus**	
ĂNG′ki	prankless	anxious	**ĂNG″l**
cranky	rankless	**ĂNGK′tum**	angle
hanky	shankless	sanctum	bangle
hanky-panky	spankless		bemangle
lanky	thankless	**ĂNGK′wet**	bespangle
planky		banquet	brangle
pranky	**ĂNGK′let**		dangle
Yankee	anklet	**ĂNGK′wil**	disentangle
		tranquil	embrangle

ĂNG'l

entangle
interjangle
intertangle
jangle
mangle
mingle-mangle
phalangal
quadrangle
sea-tangle
spangle
strangle
tangle
triangle
twangle
untangle
Wrangel
wrangle

ĂNG"ld

new-fangled
star-spangled
angled, etc.

ĂNG'les

fangless
pangless

ĂNG'li

spangly
tangly

ĂNG'ling

angling
dangling, etc.

ĂNG'lur

angler
dangler, etc.

ĂNG'man

hangman

ĂNG'o

contango
fandango
mango
Pago Pago
tango

ĂNG'gri

angry

ĂN'grov

mangrove

ĂNG'stur

gangster

ĂNG'ur

banger
clangor
ganger
hangar
hanger
haranguer
paper-hanger
slang-whanger
straphanger

ĂN'hood

manhood

ĂN'i

Allegheny
brainy
Cheyney
Delaney
Eugenie
grainy
Rainey
rainy
veiny
zany

ĂN'i

Annie
branny
canny
cranny
Fannie
granny
mannie
Nannie
uncanny

ĂN'i

frangipani
Galvani
Hindustani
rani
soprani

ĂN'id

crannied

ĂN'ij

cranage
drainage

ĂN'ij

manage
pannage
tannage

ĂN'ik

Alcoranic
aldermanic
Alemannic
Aristophanic
botanic
Brahmanic
Britannic
charlatanic
diaphanic
ferricyanic

galvanic
Germanic
hydrocyanic
Indo-Germanic
interoceanic
lexiphanic
Magellanic
mechanic
Messianic
montanic
Mussulmanic
oceanic
organic
Ossianic
paganic
panic
Puranic
Puritanic
quercitannic
rhodanic
Romanic
satanic
stannic
sultanic
talismanic
tannic
tetanic
Theophanic
titanic
tympanic
tyrannic
Uranic
valerianic
volcanic
vulcanic

ĂN'iks

humanics
mechanics
panics

ĂN'ĭl	obtaining	tanning	ĂN'jest
anil	ordaining	trepanning	*arrangest*
	paining	unmanning	*changest*
ĂN'ĭl	pertaining		*derangest*
anile	plaining	ĂN'is	*disarrangest*
	planing	anise	*estrangest*
Ā'nim	preordaining		*exchangest*
paynim	profaning	ĂN'ish	*rangest*
	raining	Danish	strangest
ĂN'ing	refraining	sanish	
abstaining	regaining	urbanish	ĂN'jeth
airplaning	reigning	vainish	*arrangeth*
appertaining	reining		*changeth*
arraigning	remaining	ĂN'ish	*derangeth*
ascertaining	restraining	Alcoranish	*disarrangeth*
attaining	retaining	banish	*estrangeth*
bestaining	spraining	clannish	*exchangeth*
braining	staining	evanish	*interchangeth*
campaigning	straining	fannish	*rangeth*
caning	sustaining	mannish	
chaining	training	Mussulmanish	ĂN'jez
complaining	unchaining	planish	arranges
constraining	uncomplaining	Spanish	changes
containing	unfeigning	vanish	deranges
craning	uptraining		disarranges
deigning	veining	ĂN'ïst	enranges
deraigning	waning	Alcoranist	estranges
detaining		pianist	exchanges
disdaining	ĂN'ing	tanist	granges
draining	banning		interchanges
enchaining	canning	ĂN'jel	ranges
entertaining	fanning	angel	
entraining	flanning		ĂN'jez
explaining	inspanning	ĂN'jel	flanges
feigning	japanning	evangel	Ganges
foreordaining	manning		phalanges
gaining	outspanning	ĂN'jent	
graining	panning	frangent	ĂN'ji
hydroplaning	planning	plangent	mangy
ingraining	scanning	tangent	rangy
maintaining	spanning		

ĂN'jing
arranging
changing
counter-
  changing
deranging
disarranging
estranging
exchanging
interchanging
ranging
unchanging

ĂNJ'ling
changling

ĂNJ'les
changeless
rangeless

ĂNJ'li
strangely

ĂNJ'ment
arrangement
derangement
disarrangement
estrangement
exchangement
interchange-
  ment

ĂNJ'nes
strangeness

ĂN'jur
arranger
bushranger
changer
danger
deranger

disarranger
endanger
estranger
exchanger
granger
interchanger
manger
money-changer
ranger
stranger

**ĂN'ka or
  ĂN'ka**
Bianca

ĂN'kin
Hankin
Rankin

ĂN'king
Nanking

ĂN'kinz
Hankins
Rankins

ĂN'kok
Hancock

ĂN'land
mainland

ĂN'les
brainless
caneless
chainless
craneless
domainless
drainless
gainless
grainless
maneless

painless
rainless
stainless
swainless
vaneless

ĂN'les
banless
clanless
fanless
manless
planless
spanless
tanless

ĂN'li
gainly
humanely
inanely
insanely
mainly
plainly
profanely
sanely
vainly

ĂN'li
Danley
Manley
manly
spick-and-
  spanly
Stanley
unmanly

ĂN'ling
manling
tanling

ĂN'ment
arraignment

ascertainment
attainment
obtainment
ordainment

ĂN'nes
humaneness
inaneness
insaneness
plainness
profaneness
saneness

Ā'no
volcano

ĂN'o
piano
Hanno
soprano

Ā'no
guano
Montesano
piano
soprano

ĂN'ok
bannock
jannock

ĂN'on
Balleyshannon
cannon
canon
fanon
Shannon

ĂN'sa
gainsay

ĂN'sal
mainsail

ĂN'sel
cancel
chancel
handsel

ĂN'sest
advancest
chancest
dancest
enhancest
entrancest
glancest
prancest
romancest

ĂN'set
lancet

ĂN'seth
advanceth
chanceth
danceth
enhanceth
entranceth
glanceth
pranceth
romanceth

ĂN'sez
advances
chances
dances
enhances
entrances
expanses
finances
glances
lances

mischances
prances
romances
trances

ĂNS'fur
transfer

ĂN'shal
circumstantial
financial
substantial
supersubstan-
tial

ĂN'she
banshee

ĂN'shent
ancient

ĂN'shent
transient

ĂN'shun
expansion
mansion
scansion
stanchion

ĂN'si
aeromancy
aldermancy
alectoromancy
alectryomancy
aleuromancy
alphitomancy
anthropomancy
astragalo-
    mancy
austromancy

axinomancy
belomancy
bibliomancy
botanomancy
capnomancy
catoptromancy
ceromancy
chancy
chiromancy
cleromancy
consonancy
coscinomancy
crithomancy
crystallomancy
dactyliomancy
dancy
Delancey
enoptromancy
exorbitancy
extravagancy
exuberancy
fancy
gastromancy
geomancy
gyromancy
halomancy
hesitancy
hieromancy
hydromancy
ichthyomancy
lecanomancy
lithomancy
mendicancy
meteoromancy
mischancy
Miss Nancy
militancy
myomancy
Nancy
necromancy
occupancy

œnomancy
oneiromancy
onomancy
onychomancy
ophiomancy
ornithomancy
pedomancy
petulancy
precipitancy
pyromancy
psephomancy
psychomancy
sciomancy
sibilancy
sideromancy
significancy
spodomancy
stichomancy
supplicancy
sycophancy
tephramancy
termagancy
unchancy

ĂN'sid
fancied
rancid

ĂN'sing
advancing
chancing
dancing
enhancing
entrancing
fiancing
glancing
lancing
Lansing
necromancing
prancing
romancing

ĂN'sis
Frances
Francis

ĂN'sist
romancist

ĂN'siv
advancive
expansive

ĂNS'ment
advancement
enhancement
entrancement

ĂN'som
handsome
hansom
ransom
transom
unhandsome

ĂN'son
Anson
Hanson

ĂN'sta
main-stay

ĂN'sur
advancer
Anser
answer
cancer
chancer
chiromancer
dancer
enhancer
entrancer
geomancer

glancer
lancer
merganser
necromancer
prancer
romancer

ĂN'tā
infante

ĂN'ta
anta
Atalanta
Atlanta
infanta
Santa
Vedanta

ĂN'ta
Vedanta

ĂN'tal
consonantal
gigantal
quadrantal

ĂN'tam
bantam
phantom

ĂN'tans
acquaintance

ĂN'tazm
phantasm

ĂN'te
ante
Dante
dilettante

pococurante
zante

ĂN'te
andante
Dante
(cf. chianti)

ĂN'ted
acquainted
attainted
bepainted
besainted
depainted
fainted
feinted
painted
sainted
tainted
unacquainted
unattainted
unsainted
untainted

ĂN'ted, ĂN'ted
canted
chanted
decanted
enchanted
granted
implanted
panted
planted
ranted
recanted
slanted
supplanted

ĂN'test
acquaintest
faintest

feintest
paintest
quaintest
taintest

ĂN'test,
ĂN'test
cantest
chantest
decantest
enchantest
grantest
implantest
pantest
plantest
rantest
recantest
scantest
supplantest

ĂN'teth
acquainteth
feinteth
painteth
tainteth

ĂN'teth,
ĂN'teth
canteth
chanteth
decanteth
enchanteth
granteth
implanteth
panteth
planteth
recanteth
supplanteth

ĂN'tez
atlantes

corybantes
(cf. ĂN'ti + s)

ĂN'them
anthem

ĂNT'hood
sainthood

ĂN'thik
œnanthic
xanthic

ĂN'thin
acanthine
amaranthine
anthine
Rhadamanthine
tragacanthin
xanthin

ĂN'thur
anther
panther

ĂN'thus
acanthous
acanthus
Agapanthus
ailanthus
amianthus
anacanthous
ananthous
canthus
Chimonanthus
dianthus
epanthous
Galanthus
Hæmanthus
hysteranthous

polyanthus
synanthous

ĂN'ti
dainty

ĂN'ti
bacchante
canty
panty
scanty
shanty

ĂN'ti
aunty

ĂN'tif
plaintiff

ĂN'tij
advantage
disadvantage
plantage
vantage

ĂN'tik
antic
Atlantic
chiromantic
consonantic
corybantic
frantic
geomantic
gigantic
hierophantic
hydromantic
mantic
necromantic
onomantic
pedantic
pyromantic

romantic
spodomantic
sycophantic
transatlantic

ĂN'tik
Vedantic

ĂN'tin
adamantine
Brabantine
Byzantine
chrysele-
    phantine
Diophantine
elephantine
gigantine
Levantine

ĂN'ting
acquainting
attainting
fainting
feinting
painting
tainting
word-painting

ĂN'ting,
    ĂN'ting
Banting
canting
chanting
decanting
descanting
disenchanting
enchanting
granting
hanting
implanting

panting
planting
ranting
recanting
slanting
supplanting
transplanting

ĂN'tist
ignorantist
Kantist

ĂN'tist
Vedantist

ĂN'tiv
constraintive
plaintive

ĂN'tizm
dilettantism
ignorantism
Kantism
obscurantism
pococurantism
rantism

ĂN't'l
cantle
dismantle
immantle
mantel
mantle
scantle

ĂN't'ld
dismantled
ivy-mantled
mantled

ĂNT'let
cantlet

āle, câre, ădd, ārm, ăsk;   mē, hĕre, ĕnd;   īce, ĭll;

mantelet	ĂN'to or ĂN'to	ĂN'tur or	disdainer
plantlet	canto	ĂN'tur	drainer
	coranto	banter	enchainer
ĂNT'let	portmanteau	canter	entertainer
gauntlet	pro tanto	chanter	explainer
	quo warranto	decanter	feigner
ĂNT'let		descanter	gainer
gantlet	ĂN'tom	enchanter	grainer
	(see ĂN'tam)	granter	inaner
ĂNT'li		implanter	maintainer
quaintly	ĂN'ton	instanter	nonabstainer
saintly	Canton	Levanter	obtainer
unsaintly	Clanton	panter	ordainer
	Danton	planter	plainer
ĂNT'li	Scranton	ranter	profaner
aslantly	Stanton	recanter	refrainer
scantly		supplanter	regainer
	ĂN'tor	transplanter	restrainer
ĂNT'lik	cantor	trochanter	retainer
saintlike	grantor		saner
		ĂN'tur	stainer
ĂNT'ling	ĂN'tres	chanter	strainer
bantling	chantress	disenchanter	sustainer
mantling	enchantress	enchanter	trainer
scantling			unchainer
	ĂN'tri	ĂN'turn	uptrainer
ĂNT'lur	pantry	lantern	vainer
antler			
dismantler	ĂN'tri	ĂN'ur	ĂN'ur
mantler	chantry	abstainer	banner
pantler		appertainer	canner
	ĂN'tu	arraigner	fanner
ĂNT'ment	Bantu	ascertainer	japanner
disenchantment		attainer	lanner
enchantment	ĂN'tur	bestainer	manner
	acquainter	campaigner	manor
ĂNT'nes	fainter	complainer	planner
faintness	painter	constrainer	scanner
quaintness	quainter	container	spanner
	tainter	cordwainer	tanner
ĂNT'nes	word-painter	detainer	
scantness			

ōld, ôr, ŏdd, oil, fŏŏt, out; ūse, ûrn, ŭp; THis, thin

trepanner	Nathaniel	**ĂP'en**	*enwrappeth*
vanner	spaniel	happen	*flappeth*
	staniel		*lappeth*
ĂN'urd	water-spaniel	**ĂP'est**	*mappeth*
bannered		*apest*	*nappeth*
ill-mannered	**ĂN'yur**	*drapest*	*rappeth*
mannered	pannier	*escapest*	*sappeth*
unmannered		*gapest*	*slappeth*
well-mannered	**ĂN'za**	*rapest*	*snappeth*
	bonanza	*scrapest*	*trappeth*
ĂN'us	extravaganza	*shapest*	*wrappeth*
heinous	ganza		
incanous	stanza	**ĂP'est**	**ĂP'got**
Janus		*clappest*	scape-goat
Silvanus	**ĂNZ'feld**	*enwrappest*	
veinous	Mansfield	*flappest*	**ĂP'gras**
		lappest	scape-grace
ĂN'vas	**ĂN'zi**	*mappest*	
canvas	chimpanzeee	*nappest*	**ĂP'i**
canvass	pansy	*rappest*	crapy
	tansy	*sappest*	gapy
ĂN'vil		*slappest*	red-tapy
anvil	**ĂN'zvil**	*snappest*	scrapy
Danville	Janesville	*trappest*	
Granville	Zanesville	*wrappest*	**ĂP'i**
			chappy
ĂN'wurk	**Ā'o**	**ĂP'et**	gappy
brainwork	cacao	lappet	gapy
chainwork	tetrao	tappet	happy
plain-work			knappy
	Ā'on	**ĂP'eth**	nappy
ĂN'yan	crayon	*apeth*	pappy
banyan		*drapeth*	sappy
canyon	**Ā'on**	*escapeth*	scrappy
companion	gaon	*gapeth*	snappy
		rapeth	
ĂN'yard	**Ā'os**	*scrapeth*	**ĂP'id**
lanyard	chaos	*shapeth*	rapid
Spaniard			sapid
	Ā'oth	**ĂP'eth**	vapid
ĂN'yel	Ā'oth	*clappeth*	
Daniel	Sabaoth		

ĂP'ik
jalapic
Lappic

ĂP'in
rapine

ĂP'ing
aping
draping
escaping
gaping
raping
scraping
shaping

ĂP'ing
capping
clapping
dapping
entrapping
enwrapping
flapping
gaping
handicapping
lapping
mapping
napping
overlapping
rapping
sapping
scrapping
slapping
snapping
strapping
tapping
trapping
understrapping
unwrapping
wrapping
yapping

ĂP'is
apis
lapis
Serapis
tapis

ĂP'is
lapis
tapis

ĂP'ish
apish
papish

ĂP'ish
knappish
snappish

ĂP'ist
lanscapist
papist
redtapist

ĂP'izm
papism
red-tapism

ĂP"l
anti-papal
capel
maple
papal
staple
wool-staple

ĂP"l
ante-chapel
apple
chapel

dapple
grapple
knapple
love-apple
rappel
scapple
scrapple
thrapple

ĂP'les
apeless
capeless
crapeless
escapeless
grapeless
napeless
scrapeless
shapeless
tapeless

ĂP'les
capless
hapless
napless
sapless

ĂP'let
chaplet

ĀP'li
shapely

ĂP'li
haply

ĂP'lin
chaplain
Chaplin

ĂP'ling
dappling

grappling
lapling
sapling

ĀP'l'z
Naples
Staples

ĂP'man
Capman
Chapman
Knapman

ĂP'nel
grapnel
shrapnel

ĂP'on
capon
misshapen
tapen
unshapen

ĀP'ril
April

ĂP'shun
caption
collapsion
contraction
elapsion
recaption

ĂP'shus
captious

ĂP'sing
collapsing
lapsing
relapsing

ĂP'stan
capstan

ĂP'stur
tapster

ĂP'ted
adapted

ĂP'test
adaptest
aptest
inaptest
raptest

ĂP'tin
captain

ĂP'tiv
adaptive
captive

ĂP'tizm
anabaptism
baptism

ĂPT'li
aptly
inaptly
raptly

ĂPT'nes
aptness
inaptness
raptness
unaptness

ĂP'trap
clap-trap

ĂP'tūr
capture

enrapture
rapture
recapture

ĂP'tūr
adapter
apter
captor
chapter
rapter
recaptor

ĂP'ur
aper
caper
draper
escaper
gaper
landscaper
paper
raper
sapor
scraper
shaper
sky-scraper
taper
tapir
undraper
vapor

ĂP'ur
capper
clapper
dapper
entrapper
enwrapper
flapper
fly-flapper
gaper
handicapper
lapper

mapper
napper
overlapper
rapper
sapper
slapper
snapper
snippersnapper
strapper
tapper
trapper
understrapper
unwrapper
whipper-
snapper
wrapper
yapper

ĂP'urz
walking-papers
capers, etc.

ĂP'us
pappus
trappous

ĂP'wing
lapwing

Ā'ra
cordillera
dulcamara
Marah
Sara
Sarah

ĂR'a
Sahara
tiara

Ä'ra
Bara
Clara

Ä'ra
caracara
Ferrara
Gemara
Sahara
solfatara
tiara

ĂR'ab
Arab
scarab

ĂR'ak
arrack
barrack
carrack

Ā'rans
abearance
forbearance
(cf. apparence)

Ā'rant
declarant
forbearant
(cf. parent,
etc.)

ĂR'ant
arrant

ĂR'ant
warrant
(see ŎR'ent)

ĂR'as
arras

debarrass
disembarrass
embarrass
harass

ÄR'bel

harebell
prayer-bell

ÄR'bi

Darby
Derby

ÄR'bij

garbage

ÄR'b'l

barbel
emmarble
garbel
garble
marble

ÄR'blur

garbler
marbler

ÄR'bling

garbling
marbling

ÄR'bord

larboard
starboard

ÄR'boil

parboil

ÄR'bon

carbon
charbon

ÄR'bur

arbor
barber
Barbour
enharbor
harbor
unharbor

ÄR'chest

archest
enarchest
marchest
parchest
starchest

ÄR'cheth

archeth
enarcheth
marcheth
parcheth
starcheth

ÄR'chez

arches
counter-
   marches
larches
marches
outmarches
overarches
parches
starches

ÄR'chi

archy
larchy
starchy

ÄR'ching

arching
counter-
   marching

marching
outmarching
overarching
overmarching
parching
starching

ÄRCH'ment

archment
emparchment
parchment

ÄRCH'nes

archness

ÄR'chur

archer
clear-starcher
Larcher
marcher
starcher

ÄRCH'wa

archway

ÄR'dant

gardant
regardant
(cf. ardent)

ÄRD'arm

yard-arm

ÄR'ded

bombarded
carded
discarded
disregarded
guarded
larded
regarded

retarded
sharded
unguarded
unregarded
unretarded

ÄR'del

fardel

**ÄR'den,
  ÄR'don**

beergarden
bombardon
caseharden
enharden
garden
harden
pardon

**ÄR'dend,
  ÄR'dond**

case-hardened
hardened
pardoned
weather-
  hardened

ÄR'dent

ardent
(cf., ÄR'dant)

ÄR'dest

bombardest
discardest
disregardest
guardest
hardest
lardest
regardest
retardest

ÄR′deth

discardeth
disregardeth
guardeth
lardeth
regardeth
retardeth

ÄRD′ful

disregardful
guardful
regardful

ÄR′di

foolhardy
hardy
tardy

ÄRD′ik

anacardic
bardic
bezoardic
Lombardic
pericardic

ÄR′din

nardine
sardine

ÄR′ding

bombarding
carding
discarding
disregarding
guarding
Harding
larding
placarding
regarding
retarding

unguarding
wool-carding

ÄR′d′l

Bardle
McArdle

ÄRD′les

cardless
guardless
regardless

ÄRD′li

hardly

ÄRD′ment

bombardment
retardment

ÄRD′nes

hardness

ÄRD′ning

gardening
hardening
pardoning

ÄRD′nur

gardener
hardener
pardner
pardoner

ÄR′do

bocardo
bombardo

ÄR′dom

backstairdom
heirdom

ÄRD′ship

guardship
hardship

ÄRDZ′man

guardsman

ÄR′dur

ardor
bombarder
carder
discarder
disregarder
guarder
harder
larder
regarder
retarder

ÄR′e

shikaree
(cf. ÄR′i)

ÄR′el

apparel
barrel
carol
Carroll
disapparel
Farrell
Harrell
parrel
pork barrel

ÄR′eld

apparelled
carolled
double-
  barrelled

ÄR′em

harem

ÄR′en

Karen
McLaren

ÄR′ens

apparence
Clarence
transparence
(cf. forbear-
  ance)

ÄR′ent

apparent
celarent
parent
transparent
(cf. declarant,
  etc.)

ÄR′es

heiress

ÄR′est

airest
barest
bearest
carest
comparest
darest
declarest
despairest
ensnarest
fairest
farest
forbearest
glarest
impairest
outdarest
pairest
parest
preparest

rarest
repairest
sharest
snarest
sparest
squarest
starest
swearest
tearest
unfairest
wearest

ÄR'est

barrest
debarrest
jarrest
marrest
scarrest
sparrest
starrest
tarrest

ÄR'et

carat
carrot
claret
garret
Garrett
parrot

ÄR'eth

aireth
bareth
beareth
careth
compareth
dareth
declareth
despaireth
ensnareth

fareth
flareth
forbeareth
forsweareth
glareth
impaireth
outdareth
paireth
pareth
prepareth
repaireth
shareth
snareth
spareth
squareth
stareth
sweareth
teareth
wearth

ÄR'eth

barreth
debarreth
marreth
scarreth
sparreth
starreth
tarreth

ÄR'ez

Benares
Buenos Ayres

ÄR'fasd

barefaced
fair-faced

ÄR'fish

garfish
starfish

ÄR'for

wherefore
(cf. therefore,
  ŪR'for).

ÄR'ful

careful
prayerful
uncareful

ÄR'gan

Dargan

ÄR'gēt

target

ÄR'gin

bargain

ÄR'g'l

argle-bargle
gargle

ÄR'go

Argo
argot
botargo
cargo
Dargo
embargo
Fargo
largo
Spargo
supercargo

ÄR'gon

argon
jargon

ÄR'gu

argue

ÄR'ï

ablutionary
accessary
accidentiary
accustomary
actuary
additionary
adminculary
adversary
airy
ancillary
antiquary
apothecary
arbitrary
Ave Mary
beneficiary
bicentenary
canary
capillary
Carey
cassowary
cautionary
centenary
chary
commentary
commissary
confectionary
constabulary
contemporary
contrary
contributary
corollary
culinary
customary
dairy
depositary
dictionary
dietary
dignitary
disciplinary
discretionary

dromedary	passionary	sumptuary	parry
eleemosynary	pecuniary	supernumerary	tarry
elocutionary	pensionary	temporary	
epistolary	petitionary	tertiary	**ĂR'ĭ**
estuary	planetary	Tipperary	araçari
evolutionary	prairie	titulary	barry
extraordinary	prebendary	traditionary	carbonari
fairy	processionary	tributary	charry
February	prolegomenary	tuitionary	scarry
fiduciary	proprietary	tumulary	sparry
formulary	prothonotary	tumultuary	starry
fragmentary	provisionary	tutelary	tarry
functionary	pulmonary	ubiquitary	(cf. shikaree)
ganglionary	quandary	unchary	
glairy	questionary	unwary	**ĂR'ĭd**
hairy	questuary	vagary	varied
hebdomadary	reactionary	valetudinary	
hereditary	reliquary	vairy	**ĂR'ĭd**
honorary	residuary	vary	arid
imaginary	reversionary	veterinary	carried
incendiary	revolutionary	vicissitudinary	harried
insurrectionary	rosemary	visionary	intermarried
intermediary	salivary	vocabulary	married
janissary	salutary	voluntary	miscarried
January	sanctuary	voluptuary	parried
legendary	sanguinary	vulnerary	tarried
legionary	sanitary	wary	
literary	scapulary	(cf. ẼR'ĭ)	**ĂR'ĭf, ĂR'ĭf**
luminary	scary		hairif
Mary	secondary	**ĂR'ĭ**	
maxillary	secretary	Barrie	**ĂR'ĭf**
mercenary	sedentary	Carrie	harif
military	seditionary	carry	tariff
millenary	seminary	charivari	
missionary	snary	harri-karri	**ĂR'ĭj**
momentary	solitary	harry	carriage
monetary	stationary	intermarry	disparage
mortuary	statuary	Larry	intermarriage
necessary	stipendiary	marry	marriage
obituary	sublunary	miscarry	miscarriage

railway-
   carriage
water-carriage

ÄR'ik

agaric
Amharic
Balearic
barbaric
baric
Bulgaric
cinnabaric
Garrick
isobaric
Megaric
pimaric
Pindaric
polaric
saccharic
stearic
tartaric

ÄR'ik

Amharic

ÄR'ing

airing
baring
bearing
blaring
caring
chairing
charing
cheese-paring
comparing
daring
declaring
despairing
ensnaring
fairing
faring

flaring
forbearing
forswearing
glaring
impairing
outdaring
outstaring
outswearing
outwearing
overbearing
pairing
paring
preparing
repairing
scaring
sea-faring
sharing
snaring
sparing
squaring
staring
swearing
tale-bearing
tearing
unbearing
underbearing
unsparing
upbearing
upstaring
uptearing
wayfaring
wearing

ÄR'ing

barring
charring
debarring
disbarring
jarring
marring
scarring

sparring
starring
tarring
unbarring

ÄR'ingks

larynx
pharynx

ÄR'is

Farris
Harris
Paris
phalaris
polaris

ÄR'ish

bearish
debonairish
fairish
garish
marish
squarish
tarish

ÄR'ish

marish
parish

ÄR'izm

proletairism
Voltairism

ÄR'jent

argent
sergeant

ÄR'jest

chargest
dischargest

enlargest
largest
overchargest

ÄR'jet

garget
parget

ÄR'jeth

chargeth
dischargeth
enlargeth
overchargeth

ÄR'jez

barges
charges
discharges
enlarges
marges
targes

ÄR'jik

lethargic

ÄR'jin

margin

ÄR'jing

barging
charging
discharging
enlarging
overcharging

ÄRJ'li

largely

ÄRJ'ment

enlargement

ÄRJ'ur
barger
charger
discharger
enlarger
larger
sparger
surcharger
undercharger

ÄR'kal
anarchal
hierarchal
monarchal
oligarchal
patriarchal
squirearchal

ÄR'kazm
sarcasm

ÄR'ken
bedarken
darken
endarken
hearken

ÄR'kest
barkest
darkest
embarkest
markest
remarkest
starkest

ÄR'ket
market

ÄR'keth
barketh
embarketh

marketh
remarketh

ÄR'ki
barky
darky
heterarchy
hierarchy
larky
oligarchy
patriarchy

ÄR'kik
anarchic
antianarchic
climatarchic
heptarchic
hierarchic
monarchic
oligarchic
patriarchic

ÄR'kin
Larkin

ÄR'king
barking
carking
disembarking
embarking
harking
larking
marking
parking
remarking
sky-larking

ÄR'kish
darkish
larkish
sparkish

ÄR'kist
heptarchist
oligarchist, etc.

ÄR'kivs
archives

ÄR'k'l
darkle
sparkle

ÄRK'let
parklet
sparklet

ÄRK'li
clarkly
darkly
starkly

ÄRK'ling
darkling
sparkling

ÄRK'nes
darkness

ÄRK'nur
darkener
hearkener

ÄR'kol
charcoal

ÄRK'som
darksome

ÄRK'spur
larkspur

ÄRK'tik
Antarctic
Arctic

ÄR'kur
barker
darker
embarker
harker
larker
marcor
marker
parker
sharker
sparker
starker

ÄRK'wis
marquis

ÄR'land
engarland
Farland
garland

ÄR'les
airless
careless
hairless
heirless
pairless
prayerless
snareless
tareless

ÄR'les
scarless
starless, etc.

ÄR'let
carlet
scarlet
starlet
varlet
(cf. harlot)

ÄR'li
barely
fairly
rarely
unfairly
yarely

ÄR'li
Arleigh
barley
Charley
Farley
gnarly
Harley
marli
McCarley
parley

ÄR'lĭk
starlike, etc.

ÄR'lĭk
garlic
pilgarlick
sarlyk

ÄR'lin
air-line
hair-line

ÄR'lind
carelined
hair-lined

ÄR'ling
darling
Harling
snarling
sparling
starling

ÄR'lĭt
starlight

ÄR'lĭt
far-lit
starlit

ÄR'lok
charlock
harlock
(cf. Harlech)

ÄR'lot
Charlotte
harlot
(cf. scarlet)

ÄR'lum
heirloom

ÄR'lur
gnarler
parlor
snarler

ÄR'lus
parlous

ÄR'mad
barmaid

ÄR'man
chairman

ÄR'men
carmen

ÄR'ment
debarment
disbarment
garment
sarment

ÄR'mest
alarmest
armest
charmest
disarmest
farmest
harmest

ÄR'met
armet

ÄR'meth
alarmeth
armeth
charmeth
disarmeth
farmeth
harmeth

ÄRM'ful
armful
charmful
harmful
unharmful

ÄR'mi
army
barmy

ÄR'mik
alexipharmic
lexipharmic
ptarmic

ÄR'min
carmine
harmine

ÄR'ming
alarming
arming

baby-farming
charming
disarming
farming
forearming
harming
unalarming
unarming
uncharming
unharming

ÄRM'les
armless
charmless
harmless

ÄRM'let
armlet
charmlet

ÄR'mot
carmot
marmot

ÄR'mur
alarmer
armor
baby-farmer
charmer
disarmer
farmer
harmer
plate-armor
serpent-
   charmer

ÄR'nal
carnal
carnel
charnel
darnel
uncharnel

ÄR′nard
Barnard

ÄR′nat
incarnate

ÄR′nes
bareness
debonairness
fairness
rareness
spareness
squareness
threadbare-
   ness
unfairness
whereness

ÄR′nes
farness
harness

ÄRN′ham
Farnham
(cf. Farnum,
   Barnum)

ÄR′ni
blarney
carney
Killarney

ÄR′nij
carnage

ÄR′nish
garnish
tarnish
varnish

ÄR′nisht
garnished

tarnished
ungarnished
untarnished
unvarnished
varnished

ÄR′nold
Arnold

ÄRN′li
Darnley

ÄR′nur
darner
garner
yarner

ÄR′o
pharaoh
Rio de Janeiro

ÄR′o
bolero
caballero
faro
llanero
sombrero
vaquero

ÄR′o
arrow
barrow
farrow
harrow
marrow
narrow
sparrow
yarrow

ÄR′o
carbonaro

claro
taro

ÄR′on
Aaron
Charon

ÄR′old
Harold
carolled, etc.

ÄR′on
baron
barren

ÄR′pest
carpest
harpest
sharpest

ÄR′pet
carpet

ÄR′peth
carpeth
harpeth

ÄR′pi
carpy
harpy

ÄR′ping
carping
harping
sharping

ÄR′pist
harpist

ÄRP′nes
sharpness

ÄR′pur
carper
harper
sharper

ÄR′sal
metatarsal
tarsal
varsal

ÄR′sel
parcel
sarcel

ÄR′sez
farces
parses
sarses

ÄR′shal
earl-marshal
field-marshal
immartial
impartial
marshal
Marshall
martial
partial
unmartial

ARS′li
scarcely

ARS′ness
scarceness

ÄR′son
arson
Carson
Larsen

Larson	leaden-hearted	**ÄR'test**	**ÄR'ti**
parson	light-hearted	*cartest*	Astarte
	lion-hearted	*dartest*	charter-party
ÄR'sur	marble-hearted	*departest*	ex parte
parser	open-hearted	*impartest*	hearty
sparser	pale-hearted	*partest*	McCarty
	parted	smartest	party
ÄR'tan	pigeon-hearted	*startest*	
Spartan	proud-hearted	*upstartest*	**ÄR'tin**
tartan	public-hearted		martin
(cf. marten)	right-hearted	**ÄR'teth**	
	sad-hearted	*carteth*	**ÄR'ting**
ÄR'ted	shallow-hearted	*darteth*	carting
broken-hearted	simple-hearted	*departeth*	darting
carted	single-hearted	*imparteth*	departing
charted	smarted	*parteth*	hearting
chicken-hearted	soft-hearted	*smarteth*	imparting
cold-hearted	started	*starteth*	smarting
darted	stony-hearted	*upstarteth*	starting
departed	stout-hearted		sweet-hearting
double-hearted	tender-hearted	**ÄRT'ful**	uncarting
down-hearted	traitor-hearted	artful	upstarting
faint-hearted	triparted		
false-hearted	truehearted	**ÄR'tha**	**ÄR'tist**
flint-hearted	unhearted	Martha	artist
frank-hearted	unimparted		Chartist
free-hearted	upstarted	**ÄR'thest**	
full-hearted	warm-hearted	farthest	**ÄR'tit**
gentle-hearted	weak-hearted		bipartite
great-hearted	wise-hearted	**ÄR'thi**	
half-hearted		McCarthy	**ÄR't'l**
hard-hearted	**ÄR'ten, Är'ton**		dartle
hare-hearted	barton	**ÄR'thing**	startle
hearted	carton	farthing	
hen-hearted	dishearten		**ÄRT'les**
high-hearted	enhearten	**ÄR'THur**	artless
imparted	hearten	farther	chartless
iron-hearted	kindergarten		heartless
kind-hearted	marten	**ÄR'thur**	
large-hearted	smarten	Arthur	**ÄRT'let**
			heartlet

martlet
tartlet

ÄRT'li

partly
smartly
tartly

ÄRT'ling

startling

ÄRT'ment

apartment
compartment
department
impartment

ÄRT'nes

smartness
tartness

ÄRT'rij

cartridge
partridge

ÄRT'wa

cartway
part-way

ÄR'tur

barter
bemartyr
carter
charter
darter
departer
garter
imparter
martyr
parter
protomartyr

smarter
starter
tartar
tarter
unmartyr
upstarter

ÄR'um

arum
carrom
harum-scarum
larum
marum

ÄR'um

alarum

ÄR'ur

airer
armor-bearer
barer
bearer
blarer
comparer
darer
declarer
despairer
ensnarer
fairer
flarer
forbearer
forswearer
glarer
impairer
mace-bearer
outdarer
outstarer
overbearer
parer
preparer

rarer
repairer
sea-farer
sharer
snarer
sparer
squarer
standard-
    bearer
starer
swearer
sword-bearer
tale-bearer
tankard-bearer
tearer
train-bearer
upbearer
way-farer
wearer

ÄR'ur

barrer
bizarrer
debarrer
marrer
sparrer
tarrer

ÄR'val

larval

ÄR'vel

carvel
marvel

ÄR'veld

marvelled

ÄR'ven

carven

ÄR'vest

harvest
starvest

ÄR'vi

Garvey
Harvey

ÄR'ving

carving
starving

ÄRV'ling

marvelling
starveling

ÄR'vur

carver
marver
starver

ÄR'wavs

air-waves

ÄR'wel

farewell

ÄR'whil

erewhile

ÄR'worn

careworn
prayerworn

ÄS'a

Amasa
Asa

ÄS'a

Hadasseh
Manasseh

Ā'sal
basal
casal

ĂS'at
cassate
incrassate

Ā'sens, Ā'sans
abaisance
adjacence
complacence
connascence
interjacence
obeisance
renascence

Ā'sent, Ā'sant
adjacent
circumjacent
complacent
connascent
"daycent"
enascent
indurascent
interjacent
jacent
naissant
nascent
renaissant
renascent
"raycent"
subjacent
superjacent

ĂS'est
abasest
basest
begracest
belacest

bracest
chasest
debasest
defacest
disgracest
displacest
effacest
embracest
enlacest
erasest
facest
gracest
interlacest
lacest
outpacest
pacest
placest
racest
replacest
retracest
spacest
tracest
unlacest

ĂS'est
amassest
classest
crassest
massest
passest
surpassest

ĂS'et
asset
basset
brasset
facet
fascet
placet
(cf. tacit)

ĂS'eth
abaseth
baseth
begraceth
belaceth
braceth
chaseth
debaseth
defaceth
disgraceth
displaceth
effaceth
embraceth
enlaceth
eraseth
faceth
graceth
interlaceth
laceth
outpaceth
paceth
placeth
raceth
replaceth
retraceth
spaceth
traceth
unlaceth

ĂS'eth
amasseth
classeth
masseth
passeth
surpasseth

ĂS'ez
aces
bases
begraces
belaces

braces
breathing-
   spaces
cases
chariot-traces
chases
commonplaces
debases
defaces
disgraces
displaces
effaces
embraces
enlaces
faces
footpaces
footraces
graces
grimaces
hiding-places
horse-races
interlaces
interspaces
laces
maces
misplaces
outfaces
outpaces
paces
places
races
replaces
resting-places
retraces
spaces
steeple-chases
traces
trysting-places
ukases
uncases

unlaces	**ĂSH'bord**	**ĂSH'ez**	balderdashing
vases	dashboard	abashes	cashing
	splashboard	ashes	clashing
ĀS'ez		caches	crashing
amasses	**Ā'shens**	cashes	dashing
asses	patience	clashes	fashing
brasses		crashes	flashing
classes	**Ā'shent**	dashes	gashing
gases	impatient	flashes	gnashing
glasses	patient	gashes	hashing
grasses		gnashes	lashing
lasses	**ĂSH'est**	hashes	mashing
masses	*cashest*	lashes	plashing
molasses	*clashest*	mashes	slashing
morasses	*crashest*	mustaches	smashing
passes	*dashest*	rashes	splashing
surpasses	*flashest*	rehashes	thrashing
	gashest	sashes	unlashing
ĀS'ful	*gnashest*	slashes	
disgraceful	*lashest*	smashes	**ĂSH'li**
graceful	*mashest*	splashes	Ashley
ungraceful	*slashest*	unlashes	flashly
	smashest		gashly
ĂSH'a	*splashest*	**ĂSH'ful**	
attaché	*thrashest*	bashful	**ĂSH'man**
cachet		gashful	ashman
sachet	**ĂSH'eth**	rashful	"flashman"
	casheth	unbashful	
Ā'shal	*clasheth*		**Ā'sho**
abbatial	*crasheth*	**ĂSH'i**	Horatio
craniofacial	*dasheth*	ashy	
facial	*flasheth*	flashy	**Ā'shun**
glacial	*gasheth*	hashy	abalienation
palatial	*gnasheth*	mashie	abacination
prelatial	*lasheth*	mashy	abbreviation
racial	*masheth*	plashy	abdication
spatial	*slasheth*	slashy	aberration
unifacial	*smasheth*	splashy	abjudication
(cf. basial)	*splasheth*	trashy	abjuration
	thrasheth		ablactation
Ā'shan		**ĂSH'ing**	ablation
(cf. Ā'shun)		abashing	

āle, câre, ădd, ärm, ȧsk; mē, hẽre, ĕnd; īce, ĭll;

abnegation
abomination
abrogation
absentation
acceleration
acceptation
acclamation
acclimatation
acclimation
acclimatization
accommodation
accreditation
accrimination
accubation
accumulation
accusation
acervation
acidification
activation
actualization
actuation
acumination
acupunctuation
adaptation
adequation
adhortation
adjudication
adjuration
administration
admiration
adoration
adornation
adulation
adulteration
adumbration
adversation
advocation
aëration
aërostation
affectation
affiliation

affirmation
afflation
afforestation
aggeration
agglomeration
agglutination
aggrandization
aggravation
aggregation
agitation
agnation
agnomination
alcoholization
alienation
alimentation
alkalization
allegation
allegorization
alleviation
alligation
alliteration
allocation
alteration
altercation
alternation
amalgamation
ambulation
amelioration
Americaniza-
     tion
ampliation
amplification
amputation
analysation
anathematiza-
     tion
anglicization
Anglification
angulation
animalization
animation

annexation
annihilation
annomination
annotation
annulation
annumeration
annunciation
anticipation
antilibration
appellation
application
appreciation
approbation
appropriation
approximation
aration
arbitration
arcuation
argentation
argumentation
aromatization
arrestation
arrogation
articulation
Asian
asphyxiation
aspiration
assassination
assentation
asseveration
assignation
assimilation
assimulation
association
atomization
attenuation
attestation
attrectation
augmentation
auguration
auscultation

authentication
authorization
averruncation
aviation
avocation
backwardation
basification
beatification
beautification
bifurcation
blood-relation
blusteration
bombilation
botheration
brutalization
brutification
cachinnation
calcification
calcination
calculation
calorification
calumniation
cameration
canalization
cancellation
canonization
cantillation
capitalization
capitation
capitulation
caprification
captivation
carbonization
carbunculation
carnation
cassation
castellation
castigation
castrametation
catechization
causation

cauterization
celebration
cementation
centralisation
cerebration
certification
cessation
cetacean
chain station
characteriza-
    tion
chrismation
Christian-
    ization
cineration
circulation
circumgyration
circumnaviga-
    tion
circumnutation
circumvallation
circumvolation
citation
civilization
clarification
classification
coagulation
coaxation
codification
cogitation
cognation
cohabitation
collation
colligation
collocation
colonization
coloration
columniation
combination
commemora-
    tion

commendation
commensura-
    tion
communication
commination
commiseration
communication
commutation
compellation
compensation
compilation
complication
compotation
compurgation
computation
concentration
concertation
conciliation
condemnation
condensation
condonation
confabulation
confederation
configuration
confirmation
confiscation
conflagration
conformation
confrontation
confutation
congelation
conglomeration
congratulation
congregation
conjugation
conjuration
connotation
consecration
conservation
consideration
consolation

consolidation
constellation
consternation
consubstantia-
    tion
consultation
consummation
contamination
contemplation
continuation
contravallation
conversation
convocation
co-operation
co-optation
co-ordination
copulation
cornification
coronation
corporation
correlation
corroboration
corrugation
coruscation
creation
cremation
crenellation
crepitation
crimination
crustacean
crustation
crystallization
cubation
culmination
cultivation
cupellation
curvation
Dalmatian
damnation
damnification
debarkation

debilitation
decalcification
decantation
decapitation
decentraliza-
    tion
decimation
declamation
declaration
declination
decollation
deconsecration
decoration
decortication
decrepitation
decubation
decussation
dedication
defalcation
defamation
defecation
deflagration
defloration
deformation
defraudation
degeneration
degradation
degustation
dehortation
deification
delation
delectation
delegation
deliberation
delimitation
delineation
deliration
deltafication
demarcation
dementation
demonetization

demonstration
demoralization
denationaliza-
    tion
denization
denomination
denotation
dentation
denticulation
dentilation
denudation
denunciation
deodorization
deoppilation
deosculation
deoxidation
deoxygenation
depilation
deploration
depopulation
deportation
depositation
depravation
deprecation
depreciation
depredation
deprivation
depuration
deputation
derivation
derogation
desecration
desiccation
desideration
designation
desolation
desperation
despoliation
desquamation
destination
deterioration

determination
deterration
detestation
detonization
detruncation
devastation
deviation
devirgination
dictation
diffarreation
differentiation
digitation
dilapidation
dilatation
dilation
dimidiation
disapprobation
discoloration
discontinuation
discrimination
disculpation
disfiguration
disinclination
disintegration
dislocation
dispensation
disputation
disqualification
dissemination
dissentation
dissertation
disseveration
dissimulation
dissipation
dissociation
distillation
divagation
divarication
diversification
divination
divulgation

documentation
domestication
domiciliation
domination
donation
dotation
dulcification
duplication
duration
economization
edification
education
edulcoration
effectuation
effemination
effeminization
efflation
effoliation
ejaculation
ejulation
elaboration
elation
electrification
electrization
electrolyzation
elevation
elimination
elixation
elucidation
emaciation
emanation
emancipation
emasculation
embrocation
emendation
emigration
emulation
endenization
enervation
enthronization
enucleation

enumeration
enunciation
equalization
equation
equilibration
equitation
equivocation
eradication
eructation
estimation
estivation
eternization
etherealization
etiolation
evacuation
evangelization
evaporation
eventuation
evisceration
evocation
evolation
exacerbation
exaggeration
exaltation
examination
exasperation
excavation
excitation
exclamation
excogitation
excommuni-
    cation
excoriation
excruciation
exculpation
execration
exemplification
exercitation
exfoliation
exhalation
exhilaration

exhortation
exhumation
exoneration
expatiation
expatriation
expectation
expectoration
experimen-
  tation
expiation
expiration
explanation
explication
exploitation
exploration
expoliation
exportation
expostulation
expropriation
expugnation
expurgation
exsiccation
exsufflation
extemporiza-
  tion
extenuation
extermination
externalization
extirpation
extravasation
extrication
exudation
exultation
fabrication
facilitation
falcation
falsification
familiarization
fasciation
fascination
fecundation

federation
felicitation
feneration
fenestration
fermentation
ferrumination
fertilization
feudalization
fibrination
figuration
filiation
filtration
fissiparation
fixation
flagellation
flagitation
flirtation
floccillation
florification
flossification
flotation
fluctuation
flusteration
fluxation
foliation
fomentation
forcipation
foreordination
formation
formulization
fortification
fossilification
fossilization
foundation
fraternation
fraternization
frequentation
friation
frication
frondation
fructification

frumentation
frustration
fulguration
fulmination
fumigation
furcation
furfuration
galvanization
gasification
gelatination
gelatinization
gemination
gemmation
generalisation
generation
generification
geniculation
germination ·
gestation
gesticulation
glaciation
glandulation
glomeration
gloriation
glorification
glutination
gradation
graduation
granitification
granulation
graticulation
gratification
gratulation
gravidation
gravitation
gunation
gustation
gyration
habilitation
habitation
habituation

hallucination
hariolation
harmonization
hebetation
hellenization
hepatization
hesitation
hibernation
Hibernization
homologation
horrification
hortation
humanization
humectation
humiliation
hybridization
hydration
hypothecation
idealization
ideation
identification
illaqueation
illation
illustration
imagination
imbrication
imitation
immaculation
immanation
immigration
immoderation
immolation
immortalization
impanation
impersonation
implication
imploration
importation
imprecation
impregnation
improvisation

āle.   câre,   ădd,   ārm,   åsk;   mē,   hĕre,   ĕnd;   īce,   ĭll;

impugnation
imputation
inadequation
inaffectation
inanimation
inapplication
inappreciation
inarticulation
inauguration
inauration
incameration
incantation
incapacitation
incarceration
incarnation
incarnification
inchoation
incineration
incitation
incivilization
inclination
incommodation
inconsideration
incorporation
incrassation
incremation
incrustation
incubation
inculcation
inculpation
incultivation
incurvation
indemnification
indentation
indetermination
indication
indigitation
indignation
indiscrimina-
tion

individualiza-
tion
individuation
indoctrination
induration
inebriation
inequation
infatuation
infestation
infeudation
infiltration
inflammation
inflation
information
ingemination
ingratiation
ingravidation
ingurgitation
inhabitation
inhalation
inhumation
initiation
innervation
innovation
inoculation
inordination
inosculation
insinuation
inspiration
inspissation
installation
instauration
instigation
instillation
instrumentation
insubordination
insufflation
insulation
insultation
integration

integumenta-
tion
inteneration
intensation
intensification
intercalation
intercolumni-
ation
intercommu-
nication
interdigitation
interlineation
interlocation
intermediation
intermigration
intermutation
interpellation
interpenetra-
tion
interpolation
interpretation
interrelation
interrogation
interstratifi-
cation
intimation
intimidation
intoleration
intonation
intoxication
intrication
inundation
invalidation
investigation
invigoration
invitation
invocation
irradiation
irrigation
irritation
isolation

iteration
jactitation
jaculation
jobation
jollification
jubilation
Judaization
justification
laceration
lachrymation
lactation
lallation
lamentation
lamination
lancination
laniation
lapidation
lapidification
Latinization
laudation
laureation
lavation
laxation
legalization
legation
legislation
legitimation
levation
levigation
levitation
libation
liberation
libration
licentiation
lignification
limitation
lineation
liquation
liquidation
literalization
litigation

ōld, ôr, ŏdd, oil, fŏŏt, out; ūse, ûrn, ŭp; THis, thin

lixiviation
localization
location
lubrication
lucubration
lunation
lustration
luxation
luxuriation
macadam-
  ization
maceration
machicolation
machination
maculation
magnetization
magnification
maladmin-
  istration
maleficiation
malformation
malleation
malversation
manifestation
manipulation
marmoration
martyrization
mastication
materialization
materiation
matriculation
maturation
maximization
mediation
mediatization
medication
meditation
melioration
mellification
mendication
mensuration

mesmerization
metallization
methodization
migration
ministration
miscegenation
mitigation
mobilization
moderation
modernization
modification
modulation
molestation
mollification
monetization
monstration
moralization
mortification
multiplication
mummification
mundification
murmuration
mutation
mutilation
mutuation
mystification
narration
nasalization
natation
nation
naturalization
navigation
necessitation
negation
negotiation
neologization
nervation
neutralization
nictation
nictitation
nidification

nidulation
nigrification
nitrification
nobilitation
noctambulation
noctivagation
nodation
nomination
normalization
notation
notification
Novatian
novation
nudation
nudification
nugation
nullification
numeration
obfuscation
objurgation
oblation
oblatration
obligation
obliteration
obnubilation
obscuration
obsecration
observation
obstination
obviation
occultation
occupation
oneration
operation
oppugnation
oration
orbiculation
orchestration
ordination
organization
orientation

origination
ornamentation
oscillation
oscitation
osculation
ossification
ostentation
otiation
ovation
oxidation
oxygenation
ozonation
ozonification
ozonization
pacation
pacification
pagination
palification
palliation
palpation
palpitation
pandiculation
panification
paralysation
participation
patronization
pauperization
pausation
pectination
peculation
penetration
perambulation
percolation
peregrination
perfectation
perfectionation
perforation
perlustration
permeation
permutation
pernoctation

āle,   câre,   ădd,   ārm,   ȧsk;   mē,   hęre,   ĕnd;   īce,   ĭll;

peroration
perpetration
perpetuation
perscrutation
personation
personification
perspiration
perturbation
pestillation
petrification
philosophation
phonation
phonetization
piscation
placation
plantation
plebification
plication
pluralization
polarization
police-station
pollicitation
pollination
polling-station
population
porphyrization
postillation
postulation
potation
precipitation
predacean
predation
predestination
predication
predomination
premeditation
pre-occupation
preparation
preponderation
presensation
presentation

preservation
prestidigitation
prevarication
privation
probation
proclamation
procrastination
procreation
procuration
profanation
profligation
prognosticion
prolation
prolification
prolongation
promulgation
pronation
pronunciation
propagation
propination
propitiation
propugnation
prorogation
prostration
protestation
protuberation
provocation
publication
pullulation
pulsation
pulverization
punctuation
purgation
purification
quadruplica-
    tion
qualification
quantification
quartation
quassation
quotation

racemation
radiation
radication
ramification
ratification
ratiocination
ration
realization
recalcitration
recantation
recapitulation
recidivation
reciprocation
recitation
reclamation
recognization
recommenda-
    tion
reconciliation
recordation
recreation
recrimination
rectification
recubation
recuperation
recurvation
recusation
redintegration
reformation
refrigeration
refutation
regelation
regeneration
registration
regulation
rehabilitation
reiteration
rejuvenation
relation
relaxation
relegation

relocation
remanation
remonetization
remonstration
remuneration
renegation
renovation
renunciation
reparation
repatriation
replication
representatiou
reprobation
reptation
repudiation
reputation
reservation
resignation
resinification
respiration
restoration
resupination
resuscitation
retaliation
retardation
reticulation
retractation
retrogradation
revelation
reverberation
revibration
revivification
revocation
rhetorication
roboration
rogation
rose-carnation
rotation
rubification
ruination
rumination

rustication
saburration
sacrification
salification
salination
salivation
saltation
salutation
salvation
sanctification
sanguification
sanitation
saponification
satiation
sation
saturation
scarification
scintillation
sciscitation
scorification
scrutation
secularization
secundation
sedimentation
segmentation
segregation
self-centration
self-
  preservation
self-
  renunciation
semination
sensation
sensualization
separation
sequestration
serration
serrulation
sibilation
siccation
sideration

signation
signification
silicification
simplification
simulation
sinuation
situation
solarization
solemnization
solicitation
solidification
somnambula-
  tion
sophistication
specialization
specification
speculation
speechification
spiflication
spiritualization
spoliation
sputation
stagnation
starvation
station
stellation
sternutation
stigmatization
stimulation
stipulation
strangulation
stratification
striation
stridulation
stultification
stupration
subarrhation
subjugation
sublation
sublevation
subligation

sublimation
sublimification
sublimitation
sublineation
subordination
subornation
subrogation
substantiation
subtilization
succussation
sudation
sufflation
suffocation
suggilation
sulcation
sulphuration
summation
superannuation
supererogation
supination
supplantation
supplementa-
  tion
supplication
supportation
suppuration
surrogation
suspensation
suspiration
sustentation
susurration
syllabication
syllogization
symbolization
synchroniza-
  tion
syncopation
systematiza-
  tion
tabularization
tabulation

tantalization
tarnation
tartarization
taxation
temeration
temporization
temptation
terebration
tergiversation
termination
tessellation
testacean
testamentation
testation
testification
theorization
Thracian
thurification
tintinnabula-
  tion
titillation
titration
titteration
titubation
toleration
trabeation
tractation
tractoration
tralation
tranquillization
transanimation
transcolation
transfiguration
transformation
translation
transliteration
translocation
transmigration
transmogrifica-
  tion
transmutation

---

transpiration
transplantation
transportation
transubstantia-
  tion
transudation
tremulation
trepidation
triangulation
tribulation
triplication
tripudiation
trituration
trucidation
trullization
truncation
tubulation
tumultuation
turbination
typification
ulceration
ultimation
ululation
undulation
unification
ustulation
usurpation
utilization
vacation
vaccination
vacillation
vacuolation
validation
valuation
vaporation
vaporization
vapulation
variation
variegation
vaticination
vegetation

vellication
venation
venenation
veneration
ventilation
verbalization
verberation
verification
vermiculation
vernation
versification
vesication
vexation
vexillation
vibration
vigesimation
vilification
vindemiation
vindication
violation
visitation
vitalization
vitiation
vitrification
vitriolation
vitriolization
vituperation
vivification
vocalization
vocation
vociferation
volatilization
volcanization
vulcanization
(cf. ĀSH'i-an)
  words

ĀSH'en,
  ĀSH'un

ashen
compassion

fashion
impassion
master-passion
passion
(cf. Circassian,
  and ĀSH'i-
  an words)

ĀSH'und
dispassioned
fashioned
impassioned
old-fashioned
passioned
unfashioned
unimpassioned
unpassioned

ĀSH'ur
Asher
baggage-
  smasher
Brasher
casher
clasher
crasher
dasher
flasher
gasher
haberdasher
lasher
masher
rasher
slasher
smasher
splasher
thrasher
unlasher

Ā'shus
audacious

bibacious
capacious
contumacious
disgracious
disputatious
edacious
efficacious
execratious
fallacious
feracious
flirtatious
fugacious
fumacious
gracious
incapacious
inefficacious
linguacious
loquacious
mendacious
minacious
misgracious
mordacious
ostentatious
palacious
perspicacious
pertinacious
pervicacious
predacious
procacious
pugnacious
rampacious
rapacious
sagacious
salacious
sequacious
spacious
tenacious
ungracious
veracious
vexatious

vivacious
voracious
acanaceous
acanthaceous
alliaceous
amylaceous
arenaceous
bulbaceous
cactaceous
camphoraceous
capillaceous
carbonaceous
cetaceous
corallaceous
coriaceous
cretaceous
crustaceous
cylindraceous
erinaceous
fabaceous
farinaceous
ferulaceous
filaceous
foliaceous
frumentaceous
fungaceous
furfuraceous
gallinaceous
gemmaceous
herbaceous
lappaceous
lardaceous
liliaceous
marlaceous
micaceous
olivaceous
orchidaceous
palmaceous
pectinaceous
perdaceous

perlaceous
piperaceous
pomaceous
porraceous
psittaceous
pulveraceous
ranunculaceous
resinaceous
rosaceous
rutaceous
sabaceous
salicaceous
saponaceous
sarmentaceous
saxifragaceous
schorlaceous
scoriaceous
sebaceous
setaceous
stercoraceous
testaceous
tophaceous
torfaceous
truttaceous
turbinaceous
vinaceous
violaceous

ĂSH'vil
Ashville
Nashville

ĀS'ĭ
Gracie
Lacey
lacy
précis
racy

ĀS'ĭ
brassie

brassy
classy
gassy
glassy
grassy
lassie
Malagasy
massy
morassy
sassy
Tallahassee

Ā'sid
bayside
braeside
wayside

ĂS'ĭd
acid
placid

ĂS'ij
brassage
passage

ĂS'ĭk
aphasic
basic
bibasic
dibasic
quadribasic
tribasic

ĂS'ĭk
boracic
classic
Jurassic
Liassic
potassic
sebacic

thoracic
Triassic

ĂS'ĭl
facile
gracile

ĂS'ĭn
basin
(cf. ĂS'n)

ĂS'ĭn
assassin

ĂS'ĭn
spadassin

ĀS'ing
abasing
basing
begracing
belacing
bracing
casing
chasing
debasing
defacing
disgracing
displacing
effacing
embracing
enlacing
erasing
facing
foot-racing
gracing
horse-racing
interlacing
interspacing
lacing
misplacing

outfacing
outpacing
pacing
placing
racing
replacing
retracing
self-abasing
spacing
steeple-chasing
tight-lacing
tracing
uncasing
underbracing
unlacing

ĀS'ing

amassing
classing
gassing
massing
overpassing
passing
surpassing
underclassing

ĀS'is

basis
crasis
glacis
oasis
phasis

ĂS'is

chassis

ĂS'it

tacit
(cf. ĂS'et)

ĀS'iv

assuasive

dissuasive
evasive
invasive
persuasive
pervasive
suasive

ĂS'iv

impassive
massive
passive

ĂS'ka

Alaska
Athabaska
Nebraska

ĂS'kal

mascle
paschal
rascal
(cf. Haskell,
   etc.)

ĂS'kar

Lascar
Madagascar

ĂS'kest

askest
baskest
bemaskest
maskest
taskest
unmaskest

ĂS'ket

basket
bread-basket
casket
flasket

gasket
lasket

ĂS'keth

asketh
basketh
bemasketh
masketh
tasketh
unmasketh

ĂS'king

asking
basking
bemasking
masking
overtasking
tasking
unmasking

ĂS'ko

Belasco
fiasco
tabasco
tasco

ĂS'kur

asker
basker
casquer
masker

ĂS'kus

Damascus

ASK'with

Asquith

ĂS' 'l

castle
entassel

envassal
tassel
vassal
wrastle

ĀS'les

aceless
baseless
caseless
faceless
graceless
laceless
maceless
paceless
placeless
raceless
spaceless
traceless

ĀS'let

bracelet

ĂS'let

haslet
taslet

ĀS'li

basely
commonplacely

ĀS'man

baseman
first baseman
laceman
paceman
placeman
raceman
second baseman
third baseman

ĂS'man

classman

ōld, ôr, ŏdd, oil, fŏŏt, out; ūse, ûrn, ŭp; THis, thĭ-

gasman
glassman

ĂS'ment

abasement
basement
begracement
belacement
casement
debasement
defacement
displacement
effacement
embracement
encasement
enlacement
erasement
interlacement
misplacement
placement
replacement
retracement
self-abasement

ĂS'ment

amassment

ĂS'min or
ĂZ'min

jasmine

ĂS' 'n

chasten
enchasten
hasten
(cf. ĀS'in,
Ăs'on)

ĂS' 'n

fasten
(cf. casson)

ĀS'nur

chastener
hastener

ĂS'nes

crassness

ĂS'o

say-so

ĂS'o, ĂS'o

basso
lasso
Sargasso
Tasso

ĂS'ok

cassock
hassock

ĂS'on

caisson
Grayson
Jason
mason
(cf. ĂS'n)

ĂS'on

casson
(cf. fasten)

ĂS'pen

aspen

ĂS'pest

claspest
enclaspest
gaspest
graspest
raspest
unclaspest

ĂS'peth

claspeth
enclaspeth
gaspeth
graspeth
raspeth
unclaspeth

ĂS'pik

aspic

ĂS'ping

clasping
enclasping
engrasping
gasping
grasping
rasping
unclasping

ĂS'pur

asper
Caspar
Casper
clasper
gasper
grasper
jasper
rasper

ĂS'ta

Shasta

Ā'star

day-star

ĀS'ted

basted
hasted
long-waisted
pasted

short-waisted
tasted
untasted
unwasted
war-wasted
wasted

ĂS'ted

blasted
contrasted
fasted
flabbergasted
lasted
masted
outlasted
unblasted
undermasted

ĂS'tel

pastel

ĀST'est

bastest
chastest
foretastest
hastest
pastest
tastest
wastest
wastest

ĂST'est

castest
contrastest
fastest
lastest
outlastest
vastest

ĀST'eth

basteth

foretasteth	antonomastic	sarcastic	hasteless
hasteth	bioplastic	scholastic	pasteless
pasteth	bombastic	scholiastic	tasteless
tasteth	ceroplastic	spastic	waistless
wasteth	chiliastic	tetrastich	wasteless
	clastic		
ĂST'eth	deutoplastic	**ĂS'tiks**	**ĂST'li**
casteth	dichastic	ecclesiastics	ghastly
contrasteth	docimastic	elastics	lastly
fasteth	drastic	fantastics	steadfastly
lasteth	dynastic	gymnastics	vastly
outlasteth	ecclesiastic	phelloplastics	
	elastic		**ĂST'ment**
ĂST'ful	emplastic	**ĂS'tim**	blastment
distasteful	encomiastic	pastime	contrastment
tasteful	enthusiastic		
wasteful	esemplastic	**ĂST'ing**	**ĂST'nes**
	fantastic	basting	fastness
ĂS'ti	galvanoplastic	foretasting	vastness
hasty	gelastic	hasting	
pasty	gymnastic	pasting	**ĂST'ning**
tasty	Hudibrastic	tasting	fastening
	iconoclastic	unwasting	
ĂS'ti	inelastic	wasting	**ĂS'ton**
blasty	mastic		Aston
epinasty	metaphrastic	**ĂST'ing**	Gaston
genioplasty	monastic	blasting	
masty	neoplastic	casting	**ĂS'tral**
nasty	onomastic	contrasting	astral
vasty	orgiastic	everlasting	cadastral
	paraphrastic	fasting	subastral
ĂS'tif	parasceuastic	flabbergasting	
mastiff	paronomastic	forecasting	**ĂS'tri**
	peirastic	lasting	pastry
ĂS'tij	periphrastic	recasting	
wastage	phelloplastic		**ĂS'trik**
	plagioclastic	**ĂS'tingz**	cacogastric
ĂS'tik	plastic	Hastings	digastric
amphiblastic	pleonastic	bastings, etc.	gastric
anaclastic	proplastic		hypogastric
antiphrastic	protoplastic	**ĂST'les**	perigastric
		basteless	

AS'tron
apastron
plastron

AS'trus
disastrous

AS'tur
baster
chaster
foretaster
paster
taster
waster

AS'tūr
pasture

AS'tūr, AS'tur
alabaster
aster
Astor
band-master
barrack-master
beplaster
blaster
burgomaster
bushmaster
cadastre
canaster
caster
castor
china-aster
contraster
courtplaster
criticaster
disaster
faster
flabbergaster
forecaster
Goniaster

grammaticaster
grand-master
interpilaster
Latinitaster
master
medicaster
oleaster
overmaster
pastor
piaster
pilaster
plaster
poetaster
postmaster
quarter-master
schoolmaster
shin-plaster
sticking-plaster
taskmaster
vaster

AS'tur
shaster

AS'turd,
    AS'turd
bastard
beplastered
dastard
mastered
overmastered
pilastered
plastered
unmastered

AS'tus
Erastus
Rastus

AS'tyun
bastion
(cf. Erastian)

AS'ur
abaser
ambulance-
    chaser
baser
begracer
belacer
bracer
chaser
debaser
defacer
disgracer
displacer
effacer
embracer
encaser
eraser
facer
footracer
gracer
grimacer
horse-racer
interlacer
lacer
macer
misplacer
outpacer
pacer
placer
racer
replacer
retracer
spacer
steeple-chaser
tracer
unlacer

ÄS'ur
amasser
antimacassar
masser

passer
placer
surpasser

ÄS'ur
kirsh-wasser

Ā'ta
albata
data
dentata
errata
Invertebrata
postulata
pro rata
strata
ultimata
Vertebrata

ÄT'a
matamata
regatta
strata
(cf. yerba-
    mata)

Ä'ta
a ballata
batata
cantata
data
imbrocata
inamorata
Mahratta
pro rata
reata
serenata
sonata
(cf. yerba-
    mata)

āle. câre. ădd, ärm, ȧsk; mē, hẹre, ĕnd; īce, ĭll;

ĀT′al

fatal
natal
prenatal
post-natal
Statal

ĀT′an

Satan
(cf. ĀT′on)

ĀT′ant

blatant
latent
natant
patent
statant

ĀT′ed

abated
abbreviated
abdicated
ablocated
abnegated
abominated
abrogated
accelerated
accentuated
accommodated
accumulated
acidulated
actuated
addle-pated
adjudicated
adulterated
advocated
aërated
affiliated
agglomerated
aggravated
aggregated

agitated
alienated
alleviated
allocated
alternated
amalgamated
ameliorated
ampliated
amputated
annihilated
annotated
annulated
annumerated
annunciated
antedated
anticipated
antiquated
appreciated
approbated
appropriated
approximated
arbitrated
armillated
armor-plated
arrogated
articulated
asphyxiated
aspirated
assassinated
asseverated
assimilated
assimulated
associated
asteriated
attenuated
augurated
aurated
authenticated
awaited
baited
bated

belated
berated
bifurcated
calculated
calumniated
camphorated
capacitated
capitulated
captivated
carbonated
castellated
castigated
celebrated
certificated
circulated
circumstanti-
    ated
coagulated
cogitated
collated
collocated
commemo-
    rated
comminated
commiserated
communicated
compensated
complicated
concentrated
conciliated
confabulated
confederated
confiscated
conglomerated
congratulated
congregated
conjugated
consecrated
consolidated
consummated
contaminated

contemplated
co-operated
co-ordinated
copper-plated
copulated
coronated
correlated
corroborated
corrugated
created
cremated
crenellated
crepitated
culminated
cultivated
dated
debated
debilitated
decapitated
decimated
decorated
dedicated
degenerated
delegated
deliberated
delineated
demonstrated
denominated
depopulated
deprecated
depreciated
derogated
desecrated
desiderated
designated
desolated
deteriorated
detonated
devastated
deviated
dictated

differentiated
dilapidated
dilated
discriminated
disintegrated
dislocated
disseminated
dissimulated
dissipated
dissociated
domesticated
dominated
dunder-pated
duplicated
educated
effectuated
efflated
ejaculated
elaborated
elated
electro-plated
elevated
eliminated
elucidated
emaciated
emanated
emancipated
emasculated
emigrated
emulated
enumerated
enunciated
equivocated
eradicated
estimated
evacuated
evaporated
eventuated
exaggerated
exasperated
excavated

excommuni-
   cated
excoriated
execrated
exhilarated
exonerated
exorbitated
expatiated
expatriated
expectorated
expiated
expostulated
extenuated
exterminated
extricated
fabricated
facilitated
fascinated
fated
federated
felicitated
fêted
flagellated
fluctuated
foreordinated
formulated
freighted
frustrated
fulminated
fumigated
gaited
gated
generated
germinated
gesticulated
graduated
granulated
grated
gratulated
gravitated
habituated

hated
heavy-gaited
heavy-
   weighted
hesitated
humiliated
idle-pated
ill-fated
illuminated
illustrated
imitated
immigrated
immolated
impersonated
implicated
imprecated
impropriated
inaugurated
incapacitated
incarcerated
incastellated
incinerated
incorporated
incriminated
incubated
indicated
indoctrinated
indurated
inebriated
infatuated
inflated
infuriated
ingratiated
initiated
innovated
inoculated
insinuated
instated
instigated
insulated
interpolated

interrogated
intimated
intimidated
intoxicated
inundated
invalidated
investigated
invigorated
invocated
irradiated
irrigated
irritated
isolated
iterated
jasperated
legislated
levigated
liberated
liquidated
located
lubricated
luxuriated
macerated
manipulated
marinated
masticated
mated
matriculated
medicated
meditated
methylated
migrated
militated
mitigated
moderated
modulated
mutilated
narrated
navigated
necessitated
negotiated

nickle-plated	propagated	simulated	unmitigated
nominated	propitiated	situated	unpremedi-
nucleolated	punctuated	skated	tated
obligated	radiated	slated	unrelated
obliterated	rated	sophisticated	unsophisti-
obviated	rattle-pated	speculated	cated
officiated	recapitulated	spifflicated	unstated
operated	reciprocated	stated	vacated
opinionated	recreated	stimulated	vaccinated
originated	recriminated	stipulated	vacillated
oscillated	recuperated	subjugated	validated
osculated	refrigerated	sublimated	variated
overrated	regenerated	subordinated	variegated
overstated	regulated	substantiated	vegetated
palliated	rehabilitated	suffocated	venerated
palpitated	reinstated	superannuated	ventilated
participated	reiterated	supplicated	vindicated
penetrated	rejuvenated	syncopated	violated
perambulated	related	syndicated	vitiated
percolated	relegated	tabulated	vituperated
peregrinated	remunerated	tergiversated	vociferated
perforated	renovated	terminated	waited
permeated	Reno-vated	tessellated	weighted
perpetrated	repatriated	titillated	
perpetuated	repudiated	tittivated	ĂT'ed
personated	resuscitated	tolerated	batted
placated	retaliated	translated	chatted
plaited	reverberated	triangulated	dratted
plated	ruminated	triturated	fatted
plicated	rusticated	ululated	hatted
populated	salivated	unabated	matted
postulated	sated	unappropri-	patted
prated	satiated	ated	plaited
precipitated	saturated	unauthenti-	platted
predestinated	scintillated	cated	(cf. caryatid)
predicated	segregated	uncreated	
predominated	separated	undecorated	ĂT'en
premeditated	shallow-pated	underrated	batten
prevaricated	sibilated	understated	fatten
procrastinated	silicated	undulated	flatten
prognosticated	silver-plated	unilluminated	

paten	decoratest	**ĂT'est**	debateth
ratten	deprecatest	battest	decorateth
	devastatest	chattest	dedicateth
ĂT'ent or	dictatest	fattest	depopulateth
ĂT'ent	dilatest	flattest	devastateth
patent	ejaculatest	pattest	dictateth
	elevatest		dilateth
ĂT'est	emulatest	**ĂT'eth**	dissipateth
abatest	exaggeratest	abateth	dominateth
abdicatest	fascinatest	abdicateth	educateth
accommodatest	frustratest	accelerateth	ejaculateth
accumulatest	graduatest	accommodateth	elevateth
adulteratest	greatest	accumulateth	emulateth
advocatest	hatest	adulterateth	estimateth
aggravatest	hesitatest	advocateth	exaggerateth
agitatest	imitatest	agitateth	excavateth
alleviatest	indicatest	alleviateth	excommuni-
animatest	irritatest	ameliorateth	cateth
annihilatest	latest	animateth	exhilarateth
anticipatest	liberatest	annihilateth	expiateth
appreciatest	matest	anticipateth	extenuateth
articulatest	narratest	appropriateth	extricateth
assimilatest	necessitatest	arbitrateth	fabricateth
associatest	overratest	articulateth	fascinateth
awaitest	plaitest	associateth	frustrateth
baitest	pratest	awaiteth	hateth
beratest	radiatest	baiteth	hesitateth
calculatest	ratest	calculateth	imitateth
captivatest	regulatest	cancellateth	indicateth
celebratest	relatest	captivateth	irritateth
cogitatest	repudiatest	celebrateth	liberateth
commemoratest	skatest	circulateth	locateth
communicatest	slatest	conciliateth	luxuriateth
conjugatest	statest	confiscateth	mateth
consecratest	toleratest	congratulateth	meditateth
contaminatest	translatest	consecrateth	narrateth
contemplatest	underratest	contaminateth	operateth
createst	vacatest	contemplateth	overrateth
cultivatest	violatest	createth	prateth
debatest	waitest	cremateth	rateth
		cultivateth	regulateth

relateth	Ăth'en	Ăth'ing	rather
separateth	lathen	bathing	(cf. bother,
skateth		lathing	etc.)
stateth	Ăth'ful		
suffocateth	faithful	Ăth'les	ĂTH'urz
underrateth		faithless	slathers
vaccinateth	Ăth'ful, Ath'ful	scatheless	gathers, etc.
violateth	wrathful		
waiteth		Ăth'les	ĂT'i
	Ăth'ik	bathless	Ate
ĂT'eth	allopathic	pathless	eighty
batteth	antipathic	wrathless	ex necessitate
chatteth	chrestomathic		Haiti
fatteth	electropathic	ĂTH'om	Jubilate
patteth	felspathic	fathom	maty
	heteropathic		platy
ĂT'ez	homeopathic	ĂTH'omd	slaty
penates	hydropathic	unfathomed	weighty
	idiopathic		
ĂT'foot	kinemato-	Ăth'os	ĂT'ī
flatfoot	graphic	bathos	antenati
	neuropathic	pathos	illuminati
ĂT'form	orthognathic		literati
platform	osteopathic	Ăth'u	
	philomathic	Matthew	ĂT'i
ĂT'ful	polymathic		batty
fateful	prognathic	ĂTH'ur	catty
grateful	psycopathic	bather	chatty
hateful	spathic	swather	Cincinnati
ungrateful	telepathic		fatty
	theopathic	ĂTH'ur	Hattie
ĂT'ha		blather	Mattie
Jagannatha	ĂTH'ing	forgather	matty
(cf. marana-	bathing	gather	natty
tha)	swathing	lather	patty
	unswathing	ungather	Pattie
Ăth'an		upgather	ratty
Elnathan	Ă'thing		
Nathan	plaything	ĂTH'ur,	ĂT'īd
	(cf. scathing)	ĂTH'ur	bat-eyed
ĂT'hed		father	cat-eyed
fathead			
flathead			

ōld, ôr, ŏdd, oil, fŏŏt, out; ūse, ûrn, ŭp; THis, thin

ĂT'ĭd

caryatid

(cf. batted, etc.)

ĂT'if

caitiff

ĂT'ik

achromatic
acousmatic
acroatic
acrobatic
acromono-
  grammatic
adiabatic
Adriatic
aerostatic
agnatic
anagram-
  matic
anastatic
aphorismatic
aplanatic
apophtheg-
  matic
aquatic
aristocratic
arithmocratic
aromatic
Asiatic
astatic
asthmatic
attic
autocratic
automatic
axiomatic
bureaucratic
caryatic
categorematic
chromatic
climatic

commatic
dalmatic
democratic
diagrammatic
diaphragmatic
dichromatic
dilemmatic
diplomatic
dogmatic
dramatic
ecbatic
ecstatic
Eleatic
emblematic
emphatic
endermatic
enigmatic
epigrammatic
erratic
fanatic
fluviatic
geostatic
grammatic
hallelujatic
Hanseatic
hepatic
hieratic
hierogram-
  matic
hydrostatic
hyperbatic
hypostatic
idiocratic
idiomatic
idiosyncratic
isochromatic
isodiabatic
kinematic
lavatic
lipogrammatic
lymphatic

magistratic
majestatic
mathematic
melodramatic
miasmatic
mobocratic
monochro-
  matic
monogram-
  matic
morganatic
muriatic
noematic
numismatic
ochlocratic
operatic
palatic
pancratic
pancreatic
pantisocratic
paradigmatic
parallelo-
  grammatic
pathematic
phantomatic
phlegmatic
phosphatic
piratic
platic
pleochromatic
plutocratic
pneumatic
poematic
polychromatic
pragmatic
prelatic
prismatic
problematic
proceleus-
  matic
prostatic

protatic
quadratic
rhematic
rheumatic
sabbatic
Sarmatic
schematic
schismatic
sciatic
smegmatic
Socratic
somatic
static
stigmatic
stromatic
subaquatic
sulphatic
sylvatic
symptomatic
systematic
thematic
theocratic
theorematic
thermostatic
timocratic
traumatic
trigrammatic
truismatic
vatic
viatic
villatic
zeugmatic
zygomatic

ĂT'ik

aquatic
(see chaotic,
  etc.)

ĂT'iks

aerostatics

---

electro-statics
hydrostatics
hygrostatics
mathematics
pneumatics
statics
attics, etc.

Ā′tim

daytime
playtime

ĂT′im

literatim
seriatim
verbatim

ĂT′in

Latin
matin
patine
platen
satin

ĂT′ing

abating
abbreviating
abdicating
abnegating
abominating
accelerating
accentuating
accommodating
accumulating
adulterating
advocating
aërating
aggravating
aggregating
agitating
alienating

alleviating
alternating
amalgamating
ameliorating
amputating
animating
annihilating
annumerating
anticipating
appreciating
appropriating
approximating
arbitrating
armor-plating
articulating
assassinating
assimilating
associating
attenuating
augurating
authenticating
awaiting
baiting
bating
berating
calculating
calumniating
capitulating
castigating
celebrating
circulating
coagulating
cogitating
collocating
commemorat-
    ing
commiserating
communicating
compensating
complicating
concentrating

conciliating
confabulating
confederating
confiscating
congratulating
congregating
conjugating
consecrating
consolidating
consummating
contaminating
contemplating
co-operating
corroborating
corrugating
creating
cremating
criminating
culminating
cultivating
dating
debating
debilitating
decapitating
decimating
decorating
dedicating
degenerating
delegating
deliberating
delineating
demonstrating
denominating
depopulating
deprecating
depreciating
derivating
derogating
desecrating
designating
deteriorating

determinating
detonating
devastating
deviating
dictating
differentiating
dilapidating
dilating
discriminating
disintegrating
dislocating
disseminating
dissimulating
dissipating
dissociating
dominating
duplicating
educating
ejaculating
elaborating
electro-plating
elevating
eliminating
elucidating
emaciating
emanating
emancipating
emigrating
emulating
enumerating
equivocating
eradicating
estimating
evacuating
evaporating
exaggerating
exasperating
excavating
excommunica-
    ting
excruciating

execrating
exhilarating
exonerating
expatiating
expectorating
expiating
expostulating
extenuating
extricating
fabricating
facilitating
fascinating
federating
felicitating
fêting
flagellating
fluctuating
formulating
fornicating
freighting
frustrating
fulminating
fumigating
generating
germinating
gesticulating
graduating
granulating
grating
gratulating
gravitating
hating
hesitating
humiliating
illuminating
illustrating
imitating
immigrating
immolating
impersonating
implicating

imprecating
inaugurating
incapacitating
incarcerating
incriminating
incubating
indicating
indiscrimi-
    nating
inebriating
infanticipating
infatuating
inflating
infuriating
ingratiating
initiating
innovating
inoculating
insinuating
instigating
insulating
interpolating
interrogating
intimating
intimidating
intoxicating
inundating
invalidating
investigating
invigorating
invocating
irradiating
irrigating
irritating
isolating
iterating
legislating
liberating
liquidating
locating
lubricating

luxuriating
manipulating
masticating
mating
matriculating
mediating
meditating
migrating
militating
mitigating
moderating
modulating
mutilating
narrating
navigating
necessitating
negotiating
nickle-plating
nominating
obliterating
obviating
operating
originating
oscillating
osculating
overrating
overstating
palliating
palpitating
participating
penetrating
perambulating
percolating
peregrinating
perforating
permeating
perpetrating
perpetuating
personating
plaiting
plating

populating
postulating
prating
precipitating
predominating
premeditating
prevaricating
prognosticat-
    ing
promulgating
propagating
propitiating
punctuating
quadrupli-
    cating
radiating
rating
rebating
recapitulating
reciprocating
recreating
recriminating
recuperating
refrigerating
regulating
reinstating
reiterating
rejuvenating
relating
relegating
remunerating
renovating
repudiating
resuscitating
retaliating
reverberating
ruminating
rusticating
satiating
saturating
scintillating

separating
simulating
skating
slating
sophisticating
speculating
stating
stimulating
stipulating
subjugating
suffocating
supplicating
syncopating
tabulating
terminating
titillating
tittivating
tolerating
translating
unabating
unaccommo-
  dating
underrating
understating
undeviating
undiscrimi-
  nating
undulating
vacating
vaccinating
vacillating
validating
variegating
vegetating
venerating
ventilating
verberating
vindicating
violating
vitiating
vituperating

vociferating
waiting
weighting

ĀT'ing

batting
chatting
fatting
matting
patting
platting
ratting
tatting
vatting

ĀT'ir

satire

ĀT'is

gratis

ĀT'is

brattice
lattice

ĀT'ish

cattish
fattish
flattish

ĀT'iv

abrogative
accelerative
accumulative
administrative
agglomerative
agglutinative
aggregative
agitative
alleviative
alliterative

alterative
ameliorative
animative
anticipative
annunciative
appreciative
approbative
appropriative
approximative
assimilative
associative
authoritative
coagulative
cogitative
collative
commemora-
  tive
commiserative
communica-
  tive
confederative
consolidative
contaminative
continuative
co-operative
co-ordinative
copulative
corroborative
creative
criminative
cumulative
dative
decorative
degenerative
deliberative
denominative
denunciative
deprecative
depreciative
desiderative
designative

determinative
dilative
discriminative
disseminative
dominative
duplicative
edulcorative
elaborative
elucidative
emanative
emulative
enumerative
enunciative
eradicative
estimative
evaporative
exaggerative
execrative
exonerative
explicative
federative
generative
germinative
glutinative
gravitative
hesitative
illuminative
imaginative
imbricative
imitative
implicative
incogitative
incommunica-
  tive
incorporative
incriminative
incubative
indiscrimina-
  tive
initiative
innovative

inoperative	regenerative	embattle	effeminately
insinuative	reiterative	prattle	elaborately
interpenetra-	remunerative	rattle	extortionately
tive	replicative	Seattle	fortunately
interpretative	reprobative	tattle	greatly
investigative	resuscitative	tittle-tattle	illiterately
irritative	retaliative		immaculately
iterative	reverberative	**ĂT'las, ĂT'les**	immoderately
justificative	*sative*	atlas	inarticulately
lacerative	separative	cravatless	inconsider-
legislative	significative	hatless	ately
manipulative	speculative	(see ĂT + less)	intemperately
meditative	stative		intimately
ministrative	stimulative	**ĂT'les**	irately
mitigative	subordinative	baitless	lately
modificative	suffocative	dateless	legitimately
native	supplicative	estateless	moderately
operative	suppurative	freightless	sedately
opinionative	terminative	gaitless	stately
originative	translative	gateless	straitly
oscillative	undulative	grateless	ultimately
palliative	vegetative	hateless	
participative	velicative	mateless	**ĂT'li**
penetrative	ventilative	rateless	fatly
perforative	verificative	stateless	flatly
predestinative	vindicative	weightless	patly
procreative	violative		rattly
prognostica-	vituperative	**ĂT'li (ĬT'li)**	
tive	vivificative	accurately	**ĂT'ling**
pronunciative		adequately	battling
propagative	**ĂT'kins**	affectionately	catling
purificative	Atkins	alternately	fatling
qualificative	Batkins	appropriately	gatling
qualitative	(cf. Watkins)	approximately	prattling
quantitative		compassion-	rattling
radiative	**ĂT' 'l**	ately	tattling
ratiocinative	battel	consummately	
recreative	battle	delicately	**ĂT'lur**
recriminative	cattle	desolately	battler
recuperative	chattel	desperately	prattler
refrigerative	death-rattle	disconsolately	rattler

āle, câre, ădd, ärm, åsk; mē, hęre, ĕnd; īce, ĭll;

Statler	Ă'to	ĂT'res	ĂT'u
tattler	annatto	mattress	statue
	chateau	mulattress	
ĂT'ment	enamorato		ĂT'um
abatement	legato	ĂT'rik	datum
affreightment	obbligato	hippiatric	desideratum
instatement	pizzicato	iatric	erratum
overstatement	pomato	kinesiatric	pomatum
reinstatement	staccato	matric	postulatum
statement	tomato	Patrick	stratum
understate-		theatric	substratum
ment	ĂT'om		superstratum
	atom	ĂT'riks	ultimatum
ĂT'nes		administratrix	
appropriate-	ĂT'on	aviatrix	ĂT'um
ness	Clayton	cicatrix	stratum
considerate-	Dayton	generatrix	
ness	Leighton	imitatrix	ĂT'um
greatness	peyton	impropriatrix	datum
innateness	Satan	matrix	pomatum
lateness		mediatrix	
ornateness	ĂT'on	spectatrix	ĂT'ūr
sedateness	baton	testatrix	good-nature
straightness	Hatton		ill-nature
		ĀT'ris, ĂT'ris	legislature
ĂT'nes	ĂT'ra	matrice	nature
fatness	Cleopatra		nomenclature
flatness		ĂT'ron	plicature
patness	Ā'tre	matron	unnature
	baytree	natron	
ĂT'o	maytree	patron	ĂT'ŭr
literato			abator
Plato	ĀT'red	ĂTS'man	abbreviator
pomato	hatred	statesman	abdicator
potato			abnegator
tomato	ĂT'res	ĂTS'man	abrogater
	dictatress	batsman	accelerator
ĂT'o	imitatress		accumulator
chateau	spectatress	ĂT'son	adjudicator
mulatto	traitress	Batson	administrator
plateau	waitress	Matson	

ōld, ôr, ŏdd, oil, fŏŏt, out; ūse, ûrn, ŭp; THis, thin

adulator
affreighter
aggravator
agitator
alienator
alleviator
alligator
alma mater
amalgamator
ameliorator
annihilator
annotator
annunciator
appropriator
arbitrator
arch-traitor
aspirater
asseverator
assimilator
authenticator
aviator
awaiter
baiter
berater
calculator
calumniator
captivator
castigator
cater
cogitator
collaborator
commemo-
   rator
commentator
comminator
commiserator
compotator
compurgator
computator
concentrator
conciliator

confiscator
conjugator
consecrator
conservator
consolidator
contaminator
contemplator
co-operator
corroborator
crater
creator
cremator
criminator
cultivator
dater
debater
decapitator
decorator
dedicator
deliberator
delineator
demonstrator
denominator
denunciator
depopulator
depreciator
depredator
designator
devastator
deviator
dictater
dictator
disintegrator
disseminator
dissimulator
duplicator
dura mater
educater
ejaculator
elaborator
elevator

eliminator
elucidator
emanator
emancipator
emendator
emulator
enumerator
enunciator
equator
equivocator
eradicator
evaporator
exaggerator
excavator
execrator
exhilarator
exonerator
expatiator
expectorator
expiator
extenuator
exterminator
extricator
fabricator
facilitator
fascinator
federator
felicitator
first-rater
flagellator
formulator
fornicator
frater
freighter
frustrator
fumigator
gaiter
generator
germinator
gesticulator
gladiator

grater
greater
hater
hesitater
humilater
hypothecator
illuminator
illustrator
imitator
imperator
impersonator
imprimatur
incarcerator
incorporator
incriminator
incubator
indicator
inflater
initiator
innovator
inoculator
insinuator
instigator
insulator
interpolator
interrogator
intimidator
investigator
invigorator
invocator
irrigator
irritator
later
laudator
legislator
liberator
liquidator
litigator
locater
lubricator
manipulator

āle, câre, ădd, ärm, ăsk; mē, hẹre, ĕnd; īce, ĭll;

masticator
mater
mediator
meditator
migrater
mitigator
moderator
modulator
mutilator
narrator
navigator
negotiator
nominator
obliterator
officiator
operator
originator
oscillator
pacificator
palliator
palpitator
pater
perambulator
percolator
peregrinator
perforator
permeator
perpetrator
personator
pia mater
piscator
plaiter
plater
prater
precipitator
predominator
prestidigitator
prevaricator
procrastinator
procurator
prognosticator

promulgator
propagator
propitiator
radiator
rater
reciprocator
refrigerator
regenerator
regrater
regulator
reinstater
reiterator
relater
remonstrator
renovator
repudiator
respirator
resuscitator
retaliator
ruminator
rusticator
satyr
scintillator
scrutator
second-rater
sedater
separator
simulator
skater
slater
sophisticator
spectator
speculator
Stabat Mater
stater
stimulator
stipulator
straighter
straiter
subjugator
supererogator

supplicator
tabulator
"tater"
tergiversator
testator
third-rater
titillator
tittivator
traitor
translator
vaccinator
vacillator
vaticinator
venerator
ventilator
versificator
vindicator
violator
vituperator
vociferator
waiter

ĀT'ūr

stature

ĀT'ŭr

attar
batter
beflatter
bepatter
bescatter
bespatter
blatter
chatter
clatter
clitter-clatter
fatter
flatter
hatter
latter
matter

patter
platter
ratter
satyr
scatter
shatter
smatter
spatter
splatter
subject-matter
tatter

ĂT'ur

alma mater
mater
pater
Stabat Mater

ĂT'urn

pattern
Saturn
slattern
willow-pattern

ĀT'us

afflatus
apparatus
hiatus
literatus
saleratus
senatus
status
stratous
stratus

ĂT'us

apparatus

ĂT'ut

statute

ōld, ôr, ŏdd, oil, fŏŏt, out; ūse, ûrn, ŭp; THis, thin

ĀT'wa	player	**ĀV'el**	**ĀV'eth**
gateway	portrayer	gavel	*behaveth*
straitway	prayer	gravel	*beslaveth*
	preyer	ravel	*braveth*
Ā'ur	prepayer	travel	*craveth*
affrayer	purveyor	unravel	*depraveth*
allayer	relayer	(cf. cavil)	*engraveth*
arrayer	repayer		*enslaveth*
assayer	slayer	**ĀV'eld**	*forgaveth*
belayer	soothsayer		*gaveth*
betrayer	sprayer	gravelled	*laveth*
brayer	stayer	ravelled	*paveth*
conveyer	strayer	travelled	*raveth*
defrayer	surveyer	untravelled	*saveth*
delayer	swayer		*shaveth*
disarrayer	underpayer	**ĀV'en**	*slaveth*
dismayer	underplayer	craven	*waiveth*
disobeyer	viséer	*engraven*	*waveth*
displayer	waylayer	graven	
essayer	weigher	haven	**ĀV'ez**
flayer		shaven	Davies
gainsayer	**Ă'va**		
gayer	brava	**ĀV'est**	**ĀV'i**
grayer	cassava	*behavest*	affidavy
greyer	guava	*beslavest*	cavy
hoorayer	Java	bravest	Davie
inlayer	lava	*cravest*	Davy
interlayer		*depravest*	gravy
inveigher	**ĀV'al**	*engravest*	navy
layer	travail	*enslavest*	peccavi
matineer		*forgavest*	ravy
mayor	**ĀV'e**	*gavest*	slavey
mislayer	agave	*gravest*	wavy
missayer	ave	*lavest*	
neigher		*pavest*	**ĀV'id**
obeyer	**Ă've**	*ravest*	David
outlayer	ave	*savest*	*engraved*, etc.
outstayer		*shavest*	
outweigher	**ĀV'el**	*slavest*	**ĀV'id**
overlayer	gavel	suavest	avid
payer	naval	*waivest*	gravid
	navel	*wavest*	

impavid
pavid

ĂV'ĭj
ravage
savage
scavage

ĂV'ĭk
gravic
Pan-Slavic
Slavic

ĂV'ĭn
savin
spavin

ĀV'ĭng
behaving
belaving
beslaving
braving
caving
craving
depraving
engraving
enslaving
graving
labor-saving
laving
misbehaving
outbraving
paving
raving
saving
shaving
slaving
staving
steel-engrav-
  ing
waiving

waving
wood-engrav-
  ing

ĂV'ĭng
having
salving

ĂV'ĭng
calving
halving
salving

ĀV'ĭs
clavis
Davis
mavis
rara avis

ĂV'ĭsh
bravish
knavish
slavish

ĂV'ĭsh
enravish
lavish
McTavish
ravish

ĀV'ĭt
affidavit
indicavit

ĂV'ĭt
davit

ĀV'les
caveless
graveless
slaveless

staveless
waveless

ĀV'lĭ
bravely
gravely
knavely
suavely

ĂV'lĭn
javelin
ravelin

ĀV'lĭng
shaveling

ĀV'ment
depravement
engravement
enslavement
lavement
pavement

ĀV'nes
braveness
graveness
suaveness

ĀV'o
bravo
octavo

ĂV'o
bravo
octavo

ĂV'ok
havoc

ĀV'ur
braver

cadaver
claver
craver
demiquaver
depraver
disfavor
engraver
enslaver
favor
flavor
graver
laver
marriage-
  favor
Papaver
paver
quaver
raver
saver
savor
semiquaver
shaver
slaver
suaver
waiver
waver
wood-engraver

ĂV'ur
beslaver
cadaver
palaver
haver

ĂV'ur
palaver
suaver

ĀV'urd
favored
flavored

ill-favored
quavered
savored
wavered
well-favored

ĀV'urn
cavern
tavern

ĀV'us
Gustavus

ĀV'yur
behavior
havior
misbehavior
Pavier
pavior
savior
Xavier

Ā'ward
wayward

Ā'ward
vaward

Ā'wir
haywire

Ā'worn
sprayworn
wayworn

Ā'ya
Aglaia
ayah
calisaya
Isaiah
naia

Ā'yan
Altaian
Cataian
Himalayan
Malayan

Ā'yan
Himalayan

Ā'yard
Bayard

Ā'yo
K.O.
kayo
Mayo

Ā'yu
gay-you
Vayu

ĀZ'a
Gaza

ĂZ'a
cazazza
piazza
plaza

ĀZ'al
appraisal
hazel
nasal
witch-hazel

ĂZ'ard
haphazard
hazard
mazard
mazzard

ĀZ'est
amazest
braisest
bepraisest
blazest
dazest
gazest
hazest
glazest
paraphrasest
phrasest
praisest
raisest
razest
upraisest

ĀZ'eth
amazeth
bepraiseth
blazeth
braiseth
dazeth
gazeth
glazeth
hazeth
paraphraseth
phraseth
praiseth
raiseth
razeth
upraiseth

ĀZ'ez
amazes
bemazes
blazes
braises
brazes
chaises
crazes
daisies

dazes
gazes
glazes
grazes
hazes
mayonnaises
mazes
paraphrases
phases
phrases
praises
raises
razes

Ā'zhun
abrasion
dissuasion
erasion
evasion
invasion
occasion
persuasion
suasion
(cf. Caucasian,
    and Ā'zhi-an
    words)

Ā'zhur
azure
brazier
embrasure
erasure
Frazier
glazier
grazier
razure

ĂZH'ur
azure

ĀZ'ĭ
blazy

āle, câre, ădd, ärm, åsk; mē, hĕre, ĕnd; īce, ĭll;

crazy
daisy
hazy
jasey
lackadaisy
lazy
mazy
phrasey
paraphrasey

ĂZ'i

ghawazi
ghazi

ĂZ'il

Basil
(cf. ĂZ''l)

ĂZ'in

raisin

ĂZ'ing

ʌblazing
amazing
bemazing
bepraising
blazing
braising

brazing
dazing
gazing
glazing
grazing
hazing
lazing
outblazing
outgazing
paraphrasing
phrasing
praising
raising
self-praising
star-gazing
upblazing
upraising

ĂZ''l

Basil
bedazzle
dazzle
frazzle
razzle-dazzle

ĂZ'les

praiseless

ĂZ'ling

dazzling
frazzling

ĂZ'ma

asthma
miasma
phantasma
Phasma
plasma
protoplasma

ĂZ'mal

miasmal
phantasmal
protoplasmal

ĂZ'ment

amazement
appraisement
praisement

ĂZ'mi

chasmy

ĂZ'mik

bioplasmic
miasmic
protoplasmic

ĂZ'mus

Erasmus

ĂZ'on

blazon
brazen
diapason
emblazon
glazen
scazon

ĂZ'ur

appraiser
blazer
dispraiser
Eleazer
Fraser
gazer
geyser
lazar
paraphraser
phraser
praiser
raiser
razer
razor
self-praiser
star-gazer
upgazer
upraiser

E

For a discussion of words included under the accented vowels following, see the beginning of E rhymes in Section I.

Ē'a
Althæa
Astræa
Ave Maria
Cassiopea

cavalleria
Crimea
Cypræa
dahabeah
Dorothea

dyspnea
Hosea
Hygeia
idea
Latakia

Lucia
Maria
Medea
melopœia
obeah

onomatopœia
panacea
pathopœia
pharmacopœia
ratafia
Rhea
spiræa
Zea

Ē'al

Arctogaeal
beau ideal
empyreal
hymeneal
ideal
laryngeal
real
unideal
unreal

Ē'an

Achean
adamantean
Adonean
Ægean
amœbean
amphigean
Andean
Anomoean
antipodean
apogean
Archimedean
Argean
Assidean
astraean
Atlantean
Augean
Berean
Cadmean
Caribbean
Chaldean

Circean
colossean
Crimean
cyclopean
Cytherean
ditrochean
empyrean
epicurean
Etnean
European
Galilean
gigantean
Hasmonaean
Hyblæan
hymenean
Indo-European
Judean
Laodicean
laryngean
lethean
Linnaean
lyncean
Maccabean
Manichaean
mausolean
Medicean
Melibean
Nemean
Niobean
nymphean
Orphean
pæan
Palæogæan
pampean
Pandean
perigean
phalangean
Pharisean
plebeian
protean
Pyrenean

Pythagorean
Sabæan
Sadducean
Sisyphean
terpsichorean
theodicean
Vendean
Zoilean

Ē'as

Aeneas
Zaccheus

Ē'ba

amœba
Reba
Seba
Sheba
zareba

Ē'be

Hebe
Phoebe
T.B.

ĒB'en

Eben

ĔB'ing

ebbing
unebbing
webbing

ĒB"l

enfeeble
feeble

ĔB"l

arch-rebel
djebel
pebble

rebel
treble

Ē'bo

gazeebo
Nebo
placebo

ĔB'on

ebon

Ē'bord

free-board
key-board
seaboard

Ē'born

free-born
sea-born

ĔB'ra

zebra

ĔB'rok

pibroch

ĔB'ru

Hebrew

ĒB'ur

Gheber

ĔB'ur

ebber
webber
Weber

Ē'bus

glebous
Phoebus
rebus

ĔCH'ed

wretched
(see ĔCH+ed)

ĔCH'est

beseechest
bleachest
foreachest
impeachest
overreachest
preachest
reachest
screechest
sea-chest
tea-chest
teachest

ĔCH'eth

beseecheth
bleacheth
forereacheth
impeacheth
overreacheth
preacheth
reacheth
screecheth
teacheth

ĔCH'ez

beaches
beeches
beseeches
bleaches
breaches
breeches
forereaches
impeaches
leeches
overreaches
peaches
preaches

reaches
screeches
sea-reaches
speeches
teaches

ĔCH'i

beachy
Beatrice
beechy
bleachy
breachy
campeachy
peachy
preachy
reachy
queachy
reechy
screechy
speechy

ĔCH'i

fetchy
sketchy
stretchy
tetchy
vetchy

ĔCH'ing

beaching
beseeching
bleaching
breaching
breeching
forereaching
foreteaching
impeaching
leaching
leeching
overreaching
peaching

preaching
reaching
screeching
teaching

ĔCH'ing

etching
fetching
sketching
stretching

ĔCH'les

beachless
beechless
breachless
peachless
reachless
speechless
teachless

ĔCH'ment

beseechment
impeachment
preachment

ĔCH'up

catchup
ketchup

ĔCH'ur

Beecher
beseecher
bleacher
breacher
breecher
forereacher
impeacher
leacher
leecher
overreacher
peacher

preacher
reacher
screecher
teacher
(cf. Ē'tŭr)

ĔCH'ur

etcher
fetcher
fletcher
lecher
retcher
sketcher
stretcher
treacher

Ē'da

Leda
olla podrida
Theda
Veda
Vida

ĔD'a

Edda
Nedda

ĔD'ant

pedant

ĔD'bed

reedbed
seedbed
weedbed

ĔD'bet

deadbeat

ĔD'breast

redbreast

ĔD'bug
bedbug
redbug

ĒD'ed
acceded
anteceded
beaded
ceded
conceded
deeded
exceeded
heeded
impeded
interceded
kneaded
needed
pleaded
preceded
proceeded
receded
reeded
retroceded
seceded
seeded
stampeded
succeeded
superseded
unheeded
unweeded
weeded

ĔD'ed
addle-headed
arrow-headed
bare-headed
bedded
beetle-headed
beheaded
blunderheaded
bullheaded

chuckle-
    headed
clear-headed
dreaded
dunder-headed
embedded
fat-headed
feather-headed
fiddle-headed
flat-headed
giddy-headed
gross-headed
headed
heavy-headed
hoary-headed
hot-headed
hydra-headed
idle-headed
Janus-headed
leaded
light-headed
longheaded
many-headed
muddle-
    headed
pig-headed
pudding-
    headed
puzzle-headed
rattle-headed
shock-headed
shredded
sleek-headed
soft-headed
thick-headed
threaded
trundle-
    headed
unbedded
undreaded
unthreaded

unwedded
warm-headed
weak-headed
wedded
wrong-headed

ĒD'en
Eden
reeden
Sweden

ĔD'en
deaden
leaden
redden
threaden

ĔD'ens
antecedence
credence
intercedence
precedence
(cf. antece-
    dents)

ĔD'ent
antecedent
credent
decedent
intercedent
needn't
precedent
retrocedent
sedent

Ē'dep
knee-deep
sea-deep
three-deep

ĒD'est
accedest

bleedest
breedest
cedest
concedest
exceedest
feedest
heedest
impedest
intercedest
kneadest
leadest
misleadest
needest
overfeedest
pleadest
precedest
proceedest
readest
recedest
secedest
seedest
speedest
stampedest
succeedest
supersedest
weedest

ĔD'est
beheadest
dreadest
outspreadest
reddest
sheddest
spreadest
threadest
treadest
weddest

ĒD'eth
accedeth
bleedeth

breedeth
cedeth
concedeth
exceedeth
feedeth
heedeth
impedeth
intercedeth
kneadeth
leadeth
misleadeth
needeth
overfeedeth
pleadeth
precedeth
proceedeth
readeth
recedeth
secedeth
seedeth
speedeth
stampedeth
succeedeth
supersedeth
weedeth

ĔD′eth
beheadeth
dreadeth
headeth
outspreadeth
overspreadeth
sheddeth
shreddeth
spreadeth
threadeth
treadeth
weddeth

ĔD′fast
steadfast

ĒD′ful
deedful
heedful
meedful
needful
speedful
unheedful
unneedful

ĔD′ful
dreadful

ĒD′gron
reed-grown
seed-grown
weed-grown

ĔD′hed
deadhead
redhead

ĔD′het
dead-heat
red-heat

ĒD′i
beady
creedy
deedy
encyclopedy
greedy
heedy
indeedy
Leedy
needy
predy
reedy
seedy
speedy
unheedy
weedy

ĔD′i
already
Eddie
eddy
Freddie
heady
leady
ready
reddy
shreddy
steady
thready
unready
unsteady

ĒD′ik
comedic
cyclopædic
encyclopædic
Vedic

ĔD′ik
Eddic
Samoyedic

ĔD′ikt
edict

ĒD′ing
acceding
beading
bleading
breeding
ceding
conceding
exceeding
feeding
God-speeding
heeding
impeding
interbreeding

interceding
interpleading
kneading
leading
love-lies-
   bleeding
misleading
misreading
needing
outspeeding
over-feeding
pleading
preceding
proceeding
reading
receding
reeding
retroceding
seceding
seeding
speeding
stampeding
succeeding
superseding
unbleeding
underfeeding
unheeding
weeding

ĔD′ing
bedding
beheading
bespreading
dreading
embedding
heading
leading
outspreading
overspreading
redding
shedding

shredding
sledding
spreading
steading
tedding
threading
treading
wedding

ĔD'ish

deadish
eddish
reddish

ĔD'it

accredit
credit
discredit
edit
miscredit
subedit
you said it

ĒD'ith

Edith
(cf. needeth,
etc.)

ĔD'iz

teddies
(see ĔD'i+s)

ĒD''l

beadle
bi-pedal
centipedal
dædal
needle
pedal
semipedal
tweedle
wheeled

ĔD''l

bi-pedal
heddle
intermeddle
medal
meddle
pedal
peddle
reddle
treadle
tripedal

ĔD'lam

Bedlam

ĔD'land

headland

ĔD'les

breedless
creedless
deedless
heedless
needless
seedless
speedless
steedless
weedless

ĔD'les

bedless
breadless
dreadless
headless
leadless

ĔD'li

chance-medley
deadly
medley
redly

ĔD'lin

breadline
dead-line
head-line

ĒD'ling

needling
reedling
seedling
wheedling

ĔD'ling

intermeddling
meddling
peddling

ĔD'lit

dead-light
red-light

ĔD'lok

deadlock
wedlock

ĒD'lur

needler
wheedler

ĔD'lur

intermeddler
meddler
medlar
peddler
treadler

ĔD'man

Friedman

ĔD'man

dead-man
Edman

headman
red-man

ĔD'na

Edna

ĔD'nes

deadness
redness

Ē'do

credo
Lido
stampedo
teredo
Toledo
torpedo

ĔD'o

meadow

ĔD'ra

ex cathedra
exedra

ĒD'ral

cathedral
decahedral
didecahedral
diedral
dihedral
pro-cathedral

ĔD'rest

bed-rest
head-rest

ĔD'ston

headstone

ĒD'tim

feed-time
seed-time

Ē'dum
freedom
(cf. sedum)

ĒD'ūr
procedure
supersedure

ĒDŭr
acceder
anteceder
breeder
cedar
ceder
conceder
exceeder
feeder
heeder
impeder
impleader
interceder
interpleader
kneader
leader
misleader
needer
overfeeder
pleader
preceder
proceeder
reader
receder
retroceder
ring-leader
scripture-
   reader
seceder
seeder
speeder
stampeder

succeeder
superseder
weeder

ĔD'ur
bedder
beheader
bespreader
Cheddar
deader
double-header
dreader
edder
embedder
header
leader
redder
shedder
shredder
spreader
tedder
threader
treader
unthreader

ĔD'wa
headway

ĔD'ward
bedward
Edward

ĔD'wood
dead-wood
redwood

ĒDZ'man
beadsman
bedesman
seedsman

ĔDZ'man
headsman
leadsman

ĔD'zo
intermezzo
mezzo

Ē'est
agreest
feest
fleest
foreseest
freest
overseest
refereest
seest
weest

Ē'eth
agreeth
feeth
fleeth
foreseeth
freeth
overseeth
seeth

ĒF'as
Cephas
(cf. Josephus)

ĒF'dom
chiefdom

ĒF'en
deafen
(cf. Strephon)

ĒF'i
beefy

leafy
reefy
sheafy

ĒF'ij
leafage

ĒF'ik
malefic
peristrephic

ĒF'les
briefless
chiefless
griefless
leafless
sheafless

ĔF'nes
deafness

Ē'fom
sea-foam

Ē'foul
pea-fowl
sea-fowl

ĔFT'nes
deftness

ĔF'ri
Geoffrey
Jeffrey

ĒF'stak
beefsteak

ĒF'tin
chieftain

ĔF′uj	ĔG′ ′l	ĔG′ur	foreseeing
refuge	bald eagle	beleaguer	freeing
	beagle	eager	guaranteeing
Ē′ful	eagle	eagre	inbeing
gleeful	gregal	fatiguer	overseeing
	illegal	intriguer	refereeing
ĔF′ur	inveigle	leaguer	seeing
beefer	kleagle	meagre	spreeing
briefer	legal	overeager	teeing
chiefer	regal		unforeseeing
liefer	vice-regal	ĔG′ur	unseeing
reefer	(cf. sea-gull)	beggar	well-being
		booklegger	
ĔF′ur	ĔG′lur	bootlegger	Ē′ist
deafer	beagler	egger	antitheist
feoffor	inveigler	legger	deist
heifer		pegger	hylotheist
zephyr	ĔG′ment	seggar	manicheist
	segment		monotheist
Ē′ga		Ē′gurt	polytheist
omega	ĔG′nant	sea-girt	theist
Riga	impregnant		
Talladega	pregnant	Ē′ik	Ē′it
Vega	queen-regnant	caffeic	albeit
	regnant	mythopœic	sobeit
ĔG′i		rheic	
dreggy	Ē′go	xanthoproteic	Ē′izm
eggy	ego		absenteeism
leggy	Oswego	Ē′in	antitheism
Peggy	Otsego	caffeine	autotheism
		codeine	cosmotheism
ĔG′ing	Ē′gren	zein	deism
fatiguing	pea-green		henotheism
intriguing	sea-green	Ē′ing	hylotheism
leaguing		agreeing	manicheism
	ĔG′res	being	monotheism
ĔG′ing	egress	clear-seeing	Parseeism
begging	negress	decreeing	Phariseeism
egging	regress	disagreeing	polytheism
legging		feeing	Sadduceeism
pegging	ĔG′ro	fleeing	sciotheism
unpegging	negro		

Sutteeism
theism
weism

Ē'jance
allegiance

ĔJ'burd
hedge-bird
sedge-bird

ĔJ'end
legend

ĔJ'ent
regent

ĔJ'est
allegest
dredgest
fledgest
hedgest
impledgest
◦ledgest
◦wedgest

ĔJ'eth
allegeth
dredgeth
fledgeth
hedgeth
impledgeth
pledgeth
wedgeth

ĔJ'ez
alleges
dredges
edges
hedges
kedges

ledges
pledges
sledges
wedges

ĔJ'i
cledgy
edgy
hedgy
ledgy
sedgy
wedgy

ĔJ'ing
alleging
dredging
edging
enhedging
fledging
hedging
kedging
impledging
interpledging
pledging
sledging
wedging

ĔJ'ling
fledgeling

ĔJ'man
liegeman

ĔJ'ment
besiegement

ĔJ'un
legion
region
under-region
(cf. collegian

and Ē'ji-an
words)

ĔJ'ur
alleger
dredger
edger
hedger
ledger
leger
pledger
sledger

ĔJ'us
egregious
sacrilegious

ĔJ'wood
Edgewood
Wedgewood

Ē'ka
bibliotheca
chica
Costa Rica
Dominica
eureka
Frederica
Fredrika
glyptotheca
Meeka
Tanganyika
Topeka
Ulrica
zotheca

ĔK'a
Rebecca
Mecca

ĔK'ad
decade

ĔK'al
bibliothecal
cæcal
fæcal
thecal
treacle

ĔK'ant
piquant
precant
secant

ĔK'ant
impeccant
peccant

ĔK'en
weaken
(see ĔK'on)

ĔK'est
bespeakest
bleakest
meekest
leakest
reekest
seekest
shriekest
sneakest
speakest
squeakest
streakest
uniquest
weakest
wreakest

ĔK'est
bedeckest
checkest
deckest
reckest
wreckest

ĒK'eth	ĒK'ing	ĒK"l	heckling
bespeaketh	bespeaking	treacle	keckling
leaketh	cheeking	(see ĒK'al)	speckling
reeketh	creaking		
seeketh	eking	**ĔK"l**	**ĔK'lur**
shrieketh	forespeaking	befreckle	heckler
sneaketh	leaking	bespeckle	freckler, etc.
speaketh	reeking	deckle	
squeaketh	seeking	freckle	**ĔK'mat**
streaketh	self-seeking	heckle	checkmate
wreaketh	sheiking	Jeckyll	deck-mate
	shrieking	keckle	
ĔK'eth	sneaking	Seckel	**ĔK'nes**
bedecketh	speaking	shekel	antiqueness
checketh	squeaking	speckle	bleakness
decketh	tweaking		meekness
recketh	wreaking	**ĔK'les**	obliqueness
wrecketh		feckless	sleekness
	ĔK'ing	fleckless	uniqueness
ĒK'i	bedecking	necklace	weakness
bleaky	bewrecking	reckless	
Bolsheviki	checking	speckless	**ĔK'nik**
cheeky	decking		philotechnic
cliquey	flecking	**ĒK'li**	polytechnic
cockaleekie	henpecking	bleakly	pyrotechnic
creaky	pecking	meekly	technic
leaky	recking	obliquely	theotechnic
Mensheviki	trekking	sleekly	
peeky	wrecking	treacly	**ĔK'ning**
reeky		uniquely	beckoning
sheiky	**ĔK'ish**	weakly	reckoning
sleeky	bleakish	weekly	unreckoning
sneaky	cliquish		
squeaky	freakish	**ĔK'li**	**Ē'ko**
streaky	Greekish	freckly	beccafico
	meekish	speckly	fico
ĒK'id	peakish		
meek-eyed	sneakish	**ĔK'ling**	**ĔK'o**
oblique-eyed	weakish	weakling	echo
weak-eyed			gecko
	ĔK'ish	**ĔK'ling**	re-echo
	peckish	freckling	secco

āle, cârǫ, ădd, ärm, åsk; mē, hĕre, ĕnd; īce, ĭll;

Ē'kok	*flexeth*	insection	prexy
Leacock	*perplexeth*	inspection	pyrexy
meacock	*unsexeth*	insubjection	
peacock	*vexeth*	insurrection	**ĔK'sil**
		intellection	exile
ĔK'on	**ĔK'shun**	interjection	flexile
archdeacon	abjection	intersection	
beacon	adjection	introspection	**ĔK'sing**
deacon	affection	irreflection	annexing
meeken	bisection	lection	flexing
weaken	by-election	misdirection	inflexing
	circumspection	objection	perplexing
ĔK'on	circumvection	perfection	unsexing
beckon	collection	predilection	vexing
reckon	complexion	prelection	
	confection	projection	**ĔK'sis**
ĔK'ond	connection	prospection	Alexis
second	convection	protection	
unreckoned,	correction	provection	**ĔK'sit**
etc.	defection	recollection	exit
	deflection	rection	
Ē'krab	dejection	re-election	**ĔK'stant**
pea-crab	detection	reflection	extant
sea-crab	dilection	rejection	sextant
tree-crab	direction	resurrection	
	disaffection	retrospection	**ĔK'stil**
ĔK'ret	disinfection	section	bissextile
secret	dissection	selection	sextile
	effection	subjection	textile
ĔK'sas	ejection	trajection	
Texas	election	trisection	**ĔK'ston**
	erection	venesection	sexton
ĔK'sest	evection	vivisection	
annexest	flection		**ĔK'strin**
flexest	genuflexion	**ĔK'shus**	dextrin
perplexest	imperfection	infectious	textrine
unsexest	incorrection		
vexest	indirection	**ĔK'si**	**ĔK'strus**
	infection	apoplexy	ambidextrous
ĔK'seth	inflection	kexy	ambisextrous
annexeth	injection	kyriolexy	dextrous

ōld, ôr, ŏdd, oil, fŏŏt, out; ūse, ûrn, ŭp; THis, thin

ĔK'stūr	bisected	resurrected	*subjectest*
intertexture	collected	selected	*suspectest*
texture	complected	subjected	
	confected	suspected	**ĔK'teth**
ĔK'stŭr	connected	unaffected	*affecteth*
ambidexter	corrected	unconnected	*bisecteth*
dexter	defected	unexpected	*collecteth*
	deflected	unprotected	*connecteth*
ĔK'sūr	dejected	unsuspected	*detecteth*
deflexure	detected		*directeth*
flexure	directed	**ĔK'test**	*disinfecteth*
inflexure	disaffected	abjectest	*dissecteth*
plexure	disconnected	*affectest*	*effecteth*
	disinfected	*bisectest*	*ejecteth*
ĔK'sŭr	dissected	*collectest*	*electeth*
annexer	effected	*connectest*	*erecteth*
flexor	ejected	*detectest*	*expecteth*
perplexer	elected	directest	*infecteth*
unsexer	erected	*disinfectest*	*injecteth*
vexer	expected	*dissectest*	*inspecteth*
	flected	*effectest*	*interjecteth*
ĔK'sus	ill-affected	*ejectest*	*misdirecteth*
nexus	infected	*electest*	*neglecteth*
plexus	inflected	*erectest*	*objecteth*
(cf. Texas)	injected	*expectest*	*projecteth*
	inspected	*infectest*	*protecteth*
ĔK'tant	interjected	*injectest*	*recollecteth*
amplectant	intersected	*inspectest*	*reflecteth*
annectent	invected	*interjectest*	*rejecteth*
aspectant	misdirected	*neglectest*	*respecteth*
disinfectant	neglected	*objectest*	*resurrecteth*
expectant	objected	*projectest*	*selecteth*
humectant	obtected	*protectest*	*subjecteth*
inexpectant	perfected	*recollectest*	*suspecteth*
reflectant	prelected	*reflectest*	*trisecteth*
respectant	projected	*rejectest*	
suspectant	protected	*respectest*	**ĔKT'ful**
unexpectant	recollected	*resurrectest*	disrespectful
	reflected	*resurrectest*	neglectful
ĔK'ted	rejected	*resurrectest*	respectful
affected	respected	selectest	

āle, câre, ădd, ärm, åsk; mē, hĕre, ĕnd; īce, ĭll;

ĔK'tik
acatalectic
analectic
apoplectic
brachycatalec-
    tic
cachectic
catalectic
dialectic
eclectic
hectic
hypercatalectic
pectic

ĔK'tiks
dialectics

ĔK'til
insectile
projectile
sectile

ĔK'ting
affecting
bisecting
collecting
connecting
deflecting
detecting
directing
disconnecting
disinfecting
dissecting
effecting
ejecting
electing
erecting
expecting
infecting
injecting
inspecting

interjecting
misdirecting
neglecting
objecting
projecting
protecting
recollecting
reflecting
rejecting
respecting
resurrecting
selecting
self-respecting
subjecting
suspecting
trisecting
unsuspecting

ĔK'tiv
affective
circumspective
collective
connective
corrective
defective
deflective
detective
directive
effective
elective
erective
humective
ineffective
infective
inflective
injective
inspective
introspective
invective
irreflective
irrespective

neglective
objective
perfective
perspective
prospective
protective
recollective
refective
reflective
rejective
respective
retrospective
sective
selective
subjective

ĔK'tizm
eclectism
sectism

ĔKT'ment
ejectment
projectment
rejectment

ĔKT'nes
abjectness
correctness
directness
erectness
incorrectness
indirectness
selectness

ĔK'tor
Hector
nectar
rector
sector
vector

vivisector
(cf. ĔK'tur)

ĔK'tord
hectored
nectared
rectored

ĔK'tral
spectral

ĔK'tres
directress
electress
inspectress
protectress
rectress

ĔK'tric
anelectric
dielectric
electric
idioelectric

ĔK'tron
electron

ĔK'trum
electrum
plectrum
spectrum

ĔK'tūr
architecture
belecture
confecture
conjecture
lecture
projecture

ĔK'tur
bisecter
collector

connector
corrector
deflector
detector
director
disrespector
dissector
ejector
elector
erecter
expecter
flector
hector
infecter
injecter
inspector
interjecter
lector
misdirecter
nectar
neglecter
objector
prelector
projector
prospector
protector
recollecter
rector
reflector
rejecter
respecter
resurrecter
sector
selector
spectre
subjecter
suspecter
trisecter

ĔK'tus
conspectus

pectous
prospectus

ĔK'um
cæcum
vade-mecum

ĔK'und
fecund
infecund

ĔK'ur
beaker
bespeaker
bleaker
Bleecker
cheeker
creaker
meeker
peeker
reeker
seeker
self-seeker
shrieker
sleeker
sneaker
speaker
squeaker
stump-speaker
tweaker
weaker

ĔK'ur
bedecker
brekker
checker
chequer
decker
exchequer
flecker
henpecker

pecker
three-decker
trekker
woodpecker
wrecker

ĔK'urz
sneakers
beakers, etc.

ĔK'urz
checkers
henpeckers, etc.

ĔK'wal
coequal
equal
inequal
sequel

ĔK'wence
frequence
infrequence
sequence

ĔK'went
frequent
infrequent
sequent

Ē'la
gila
philomela
sequela
stele
seguidilla
Venezuela

ĔL'a
a capella
Adela

Bella
capella
Della
Ella
fellah
fenestella
gentianella
Isabella
lamella
lirella
Littorella
Marcella
patella
Pimpinella
prunella
Rosabella
scutella
stella
tarantella
umbella
umbrella

ĔL'an
Atellan
Magellan
McClellan

ĔL'ant
appellant
divellent
impellent
interpellant
propellent
repellent
revellent

ĔL'arz
Sellars
(cf. Sellers)

ĔL'at
appellate

constellate	Nelda	ĔL'dom	*impellest*
debellate	Zelda	seldom	*knellest*
flabellate		swelldom	*propellest*
interpellate	ĒL'dans		*quellest*
ocellate	yieldance	ĔL'en	*rebellest*
prelate		Ellen	*repellest*
stellate	ĔL'ded	Helen	*sellest*
	fielded	Llewellyn	*shellest*
	shielded	Mellen	*smellest*
ĔL'ba	unshielded	(cf. Mellon)	*spellest*
Elba	wielded		*swellest*
Melba	yielded	ĔL'est	*tellest*
		annealest	*undersellest*
ĔL'born	ĔL'dest	*appealest*	*yellest*
hell-born	eldest	*concealest*	
well-born	*heldest*	*congealest*	ĔL'eth
	weldest	*dealest*	*annealeth*
ĔL'bound		*feelest*	*appealeth*
hell-bound	ĔL'dur	*genteelest*	*concealeth*
spell-bound	elder	*healest*	*congealeth*
	Gelder	*kneelest*	*dealeth*
ĔL'burt	Melder	*lealest*	*feeleth*
Elbert	Van Gelder	*pealest*	*healeth*
	welder	*peelest*	*kneeleth*
ĔL'chest		*reelest*	*pealeth*
belchest, etc.	ĒLD'far	*repealest*	*peeleth*
	fieldfare	*revealest*	*reeleth*
ĔL'cheth		*sealest*	*repealeth*
belcheth, etc.	ĔL'di	*squealest*	*revealeth*
	unwieldy	*stealest*	*sealeth*
ĔL'ching		*steelest*	*squealeth*
belching	ĔL'ding	*wheelest*	*stealeth*
squelching	enshielding		*steeleth*
welching	fielding	ĔL'est	*wheeleth*
	shielding	*compellest*	
ĔL'chur	unshielding	*dispellest*	ĔL'eth
belcher	unyielding	*dwellest*	*compelleth*
squelcher	wielding	*excellest*	*dispelleth*
welsher	yielding	*expellest*	*dwelleth*
	ĔL'ding	*fellest*	*excelleth*
ĔL'da	gelding	*foretellest*	*expelleth*
Griselda	welding		

felleth	ĔL'ful	ĔL'ij	healing
foretelleth	seelful	pellage	heeling
impelleth	wealful		interdealing
knelleth	zealful	ĔL'ik	keeling
propelleth		parhelic	kneeling
quelleth	Ē'lī		misdealing
rebelleth	Eli	ĔL'ik	pealing
repelleth		angelic	peeling
selleth	Ēl'ĭ	archangelic	reeling
shelleth	Ealey	Aristotelic	repealing
smelleth	freely	bellic	revealing
spelleth	Healey	evangelic	sealing
swelleth	Keeley	melic	self-healing
telleth	mealy	nickelic	shealing
underselleth	seely	parhelic	squealing
yelleth	steely	Pentelic	stealing
	wheely	pimelic	steeling
ĔL'far	(cf. genteelly)	relic	uncongealing
welfare		superangelic	underdealing
	Ĕ'li	telic	unfeeling
ĔL'fik	belly		unsealing
Delphic	cancelli	ĔL'iks	wheeling
Guelphic	Donatelli	Felix	
	felly	helix	ĔL'ing
ĔL'fin	*helly*		belling
delphin	jelly	Ē'lin	cloud-
delphine	Kelly	bee-line	compelling
elfin	O'Delly	feline	compelling
	rakehelly	sea-line	dispelling
ĔL'fir	Shelley		dwelling
hellfire	shelly	ĔL'ing	excelling
	Skelly	annealing	expelling
ĔL'fish	smelly	appealing	felling
elfish	vermicelli	automobiling	foretelling
pelfish		ceiling	fortune-telling
selfish	ĔL'id	concealing	impelling
shellfish	bellied	congealing	knelling
unselfish	gelid	dealing	misspelling
	jellied	double-dealing	paralleling
ĔL'fri		feeling	propelling
belfry	ĔL'ij	fellow-feeling	quelling
pelfry	keelage		
	wheelage		

rebelling
repelling
selling
sentinelling
shelling
smelling
spelling
swelling
telling
underselling
welling
yelling

ĔL'is
Ellis
trellis

ĔL'ish
disrelish
embellish
hellish
relish
swellish

ĔL'kom
welcome

ĔL'ma
Elma
Selma
Thelma
Velma

ĔL'man
bellman
Elman
Wellman

ĔL'ment
concealment
congealment

repealment
revealment

ĔL'met
helmet

ĔL'ming
dishelming
helming
overwhelming
unhelming
whelming

ĔL'mur
Elmer

ĔL'nes
genteelness
lealness

ĔL'nes
fellness
wellness

ĔL'o
bellow
brocatello
cobra-de-
   capello
cello
duello
felloe
fellow
good-fellow
mellow
morello
niello
play-fellow
prunello
punchinello
saltarello

scrivello
violoncello
yellow

ĔL'od
unmellowed
bellowed, etc.

ĔL'on
enfelon
felon
melon
water-melon

ĔL'op
develop
envelop

ĔL'ot
helot
zealot

ĔL'oz
bellows
fellows, etc.

ĔLP'ful
helpful
self-helpful
unhelpful

ĔL'pi
kelpie

ĔL'ping
helping
yelping

ĔLP'les
helpless
whelpless
yelpless

ĔL'pur
helper
self-helper
yelper

ĔL'sa
Elsa

ĔL'skin
eel-skin
seal-skin

ĔL'son
kelson
Nelson

ĔL'ta
delta
pelta

ĔL'ted
belted
felted
melted
pelted
smelted
unbelted
welted

ĔL'test
beltest, etc.

ĔL'teth
belteth, etc.

ĔL'thi
healthy
stealthy
wealthy

ĔL'tik
Celtic
Keltic

ōld, ôr, ŏdd, ⌐il, fŏŏt, out; ūse, ûrn, ŭp; THis, thin

ĔL'ting
belting
felting
melting
pelting
smelting
unbelting
welting

ĔLT'les
beltless
Celtless
feltless
peltless
weltless

ĔL'tri
peltry
sweltry

ĔL'tur
belter
felter
helter-skelter
inshelter
kelter
melter
pelter
shelter
smelter
spelter
swelter
welter

ĔL'turd
unsheltered
sheltered, etc.

ĔL'ud
prelude

ĔL'ug
deluge

ĔL'um
cerebellum
flabellum
flagellum
vellum

ĔL'ur
annealer
appealer
concealer
congealer
dealer
double-dealer
feeler
four-wheeler
healer
heeler
interdealer
keeler
kneeler
misdealer
pealer
peeler
reeler
repealer
revealer
sealer
squealer
stealer
steeler
ward heeler
wheeler

ĔL'ur
appellor
cave-dweller
cellar

cloud-com-
    peller
compeller
dispeller
dweller
exceller
expeller
feller
foreteller
fortune-teller
Geller
impeller
interstellar
Keller
lamellar
"meller"
propeller
queller
rebeller
repeller
screw propeller
Sellar
seller
sheller
smeller
speller
stellar
sweller
tale-teller
teller
twin propeller
underseller
Weller
wine-cellar
yeller

ĔL'us
apellous
entellus
jealous
overzealous

procellous
vitellus
zealous

ĔL'vet
velvet

ĔL'ving
delving
helving
shelving

ĔL'vish
elvish

ĔL'vur
delver
helver
shelver

ĔL'ya
Amelia
Aurelia
Bedelia
camellia
Cecelia
Celia
Cordelia
Cornelia
Delia
Lelia
lobelia

ĔL'yal
Belial

ĔL'yon
chameleon
(see Ē'li+on)

ĔL'yon
rebellion

(cf. rhymes on
ĔL'+on)

ĔL'yus
rebellious

ĔL'za
Elsa

ĒM'a
bema
blastema
eczema
edema
empyema
erythema
Fatima
Lima
myxedema
schema
seriema
terza-rima

ĔM'a
analemma
dilemma
Emma
gemma
lemma
maremma
neurilemma
stemma
trilemma

Ē'māl
female
she-male

ĔM'ăl
blastemal
hemal

Ē'man
able-seaman
beeman
freeman
G-man
gleeman
he-man
leman
merchant-sea-
man
seaman
teaman
(cf. Bremen)

ĔM'b'l
assemble
dissemble
resemble
semble
tremble

ĔM'blans
assemblance
dissemblance
resemblance
semblance

ĔM'blant
resemblant
semblant

ĔM'b'ld
undissembled
assembled, etc.

ĔM'blem
emblem

ĔM'bli
assembly
trembly

ĔM'blij
assemblage

ĔM'bling
assembling
dissembling
resembling
trembling

ĔM'blur
assembler
dissembler
resembler
trembler

ĔM'bral
bimembral
trimembral

ĔM'brans
remembrance

ĔM'bur
December
dismember
disremember
ember
member
November
remember
September

ĔM'burd
dismembered
unremembered,
etc.

ĔM'ens
Clemens

Ē'ment
agreement

decreement
disagreement

ĔM'ent
clement
inclement

ĔM'est
beamest
blasphemest
deemest
dreamest
esteemest
extremest
gleamest
misdeemest
reedemest
schemest
screamest
seemest
steamest
streamest
supremest

ĔM'est
begemmest
condemnest
hemmest
stemmest

ĔM'et
Emmett

ĔM'eth
beameth
blasphemeth
deemeth
dreameth
esteemeth
gleameth
redeemeth

ōld, ôr, ŏdd, oil, fŏŏt, out; ūse, ûrn, ŭp; THis, thin

schemeth
screameth
seemeth
steameth
streameth

ĔM'eth

begemmeth
condemneth
contemneth
hemmeth
stemmeth

ĒM'ful

beamful
dreamful
schemeful
teemful

ĒM'i

beamy
creamy
daydreamy
dreamy
gleamy
screamy
seamy
steamy
streamy
teemy
(cf. Mimi)

ĔM'i

demi
gemmy
jemmy
semi

ĔM'ik

anemic
racemic
systemic

ĔM'ik

academic
alchemic
chemic
endemic
epidemic
pandemic
polemic
stratagemic
systemic
theoremic
totemic

ĒM'ing

beaming
beseeming
blaspheming
creaming
daydreaming
deeming
dreaming
esteeming
gleaming
overstreaming
redeeming
scheming
screaming
seeming
steaming
streaming
summer-
   seeming
teeming
unbeseeming

ĔM'ing

begemming
condemning
contemning
Fleming
gemming

hemming
leming
self-condemn-
   ing
stemming

ĔM'ish

blemish
Flemish
unblemish

ĔM'isht

blemished
unblemished

ĔM'ist

extremist
schemist

ĔM'ist

chemist

ĔM'it, ĒM'it

Semite

ĔM'land

dreamland

ĒM'less

beamless
creamless
dreamless
schemeless
seamless
streamless

ĒM'let

streamlet

ĒM'li

extremely

seemly
supremely
unseemly

ĔM'non

Agamemnon
Memnon

ĒM'o

a tempo primo
Cremo
primo

ĒM'o

memo

ĔM'on

agathodæmon
cacodemon
demon
eudæmon

ĔM'on

lemon
(cf. "gem-
   man")

ĔM'pest

tempest

ĔM'pir

empire

ĔM'p'l

Semple
stemple
temple

ĔM'plar

exemplar
templar

ĔM'plat

contemplate
template

ĔMP'shun

ademption
coemption
diremption
emption
exemption
pre-emption
redemption

ĔMP'stur

dempster
sempster

ĔMP'ted

attempted
exempted
pre-empted
tempted
unattempted
untempted

ĔMP'test

attemptest
exemptest
temptest

ĔMP'teth

attempteth
exempteth
tempteth

ĔMP'ti

empty

ĔMP'ting

attempting
exempting

pre-empting
tempting

ĔMP'tiv

pre-emptive
redemptive

ĔMP'tres

temptress

ĔMP'tur

attempter
exempter
pre-emptor
tempter
unkempter

ĔM'pur

attemper
distemper
Semper
temper
untemper

ĔM'purd

ill-tempered
tempered
untempered

ĔM'son

Clemson
Empson

ĔM'song

theme-song

ĔM'stur

deemster
seamster
teamster

ĒM'ur

beamer
blasphemer
daydreamer
dreamer
femur
lemur
reamer
redeemer
schemer
screamer
seamer
seemer
steamer
streamer
teemer

ĔM'ur

begemmer
condemner
contemner
hemmer
stemmer

ĒM'us

Nicodemus
Remus

ĔM'yer

premier

ĒN'a

arena
Alexandrina
Argentina
Athena
catena
cavatina
Celestina
Christina
Clementina

concertina
Czarina
farina
Faustina
galena
gena
Georgina
Helena
hyena
Justina
Lena
Magdalena
maizena
Medina
Messina
Modena
Paulina
philopena
scarlatina
scena
Selena
semolina
Serena
signorina
subpœna
Tsarina
verbena
Wilhelmina

ĔN'a

antenna
duenna
Gehenna
henna
Ravenna
senna
Sienna
Vienna

ĒN'al

machinal

penal
plenal
renal
venal
weanel

ĔN'al
antennal

ĔN'ant
lieutenant
pennant
sub-lieutenant
tenant

ĔN'ard
Leonard

Ē'nas
Enas
Zenas

ĔN'as
menace
tenace
(cf. tennis)

ĔN'at
brevipennate
impennate
longipennate
pennate
tripennate

ĔN'chant
trenchant

ĔN'chest
bedrenchest
blenchest
clenchest

drenchest
flenchest
intrenchest
quenchest
retrenchest
trenchest
unclenchest
wrenchest

ĔN'cheth
bedrencheth
blencheth
clencheth
drencheth
flencheth
intrencheth
quencheth
retrencheth
trencheth
unclencheth
wrencheth

ĔN'ching
bedrenching
benching
blenching
clenching
drenching
flenching
intrenching
quenching
retrenching
trenching
unclenching
unquenching
wrenching

ĔNCH'les
quenchless
(see ĔNCH +
less)

ĔNCH'man
Frenchman
henchman

ĔNCH'ment
intrenchment
retrenchment

ĔN'chur
bedrencher
bencher
blencher
clencher
drencher
intrencher
quencher
retrencher
trencher
unclencher
wrencher

ĔN'da
agenda
Benda
Brenda
corrigenda
delenda
hacienda
Zenda

ĔN'dal
prebendal
sendal
trendle

ĔN'dans
ascendance
attendance
condescendence
dependence
descendance

impendence
independence
interdepend-
ence
pendence
resplendence
superintend-
ence
tendance
transcendence
(cf. attendant
+ s)

ĔN'dant,
ĔN'dent
appendant
ascendant
attendant
contendant
defendant
dependant
dependent
descendant
descendent
equipendent
impendent
independent
intendant
interdependent
pendant
pendent
resplendent
splendent
superintendent
transcendent
transplendent

ĔN'ded
amended
appended
apprehended

ascended
attended
befriended
bended
blended
commended
comprehended
condescended
contended
defended
depended
descended
distended
emended
ended
expended
extended
fended
friended
impended
inextended
intended
interblended
mended
misappre-
  hended
offended
portended
pretended
reascended
recommended
reprehended
subtended
superintended
suspended
tended
transcended
trended
unattended
unbefriended
unblended

undefended
unextended
unfriended
wended
(cf. splendid)

ĔN'dest

amendest
appendest
apprehendest
ascendest
attendest
befriendest
bendest
blendest
commendest
comprehendest
condescendest
contendest
defendest
dependest
descendest
emendest
endest
expendest
extendest
fendest
intendest
interblendest
lendest
mendest
offendest
pretendest
recommendest
rendest
reprehendest
sendest
spendest
subtendest
superintendest
suspendest

tendest
unbendest
vendest
wendest

ĔN'deth

amendeth
appendeth
apprehendeth
ascendeth
attendeth
befriendeth
bendeth
blendeth
commendeth
comprehendeth
condescendeth
contendeth
defendeth
dependeth
descendeth
emendeth
endeth
expendeth
extendeth
fendeth
impendeth
intendeth
interblendeth
lendeth
mendeth
misapprehendeth
offendeth
portendeth
pretendeth
reascendeth
recommendeth
rendeth
reprehendeth
sendeth
spendeth

subtendeth
suspendeth
tendeth
transcendeth
vendeth
wendeth

ĔN'di

bendy
Effendi

ĔN'dik

Wendic
zendik

ĔN'ding

amending
appending
apprehending
ascending
attending
befriending
bending
blending
commending
comprehending
condescending
contending
defending
depending
descending
distending
emending
ending
expending
extending
forfending
forelending
forespending
heart-rending
impending

ōld, ôr, ŏdd, oil, foŏt, out; ūse, ûrn, ŭp; THis, thin

intending
interblending
lending
mending
misspending
offending
pending
perpending
portending
pretending
recommending
rending
reprehending
sending
spending
subtending
superintending
suspending
tending
transcending
trending
unattending
unbending
unending
unfriending
unoffending
unpretending
vending
wending

ĒN'dish

fiendish

ĔND'les

endless
friendless

ĔND'li

friendly
unfriendly

ĔND'ment

amendment
befriendment
intendment

ĔN'do

cresendo
decrescendo
diminuendo
innuendo

ĔN'dron

liriodendron
lithodendron
rhododendron

ĔND'ship

friendship

ĔN'dum

addendum
agendum
corrigendum
credendum
referendum

ĔN'dur

amender
apprehender
ascender
attender
befriender
bender
blender
commender
comprehender
contender
defender
depender
descender
emender

ender
engender
entender
expender
extender
fender
gender
intender
interblender
lender
mender
money-lender
offender
perpender
pretender
recommender
render
reprehender
sender
slender
spender
splendor
surrender
suspender
tailender
tender
vendor
week-ender
wender

ĔN'durd

unsurrendered
tendered, etc.

ĔN'dus, not
  ĔN'jus

stupendous
tremendous

ĔND'waz

endways

ĔN'el

fennel
Fennell
kennel
unkennel

ĒN'elm

Kenelm

ĒN'est

bescreenest
cleanest
contravenest
convenest
demeanest
gleanest
greenest
intervenest
keenest
leanest
meanest
screenest
serenest
supervenest
weanest
weenest

ĔN'et

Bennett
jennet
rennet
senate
tenet

ĒN'eth

bescreeneth
cleaneth
contraveneth
conveneth
demeaneth
gleaneth

interveneth
keeneth
leaneth
meaneth
screeneth
superveneth
weaneth
weeneth

ĔN'eth
Kenneth
penneth, etc.

ĔNG'then
lengthen
strengthen

ĔNG'thi
lengthy

ĔN'horn
greenhorn

ĔN'i
Cheney
Cheyney
fantoccini
genie
greeny
Hippocrene
meany
Selene
sheeny
spleeny
Sweeney
teeny
visne
weeny

ĔN'i
any

Benny
fenny
Jenny
Kilkenny
Penney
many
penny
Rennie
spinning-jenny
tenney
true-penny
wenny

ĔN'id
green-eyed
keen-eyed

ĔN'ij
careenage
greenage
teenage

ĔN'ik
phenic
scenic

ĔN'ik
alphenic
anthropogenic
asthenic
callisthenic
chromogenic
crystallogenic
Demosthenic
deuterogenic
Diogenic
diplogenic
ecumenic
Edenic
embryogenic
eugenic

galenic
geoselenic
glycogenic
Hellenic
hygienic
hysterogenic
irenic
lichenic
metagenic
neurasthenic
nitrogenic
organogenic
oxygenic
Panhellenic
paragenic
parthenic
parthenogenic
pathogenic
phenic
Philhellenic
phosphorogenic
photogenic
phrenic
protogenic
Prutenic
pyrogenic
pythogenic
Saracenic
scenic
selenic
splenic
sthenic
thermogenic
tungstenic
zoogenic

ĔN'im
denim

ĔN'in
Lenin

ĔN'ing
advening
bemeaning
cleaning
contravening
convening
demeaning
double-mean-
   ing
eaning
gleaning
greening
intervening
keening
leaning
machining
meaning
overweening
preening
queening
screening
shebeening
subvening
supervening
unmeaning
upleaning
weaning
weening
well-meaning
yeaning

ĔN'ingz
screenings
cleanings, etc.

ĔN'ingz
Jennings
pennings, etc.

ĔN'is
Dennis

tennis
(cf. menace,
　tenace)

ĚN'ish

cleanish
greenish
keenish
leanish
meanish
queenish
spleenish

ĚN'ish

plenish
replenish
Rhenish
wennish

ĚN'ist

machinist
magazinist
plenist
routinist

ĚN'iz

bennies
pennies
spinning-jen-
　nies

ĚN'jans

vengeance

ĚN'jin

engine

ĚN'jing

avenging
revenging
venging

ĚN'jur

avenger

ĚN'li

cleanly
greenly
keenly
leanly
meanly
obscenely
queenly
serenely

ĚN'li

cleanly
Henley
Schenley
Senley
uncleanly

ĚN'ling

weanling
yeanling

ĚN'man

fenman
penman

ĚN'nes

cleanness
greenness
keenness
leanness
meanness
obsceneness
sereneness
uncleanness

ĚN'o

andantino
baldachino

bambino
casino
festino
Filipino
keno
maraschino
merino
peacherino
peperino
pianino
Reno
San Marino
Sereno
tondino
Valentino
vetturino

ĚN'ok

Enoch

ĚN'old

Reynold

ĚN'olz

Reynolds

ĚN'om

envenom
venom

ĚN'on

pennon
tenon

ĚN'os

Enos

ĚN'ri

Denry
Henry

ĚN'sal

bimensal
commensal
forensal
mensal

ĚN'sat

compensate
condensate
insensate
intensate

ĚN'sest

commencest
condensest
densest
dispensest
fencest
incensest
intensest
recompensest

ĚN'seth

commenceth
condenseth
dispenseth
fenceth
incenseth
recompenseth

ĚN'sez

Albigenses
amanuenses
menses

ĚNS'forth

henceforth
thenceforth
whenceforth

ĚN'shal

agential

bigential
coessential
conferential
confidential
consequential
credential
deferential
differential
equipotential
essential
evidential
existential
expediential
experiential
exponential
inconsequential
indulgential
inessential
inferential
influential
intelligential
irreverential
jurisprudential
nonessential
obediential
omnipresential
penitential
pestilential
potential
precedential
preferential
presidential
Provencial
providential
prudential
querulential
quintessential
referential
reminiscential
residential
reverential

rodential
sapiential
sciential
sentential
sequential
superessential
tangential
torrential
transferential
unessential

ĔN'ship

deanship
queenship

ĔN'shun

abstention
accension
apprehension
ascension
attention
circumvention
coextension
comprehension
condescension
contention
contravention
convention
declension
deprehension
descension
detention
dimension
dissension
distention
extension
inapprehension
inattention
incomprehen-
    sion
inextension

intension
intention
intervention
invention
mention
misapprehen-
    sion
obtention
obvention
ostension
pension
portention
preapprehen-
    sion
prehension
presention
pretension
prevention
propension
recension
reprehension
retention
subvention
supervention
suspension
tension
thermo-tension

ĔN'shund

unmentioned
unpensioned
well-inten-
    tioned

ĔN'shus

conscientious
contentious
dissentious
licentious
pestilentious
pretentious

sententious
silentious

ĔN'sil

extensile
pencil
pensile
prehensile
stencil
tensile
utensil

ĔN'sild

pencilled
stencilled

ĔN'sing

commencing
condensing
dispensing
fencing
incensing
recompensing

ĔN'siv

apprehensive
ascensive
comprehensive
condensive
condescensive
defensive
descensive
distensive
expensive
extensive
inapprehensive
incensive
incomprehen-
    sive
indefensive
inexpensive

ōld, ôr, ŏdd, oil, fŏŏt, out; ūse, ûrn, ŭp; THis, thin

influencive
inoffensive
intensive
offensive
ostensive
pensive
protensive
recompensive
reprehensive
self-defensive
suspensive
tensive
unapprehen-
   sive

ĔNS'les

defenceless
expenseless
fenceless
offenceless
senseless

ĔNS'ment

commencement
incensement

ĔNS'nes

denseness
immenseness
intenseness
propenseness
tenseness

ĔN'son

Benson
Henson

ĔN'sŭr

censure

ĔN'sŭr

censer

censor
commencer
condenser
denser
dispenser
extensor
fencer
incensor
intenser
prehensor
recompenser
spencer
Spenser
tensor

ĔN'sus

census

ĔN'ta

magenta
Pimenta
polenta

ĔN'tal

accidental
alimental
antecedental
argental
argumental
atramental
bidental
cental
coincidental
complemental
complimental
continental
dental
dentil
dentile
departmental
detrimental

developmental
documental
elemental
experimental
falcon-gentle
firmamental
fragmental
fundamental
gentle
governmental
impedimental
incidental
instrumental
intercontin-
   ental
kentle
labiodental
Lental
ligamental
linguadental
medicamental
mental
monumental
nutrimental
occidental
oriental
ornamental
parental
parliamental
pedimental
pigmental
placental
predicamental
recremental
regimental
rental
rudimental
sacramental
segmental
sentimental
supplemental

temperamental
tenemental
testamental
transcendental
trental
tridental
ungentle
(cf. ĔN'til)

ĔN'tans

repentance
sentence
unrepentance

ĔN'tant

repentant
representant
unrepentant

ĔN'tat

bidentate
commentate
dementate
dentate
edentate
quadridentate
tridentate

ĔN'te

aguardiente
cognoscente
diapente

ĔN'ted

absented
accented
assented
augmented
battlemented
cemented
circumvented

commented
complimented
consented
contented
demented
dented
discontented
dissented
fermented
frequented
fomented
ill-contented
indented
invented
lamented
misrepresented
ornamented
presented
prevented
relented
rented
repented
represented
resented
scented
supplemented
sweet-scented
tented
tormented
unlamented
unornamented
unprecedented
unprevented
unrepented
untented
untormented
vented
well-contented

ĔN'test
absentest

accentest
assentest
augmentest
cementest
circumventest
commentest
complimentest
consentest
contentest
dissentest
fermentest
fomentest
frequentest
indentest
inventest
lamentest
misrepresentest
ornamentest
presentest
preventest
relentest
rentest
repentest
representest
resentest
sentest
scentest
supplementest
tormentest
ventest

ĔN'teth
absenteth
accenteth
assenteth
augmenteth
cementeth
circumventeth
commenteth
complimenteth
consenteth

contenteth
dissenteth
fermenteth
fomenteth
frequenteth
indenteth
inventeth
lamenteth
misrepreseneth
ornamenteth
presenteth
preventeth
relenteth
renteth
repenteth
representeth
resenteth
scenteth
supplementeth
tormenteth
venteth

ĔNT'ful
eventful
resentful
uneventful

ĔNT'hous
penthouse

ĔN'ti
dolce far niente
Henty
plenty
presidente
tormenty
twenty

ĔN'tij
percentage
ventage

ĔN'tik
argentic
authentic
identic

ĔN'tīl
Gentile

ĔN'tĭl
lentil
(cf. ĔN'tal)

ĔN'tin
dentine
Quentin
San Quentin
torrentine
tridentine

ĔN'ting
absenting
accenting
assenting
augmenting
cementing
circumventing
commenting
complimenting
consenting
contenting
denting
dementing
dissenting
fermenting
fomenting
frequenting
indenting
inventing
lamenting
misrepresent-
  ing

ornamenting
presenting
preventing
relenting
renting
repenting
representing
resenting
scenting
self-tormenting
suppplement-
    ing
tenting
tormenting
unconsenting
unrelenting
unrepenting
venting

ĔN'tis

appentice
apprentice
non compos
    mentis
pentice
prentice

ĔN'tist

apprenticed
dentist
preventist

ĔN'tiv

adventive
assentive
attentive
circumventive
inattentive
incentive
inventive
irretentive

pendentive
presentive
preventive
resentive
retentive

ĔNT'les

cementless
centless
dentless
lamentless
relentless
rentless
scentless
tentless, etc.

ĔNT'li

eminently
evidently
gently
impotently
innocently
insolently
intently
(see ĔNT+ly)

ĔNT'ment

contentment
discontentment
presentment
relentment
representment
resentment

ĔNT'nes

intentness

ĔN'to

cento
cinque-cento
divertimento

lento
memento
pimento
polento
portamento
pronuncia-
    mento
quattrocento
rifacimento
Sacramento

ĔN'ton

Benton
Denton
Fenton
Trenton

ĔN'tor

bucentaur
centaur
mentor
stentor
succentor
(cf. ĔN'tur)

ĔN'tral

central
ventral

ĔN'trans

entrance

ĔN'trat

concentrate

ĔNT'res

inventress
tormentress

ĔN'tri

entry

gentry
sentry

ĔN'trik

acentric
anthropocen-
    tric
barycentric
centric
concentric
eccentric
geocentric
gynecocentric
heliocentric
paracentric
selenocentric

ĔN'tum

momentum
sarmentum

ĔN'tūr

adventure
debenture
indenture
misadventure
peradventure
tenture
venture

ĔN'tŭr

assenter
augmenter
cementer
center
circumventor
commenter
concenter
consenter
contenter
dead-center

denter
dissenter
enter
experimenter
fermenter
fomenter
frequenter
indenter
inventor
lamenter
lentor
misrepresenter
ornamenter
precentor
presenter
preventer
re-enter
relenter
renter
repenter
representer
resenter
supplementer
tenter
tormenter
venter
(cf. centaur,
   etc.)

ĔN'turd

entered
self-centered
centered, etc.

ĔN'tus

immomentous
ligamentous
momentous
pedetentous
pigmentous
portentous

sarmentous
unguentous

ĔN'um

frenum
plenum

ĔN'ur

cleaner
contravener
convener
demeanor
gleaner
greener
intervener
keener
leaner
machiner
magaziner
meaner
misdemeanor
obscener
screener
seiner
serener
shebeener
supervener
weaner
wiener

ĔN'ur

Fenner
penner
tenner
tenor
Venner

ĔN'us

genus
Silenus

venous
Venus

ĔN'vi

envy

ĔN'vil

Bienville
Glenville
Grenville

ĔN'yal

congenial
(see ĔN'i-al)

ĔN'yan

Armenian
(see ĔN'i-an)

ĔN'yens

lenience
(see ĔN'i-ens)

ĔN'yent

convenient
(see ĔN'i-ent)

ĔN'yor

monsignor
seignior
senior
signor

ĔN'yus

genius
(see ĔN'i-us)

ĔN'za

cadenza
influenza

ĔNZ'da

Wednesday

ĔN'zes

cleanses
lenses

ĔN'zi

frenzy
McKenzie

ĔN'zo

Lorenzo

ĔN'zon

tenzon
venison

Ē'o

Cleo
Leo
Theo
trio

Ē'on

æon
Creon
Leon
neon
odeon
pæon
pantræon
peon
pheon

ĔP'ard

jeopard
leopard
peppered
shepherd

ōld, ôr, ŏdd, oil, fŏŏt, out; ūse, ûrn, ŭp; THis, thin

ĒP'en
cheapen
deepen
steepen

ĒP'est
cheapest
cheepest
creepest
deepest
heapest
keepest
leapest
outsleepest
overleapest
oversleepest
peepest
reapest
sleepest
steepest
sweepest
weepest

ĒP'eth
cheepeth
creepeth
heapeth
keepeth
leapeth
outsleepeth
overleapeth
oversleepeth
peepeth
reapeth
sleepeth
sweepeth
weepeth

ĒP'i
cheepy
creepy

heapy
kepi
seepy
sleepy
steepy
sweepy
tepee
weepy

ĔP'i
tepee

ĔP'id
intrepid
lepid
tepid
trepid

ĒP'ij
seepage
sweepage

ĔP'ik
epic
orthoepic

ĒP'ing
cheeping
creeping
heaping
house-keeping
keeping
leaping
outsleeping
overleaping
oversleeping
peeping
reaping
safe-keeping
sleeping
steeping

sweeping
unsleeping
unweeping
weeping

ĒP'ish
deepish
sheepish
steepish

ĒP' 'l
empeople
people
steeple
unpeople

ĒP'les
sleepless
weepless

ĒP'nes
cheapness
deepness
sleepness

ĔP'on
weapon

ĔP'shun
abreption
apperception
arreption
conception
contraception
deception
ereption
exception
imperception
inception
interception
introsusception

intussusception
misconception
obreption
perception
preconception
preperception
reception
self-deception
subreption
surreption

ĔP'si
apepsy
catalepsy
dyspepsy
epilepsy
eupepsy

ĔP'sis
asepsis
analepsis
epanalepsis
metalepsis
paralepsis
prolepsis
scepsis
syllepsis

ĔP'skin
sheepskin

ĔP'tans
acceptance

ĔP'tant
acceptant
exceptant
reptant

ĔP'ted
accepted

excepted
intercepted

ĔP'test
acceptest
adeptest
exceptest
interceptest

ĔP'teth
accepteth
excepteth
intercepteth

ĔP'tĭk
acataleptic
analeptic
antiseptic
aseptic
bradypeptic
cataleptic
dyspeptic
epileptic
eupeptic
metaleptic
nympholeptic
organoleptic
peptic
proleptic
sceptic
septic
sylleptic

ĔP'tĭng
accepting
excepting
incepting
intercepting

ĔP'tĭv
acceptive

conceptive
deceptive
exceptive
imperceptive
inceptive
insusceptive
interceptive
intussusceptive
irreceptive
perceptive
preceptive
receptive
susceptive

ĔPT'nes
ineptness

ĔP'tun
Neptune

ĔP'tur
accepter
adepter
excepter
inceptor
intercepter
preceptor
sceptre
susceptor

Ē'P'ur
cheaper
cheeper
creeper
deeper
heaper
hedge-keeper
housekeeper
keeper
leaper
peeper

reaper
shopkeeper
sleeper
steeper
sweeper
wall-creeper
weeper
wicket-keeper

ĔP'ur
hepper
high-stepper
leper
overstepper
pepper
stepper

ĔP'wôk
sheep-walk
sleep-walk

Ē'ra
Ça ira
chimera
era
gerah
Hera
lira
Madeira
Vera

ĔR'af
seraph
teraph

Ē̤R'al
feral
spheral

ĔR'ald
Gerald

herald
Herrold

ĔR'ans
aberrance

ĔR'ant
aberrant

ĔR'as
terrace
(cf. ĔR'is)

ĔR'at
serrate

Ē̤R'ded
bearded

Ē̤RD'li
weirdly

Ē̤R'ens
adherence
appearance
arrearance
clearance
coherence
disappearance
incoherence
inherence
interference
perseverance
reappearance

Ē̤R'ent
adherent
coherent
inadherent
incoherent
inherent
perseverant

ōld, ôr, ŏdd, oil, fŏŏt, out; ūse, ûrn, ŭp; THis, thin

querent	*spearest*	**ĘR'ful**	cemetery
vicegerent	steerest	cheerful	cherry
	unrearest	earful	Derry
ĘR'est	*veerest*	fearful	ferry
adherest		sneerful	Gerry
appearest	**ĔR'et**	tearful	Kerry
austerest	ferret	uncheerful	lamasery
besmearest	terret	unfearful	merry
careerest			millinery
cheerest	**ĘR'eth**	**Ę'ri, Ē'ri**	monastery
clearest	*adhereth*	ærie	perry
coherest	*appeareth*	aweary	Pondicherry
dearest	*besmeareth*	beery	presbytery
disappearest	*careereth*	bleary	sherry
drearest	*cheereth*	cheery	skerry
endearest	*cleareth*	deary	stationery
fearest	*disappeareth*	dreary	very
gearest	*endeareth*	eerie	wherry
hearest	*feareth*	Erie	(cf. ÂR'i)
insincerest	*geareth*	*forweary*	
interferest	*heareth*	hara-kiri	**ĘR'ĭd**
jeerest	*interfereth*	jeery	blear-eyed
leerest	*jeereth*	leary	clear-eyed
merest	*leereth*	life-weary	tear-eyed
nearest	*overheareth*	miserere	
overhearest	*peereth*	overweary	**ĘR'ĭd**
peerest	*persevereth*	peri	queried
perseverest	*reappeareth*	quære	unwearied
queerest	*reareth*	query	war-wearied
reappearest	*revereth*	smeary	wearied
rearest	*seareth*	sneery	world-wearied
reverest	*sheareth*	sphery	(cf. virid)
searest	*smeareth*	teary	
serest	*sneereth*	uncheery	**ĔR'ĭd**
severest	*speareth*	veery	berried
uprearest	*steereth*	weary	buried
shearest	*upreareth*		cherried
sheerest	*veereth*	**ĔR'i**	ferried
sincerest		beriberi	serried
smearest	**ĘR'fon**	berry	unburied
sneerest	earphone	bury	

āle,   câre,   ădd,   ärm,   åsk;   mē,   hĕre,   ĕnd;   īce,   ĭll;

ĔR'if

sheriff

(cf. ĔR'af)

ȖR'ij

arrearage

clearage

peerage

pierage

steerage

ĔR'ik

alexiteric

amphoteric

anisomeric

atmospheric

chimeric

chromospheric

cleric

climacteric

derrick

enteric

Eric

esoteric

exoteric

ferric

generic

helispheric

hemispheric

Herrick

Homeric

hysteric

icteric

isomeric

masseteric

mesmeric

neoteric

numeric

peripheric

perispheric

phylacteric

piperic

spheric

suberic

valeric

ĔR'iks

esoterics

hysterics

clerics, etc.

ĔR'il

beryl

chrysoberyl

peril

sterile

ȖR'in

Erin

ȖR'ing

adhering

appearing

auctioneering

Bering

besmearing

blearing

cannoneering

careering

cashiering

cheering

clearing

cohering

Dearing

disappearing

domineering

earing

electioneering

endearing

engineering

fearing

gearing

gondoliering

hearing

interfering

jeering

leering

mountaineering

nearing

overhearing

peering

persevering

pioneering

privateering

queering

reappearing

rearing

rehearing

revering

searing

shearing

skeering

sneering

spearing

steering

ungearing

upcheering

uprearing

veering

venecring

volunteering

(cf. earring)

ĔR'is

ferris

terrace

Terris

ĔR'ish

cherish

perish

ĔR'it

demerit

disherit

disinherit

immerit

inherit

merit

ȖR'iz

dearies

overwearies

queries

series

wearies

ĔR'iz

berries

buries

cherries

ferries

sherries

wherries

ȖR'les

cheerless

earless

fearless

gearless

peerless

spearless

tearless

yearless

ȖR'li

austerely

cavalierly

cheerly

clearly

dearly

merely

nearly

queerly

severely

ōld, ôr, ŏdd, oil, fŏŏt, out; ūse, ûrn, ŭp; THis, thin

sincerely
yearly

ĔR'ling

shearling
steerling
yearling

ĔR'ment

cerement
endearment

ĔR'nes

austereness
clearness
dearness
nearness
queerness
severeness
sincereness

ĔR'o, Ē'ro

hero
lillibullero
zero

ĔR'on

heron

Ē'room

sea-room
tea-room

ĔR'or

error
terror

ĔR'os, ĔR'os

Eros

ĔRS'nes

fierceness

ĔR'sur

fiercer
piercer

ĔR'sing

ear-piercing
piercing
transpiercing

ĔR'son

Grierson
Pearson

ĔR'ub

cherub

ĔR'ul

ferrule
ferule
perule
spherule

ĔR'ur

adherer
appearer
austerer
besmearer
cheerer
clearer
dearer
disappearer
electioneerer
endearer
fearer
fleerer
hearer
interferer
jeerer
leerer
nearer
overhearer

peerer
perseverer
queerer
rearer
reverer
severer
shearer
sneerer
spearer
steerer
teerer
ungearer
veerer
(cf. mirror)

ĔR'us

sclerous
serous

ĔR'us

ferrous

ĔRZ'man

privateersman
steersman

Ē'sa

Felica
mesa
Theresa

Ē'saj

presage

ĔS'chun

congestion
digestion
indigestion
ingestion
question
suggestion

ĔS'chund

questioned
unquestioned

ĔS'ed

blessed
(see ĔS+ed)

ĔS'el

Diesel

ĔS'en

lessen

ĔS'ens

indecence

ĔS'ens

accrescence
acquiescence
adolescence
arborescence
calescence
calorescence
candescence
coalescence
concrescence
contabescence
convalescence
defervescence
deliquescence
delitescence
effervescence
efflorescence
emollescence
erubescence
essence
evanescence
exacerbescence
excrescence
florescence

fluorescence
fremescence
frondescence
fructescence
frutescence
glaucescence
hyalescence
incalescence
incandescence
incoalescence
ineffervescence
inflorescence
intumescence
iridescence
juvenescence
lactescence
lapidescence
latescence
obsolescence
opalescence
petrescence
phosphor-
  escence
pubescence
putrescence
quiescence
quintessence
recrudescence
reflorescence
rejuvenescence
revalescence
revirescence
rubescence
senescence
spumescence
supercrescence
torpescence
tumescence
turgescence
viridescence

virilescence
vitrescence

ĔS'ent
decent
indecent
recent

ĔS'ent
accrescent
acquiescent
adolescent
albescent
alkalescent
arborescent
cessant
coalescent
convalescent
crescent
decrescent
deliquescent
delitescent
depressant
effervescent
efflorescent
erubescent
evanescent
excrescent
fervescent
flavescent
florescent
fluorescent
fremescent
fructescent
frutescent
gangrenescent
glaucescent
herbescent
ignescent
incalescent
incandescent

incessant
increscent
ineffervescent
iridescent
jessant
juvenescent
lactescent
languescent
lapidescent
latescent
liquescent
lutescent
marcescent
maturescent
nigrescent
obsolescent
opalescent
petrescent
phosphorescent
pubescent
putrescent
quiescent
rancescent
recrudescent
rejuvenescent
revalescent
rubescent
rufescent
senescent
spinescent
spinulescent
spumescent
suffrutescent
sugescent
supercrescent
torpescent
turgescent
violescent
virescent
viridescent
vitrescent

ĔS'ept
precept

ĔS'est
ceasest
creasest
decreasest
fleecest
greasest
increasest
leasest
releasest

ĔS'est
acquiescest
addressest
assessest
blessest
caressest
compressest
confessest
depressest
digressest
distressest
dressest
expressest
guessest
impressest
oppressest
possessest
pressest
professest
progressest
redressest
repressest
suppressest
trangressest
undressest

ĔS'eth
ceaseth

ōld, ôr, ŏdd, oil, fŏŏt, out; ūse, ûrn, ŭp; THis, thin

creaseth
decreaseth
fleeceth
greaseth
increaseth
leaseth
releaseth

ĔS'eth
acquiesceth
addresseth
assesseth
blesseth
caresseth
compresseth
confesseth
depresseth
digresseth
distresseth
dresseth
expresseth
guesseth
impresseth
oppresseth
possesseth
presseth
professeth
progresseth
redresseth
represseth
suppresseth
transgresseth
undresseth

ĔS'ez
battlepieces
caprices
ceases
creases
decreases
fleeces

greases
increases
leases
mantel-pieces
master-pieces
nieces
peaces
pelisses
pieces
releases

ĔS'ez
dresses
presses, etc.

ĔS'ful
capriceful
peaceful
unpeaceful

ĔS'ful
successful
(see ĔS+ful)

ĔSH'al
especial
special

ĔSH'an
Grecian
(see ĔSH'un)

ĔSH'est
enmeshest
freshest
immeshest
refreshest
threshest

ĔSH'eth
enmesheth

immesheth
mesheth
refresheth
thresheth

ĔSH'ez
species

ĔSH'i
fleshy
meshy

ĔSH'ing
meshing
refreshing
threshing

ĔSH'ingz
fleshings
meshings, etc.

ĔSH'les
fleshless
meshless

ĔSH'li
fleshly
freshly
unfleshly

ĔSH'man
freshman

ĔSH'ment
refreshment

ĔSH'nes
freshness

Ē'shor
sea-shore

Ē'shun
accretion
completion
concretion
deletion
depletion
Grecian
impletion
incompletion
internecion
repletion
secretion
(cf. Ē'shi-an,
etc.)

ĔSH'un
accession
aggression
cession
compression
concession
confession
depression
digression
discretion
dispossession
egression
expression
freshen
impression
indiscretion
ingression
insession
intercession
introgression
intropression
obsession
oppression
possession
precession
prepossession

procession
profession
progression
recession
regression
repossession
reimpression
repossession
repression
retrocession
retrogression
secession
self-possession
session
succession
supersession
suppression
transgression
(cf. Hessian,
  etc.)

ĔSH'unz

quarter-ses-
  sions, acces-
  sions, etc.

ĔSH'ur

flesher
fresher
mesher
pressure
refresher
thresher
tressure

Ē'shus

facetious
specious

ĔSH'us

precious

ĒS'ĭ

creasy
fleecy

ĔS'ĭ

Bessie
Cressy
dressy
Jesse
Jessie
messy
Tessie
tressy
(cf. in esse)

Ē'sid

lee-side
sea-side

ĔS'ij

expressage
message
pesage
presage

ĔS'ik

eugenesic
geodesic

**Ē'sil, ĔS'il or
  ĬS'il**

Cecil

ĒS'ing

ceasing
creasing
decreasing
fleecing
greasing
increasing
leasing

piecing
policing
releasing
surceasing
unceasing

ĔS'ing

acquiescing
addressing
assessing
blessing
caressing
coalescing
compressing
confessing
convalescing
depressing
digressing
dispossessing
distressing
dressing
excessing
expressing
guessing
impressing
messing
oppressing
possessing
prepossessing
pressing
professing
progressing
redressing
repressing
retrogressing
suppressing
undressing
unprepos-
  sessing
water-dressing

ĒS'is

anamnesis
anesthesis
anthesis
aposiopesis
catachresis
deesis
diaphoresis
diesis
erotesis
exegesis
hyperesthesis
mathesis
mimesis
ochlesis
paracentesis
perichoresis
schesis
synteresis
thesis
tmesis

ĒS'iv

adhesive
cohesive

ĔS'iv

accessive
aggressive
compressive
concessive
concrescive
congressive
crescive
depressive
digressive
excessive
expressive
impressive
inexpressive
oppressive

possessive
progressive
recessive
redressive
regressive
repressive
retrogressive
successive
suppressive
transgressive
unexpressive

ĔS'kĭ
de Reszke
pesky

ĔSK'nĕs
grotesqueness
picturesqueness
statuesqueness

ĔS'kō
al fresco
fresco
tedesco

ĔS'kū
fescue
rescue

Ē'skwär
T-square

ĔS"l
Cecil
chessel
nestle
pestle
redressal
trestle
unnestle

vessel
wrestle

ĔS'lĕs
capriceless
ceaseless
creaseless
fleeceless
leaseless
peaceless

ĔS'lĭng
nestling
pestling
wrestling

ĔS'lur
nestler
wrestler

ĔS'man
policeman

ĔS'man
pressman
yes man

ĔS'mat
mess-mate

ĔS'mĕl
piecemeal

ĔS'mĕnt
assessment
impressment
redressment

ĔS'nĕs
obeseness

ĔS'on
Gleason
Leisen

ĔS'on
lessen
lesson

ĔS'pĭt
respite

ĔS'pur
Hesper
vesper

ĔS'ta
podesta
siesta
Vesta
Zend-Avesta

ĔS'tal
festal
vestal

ĔS'tan
Avestan
sebesten

ĔS'tant
contestant
gestant

ĔS'tat
intestate
testate

ĔS'tĕd
arrested
attested
bested

breasted
castle-crested
chested
chicken-
  breasted
congested
contested
crested
detested
digested
disinterested
divested
double-breasted
foam-crested
indigested
infested
ingested
interested
invested
jested
manifested
marble-
  breasted
molested
nested
pigeon-
  breasted
predigested
protested
redigested
requested
rested
sable-vested
single-breasted
suggested
tested
unbreasted
undigested
unmolested
unrested

āle, câre, ădd, ärm, ȧsk; mē, hĕre, ĕnd; īce, ĭll;

vested
wrested

ĔS'test

arrestest
attestest
bestest
breastest
contestest
crestest
detestest
digestest
divestest
infestest
interestest
investest
jestest
manifestest
molestest
protestest
requestest
restest
suggestest
testest
wrestest

ĔS'teth

arresteth
attesteth
breasteth
contesteth
cresteth
detesteth
digesteth
divesteth
infesteth
interesteth
investeth
jesteth
manifesteth
molesteth

nesteth
protesteth
requesteth
resteth
suggesteth
testeth
wresteth

ĔS'tez

Estes

ĔST'ful

blestful
jestful
restful
unrestful

ĔS'ti

beastie
bheesty
yeasty

ĔS'ti

chesty
cresty
resty
testy
yesty

ĔS'tij

prestige
vestige

ĔS'tik

agrestic
alkahestic
anamnestic
anapestic
aposiopestic
asbestic
catachrestic

domestic
gestic
majestic
telesic
telestich

ĔS'tin

asbestine
clandestine
destine
intestine
predestine
sestine

ĔS'tind

destined
predestined
undestined

ĔS'ting

easting
feasting
unpriesting
yeasting

ĔS'ting

arresting
attesting
besting
breasting
congesting
contesting
cresting
detesting
digesting
disinteresting
divesting
infesting
ingesting
interesting
investing
jesting

manifesting
molesting
nesting
protesting
questing
reinvesting
requesting
resting
suggesting
testing
uninteresting
unresting
vesting
westing
wresting

ĔS'tiv

attestive
congestive
digestive
festive
infestive
restive
suggestive
tempestive

ĔST'les

breastless
crestless
guestless
jestless
questless
restless

ĔST'li

beastly
priestly

ĔST'ling

nestling
westling

ĔST'ment

arrestment
divestment
investment
vestment

ĔS'to

manifesto
presto

Ē'ston

freestone
keystone

ĔS'ton

Weston

ĔS'tral

ancestral
campestral
fenestral
kestrel
orchestral
trimestral

ĔS'trat

fenestrate
sequestrate

ĔS'trik

orchestric
palaestric

ĔS'tur

divesture
gesture
investure
purpresture
revesture
vesture

ĔS'tus

asbestus
cestus

ĒST'ward

eastward

ĒST'ward

westward

ĔS'ter

Dniester
down-easter
Easter
feaster
north-easter
south-easter

ĔS'tur

arrester
attester
Bester
Bestor
breaster
Chester
contester
digester
divester
Dnestr
Esther
fester
Hester
infester
investor
jester
Leicester
Lester
mid-sementer
molester
nester

nor'-wester
pester
prester
protester
requester
rester
semester
sequester
sou'-wester
suggester
Sylvester
tester
trimester
vester
wrester
yester

ĔS'turd

sequestered
unsequestered
festered, etc.

ĔS'turn

eastern

ĔS'turn

hestern
north-western
south-western
western
yestern

ĒS'ur

creaser
decreaser
fleecer
greaser
increaser
leaser

piecer
releaser

ĔS'ŭr

acquiescer
addresser
aggressor
antecessor
assessor
blesser
caresser
cesser
compressor
confessor
depressor
digresser
distresser
dresser
excesser
guesser
impresser
intercessor
lesser
messer
oppressor
possessor
predecessor
presser
professor
progressor
redresser
represser
successor
suppressor
transgressor

ĒT'a

cheetah
Chiquita
Juanita

Rita	reheated	eaten	*receiptest*
zeta	repeated	moth-eaten	*repeatest*
	retreated	overeaten	*repletest*
ĒT'a	seated	storm-beaten	*retreatest*
animetta	secreted	sweeten	*seatest*
arietta	self-conceited	tempest-beaten	*sweetest*
biretta	sheeted	unbeaten	*treatest*
burletta	sleeted	weather-beaten	(cf. defeatist,
codetta	treated	wheaten	etc.)
comedietta	unmeeted	worm-eaten	
Etta	unseated	(cf. ĒT'on)	**ĒT'est**
Henrietta	wine-heated		*abettest*
lametta	(cf. fetid)	**ĒT'en**	*backsettest*
mozetta		*fretten*	*bayonettest*
operetta	**ĒT'ed**	threaten	*begettest*
Retta	abetted	(cf. Bretton)	*benettest*
Rosetta	benetted		*besettest*
vendetta	betted	**ĒT'est**	*bettest*
Yetta	brevetted	*beatest*	*coquettest*
	coquetted	*bleatest*	*forgettest*
ĒT'ed	coroneted	*cheatest*	*frettest*
accreted	curvetted	*competest*	*gettest*
bleated	fretted	completest	*lettest*
cheated	gazetted	*defeatest*	*nettest*
competed	indebted	*deletest*	*oversettest*
completed	interfretted	*depletest*	*pettest*
conceited	jetted	discreetest	*regrettest*
defeated	netted	*eatest*	*settest*
deleted	petted	*effetest*	*upsettest*
depleted	pirouetted	elitest	*wettest*
entreated	regretted	*entreatest*	*whettest*
escheated	sweated	fleetest	
evil-treated	unfretted	*greetest*	**ĒT'eth**
excreted	unnetted	*heatest*	*beateth*
greeted	wetted	*ill-treatest*	*bleateth*
heated	whetted	incompletest	*cheateth*
ill-treated	(cf. fetid)	*maltreatest*	*competeth*
incompleted		*meetest*	*completeth*
maltreated	**ĒT'en**	neatest	*defeateth*
meted	beaten	*overeatest*	*deleteth*
receipted	Cretan	*pleatest*	*depleteth*

eateth	**Ēth'al**	¯teething	**Ēth'ur**
entreateth	ethal	terror-	ether
greeteth	lethal	breathing	
heateth		unsheathing	**ĔTH'ur**
maltreateth	**Ēth'an**	wreathing	altogether
meeteth	Ethan		aweather
overeateth		**Ēth'les**	blether
pleateth	**Ēth'el**	sheathless	feather
receipteth	Bethel	wreathless	heather
repeateth	ethal		leather
retreateth	Ethel	**Ēth'les**	nether
seateth	(cf. Ēth'il)	breathless	patent-leather
treateth		deathless	pinfeather
	ĔTH'en		tether
ĔT'eth	heathen	**Ēth'li**	¯together
abetteth	wreathen	deathly	weather
begetteth			wether
benetteth	**Ēth'i**	**ĒTH'ment**	white-feather
betteth	heathy	bequeathment	whitleather
bewetteth	Lethe	ensheathment	whether
coquetteth	lethy	enwreathment	
forgetteth			**ĔTH'urd**
fretteth	**Ĕth'i**	**Ĕth'nĭk**	unfeathered
getteth	deathy	ethnic	weathered
letteth		holethnic	feathered, etc.
netteth	**Ĕth'il**		
petteth	ethyl	**Ĕth'od**	**ĔT'i**
regretteth	methyl	method	entreaty
setteth			meaty
whetteth	**ĔTH'ing**	**ĔTH'ren**	peaty
	bequeathing	brethren	sleety
ĔT'ful	breathing		spermaceti
deceitful	ensheathing	**ĔTH'ur**	sweetie
	enwreathing	bequeather	sweety
ĔT'ful	inbreathing	breather	treaty
forgetful	incense-	either	
fretful	breathing	¯enwreather	**ĔT'i**
regretful	interwreathing	neither	Alligretti
	inwreathing	seether	Bettie
ĒTH'al	seething	sheather	betty
bequeathal	sheathing	wreather	confetti

āle,   câre,   ădd,   ärm,   åsk;   mē,   hēre,   ĕnd;   īce,   ĭll;

fretty
Hettie
Hetty
Irish confetti
jetty
Lettie
Letty
libretti
netty
Nettie
petit
petty
Rossetti
spaghetti
spermaceti
Vanizetti
sweaty

ĔT'id, ĔT'id

fetid
(cf. ĔT'ed,
   ĔT'ed)

ĔT'ij

cheatage
cleatage
eatage
escheatage
metage

ĔT'ik

acetic
cetic
Cretic
Rhætic

ĔT'ik

abietic
abiogenetic
æsthetic
agamogenetic

alexipyretic
allopathetic
aloetic
alphabetic
amuletic
anesthetic
anchoretic
antipathetic
antithetic
apathetic
apologetic
arithmetic
ascetic
athletic
auletic
Baphometic
bathetic
biogenetic
biomagnetic
catechetic
colletic
cometic
cosmetic
diamagnetic
dianoetic
diaphoretic
dietetic
docetic
electro-
   magnetic
emetic
emporetic
energetic
epigenetic
epithetic
erotetic
eugenetic
exegetic
frenetic
galactopoietic
Gangetic

genetic
geodetic
Helvetic
hermetic
histogenetic
homiletic
homogenetic
hypothetic
idiopathetic
inergetic
Japhetic
kinetic
Lettic
logarithmetic
magnetic
Masoretic
metic
mimetic
mythopoetic
noetic
nomothetic
ochletic
onomatopoetic
ontogenetic
palingenetic
pangenetic
parathetic
parenthetic
paretic
partheno-
   genetic
pathetic
pathogenetic
peripatetic
phonetic
phrenetic
phylogenetic
plethoretic
poetic
polygenetic
polysynthetic

prophetic
quercetic
quodlibetic
splenetic
strategetic
sympathetic
syncretic
synthetic
tabetic
theopathetic
theoretic
threnetic
zetetic

ĔT'iks

apologetics
dietetics
exegetics
homiletics
poetics
aesthetics, etc.

ĔT'ing

beating
bitter-
   sweeting
bleating
cheating
competing
completing
concreting
defeating
eating
entreating
fleeting
flesh-eating
greeting
heating
ill-treating
maltreating
meeting

meting
overeating
receipting
repeating
retreating
seating
secreting
sheeting
sweeting
toad-eating
treating
unseating

ĔT'ing

abetting
backsetting
begetting
benetting
besetting
betting
brevetting
coquetting
curvetting
forgetting
fretting
gazetting
getting
intersetting
jetting
letting
minuetting
netting
oversetting
petting
regretting
retting
setting
somersetting
sweating
undersetting
upsetting

wetting
whetting

ĔT'is

Thetis

ĔT'is

lettuce

ĔT'ish

coquettish
fetish
Lettish
pettish
wettish

ĔT'ist

defeatist, etc.

ĔT'it

beat it

ĔT'iv

accretive
completive
concretive
decretive
depletive
discretive
repletive
secretive

ĔT'iz

entreaties
sweeties
treaties
treatise

ĔT''l

beetle
betel

decretal
fetal

ĔT''l

abettal
Babbitt metal
Chettle
fettle
kettle
metal
mettle
Monel metal
nettle
petal
Popocatapetl
resettle
settle
type-metal
white-metal

ĔT''ld

high-mettled
nettled
petalled
unsettled
mettled, etc.

ĔT'les

debtless
threatless

ĔT'li

completely
concretely
discreetly
featly
fleetly
indiscreetly
meetly
neatly
obsoletely

sweetly
unmeetly

ĔT'ling

nettling
settling
unsettling

ĔT'ment

entreatment
ill-treatment
maltreatment
treatment

ĔT'ment

abetment
besetment
indebtment
revetment

ĒT'nes

completeness
concreteness
discreetness
effeteness
featness
fleetness
incompleteness
meetness
neatness
obsoleteness
repleteness
sweetness

ĔT'nes

setness
wetness

ĒT'o

bonito
mosquito

san-benito
veto

ĒT'o

allegreto
amoretto
falsetto
ghetto
lazaretto
libretto
palmetto
stiletto
terzetto
zucchetto

ĒT'on

Beaton
Eaton
Eton
Keaton
Keyton
Seaton
Seyton
Zyzzogeton
(cf. ĒT'en)

ĔT'on

Bretton

ĔT'ral, ĔT'rel

diametral
petrel

ĒT'ri

Petrie

ĔT'rik

actinometric
alkalimetric
anemometric
anisometric

audiometric
barometric
bathymetric
calorimetric
clinometric
chlorometric
chronometric
diametric
dimetric
electrometric
endosmometric
eudiometric
gasometric
geometric
goniometric
gravimetric
hexametric
hydrometric
hygrometric
hypsometric
isobarometric
isometric
logometric
magnetometric
metric
micrometric
monometric
obstetric
ozonometric
pedometric
photometric
stereometric
symmetric
tasimetric
thermometric
trigonometric
trimetric
volumetric

ĔT'rok

sheetrock

ĔT'rus, ĔT'rus

petrous
saltpetrous
triquetrous

ĒT'um

arboretum
fretum
pinetum
zibetum

ĒT'ūr

creature
feature
(cf. ĒCH'ur)

ĒT'ur

beater
beefeater
bleater
cake-eater
cheater
centimeter
competer
completer
decaliter
defeater
Demeter
depleter
eater
entreater
escheator
fire-eater
fleeter
frog-eater
gas-meter
goldbeater
greeter
heater
hectoliter
ill-treater

kilometer
liter
lotus-eater
meeter
meter
metre
neater
overeater
Peter
prætor
receipter
repeater
retreater
saltpeter
seater
secreter
skeeter
smoke-eater
superheater
sweeter
teeter
toad-eater
treater
unseater
water-meter

ĔT'ur

abettor
begetter
besetter
better
carburetor
coquetter
curvetter
dead-letter
debtor
enfetter
fetter
forgetter
fretter
getter

go-getter
jetter
letter
netter
petter
red-letter
regretter
resetter
setter
somersetter
sweater
type-setter
wetter
whetter

ĔT′urd

featured

ĔT′urd

fettered
unfettered
unlettered
bettered, etc.

ĔT′urz

Peters

ĔT′us

acetous
Cetus
fetus
quietus

ĔT′wurk

fretwork
network

Ē′um

amœbæum
athenæum
bronteum

colosseum
lyceum
mausoleum
museum
peritoneum
prytaneum
Te Deum

Ē′ur

agreer
feer
fleer
freer
over-seer
seer
sight-seer

Ē′us

choreus
corypheus
gluteus
onomatopœous
plumbeous
scarabæus

Ē′va

diva
Eva
Geneva
Kamadeva
Kivah
Mahadeva
viva

ĒV′al

coeval
longeval
medieval
primeval
retrieval
shrieval

upheaval
(cf. weevil)

ĔV′an

Evan
Devon
(cf. Ĕv′en)

ĔV′ans

achievance
grievance
perceivance
retrievance

ĔV′el, ĔV′l

bedevil
bevel
devil
dishevel
Greville
kevel
level
Neville
revel
sea-level
spirit-level
water-level

ĔV′en

even
good-even
Hallow-even
Stephen
Steven
unbereaven
uneven
yester-even

ĔV′en

eleven
heaven

leaven
seven

ĔV′end

leavened
unleavened

ĔV′enth

eleventh
seventh

ĔV′enz

Stevens

ĔV′est

achievest
believest
bereavest
cleavest
conceivest
deceivest
disbelievest
grievest
heavest
inweavest
leavest
perceivest
receivest
relievest
reprievest
retrievest
thievest
upheavest
weavest

ĔV′eth

achieveth
believeth
bereaveth
cleaveth
conceiveth

āle, câre, ădd, ärm, åsk; mē, hĕre, ĕnd; īce, ĭll;

deceiveth
disbelieveth
grieveth
heaveth
inweaveth
leaveth
perceiveth
receiveth
relieveth
reprieveth
retrieveth
thieveth
upheaveth
weaveth

Ē'vī

Levi

Ē'vĭ

Levy

ĔV'ĭ

bevy
chevy
clevy
heart-heavy
heavy
levee
levy
nevvy
top-heavy

ĔV'ij

cleavage
leavage

ĔV'il

evil
king's-evil
weevil

ĔV'il

devil
Neville
(see ĔV'el)

ĔV'ilz

blue-devils
devils, etc.

ĔV'in

levin
replevin

ĔV'ing

achieving
aggrieving
believing
bereaving
cleaving
conceiving
deceiving
disbelieving
grieving
heaving
interweaving
inweaving
leaving
misconceiving
perceiving
preconceiving
receiving
relieving
reprieving
retrieving
sheaving
steeving
thieving
unbelieving
undeceiving
unweaving

upheaving
weaving

ĔV'ingz

leavings, etc.

ĔV'ish

peevish
thievish

ĔV'les

leaveless
sheaveless
sleeveless

ĔV'ment

achievement
bereavement
retrievement

ĔV'ning

evening

ĔV'ri

every

ĔV'ur

achiever
aggriever
ballast-heaver
beaver
believer
bereaver
brever
cantilever
cleaver
coal heaver
conceiver
deceiver
Deever
disbeliever

enfever
fever
griever
Guadalquivir
heaver
interleaver
interweaver
jungle-fever
keever
leaver
lever
liever
livre
makebeliever
misconceiver
naïver
perceiver
preconceiver
reaver
reever
receiver
reiver
reliever
repriever
retriever
sheaver
unbeliever
undeceiver
upheaver
weaver
weever
yellow-fever

ĔV'ur

assever
cantilever
clever
dissever
endeavor
ever
forever

ōld, ôr, ŏdd, oil, fŏŏt, out; ūse, ûrn, ŭp; THis, thin

however	**Ē'ya**	teasel	pleasure
howsoever	Cassiopeia	Teazle	treasure
lever	(cf. Ē'a)	weasel	**Ē'zhurd**
never			
sever	**Ē'yan**	**ĔZ'el**	unleisured
unsever	Tarpeian	bezel	**Ē'zhurd**
whatever	(cf. Ē'an)	(cf. ĔZ"l)	immeasured
whatsoever			unleisured
whencesoever	**ĒZ'a**	**ĒZ'els**	unmeasured
whenever	Liza	easels	untreasured
whensoever	Louisa	measles, etc.	measured, etc.
wheresoever	Pisa	**Ē'zha**	
wherever		magnesia	**ĒZ'i**
whichever	**ĒZ'ans**	(see Ĕz'i-a)	breezy
whichsoever	defeasance		cheesy
whithersoever	easance	**Ē'zhan**	easy
whoever	malfeasance	Milesian	free-and-easy
whomsoever	misfeasance	(see ĒZ'i-an)	freezy
whosesoever	**ĔZ'ans, ĔZ'ens**		greasy
whosoever	omnipresence	**Ē'zhun**	queasy
	pleasance	adhesion	sleazy
ĔV'urd	presence	cohesion	sneezy
unsevered	peasants, etc.	inadhesion	speakeasy
dissevered, etc.		inhesion	uneasy
	ĔZ'ant, ĔZ'ent	lesion	wheezy
ĔV'us	displeasant	Silesian	Zambezi
grievous	omnipresent	trapezian	**ĒZ'iks**
longevous	peasant	(cf. ĒZ'i-on)	skeeziks
primevous	pheasant		
	pleasant	**Ē'zhur**	**ĒZ'in**
Ē'wa	present	leisure	seizin
leeway	unpleasant	seizure	
seaway	**ĒZ'dal**	**ĔZH'ur**	**ĒZ'ing**
Ē'ward	Teasdale	admeasure	appeasing
leeward	**ĔZ'dal**	displeasure	breezing
seaward	Esdale	entreasure	displeasing
		leisure	easing
Ē'wit	**ĒZ'el**	measure	foreseizing
peewit	easel	outmeasure	freezing
			greasing

āle,   câre,   ădd,   ärm,   àsk;   mē,   hęre,   ĕnd;   īce,   ĭll;

pleasing	**ĔZ'lur**	**ĔZ'ra**	sneezer
seizing	embezzler	Ezra	squeezer
self-pleasing			teaser
sneezing	**ĔZ'ment**	**ĔZ'ur**	tweezer
squeezing	appeasement	appeaser	wheezer
teasing	easement	Cæsar	
unpleasing		easer	**ĔZ'urt**
wheezing	**ĔZ'on**	Ebenezer	desert
	reason	freezer	
ĒZ'it	season	friezer	**ĔZ'urz**
cheese it	treason	geezer	tweezers, etc.
	unreason	greaser	
ĔZ"l	unseason	leaser	**ĔZ'us**
embezzle		pleaser	Jesus
(cf. ĔZ'el)			

I

For a discussion of words included under the accented vowels following, see the beginning of I rhymes in Section I.

Ī'a	Sophia	**Ī'adz**	retrial
Amariah	stria	Hyads	*rial*
asthenia	Thalia	dryads, etc.	self-denial
Ave Maria	Tobiah		supplial
Azariah	Uriah	**Ī'ak**	trial
Beniah	via	elegiac	vial
Beriah	Zachariah	guiac	viol
Black Maria	Zebediah	kayak	
gorgoneia	Zedekiah	phrenesiac	**Ī'am**
Hezekiah	Zephaniah		Priam
Isaiah		**Ī'al, Ī'ol**	Siam
Jedediah	**Ī'ad**	basihyal	
Jeremiah	dryad	bass-viol	**Ī'amb**
Josiah	dyad	decrial	iamb
Keziah	hamadryad	denial	
latria	Jeremiad	dial	**Ī'an**
Maria	Pleiad	espial	Altaian
messiah	triad	genial	Brian
Obadiah		phial	Bryan

ōld, ôr, ŏdd, oil, fŏŏt, out; ūse, ûrn, ŭp; THis, thin

Chian
genian
Orion
O'Ryan
Ryan
styan
thalian
(cf. Ī'on)

Ī'and
viand

Ī'andz
viands

Ī'ans

affiance
alliance
appliance
compliance
defiance
incompliance
misalliance
reliance
science
self-reliance
suppliance
(cf. giants,
    etc.)

Ī'ant
affiant
alliant
calorifient
client
compliant
defiant
giant
pliant
reliant

scient
self-reliant

Ī'as
Ananias
bias
Elias
eyas
Jeremias
Josias
Lias
Matthias
Messias
Tobias, etc.
unbias
(see Ī'us)

Ī'at
fiat

Ī'azm
miasm

Ī'ba
capaiba
Ziba

ĬB'ald
ribald
Theobald

ĬB'dis
Charybdis

ĬB'est
ascribest
bribest
circumscribest
describest
gibest
imbibest

inscribest
prescribest
proscribest
subscribest
superscribest
transcribest

ĬB'est
fibbest
glibbest
jibbest

ĬB'et
flibbertigibbet
gibbet
Tibbett
zibet
(cf. ĬB'it)

ĬB'eth
ascribeth
bribeth
circumscribeth
describeth
gibeth
imbibeth
inscribeth
prescribeth
proscribeth
subscribeth
superscribeth
transcribeth

ĬB'eth
fibbeth
jibbeth

ĬB'ĭ
Kibbee
Libbey

Libby
Tibbie

ĪB'ing
ascribing
bribing
circumscribing
describing
gibing
imbibing
inscribing
prescribing
proscribing
subscribing
transcribing

ĬB'ing
fibbing
jibbing
ribbing
squibbing

ĬB'it
adhibit
cohibit
exhibit
inhibit
prohibit

Ī'b'l
Bible
libel
tribal

ĬB"l
cribble
dibble
dribble
fribble
gribble
ish ka bibble

āle, câre, ădd, ärm, åsk; mē, hĕre, ĕnd; īce, ĭll;

kibble	fribbling	ĬB′rant	cribber
nibble	kibbling	vibrant	dibber
quibble	nibbling		fibber
scribble	quibbling	ĬB′rat	flibbergibber
sibyl	scribbling	equilibrate	gibber
thribble	tribbling	librate	glibber
		vibrate	jibber
ĬB″ld	Ĭ′blo		nibber
cribbled	by-blow	Ĭ′brou	quibber
ribald	fly-blow	eyebrow	squibber
dibbled, etc.		high-brow	wine-bibber
	ĬB′lur		
ĬB′lest	cribbler	ĬB′sen	ĬB′ut
dribblest	dibbler	Ibsen	attribute
scribblest, etc.	dribbler		contribute
	fribbler	ĬB′son	distribute
ĬB′let	kibbler	Ibson	redistribute
driblet	nibbler	Gibson	retribute
giblet	quibbler		tribute
triblet	scribbler	ĬB′un	
	transcribbler	tribune	ĬCH′ard
ĬB′leth			Pritchard
dribbleth	Ĭ′bôl	ĬB′ur	Richard
scribbleth, etc.	eye-ball	ascriber	
	high-ball	briber	ĬCH′el
ĬB′li	sky-ball	circumscriber	Kitchell
dribbly		describer	Mitchell
glibly	Ĭ′bôld	fiber	Turchell
nibbly	piebald	giber	switchel
quibbly		imbiber	
scribbly	ĬB′on	inscriber	ĬCH′en
thribbly	gibbon	Leiber	kitchen
tribbly	ribbon	liber	lichen
		prescriber	
ĬB′lik	ĬB′onz	proscriber	ĬCH′est
niblick	Gibbons	scriber	bewitchest
	ribbons, etc.	subscriber	enrichest
ĬB′ling		Tiber	hitchest
cribbling	Ĭ′born	transcriber	pitchest
dibbling	high-born		richest
dribbling	sky-born	ĬB′ur	stitchest
		bibber	

ōld, ôr, ŏdd, oil, fŏŏt, out; ūse, ûrn, ŭp; THis, thin

switchest
twitchest

ĬCH′et

fitchet
Fitchett
Pritchett
Twichett
witchet

ĬCH′eth

bewitcheth
enricheth
hitcheth
pitcheth
stitcheth
switcheth
twitcheth

ĬCH′ez

bewitches
bitches
breeches
ditches
enriches
flitches
hitches
itches
niches
pitches
riches
scritches
stitches
switches
twitches
witches

ĬCH′i

fitchy
itchy
pitchy

Richie
stitchy
witchy

ĬCH′ing

bewitching
ditching
enriching
hitching
itching
miching
pitching
stitching
switching
twitching
witching

ĬCH′les

hitchless
itchless
stitchless
switchless
witchless

ĬCH′ment

bewitchment
enrichment

ĬCH′nes

richness

ĬCH′ur

bewitcher
ditcher
enricher
hitcher
itcher
pitcher
richer
stitcher
switcher
twitcher

ĬCH′us

righteous

Ī′da

Ida
Lida
Oneida

ĪD′ans

abidance
guidance
misguidance
subsidence

ĪD′ans

forbiddance
riddance

ĪD′ant

dividant
guidant

ĪD′ed

backslided
betided
bided
chided
coincided
collided
confided
decided
derided
divided
elided
glided
guided
lopsided
many-sided
misguided
one-sided
presided

prided
provided
resided
sided
slab-sided
subdivided
subsided
tided
undecided
undivided
unguided
unprovided
(cf. tidied)

ĬD′ed

kidded
lidded, etc.

ĪD′en

Dryden
widen
(cf. ĪD′on)

ĬD′en

bidden
chidden
forbidden
hag-ridden
hidden
kitchen-midden
midden
overridden
priest-ridden
ridden
slidden
stridden
unbidden
unforbidden
wife-ridden

ĪD′ent

bident

āle, câre, ădd, ärm, åsk; mē, hęre, ĕnd; īce, ĭll;

rident	chideth	middy	outriding
strident	coincideth	stiddy	outstriding
trident	collideth	"widdy"	overriding
	confideth		presiding
ĪD'est	decideth	**ĪD'id**	priding
abidest	derideth	tidied	providing
backslidest	divideth	(cf. ĪD'ed)	residing
bidest	elideth		riding
chidest	glideth	**ĪD'ij**	siding
coincidest	guideth	guidage	sliding
collidest	hideth	hidage	striding
confidest	overrideth		subsiding
decidest	presideth	**ĪD'ik**	
deridest	prideth	druidic	**ĪD'ing**
dividest	provideth	fatidic	bidding
elidest	resideth	juridic	forbidding
glidest	rideth	pyramidic	kidding
guidest	sideth		lidding
hidest	slideth	**ĪD'il or ĬD'il**	outbidding
overridest	strideth	idyll	overbidding
presidest	subdivideth		ridding
pridest	subsideth	**ĪD'ing**	skidding
providest	tideth	abiding	unforbidding
residest		backsliding	
ridest	**ĬD'eth**	bestriding	**ĬD'ingz**
sidest	biddeth	betiding	tidings
slidest	forbiddeth, etc.	biding	backslidings,
stridest		chiding	etc.
subdividest	**ĪD'i**	coinciding	
subsidest	bonafide	colliding	**ĪD'l**
tidest	Friday	confiding	bridal
widest	sidy	deciding	bridle
	tidy	deriding	fratricidal
ĬD'est	untidy	dividing	homicidal
biddest	vide	eliding	idle
forbiddest, etc.		gliding	idol
	ĬD'i	guiding	infanticidal
ĬD'eth	biddy	hiding	matricidal
abideth	chickabiddy	law-abiding	parricidal
betideth	giddy	misguiding	patricidal
bideth	kiddy	niding	regicidal

ōld, ôr, ŏdd, oil, fŏŏt, out; ūse, ûrn, ŭp; THis, thin

sidle
suicidal
tidal
tyrannicidal

ĪD"l

Biddle
fiddle
diddle
flumadiddle
griddle
Liddle
middle
quiddle
riddle
rum-tum-tiddle
tiddle
twiddle
unriddle

ĪD"ld

unbridled
bridled, etc.

ĪD'ld

fiddled, etc.

ĪD'lest

idlest, etc.

ĪD'lest

fiddlest, etc.

ĪD'leth

idleth, etc.

ĪD'leth

fiddleth, etc.

ĪD'li

bridely
widely

ĪD'ling

bridling
idling
sidling

ĪD'ling

diddling
fiddling
kidling
middling
riddling
twiddling

ĪD'lings

middlings
kidlings, etc.

ĪD'lit

guide-light
side-light

ĪD'lur

bridler
idler

ĪD'lur

fiddler
quiddler
riddler
tiddler
twiddler

ĪD'nes

piedness
wideness

ĪD'ni

kidney
Sidney
Sydney

ĪD'o

Dido
Fido

ĪD'o

kiddo
widow

ĪD'on

guidon
Poseidon
Sidon
(cf. widen)

ĪD'or

nidor
stridor
(cf. ĪD'ur)

ĪD'rule

slide rule

ĪD'ur

backslider
bestrider
chider
cider
coincider
collider
confider
decider
derider
divider
eider
elider
Fulenwider
glider
guider
hider
insider
misguider

one-sider
outrider
outsider
presider
provider
resider
rider
rough-rider
Schneider
sider
slider
Snider
Snyder
spider
strider
subdivider
subsider
wider

ĪD'ur

bidder
consider
forbidder
kidder
outbidder
overbidder
ridder
skidder

ĪD'urd

considered
ill-considered
unconsidered

Ī'ens

science
(see Ī'ans)

Ī'ent

calorifient
client

inscient
scient
(see affiant,
  etc.)

Ī'est

alliest
amplifiest
appliest
awryest
beautifiest
bedyest
beliest
bespyest
brutifiest
buyest
certifiest
clarifiest
classifiest
compliest
criest
crucifiest
decriest
defiest
deifiest
deniest
descriest
diest
dignifiest
diversifiest
driest
dyest
edifiest
electrifiest
espiest
eyest
falsifiest
fliest
fortifiest
friest
glorifiest

gratifiest
hiest
highest
horrifiest
identifiest
impliest
justifiest
liest
liquefiest
magnifiest
modifiest
mollifiest
mortifiest
multipliest
mystifiest
nighest
notifiest
nullifiest
occupiest
ossifiest
outviest
pacifiest
personifiest
pliest
prophesiest
pryest
purifiest
qualifiest
ratifiest
rectifiest
reliest
repliest
sanctifiest
satisfiest
shyest
sighest
signifiest
simplifiest
slyest
specifiest
spryest

spyest
stupefiest
suppliest
terrifiest
testifiest
tiest
tryest
typifiest
untiest
verifiest
versifiest
viest
vilifiest
vitrifiest
wryest

Ī'et

diet
inquiet
piet
quiet
(cf. riot)

Ī'eth

allieth
amplifieth
applieth
bedyeth
belieth
bespyeth
buyeth
certifieth
clarifieth
classifieth
complieth
crieth
crucifieth
decrieth
defieth
deif:eth
denieth

descrieth
dieth
dignifieth
diversifieth
drieth
dyeth
edifieth
electrifieth
espieth
eyeth
falsifieth
flieth
fortifieth
frieth
glorifieth
gratifieth
hieth
horrifieth
identifieth
implieth
justifieth
lieth
liquefieth
magnifieth
modifieth
mollifieth
mortifieth
multiplieth
mystifieth
notifieth
nullifieth
occupieth
outvieth
pacifieth
personifieth
plieth
prophesieth
purifieth
qualifieth
ratifieth
rectifieth

relieth
replieth
sanctifieth
satisfieth
sigheth
signifieth
simplifieth
specifieth
spyeth
stupefieth
supplieth
terrifieth
testifieth
tieth
trieth
typifieth
untieth
verifieth
versifieth
vieth
vilifieth
vitrifieth
vivifieth

ĪF'en, ĪF'on

hyphen
siphon
Typhon

ĪF'en, ĪF'on

griffon
stiffen

ĬF'est

sniffest
stiffest
whiffest

ĬF'et

whiffet

ĬF'eth

sniffeth, etc.

ĬF'i

cliffy
jiffy
sniffy
spiffy
squiffy

ĬF'ik

acidific
algific
anaglyphic
aurific
beatific
calorific
classific
colorific
cornific
damnific
deific
diaglyphic
dolorific
finific
frigorific
glyphic
grandific
hieroglyphic
honorific
horrific
humorific
incoherentific
lactific
lapidific
lithoglyphic
lucific
magnific
mellific
mirific
morbific

mucific
omnific
ossific
pacific
petrific
petroglyphic
photoglyphic
phytoglyphic
pontific
prolific
pulsific
rubific
sacrific
salvific
saporific
scientific
sensific
siccific
somnific
sonorific
soporific
specific
sudorific
tabific
tenebrific
terrific
torporific
triglyphic
vaporific
vivific
vulnific

ĬF'in

biffin
griffin
tiffin
(cf. stiffen,
etc.)

ĬF'ing

sniffing

tiffing
whiffing

ĬF'ish

miffish
sniffish
stiffish
tiffish

Ĭ'f'l

Eiffel
rifle
stifle
trifle

ĬF''l

piffle
riffle
sniffle
whiffle

ĪF'les

fifeless
knifeless
lifeless
strifeless
wifeless

ĪF'li

rifely
wifely

ĪF'lik

lifelike
wifelike

ĪF'ling

rifling
stifling
trifling

ĬF'ling
piffling
riffling
sniffling
whiffling

ĬF'lur
rifler, etc.

ĬF'lur
piffler
riffler
sniffler
whiffler

ĬF'on, ĬF'en
hyphen
siphon
Typhon

ĬF'ted
drifted
gifted
lifted
rifted
shifted
sifted
ungifted
uplifted

ĬF'test
driftest
liftest
riftest
shiftest
siftest
swiftest
upliftest

ĬF'teth
drifteth

lifteth
rifteth
shifteth
sifteth
uplifteth

ĬF'ti
clifty
drifty
fifty
fifty-fifty
nifty
rifty
shifty
thrifty

ĬF'ting
drifting
lifting
rifting
shifting
shop-lifting
sifting
uplifting

ĬFT'les
driftless
riftless
shiftless
thriftless

ĬFT'nes
swiftness

ĬF'ton
Clifton

ĬF'thong
diphthong
triphthong

ĬFT'ur
drifter
lifter
scene-shifter
shifter
shop-lifter
sifter
swifter
uplifter

ĬF'ur
cipher
decipher
fifer
lifer
knifer
rifer

ĬF'ur
differ
sniffer
stiffer

Ī'ga
saiga

ĬG'and
brigand

ĬG'at
frigate
(cf. bigot)

ĬG'bi
Digby

ĬG'est
biggest
diggest
riggest
triggest

ĬG'eth
diggeth, etc.

ĬG'i
biggy
piggy
piggy-wiggy
spriggy
twiggy

ĬG'ing
digging
gigging
jigging
rigging
sprigging
swigging
thimblerigging
trigging
twigging
unrigging
wigging

ĬG'inz
Dwiggins
Higgins
Wiggins

ĬG'ish
piggish
priggish
whiggish

ĬG″'l
giggle
higgle
jiggle
niggle
sniggle
squiggle
wiggle
wriggle

ōld, ôr, ŏdd, oil, fŏŏt, out; ūse, ûrn, ŭp; THis, thin

Ĭ'glas

eye-glass
spy-glass

ĬG''ld

giggled, etc.

ĬG'lest

gigglest, etc.

ĬG'leth

giggleth, etc.

ĬG'li

Piggly-Wiggly
giggly, etc.

ĬG'lif

diglyph
monotriglyph
triglyph

ĬG'ling

giggling
higgling, etc.

ĬG'lur

giggler
higgler, etc.

ĬG'ma

enigma
sigma
stigma

ĬG'ment

figment
pigment

ĬG'mi

pygmy

ĬG'nal

signal

ĬG'nans

malignance

ĬG'nant

benignant
indignant
malignant

ĬG'net

cygnet
signet

ĬG'nit

lignite

ĬG'num

ecce signum
lignum

Ĭ'go

caligo
fuligo
impetigo
Loligo
vertigo

Ĭ'gon

bygone
trigone

ĬG'on

big 'un
Ligon

Ĭ'gor

rigor
vigor
(cf. ĬG'ur)

Ĭ'got

bigot
gigot
spigot
(cf. frigate)

ĬG'res

tigress

Ĭ'gur

Niger
tiger

ĬG'ūr

configure
disfigure
figure
ligure
prefigure
transfigure

ĬG'ur

bigger
chigger
digger
"figger"
gold-digger
grave-digger
gigger
jigger
ligger
market-rigger
nigger
outrigger
prigger
rigger
snigger
sprigger
swigger
thimblerigger
trigger
twigger

(cf. rigor
and vigor)

ĬG'urd

"figgered"
jiggered
niggard
sniggered
unniggard

Ĭ'ing

acidifying
adrying
alibing
allying
amplifying
applying
beatifying
beautifying
bedying
belying
bespying
brutifying
butterflying
buying
candifying
certifying
clarifying
classifying
codifying
complying
countrifying
crucifying
crying
damnifying
dandifying
decrying
defying
deifying
denying
descrying

āle, câre, ădd, ärm, åsk; mē, hẹre, ĕnd; īce, ĭll;

dignifying	mystifying	specifying	ĬJ'il
disqualifying	notifying	spying	sigil
dissatisfying	nullifying	stultifying	strigil
diversifying	occupying	stupefying	vigil
drying	ossifying	supplying	
dulcifying	outcrying	terrifying	ĬJ'ing
dyeing	outflying	testifying	disobliging
dying	outlying	torpifying	obliging
edifying	outvying	torrefying	
electrifying	pacifying	trying	ĬJ'ing
emulsifying	personifying	typifying	abridging
espying	petrifying	uncomplying	bridging
exemplifying	piing	under-buying	ridging
eyeing	plying	underlying	
falsifying	preachifying	undying	ĬJ'it
fying	preoccupying	unifying	Bridget
fortifying	prophesying	unsatisfying	Brigit
Frenchifying	prying	untying	digit
fructifying	purifying	verifying	fidget
frying	putrefying	versifying	"ijjit"
glorifying	qualifying	vieing	midget
gratifying	ramifying	vilifying	
guying	rarefying	vitrifying	ĬJ'on
hieing	ratifying	vivifying	irreligion
horrifying	rectifying		pigeon
humanifying	relying	Ī'ja	religion
hushabying	replying	Abijah	widgeon
identifying	revivifying	Elijah	
implying	sanctifying		ĬJ'ur
indemnifying	satisfying	Ī'jak	abridger
intensifying	scarifying	highjack	bridger
justifying	scorifying		
kite-flying	self-denying	ĬJ'est	ĬJ'us
labifying	self-relying	digest	irreligious
liquefying	self-satisfying	disobligest	litigious
lying	shying	obligest	prodigious
magnifying	sighing		religious
modifying	signifying	ĬJ'id	sacrilegious
mollifying	simplifying	frigid	
mortifying	skying	rigid	ĬK'a
multiplying	solidifying		balalaika

ōld, ôr, ŏdd, oil, fŏŏt, out; ūse, ûrn, ŭp; THis, thin

lorica
mica
Micah
pica
pika

I'kal
Michael

ĬK'ard
Pickard
Rickard

ĬK'at
exsiccate
siccate

Ĭk'ed
wicked
(see ĬK+ed)

ĬK'en
lichen
liken
unliken

ĬK'en
chicken
horror-stricken
quicken
sicken
stricken
terror-stricken
thicken
wicken
wonder-
  stricken

ĬK'enz
chickens
slickens
the dickens

ĬK'est
dislikest
likest
obliquest
spikest
strikest

ĬK'est
clickest
flickest
kickest
lickest
pickest
prickest
slickest
stickest
thickest
tickest
trickest

Ĭk'et
clicket
cricket
midwicket
picket
Pickett
pricket
Prickett
Rickett
thicket
ticket
walking-ticket
wicket

ĬK'eth
disliketh
liketh
spiketh
striketh

ĬK'eth
clicketh

---

flicketh
kicketh
licketh
picketh
pricketh
sticketh
ticketh
tricketh

ĬK'ets
rickets
crickets, etc.

ĬK'i
spiky
(cf. Psyche)

ĬK'i
bricky
dickey
do-hickey
Ficke
gin-rickey
quickie
rickey
sticky
tricky

ĬK'ik
psychic

ĬK'iks
psychics

ĬK'ing
biking
disliking
dyking
misliking
piking
spiking

---

striking
viking
well-liking

ĬK'ing
besticking
bricking
clicking
cricking
flicking
kicking
licking
picking
pocket-picking
pricking
snicking
sticking
thicking
ticking
tricking
wicking

ĬK'ish
brickish
sickish
slickish
thickish

ĬK"l
cycle
epyicycle
psychal

ĬK"l
fickle
mickle
nickel
pickle
prickle
sickle
stickle

āle, câre, ădd, ärm, ȧsk; mē, hẽre, ĕnd; īce, ĭll;

strickle
tickle
trickle

ĬK′lest
ficklest
picklest
ticklest
tricklest

ĬK′leth
pickleth
prickleth
tickleth
trickleth

ĬK′li
belikely
likely
obliquely
unlikely

ĬK′li
prickly
quickly
sickly
slickly
stickly
thickly
trickly

ĬK′lik
bicyclic
cyclic
encyclic
epicyclic
geocyclic

ĬK′ling
cycling

ĬK′ling
chickling
pickling
prickling
tickling
trickling

ĬK′lish
pricklish
ticklish

ĬK′list
cyclist

ĬK′lon
cyclone

ĬK′lur
fickler
prickler
stickler
strickler
tickler

ĬK′nes
likeness
obliqueness
unlikeness

ĬK′nes
love-sickness
quickness
sickness
slickness
thickness

ĬK′nik
picnic
strychnic

ĬK′nin
strychnine

ĬK′ning
quickening
sickening
thickening

ĬK′on
icon

ĬK′or
ichor

Ĭ′kount
viscount

ĬK′sen
mixen
vixen

ĬK′sest
affixest
fixest
intermixest
mixest
prefixest
transfixest

ĬK′set
quickset
thick-set

ĬK′seth
affixeth
fixeth
intermixeth
mixeth
prefixeth
transfixeth

ĬK′shun
abstriction
addiction

affixion
affliction
affriction
benediction
confliction
constriction
contradiction
conviction
crucifixion
depiction
dereliction
diction
eviction
fiction
friction
indiction
infliction
interdiction
jurisdiction
malediction
obstriction
prediction
prefixion
reliction
restriction
suffixion
transfixion
valediction

ĬK′shus
contradictious
fictious

ĬK′si
Dixey
Dixie
nixie
pixie
tricksy
Trixie
water-nixie

ĬK'sing

admixing
affixing
fixing
intermixing
mixing
prefixing
transfixing

ĬK'son

Dickson
Dixon
Hickson
Hixon

ĬK'sti

sixty

ĬK'stŭr

admixture
affixture
fixture
immixture
incommixture
intermixture
mixture

ĬK'stŭr

trickster

ĬK'sur

affixer
elixir
fixer
intermixer
mixer
prefixer
transfixer

ĬK'tat

dictate
uictate

ĬK'ted

addicted
afflicted
conflicted
constricted
contradicted
convicted
depicted
evicted
inflicted
interdicted
predicted
relicted
restricted
self-inflicted
unrestricted

ĬK'test

addictest
afflictest
conflictest
contradictest
convictest
depictest
evictest
inflictest
predictest
restrictest
strictest

ĬK'teth

addicteth
afflicteth
conflicteth
contradicteth
convicteth
depicteth
evicteth
inflicteth
predicteth
restricteth

ĬK'tik

apodictic
deictic
endeictic
epideictic
ictic

ĬK'tim

victim

ĬK'ting

addicting
afflicting
conflicting
constricting
contradicting
convicting
depicting
evicting
inflicting
interdicting
predicting
restricting

ĬK'tiv

addictive
afflictive
benedictive
conflictive
constrictive
contradictive
convictive
depictive
fictive
indictive
inflictive
interdictive
jurisdictive
predictive
restrictive
vindictive

ĬKT'li

derelictly
strictly

ĬKT'nes

strictness

ĬK'tor

(see ĬK'tur)

ĬK'tum

dictum

ĬK'tūr

depicture
impicture
picture
stricture
word-picture

ĬK'tŭr

afflicter
boa-constrictor
conflicter
constrictor
contradicter
depicter
fictor
inflicter
lictor
Pictor
predicter
restricter
stricter
victor

ĬK'tus

acronyctous
Benedictus
ictus

ĪK'ur

biker

Diker	**ĪL'a**	**ĪL'an**	**ĪL'dest**
hiker	Hyla	arch-villain	mildest
liker	Lila	villain	wildest
obliquer		villein	
piker	**ĪL'a**		**ĪL'dest**
Riker	anilla	**Ī'land**	*begildest*
spiker	armilla	highland	*buildest*
striker	barilla	island	*gildest*
	bismillah	Rhode Island	
ĪK'ur	camarilla		**ĪL'deth**
bicker	Camilla	**Ī'lark**	*begildeth*
clicker	cascarilla	phylarch	*buildeth*
dicker	cedilla	sky-lark	*gildeth*
flicker	chinchilla		
kicker	codilla	**ĪL'as**	**ĪLD'hood**
knicker	Drusilla	Silas	childhood
licker	flotilla	Vilas	
liquor	gorilla		**ĪL'ding**
nicker	granadilla	**Ī'lash**	childing
picker	granilla	eyelash	wilding
pricker	guerrilla		
quicker	Lilla	**ĪL'at**	**ĪL'ding**
sicker	Manila	distillate	begilding
slicker	manilla	penicillate	building
snicker	mantilla		castle-building
sticker	maxilla	**ĪL'burt**	gilding
thicker	Priscilla	filbert	rebuilding
ticker	sabadilla	Gilbert	unbuilding
tricker	sapodilla	Wilbert	ungilding
vicar	sarsaparilla		
wicker	seguidilla	**ĪL'da**	**ĪL'dish**
	Sybilla	Hilda	childish
ĪK'urz	vanilla	Mathilda	mildish
knickers	villa	Matilda	wildish
bickers, etc.			
	ĪL'ak	**ĪL'ded**	**ĪLD'les**
ĪK'us	lilac	begilded	childless
Picus		builded	mildless
spicous	**ĪL'aks**	gilded	
	lilacs	ungilded	**ĪLD'li**
ĪK'wid	smilax		childly
liquid			

mildly	ĪL'est	pilot	*'tilleth*
wildly	*beguilest*	sky-pilot	*trilleth*
	compilest	stylet	*willeth*
ĪLD'lik	*defilest*		
childlike	*filest*	ĪL'et	ĪL'ful
	pilest	billet	guileful
ĪLD'nes	*reconcilest*	fillet	smileful
mildness	*revilest*	millet	wileful
riledness	*rilest*	rillet	
unmildness	*smilest*	skillet	ĪL'ful
wildness	*stylest*	willet	skilful
	vilest		wilful
ĪL'dred	*whilest*	ĪL'eth	unskilful
Mildred	*wilest*	*beguileth*	
		compileth	ĪL'fur
ĪLD'ren	ĪL'est	*defileth*	pilfer
children	*befrillest*	*fileth*	
	chillest	*pileth*	ĪL'grim
ĪL'dur	*distillest*	*reconcileth*	pilgrim
milder	*drillest*	*revileth*	
wilder	*enthrillest*	*rileth*	Ī'li
	fillest	*smileth*	ancile
ĪL'dur	*frillest*	*styleth*	drily
begilder	*fulfillest*	*tileth*	highly
bewilder	*grillest*	*up-pileth*	O'Reilly
builder	illest	*whileth*	Reilly
castle-builder	*instillest*	*wileth*	Riley
gilder	killest		shyly
guilder	*millest*	ĪL'eth	slily
rebuilder	shrillest	*chilleth*	wily
wilder	*spillest*	*distilleth*	wryly
	stillest	*drilleth*	
ĪLD'wood	*swillest*	*enthrilleth*	ĪL'i
wildwood	*thrillest*	*filleth*	Billee
	tillest	*fulfilleth*	Billie
ĪL'ens	*trillest*	*instilleth*	billy
silence	*willest*	*killeth*	Chile
		milleth	chili
ĪL'ent	Ī'let, Ī'lot	*spilleth*	chilly
silent	eyelet	*stilleth*	daffy-down-
si'lent	islet	*thrilleth*	dilly

filly
frilly
gillie
grilly
hilly
illy
lily
Millie
Milly
Piccadilly
piccalilli
silly
shrilly
skilly
stilly
tiger-lily
Tillie
Tilly
water-lily
Willie
Willy
willy-nilly

Ī'lid
eyelid

ĬL'id
lilied

ĬL'ij
grillage
pillage
tillage
village
thrillage, etc.

ĬL'ik
amylic
basilic
Cyrillic
dactylic

idyllic
macrodactylic
methylic
odylic
salicylic
zygodactylic

Ī'lin
sky-line
styline

ĬL'in
MacMillin
McQuillin
(cf. McMillan,
   Dillon, etc.)

ĬL'ing
beguiling
compiling
defiling
filing
piling
reconciling
reviling
riling
smiling
styling
tiling
time-beguiling
up-piling
whiling
wiling

ĬL'ing
befrilling
billing
chilling
distilling
drilling
enthrilling

filling
frilling
fulfilling
grilling
instilling
killing
milling
shilling
shrilling
skilling
spilling
stilling
swilling
thrilling
tilling
trilling
unwilling
upfilling
willing

ĬL'ingz
Billings
drillings, etc.

ĬL'ip
Philip

ĬL'ips
Philips

ĬL'is
Amaryllis
Myrtillis
Phyllis
Willis
Wyllis

ĬL'ish
stylish

Ī'lit
dry-light

high-light
skylight
stylite
twilight
xylite

ĬL'iz
chilies
fillies
gillies
lilies
sillies
the Willies

ĬL'izm
Carlylism
hylism

ĬL'joy
killjoy

ĬL'ken
milken
silken

ĬL'ki
milky
silky

ĬL'king
bilking
milking

ĬL'koks
Philcox
Silcox
Wilcox

ĬL'les
guileless
smileless
wileless

ĬL'man	**ĪL'o**	sky-pilot	*kilteth*
billman	high-low	(cf. islet)	*lilteth*
Gilman	milo		*quilteth*
grillman	silo	**ĬL'pin**	*tilteth*
hill-man		Gilpin	*wilteth*
mill-man	**ĬL'o**		
Stillman	armadillo	**ĬL'room**	**ĬL'thi**
	billow	grill-room	filthy
ĪL'ment	embillow	still-room	
beguilment	grenadillo		**ĬL'ti**
defilement	*killow*	**ĬL'sid**	guilty
exilement	kilo	hillside	silty
irreconcilement	negrillo	rill-side	stilty
reconcilement	peccadillo		
revilement	pillow	**ĬL'son**	**ĬL'ting**
	pulvillo	Gilson	jilting
ĬL'ment	weeping-	Stillson	kilting
distilment	willow	Wilson	lilting
fulfilment	willow		quilting
instilment		**ĬL'ted**	silting
	ĬL'od	hilted	tilting
ĬL'mi	unpillowed	jilted	wilting
filmy	billowed, etc.	kilted	
		lilted	**ĬL'ton**
ĬL'mor	**ĬL'oid**	overtilted	Chilton
Filmore	styloid	quilted	Hilton
Gilmore	xyloid	silted	Milton
		stilted	Stilton
ĬL'nes	**Ī'lok**	tilted	Tilton
juvenileness	Shylock	tip-tilted	
vileness		wilted	**ĬL'tur**
	ĬL'ok		filter
	hillock	**ĬL'test**	infilter
ĬL'nes		*jiltest*	jilter
chillness	**ĬL'om**	*kiltest*	kilter
illness	whilom	*liltest*	philter
shrillness		*quiltest*	quilter
stillness	**ĬL'on**	*tiltest*	tilter
	Dillon	*wiltest*	wilter
ĬL'nur	**ĬL'ot**	**ĬL'teth**	**ĪL'um**
Milner	pilot	*jilteth*	asylum

phylum	lady-killer	(cf. ÎL'i-ant,	ÎM'a
Wylam	man-killer	ÎL'i-ent)	cyma
	maxillar		Jemima
ÎL'ur	miller	**ÎL'yar**	Lima
beguiler	pillar	atrabiliar	
bifilar	Schiller	*auxiliar*	**ÎM'aks**
compiler	shriller	conciliar	anti-climax
defiler	siller	domiciliar	climax
filar	spiller	familiar	
filer	stiller	(cf. ÎL'i-ur)	**ÎM'al**
Huyler	swiller		isocheimal
piler	thiller	**ÎL'yardz**	isocrymal
reconciler	thriller	billiards	primal
reviler	tiller	milliards	
riler	willer		**Î'man**
Schuyler		**ÎL'yun**	Hymen
smiler	**ÎL'us**	billion	pieman
stylar	aspergillus	carillon	Simon
tiler	bacillus	cotillion	Wyman
Tyler	favillous	decillion	
up-piler	fibrillous	mandillon	**ÎM'at**
viler	orgillous	million	acclimate
wiler	villus	modillion	climate
Zuyler		nonillion	primate
	ÎL'van	octillion	
ÎL'ur	sylvan	pavilion	**ÎM'bal**
befriller		pillion	cymbal
biller	**ÎL'vur**	postillion	fimble
caterpillar	silver	quadrillion	gimbal
chiller		quintillion	nimble
distiller	**ÎL'yam**	sextillion	symbol
driller	Gilliam	stillion	thimble
filler	William	trillion	tymbal
friller		tourbillion	wimble
fulfiller	**ÎL'yans**	vermilion	
griller	brilliance	(cf. ÎL'i-an)	**ÎM'bo**
iller	(cf. ÎL'i-ans,		akimbo
ill-willer	ÎL'i-ens)	**ÎL'yunth**	bimbo
instiller		billionth	kimbo
Joe-Miller	**ÎL'yant**	millionth	limbo
killer	brilliant	trillionth, etc.	

ōld, ôr, ŏdd, oil, fŏŏt, out; ūse, ûrn, ŭp; THis, thin

ĬM'brel
timbrel
whimbrel

ĬM'bur
imber
limber
timber
timbre
unlimber

ĬM'burd
untimbered
limbered, etc.

ĬM'bus
limbus
nimbus

ĬM'el
Friml
gimmal
Grimmell
Himmel
kümmel

Ī'men
Hymen
(see Ī'man)

ĬM'en
women
(cf. persim-
  mon)

ĬM'est
begrimest
berhymest
beslimest
chimest
climbest

primest
rhymest
sublimest

ĬM'est
brimmest
dimmest
grimmest
primmest
skimmest
slimmest
swimmest
trimmest

ĪM'eth
begrimeth
berhymeth
beslimeth
chimeth
climbeth
rhymeth

ĬM'eth
brimmeth
dimmeth
skimmeth
swimmeth
trimmeth

ĬM'flam
flimflam

ĪM'i
beslimy
blimy
grimy
limy
rimy
rhymy
slimy

stymie
thymy

ĬM'i
gimme
jimmy
shimmy
whimmy

ĬM'id
timid

ĬM'ij
image
scrimmage

ĬM'ik
alchimic
cacochymic
cherubimic
eponymic
etymic
homonymic
lipothymic
metonymic
metronymic
mimic
pantomimic
patronymic
synonymic
zymic (also
  ĬM'ik)

ĪM'ing
begriming
beliming
berhyming
besliming
chiming
climbing
griming

liming
priming
rhyming
sliming
timing

ĬM'ing
bedimming
betrimming
brimming
dimming
grimming
skimming
slimming
swimming
trimming

ĪM'ist
rhymist
timist

ĬM'it
limit

ĬM'jams
jimjams

ĬM'krak
gimcrack

ĬM'les
chimeless
crimeless
grimeless
limeless
rhymeless
rimeless
slimeless
thymeless
timeless
overtimeless

āle, câre, ădd, ärm, ȧsk; mē, hĕre, ĕnd; īce, ĭll;

ĬM'les
brimless
hymnless
limbless
rimless
swimless
vimless
whimless

ĬM'li
primely
sublimely
timely
untimely

ĬM'li
dimly
grimly
primly
slimly
trimly

ĬM'nal, ĬM'nel
hymnal
simnel

ĬM'nes
primeness
sublimeness

ĬM'nes
dimness
grimness
primness
slimness
trimness

ĬM'ni
chimney

Ī'mon
Simon

Timon
(see Ī'man)

ĬM'on
persimmon
Rimmon
(cf. women)

ĬM'onz
Simmons
persimmons

ĬM'pet
limpet

ĬM'pi
crimpy
impi
impy
skimpy

ĬM'ping
blimping
crimping
imping
limping
primping
scrimping
shrimping
skimping

ĬM'pish
impish

ĬM'pit
lime-pit
slime-pit

ĬM'p'l
bewimple
crimple
dimple

pimple
rimple
simple
wimple

ĬM'plest
crimplest
dimplest
pimplest
rimplest
simplest
wimplest

ĬM'pleth
crimpleth, etc.

ĬM'pli
crimply
dimply
limply
pimply
simply

ĬM'pling
crimpling
dimpling
impling
pimpling
rimpling
shrimpling
wimpling

ĬM'plur
crimpler
dimpler
rimpler
simpler
wimpler

ĬM'pur
crimper

limper
scrimper
shrimper
simper
skimper
whimper

ĬM'ros
primrose

ĬM'shi
imshi

ĬM'son
jimson

ĬM'stur
rhymester

ĬM'ur
begrimer
chimer
climber
Hergesheimer
old-timer
primer
rhymer
timer
sublimer

ĬM'ur
brimmer
dimmer
gimmer
glimmer
grimmer
primer
primmer
shimmer
simmer
skimmer

ōld, ôr, ŏdd, oil, fŏŏt, out; ūse, ûrn, ŭp; THis, thin

slimmer
swimmer
trimmer
Zimmer

ĬM'us

primus
rimous
simous
timeous
untimeous

ĬM'zi

flimsy
slimsy
whimsey

ĬM'zon

crimson
encrimson

Ī'na

Adelina
Angelina
Carolina
Catalina
China
Dinah
Evelina
farina
Jaina
Lucina
Meleagrina
Messalina
Platyrhina
Regina
Sabina
Sabrina
salina
semolina

Shekinah
trichina

Ĭn'a

Corinna
Erinna
Minna

ĬN'al

acclinal
anticlinal
binal
caninal
cerebro-spinal
crinal
declinal
endocrinal
equinal
final
isoclinal
matutinal
officinal
periclinal
piscinal
rhinal
spinal
synclinal
trinal
Vinal

ĬN'as

pinnace

ĬN'at

binate
quinate

ĬN'chest

clinchest
flinchest

lynchest
pinchest

ĬN'cheth

clincheth
flincheth
lyncheth
pincheth

ĬN'ching

clinching
flinching
lynching
pinching
unflinching

ĬN'chur

clincher
flincher
lyncher
pincher

ĬN'churz

pinchers, etc.

ĬN'da

Belinda
Chlorinda
Dorinda
Ethelinda
Lucinda

ĬN'ded

alike-minded
blinded
bloody-minded
carnal-minded
double-minded
even-minded
earthly-minded
evil-minded

fair-minded
feeble-minded
fleshly-minded
free-minded
high-minded
light-minded
like-minded
low-minded
minded
narrow-minded
public-minded
reminded
rinded
self-blinded
simple-minded
single-minded
snow-blinded
soberminded
strongminded
winded
worldly-minded

ĬN'ded

abscinded
brinded
broken-winded
exscinded
interscinded
long-winded
rescinded
short-winded
winded

ĬN'den

linden
Lindon
Minden

ĬN'dest

bindest
blindest

findest   unbinding   kindler   **ĪN'en**
grindest   unwinding   swindler, etc.   linen
kindest   upbinding
remindest   upwinding   **ĪND'nes**   **Ī'nes**
windest   winding   blindness   dryness

                            color-blindness   highness

ĪN'deth   **ĬN'd'l**   kindness   nighness

bindeth   brindle   loving-kindness   shyness
blindeth   dwindle   slyness
findeth   enkindle   **ĪN'do**   spryness
grindeth   kindle   window   wryness
mindeth   rekindle
remindeth   spindle   **ĪN'drans**   **ĬN'es**
windeth   swindle   hindrance   Inness

                                      Guinness

ĪND'ful   **ĬN'd'ld**   **ĬN'dred**   (cf. pinnace)

mindful   brindled, etc.   kindred
remindful   **ĪN'est**
unmindful   **ĬN'dlest**   **ĬN'dur**   *assignest*
               brindlest, etc.   binder   *benignest*

ĬN'di   blinder   *combinest*

Lindy   **ĬN'dleth**   faultfinder   *condignest*
Lucindy   *brindleth,* etc.   finder   *confinest*
shindy   grinder   *consignest*
windy   **ĪND'li**   hinder   *countersignest*
            blindly   kinder   *declinest*
ĬN'dig   kindly   minder   *definest*
shindig   unkindly   pathfinder   *designest*
             ĬND'li   reminder   *dinest*
ĬN'dik   Hindley   spellbinder   *divinest*
indic   spindly   stem-winder   *enshrinest*
syndic   water-finder   *entwinest*
             ĬND'ling   winder   finest
ĬN'ding   brindling   *inclinest*
binding   dwindling   **ĬN'dur**   *intertwinest*
blinding   enkindling   cinder   *malignest*
finding   kindling   flinder   *minest*
grinding   rekindling   hinder   *outlinest*
inbinding   swindling   pinder   *outshinest*
minding   **ĬND'lur**   rescinder   *overtwinest*
reminding   dwindler   tinder   *pinest*

ōld, ôr, ŏdd, oil, fŏŏt, out: ūse, ûrn, ŭp: THis, thin

reassignest

reclinest

refinest

resignest

shinest

signest

superfinest

supinest

twinest

underlinest

underminest

undersignest

untwinest

whinest

winest

ĬN'est

beginnest

dinnest

grinnest

pinnest

sinnest

skinnest

spinnest

thinnest

winnest

ĬN'et

linnet

minute

spinet

ĬN'eth

assigneth

combineth

confineth

consigneth

countersigneth

declineth

defineth

designeth

dineth

divineth

enshrineth

entwineth

inclineth

intertwineth

maligneth

mineth

outlineth

outshineth

overtwineth

pineth

reassigneth

reclineth

refineth

resigneth

shineth

signeth

twineth

underlineth

undermineth

undersigneth

untwineth

whineth

wineth

ĬN'eth

beginneth

dinneth

ginneth

grinneth

pinneth

sinneth

skinneth

spinneth

winneth

ĬN'fant

infant

ĬN'ful

sinful

ĬNG'am

Bingham

ĬNG'bolt

king-bolt

ring-bolt

wring-bolt

ĬNG'dom

kingdom

ĬNG'duv

ring-dove

ĬNG'ed

winged

(see ĭng + ed)

ĬNG'est

bringest

clingest

flingest

outwingest

ringest

singest

slingest

springest

stingest

stringest

swingest

wingest

wringest

ĬNG'eth

bringeth

clingeth

flingeth

outwingeth

ringeth

singeth

slingeth

springeth

stingeth

stringeth

swingeth

unslingeth

wingeth

wringeth

ĬNG'ga

anhinga

ĬNG'gi

dinghy

(cf. Feringhee)

ĬNG'g'l

commingle

cringle

dingle

immingle

intermingle

jingal

jingle

Kriss Kringle

mingle

shingle

single

springal

surcingle

swingle

tingle

tringle

ĬNG'g'ld

unmingled

commingled,

etc.

ĬNG'glest

jinglest

minglest

tinglest

ĬNG'gleth

jingleth
mingleth
tingleth

ĬNG'gli

jingly
mingly
shingly
singly
tingly

ĬNG'gling

intermingling
jingling
kingling
mingling
singling
tingling
wingling

ĬNG'glish

English
tinglish

ĬNG'glur

intermingler
jingler
mingler
shingler
tingler

ĬNG'go

dingo
flamingo
gringo
jingo
lingo
stingo

ĬNG'gur

finger

forefinger
index-finger
linger
malinger

ĬNG'gurd

light-fingered
rosy-fingered
web-fingered
fingered, etc.

ĬNG'gus

dingus

ĬNG'gwal

bilingual
lingual

ĬNG'gwish

contradistin-
  guish
distinguish
extinguish

ĬNG'i

clingy
springy
stingy
stringy
swingy
wingy

ĬNG'ing

bringing
clinging
dinging
enringing
flinging
outwinging
plainsinging
ringing

singing
slinging
springing
stinging
stringing
swinging
unslinging
unstringing
upbringing
upstringing
winging
wringing

ĬNGK'est

bethinkest
blinkest
chinkest
clinkest
drinkest
hoodwinkest
inkest
linkest
pinkest
shrinkest
sinkest
slinkest
stinkest
thinkest
winkest

ĬNGK'et

trinket

ĬNGK'eth

bethinketh
blinketh
chinketh
clinketh
drinketh
hoodwinketh
inketh

linketh
pinketh
shrinketh
sinketh
slinketh
stinketh
thinketh
winketh

ĬNGK'go

ginkgo

ĬNGK'i

blinky
inky
kinky
pinky
zincky

ĬNGK'id

blink-eyed
pink-eyed

ĬNGK'ing

bethinking
blinking
chinking
clinking
drinking
enlinking
free-thinking
hoodwinking
inking
interlinking
linking
pinking
rinking
shrinking
sinking
slinking
stinking

thinking
unblinking
unlinking
unshrinking
unthinking
unwinking
winking

ĬNGK"l
besprinkle
crinkle
inkle
periwinkle
sprinkle
tinkle
twinkle
winkle
wrinkle

ĬNGK"ld
unwrinkled
besprinkled,
   etc.

ĬNGK'lest
crinklest
sprinklest
tinklest
twinklest
wrinklest

ĬNGK'leth
crinkleth
sprinkleth
tinkleth
twinkleth
wrinkleth

ĬNGK'li
crinkly
pinkly

tinkly
twinkly
wrinkly

ĬNGK'ling
besprinkling
crinkling
inkling
sprinkling
tinkling
twinkling
wrinkling

ĬNGK'lur
sprinkler
tinkler
twinkler
wrinkler

ĬNGK'o
stinko

ĬNGK'on
Lincoln
pink 'un

ĬNGK'shun
contradistinc-
   tion
distinction
extinction
indistinction
intinction

ĬNGK'tiv
contradistinc-
   tive
distinctive
instinctive

ĬNGK'tnes
distinctness

indistinctness
succinctness

ĬNGK'tur
cincture
encincture
tincture

ĬNGK'turd
cinctured
encinctured
uncinctured
untinctured

ĬNGK'ur
bethinker
blinker
clinker
drinker
enlinker
free-thinker
hoodwinker
inker
linker
pinker
prinker
rinker
shrinker
sinker
slinker
stinker
thinker
tiddledewinker
tinker
winker

ĬNGK'us
ornithorhyn-
   chus
oxyrhynchus
scincus
zincous

ĬNG'les
kingless
ringless
springless
stingless
wingless

ĬNG'let
kinglet
ringlet
springlet
winglet

ĬNG'lik
kinglike
springlike
winglike

ĬN'gram
Ingram

ĬNG'song
singsong
spring-song

ĬNG'tim
ring-time
spring-time

ĬNG'ur
ballad-singer
bringer
clinger
dinger
flinger
humdinger
master-singer
Meistersinger
minnesinger
ringer
singer

āle, câre, ădd, ärm, åsk; mē, hēre, ĕnd; īce, ĭll;

slinger
springer
stinger
stringer
swinger
unslinger
unstringer
whinger
winger
wringer

ĬN′i

briny
Heine
liney
miny
moonshiny
outliney
piney
shiny
spiny
sunshiny
tiny
twiney
viny
whiney
winy

ĬN′i

finny
guinea
hinny
ignominy
jinny
Minnie
ninny
pickaninny
pinny
Pliny
shinney
skinny

spinney
squinny
tinny
vinny
whinny

ĬN′ik

kinic
pinic
vinic

ĬN′ik

aclinic
actinic
adiactinic
Brahminic
clinic
cynic
delphinic
diactinic
finic
Franklinic
fulminic
isoclinic
Jacobinic
mandarinic
monoclinic
narcotinic
Odinic
pinic
platinic
polygynic
quinic
rabbinic
vinic

ĬN′im

minim
(cf.
    houyhnhmn)

ĬN′ing

aligning
assigning
beshining
combining
confining
consigning
countermining
countersigning
declining
defining
designing
dining
divining
enshrining
entwining
fining
inclining
interlining
intermining
intertwining
lining
maligning
mining
moonshining
opining
outlining
outshining
overtwining
pining
reclining
refining
repining
resigning
shining
signing
subsigning
trephining
twining
underlining
undermining

untwining
whining
wining

ĬN′ing

beginning
chinning
dinning
grinning
inning
pinning
shinning
sinning
skinning
spinning
thinning
tinning
underpinning
unpinning
unsinning
winning

ĬN′ingz

innings
beginnings, etc.

ĬN′ish

diminish
finish
Finnish
thinnish
tinnish

ĬN′ist

violinist

ĬN′it

crinite
finite

ĬN′jens

contingence

(cf. astringents,
etc.)

ĬN'jent

astringent
constringent
contingent
fingent
impingent
refringent
restringent
ringent
stringent
tingent

ĬN'jest

befringest
cringest
fringest
hingest
imfringest
infringest
singest
swingest
tingest
twingest
unhingest

ĬN'jeth

befringeth
cringeth
fringeth
hingeth
impingeth
infringeth
singeth
swingeth
tingeth
twingeth
unhingeth

ĬN'jez

befringes
constringes
cringes
fringes
hinges
impinges
infringes
perstringes
scringes
singes
springes
swinges
tinges
twinges
unhinges

ĬN'ji

cringy
dingy
fringy
stingy
swingy
twingy

ĬN'jing

cringing
fringing
hinging
infringing
singeing
swingeing
tingeing
twingeing

ĬNJ'les

fringeless
hingeless
swingeless
tingeless
twingeless

ĬNJ'ment

impingement
infringement
unhingement

ĬNJ'ur

cringer
fringer
ginger
hinger
infringer
injure
singer
swinger
twinger

ĬN'ka

Inca
Katinka

ĬN'klad

pine-clad
vine-clad

ĬN'kom

income

ĬN'kres

increase

ĬN'kround

pine-crowned
vine-crowned

ĬN'kwent

delinquent
relinquent

ĬN'kwish

relinquish
vinquish

ĬN'les

dinless
finless
ginless
kinless
pinless
sinless
skinless
tinless
winless

ĪN'li

aquilinely
benignly
caninely
condignly
divinely
finely
malignly
saturninely
superfinely
supinely

ĬN'li

Finley
inly
McGinley
McKinley
thinly

ĬN'ment

alignment
assignment
confinement
consignment
designment
entwinement
inclinement
interlinement
refinement
resignment

ĪN'nes
condignness
divineness
fineness
salineness
superfineness
supineness

ĬN'nes
thinness
(cf. ĬN'es)

ĪN'o
Aino
albino
jure divino
rhino

ĬN'o
minnow
winnow

ĬN'of
sign-off

ĬN'sel
tinsel
(cf. Insull)

ĬN'sens
incense

ĬN'sent
St. Vincent
vincent

ĬN'ses
princess

ĬN'sest
convincest

evincest
mincest
rinsest
wincest
(cf. incest)

ĬN'ceth
convinceth
evinceth
minceth
rinseth
winceth

ĬN'shal
provincial

ĬN'si
Quincy
rinsey

ĬN'sing
convincing
evincing
mincing
rinsing
unconvincing
wincing

ĬN'siv
evincive

ĬNS'li
princely

ĬNS'ment
convincement
evincement

ĬN'som
winsome

ĬN'strel
minstrel

ĬN'stur
minster
spinster

ĬN'sur
convincer
mincer
rinser
wincer

ĬN'surz
pincers
convincers, etc.

ĬN'ted
dinted
glinted
hinted
imprinted
minted
misprinted
printed
rainbow-tinted
rosy-tinted
sprinted
squinted
stinted
tinted
vinted

ĬN'test
glintest
hintest
imprintest
mintest
printest
sprintest
squintest
stintest
tintest

ĬN'teth
glinteth
hinteth
imprinteth
minteth
printeth
sprinteth
squinteth
stinteth
tinteth

ĬN'ti
ninety

ĬN'ti
Dinty
flinty
glinty
linty
McGinty
squinty

ĬNT'id
flint-eyed
squint-eyed

ĬN'tij
mintage
vintage

ĬN'thick
absinthic
labyrinthic

ĬN'thin
hyacinthine
labyrinthine
terebinthine

ĬN'ting
aquatinting

---

dinting
glinting
hinting
imprinting
minting
misprinting
printing
sprinting
squinting
stinting
tinting

ĬN't'l

lintel
pintle
quintal

ĬN'to

mezzotinto
Shinto

ĬN'trest

interest
self-interest
winterest

ĬN'tri

splintry
vintry
wintry

ĬN'tur

aquatinter
dinter
hinter
imprinter
minter
printer
splinter
sprinter
squinter

stinter
tinter
winter

ĬN'u

continue
discontinue
retinue
sinew
unsinew

ĬN'ud

continued
discontinued
sinewed
unsinewed

ĬN'ur

arch-designer
assigner
benigner
calciner
combiner
confiner
consigner
decliner
definer
designer
diner
diviner
enshriner
entwiner
finer
incliner
intertwiner
liner
maligner
miner
minor
penny-a-liner
decliner

refiner
repiner
shiner
signer
Steiner
supiner
twiner
underliner
underminer
whiner

ĬN'ur

beginner
bread-winner
Bynner
dinner
finner
grinner
inner
pinner
shinner
sinner
skinner
spinner
thinner
tinner
twinner
winner

ĬN'us

binous
echinus
linous
Linus
Lupinus
minus
Pinus
salinous
sinus
spinous
vinous

ĬN'ward

inward

ĬN'yon

dominion
minion
opinion
pinion
(cf. ĬN'i-an)

ĬN'yond

dominioned
opinioned
pinioned
self-opinioned

ĬN'zi

Lindsay
Lindsey
linsey
quinsey
thinsey

ĬN'zik

extrinsic
intrinsic

ĬN'zman

kinsman

ĬN'zor

Windsor

Ī'o

Clio
Io
trio

Ī'ol

bass-viol
(see Ī'al)

Ī'on
dandelion
ion
Ixion
lion
Orion
scion
sea-lion
Zion

Ī'or
prior
(see Ī'ur)

Ī'ot
eyot
piot
riot
Sciot
(cf. quiet)

ĬP'a
Philippa

Ī'pal, Ī'p'l
disciple
ectypal

ĬP'ant
flippant
trippant

ĬP'en
enripen
ripen

ĬP'end
ripened
stipend

ĬP'est
pipest

ripest
typest
wipest
(cf. typist)

ĬP'est
chippest
clippest
dippest
drippest
equippest
flippest
grippest
gyppest
horsewhippest
nippest
outstrippest
rippest
shippest
sippest
skippest
slippest
snippest
strippest
tippest
trippest
whippest

ĬP'et
sippet
skippet
snippet
tippet
(cf. skip it)

ĬP'eth
gripeth
pipeth
typeth
wipeth

ĬP'eth
chippeth
clippeth
dippeth
drippeth
equippeth
flippeth
grippeth
gyppeth
horsewhippeth
nippeth
outstrippeth
rippeth
shippeth
sippeth
skippeth
slippeth
snippeth
strippeth
tippeth
trippeth
whippeth

ĬP'i
pipy
swipey
(cf. I.P.)

ĬP'i
chippy
dippy
grippy
Lippo Lippi
lippy
Mississippi
nippy
shippy
snippy
zippy

ĬP'id
insipid

ĬP'ij
kippage
scrippage
strippage

ĬP'ik
daguerreotypic
electrotypic
hippic
homotypic
idiotypic
monotypic
philippic
phonotypic
stereotypic
typic

ĬP'in
pippin

ĬP'ing
griping
Peiping
piping
stereotyping
striping
swiping
typing
wiping

ĬP'ing
atripping
chipping
clipping
dipping
dripping
equipping
flipping
gripping
nipping
outstripping

overtripping
quipping
ripping
shipping
sipping
skipping
slipping
snipping
stripping
tipping
transhipping
tripping
whipping

ĬP'ish

grippish
hippish
hyppish
snippish

ĬP"l

becripple
cripple
grippal
nipple
ripple
sipple
stipple
swiple
tipple
triple

ĬP'let

liplet
ripplet
siplet
triplet

ĬP'li

cripply
ripply

stipply
triply

ĬP'ling

crippling
Kipling
rippling
stippling
stripling
tippling

ĬP'lur

crippler
tippler

ĬP'ment

equipment
shipment
transhipment

ĪP'nes

dead-ripeness
overripeness
ripeness

ĬP'o

hippo
gippo

ĪP'res

cypress

ĬP'shun

ascription
circumscription
conniption
conscription
description
Egyptian
inscription
prescription

proscription
rescription
subscription
superscription
transcription

ĬP'si

gypsy
Poughkeepsie
Skipsey
tipsy

ĬP'sis

ellipsis
tripsis

ĬP'tik

anaglyptic
apocalyptic
cryptic
diptych
ecliptic
elliptic
glyptic
holocryptic
iatraliptic
styptic
triptych

ĬP'tiv

adscriptive
ascriptive
circumscriptive
descriptive
indescriptive
inscriptive
prescriptive
proscriptive
rescriptive
transcriptive

ĬP'tur

scripture

ĪP'ur

bag-piper
daguerreotyper
electrotyper
griper
linotyper
monotyper
piper
riper
stereotyper
sniper
striper
swiper
typer
viper
wiper

ĬP'ur

chipper
clipper
dipper
dripper
flipper
fripper
gallinipper
gripper
kipper
lady's-slipper
nipper
outstripper
ripper
shipper
sipper
skipper
slipper
snipper
stripper
swipper

āle, câre, ădd, ärm, åsk; mē, hēre, ĕnd; īce, ĭll;

tipper	**ĬR'āt**	*bemirest*	*tireth*
tripper	circumgyrate	*conspirest*	*transpireth*
whipper	dextro-gyrate	*desirest*	*umpireth*
	gyrate	*direst*	*wireth*
ĬP'urd	irate	*enquirest*	
kippered	lyrate	*expirest*	**ĬR'fli**
skippered		*firest*	firefly
slippered	**ĬR'ăt**	*hirest*	
	pirate	*inquirest*	**ĬR'ful**
Ī'ra		*inspirest*	direful
Almira	**ĬR'e**	*mirest*	ireful
Elmira	Dies Irae	*perspirest*	
Elvira	præmunire	*requirest*	**ĬR'i**
Ira	(cf. ĬR'i)	*respirest*	*acquiry*
Lyra		*retirest*	dairi
Myra	**ĬR'el**	*suspirest*	enquiry
Palmyra	squirrel	*tirest*	inquiry
Thyra		*transpirest*	miry
	Ī'rem	*umpirest*	spiry
ĬR'ah	bireme	*wirest*	squiry
sirrah	trireme		wiry
		ĬR'eth	(cf. ĬR'e)
ĬR'al	**Ī'rēn**	*acquireth*	
gyral	pyrene	*admireth*	**ĬR'ï**
retiral	squireen	*aspireth*	eyrie
spiral		*attireth*	
	Ī'rĕn	*bemireth*	**ĬR'id**
ĬR'am	lepidosiren	*conspireth*	irid
Hiram	siren	*desireth*	
		enquireth	**ĬR'ïk**
ĬR'ant	**ĬR'ent**	*expireth*	butyric
arch-tyrant	inquirent	*fireth*	empiric
aspirant	sempervirent	*hireth*	lyric
conspirant	virent	*inquireth*	panegyric
expirant	(cf. tyrant, etc.)	*inspireth*	Pyrrhic
gyrant		*mireth*	satiric
spirant	**ĬR'est**	*perspireth*	satyric
tyrant	*acquirest*	*requireth*	
(cf. inquirent,	*admirest*	*respireth*	**ĬR'il**
etc.)	*aspirest*	*retireth*	Cyril
	attirest	*suspireth*	virile

ĪR'ing
acquiring
admiring
aspiring
attiring
bemiring
conspiring
desiring
enquiring
expiring
firing
hiring
inquiring
inspiring
miring
perspiring
requiring
respiring
retiring
squiring
suspiring
tiring
transpiring
unaspiring
undesiring
untiring
wiring

ĪR'is
iris
Osiris

ĪR'ish
Irish

ĪR'ist
irised
lyrist

ĪR'ist
lyrist
panegyrist

ĪR'it
dispirit
inspirit
master-spirit
party-spirit
spirit

ĪR'ling
hireling
squireling

ĪR'man
fireman

ĪR'ment
acquirement
aspirement
bemirement
requirement
retirement

ĪR'nes
direness
entireness

ĪR'o
Cairo
tyro

Ī'rod
byroad
highroad

ĪR'on
Byron
Chiron
environ
gyron

ĪR'os
gyrose
virose

ĪR'sid
fireside

ĪR'som
iresome
tiresome

ĪR'up
chirrup
stirrup
syrup

ĪR'ur
acquirer
admirer
aspirer
attirer
bemirer
conspirer
desirer
direr
enquirer
expirer
firer
hirer
inquirer
inspirer
mirer
perspirer
requirer
respirer
retirer
suspirer
tirer
wirer

ĪR'us
apyrous
Cyrus
desirous
Epirus

papyrus
virus

ĪR'wurks
fire-works
wire-works

ĬS'a
Clarissa
Lissa
Melissa
Nerissa

Ī'sal
sky-sail
try-sail

ĪS'al
paradisal

ĬS'chif
mischief

ĬS'chan
anti-Christian
Christian

ĬS'ens
license

ĬS'ens
dehiscence
fatiscence
indehiscence
reminiscence
resipiscence
reviviscence

ĬS'ent
dehiscent
indehiscent

āle, câre, ădd, ärm, åsk; mē, hẹre, ĕnd; īce, ĭll;

reminiscent
reviviscent

ĬS'est
bespicest
concisest
enticest
nicest
precisest
pricest
sacrificest
slicest
spicest
splicest
sufficest

ĬS'est
dismissest
hissest
kissest
missest

ĬS'eth
bespiceth
enticeth
priceth
sacrificeth
sliceth
spiceth
spliceth
sufficeth

ĬS'eth
dismisseth
hisseth
kisseth
misseth

ĬS'ēz
Ulysses

ĬS'ĕz
abysses
artifices
benefices
blisses
cockatrices
dismisses
edifices
hisses
kisses
misses
precipices
prejudices
Swisses

ĬS'ful
blissful
remissful
unblissful

ĪSH'a
Elisha

ĬSH'a
Delicia
Letitia

ĬSH'al
accrementitial
artificial
beneficial
comitial
edificial
exitial
extrajudicial
gentilitial
inartificial
initial
interstitial
judicial
natalitial

official
policial
prejudicial
recrementitial
rusticial
sacrificial
solstitial
superficial
tribunitial
veneficial

ĬSH'an
academician
logician
magician
optician, etc.
(see ĬSH'un)

ĬSH'ens
deficience
efficience
insufficience
maleficience
omniscience
perspicience
proficience
prospicience
self-sufficience

ĬSH'ent
beneficient
calorificent
co-efficient
deficient
efficient
indeficient
inefficient
insufficient
maleficient
objicient
omniscient

perficient
proficient
self-sufficient
sufficient
volitient

ĬSH'est
dishest
fishest
swishest
wishest

ĬSH'eth
disheth
fisheth
swisheth
wisheth

ĬSH'ful
dishful
wishful

ĬSH'i
fishy
swishy

ĬSH'ing
dishing
fishing
ill-wishing
swishing
well-wishing
wishing

ĬSH'op
bishop

ĬSH'un
abannition
abligurition
abolition

academician	disposition	mathematician	recognition
accrementition	disquisition	mechanician	recomposition
acoustician	ebullition	metaphysician	reddition
acquisition	edition	metrician	*redition*
addition	electrician	mission	remission
adhibition	emission	monition	rendition
admission	epinician	munition	repetition
admonition	erudition	musician	reposition
affinition	exhibition	Neoplatonician	requisition
aglutition	expedition	nolition	resilition
ambition	exposition	nutrition	reunition
ammunition	extradition	obdormition	rhetorician
Apician	fission	obstetrician	rubrician
apparition	fruition	omission	sedition
apposition	futurition	opposition	*simplician*
arithmetician	Galician	optician	sortition
atomician	geometrician	partition	statistician
attrition	Hebrician	parturition	submission
audition	hydrostatician	patrician	submonition
bipartition	ignition	Paulician	superaddition
circuition	illinition	perdition	superposition
coalition	imbibition	permission	superstition
cognition	immission	perquisition	supposition
commission	imposition	petition	suspicion
competition	inanition	Phenician	tactician
composition	indisposition	physician	tradition
condition	inhibition	politician	tralatition
contraposition	*inition*	position	transition
contrition	inquisition	practician	transmission
decomposition	*insition*	precognition	transposition
definition	insubmission	precondition	tribunitian
deglutition	intermission	predisposition	tripartition
demission	interposition	premonition	tuition
demolition	intromission	preposition	vendition
dentition	intuition	presupposition	volition
departition	irremission	preterition	vomition
deperdition	juxtaposition	prohibition	
deposition	logician	proposition	**ISH'und**
detrition	magician	punition	ill-conditioned
dialectician	magnetician	pyrotechnician	uncommis-
dismission	manumission	readmission	sioned

āle, câre, ădd, ärm, åsk; mē, hęre, ĕnd; īce, ĭll;

conditioned,
etc.

ĬSH'ur

disher
Fischer
fisher
fissure
ill-wisher
kingfisher
swisher
well-wisher
wisher

ĬSH'us

addititious
adjectitious
adscititious
advectitious
adventitious
ambitious
arreptitious
ascititious
ascriptitious
auspicious
avaricious
capricious
cilicious
deglutitious
delicious
exitious
expeditious
factitious
fictitious
flagitious
gentilitious
inauspicious
injudicious
inofficious
judicious
lateritious

malicious
meretricious
multiplicious
natalitious
nutritious
obreptitious
obstetricious
officious
pernicious
piceous
profectitious
propitious
pumiceous
puniceous
satellitious
secretitious
seditious
sericeous
silicious
stillatitious
superstitious
supposititious
surreptitious
suspicious
tralatitious
veneficious
vermicious
vicious

ĬS'i

Datisi
icy
nisi
spicy

ĬS'i

missy
sissy

ĬS'ik

masticic
silicic

ĬS'il

fissile
missile
scissile
(cf. abyssal,
    scissel, etc.)

ĬS'id

viscid

ĬS'in

datiscin
viscin

ĬS'ing

bespicing
dicing
enticing
icing
pricing
sacrificing
self-sacrificing
self-sufficing
slicing
spicing
splicing
sufficing

ĬS'ing

dehiscing
dismissing
hissing
kissing
missing

ĬS'is

crisis
Isis
phthisis

ĬS'ish

missish

ĬS'it

elicit
explicit
illicit
implicit
licit
solicit

ĬS'iv

cicatrisive
collisive
decisive
derisive
divisive
incisive
indecisive
precisive

ĬS'iv

admissive
commissive
demissive
emissive
intermissive
irremissive
missive
nonsubmissive
omissive
permissive
promissive
remissive
submissive
transmissive

ĬS'ka

Mariska

ĬS'kal

discal
fiscal
obeliscal

ōld, ôr, ŏdd, oil, fŏŏt, out; ūse, ûrn, ŭp; THis, thin

ĬS'kat
confiscate
inviscate

ĬS'kest
briskest
friskest
riskest
whiskest

ĬS'ket
brisket
frisket

ĬS'keth
frisketh
risketh
whisketh

ĬSK'ful
friskful
riskful

ĬS'ki
frisky
risky
whiskey

ĬS'kin
griskin
siskin

ĬS'king
brisking
frisking
risking
whisking

ĬS'kit
biscuit

ĬS'ko
Crisco
Francisco
San Francisco

ĬS'kur
bewhisker
brisker
frisker
risker
whisker

ĬS'kus
abaciscus
discous
discus
hibiscus
lemniscus
lentiscus
meniscus
trochiscus
viscous

ĬS''l
abyssal
bristle
dismissal
epistle
gristle
missal
scissel
thistle
whistle
(cf. missile,
    etc.)

ĬS'les
adviceless
diceless
iceless
miceless

priceless
spiceless
spliceless
viceless, etc.

ĬS'li
Cicely
concisely
nicely
precisely

ĬS'li
bristly
gristly
thistly

ĬS'ling
bristling
whistling

ĬS'ment
enticement
sufficement

ĬS'mus
isthmus
(see Christmas)

ĬS''n
christen
glisten
listen
relisten

ĬS'nes
conciseness
niceness
overniceness
preciseness

ĬS'nes
remissness
thisness

ĬS'ning
Christening
glistening
listening

ĬS'om
lissome

ĬS'on
bison
Dyson
grison
hyson
Tyson
vison

ĬS'pest
crispest
lispest

ĬS'peth
crispeth
lispeth

ĬS'pi
crispy

ĬS'pin
Crispin
St. Crispin

ĬS'ping
crisping
lisping

ĬS'pur
crisper
lisper
stage-whisper
whisper

ĬS'ta

ballista
genista
vista

ĬS'tal, ĬS't'l

crystal
listel
pistol
pocket-pistol

ĬS'tan

Tristan

ĬS'tans

assistance
coexistence
consistence
desistance
distance
equidistance
existence
inconsistence
inexistence
insistence
nonexistence
persistence
pre-existence
resistance
subsistence
(cf. assitants,
    etc.)

ĬS'tant, ĬS'tent

assistant
coexistent
consistent
distant
equidistant
existent
inconsistent

inexistent
insistent
nonexistent
nonresistant
persistent
pre-existent
resistant
subsistent

ĬST'dom

Christdom

ĬS'ted

assisted
black-listed
close-fisted
consisted
cysted
desisted
encysted
enlisted
entwisted
existed
fisted
hard-fisted
insisted
intertwisted
iron-fisted
listed
misted
persisted
resisted
subsisted
twisted
unassisted
unresisted
untwisted
white-listed

ĬS'tem

system

ĬS'test

assistest
consistest
desistest
enlistest
existest
insistest
listest
persistest
resistest
subsistest
twistest

ĬS'teth

assisteth
consisteth
desisteth
enlisteth
existeth
insisteth
listeth
misteth
persisteth
resisteth
resisteth
subsisteth
twisteth

ĬST'ful

mistful
wistful

ĬS'tik

absolutistic
adiaphoristic
agonistic
alchemistic
altruistic
anabaptistic
anachronistic
animistic

annalistic
anomalistic
antagonistic
anarchistic
aoristic
aphlogistic
aphoristic
artistic
atheistic
ballistic
baptistic
belletristic
bibliopegistic
bibliopolistic
Buddhistic
cabalistic
Calvinistic
cameralistic
canonistic
casuistic
catechistic
characteristic
Chauvinistic
communalistic
communistic
curialistic
cystic
deistic
dialogistic
dualistic
egoistic
egotistic
eleetro-
    ballistic
Elohistic
epilogistic
eristic
Eucharistic
eudemonistic
euhemeristic
eulogistic

euphemistic
euphuistic
evangelistic
familistic
fatalistic
fetichistic
fistic
formularistic
Hebraistic
Hellenistic
humanistic
humoristic
idealistic
illuministic
individualistic
interimistic
Jehovistic
journalistic
Judaistic
juristic
Latinistic
liberalistic
linguistic
logistic
materialistic
methodistic
monistic
monotheistic
mystic
naturalistic
neologistic
nihilistic
nominalistic
optimistic
palæocrystic
pantheistic
papistic
parallelistic
patristic
pessimistic

philanthropis-
tic
philosophistic
phlogistic
pietistic
polaristic
polytheistic
pugilistic
puristic
quietistic
rationalistic
realistic
ritualistic
schistic
sciolistic
sensualistic
simplistic
socialistic
solecistic
somnambu-
listic
sophistic
spiritualistic
stylistic
syllogistic
synchronistic
talmudistic
theistic
touristic
tritheistic
unionistic
universalistic

ĬS'tiks

agonistics
mystics
sphragistics
statistics

ĬS'til

pistil

ĬS'tin

amethystine
Philistine
pristine
Sistine

ĬS'ting

assisting
consisting
desisting
enlisting
entwisting
existing
insisting
intertwisting
listing
misting
pre-existing
persisting
resisting
subsisting
twisting
unresisting
untwisting

ĬS'tiv

persistive
resistive

ĬST'les

listless
resistless
twistless

ĬST'mus

Christmas
cf. isthmus

ĬST'ment

agistment
enlistment

ĬS'tral

mistral

ĬS'tram

Tristram

ĬS'tres

mistress

ĬS'tur

agistor
assister
bister
blister
enlister
exister
foster-sister
glister
insister
intertwister
lister
magister
mister
passive-resister
persister
resister
sister
subsister
twister

ĬS'turn

cistern

ĬS'tus

acathistus
schistous

ĬS'u

issue
tissue

āle, câre, ădd, ärm, åsk; mē, hẹre, ĕnd; īce, ĭll;

ĪS'ur
conciser
dicer
enticer
geyser
nicer
preciser
sacrificer
slicer
spicer
splicer

ĬS'ŭr
dehiscer
dismisser
hisser
kisser
misser
remisser

ĬS'us
byssus
Issus
"missus"
narcissus

ĬT'al
cital
detrital
entitle
parasital
recital
requital
title
vital

ĬT'alz
vitals
recitals, etc.

ĬT'an
Titan

ĬT'an, ĬT'en
Britain
Britten
(cf. Briton)

ĬT'ans
acquittance
admittance
omittance
permittance
pittance
quittance
remittance
transmittance

ĬT'e
Amphitrite
Aphrodite
arbor-vitæ
lignum-vitæ
(cf. ĬT'i)

ĬT'ed
affrighted
alighted
attrited
bedighted
beknighted
benighted
blighted
cited
clear-sighted
delighted
despited
detrited
dighted
eagle-flighted
eagle-sighted
excited
far-sighted
foresighted

frighted
ignited
incited
indicted
indited
invited
knighted
lighted
long-sighted
near-sighted
nighted
oversighted
plighted
quick-sighted
recited
requited
reunited
righted
second-sighted
sharp-sighted
short-sighted
sighted
sited
slighted
spited
troth-plighted
unaffrighted
unbenighted
undighted
unfrighted
united
unplighted
unrequited
unrighted
unsighted

ĬT'ed
acquitted
admitted
after-witted
befitted

benefited
bitted
blunt-witted
committed
counterfeited
emitted
fat-witted
fitted
flitted
gritted
half-witted
interknitted
intermitted
knitted
lean-witted
manumitted
nimble-witted
omitted
outwitted
permitted
pitted
quick-witted
quitted
ready-witted
recommitted
refitted
remitted
sharp-witted
short-witted
slitted
spitted
submitted
subtle-witted
transmitted
twitted
unbenefited
unbitted
underwitted
unfitted
unremitted
witted

writted
(cf. pitied, etc.)

ĬT'em
item

ĬT'en
brighten
enlighten
frighten
heighten
lighten
tighten
Titan
whiten
(cf. Ĭ'ton)

ĬT'en
bitten
Briton
conscience-
　smitten
flea-bitten
fly-bitten
hunger-bitten
kitten
mitten
smitten
sun-smitten
terror-smitten
underwritten
unsmitten
unwritten
weather-bitten
written

ĬT'ent
emittent
intermittent
intromittent
remittent

ĬT'est
affrightest
alightest
beknightest
bitest
blightest
brightest
citest
delightest
excitest
fightest
impolitest
incitest
inditest
invitest
knightest
lightest
mightest
plightest
politest
recitest
requitest
reunitest
rightest
sightest
sleightest
slightest
smitest
spitest
tightest
tritest
unitest
uprightest
whitest
writest

ĬT'est
acquittest
admittest
benefitest

committest
fittest
flittest
hittest
knittest
omittest
outwittest
permittest
pittest
quittest
refittest
remittest
sittest
slittest
spittest
splittest
submittest
twittest

ĬT'eth
affrighteth
alighteth
beknighteth
biteth
blighteth
citeth
delighteth
exciteth
fighteth
igniteth
inciteth
inditeth
inviteth
plighteth
reciteth
requiteth
righteth
sighteth
sleighteth
smiteth

spiteth
uniteth
writeth

ĬT'eth
acquitteth
admitteth
befitteth
benefiteth
committeth
fitteth
flitteth
hitteth
knitteth
omitteth
out-witteth
permitteth
pitteth
quitteth
refitteth
remitteth
sitteth
slitteth
spitteth
splitteth
submitteth
twitteth

ĬT'ez
pyrites
sorites

ĬT'ful
delightful
despiteful
frightful
mightful
rightful
spiteful
sprightful

āle, câre, ădd, ärm, àsk; mē, hēre, ĕnd; īce, ĭll;

ĬT'ful
fitful
witful

ĬTH'ee
prithee

ĬTH'en
battle-writhen
writhen

ĬTH'est
blithest
lithest
writhest

ĬTH'eth
writheth

ĬTH'ful
blitheful
litheful

ĬTH'ĭ
blithy
lithy

Ĭth'ĭ
pithy
smithy
stithy
withy

Ĭth'ik
eolithic
lithic
megalithic
microlithic
monolithic
mythic
neolithic
ornithic

palæolithic
trilithic

ĬTH'ing
nithing
scything
tithing
trithing
writhing

ĬTH''m
rhythm

ĬTH'mik
logarithmic
polyrhythmic
rhythmic

ĬTH'nes
blitheness
litheness

Ĭ'thon
python

ĬTH'som
blithesome
lithesome

ĬTH'ur
blither
either
neither
tither
writher

ĬTH'ur
anywhither
behither
blither
dither

hither
nowhither
slither
somewhither
swither
thither
whither
wither

ĬTH'urd
withered
unwithered

ĬTH'urz
withers

ĬT'ĭ
almighty
blighty
flighty
highty-tighty
mighty
mity
whity
(cf. Aphrodite,
etc.)

ĬT'ĭ
banditti
city
committee
ditty
flitty
Giovanitti
gritty
kitty
pity
pretty
self-pity
witty

ĬT'id
citied
pitied
unpitied
(cf. acquitted,
etc.)

ĬT'ik
aconitic
actinolitic
Adamitic
aerolitic
analytic
anthracitic
anthropomor-
phitic
arthritic
biolytic
Cabiritic
catalytic
cenobitic
conchitic
critic
dendritic
diacritic
dialytic
diphtheritic
dolomitic
electrolytic
enclitic
eophytic
epiphytic
eremitic
gingitic
granitic
Hamitic
hematitic
hermaphro-
ditic
heteroclitic
hypercritic

hypocritic
Islamitic
Israelitic
Jacobitic
Jesuitic
Levitic
lignitic
margaritic
mephitic
Nazaritic
nummulitic
oneirocritic
oolitic
palmitic
paralytic
parasitic
phosphoritic
pleuritic
porphyritic
preadamitic
proclitic
rachitic
sagenitic
selenitic
Semitic
Shemitic
Sinaitic
stalactitic
stalagmitic
steatitic
strontitic
sybaritic
syenitic
theodolitic
Titanitic
tonsilitic
toxophilitic
trilobitic
trogodytic
tympanitic
uranitic

variolitic
zeolitic
zoophytic

ĬT'iks

analytics
critics, etc.

ĬT'in

chitin
(cf. ĬT'en,
   ĬT'on)

ĬT'ing

affrighting
alighting
back-biting
beknighting
biting
blighting
citing
copyrighting
delighting
disuniting
dynamiting
exciting
expediting
fighting
frighting
hand-writing
igniting
inciting
indicting
inditing
inviting
kiting
knighting
lighting
plighting
reciting
requiting

reuniting
righting
sighting
slighting
smiting
spiting
underwriting
uniting
whiting
writing

ĬT'ing

acquitting
admitting
befitting
benefiting
bitting
committing
counterfeiting
emitting
fitting
flitting
gritting
hair-splitting
hitting
knitting
manumitting
misfitting
omitting
outsitting
outwitting
permitting
pitting
pretermitting
quitting
recommitting
refitting
remitting
sitting
skitting

slitting
spitting
splitting
submitting
transmitting
twitting
unbefitting
unfitting
unremitting
unsubmitting
unwitting
witting

ĬT'is

appendicitis
arthritis
bronchitis
carditis
colitis
endocarditis
gastritis
hyalitis
laryngitis
meningitis
neuritis
pericarditis
pharyngitis
rachitis
tonsillitis
trachitis

ĬT'ish

anchoritish
Canaanitish
eremitish
Ishmaelitish
Israelitish
lightish
tightish
whitish

āle,   câre,   ădd,   ärm,   ȧsk;   mē,   hẽre,   ĕnd;   īce,   ĭll;

ĬT'ish
British
skittish

ĬT'iv
appetitive
expeditive

ĪT"l
entitle
title
(cf. ĪT'al)

ĬT"l
acquittal
belittle
brittle
committal
knittle
lickspittle
little
non-committal
remittal
skittle
spital
spittle
tittle
transmittal
victual
whittle

ĪT'les
delightless
fightless
frightless
heightless
knightless
lightless
nightless
riteless
sightless

spiteless
sprightless

ĬT'les
witless
(see ĬT+less)

ĬT'lest
brittlest
littlest
belittlest, etc.

ĬT'leth
belittleth, etc.

ĪT'li
brightly
impolitely
Kneightly
knightly
lightly
nightly
politely
rightly
sightly
slightly
sprightly
tightly
tritely
unknightly
unsightly
uprightly
whiteley
whitely

ĬT'li
fitly
unfitly

ĪT'ling
entitling
titling

ĪT'ling
kitling
titling
witling
whittling

ĬT'lur
brittler
littler
victualler
whittler

ĬT"lz
skittles
victuals
belittles, etc.

ĪT'ment
affrightment
excitement
frightment
incitement
indictment
invitement

ĬT'ment
acquitment
commitment
fitment
refitment
remitment

ĬT'nes
brightness
impoliteness
lightness
politeness
rightness
slightness

tightness
triteness
uprightness
whiteness

ĬT'nes
eye-witness
fitness
unfitness
witness

ĬT'ni
jitney
Mt. Whitney
Whitney

ĪT'ning
brightening
frightening
heightening
lightening
lightning
sheet-lightning
tightening
whitening

ĪT'nur
brightener
frightener
heightener
lightener
whitener

ĪT'on
chiton
triton
(cf. whiten,
chitin, etc.)

ĪT'rat
nitrate
titrate

ĬT'ri	sighter	quitter	itsy-bitsy
mitry	slighter	recommitter	Ritzy
nitry	smiter	refitter	
	tighter	remitter	Ī'umf
ĬT'rik	triter	sitter	triumph
nitric	typewriter	slitter	
	underwriter	spitter	Ī'un
ĬT'rik	uniter	splitter	triune
citric	unmiter	submitter	
vitric	whiter	titter	Ī'ur
	writer	transmitter	amplifier
ĬT'ur		twitter	applier
alighter	ĬT'ur	unfitter	Bayer
arbeiter	acquitter	Witter	beautifier
back-biter	admitter		Biedermeier
bemitre	befitter	ĬT'urd	briar
biter	benefitter	unembittered	brier
blighter	bitter	frittered, etc.	buyer
brighter	committer		certifier
citer	counterfeiter	ĬT'urn	clarifier
delighter	critter	bittern	classifier
dynamiter	embitter	flittern	codifier
exciter	emitter	gittern	complier
fighter	fitter		crier
flighter	flitter	ĬT'urz	crucifier
igniter	fritter	bitters	cryer
impoliter	glitter	glitters, etc.	decryer
inciter	gritter		defier
indicter	hitter	ĬT'us	defyer
inditer	intermitter	St. Vitus	deifier
inviter	intromitter	Titus	denier
lamplighter	knitter	Vitus	descrier
lighter	litter		dignifier
miter	manumitter	ĬT'wat	disqualifier
moonlighter	misfitter	lightweight	diversifier
niter	omitter		drier
plighter	outsitter	ĬT'wit	dyer
politer	outwitter	nitwit	edifier
reciter	permitter		electrifier
requiter	pitter	ĬT'zi	exemplifier
righter	pretermitter	Fritzy	eyer

falsifier
flier
fortifier
friar
frier
fructifier
glorifier
gratifier
hier
higher
horrifier
identifier
implier
indemnifier
intensifier
justifier
kite-flier
lammergeier
liar
lier
liquefier
magnifier
Mayer
Meier
Meyer
modifier
mollifier
mortifier
multiplier
Myer
mystifier
nigher
notifier
nullifier
occupier
pacifier
personifier
petrifier
plyer
prior
prophesier

pryer
purifier
putrifier
qualifier
ramifier
ratifier
rectifier
relier
replier
revivifier
sanctifier
satisfier
scarifier
scorifier
shyer
sigher
signifier
simplifier
skyer
slyer
specifier
speechifier
spryer
spyer
stultifier
stupefier
supplier
sweet-briar
terrifier
testifier
tier
town-crier
trier
trior
tyer
typifier
Untermyer
untier
verifier
versifier
vier

vilifier
vivifier
white-friar
wryer
(cf. tiar)
(cf. fire, etc.)

Ī'urn

grappling-iron
iron
lofting-iron

Ī'urz

Meyers
Myers
pliers
briers, etc.

Ī'us

bacchius
Darius
nisi prius
pious
Pius
(see Ī'as)

ĪV'a

Saiva
saliva
Siva

ĪV'al

adjectival
archival
arrival
conjunctival
estival
imperatival
nominatival
outrival
revival

rival
salival
survival

ĪV'an

Ivan
(cf. ĪV'en)

ĪV'ans

arrivance
connivance
contrivance
survivance

ĪV'ant

trivant

ĪV'at

private

ĪV'en

enliven

ĪV'en

driven
forgiven
given
overdriven
riven
scriven
shriven
stormdriven
thriven
undriven
unforgiven
unshriven
weather-
  driven

ĪV'ent

connivent

ĬV′est	striveth	ĬV′ing	ĬV′ment
arrivest	*surviveth*	arriving	deprivement
connivest	*thriveth*	conniving	revivement
contrivest		contriving	
deprivest	**ĬV′eth**	depriving	**ĬV′nes**
derivest	*forgiveth*	deriving	forgiveness
divest	*giveth*	diving	
drivest	*liveth*	driving	**ĬV′ot**
livest	*misgiveth*	hiving	divot
revivest	*outliveth*	reviving	pivot
rivest		shriving	
shrivest	**ĬV′i**	striving	**ĬV′ring**
strivest	ivy	surviving	delivering
survivest		thriving	quivering
thrivest	**ĬV′i**	uncontriving	shivering
	chivvy	wiving	slivering
ĬV′est	divi-divi		
forgivest	divvy	**ĬV′ing**	**ĬV′ur**
givest	Livy	ever-living	arriver
livest	privy	forgiving	conniver
misgivest	tantivy	giving	contriver
outlivest	tivy	lawgiving	depriver
		life-giving	deriver
ĬV′et	**ĬV′id**	living	diver
civet	ivied	misgiving	driver
grivet		outliving	fiver
privet	**ĬV′id**	thanksgiving	hiver
rivet	livid	unforgiving	liver
trivet	vivid		pearl-diver
unrivet			reviver
	ĬV′ik	**ĬV′li**	river
ĬV′eth	civic	lively	shriver
arriveth			skiver
conniveth	**ĬV′il, ĬV′el**	**ĬV′li**	slave-driver
contriveth	civil	absotively	sliver
depriveth	drivel	positively	stiver
deriveth	*rivel*		striver
diveth	shrivel	**ĬV′ling**	surviver
driveth	snivel	shrivelling	thriver
reviveth	swivel	snivelling	**ĬV′ur**
shriveth	uncivil		cantaliver

deliver	highway	mizzen	*solemnizest*
flivver	skyway	prison	*supervisest*
forgiver		risen	*surmisest*
freeliver	**Ī'za**	ptisan	*surprisest*
giver	Eliza	wizen	*sympathizest*
Indian giver	Isa		*theorizest*
liver		**ĪZ'est**	*tyrannizest*
misgiver	**ĪZ'ak**	*advertisest*	*uprisest*
outliver	Isaac	*advisest*	*wisest*
quiver		*agonizest*	
river	**ĪZ'al**	*apologizest*	**ĬZ'est**
shiver	comprisal	*arisest*	*fizzest, etc.*
skiver	revisal	*baptizest*	
sliver	surprisal	*catechizest*	**ĪZ'eth**
Spoon River		*chastisest*	*advertiseth*
stiver	**ĬZ'ard**	*civilizest*	*adviseth*
tiver	blizzard	*comprisest*	*agonizeth*
	gizzard	*compromisest*	*apologizeth*
ĬV'urd	izzard	*criticizest*	*ariseth*
delivered	lizard	*despisest*	*baptizeth*
lily-livered	lounge-lizard	*devisest*	*catechizeth*
pigeon-livered	scissored	*disguisest*	*chastiseth*
quivered	visored	*dramatizest*	*civilizeth*
shivered	vizard	*emphasizest*	*compriseth*
slivered	wizard	*eulogizest*	*compromiseth*
unshivered		*excisest*	*criticizeth*
white-livered	**ĬZ'dal**	*exercisest*	*despiseth*
	Grisdale	*exorcisest*	*deviseth*
ĬV'us		*improvisest*	*disguiseth*
acclivous	**ĬZ'dom**	*merchandisest*	*dramatizeth*
declivous	wisdom	*mobilizest*	*emphasizeth*
proclivous		*monopolizest*	*eulogizeth*
salivous	**ĪZ'en**	*organizest*	*exerciseth*
	bedizen	*patronizest*	*exorciseth*
	dizen	*premisest*	*improviseth*
ĬV'yal		*prizest*	*merchandiseth*
trivial	**ĪZ'en, ĪZ'on**	*realizest*	*mobilizeth*
(see ĬV'i-al)	arisen	*recognizest*	*monopolizeth*
	bedizen	*revisest*	*organizeth*
Ī'wa	dizen	*risest*	*patronizeth*
byway	imprison	*sizest*	*premiseth*

ōld, ôr, ŏdd, oil, fŏŏt, out; ūse, ûrn, ŭp; THis, thin

prizeth
realizeth
recognizeth
reviseth
riseth
sizeth
solemnizeth
superviseth
surmiseth
surpriseth
sympathizeth
theorizeth
tyrannizeth
upriseth

ĪZ'eth

fizzeth, etc.

ĪZH'un

abscission
allision
collision
concision
decision
derision
division
elision
envision
excision
illision
imprecision
incision
indecision
irrision
misprision
precision
prevision
provision
recision
rescission
revision

scission
subdivision
supervision
television
transition
vision
(cf. ĪZ'i-an)

ĪZH'und

provisioned
visioned

ĪZH'ur

scissure

ĪZ'i

sizy

ĪZ'i

busy
dizzy
frizzy
jizzy
Lizzy
tin-lizzie
tizzy

ĪZ'id

busied
dizzied
unbusied

ĪZ'ij

visage

ĪZ'ik

metaphysic
paradisic
phthisic
physic

ĪZ'iks

physics

ĪZ'ing

advertising
advising
aggrandizing
agonizing
analyzing
anglicizing
antagonizing
apologizing
apostatizing
appetizing
apprising
arising
authorizing
baptizing
brutalizing
canonizing
capitalizing
capsizing
catechizing
Catholicizing
cauterizing
centralizing
characterizing
chastising
civilizing
colonizing
comprising
compromising
criticizing
crystallizing
demising
demoralizing
deodorizing
despising
devising
disguising
disorganizing

dramatizing
economizing
emphasizing
enterprising
equalizing
eternalizing
eulogizing
evangelizing
exercising
exorcising
familiarizing
fertilizing
galvanizing
generalizing
gormandizing
harmonizing
Hebraizing
humanizing
hybridizing
hypnotizing
idealizing
idolizing
immortalizing
improvising
italicizing
jeopardizing
journalizing
localizing
macadamizing
magnetizing
materializing
mesmerizing
methodizing
minimizing
mobilizing
modernizing
monopolizing
moralizing
neutralizing
organizing
paralyzing

āle, câre, ădd, ärm, åsk; mē, hēre, ĕnd; īce, ĭll;

patronizing
pauperizing
plagiarizing
premising
prizing
pulverizing
rationalizing
realizing
recognizing
revising
revolution-
  izing
rising
ruralizing
scandalizing
scrutinizing
secularizing
sermonizing
signalizing
sizing
solemnizing
soliloquizing
specializing
standardizing
sterilizing
stigmatizing
subsidizing
summarizing
supervising
surmising
surprising
symbolizing
sympathizing
systematizing
tantalizing
temporizing
terrorizing
theorizing
totalizing
tranquillizing
tyrannizing

uncompromis-
  ing
underprizing
uprising
utilizing
vaporizing
visualizing
vitalizing
vocalizing
volatilizing
vulgarizing

ĬZ'ing

befrizzing
fizzing
frizzing
phizzing
quizzing
whizzing

ĬZ'it

visit
what-is-it

ĬZ'krak

wisecrack

ĬZ"l

drizzle
chisel
crizzle
enchisel
fizzle
frizzle
grizzle
mizzle
sizzle
swizzle
twizzle

ĬZ"ld

grizzled
drizzled, etc.

ĬZ'li

chiselly
drizzly
frizzly
grisly
grizzly

ĬZ'ling

chiseling
drizzling
fizzling
frizzling
grizzling
mizzling
sizzling
swizzling

ĬZ"m

izzum-wizzum

ĬZ'mal

abysmal
aneurismal
baptismal
cataclysmal
catechismal
chrismal
dismal
embolismal
paroxysmal
rheumatismal

ĪZ'man

exciseman
prizeman

ĪZ'ment

aggrandize-
  ment

apprizement
assizement
baptizement

ĬZ'met

kismet

ĬZ'mi

prismy

ĬZ'mik

aphorismic
cataclysmic
clysmic
embolismic
paroxysmic

ĬZ'mus

accismus
strabismus
tarantismus
trismus

ĪZ'nes

wiseness

ĬZ'nes

business

ĬZ'om

chrisom
(cf. schism)

ĪZ'on

horizon
Kyrie eleison

ĪZ'ord

visored

ĪZ'ord

(see ĪZ'ard)

ĪZ′ur
advertiser
adviser
aggrandizer
agonizer
analyzer
apologizer
appetizer
apprizer
assizer
atomizer
authorizer
baptizer
canonizer
capsizer
catechizer
cauterizer
chastiser
civilizer
colonizer
deodorizer
despiser
deviser
devisor
dialyser

disguiser
disorganizer
divisor
dogmatizer
economizer
elisor
epitomizer
equalizer
eulogizer
exerciser
exorciser
extemporizer
fertilizer
galvanizer
generalizer
geyser
gormandizer
guiser
harmonizer
humanizer
hybridizer
idolizer
improviser
incisor
itemizer
Kaiser

Keyser
Kyser
lionizer
magnetizer
miser
moralizer
organizer
pauperizer
polarizer
prizer
proselytizer
pulverizer
realizer
reviser
riser
scandalizer
scrutinizer
sermonizer
sizer
solemnizer
sterilizer
stigmatizer
supervisor
surmiser
surpriser
sympathizer

synchronizer
tantalizer
temporizer
terrorizer
theorizer
tranquillizer
tyrannizer
upriser
vaporizer
victimizer
vitalizer
vocalizer
vulgarizer
vulcanizer
wiser

ĬZ′ur
befrizzer
frizzer
quizzer
scissor
vizor

ĬZ′urz
scissors, etc.

O

For a discussion of words included under the accented vowels following, see the beginning of O rhymes in Section I.

Ō′a
boa
entozoa
epizoa
Genoa
Gilboa
jerboa
metazoa

moa
Noah
proa
protozoa
quinoa
Samoa
spermatazoa
(cf. aloha)

Ō′ab
Joab
Moab

Ō′al
bestowal

Ô′al
withdrawal

Ō′ba
arroba
bona-roba
dagoba

Ô′ba
Cahaba
Catawba

Ō'ball
no-ball
snow-ball

Ō'bat
globate
lobate
probate

ŎB'est
disrobest
enrobest
probest
robest
unrobest

ŎB'est
daubest, etc.

ŎB'est
robbest
sobbest
throbbest

ŎB'eth
disrobeth
enrobeth
probeth
robeth
unrobeth

ŎB'et
Cobbett

ŎB'eth
daubeth, etc.

ŎB'eth
robbeth
sobbeth
throbbeth

Ō'bī
go-by

ŌB'ĭ, ŌB'e
adobe
globy
Gobi
hydrophoby
Kobe
obi

ŎB'ĭ
bobby
cobby
hobby
knobby
lobby
mobby
nobby
scobby
snobby
squabby

ŎB'ĭl, ŎB'ēl
automobile
immobile
mobile

ŎB'in
bobbin
dobbin
ragged-robin
robbin
robin
round robin

ŌB'ing
disrobing
enrobing
globing
probing

robing
unrobing

ŎB'ing
blobbing
bobbing
cobbing
hobnobbing
jobbing
knobbing
lobbing
mobbing
robbing
snobbing
sobbing
swabbing
throbbing

ŎB'inz
Jobbins
Robbins
bobbins, etc.

ŎB'ish
bobbish
mobbish
nobbish
snobbish
squabbish

ŎB'jekt
object

ŎB''l
ennoble
ignoble
noble
unnoble

ŎB''l
bauble

ŎB''l
cobble
coble
gobble
hobble
nobble
squabble
wabble

ŎB'li
cobbly
squabbly
wabbly
Wobbly

ŎB'lin
goblin

ŎB'ling
cobbling
gobbling
hobbling
nobbling
snobling
squabbling
wabbling

ŎB'lur
cobbler
gobbler
hobbler
knobbler
nobbler
sherry-cobbler
squabbler
wabbler

ŌB'o
hobo
lobo
zobo

Ō'boi
doughboy

Ó'bonz
jawbones
sawbones

ōB'ra
cobra

Ó'brou
lowbrow

ōB'son
Jobson
Robeson
Robson

ōB'son
dobson
Jobson
Robson

ōB'stur
lobster

ŏB'ul
globule
lobule

ōB'ur
disrober
enrober
October
prober
rober
sober

ōB'ur
bedauber
dauber

ŏB'ur
beslobber
blobber
clobber
cobber
jobber
knobber
lobber
robber
slobber
snobber
sobber
swabber
throbber

ōB'urn
auburn

ōB'us
globus
jacobus
obus

ŏB'web
cobweb

ōCH'est
approachest
broachest
encroachest
poachest
reproachest

ŏCH'est
blotchest, etc.

ŏCH'et
crotchet
rotchet

ōCH'eth
approacheth

broacheth
encroacheth
poacheth
reproacheth

ŏCH'eth
blotcheth, etc.

ōCH'ez
approaches
broaches
brooches
coaches
encroaches
loaches
poaches
reproaches
roaches
self-reproaches

ōCH'ful
reproachful

ŏCH'i
blotchy
botchy
notchy
splotchy

ōCH'ing
approaching
broaching
coaching
encroaching
poaching
reproaching

ŏCH'ing
blotching
botching
notching

scotching
splotching
watching

ŏCH'man
Scotchman
watchman

ōCH'ment
approachment
encroachment

ōCH'ur
approacher
broacher
encroacher
poacher
reproacher
self-reproacher

ŏCH'ur
blotcher
botcher
notcher
splotcher
watcher

ŏCH'wurd
watchword

ōD'a
coda
pagoda
Rhoda
soda
trinoda

ōD'al
internodal
modal
nodal

---

trinodal
yodel

ŌD'al
bicaudal
caudal
caudle
dawdle

ŌD'ard
Goddard
Stoddard
(cf. foddered)

ŌD'ed
boded
coded
corroded
eroded
exploded
foreboded
goaded
loaded
outmoded
overloaded
unloaded
woaded

ŎD'ed
nodded
plodded
podded
prodded
sodded
wadded
(cf. bodied, etc.)

ŌD'el
yodel
(cf. ŌD'al)

ŌD'en
foreboden
Woden

ŌD'en
broaden

ŎD'en
hodden
sodden
trodden
untrodden
water-sodden
(cf. ÄD'en)

ŎD'ent
corrodent
erodent
explodent
rodent

ŎD'es
goddess
(cf. bodice)

ŎD'est
bodest
corrodest
explodest
forebodest
goadest
loadest
unloadest

ŎD'est
applaudest
belaudest
broadest
defraudest
laudest
maraudest

ŎD'est
immodest
modest
noddest
oddest
ploddest
proddest

ŌD'eth
bodeth
corrodeth
explodeth
forebodeth
goadeth
loadeth
unloadeth

ŎD'eth
applaudeth
belaudeth
defraudeth
laudeth
maraudeth

ŎD'eth
noddeth, etc.

ŌD'i
toady

ôD'i
bawdy
dawdy
gaudy

ŎD'i
body
busy-body
cloddy
embody
hoddy

noddy
roddy
shoddy
soddy
somebody
squaddy
toddy
waddy
(cf. ÄD'i)

ŎD'id
ablebodied
bodied
disembodied
unbodied
unembodied
(cf. ŎD'ed)

ŎD'ik
odic

ŎD'ik
anodic
episodic
exodic
hellanodic
hydriodic
iodic
kinesodic
melodic
methodic
odic
parodic
periodic
rhapsodic
sarcodic
spasmodic
synodic

ŌD'in
Odin
Wodin

ōld, ôr, ŏdd, oil, fŏŏt, out; ūse, ûrn, ŭp; THis, thin

ŎD′ing
boding
corroding
exploding
foreboding
goading
loading
outmoding
overloading
unloading

ŎD′ing
applauding
belauding
defrauding
lauding
marauding

ŎD′ing
codding
nodding
plodding
podding
prodding
wadding

ŎD′is
bodice
(cf. goddess)

ŎD′ish
cloddish
goddish

ŎD′ist
codist
modist
palinodist

ŎD′it
audit
plaudit

ŎD′kast
broadcast

ŎD′l
coddle
model
mollycoddle
noddle
remodel
swaddle
toddle
twaddle
waddle

ŎD′li
godly
twaddly
ungodly
waddly

ŎD′lin
maudlin

ŎD′ling
coddling
codling
godling
modelling
remodelling
swaddling
toddling
twaddling
waddling

ŎD′lur
coddler
modeller
mollycoddler
swaddler
toddler

twaddler
waddler

ŎD′nes
oddness

Ō′do
dodo
quasimodo

ŎD′om
Sodom

ŎD′ri
bawdry
tawdry

ŎD′ron
squadron

ŎD′son
Dodson
Hodson

ŎD′ston
loadstone
lodestone
toad-stone

ŎD′stur
goadster
roadster

ŎD′ukt
product

ŎD′ul
module
nodule

ŎD′ur
corroder

exploder
foreboder
goader
loader
malodor
muzzle-loader
Oder
odor
unloader

ŎD′ur
applauder
belauder
broader
defrauder
lauder
marauder
sawder
soft-sawder

ŎD′ur
codder
dodder
fodder
nodder
odder
plodder
podder
prodder
solder

ŎD′urn
modern

ŎD′us
modus
nodous

Ō′ed
coed

āle, câre, ădd, ärm, åsk; mē, hĕre, ĕnd; īce, ĭll;

Ō′el
Crowell
Joel
Lowell
Noel

Ō′em
poem
proem

Ō′en
Bowen
Cohen
Owen

Ō′est
bestowest
blowest
crowest
flowest
foregoest
foreknowest
foreshowest
glowest
goest
growest
hoest
knowest
lowest
mowest
outgoest
overflowest
overgrowest
overthrowest
owest
rowest
sewest
showest
slowest
snowest
sowest

stowest
throwest
towest
undergoest
undertowest
upthrowest

Ō′est
awest
drawest
overawest
rawest
withdrawest

Ō′et
poet

Ō′eth
bestoweth
bloweth
croweth
floweth
foregoeth
foreknoweth
foreshoweth
gloweth
goeth
groweth
hoeth
knoweth
loweth
moweth
outgoeth
overfloweth
overgroweth
overthroweth
oweth
roweth
seweth
showeth
snoweth

soweth
stoweth
throweth
toweth
undergoeth

Ō′eth
aweth, etc.

Ō′fa
sofa

Ō′fet
Tophet

ŎF′et, ŎF′it
archprophet
profit
prophet
soffit
weather-
   prophet

ŌF′i
Sophie
strophe
trophy

ŎF′i
coffee
spoffy
toffy

ŎF′ik
antistrophic
apostrophic
catastrophic
hypertrophic
philosophic
theosophic
theophilosophic

ŌF′il
profile

ŎF′in
coffin
encoffin

ŎF′ing
coughing
doffing
golfing
offing
scoffing

ŎF′is
office

ŎF′ish
crawfish
standoffish

ŎF′ish
offish
spoffish

ŎF″l
offal
waffle

ŎF″n
often
soften

ŎF′ted
lofted

ŎF′test
softest

ŎF′ti
lofty
softy

ŎFT'li
softly

ŎF'tur
crofter
lofter
softer

Ō'ful
woeful

Ô'ful
awful
lawful
unlawful

ŌF'ur
chauffeur
gopher
loafer
Ophir

ŎF'er
coffer
cougher
doffer
goffer
golfer
offer
proffer
scoffer

ŌG'a
Saratoga
snoga
Ticonderoga
toga
yoga

ŎG'a
Chicamauga
Sylacauga

ŌG'al
dogal

ŌG'al
synagogal

ŌG'an
brogan
Hogan
slogan

ŎG'an
toboggan

ŌG'i
bogey
bogie
dogie
fogey
stogie
yogi

ŎG'i
boggy
cloggy
doggy
foggy
froggy
groggy
joggy
soggy

ŎG'in
noggin

ŎG'ing
befogging
bogging
clogging
cogging
dogging

flogging
fogging
jogging
nogging
slogging
togging
unclogging

ŎG'ish
doggish
hoggish

ŌG'ish
roguish

ŌG"l
bogle
fogle
ogle

ŎG"l
boondoggle
boggle
coggle
goggle
joggle
toggle

ŎG'ling
boondoggling
boggling
goggling
joggling

ŌG'lur
ogler

ŎG'lur
boondoggler
boggler
goggler
joggler

ŎG'mir
quagmire

ŌG'ram
programme

ŌG'res
ogress
progress

ŎG'res
progress

ŎG'trot
dog-trot
jog-trot

ŌG'ur
ogre

ŌG'ur
auger
augur
inaugur
mauger

ŎG'ur
befogger
clogger
cogger
dogger
flogger
hogger
jogger
logger
pettifogger
slogger
togger
wholehogger

ŌG'us
bogus

ÔG′ust
August

ŎG′wood
bog-wood
dog-wood
logwood

Ō′hen
Cohen

Ō′hunk
Bohunk

Ō′i
blowy
Bowie
Chloe
doughy
Floey
glowy
Joey
showy
snowy
towy
Zoe

Ô′i
flawy
jawy
strawy
thawy
(cf. Ä′i)

OI′al
chapel-royal
disloyal
loyal
pennyroyal
royal
sur-royal

OI′ans
annoyance
buoyance
clairvoyance
joyance

OI′ant
annoyant
buoyant
chatoyant
clairvoyant
flamboyant
prevoyant

OI′b′l
foible

OID′al
asteroidal
colloidal
conchoidal
conoidal
coralloidal
crinoidal
cycloidal
dendroidal
discoidal
elephantoidal
ellipsoidal
ethnoidal
ganoidal
hemispheroidal
lithoidal
metalloidal
negroidal
ooidal
ovoidal
paraboloidal
planetoidal
prismatoidal
prismoidal

rhomboidal
saccharoidal
sigmoidal
spheroidal
trochoidal
typhoidal

OID′ans
avoidance

OID′ed
avoided
voided

OID′en
hoyden

OID′ur
avoider
broider
embroider
moider
voider

OI′e
employee

OI′est
annoyest
buoyest
cloyest
convoyest
coyest
decoyest
deployest
destroyest
employest
enjoyest
joyest
toyest

OI′eth
annoyeth
buoyeth
cloyeth
convoyeth
decoyeth
destroyeth
employeth
enjoyeth
joyeth
toyeth

OI′ful
joyful

OI′ij
alloyage
buoyage
voyage

OI′ing
annoying
buoying
cloying
convoying
decoying
deploying
destroying
employing
enjoying
joying
toying

OI′ish
boyish
coyish
toyish

Ō′ij
flowage
stowage
towage

Ō'ik	*broileth*	broiler	going
azoic	*coileth*	coiler	growing
benzoic	*despoileth*	despoiler	helloing
Cenozoic	*embroileth*	embroiler	hoeing
dichroic	*foileth*	foiler	inflowing
dyspnoic	*recoileth*	oiler	knowing
Eozoic	*roileth*	recoiler	lowing
heroic	*soileth*	soiler	mowing
hylozoic	*spoileth*	spoiler	oboeing
hypozoic	*toileth*	toiler	outflowing
melanochroic	*uncoileth*	uncoiler	outgoing
Mesozoic			outgrowing
mock-heroic	**OIL'i**	**OI'man**	overcrowing
Neozoic	coyly	decoy-man	overflowing
Palæozoic	doily	hoyman	overgrowing
pleochroic	oily	toyman	overthrowing
protozoic	roily		owing
Stoic		**OI'ment**	rowing
Troic	**OIL'ing**	deployment	sea-going
xanthochroic	assoiling	employment	self-knowing
	boiling	enjoyment	sewing
OIL'est	broiling		showing
boilest	coiling	**OIN'dur**	slowing
broilest	despoiling	rejoinder	snowing
coilest	embroiling		sowing
despoilest	foiling	**OI'nes**	stowing
embroilest	moiling	coyness	*strowing*
foilest	oiling		thorough-going
recoilest	recoiling	**Ō'ing**	throwing
roilest	soiling	bestowing	toeing
soilest	spoiling	blowing	towing
spoilest	toiling	bowing	undergoing
toilest	uncoiling	cock-crowing	undertowing
uncoilest		crowing	unknowing
	OIL'ment	easy-going	unflowing
OIL'et	despoilment	flowing	upgrowing
oillet	embroilment	foregoing	
toilet	recoilment	foreknowing	**Ō'ing**
		foreshowing	awing
OIL'eth	**OIL'ur**	glass-blowing	begnawing
boileth	boiler	glowing	cawing

clawing
clawing
drawing
gnawing
guffawing
heehawing
jawing
lawing
outlawing
overawing
overdrawing
pawing
pshawing
sawing
thawing
wiredrawing
withdrawing
yawing

OIN'ij

coinage

OIN'ing

adjoining
coining
conjoining
disjoining
enjoining
groining
joining
purloining
rejoining
subjoining

OIN'ted

anointed
appointed
conjointed
disappointed
disjointed
jointed

pointed
unanointed
unpointed
unjointed

OIN'ting

anointing
appointing
disappointing
disjointing
jointing
pointing

OINT'les

jointless
pointless

OINT'ment

anointment
appointment
disappointment
disjointment
ointment

OIN'tur

anointer
appointer
disappointer
disjointer
jointer
pointer

OIN'ur

coiner
conjoiner
enjoiner
joiner
purloiner
rejoiner

OI'ride

joyride

Ō'is

Lois

Ō'ish

showish
snowish

OIS'ing

rejoicing
voicing
unrejoicing

OIS'les

choiceless
voiceless

OI'som

noisome
toysome

OIS'ti

foisty
moisty

OI'stik

joystick

OIS'ting

foisting
hoisting
joisting

OIS'tral

cloistral
coystrel

OIS'tur

cloister
encloister
foister
hoister

moister
oyster
pearl-oyster
royster
uncloister

OIT'ed

doited
exploited

OIT'i

dacoity
hoity-toity

OIT'ring

loitering
reconnoitring

OIT'ūr

exploiture
voiture

OIT'ŭr

adroiter
exploiter
goiter
loiter
reconnoiter

OI'ur

annoyer
Boyar
Boyer
coyer
decoyer
deployer
destroyer
employer
enjoyer
self-destroyer
toyer

ōld, ôr, ŏdd, oil, fŏŏt, out; ūse, ûrn, ŭp; THis, thin

OI'us
joyous

OIZ'ez
boyses
noises
poises

OIZ'ĭ
noisy

OIZ'ing
noising
poising

OIZ'on
empoison
foison
poison
toison

OIZ'onz
foisons
poisons, etc.

Ō'jan
Trojan

ŎJ'ez
Hodges
dodges, etc.

ŌJ'e
anagoge
apagoge
èpagoge
paragoge

ŎJ'ĭ
pedagogy
podgy
stodgy

ŎJ'ik
aerologic
anagogic
anthropologic
archæologic
astrologic
biologic
chronologic
curiologic
demagogic
demonologic
dialogic
entomologic
epagogic
epilogic
ethnologic
ethologic
etymologic
eulogic
geologic
gnomologic
hierologic
histologic
horologic
ichthyologic
idealogic
isagogic
lithologic
logic
martyrologic
meteorologic
mineralogic
morphologic
mycologic
myologic
mystagogic
mythologic
necrologic
neologic
ontologic
ophiologic

paragogic
pathologic
pedagogic
philologic
phonologic
photologic
phraseologic
physiologic
psychologic
sarcologic
sociologic
tautologic
theologic
tropologic
zymologic

ŎJ'iks
pedagogics

ŎJ'ing
dislodging
dodging
lodging

ŎJ'ur
codger
dislodger
dodger
lodger
Roger

ŌJ'urn
sojourn

Ō'kā
croquet
roquet

ŌK'ă
coca
tapioca

ŌK'al
bocal
focal
local
phocal
socle
vocal
yokel

ŌK'e
troche
trochee
(cf. choky, etc.)

ŌK'en
bespoken
betoken
broken
fair-spoken
fine-spoken
forespoken
foretoken
freespoken
heart-broken
Hoboken
oaken
outspoken
soft-spoken
spoken
token
unbroken
unspoken

ŎK'en
Brocken

ŌK'est
chokest
cloakest
convokest
croakest

evokest
invokest
jokest
provokest
revokest
smokest
soakest
spokest
unyokest
yokest

ŎK′est

balkest
stalkest
talkest
walkest

ŎK′est

bemockest
blockest
dockest
flockest
knockest
lockest
mockest
rockest
sockest
shockest
smockest
stockest
unfrockest
unlockest

ŎK′et

air-pocket
brocket
cocket
crocket
Crockett
docket
impocket

locket
Lockett
pickpocket
pocket
rocket
sky-rocket
socket
sprocket

ŌK′eth

choketh
cloaketh
convoketh
croaketh
evoketh
invoketh
joketh
poketh
provoketh
revoketh
smoketh
soaketh
spoketh
unyoketh
yoketh

ŎK′eth

balketh
stalketh
talketh
walketh

ŎK′eth

bemocketh
blocketh
docketh
flocketh
knocketh
locketh
mocketh
rocketh

shocketh
smocketh
stocketh
unlocketh

ŎK′hed

blockhead
shock-head

ŌK′i

choky
cokey
croaky
hokey
joky
Loki
moky
oaky
okey-dokey
poky
roky
slow-poky
smoky
soaky
yoky
(cf. troche and
trochee)

ŎK′i

balky
chalky
gawky
Milwaukee
pawky
squawky
stalky
talkie
talky
walkie

ŎK′i

cocky

crocky
flocky
hockey
jockey
locky
rocky
stocky

ŎK′id

cockeyed

ŌK′ij

brokage
cloakage
soakage

ŎK′ij

dockage
lockage
soccage

ŌK′ing

besmoking
choking
cloaking
convoking
croaking
evoking
invoking
joking
poking
provoking
revoking
smoking
soaking
stoking
stroking
troching
uncloaking
yoking

ÔK'ing	**ŎK''l**	rococo	orthodoxy
balking	cockle	troco	paradoxy
calking	hockle		proxy
hawking	socle	**ŎK'o**	
jaywalking	strockle	Morocco	**ŎK'sid**
squawking		sirocco	fox-eyed
stalking	**ŎK'les**		ox-eyed
talking	cloakless	**ŎK'port**	oxide
walking	jokeless	Brockport	
	smokeless	Lockport	**ŎK'sin**
ŎK'ing	yokeless	Stockport	tocsin
bemocking	yolkless		
blocking		**ŎK'ra**	**ŌK'sing**
clocking	**ŎK'ling**	okra	coaxing
cocking	cockling		hoaxing
docking	flockling	**ŎK'sen, ŎK's'n**	
flocking	rockling	cockswain	**ŎK'sing**
hocking		oxen	boxing
interlocking	**ŎK'lor**		foxing
knocking	folklore	**ŎK'shal**	
locking		equinoctial	**ŌKS'man**
mocking	**ŎK'man**	trinoctial	spokesman
rocking	Brockman		strokesman
shocking	lockman	**ŎK'shun**	
smocking	socman	auction	**ŎK'smith**
stocking			jokesmith
unlocking	**ŎK'ment**	**ŎK'shun**	
	invokement	concoction	**ŎK'sur**
ÔK'inz	provokement	decoction	coaxer
Dawkins	revokement		hoaxer
Hawkins		**ŎK'shus**	
	ŎK'ni	innoxious	**ŎK'sur**
ÔK'ish	cockney	noxious	boxer
hawkish		obnoxious	oxer
mawkish	**Ō'ko**		
	baroco	**ŎK'si**	**ŎK'til**
ŎK'ish	coco	cacodoxy	coctile
blockish	cocoa	Coxey	trioctile
cockish	koko	doxy	
mockish	loco	foxy	**ŎK'tiv**
stockish	locofoco	heterodoxy	concoctive
			decoctive

ŎK'ton
Blockton
Brockton
Stockton

ŎK'trin
doctrine

ŎK'tur
concocter
doctor
proctor

ŎK'turn
nocturne

Ō'kum
hokum
oakum

Ō'kund
jocund

ŎK'ur
broker
choker
cloaker
convoker
croaker
evoker
invoker
joker
mediocre
ocher
poker
provoker
revoker
smoker
soaker
stoker
stroker

uncloaker
yoker

ŎK'ur
balker
calker
deer-stalker
gawker
hawker
jaywalker
shop-walker
sleep-walker
squawker
stalker
street-walker
talker
tomahawker
walker

ŎK'ur
blocker
cocker
docker
Fokker
hougher
Knickerbocker
knocker
locker
mocker
rocker
shocker
soccer
socker
stocker

ŎK'urz
knickerbockers
dockers, etc.

Ō'kus
crocus

focus
hocus
hocus-pocus
Hohokus
locus

ŎK'us
caucus
Daucus
glaucous
raucous

Ō'kust
locust
focussed, etc.

ŎK'ward
awkward

Ō'la
Angola
Appalachicola
carambola
coca-cola
gola
gondola
Gorgonzola
kola
Leola
Maizola
Pensacola
Ramola
scagliola
stola
Viola
Zola

ŎL'a
Eufaula
Guatamala
Paula

ŌL'a
corolla
holla
mollah

ŌL'ak
Polack

ŌL'an
Dolan
Nolan

Ō'land
Boland
Bowland
lowland
Noland
Roland
Rowland

ŌL'ar
(see ŌL'ur)

ŌL'ard
bollard
collard
collared
dollared
Lollard
pollard
scollard

ŌL'as
solace

ŌL'chun
falchion

ŌL'da
Alda

ŌL'ded
blindfolded

---

enfolded
infolded
manifolded
molded
refolded
scolded
unfolded

ŌL'den
beholden
embolden
golden
holden
misbeholden
olden
withholden

ŌL'den
Alden

ŌL'dest
beholdest
boldest
coldest
enfoldest
foldest
holdest
infoldest
interfoldest
moldest
oldest
refoldest
scoldest
unfoldest
upholdest
withholdest

ŌL'dest
baldest
scaldest

ŌL'deth
beholdeth
enfoldeth
foldeth
holdeth
infoldeth
interfoldeth
moldeth
refoldeth
scoldeth
unfoldeth
upholdeth
withholdeth

ŌL'deth
scaldeth

ŌLD'ham
Oldham

ŌL'di
foldy
moldy

ŌL'ding
beholding
enfolding
folding
holding
infolding
interfolding
molding
refolding
scolding
slave-holding
unfolding
upholding
weather-
   molding
withholding

ŌL'ding
Balding
Paulding
scalding
Spaulding

ŌL'dish
coldish
oldish

ŌLD'li
boldly
coldly
manifoldly

ŌLD'man
Goldman
Oldman

ŌLD'ment
enfoldment
withholdment

ŌLD'nes
boldness
coldness
oldness

ŌLD'ron
caldron
pauldron

ŌL'drumz
doldrums

ŌLD'smith
Goldsmith

ŌL'dur
beholder
bolder
bottleholder

boulder
colder
enfolder
freeholder
holder
householder
infolder
interfolder
landholder
leaseholder
molder
older
pattern-
   molder
polder
refolder
scolder
shareholder
shoulder
slave-holder
smolder
unfolder
upholder
withholder

ŌL'dur
alder
balder
Baldur
scalder

ŌL'durd
bouldered
broad-
   shouldered
moldered
shouldered
smoldered

ŌLD'win
Baldwin

ŎL'eg

colleague

ŎL'ej

acknowledge
college
foreknowledge
knowledge
self-knowledge

ŎL'ejd

acknowledged
unacknowl-
    edged

ŎL'em, ŎL'um

column
solemn

ŎL'en

stolen
swollen

ŎL'en

chop-fallen
fallen
wind-fallen

ŎL'ent

equipollent
prepollent

ŎL'er

(see ŎL'ur)

Ŏ'les

clawless
flawless
jawless
lawless
mawless
sawless

ŎL'est

bowlest
cajolest
condolest
consolest
controllest
dolest
drollest
enrollest
patrollest
pollest
rollest
strollest
tollest
trollest
unrollest
uprollest

ŎL'est

bawlest
bemawlest
brawlest
callest
crawlest
drawlest
enthrallest
forestallest
maulest
scrawlest
smallest
sprawlest
squallest
tallest

ŎL'et

collet
La Follette
wallet

ŎL'eth

bowleth

cajoleth
condoleth
consoleth
controlleth
doleth
enrolleth
patrolleth
polleth
rolleth
strolleth
tolleth
trolleth
unrolleth
uprolleth

ŎL'eth

bawleth
bemawleth
brawleth
calleth
crawleth
drawleth
enthralleth
forestalleth
mauleth
scrawleth
sprawleth
squalleth

ŎL'fin

dolphin

ŎL'fing

golfiing

ŎL'ful

bowlful
doleful
soulful

ŎL'fur

golfer

ŎL'fus

Adolphus
Rodolphus
Rudolphus

ŎL'hous

poll-house
toll-house

ŎL'i

coaly
holy
lowly
moly
roly-poly
shoaly
slowly
unholy
(cf. ŎL'li)

ŎL'i

Macaulay
Macauley
sprawly
squally
whally

ŎL'i

Bali
collie
dolly
folly
golly
Holley
holly
jolly
loblolly
melancholy
Molly
Polly
rolley

Tolley
trolley
volley

ŎL'ĭd
jollied
olid
solid
squalid
stolid
volleyed

Ō'lĭf
lowlife

ŎL'ĭj
hallage
haulage
stallage

ŎL'ĭk
aulic
Gallic
hydraulic
interaulic

ŎL'ĭk
Aeolic
alcoholic
apostolic
bibliopolic
bucolic
carbolic
colic
diabolic
diastolic
embolic
epipolic
epistolic
frolic
hyperbolic

melancholic
metabolic
parabolic
petrolic
rollick
symbolic
systolic
variolic
vicar-apostolic
vitriolic

ŎL'ĭn
tarpaulin

ŎL'ĭng
bolling
bowling
cajoling
caracoling
coaling
condoling
consoling
controlling
doling
drolling
enrolling
extolling
foaling
holing
inscrolling
parolling
patrolling
poling
rolling
shoaling
strolling
tolling
trolling
unrolling
uprolling

ŎL'ĭng
appalling
balling
bawling
befalling
bemawling
blackballing
brawling
calling
caterwauling
crawling
drawling
enthralling
falling
footballing
forestalling
galling
hauling
installing
mauling
miscalling
overhauling
palling
Pawling
recalling
scrawling
snow-balling
sprawling
squalling
thralling
trawling
walling

ŎL'ĭng
caracolling
extolling
lolling

ŎL'ĭnz
Collins

Hollins
Rollins

ŎL'ĭs
Collis
Cornwallis
Hollis
Wallace
Wallis

ŎL'ĭsh
drollish
Polish

ŎL'ĭsh
Gaulish
smallish
squallish
tallish

ŎL'ĭsh
abolish
demolish
polish

ŎL'ĭsht
abolished
demolished
polished
unpolished

ŎL'ĭv
olive

ŎL'jur
soldier

ŎL'ka
polka

ŎL'kon
falcon

gerfalcon
soar-falcon
sorefalcon

ÔLK'nur
falconer

ÔL'li
drolly
solely
wholly
(cf. ÔL'i)

ÔL'man
coal-man
Coleman
Colman
Holman
toll-man

ÔL'ment
cajolement
condolement
controlment
enrollment

ÔL'ment
appallment
disenthrallment
enthrallment
epaulement
instalment
installment

ÔL'most
almost

ÔL'nes
drollness
soleness
wholeness

ÔL'nes
allness
smallness
tallness

Ô'lo
polo
solo

ÔL'o
Apollo
follow
hollo
hollow
swallow
wallow

Ô'lok
Moloch
rowlock

ÔL'on
colon
eidolon
semicolon
Solon
stolon
(cf. ÔL'an,
  ÔL'en)

ÔL'op
collop
dollop
escalop
lollop
scallop
trollop
wallop

ÔL'or
dolor

ÔLS'hood
falsehood

ÔL'sid
palsied

ÔLS'nes
falseness

ÔL'so
also

ÔL'som
dolesome
wholesome

ÔL'son
Jolson
Olsen
Olson
Tolson
Toulson

ÔL'star
pole-star

ÔL'ston
gallstone

ÔL'ston
Alston
Balston
Ralston

ÔL'stur
bolster
holster
upholster

ÔL'ted
bolted

jolted
molted
revolted
unbolted

ÔL'ted
assaulted
defaulted
exalted
faulted
halted
malted
salted
vaulted

ÔL'ten
molten

ÔL'test
boltest, etc

ÔL'test
assaultest
defaultest
exaltest
haltest
vaultest

ÔL'teth
bolteth, etc.

ÔL'teth
assaulteth
defaulteth
exalteth
halteth
vaulteth

ÔL'ti
faulty
malty

ōld, ôr, ŏdd, oil, fŏŏt, out; ūse, ûrn, ŭp; THis, thin

salty
vaulty

ŌL'tij

voltage

ŌL'tij

maltage
vaultage

ŌL'tik

asphaltic
Baltic
basaltic
cobaltic
peristaltic

ŌL'ting

bolting
jolting
molting
revolting
unbolting

ŌL'ting

assaulting
defaulting
exalting
faulting
halting
malting
salting
vaulting

ŌL'tish

coltish
doltish

ŌLT'les

faultless
maltless
saltless

ŌL'ton

Bolton
Colton
Moulton

ŌL'ton

Dalton
Walton

ŌL'tri

poultry

ŌL'tur

bolter
colter
jolter
revolter
unbolter

ŌL'tur

altar
alter
assaulter
defaulter
exalter
falter
Gibraltar
halter
malter
McWalter
palter
psalter
Salter
unalter
vaulter
Walter

ŌL'turn

saltern
subaltern

ŌLT'sur

waltzer
(cf. falser)

ŌL'ūm

colyum
volume

ŌL'um

column
solemn

ŌL'ur

bowler
cajoler
circumpolar
coaler
condoler
consoler
controller
doler
dolor
droller
enroller
molar
patroller
polar
poler
poller
roller
scroller
shoaler
solar
stroller
toller
troller
unipolar
unroller
uproller

ŌL'ur

bawler

bemawler
brawler
caller
crawler
drawler
enthraller
faller
footballer
forestaller
hauler
mauler
scrawler
smaller
sprawler
squaller
taller
trawler

ŌL'ur

choler
collar
dollar
extoller
loller
scholar
sollar
squalor

ŌL'us

bolus
holus-bolus
solus

ŌL'usk

mollusk

ŌL'vent

dissolvent
evolvent
insolvent
resolvent
solvent

āle,   câre,   ădd,   ärm,   åsk;   mē,   hęre,   ěnd;   īce,   ĭll;

ŎL'vest
absolvest
devolvest
dissolvest
evolvest
involvest
resolvest
revolvest
solvest

ŎL'veth
absolveth
devolveth
dissolveth
evolveth
involveth
resolveth
revolveth
solveth

ŎL'ving
absolving
devolving
dissolving
evolving
involving
resolving
revolving
solving

ŎLV'ment
devolvement
evolvement
involvement

ŎL'vur
absolver
dissolver
evolver
involver
resolver

revolver
solver

ŎL'wart
stalwart

ŎL'waz
always

Ō'ma
aboma
aroma
coma
diploma
Natoma
sarcoma
Roma
Sonoma
Tacoma
theobroma
zygoma

ŎM'a
comma
momma

Ō'mad
nomad
ohmad

Ō'man
bowman
foeman
Roman
showman
yeoman

ŎM'as
Thomas

ŎM'bat
combat
wombat

ŎM'bi
Abercrombie
Dombey
zombie

ŎM'brus
sombrous

ŎM'bur
hombre
omber
Scomber
somber

ŎM'en, Ō'men
abdomen
agnomen
bowmen
cognomen
foemen
omen
prænomen
yeomen
(cf. gnomon)

ŎM'end
ill-omened
omened

Ō'ment
bestowment
moment

ŎM'et
comet
domett
grommet

ŎM'i
foamy

homy
loamy

ŎM'i
mommy
Tommie

ŎM'ij
homage

ŎM'ik
bromic
chromic
gnomic
hydrobromic
polychromic

ŎM'ik
agronomic
anatomic
astronomic
atomic
autonomic
cinnamomic
comic
diatomic
dystomic
economic
entomic
gastronomic
heliochromic
isonomic
metronomic
microtomic
monatomic
nomic
orthodromic
palindromic
phantomic
physiognomic
serio-comic

ōld, ôr, ŏdd, oil, fŏŏt, out; ūse, ûrn, ŭp; THis, thin

stereochromic
stereotomic
taxonomic
tragi-comic
triatomic
vomic

ŎM'iks
economics
phoronomics

ŎM'in
bromine
theobromine

ŎM'ing
befoaming
coaming
combing
foaming
gloaming
homing
roaming

ŎM'is
promise

ŎM'ish
Romish

ŎM'les
foamless
combless
homeless

ŎM'let
homelet
tomelet

ŎM'let
omelet

ŎM'li
homely

Ō'mo
chromo
Como
Ecce Homo
major-domo

ŎM'on
common

ŎM'pi
Pompey

ŎMP'ish
rompish
swampish

ŎM'plish
accomplish

ŎMP'ted
prompted
unprompted

ŎMP'ton
Brompton
Compton
Lecompton

ŎMP'us
pompous

ŎM'spun
homespun

ŎM'sted
homestead

ŎM'ur
beachcomber

comber
gomer
homer
Homer
misnomer
omer
roamer
vomer
wool-comber

ŎM'ur
bomber

ŎM'urs
commerce

ŎM'ward
homeward

Ō'na
annona
Arizona
Barcelona
Bellona
Bologna
cinchona
corona
Cremona
Desdemona
Iona
Jonah
mona
Nona
Pomona
Ramona
Zona

ŎN'a
Mauna

ŎN'a
belladonna

donna
Madonna
prima donna

ŎN'al
coronal
subumbonal
tonal
zonal

ŎN'ald
Donald
McDonald
Ronald

ŎN'ant
intersonant
sonant
(cf. deponent,
etc.)

ŎN'ark
monarch

ŎN'as
Jonas

ŎN'at
donate
zonate

ŎN'da
anaconda

ŎN'de
arrondi

ŎN'de
dispondee
spondee

ŎN'ded
absconded
bonded
corresponded
desponded
responded

ŌN'def
stone-deaf
tone-deaf

ŎN'del
rondel

ŎN'dens
correspondence
despondence
respondence

ŎN'dent
co-respondent
correspondent
despondent
frondent
respondent

ŎN'dest
abscondest
bondest
correspondest
fondest
respondest

ŎN'deth
abscondeth
bondeth
correspondeth
respondeth

ŎN'dij
bondage

frondage
vagabondage

ŎN'ding
absconding
corresponding
desponding
responding

ŎN'd'l
fondle
rondle

ŎND'li
fondly

ŎND'ling
bondling
fondling

ŎND'nes
blondness
fondness

ŎN'dur
absconder
bonder
corresponder
desponder
fonder
hypochonder
ponder
responder
squander
wander
yonder
(cf. condor)

ŎN'durz
Saunders

ŌN'e
Pawnee
Punxatawnee
Sewanee
Shawnee
Swanee
(cf. ŌN'i)

ŌN'ent
component
deponent
exponent
interponent
opponent
proponent
(cf. sonant)

Ō'nes
lowness
slowness

ŌN'est
atonest
bemoanest
condonest
dethronest
disownest
dronest
enthronest
groanest
intonest
honest
loanest
lonest
moanest
ownest
postponest
stonest
thronest
tonest

ŎN'est
connest
dishonest
donnest
honest
non-est
wannest

ŎN'et
bonnet
sonnet
unbonnet

ŌN'eth
atoneth
begroaneth
bemoaneth
condoneth
dethroneth
disowneth
droneth
enthroneth
groaneth
honeth
intoneth
loaneth
moaneth
owneth
postponeth
stoneth
throneth
toneth

ŎNG'est
longest
strongest

ŎNG'ful
songful
throngful
wrongful

ŎNG'go
Bongo
Congo

ŎNG'gur
conger
longer

ŎNG'ing
belonging
longing
prolonging
thronging
wronging

ŎNG'ish
longish
prongish
songish
strongish

ŎNG'ki
donkey

ŎNG'kur
conker
conquer

ŎNG'kurz
conquers
Yonkers

ŎNG'li
longly
wrongly

ŎNG'nes
longness
wrongness

ŎNG'stur
songster

ŎNG'ur
prolonger
wronger

ŎNG'wav
long-wave

ŌN'hed
bonehead

Ō'ni
alimony
aloney
antimony
baloney
bologney
bony
Coney
cony
crony
drony
lazzaroni
macaroni
Mahoney
Maloney
matrimony
parsimony
patrimony
phony
pony
sanctimony
stony
testimony
tony
(cf. cicerone)

ŌN'ĭ
brawny
lawny
mulligatawny
orange-tawny
sawney
scrawny
tawny
yawny

ŎN'ĭ
bonnie
bonny
Connie
Lonnie
Renee
Ronnie

ŎN'ĭk
phonic
zonic

ŎN'ĭk
Aaronic
acronyc
Adonic
agonic
Amphictyonic
anharmonic
antiphonic
architectonic
atonic
Babylonic
cacophonic
canonic
carbonic
cataphonic
Chalcedonic
chronic
colophonic
conic
crotonic
cyclonic
dæmonic
demonic
diaphonic
diatonic
draconic
embryonic
euphonic
ganglionic
geogonic
geoponic
gnominic
harmonic
hedonic
hegemonic
histrionic
homophonic
Housatonic
intergan-
  glionic
Ionic
ironic
isotonic
jargonic
laconic
macaronic
masonic
Metonic
Miltonic
mnemonic
monochronic
monophonic
monotonic
neoplatonic
Olympionic
paratonic
parsonic
pathogno-
  monic
Pharaonic
philharmonic
phonic
photophonic
Platonic
Plutonic

āle, câre, ădd, ärm, ȧsk; mē, hẹre, ĕnd; īce, ĭll;

pneumonic
polyphonic
pulmonic
Pyrrhonic
pythonic
sardonic
semitonic
sermonic
siphonic
Slavonic
Solomonic
stentoronic
stratonic
symphonic
tectonic
telephonic
Teutonic
theogonic
tonic
Tychonic
zoonic

ŎN'iks

geoponics
hedonics
histrionics
Megalonyx
mnemonics
onyx

ŌN'ing

atoning
bemoaning
boning
dethroning
disowning
droning
enthroning
groaning
intoning
moaning

owning
postponing
stoning
throning
toning

ŎN'ing

awning
dawning
fawning
pawning
spawning
undawning
yawning

ŎN'ing

conning
donning

ŎN'is

Adonis
Coronis

ŎN'ish

Babylonish
dronish

ŎN'ish

admonish
astonish
tonnish
wannish

ŎN'je

congee
pongee

ŎN'les

boneless
throneless
toneless
zoneless

ŌN'li

lonely
only

ŌN'ment

atonement
condonement
dethronement
disownment
enthronement
postponement

ŌN'nes

loneness
proneness
unknownness

ŌN'or

donor
(cf. ŌN'ur)

ŎN'rad

Conrad

ŎN'shens

conscience

ŎN'shus

conscious
self-conscious
sub-conscious

ŎN'siv

corresponsive
irresponsive
responsive

ŌN'som

lonesome

ŎN'son

Johnson

Jonson
(cf. Wiscon-
    sin)

ŎN'sor

sponsor
tonsor

ŎN'stant

constant
inconstant

ŎN'ston

Johnston

ŎN'strans

monstrance
remonstrance

ŎN'strat

demonstrate
remonstrate

ŎN'strous

monstrous

ŎN'stur

monster

ŎN'tal

fontal
frontal
horizontal
peridontal

ŎN'tan

cismontane
tramontane
ultramontane

ÔN'ted

daunted

ōld, ôr, ŏdd, oil, fŏŏt, out; ūse, ûrn, ŭp; THis, thin

flaunted
haunted
taunted
undaunted
vaunted
wanted

ŏN'ted

wanted

ŏN'test

dauntest
flauntest
hauntest
tauntest
vauntest
wantest

ŏN'teth

daunteth
flaunteth
haunteth
taunteth
vaunteth
wanteth

ÔN'ti

flaunty
jaunty

ŏN'tif

pontiff

ŏN'tij

wantage

ŏN'tij

pontage
wantage

ŏN'tik

Anacreontic

archontic
mastodontic
pontic
quantic

ŏN'tin

dracontine
Hellespontine
pontine
(cf. tontine)

ŏN'ting

daunting
flaunting
haunting
jaunting
taunting
vaunting
wanting

ŏN'ting

wanting

ONT'les

dauntless
tauntless
vauntless

ONT'let

gantlet
gauntlet

ŏN'ton

wanton
(cf. fronton)

ŏN'trit

contrite
uncontrite

ŏN'tum

quantum

ÔN'tur

daunter
flaunter
gaunter
haunter
saunter
taunter
vaunter

ŌN'ur

atoner
bemoaner
boner
condoner
dethroner
droner
groaner
honer
intoner
moaner
owner
phoner
postponer
telephoner
stoner
(cf. donor)

ÔN'ur

awner
barley-awner
brawner
fawner
pawner
spawner
yawner

ŏN'ur

Bonner
conner
Connor
dishonor

goner
honor
O'Conner
O'Connor
wanner

ŏN'urd

dishonored
honored
timehonored
unhonored

ŏN'urz

Conners
Connors
O'Connors
honors, etc.

Ō'nus

bonus
onus
tonous

ŏN'yard

poniard

ŏN'zo

Alonzo
Alphonso
Alphonzo

Ō'on

entozoon
epizoon
phytozoon
zoon

O͞OD'ed

hooded
wooded

Ŏ͞OD′en
wooden

Ŏ͞OD′i
goody
goody-goody
woody

Ŏ͞OD′ing
gooding
hooding
pudding

Ŏ͞OD′ish
goodish

Ŏ͞OD′li
goodly

Ŏ͞OD′man
goodman
hoodman
woodman

Ŏ͞OD′nes
goodness

Ŏ͞OG′ur
sugar

Ŏ͞OK′ed
crooked
(see Ŏ͞OK +
ed)

Ŏ͞OK′i
bookie
cooky
hookey

hooky
rooky

Ŏ͞OK′ing
booking
brooking
cooking
crooking
hooking
ill-looking
looking
over-looking
rooking
unhooking
well-looking

Ŏ͞OK′let
booklet
brooklet

Ŏ͞OK′up
hook-up

Ŏ͞OK′ur
cooker
hooker
looker
overlooker
stooker

Ŏ͞OL′bul
bulbul

Ŏ͞OL′en
woollen

Ŏ͞OL′et
bullet
pullet

Ŏ͞OL′i
bully
fully
pulley
woolly

Ŏ͞OL′id
bullied, etc.

Ŏ͞OL′ing
bulling
pulling

Ŏ͞OL′ish
bullish
fullish

Ŏ͞OL′man
Pullman
Woolman

Ŏ͞OL′nes
fullness

Ŏ͞OL′ur
buller
fuller
puller
wire-puller

Ŏ͞OM′an
woman

Ŏ͞O′si
pussy

Ŏ͞OT′ed
footed
nimble-footed

Ŏ͞OT′ing
footing
putting

Ŏ͞OT′ur
footer
putter

ō′pa
Europa

ō′pal, ō′p′l
Adrianople
Bhopal
Constantinople
nopal
opal

ō′paz
topaz

ō′pen
open

ŌP′est
copest
elopest
gropest
hopest
interlopest
mopest
ropest
soapest

ŎP′est
choppest
droppest
hoppest
loppest
moppest

overtoppest	mopy	hygroscopic	stoping
poppest	ropy	isotropic	toping
proppest	slopy	kaleidoscopic	
shoppest	soapy	laryngoscopic	**ŎP'ing**
stoppest		metopic	bedropping
toppest	**ŎP'ī**	metoscopic	chopping
	Pop-eye	microscopic	clip-clopping
ŎP'et		misanthropic	copping
moppet	**ŎP'ĭ**	myopic	cropping
poppet	choppy	necroscopic	dropping
	copy	pantascopic	eavesdropping
ŎP'eth	croppy	periscopic	flopping
copeth	droppy	philanthropic	hopping
elopeth	floppy	presbyopic	lopping
gropeth	hoppy	psilanthropic	mopping
hopeth	loppy	spectroscopic	overtopping
interlopeth	moppy	stereoscopic	plopping
mopeth	poppy	stethoscopic	popping
ropeth	shoppy	telescopic	propping
soapeth	sloppy	theanthropic	shopping
	soppy	theophilan-	slopping
ŎP'eth		thropic	sopping
choppeth	**ŎP'ij**	topic	stopping
droppeth	proppage	tropic	stropping
hoppeth	stoppage		swapping
loppeth		**ŎP'iks**	topping
moppeth	**ŎP'ik**	topics	Wapping
poppeth	acopic	tropics	whopping
proppeth	allotropic		
shoppeth	anthropic	**ŎP'ing**	**ŎP'ish**
stoppeth	canopic	coping	mopish
toppeth	Cyclopic	doping	popish
	dichroscopic	eloping	
ŎP'ful	eletroscopic	groping	**ŎP'ish**
hopeful	Ethiopic	hoping	foppish
unhopeful	galvanoscopic	interloping	shoppish
	geotropic	loping	
ŎP'hed	helioscopic	moping	**ŎP"l**
hophead	heliotropic	roping	estoppel
	horoscopic	sloping	hopple
ŎP'i	hydroscopic	soaping	popple
dopey			

āle, câre, ădd, ärm, ȧsk: mē, hẹre, ĕnd; īce, ĭll;

stopple	ŎP′tik	plopper	Laura
topple	autoptic	popper	Maura
ŎP′les	Coptic	proper	**ŎR′ā**
	optic	propper	
hopeless	synoptic	shopper	foray
popeless		sopper	
soapless	**ŎP′trik**	stopper	**ŎR′ă**
ŎP′ling	catadioptric	swapper	Andorra
	catoptric	tiptopper	Gomorrah
fopling	dioptric	topper	
toppling		whopper	**Ō′raks**
	ŎP′ur		borax
ŎP′ment	coper	**Ō′pus**	corax
elopement	doper	Canopus	storax
Ō′pô	eloper	lagopous	thorax
	groper	Lagopus	
pawpaw	interloper	opus	**Ō′ral**
Ō′pok	moper		auroral
	roper	**Ō′ra**	chloral
slowpoke	sloper	Angora	choral
ŎP′shun	soaper	aurora	floral
	toper	Cora	horal
adoption		Dora	oral
option	**ŎP′ur**	dumb Dora	sororal
ŎP′si	pauper	Eldora	thoral
	scauper	Endora	trifloral
copsy		flora	
dropsy	**ŎP′ur**	Floradora	**ŎR′al**
Mopsy	chopper	Leonora	aural
Topsy	clodhopper	Marmora	binaural
ŎP′sis	copper	Masora	(cf. laurel)
ampelopsis	cropper	Nora	**ŎR′al**
lycopsis	dropper	Pandora	
synopsis	eaves-dropper	passiflora	coral
thanatopsis	finale-hopper	signora	immoral
	grasshopper	Theodora	moral
ŎP′stur	hopper	Torah	quarrel
dopester	improper		sorrel
	lopper	**ŎR′a**	(cf. laurel)
ŎP′ted	mopper	aura	**ŎR′anj**
adopted	overtopper	Chamæsaura	orange
co-opted			

ŌR'ant
soarant
vorant

Ō'rat
chlorate
deflorate
perchlorate

ŌR'at
inaurate
instaurate

ŌR'bi
corbie
orby

ŌR'bid
morbid

ŌR'bing
absorbing
orbing
resorbing

ŌR'b'l
corbel
warble

ŌR'blur
warbler

**ŌR'chard, ŌR'-
churd**
orchard
tortured

ŌR'chur
scorcher
torcher

ŌR'dan
Jordan
(cf. ŌR'don)

ŌR'dans
accordance
concordance
discordance

ŌR'dant
accordant
concordant
disaccordant
discordant
inaccordant
mordant

ŌR'ded
afforded
boarded
forded
hoarded
sworded
unforded
unhoarded
uphoarded

ŌR'ded
accorded
awarded
belorded
chorded
corded
lorded
recorded
rewarded
swarded
unlorded
unrecorded
unrewarded
warded
(cf. sordid)

ŌR'den
warden
way-warden

ŌR'dest
boardest
fordest
hoardest

ŌR'dest
accordest
awardest
belordest
lordest
recordest
rewardest
wardest

ŌR'deth
boardeth
fordeth
hoardeth

ŌR'deth
accordeth
awardeth
belordeth
cordeth
lordeth
recordeth
rewardeth
wardeth

ŌRD'ful
discordful
rewardful

ŌR'did
sordid
(cf. accorded,
etc.)

ŌR'dij
boardage
bordage

ŌR'dij
cordage

ŌR'ding
affording
boarding
fording
hoarding
unhoarding
uphoarding
weather-board-
ing

ŌR'ding
according
awarding
belording
cording
lording
recording
rewarding
unrecording
unrewarding
warding

ŌRD'li
lordly
unlordly

ŌR'don
cordon
Gordon

ŌRD'ship
lordship
wardship

ŌR'dur
boarder
forder
hoarder

āle, câre, ădd, ärm, åsk; mē, hęre, ĕnd; īce, ĭll;

parlor-
  boarder

ÕR'dur

accorder
awarder
border
corder
disorder
emborder
money-order
order
recorder
reorder
rewarder
unorder
warder

ÕR'durd

bordered
disordered
ordered
reordered
well-ordered

ÕRDZ'man

swordsman

ÕR'ed

forehead

ÕR'el, ÕR'el

laurel
(cf. ÕR'al,
  ÕR'al)

ÕR'en, ÕR'an

sporran
warren

ÕR'ens

abhorrence

Lawrence
St. Lawrence

ÕR'ens

Dorrance
Florence
(cf. torrents,
  etc.)

ÕR'ent, ÕR'ant

death-warrant
horrent
torrent
warrant
(cf. abhôrrent)

ÕR'est

adorest
borest
deplorest
encorest
explorest
floorest
gorest
hoarest
ignorest
implorest
outsoarest
porest
pourest
restorest
roarest
scorest
snorest
soarest
sorest
storest

ÕR'est

abhorrest
warrest

ÕR'est

afforest
disafforest
enforest
forest

ÕR'eth

adoreth
boreth
deploreth
encoreth
exploreth
flooreth
goreth
ignoreth
imploreth
outsoareth
poreth
poureth
restoreth
roareth
scoreth
snoreth
soareth
storeth

ÕR'eth

abhorreth
warreth

ÕR'fan

orphan

ÕR'fik

allomorphic
anthropo-
  morphic
automorphic
dimorphic
endomorphic
heteromorphic

ichthyomor-
  phic
idiomorphic
isomorphic
metamorphic
morphic
ophiomorphic
Orphic
pantamorphic
polymorphic
protomorphic
pseudomor-
  phic
theormorphic
trimorphic
zoomorphic

ÕR'fing

dwarfing
wharfing

ÕR'fist

anthropomor-
  phist
metamorphist
wharfist

ÕR'fit

forfeit

ÕR'fizm

allomorphism
amorphism
anamorphism
anthropomor-
  phism
automorphism
dimorphism
isodimorphism
isomeromor-
  phism

õld, ôr, õdd, oil, fŏŏt, out; ūse, ûrn, ŭp; THis, thin

isomorphism
isotrimor-
  phism
metamorphism
monomor-
  phism
pleomorphism
polymorphism
trimorphism
zoomorphism

ŎR'fūs

Morpheus
Orpheus

ŎR'fŭs

amorphous
anthropomor-
  phous
dimorphous
isodimor-
  phous
isomorphous
isotrimorphous
ophiomorphous
paramor-
  phous
polymor-
  phous
trimorphous

ŎR'gan

barrel-organ
Dorgan
Morgan
morgen
organ

ŎR'hand

aforehand
beforehand
forehand

ŎR'hous

storehouse
whorehouse

Ō'ri

abbreviatory
abjuratory
absolutory
acceleratory
acclamatory
accusatory
additory
adhortatory
adjuratory
admonitory
adulatory
a fortiori
allegory
amatory
ambagitory
ambulatory
amendatory
annotatory
annunciatory
a posteriori
appellatory
applicatory
appreciatory
approbatory
a priori
aratory
aspiratory
asseveratory
assimilatory
auditory
auxiliatory
basement-story
bibitory
cachinnatory
calculatory
calumniatory

castigatory
category
circulatory
commandatory
commemora-
  tory
commendatory
comminatory
communicatory
compellatory
compensatory
conciliatory
condemnatory
confabulatory
confirmatory
confiscatory
congratulatory
conservatory
consolatory
contributory
corroboratory
crematory
criminatory
damnatory
declamatory
declaratory
dedicatory
defamatory
delineatory
demonstratory
denunciatory
depilatory
depository
deprecatory
depreciatory
depredatory
derogatory
designatory
desultory
dictatory
dilatory

disapprobatory
discriminatory
dispensatory
dormitory
dory
edificatory
ejaculatory
emendatory
emulatory
exaggeratory
exclamatory
exculpatory
execratory
executory
exhortatory
expiatory
expiratory
explanatory
expostulatory
expurgatory
extenuatory
exterminatory
extirpatory
feudatory
flory
frigeratory
funambulatory
gesticulatory
gladiatory
glory
gory
gradatory
grallatory
gratulatory
gustatory
gyratory
habilatory
hallucinatory
hoary
hortatory
hunky-dory

imperatory	osculatory	restoratory	**ŎR'i**
imprecatory	pacificatory	retaliatory	Laurie
improvisatory	palliatory	retardatory	Maury
incantatory	peremptory	retributory	
incriminatory	perfumatory	reverberatory	**ŎR'i**
incubatory	perspiratory	revocatory	Corrie
inculpatory	piscatory	rogatory	Florrie
indicatory	plauditory	rotatory	lorry
inflammatory	postulatory	sacrificatory	quarry
initiatory	potatory	saltatory	sorry
inspiratory	predatory	salutatory	(cf. ÄR'i)
interlocutory	predicatory	sanatory	
interrogatory	prefatory	sanitory	**ŎR'id**
inventory	premonitory	shory	gloried
investigatory	preparatory	sibilatory	storied
invitatory	probatory	signatory	
invocatory	procrastinatory	significatory	**ŎR'id**
jaculatory	procuratory	simulatory	florid
judicatory	profanatory	snory	horrid
laboratory	prohibitory	speculatory	torrid
laudatory	promissory	sternutatory	
libatory	promontory	stillatory	**ŎR'ij**
liberatory	pronunciatory	story	shorage
lory	propitiatory	stridulatory	storage
Maggiore	punitory	sublimatory	
mandatory	purgatory	sudatory	**ŎR'ij**
masticatory	purificatory	supplicatory	borage
migratory	recommenda-	terminatory	forage
monitory	tory	territory	
narratory	recriminatory	tory	**Ō'rik**
natatory	reformatory	transitory	chloric
negatory	refrigeratory	transpiratory	choric
negotiatory	refutatory	undulatory	euchloric
nugatory	regeneratory	usurpatory	hydrochloric
oary	remuneratory	vacillatory	perchloric
objurgatory	repertory	vain-glory	roric
obligatory	repository	vehiculatory	
observatory	reprobatory	vibratory	**ŎR'ik**
offertory	reptatory	vindicatory	allegoric
oratory	requisitory	vomitory	amphigoric
oscillatory	respiratory	whory	amphoric

armoric
caloric
camphoric
Doric
elydoric
historic
lithophosphoric
metaphoric
meteoric
paregoric
peloric
phantasmagoric
phosphoric
pictoric
plethoric
prehistoric
prophoric
pyloric
Pythagoric
semaphoric
sophomoric
theoric
zoophoric
zoosporic

Ō'rin
florin

ŌR'ing
adoring
boring
choring
deploring
encoring
exploring
flooring
goring
ignoring
imploring
Loring
outsoaring

poring
pouring
restoring
roaring
scoring
shoring
snoring
soaring
storing
upsoaring

ŌR'ing
abhorring
warring

ŌR'is
Doris
loris

ŌR'is
Doris

ŌR'is
doch-an-dorris
Doris
Horace
loris
morris
orris

ŌR'ja
Borgia
Georgia

ŌR'jal,
ŌRD'yal
cordial

ŌR'ji
orgy

porgy
storge

ŌR'jing
forging

ŌR'jiz
Georges
George's
orgies, etc.

ŌR'jur
forger

ŌR'jus
gorgeous

ŌR'kas
Dorcas

ŌR'ki
corky
forky

ŌR'kid
orchid

ŌR'king
corking
Dorking
forking
uncorking

ŌR'les
coreless
oarless
oreless
shoreless

ŌR'li
schorly
warly

ŌR'ling
shoreling

ŌR'lok
forelock
oarlock

ŌR'lok
warlock

ŌR'mal
abnormal
anormal
cormal
formal
informal
normal
uniformal
(cf. cormel)

ŌR'man
doorman
floorman
foreman
longshoreman
shoreman

ŌR'man,
ŌR'mon
Gorman
Mormon
Norman
O'Gorman

ŌR'mans
conformance
dormance
performance

ŌR'mant
conformant
dormant
informant

ŌR'ment
adorement
deplorement
explorement
ignorement
implorement
restorement

ÔR'ment
torment

ÔR'mest
conformest
deformest
formest
informest
performest
reformest
stormest
swarmest
transformest
warmest

ÔR'meth
conformeth
deformeth
formeth
informeth
performeth
reformeth
stormeth
swarmeth
transformeth
warmeth

ÔR'mi
dormy
stormy
swarmy

ÔR'ming
bestorming

conforming
deforming
forming
informing
nonconforming
performing
reforming
storming
swarming
transforming
warming

ÔR'mist
conformist
nonconformist
reformist

ÔRM'les
formless
stormless

ÔRM'li
warmly
uniformly

ÔR'most
foremost
head-foremost

ÔR'mur
barn-stormer
conformer
deformer
dormer
foot-warmer
former
informer
performer
reformer
stormer
swarmer

transformer
warmer

ÔR'mus
abnormous
cormous
cormus
enormous
multiformous

ÔR'na
cromorna
Lorna
Norna

ÔR'nat
ornate

ŌR'nes
soreness

ÔR'nest
adornest
bescornest
forewarnest
scornest
subornest
warnest

ÔR'net
cornet
hornet

ÔR'neth
adorneth
bescorneth
forewarneth
scorneth
suborneth
warneth

ŌRN'ful
mournful

ŌRN'ful
scornful

ÔR'ni
corny
Hornie
horny
thorny

ŌR'ning
mourning

ÔR'ning
adorning
bescorning
dehorning
dishorning
forewarning
good-morning
horning
morning
scorning
suborning
yester-morning
warning

ÔR'nis
Aepyornis
cornice
Dinornis
Gastornis
Heliornis
Ichthyornis

ÔR'nish
Cornish
hornish

ÔRN'les
hornless

scornless
thornless

ŌRN'ment
adornment

ŌR'nun
forenoon

ŌR'nur
mourner

ŌR'nur
adorner
bescorner
chimney-corner
corner
forewarner
horner
scorner
suborner
warner

Ō'ro
Moro
toro

ŏR'o
amorrow
borrow
good-morrow
morrow
sorrow
to-morrow

ŏR'od
borrowed
sorrowed
unsorrowed

ŏR'old
Thorold
(cf. quarrelled)

ŌR'or
horror

ŌR'pid
torpid

ŌR'por
torpor

ŌR'sal
dextrorsal
dorsal
dorsel
morsel
torsel

ŌR'sen
coarsen
hoarsen

ŌR'sest
coarsest
coursest
discoursest
divorcest
enforcest
forcest
hoarsest
reinforcest

ŌR'sest
endorsest, etc.

ŌR'seth
courseth
discourseth
divorceth
enforceth
forceth
reinforceth

ŌR'seth
endorseth, etc.

ŌRS'ful
forceful
resourceful

ŌRS'ful
remorseful

ŌR'shun
apportion
disproportion
portion
proportion

ŌR'shun
abortion
consortion
contortion
detortion
distortion
extorsion
intorsion
retortion
torsion

ŌR'shund
apportioned
disproportioned
portioned
proportioned
unportioned

ŌR'si
gorsy
horsy

ŌR'sing
coursing
discoursing
divorcing
enforcing
forcing
reinforcing

ŌR'siv
discoursive
divorcive
enforcive

ŌRS'les
forceless
resourceless
sourceless

ŌRS'les
horseless
remorseless

ŌRS'man
horseman
lighthorseman
Norseman

ŌRS'ment
deforcement
divorcement
enforcement
forcement
reinforcement

ŌRS'ment
endorsement

ŌRS'nes
coarseness
hoarseness

ŌR'som
foursome

ŌR'son
Orson

ŌR'song
warsong

āle, câre, ădd, ärm, åsk; mē, hĕre, ĕnd; īce, ĭll;

ŌR'sur	ŌR'ted	ŌR'test	ŌRT'gid
coarser	aborted	*assortest*	court-guide
courser	assorted	*consortest*	port-guide
discourser	consorted	*contortest*	
divorcer	contorted	*detortest*	ŌR'thi
enforcer	detorted	*distortest*	
forcer	distorted	*escortest*	swarthy
hoarser	escorted	*exhortest*	
reinforcer	exhorted	*extortest*	ŌR'ti
	extorted	*resortest*	forty
ŌR'sur	resorted	*retortest*	pianoforte
endorser	retorted	shortest	snorty
	snorted	*snortest*	sortie
ŌR'tal	sorted	*sortest*	*swarty*
portal	thwarted	*swartest*	warty
transportal	unsorted	*thwartest*	
			ŌR'tij
ŌR'tal		ŌR'teth	shortage
aortal	ŌR'teks	*courteth*	
immortal	cortex	*disporteth*	ŌR'tim
mortal	vortex	*exporteth*	aforetime
(cf. ŌRT"l)		*importeth*	beforetime
	ŌR'tem	*reporteth*	
ŌR'tans	post-mortem	*sporteth*	ŌR'ting
supportance		*supporteth*	courting
transportance	ŌR'ten	*transporteth*	deporting
	shorten		disporting
ŌR'tans		ŌR'teth	exporting
importance	ŌR'tent	*assorteth*	importing
	portent	*consorteth*	reporting
ŌR'tant		*contorteth*	sporting
important	ŌR'test	*detorteth*	supporting
	courtest	*distorteth*	transporting
ŌR'ted	*disportest*	*escorteth*	
courted	*exportest*	*exhorteth*	ŌR'ting
disported	*importest*	*extorteth*	aborting
exported	*reportest*	*resorteth*	assorting
imported	*sportest*	*retorteth*	consorting
reported	*supportest*	*snorteth*	contorting
sported	*transportest*	*sorteth*	detorting
supported		*thwarteth*	distorting
transported			escorting

exhorting
extorting
resorting
retorting
snorting
sorting
thwarting

ŌR'tiv

sportive
transportive

ŌR'tiv

abortive
contortive
distortive
ortive
retortive
tortive

ŌRT"l

chortle
whortle
(cf. ŌR'tal)

ŌRT'land

Courtland
Portland

ŌRT'li

courtly
portly
uncourtly

ŌRT'li

shortly

ŌRT'ment

comportment
deportment

disportment
transportment

ŌRT'ment

assortment

ŌRT'nes

swartness
thwartness

ŌRT'nit

fortnight

ŌR'ton

Horton
Morton
Norton

ŌR'trat

portrait

ŌR'tres

fortress

ŌRT'ship

courtship

ŌRTS'man

sportsman

ŌR'tun

befortune
enfortune
fortune
importune
misfortune

ŌR'tur

courter
disporter
exporter
importer

porter
reporter
sporter
supporter
transporter

ŌR'tūr

torture

ŌR'tūr

assorter
consorter
contorter
detorter
distorter
escorter
exhorter
extorter
mortar
quarter
resorter
retorter
shorter
snorter
sorter
thwarter
weather-
   quarter
woolsorter

**ŌR'turd,
ŌR'chard**

orchard
tortured

ŌR'turz

winter-quarters
assorters, etc.

ŌRT'wav

short-wave

Ō'rum

decorum
forum
indecorum
jorum
quorum
variorum
cf. ad valorem

ŌR'ur

adorer
borer
corer
decorer
deplorer
encorer
explorer
floorer
gorer
ignorer
implorer
outpourer
outsoarer
porer
pourer
restorer
roarer
scorer
snorer
soarer
sorer
storer

Ō'rus

canorous
chorus
decorous
Horus
imporous
indecorous
porous

pylorus
sonorous
torous
torus

ŎR'us

brontosaurus
dolichosaurus
hadrosaurus
ichthyosaurus
megalosaurus
mososaurus
nanosaurus
pleiosaurus
plesiosaurus
protosaurus
regnosaurus
Taurus
teleosaurus
thesaurus
tyranosaurus

ŌR'ward

foreward
shoreward

ŎR'ward

forward
henceforward
norward
straightforward
thenceforward

ŎR'worn

war-worn

ŌRZ'man

oarsman

Ō'sa

amorosa

Formosa
mimosa

ŎS'chun

exhaustion

ŌS'est

closest, etc.
grossest
dosest, etc.

ŎS'est

crossest
embossest
glossest
tossest

ŎS'et

faucet

ŎS'et

bosset
cosset
posset
sack-posset

ŎS'eth

crosseth
embosseth
glosseth
tosseth

Ō'shal

antisocial
intersocial
social

ŎSH'i

boshy
sloshy
squashy

swashy
toshy
washy
wishy-washy

ŎSH'ing

sloshing
squashing
swashing
washing

ŌSH'ur

gaucher
kosher

ŌSH'ur

cosher
josher
squasher
swasher
washer

Ō'shun

Bœotian
commotion
devotion
emotion
groschen
indevotion
locomotion
lotion
motion
nicotian
notion
ocean
potion
prenotion
promotion
remotion
self-devotion

ŌSH'un

caution
incaution
precaution

ŌSH'us

atrocious
ferocious
nepotious
precocious

ŌSH'us

cautious
incautious
precautious

ŎS'i

saucy

ŎS'i

bossy
drossy
Flossie
flossy
glossy
mossy
posse
tossy

ŎS'ij

sausage

ŎS'ik

fossick
glossic

ŎS'il

docile
indocile

ŎS'il

docile

dossil
fossil
(see ŎS"l)

ŎS'ing
dosing
engrossing

ŎS'ing
bossing
crossing
dossing
embossing
glossing
railway-
  crossing
tossing

ŎS'ip
gossip

Ō'sis
anadiplosis
anamorphosis
ankylosis
apotheosis
carcinosis
chlorosis
cirrhosis
diagnosis
enantiosis
endosmosis
epanadiplosis
epanorthosis
exosmosis
geognosis
heliosis
heterosis
hypnosis
hypotyposis
ichthyosis

meiosis
metasomatosis
metem-
  psychosis
metemptosis
metensomatosis
morosis
morphosis
narcosis
necrosis
neurosis
osmosis
proemptosis
prognosis
psychosis
ptosis
pyrosis
sarcosis
scirrhosis
sorosis
tuberculosis
zygosis
zymosis

ŎS'is
proboscis

ŎS'iv
corrosive
erosive
explosive
inexplosive

ŎS'kar
Oscar

ŎS'ki
bosky

ŎS"l
apostle

colossal
dosel
dossil
fossil
hypoglossal
jostle
throstle
tossel
wassail

ŎS'lur
hostler
jostler
Rossler

ŎS'li
crossly

ŎS'nes
closeness
grossness
jocoseness
moroseness
verboseness

Ō'so
amoroso
arioso
doloroso
gracioso
so-so
virtuoso

ŎS'om
blossom
odontoglossum
opossum
orangeblossom
possum

ŎS'on
Dawson

Lawson
Rawson

ŎS'pel
gospel

ŎS'pish
waspish

ŎS'pur
prosper

ŎS'tal
coastal
postal

ŎS'tal
costal
infracostal
intercostal
Pentecostal
supra-costal

ŎS'tat
apostate
laticostate
quadricostate

ŎS'ted
boasted
coasted
posted
roasted
toasted
unposted

ŎS'ted
exhausted

ŎS'ted
accosted
frosted

ŎS'tel, ŎS"l	ŎS'tik	ŎST'li	coaster
hostel	acrostic	costly	four-poster
	agnostic		poster
ŎS'ten	diagnostic	ŎST'man	roaster
Austen	*eteostic*	postman	throwster
	geognostic		toaster
ŎS'tes	gnostic	ŎST'mark	
hostess	paracrostic	postmark	ŎS'tur
	pentacostic		auster
ŎS'test	prognostic	ŎS'ton	exhauster
boastest		Boston	
coastest	ŎS'til		ŎS'tūr
postest	hostile	Ŏ'storm	imposture
roastest		snow-storm	posture
toastest	ŎS'tin		
	Austin	ŎS'tral	ŎS'tŭr
ŎS'teth		austral	accoster
boasteth	ŎS'ting	claustral	coster
coasteth	boasting		foster
posteth	coasting	ŎS'tral, ŎS'trel	Gloucester
roasteth	posting	costrel	imposter
toasteth	roasting	lamellirostral	Paternoster
	toasting	longirostral	pentecoster
ŎST'hous		rostral	roster
oasthouse	ŎS'ting	(cf. nostril)	
post-house	exhausting		ŎS'turn
		ŎS'trat	postern
ŎS'ti	ŎS'ting	prostrate	
frosty	accosting	rostrate	ŎS'tus
	costing		Faustus
ŎS'tij	frosting	ŎS'trich	
postage		ostrich	ŎS'ur
	ŎS'tiv		closer
ŎS'tij	exhaustive	ŎS'trum	doser
hostage	inexhaustive	nostrum	engrosser
		rostrum	grocer
ŎS'tik	ŎS'tiv		grosser
catacaustic	costive	ŎS'tum	jocoser
caustic		costume	moroser
diacaustic	ŎST'li		
encaustic	ghostly	ŎS'tur	ŎS'ur
	mostly	boaster	Chaucer

Naw sir
saucer

ŎS'ur
bosser
crosser
dosser
embosser
glosser
josser
tosser

ŎS'us
colossus
molossus

Ō'ta
Dakota
flota
iota
Minnesota
quota
rota

ŌT'al
anecdotal
antidotal
dotal
extradotal
notal
rotal
sacerdotal
sclerotal
teetotal
total

ŌT'ant, ŌT'ent
flotant
potent
prepotent

ŌT'at
denotate
notate
rotate

ŎT'ash
potash

ŌT'ed
bloated
boated
coated
demoted
denoted
devoted
doted
floated
gloated
misquoted
moated
noted
parti-coated
petticoated
promoted
quoted
refloated
self-devoted
throated
unnoted
voted

ŎT'ed
allotted
besotted
bespotted
blood-bespotted
blotted
cheviotted
clotted
dotted
garotted

jotted
knotted
lotted
plotted
potted
rotted
shotted
slotted
sotted
spotted
squatted
totted
trotted
unblotted
underplotted
unknotted
unspotted
wainscotted
(cf. carotid
    and parotid)

ŌT'en
oaten

ŎT'en, ŎT'on
begotten
cotton
first-begotten
forgotten
gotten
hard-gotten
ill-gotten
misbegotten
misgotten
rotten
unbegotten
unforgotten
ungotten

ŌT'est
demotest

denotest
devotest
dotest
floatest
gloatest
misquotest
notest
promotest
quotest
votest

ŎT'est
clottest, etc.

ŌT'eth
demoteth
denoteth
devoteth
doteth
floateth
gloateth
noteth
misquoteth
promoteth
quoteth
voteth

ŎT'eth
clotteth, etc.

ŎT'ful
thoughtful

Ŏth'a
quotha

Ōth'al
betrothal

Ōth'am
Gotham
Jotham

ŎTH′am
Gotham

ŎTH′est
clothest
loathest

ŎTH′eth
clotheth
loatheth

ŌTH′ful
loathful

Ŏth′ful
slothful

Ŏth′ful
wrathful

Ŏth′i
frothy
mothy

Ŏth′ik
Gothic
Mœso-gothic
Ostrogothic
Visigothic

ŌTH′ing
clothing
loathing

Ŏth′ment
betrothment

ŌT′hook
boathook
coathook

Ŏ′thorn
Cawthorn
hawthorn

ŌTH′som
loathsome

Ŏth′ur
author

ŎTH′ur
bother
fother
pother
(cf. father,
   rather)

ŌT′i
bloaty
coyote
dhoty
Doty
Doughty
floaty
goaty
throaty

ŌT′i
haughty
naughty

ŎT′i
clotty
dotty
knotty
spotty
totty

ŎT′id
carotid

parotid
(cf. ŎT+ed)

ŌT′ij
anecdotage
dotage
floatage
flotage

ŎT′ij
cottage
pottage
wattage

ŎT′ik
otic

ŎT′ik
aeronautic
argonautic
nautic

ŎT′ik
acrotic
agrypnotic
anaptotic
anecdotic
ankylotic
anti-patriotic
aptotic
aquatic
carotic
chaotic
chlorotic
cirrhotic
culottic
demotic
despotic
endosmotic
epiglottic
epizootic

erotic
escharotic
exotic
glottic
henotic
hidrotic
hypnotic
idiotic
macrobiotic
narcotic
nepotic
neurotic
Nilotic
osmotic
otic
patriotic
pyrotic
quixotic
san-culottic
sarcotic
sclerotic
semeiotic
zootic
zymotic

ŌT′ing
bloating
boating
coating
demoting
denoting
devoting
doting
floating
gloating
misquoting
noting
promoting
quoting
throating
voting

ōld, ôr, ŏdd, oil, fŏŏt, out; ūse, ûrn, ŭp; THis, thin

ŎT'ing	ŎT'iv	ŎT'li	otto
allotting	emotive	hotly	ridotto
besotting	locomotive	motley	risotto
blotting	motive		(cf. staccato)
clotting	promotive	ŎT'ling	
dotting	votive	bottling, etc.	ŎT'om
garotting			bottom
jotting	ŎT'kinz	ŎT'man	
knotting	Otkins	boatman	Ō'ton
plotting	Watkins		Croton
potting		ŎT'man	proton
rotting	ŎT''l	Cotman	(cf. oaten)
sotting	bottle	Ottman	
spotting	dottle		Ó'ton
squatting	glottal	ŎT'ment	Lawton
totting	mottle	demotement	
trotting	pottle	denotement	ŎT'on
underplotting	throttle	devotement	cotton
unknotting	tottle		Groton
yatching	twattle	ŎT'ment	(see ŎT'en)
	wattle	allotment	
ŎT'is		besotment	ŎT'rel
epiglottis	ŎT'les		Cottrell
glottis	thoughtless	ŎT'nes	dottrel
		hotness	
ŎT'ish		whatness	ŎT'si
dotish	ŎT'les		hotsy-totsy
goatish	blotless	Ō'to	
	clotless	De Soto	ŎTS'man
ŎT'ish	cotless	divoto	Scotsman
Scottish	dotless	ex voto	yachtsman
sottish	jotless	fagotto	
	knotless	in toto	ŎT'son
ŎT'ist	lotless	Kioto	Watson
anecdotist	potless	photo	
noticed	rotless		Ō'tum
Scotist	sotless	ŎT'o	quotum
unnoticed	spotless	blotto	tee-totum
	totless	grotto	
ŎT'ist	trotless	lotto	ŎT'um
sans-culottist		motto	autumn

ŌT'ur

bloater
boater
demoter
denoter
devoter
doter
fagot-voter
floater
gloater
locomotor
magnetomotor
motor
noter
promoter
quoter
rotomotor
rotor
scoter
toter
vaso-motor
voter

ŌT'ur

backwater
daughter
fire-water
fizz-water
giggle-water
milk-and-
   water
slaughter
soda-water
water

ŎT'ur

blotter
bogtrotter
clotter
complotter
cotter

dotter
garotter
globe-trotter
hotter
jotter
knotter
ottar
otter
plotter
potter
rotter
spotter
squatter
totter
trotter
underplotter
unknotter
yachter

Ō'tus

Gymnotus
lotus
macrotous

OU'al

avowal
disavowal
(cf. OU"el)

OU'an

gowan
McGowan
rowan
rowen

OU'ans

allowance
avowance
disallowance
disavowance

OU'ard

coward
Howard
(cf. OU'urd)

OUCH'est

avouchest, etc.

OUCH'eth

avoucheth, etc.

OUCH'ing

avouching
couching
crouching
grouching
pouching
slouching
vouching

OUCH'ur

avoucher
coucher
croucher
Goucher
groucher
poucher
sloucher
voucher

OU'da

howdah

OUD'ed

beclouded
clouded
crowded
enshrouded
overclouded
overcrowded
shrouded

unbeclouded
unclouded
unshrouded

OUD'est

becloudest
beshroudest
cloudest
crowdest
enshroudest
loudest
overcloudest
overcrowdest
proudest
shroudest

OUD'eth

becloudeth
beshroudeth
cloudeth
crowdeth
enshroudeth
overcloudeth
overcrowdeth
shroudeth

OUD'i

cloudy
crowdy
dowdy
Gowdy
howdie
howdy
pandowdy
proudy
rowdy
shroudy
uncloudy
(cf. summa
   cum laude)

OUD'ing
beclouding
beshrouding
clouding
crowding
enshrouding
overclouding
overcrowding
shrouding
unshrouding

OUD'ish
loudish
proudish

OUD'li
loudly
proudly

OUD'nes
loudness
proudness

OUD'ur
baking powder
clam chowder
bepowder
chowder
crowder
louder
powder
prouder
seidlitz-powder

OU'el
bowel
dowel
embowel
Howell
Powell
Prowell

rowel
towel
trowel
vowel
(cf. OU'al)

OU'es
prowess

OU'est
allowest
avowest
bowest
cowest
disallowest
endowest
ploughest
vowest

OU'et
Howett
Jowett

OU'eth
alloweth
avoweth
boweth
coweth
disalloweth
endoweth
plougheth
voweth

OU'i
Dowie
zowie

OU'ing
allowing
avowing
bowing

cowing
disallowing
endowing
ploughing
plowing
rowing
vowing

OUL'est
foulest
growlest
howlest
prowlest
scowlest

OUL'et
owlet

OUL'eth
growleth
howleth
prowleth
scowleth

OU'li
Cowley
Powley
Rowley

OUL'ing
fouling
fowling
growling
howling
prowling
scowling

OUL'ish
foulish
owlish

OUL'ur
fouler
fowler
growler
howler
prowler
scowler
yowler

OU'ment
avowment
endowment

OUN'ded
abounded
astounded
bounded
compounded
confounded
dumfounded
expounded
founded
grounded
hounded
impounded
mounded
pounded
propounded
rebounded
redounded
resounded
rounded
sounded
superabound-
ed
surrounded
unbounded
unfounded
ungrounded
unsounded

āle, câre, ădd, ärm, àsk; mē, hĕre, ĕnd; īce, ĭll;

well-founded
wounded

OUN'del
roundel

OUN'den
bounden

OUN'dest
aboundest
astoundest
boundest
compoundest
confoundest
expoundest
foundest
groundest
houndest
impoundest
poundest
profoundest
propoundest
reboundest
resoundest
roundest
soundest
superabound-
est
surroundest

OUN'deth
aboundeth
astoundeth
boundeth
compoundeth
confoundeth
dumfoundeth
expoundeth
foundeth
groundeth

houndeth
impoundeth
poundeth
propoundeth
reboundeth
redoundeth
resoundeth
roundeth
soundeth
surroundeth

OUN'dij
groundage
poundage
soundage

OUN'ding
abounding
astounding
big-sounding
bounding
compounding
confounding
dumfounding
expounding
founding
grounding
high-sounding
hounding
impounding
pounding
propounding
rebounding
redounding
resounding
rounding
sounding
superabound-
ing
surrounding

unbounding
wounding

OUND'les
boundless
groundless
soundless

OUND'li
profoundly
roundly
soundly
unsoundly

OUND'ling
foundling
groundling

OUND'nes
profoundness
roundness
soundness
unsoundness

OUN'drel
scoundrel

OUN'dri
foundry

OUN'dur
bounder
compounder
confounder
dumfounder
expounder
flounder
founder
four-pounder
impounder
iron-founder

pounder
profounder
propounder
rebounder
resounder
rounder
sounder
surrounder
type-founder

OUN'est
brownest
crownest
drownest
frownest

OUN'eth
browneth
crowneth
drowneth
frowneth

OUN'i
brownie
browny
downy
frowny
towny

OUN'ing
browning
clowning
crowning
discrowning
downing
drowning
frowning
gowning
intowning
uncrowning

OUN'ish	denouncement	*recountest*	counter
brownish	pronounce-	*remountest*	discounter
clownish	ment	*surmountest*	encounter
frownish	renouncement		mounter
		OUN'teth	recounter
OUN'jing	**OUN'sur**	*accounteth*	remounter
lounging	announcer	*amounteth*	reencounter
	bouncer	*counteth*	surmounter
OUN'les	denouncer	*discounteth*	
crownless	flouncer	*dismounteth*	**OUN'ur**
frownless	pouncer	*miscounteth*	browner
gownless	pronouncer	*mounteth*	crowner
	renouncer	*recounteth*	drowner
OUN'sest	trouncer	*remounteth*	frowner
announcest, etc.		*surmounteth*	
	OUN'ted		**OUN'ward**
OUN'seth	accounted	**OUN'ti**	downward
announceth, etc.	amounted	bounty	townward
	counted	county	
OUN'sez	discounted	mounty	**OUN'zman**
announces	dismounted	viscounty	gownsman
bounces	miscounted		townsman
denounces	mounted	**OUN'tin**	
flounces	recounted	catamountain	**Ō'ur**
ounces	remounted	fountain	bestower
pounces	surmounted	mountain	blower
pronounces	uncounted		flower
renounces	unmounted	**OUN'ting**	foregoer
trounces	unrecounted	accounting	foreknower
		amounting	foreshower
OUN'sing	**OUN'tes**	counting	glass-blower
announcing	countess	discounting	goer
bouncing		dismounting	glower
denouncing	**OUN'test**	miscounting	grower
flouncing	*accountest*	mounting	hoer
pouncing	*amountest*	recounting	knower
pronouncing	*countest*	remounting	lower
renouncing	*discountest*	surmounting	mower
trouncing	*dismountest*		outgoer
	miscountest	**OUN'tur**	overthrower
OUNS'ment	*mountest*	accounter	ower
announcement			

āle, câre, ădd, ārm, ȧsk; mē, hẹre, ĕnd; īce, ĭll;

rower
sewer
shower
slower
sower
stower
thrower
tower
undergoer
wine-grower

Ŏ'ur

cawer
clawer
drawer
gnawer
guffawer
"jawer"
overawer
pawer
rawer
sawer
tawer
wiredrawer
withdrawer

Ō'urd, Ō'ard

lowered
toward
untoward

OUR'est

bescourest
deflowerest
devourest
scourest
sourest

OUR'eth

bescoureth
deflowereth

devoureth
scoureth
soureth

OUR'i

avowry
cowrie
dowry
floury
houri
(cf. OU'ur-i)

OUR'ing

bescouring
deflowering
devouring
flouring
off-scouring
scouring
souring
(cf. OU'ur-
    ing)

OUR'li

hourly
sourly

OUR'nes

sourness

OUR'ur

deflowerer
devourer
scourer
sourer

OU'son

Dowson

OUT'ed

clouted

doubted
flouted
gouted
grouted
misdoubted
pouted
redoubted
routed
scouted
shouted
spouted
sprouted
undoubted

OUT'est

cloutest
devoutest
doubtest
floutest
poutest
scoutest
shoutest
spoutest
sproutest
stoutest

OUT'eth

clouteth
doubteth
flouteth
pouteth
scouteth
shouteth
spouteth
sprouteth

OUT'i

doughty
droughty
gouty
grouty

louty
moughty
pouty
snouty
touty

OUT'ing

beshouting
bespouting
besprouting
clouting
doubting
flouting
grouting
louting
outing
pouting
routing
scouting
shouting
spouting
sprouting
touting
undoubting

OUT'let

outlet
troutlet

OUT'li

devoutly
stoutly

OUT'nes

devoutness
stoutness

OUT'ur

devouter
doubter

down-and-
  outer
flouter
jowter
out-and-outer
pouter
router
scouter
shouter
spouter
sprouter
stouter
touter

OU'ur

allower
avower
beacon-tower
beflower
bower
Brower
candle-power
cauliflower
cower
deflower
dower
embower
empower
endower
enflower
flower
glower
horse-power
imbower
lower
overpower
overtower
passion-flower
plougher
plower
power

rower
shower
thunder-show-
  er
tower
vower
water-power
(cf. OUR)

OU'urd

unshowered
untowered
bowered, etc.
(cf. OU'ard)

OU'urz

Powers
avowers, etc.

OU'wou

bow-wow
pow-wow
wow-wow

OU'zal

arousal
carousal
espousal
housel
ousel
spousal
tousle

OU'zand

thousand

OUZ'est

arousest, etc.

OUZ'eth

arouseth, etc.

OUZ'ez

arouses
blouses
browses
carouses
espouses
houses
rouses
spouses

OUZ'i

bowsie
drowzy
frowzy
lousy
mousy

OUZ'ij

espousage
housage
spousage

OUZ'ing

arousing
blowzing
browzing
carousing
housing
rousing

OUZ'ur

arouser
browser
carouser
espouser
mouser
rouser
Towser
trouser

OUZ'urz

trousers
carousers, etc.

Ō'va

Jehovah

Ō'val

oval

ŎV'el

grovel
hovel
novel

ŌV'en

cloven
hoven
interwoven
inwoven
uncloven
woven

ŌV'i

anchovy
covy
grovy

ŌV'in

bovine
ovine

ŌV'ing

roving
shroving

ŌV'o

ab ovo
de novo

ŌV'ur

clover

āle, câre, ădd, ärm, åsk; mē, hĕre, ĕnd; īce, ĭll;

Dover	ŌZ'al	*imposest*	ŌZ'ez
drover	*desposal*	*inclosest*	Moses
flopover	disposal	*interposest*	roses, etc.
half-seas-over	interposal	*juxtaposest*	
moreover	opposal	*opposest*	ŌZ'ez
over	presupposal	*posest*	causes
plover	proposal	*presupposest*	clauses
pushover	reposal	*proposest*	gauzes
rover	rosal	*recomposest*	pauses
sea-rover	supposal	*reimposest*	vases
stover	transposal	*reposest*	
trover		*superimposest*	ŌZ'ga
walkover	ŌZ'bud	*supposest*	nosegay
	rosebud	*transposest*	
ŎV'urb			ŌZ'han
proverb	ŌZ'div	ŌZ'eth	ambrosian
	nose-dive	*closeth*	(cf. Ō'zi-an,
ŌV'urz		*composeth*	Ō'zi-on)
estovers	ŌZ'en	*decomposeth*	
drovers, etc.	chosen	*deposeth*	ŌZ'hun
	forechosen	*discloseth*	corrosion
Ō'ward	frozen	*discomposeth*	erosion
froward	*hosen*	*disposeth*	explosion
	Posen	*dozeth*	implosion
Ō'whar	*rosen*	*encloseth*	(cf. Ō'zi-an,
nowhere	squozen	*exposeth*	etc.)
		imposeth	
Ō'yez	ŎZ'enj	*incloseth*	Ō'zhur
oyez	lozenge	*intercloseth*	crosier
		interposeth	Dozier
Ō'yur	ŌZ'est	*juxtaposeth*	hosier
bowyer	*closest*	*opposeth*	osier
oyer	*composest*	*poseth*	
	decomposest	*presupposeth*	ŌZ'ĭ
Ô'yur	*deposest*	*proposeth*	cozy
lawyer	*disclosest*	*recomposeth*	dozy
sawyer	*discomposest*	*reimposeth*	nosy
topsawyer	*disposest*	*reposeth*	posy
	dozest	*superimposeth*	prosy
ŌZ'a	*enclosest*	*supposeth*	rosy
Rosa	*exposest*	*transposeth*	
Spinoza			

ōld, ôr, ŏdd, oil, fŏŏt, out; ūse, ûrn, ŭp; THis, thin

ŎZ'ĭ	prosing	ŎZ'mĭk	disposer
gauzy	recomposing	cosmic	dozer
causey	reposing	endosmic	encloser
	supposing	microcosmic	exposer
ŎZ'ĭd	transposing		forecloser
posied	unclosing	ŎZ'ō	glozer
rosied	unimposing	bozo	imposer
			incloser
ŎZ'ĭng	ŎZ'ĭng	ŎZ'ōn	interposer
closing	causing	ozone	juxtaposer
composing	pausing		opposer
decomposing		ŎZ'ūr	poser
deposing	ŎZ'ĭt	closure	predisposer
disclosing	closet	composure	presupposer
discomposing	deposit	disclosure	proposer
disposing	interposit	discomposure	roser
dozing	juxtaposit	disposure	reimposer
enclosing	posit	exposure	reposer
exposing	reposit	foreclosure	superimposer
imposing		inclosure	supposer
inclosing	ŎZ'ĭv	reposure	transposer
interposing	applausive		uncloser
juxtaposing	plausive	ŎZ'ŭr	
nosing	unapplausive	bulldozer	ŎZ'ur
opposing		closer	causer
posing	ŎZ''l	composer	hawser
predisposing	nozzle	deposer	pauser
presupposing	schnozzle	discloser	
proposing	sozzle		

āle, câre, ădd, ärm, ȧsk; mē, hẹre, ĕnd; īce, ĭll;

U

For a discussion of words included under the accented vowels following, see the beginning of U rhymes in Section I.

Ū′al
dual
eschewal
pursual
renewal
reviewal
subdual
(cf. Ū′el)

Ū′an
Chouan
duan
Peguan

Ū′ans
eschewance
pursuance
renewance

Ū′ant
pursuant
truant

Ū′ard
leeward
steward
(see Ū′urd)

Ū′ba
Cuba
juba
tuba

Ū′ben
Reuben

Steuben
(cf. Lubin)

ŪB′i
booby
looby
ruby

ŬB′i
bubby
chubby
cubby
fubby
grubby
hubby
nubby
rabi
rubby
scrubby
shrubby
stubby
tubby

ŬB′id
rubied

ŪB′ik
cherubic
cubic
pubic

ŬB′ing
cubing
tubing

ŬB′ing
blubbing
clubbing
drubbing
dubbing
grubbing
nubbing
rubbing
scrubbing
snubbing
stubbing
subbing
tubbing

ŬB′ish
clubbish
cubbish
grubbish
rubbish
tubbish

ŬB′it
cubit

ŬB′jekt
subject

Ū′b′l
ruble

ŬB″l
bubble
double
grubble
Hubbell

hubble-bubble
nubble
redouble
rubble
stubble
trouble

ŬB″ld
bubbled
doubled
redoubled
stubbled
troubled
untroubled

ŬB′lest
bubblest, etc.

ŬB′let
doublet

ŬB′leth
bubbleth, etc.

ŬB′li
bubbly
doubly
knubbly
nubbly
rubbly
stubbly

ŬB′lik
public
republic

ŬB′ling
bubbling
doubling
troubling

ŬB′lish
publish

ŬB′lur
bubbler
doubler
troubler

ŬB′lus
troublous

ŬB′orn
stubborn

ŬB′rik
lubric
rubric

ŬB′stak
grubstake

ŬB′stans
substance

ŪB′ur
goober
Huber
tuber

ŬB′ur
blubber
clubber
drubber
dubber
grubber
india-rubber

landlubber
lubber
money-grub-
    ber
rubber
scrubber
slubber
snubber
stubber
tubber
tub-drubber

ŬB′urd
blubbered
cupboard
Hubbard
mother hub-
    bard
rubbered

ŬB′urt
Hubert

ŬCH′es
archduchess
duchess
Dutchess

ŬCH′est
clutchest, etc.

ŬCH′eth
clutcheth, etc.

ŬCH′ez
clutches
crutches
hutches
retouches
scutches
smutches
touches

ŬCH′i
coochy
hoochy-coochy

ŬCH′i
archduchy
clutchy
duchy
smutchy
touchy

ŬCH′ing
clutching
retouching
scutching
smutching
touching

ŬCH′on
escutcheon

ŬCH′ur
retoucher
scutcher
smutcher
toucher

Ū′da
Barbuda
barracuda
Bermuda
Buddha
Ishkooda
Judah

Ū′dad
doodad

ŪD′al
feudal

paludal
udal

ŪD′ed
alluded
brooded
colluded
concluded
deluded
denuded
detruded
duded
eluded
excluded
extruded
exuded
illuded
included
interluded
intruded
obtruded
occluded
precluded
preluded
protruded
recluded
retruded
secluded
snooded
subtruded
transuded
undeluded

ŬD′ed
bestudded
blooded
budded
flooded
scudded
spudded
studded

thudded
(cf. muddied,
etc.)

ŬD'en

sudden

ŬD'ens

jurisprudence
prudence

ŬD'ent

concludent
imprudent
jurisprudent
occludent
prudent
student

ŬD'est

alludest
broodest
concludest
crudest
deludest
denudest
detrudest
eludest
excludest
extrudest
exudest
illudest
includest
intrudest
nudest
obtrudest
precludest
preludest
protrudest
recludest
retrudest

rudest
secludest
shrewdest
subtrudest

ŪD'eth

alludeth
broodeth
colludeth
concludeth
deludeth
denudeth
detrudeth
eludeth
excludeth
extrudeth
exudeth
illudeth
includeth
intrudeth
obtrudeth
occludeth
preludeth
protrudeth
retrudeth
recludeth
secludeth
subtrudeth
transudeth

ŪD'i

broody
moody
scudi

ŬD'i

bloody
buddy
cuddy
muddy
puddy

ruddy
studdy
study

ŬD'id

bloodied
muddied
ruddied
studied
unstudied
(cf. studded,
etc.)

ŬD'ing

abrooding
alluding
brooding
concluding
deluding
denuding
detruding
eluding
excluding
extruding
exuding
illuding
including
intruding
obtruding
occluding
precluding
preluding
protruding
recluding
retruding
secluding
snooding
subtruding
transuding

ŬD'ing

bestudding

budding
flooding
scudding
spudding
studding

ŪD'ish

prudish
rudish
shrewdish

ŬD'ith

Judith

ŪD''l

boodle
caboodle
canoodle
flapdoodle
kiyoodle
noodle
poodle
Yankee-doodle

ŬD''l

bemuddle
buddle
cuddle
fuddle
huddle
muddle
nuddle
puddle
ruddle
scuddle

ŬD'lest

bemuddlest, etc.

ŬD'leth

bemuddleth, etc.

ŬD'li

crudely
lewdly
nudely
rudely
shrewdly

ŬD'li

Dudley

ŬD'ling

bemuddling
cuddling
fuddling
huddling
muddling
puddling
scuddling

ŬD'lum

hoodlum

ŬD'lur

cuddler
fuddler
huddler
muddler
puddler

ŬD'nes

lewdness
nudeness
crudeness
rudeness
shrewdness

ŬD'ok

puddock
ruddock

ŪD'os

kudos

ŬD'son

Hudson
Judson

ŬD'ur

alluder
brooder
concluder
cruder
deluder
denuder
detruder
eluder
excluder
extruder
exuder
illuder
includer
intruder
obtruder
occluder
precluder
preluder
protruder
recluder
retruder
ruder
secluder
shrewder
subtruder
transuder
Tudor

ŬD'ur

dudder
flooder
mudder
pudder
rudder
scudder

shudder
udder

ŬD'zi

sudsy

Ū'e

cooee
(see Ū'i)

Ū'el

bejewel
crewel
cruel
duel
fuel
gruel
Hewell
jewel
newel
Reuel
Sewell
tewel
(cf. Ū'al)

Ū'es

Jewess

Ū'est

accruest
bedewest
beshrewest
bluest
brewest
chewest
cooest
doest
drewest
enduest
ensuest

eschewest
fewest
flewest
gluest
grewest
hallooest
hewest
imbrewest
imbuest
interviewest
knewest
mewest
newest
pursuest
renewest
reviewest
ruest
screwest
shampooest
shoest
shooest
spuest
stewest
strewest
subduest
suest
tattooest
threwest
truest
undoest
unscrewest
untruest
ungluest
viewest
withdrewest
wooest

Ū'et

cruet
suet

Ū′eth	*withdreweth*	ŬF′i	huffish
accrueth	*wooeth*	goofy	roughish
bedeweth		roofy	toughish
beshreweth	Ū′fa	spoofy	
breweth	chufa	woofy	ŬF″l
cheweth	stufa		bemuffle
cooeth	tufa	ŬF′i	buffle
doeth	Ufa	bluffy	double- shuffle
dreweth		buffy	duffel
endueth	Ū′feld	chuffy	muffle
ensueth	Bluefield	fluffy	ruffle
escheweth	Newfield	huffy	scuffle
glueth		pluffy	shuffle
greweth	ŬF′en	puffy	snuffle
hallooeth	roughen	sloughy	truffle
heweth	toughen	snuffy	unmuffle
imbreweth		stuffy	unruffle
imbueth	ŬF′est		
intervieweth	*bepuffest*	ŬF′in	ŬF″ld
kneweth	bluffest	muffin	bemuffled, etc.
meweth	*cuffest*	puffin	
pursueth	*gruffest*	ragamuffin	ŬF′lest
reneweth	*luffest*		*bemufflest*, etc.
revieweth	*muffest*	Ū′ing	
rueth	*puffest*	roofing	ŬF′leth
screweth	*rebuffest*	waterproofing	*bemuffleth*, etc.
shampooeth	roughest	woofing	
shoeth	*sloughest*		ŬF′li
shooeth	*snuffest*	ŬF′ing	bluffly
speweth	*stuffest*	bluffing	gruffly
steweth	toughest	cuffing	muffly
subdueth		fluffing	roughly
sueth	ŬF′et	huffing	ruffly
streweth	buffet	luffing	scuffly
tabooeth		puffing	sluffly
tattooeth	ŬF′eth	roughing	snuffly
threweth	*bluffeth*, etc.	sloughing	toughly
undoeth		stuffing	truffly
unglueth	ŬF′hous		
unscreweth	roughhouse	ŬF′ish	ŬF′ling
vieweth		gruffish	bemuffling

ōld, ôr, ŏdd, oil, fŏŏt, out; ūse, ûrn, ŭp; THis, thin

muffling
ruffling
scuffling
shuffling
snuffling
unmuffling
unruffling

ŬF′lur

muffler
ruffler
scuffler
shuffler
snuffler
unmuffler

ŬF′nes

bluffness
gruffness
roughness
toughness

ŬF′ted

tufted

ŬF′ti

mufti
tufty

ŬF′ur

aloofer
hoofer
roofer
spoofer

ŬF′ur

bluffer
buffer
cuffer
duffer
gruffer

huffer
luffer
puffer
rougher
snuffer
stuffer
suffer
tougher

Ŭ′fus

goofus
rufous
Rufus

ŬG′a

meshuggah

Ŭ′gar

cougar

ŬG′ard

sluggard

ŬG′ed

rugged
(see ŬG + ed)

ŬG′est

*drugges*t
huggest
juggest
luggest
muggest
pluggest
shruggest
sluggest
smuggest
snuggest
tuggest
(cf. druggist)

ŬG′et

drugget
nugget

ŬG′eth

druggeth
huggeth
juggeth
luggeth
muggeth
pluggeth
shruggeth
sluggeth
tuggeth

ŬG′hous

bughouse

ŬG′i

buggy
muggy
puggi
puggy
sluggy

ŬG′ij

luggage

ŬG′ing

drugging
hugging
jugging
lugging
mugging
plugging
shrugging
slugging
tugging

ŬG′ish

muggish

sluggish
smugish
snuggish

ŬG′ist

druggist

ŬG″l

bugle
febrifugal
frugal
fugal
infrugal
jugal
McDougall
vermifugal

ŬG′l

death-struggle
guggle
juggle
smuggle
snuggle
struggle

ŬG′lest

jugglest, etc.

ŬG′leth

juggleth, etc.

ŬG′li

guggly
juggly
plug-ugly
smugly
snuggly
struggly
ugly

ŬG′ling

guggling

juggling
smuggling
struggling

ŪG'lur
bugler
fugler

ŬG'lur
juggler
smuggler
snuggler
struggler

ŬG'nes
smugness
snugness

Ū'go
Hugo

ŬG'ur
drugger
hugger
hugger-
  mugger
lugger
mugger
plugger
rugger
shrugger
snugger
tugger

ŬG'wump
mugwump

Ū'i
bedewy
bluey
Bowie

buoy
chop suey
coo-ee
coue
dewy
fluey
gluey
Louis
screwy
thewy
viewy

Ū'īd
blue-eyed
true-eyed

Ū'ĭd
druid
fluid

Ū'ij
brewage
sewage

Ū'ik
catechuic
toluic

Ū'in
blue-ruin
bruin
ruin
sewen

Ū'ing
accruing
barbecuing
bedewing
bestrewing
blueing
brewing
canoeing

chewing
clewing
cooing
cueing
doing
enduing
ensuing
eschewing
eweing
gluing
hallooing
hewing
imbruing
imbuing
interviewing
mewing
mildewing
misconstruing
misdoing
mooing
outdoing
overdoing
poohpoohing
pursuing
renewing
reviewing
screwing
shampooing
shoeing
spewing
stewing
strewing
subduing
suing
tattooing
undoing
unscrewing
viewing
well-doing
wooing
wrong-doing

Ū'ingz
doings
misdoings, etc.

Ū'is
Lewis
Louis
(cf. Jewess)

Ū'ish
blueish
glueish
Jewish
newish
shrewish
truish

ŬJ'el
cudgel

ŬJ'est
begrudgest, etc.

ŬJ'et
budget

ŬJ'eth
begrudgeth, etc.

ŬJ'ez
adjudges
begrudges
budges
drudges
forejudges
fudges
grudges
judges
misjudges
nudges
prejudges

rejudges	drudger	**ŬK′est**	clucking
sludges	forejudger	*rebukest,* etc.	ducking
smudges	fudger		mucking
trudges	grudger	**ŬK′est**	plucking
	judger	*pluckest,* etc.	shucking
ŬJ′ĭ	misjudger		sucking
pudgy	nudger	**ŬK′et**	trucking
sludgy	prejudger	bucket	tucking
smudgy	rejudger	Luckett	
	sludger	Nantucket	**ŬK′ish**
ŬJ′ing	smudger	Pawtucket	buckish
adjudging	trudger	Puckett	muckish
begrudging		sucket	puckish
budging	**Ū′ka**	tucket	
drudging	bucca		**ŬK′′l**
forejudging	felucca	**ŬK′eth**	bruckle
fudging	festuca	*rebuketh,* etc.	buckle
grudging	fistuca		chuckle
judging	garookuh	**ŬK′eth**	honeysuckle
misjudging	palooka	*plucketh,* etc.	huckle
nudging	sambouka		knuckle
prejudging	yucca	**ŬK′ĭ**	muckle
rejudging		fluky	parbuckle
sludging	**Ū′kal**	snooky	suckle
smudging	archducal	spooky	truckle
trudging	ducal		unbuckle
ungrudging	noctilucal	**ŬK′ĭ**	
	nuchal	ducky	**ŬK′′ld**
ŬJ′ment	Pentateuchal	Kentucky	buckled
judgment		lucky	chuckled
	Ū′kan	mucky	knuckled
ŬJ′on	antelucan	plucky	suckled
bludgeon	toucan	unlucky	truckled
curmudgeon			unbuckled
dudgeon	**Ū′kas**	**ŬK′ing**	(cf. cuckold)
gudgeon	ukase	puking	
		rebuking	**ŬK′les**
ŬJ′ur	**ŬK′ăs**		luckless
adjudger	Clucas	**ŬK′ing**	
begrudger	Lucas	bucking	**ŬK′lest**
budger		chucking	*bucklest,* etc.

āle,　câre,　ădd,　ärm,　åsk:　mē,　hĕre,　ĕnd;　īce,　ĭll;

ŬK'leth
buckleth, etc.

ŬK'ling
buckling
chuckling
duckling
knuckling
suckling
truckling
unbuckling

ŬK'lur
buckler
chuckler
knuckler
swash-buckler
truckler

Ū'ko
Duco
Pernambuco

ŬK'old
cuckold
(cf. ŬK"ld)

ŬK'rak
muckrake

ŬK'shot
buck-shot
duck-shot

ŬK'siv
influxive

ŬK'som
buxom
lucksome

ŬK'stur
huckster

ŬK'shun
abduction
adduction
affluxion
conduction
construction
deduction
defluxion
destruction
diduction
duction
eduction
effluxion
fluxion
induction
influxion
instruction
introduction
manuduction
misconstruc-
    tion
non-conduc-
    tion
obduction
obstruction
over-produc-
    tion
production
reduction
reproduction
ruction
seduction
self-destruction
subduction
substruction
suction
superinduction

superstruction
traduction

ŬK'tans
reluctance

ŬK'tant
reluctant

ŬK'ted
abducted
conducted
constructed
deducted
fructed
inducted
instructed
miconstructed
obstructed
superstructed
unobstructed

ŬK'test
abductest
conductest
constructest
deductest
inductest
instructest
misconstructest
obstructest

ŬK'teth
abducteth
conducteth
constructeth
deducteth
inducteth
instructeth
misconstructeth
obstructeth

ŬK'til
ductile
inductile
productile

ŬK'ting
abducting
conducting
constructing
deducting
inducting
instructing
misconducting
non-conducting
non-obstruct-
    ing
obstructing

ŬK'tiv
adductive
conductive
constructive
deductive
destructive
inductive
instructive
introductive
obstructive
productive
reconductive
reconstructive
reductive
reproductive
seductive
self-destructive
superinductive
superstructive
traductive

ŬK'tres
conductress

instructress	pucker	**Ū'lep**	**ŬL'fur**
introductress	sap-sucker	julep	sulphur
seductress	seer-sucker	(cf. tulip)	(cf. Gulfer)
	shucker		
ŬK'tūr	succor	**Ū'les**	**ŬL'gar**
structure	sucker	clueless	vulgar
substructure	trucker	cueless	
superstructure	tucker	dewless	**ŬL'gat**
		Jewless	promulgate
ŬK'tŭr	**Ū'kus**	mewless	vulgate
abductor	caducous	pewless	**Ū'li**
adductor	fucus	screwless	
conductor	leucous	viewless	bluely
constructor	mucous		Cooley
destructor	noctilucous	**ŬL'est**	coolie
ductor	rukus	*befoolest*	coolly
eductor		coolest	Dooley
inductor	**Ū'la**	foolest	duly
instructor	Ashtabula	*pulest*	Gilhooley
introductor	Beulah	*rulest*	Gillooley
manuductor	Boola Boola		Gilluley
non-conductor	Eula	**ŬL'est**	*guly*
obstructor	hula-hula	*annullest*	newly
	Loula	*cullest*	patchouli
ŬK'u, ŎŎ'ku	Missoula	dullest	Thule
cuckoo	Wallula	*lullest*	truly
		scullest	tule
Ū'kur	**ŬL'a**		Ultima Thule
euchre		**ŬL'et**	unduly
fluker	ampulla	cullet	unruly
lucre	medulla	gullet	
puker	mullah	mullet	**ŬL'i**
rebuker	nullah		cully
		ŬL'eth	dully
ŬK'ur	**ŬL'da**	*befooleth*, etc.	gully
bucker	Hulda		hully
chucker		**ŬL'eth**	sully
chukker	**ŬL'en**	*annulleth*	**ŬL'id**
clucker	Cullen	*gulleth*	gullied
ducker	sullen	*lulleth*	sullied
mucker	(cf. ŬL'in)	*sculleth*	unsullied

ŬL'ij
Coolidge

ŬL'ij
gullage
sullage
ullage

ŬL'in
McMullin
mullein

ŬL'ing
befooling
cooling
drooling
fooling
mewling
misruling
overruling
puling
ruling
schooling
spooling
tooling

ŬL'ing
annulling
culling
dulling
gulling
hulling
lulling
mulling
sculling

ŬL'inz
Mullins

Ū'lip
tulip
(cf. julep)

ŬL'is
portcullis

ŬL'ish
coolish
foolish
mulish
pound-foolish
tom-foolish

ŬL'ish
dullish
gullish

Ū'liks
spondulix

ŬL'jens
effulgence
indulgence
refulgence
self-indulgence

ŬL'jent
circumfulgent
effulgent
emulgent
fulgent
indulgent
interfulgent
profulgent
refulgent
self-indulgent

ŬL'jest
indulgest, etc.

ŬL'jeth
indulgeth, etc.

ŬL'jez
bulges

divulges
effulges
indulges

ŬL'jing
bulging
divulging
effulging
indulging
promulging

ŬLJ'ment
divulgement
indulgement

ŬL'jur
divulger
indulger
promulger

ŬL'kat
inculcate
sulcate
trisulcate

ŬLK'ing
bulking
hulking
skulking
sulking

ŬLK'i
bulky
hulky
sulky

ŬLK'ur
bulker
skulker
sulker

ŬL'man
Ullman

ŬL'nes
coolness

ŬL'nes
dullness

ŬL'ok
hullock
rowlock

ŬL'pat
disculpate
exculpate
inculpate

ŬL'pest
gulpest, etc.

ŬL'peth
gulpeth, etc.

ŬL'pi
gulpy
pulpy

ŬL'pin
vulpine

ŬL'prit
culprit

ŬLP'tor
sculptor

ŬLP'tur
sculpture

ŬL'sest
repulsest, etc.

ŬL'set
dulcet

ōld, ôr, ŏdd, oil, fŏŏt, out; ūse, ûrn, ŭp; THis, thin

ŬL'seth
repulseth, etc.

ŬL'shun
appulsion
avulsion
compulsion
convulsion
demulsion
divulsion
emulsion
evulsion
expulsion
impulsion
propulsion
pulsion
repulsion
revulsion

ŬL'sing
convulsing
pulsing
repulsing

ŬL'siv
appulsive
compulsive
convulsive
divulsive
emulsive
expulsive
impulsive
propulsive
pulsive
repulsive
revulsive

ŬL'sur
repulser
ulcer

ŬL'tan
sultan

ŬL'tans
exultance
resultance

ŬL'tant
exultant
resultant

ŬL'ted
consulted
exulted
insulted
occulted
resulted

ŬL'test
consultest, etc.

ŬL'teth
consulteth, etc.

ŬL'ting
consulting
exulting
insulting
occulting
resulting

ŬL'tiv
consultive
resultive

ŬLT'nes
adultness
occultness

ŬL'tri
sultry

ŬL'tūr
agriculture
apiculture
arboriculture
aviculture
culture
floriculture
horticulture
inculture
multure
pisciculture
self-culture
sylviculture
terra-culture
viticulture
vulture

ŬL'tur
consulter
exulter
insulter
resulter

Ū'lu
Honolulu
Lulu
Zulu

Ū'lur
cooler
drooler
mewler
puler
ridiculer
ruler
spooler
wine-cooler

ŬL'ur
annulier
color

cruller
culler
discolor
duller
guller
huller
luller
medullar
miscolor
Muller
multicolor
rose-color
sculler
technicolor
tricolor
water-color

ŬL'urd
colored
discolored
dullard
high-colored
over-colored
party-colored
peach-colored
rosy-colored
sky-colored
wine-colored

Ū'lus
screw-loose

ŬL'yar
peculiar

ŬL'yun
cullion
mullion
scullion

Ū'ma
duma

mazuma	**ŬM'b'l**	**ŬM'bli**	**ŬM'bril**
Montezuma	bejumble	crumbly	tumbril
puma	bumble	humbly	
Yuma	crumble	stumbly	**ŬM'brus**
	fumble	tumbly	cumbrous
Ū'man	grumble		penumbrous
human	humble	**ŬM'bling**	slumbrous
inhuman	jumble	crumbling	unslumbrous
Newman	mumble	fumbling	
superhuman	rumble	grumbling	**ŬM'bug**
Truman	scumble	humbling	humbug
	stumble	jumbling	
ŬM'at	tumble	mumbling	**ŬM'bul**
despumate	umbel	rumbling	Trumbull
exhumate		stumbling	
inhumate	**ŬM'b'ld**	tumbling	**ŬM'bur**
	unhumbled		cumber
ŬM'at	crumbled, etc.	**ŬM'blur**	disencumber
consummate		crumbler	encumber
	ŬM'blest	drumbler	Humber
ŬM'ba, ŬM'ba	*crumblest*	fumbler	lumbar
rumba	*fumblest*	grumbler	lumber
	grumblest	humbler	number
ŬM'bat	humblest	jumbler	outnumber
combat	*jumblest*	mumbler	slumber
(cf. wombat)	*mumblest*	rumbler	number
	rumblest	stumbler	
ŬM'bel	*stumblest*	tumbler	**ŬM'burd**
dumbbell	*tumblest*		unnumbered
		ŬM'bo	cumbered, etc.
ŬM'bent		gumbo	
accumbent	**ŬM'bleth**	Jumbo	**ŬM'drum**
decumbent	*crumbleth*	Mumbo-Jumbo	humdrum
incumbent	*fumbleth*		
procumbent	*grumbleth*	**ŬM'brat**	**ŬM'el**
recumbent	*humbleth*	adumbrate	bepummel
superincum-	*jumbleth*	inumbrate	hummel
bent	*mumbleth*	obumbrate	pommel
ŬM'bik	*rumbleth*		
columbic	*stumbleth*	**ŬM'brij**	**Ū'men**
plumbic	*tumbleth*	umbrage	acumen

ōld, ôr, ŏdd, oil, fŏŏt, out; ūse, ûrn, ŭp; THis, thin

albumen
bitumen
catechumen
legumen
rumen
(cf. illumine,
etc.)

Ū'ment
accrument
eschewment
imbruement
imbuement
induement
subduement

ŬM'est
assumest
bloomest
boomest
consumest
costumest
doomest
entombest
exhumest
fumest
groomest
illumest
perfumest
plumest
presumest
resumest

ŬM'est
becomest
comest
drummest
dumbest
glummest
gummest
hummest

numbest
rummest
strummest
succumbest

ŬM'et
grummet
plummet
(cf. summit)

ŪM'eth
assumeth
bloometh
boometh
consumeth
costumeth
doometh
entombeth
exhumeth
fumeth
groometh
illumeth
perfumeth
plumeth
presumeth
resumeth

ŬM'eth
becometh
cometh
drummeth
gummeth
hummeth
strummeth
succumbeth

ŬM'fal
triumphal

ŬM'fant
triumphant

ŬM'fit
comfit

ŬM'fort
comfort

ŬM'fri
Humphrey

ŬM'friz
Humphreys

ŬM'ful
bloomful
doomful

ŪM'i
bloomy
broomy
Fiume
fumy
gloomy
plumy
rheumy
roomy
spumy

ŬM'i
crumby
crummie
dummy
gummy
lummy
mummy
plummy
rummy
scrummy
scummy
thrummy
tummy
yummy

ŪM'id
humid
tumid

ŪM'ij
fumage
plumage

ŬM'ij
chummage
rummage
scrummage

ŪM'in
illumine
relumine
(cf. acumen,
etc.)

ŬM'ing
assuming
blooming
booming
consuming
disentombing
dooming
entombing
exhuming
fuming
glooming
grooming
illuming
looming
perfuming
pluming
predooming
presuming
resuming
unassuming
unpresuming

āle, câre, ădd, ärm, ȧsk: mē, hĕre, ĕnd; īce, ĭll;

ŬM'ing

becoming
benumbing
chumming
coming
drumming
forthcoming
gumming
humming
mumming
numbing
overcoming
plumbing
plumming
scrumming
shortcoming
slumming
strumming
succumbing
summing
thumbing
unbecoming

ŬM'is

pumice

ŬM'it

summit
(cf. grummet,
   etc.)

ŬM'les

bloomless
broomless
doomless
fumeless
groomless
loomless
plumeless
roomless
tombless

ŬM'let

boomlet
groomlet
plumelet

ŬM'li

Cholmondesley
Chumley
comely
cumbersomely
dumbly
frolicsomely
glumly
humorsomely
numbly
rumly
troublesomely,
   etc.

ŬM'nal

autumnal
columnal

ŬM'nes

dumbness
glumness
numbness

ŬM'nur

Sumner

ŬM'ok

hummock
stomach

ŬM'oks

lummox
(cf. stomachs)

ŬM'on

come-on
summon

ŬM'ond

Drummond

ŬM'pas

compass
encompass
rumpus

ŬM'pest

bethumpest
bumpest
dumpest
humpest
jumpest
lumpest
plumpest
pumpest
stumpest
thumpest
trumpest

ŬM'pet

crumpet
strumpet
trumpet

ŬM'peth

bethumpeth
bumpeth
dumpeth
humpeth
jumpeth
lumpeth
pumpeth
stumpeth
thumpeth
'trumpeth

ŬM'pi

bumpy
chumpy

clumpy
crumpy
dumpy
frumpy
grumpy
humpy
jumpy
lumpy
mumpy
plumpy
slumpy
stumpy
thumpy

ŬMP'ing

bethumping
bumping
dumping
bumping
jumping
lumping
mumping
plumping
pumping
slumping
stumping
thumping
trumping

ŬMP'ir

umpire

ŬMP'ish

bumpish
dumpish
frumpish
grumpish
humpish
jumpish
lumpish
mumpish

ōld, ôr, ŏdd, oil, fŏŏt, out; ūse, ûrn, ŭp; THis, thin

plumpish
slumpish

ŬMP'kin
bumpkin
pumpkin
(cf. Lumkin)

ŬM'p'l
crumple
rumple
unrumple

ŬM'plest
crumplest, etc.

ŬM'pleth
crumpleth, etc.

ŬM'pling
crumpling
dumpling
rumpling

ŬMP'nes
plumpness

ŬM'po
Bumpo

ŬMP'shun
assumption
consumption
gumption
presumption
resumption
subsumption

ŬMP'shus
bumptious
scrumptious

ŬMP'tiv
assumptive
consumptive
presumptive
resumptive
subsumptive

ŬM'pur
bethumper
bumper
counter-jumper
dumper
jumper
lumper
mumper
plumper
pumper
stumper
thumper
trumper
tub-thumper

ŬM'pus
rumpus
(see ŬM'pas)

ŬM'ston
tombstone

ŬM'tur
Sumter

ŬM'ur
assumer
bloomer
boomer
consumer
doomer
entomber
fumer
humor

ill-humor
illumer
perfumer
plumer
presumer
resumer
roomer
rumor
tumor

ŬM'ur
comer
Cummer
drummer
dumber
glummer
grummer
gummer
hummer
incomer
midsummer
mummer
newcomer
number
plumber
rummer
scrummer
scummer
strummer
summer

ŬM'urd
good-humored
humored
ill-humored
rumored

ŬM'urz
bloomers
rumors, etc.

ŬM'urz
Somers

ŬM'us
brumous
dumous
fumous
grumous
humous
humus
implumous
plumous
spumous

ŬMZ'da
doomsday

ŬM'zi
clumsy
mumsie

ŬMZ'man
doomsman
groomsman

Ū'na
Acuna
fortuna
lacuna
luna
Peruna
Una
vicuna

Ū'nal
lacunal
tribunal

ŬN'chest
bunchest, etc.

āle, câre, ădd, ärm, àsk; mē, hęre, ĕnd; īce, ĭll;

ŬN'cheth
buncheth, etc.

ŬN'chez
brunches
bunches
crunches
hunches
lunches
munches
punches
scrunches

ŬN'chi
bunchy
crunchy
hunchy
punchy

ŬN'ching
bunching
crunching
hunching
lunching
munching
punching
scrunching

ŬN'chun
bruncheon
luncheon
nuncheon
puncheon
scuncheon
truncheon

ŬN'chur
bruncher
buncher
cruncher
huncher

luncher
muncher
puncher
scruncher

ŬN'dan
antemundane
extramundane
infra-mundane
intermundane
intramundane
mundane
supermundane
supramundane
ultramundane

ŬN'dans
abundance
redundance
sun dance
superabun-
    dance

ŬN'dant
abundant
redundant
superabundant

ŬN'dat
fecundate
secundate

ŬN'ded
unwounded
wounded

ŬN'ded
funded
refunded
retunded

ŬN'dest
woundest, etc.

ŬN'dest
fundest, etc.

ŬN'deth
woundeth, etc.

ŬN'deth
fundeth, etc.

ŬN'di
Bundy
fundi
Fundy
Grundy
Lundy
Monday
salmagundi
Sunday

ŬN'din
hirundine

ŬN'ding
funding
refunding

ŬN'dit
conduit
pundit

ŬN'd'l
bundle
trundle
unbundle

ŬN'dlest
bundlest, etc.

ŬN'dleth
bundleth, etc.

ŬN'dling
bundling
trundling, etc.

ŬN'don
London
(cf. undone)

ŬN'dred
hundred

ŬN'dri
sundry
thund'ry

ŬN'drus
wondrous

ŬN'dur
asunder
blunder
dissunder
dunder
down-under
enthunder
Gunder
plunder
refunder
rotunder
sunder
thereunder
thunder
under
wonder

ŬN'el
funnel
gunwale

runnel

trunnel

tunnel

ŬN'et

punnet

runnet

Ū'nes

blueness

fewnesss

newness

trueness

ŬN'est

attunest

communest

croonest

entunest

harpoonest

importunest

impugnest

moonest

oppugnest

prunest

soonest

spoonest

swoonest

tunest

ŬN'est

runnest, etc.

ŬN'eth

attuneth

communeth

crooneth

entuneth

harpooneth

impugneth

mooneth

oppugneth

pruneth

spooneth

swooneth

tuneth

ŬN'eth

runneth, etc.

ŬN'ful

tuneful

runeful

spoonful

UNG'g'l

bungle

jungle

ŬNG'gling

bungling

ŬNG'gur

ballad-monger

borough-

   monger

costermonger

enhunger

fishmonger

hunger

ironmonger

monger

Munger

younger

ŬNGK'al

carbuncle

caruncle

peduncle

truncal

uncle

ŬNGK'at

averruncate

detruncate

truncate

ŬNGK'en

drunken

shrunken

sunken

ŬNGK'et

junket

Plunkett

ŬNGK'i

chunky

flunkey

funky

hunky

monkey

powder-

  monkey

punkie

spunky

ŬNG'kin

punkin

(cf. ŬN'kan)

ŬNGK'ish

funkish

monkish

skunkish

ŬNGK'o

bunco

junco

ŬNGK'shun

adjunction

compunction

conjunction

defunction

disjunction

expunction

function

injunction

interjunction

interpunction

inunction

junction

punction

sejunction

subjunction

unction

ŬNGK'shus

compunctious

rambunctious

unctious

ŬNGK'tiv

abjunctive

adjunctive

compunctive

conjunctive

disjunctive

subjunctive

ŬNGK'tur

acupuncture

conjuncture

juncture

puncture

ŬNGK'um

Buncombe

bunkum

ŬNGK'ur

bunker

drunker

āle,   câre,   ădd,   ärm,   åsk;   mē,   hĕre,   ĕnd;   īce,   ĭll;

dunker
flunker
funker
hunker
junker
punker
tunker

ŬNGK'urd
bunkered
drunkard
Dunkard

ŬNGK'us
aduncous
dohunkus
juncous

ŬNG'ling
youngling

ŬN'gri
hungry

ŬNG'stur
tonguester
youngster

ŬNG'ur
lunger

ŬN'i
Dooney
loony
Mooney
moony
Mulrooney
Muni
puisne
puny
spoony

ŬN'i
acrimony
agrimony
alimony
antimony
bunny
funny
gunny
honey
matrimony
money
parsimony
patrimony
sanctimony
sonny
sunny
Tunney
tunny
unsunny

ŬN'ij
dunnage
gunnage
tonnage

ŬN'ik
Munich
Punic
runic
tunic

ŬN'in
run-in

ŬN'ing
ballooning
communing
crooning
expugning
harpooning
impugning

mooning
nooning
oppugning
pruning
spooning
swooning
tuning

ŬN'ing
cunning
dunning
funning
gunning
outrunning
overrunning
punning
running
shunning
stunning
sunning

Ū'nis
Eunice
Tunis

ŬN'ish
buffoonish
poltroonish

ŬN'ish
punish
Hunnish

ŬN'ist
balloonist
bassoonist
harpoonist
opportunist

Ū'nit
unit

ŬN'izm
buffoonism
opportunism
poltroonism

ŬN'jent
pungent

ŬN'jest
expungest, etc

ŬN'jeth
expungeth, etc.

ŬN'jez
expunges
lunges
plunges
sponges

ŬN'ji
plungy
spongy

ŬN'jing
expunging
lunging
plunging
sponging

ŬN'jun
dungeon
plungeon

ŬN'jur
blunger
expunger
lunger
plunger
sponger

ōld, ôr, ŏdd, oil, fŏŏt, out; ūse, ûrn, ŭp; THis, thin

ŬN′kan	**ŬN′stur**	*hunteth*	**ŬN′tur**
Duncan	gunster	*punteth*	affronter
(cf. ŬNG′kin)	punster	*shunteth*	blunter
		stunteth	bunter
ŬN′les	**ŬN′tal**		confronter
moonless	contrapuntal	**ŬN′ti**	fortune-hunter
runeless	frontal	punty	grunter
tuneless	gruntle	runty	Gunter
		stunty	head-hunter
ŬN′les	**ŬN′ted**		hunter
runless	affronted	**ŬN′ting**	legacy-hunter
sonless	blunted	affronting	punter
sunless	bunted	bunting	shunter
	confronted	confronting	stunter
ŬN′lit	fronted	fronting	
moonlight	grunted	grunting	**ŬNTS′vil**
noon-light	hunted	head-hunting	Blountsville
	punted	hunting	Huntsville
ŬN′man	shunted	punting	
gunman	stunted	reed-bunting	**Ū′nuk**
	unblunted	shunting	eunuch
ŬN′nes	unwonted	stunting	
inopportune-	wonted	yellow-bunting	**ŬN′ur**
ness			attuner
jejuneness	**ŬN′test**	**ŬNT′les**	ballooner
opportuneness	*affrontest*	frontless	communer
	bluntest	wontless	crooner
Ū′no	*buntest*		dragooner
Bruno	*confrontest*	**ŬNT′nes**	harpooner
Juno	*gruntest*	bluntness	importuner
	huntest	stuntness	impugner
ŬN′riz	*puntest*		interlunar
moonrise	*shuntest*	**ŬN′to**	lacunar
	stuntest	junto	lampooner
ŬN′si			lunar
Munsey	**ŬN′teth**	**ŬN′tri**	mooner
	affronteth	country	novilunar
ŬN′stan,	*blunteth*		oppugner
ŬN′ston	*bunteth*	**ŬN′tu**	piano-tuner
Dunstan	*confronteth*	unto	plenilunar
Funston	*grunteth*		pruner

schooner	ŬP'ans	ŬP'ĭ	ŬP''l
semilunar	come-uppance	croupy	octuple
sooner	thruppence	droopy	quadruple
spooner		soupy	quintuple
sublunar	ŬP'e	(cf. whoopee)	septuple
swooner	whoopee		sextuple
translunar	(cf. ŬP'ĭ)	ŬP'ĭ	scruple
tuner		cuppy	subduple
	ŬP'est	guppy	(cf. pupil)
ŬN'ur	coopest	puppy	
dunner	droopest		ŬP''l
forerunner	dupest	Ū'pĭd	couple
gunner	groupest	Cupid	supple
overrunner	loopest	stupid	
punner	recoupest		ŪP'lest
runner	scoopest	Ū'pĭl	scruplest, etc.
stunner	stoopest	pupil	
	swoopest	(cf. Ū'p''l)	ŬP'lest
ŬN'yon	troopest		couplest, etc.
communion	whoopest	ŬP'ing	
disunion		cooping	ŬP'let
excommunion	ŬP'est	drooping	octuplet
intercom-	suppest, etc.	duping	quintuplet, etc.
munion		grouping	
reunion	ŬP'et	hooping	ŪP'leth
trades-union	puppet	looping	scrupleth, etc
union		recouping	
	ŪP'eth	scooping	ŬP'leth
ŬN'yon	coopeth	stooping	coupleth, etc.
bunion	droopeth	swooping	
munnion	dupeth	trooping	ŬP'lur
onion	groupeth	whooping	coupler
ronyon	loopeth		suppler
trunnion	recoupeth	ŬP'ing	
	scoopeth	cupping	ŪP'ment
ŬN'yor	stoopeth	supping	aggroupment
junior	swoopeth	tupping	recoupment
	troopeth		
Ū'pa	whoopeth	ŬP'ish	Ū'pon
pupa	ŬP'eth	puppish	coupon
supa	suppeth, etc.	uppish	jupon

ŬP'or
stupor
(see ŬP'ur)

ŬP'shal
antenuptial
nuptial
post-nuptial

ŬP'shun
abruption
corruption
disruption
eruption
incorruption
interruption
irruption
ruption

ŬP'ted
abrupted
corrupted
disrupted
interrupted
irrupted

ŬP'test
abruptest
corruptest
interruptest

ŬP'teth
corrupteth, etc.

ŬP'ting
corrupting
erupting
interrupting

ŬP'tiv
corruptive

disruptive
eruptive
incorruptive
interruptive
irruptive

ŬPT'li
abruptly
corruptly, etc.

ŬPT'nes
abruptness
corruptness
incorruptness

ŬP'ur
cooper
drooper
duper
grouper
hooper
looper
recouper
scooper
snooper
stooper
stupor
super
swooper
trooper
whooper

ŬP'ur
crupper
cupper
scupper
supper
upper

ŬP'urt
Rupert
(cf. Newport)

ŬP'ward
upward

Ū'ra
Angostura
appoggiatura
bravura
caesura
coloratura
Cuticura
datura
fissura
flexura
Keturah
pietra-dura
pleura
purpura
sura
velatura
vettura

Ū'ral
antemural
caesural
commissural
crural
extramural
intermural
interneural
intramural
jural
mural
neural
pleural
plural
rural
sinecural
sural
tellural
Ural

ŪR'ans
allurance
assurance
durance
endurance
insurance
perdurance
reassurance

ŪR'āt
curate

ŪR'ăt
jurat

ŪR'bal
herbal
verbal

ŪR'ban
suburban
turban
urban

ŪR'bans
disturbance

ŪR'bar
durbar

ŪR'bat
acerbate
perturbate

ŪR'best
blurbest
curbest
disturbest
perturbest

ŪR'bet
sherbet

ÛR'beth
blurbeth
curbeth
disturbeth
perturbeth

ÛR'bi
Derby
herby
Iturbi
Kirby

ÛR'bid
herbid
turbid

ÛR'bin
turbine

ÛR'bing
curbing
disturbing
perturbing

ÛR'bot
burbot
turbot

ÛR'bur
Berber
blurber
curber
disturber
Ferber
Gerber
perturber
superber

ÛR'burt
Herbert

ÛR'chant
merchant
perchant

ÛR'chas
purchase

ÛR'chast
purchased

ÛR'chen
birchen
(cf. urchin)

ÛR'chest
birchest
lurchest
perchest
searchest
smirchest
(cf. purchased)

ÛR'cheth
bircheth
lurcheth
percheth
searcheth
smircheth

ÛR'chez
besmirches
birches
churches
lurches
perches
researches
searches
smirches

ÛR'chif
kerchief

ÛR'ching
besmirching
birching
churching
lurching
perching
searching
smirching

ÛRCH'les
churchless
smirchless

ÛR'chur
besmircher
bircher
lurcher
percher
researcher
searcher
smircher
(cf. nurture)

ÛRD'book
herdbook
word-book

ÛR'ded
begirded
curded
engirded
girded
herded
sherded
worded

ÛR'den
burden
disburden
overburden

unburden
(cf. ÛR'don)

ÛR'dest
absurdest
begirdest
engirdest
girdest
heardest

ÛR'deth
begirdeth, etc.

ÛR'di
birdie
curdy
hurdy-gurdy
sturdy
wordy

ÛR'dikt
verdict

ÛR'ding
begirding
engirding
girding
herding
ungirding
wording

ÛR'd'l
begirdle
curdle
engirdle
girdle
hurdle

ÛR'don
Burdon
guerdon
(cf. ÛR'den)

ÛR'dūr	**ÛR'est**	*stirrest*	*recurreth*
verdure	*abjurest*	*transferrest*	*referreth*
(cf. perjure)	*adjurest*		*spurreth*
	allurest	**ÛR'et**	*stirreth*
ÛR'dūr	*assurest*	turret	*transferreth*
absurder	*conjurest*		
Burder	*curest*	**ÛR'eth**	**ÛR'fas**
engirder	demurest	*abjureth*	surface
girder	*endurest*	*adjureth*	
herder	*ensurest*	*allureth*	**ÛR'fekt**
murder	*immurest*	*conjureth*	perfect
self-murder	impurest	*cureth*	
thirder	*insurest*	*endureth*	**ÛR'fi**
	lurest	*immureth*	Durfey
ÛRDZ'man	*maturest*	*lureth*	Murphy
herdsman	*moorest*	*matureth*	scurfy
wordsman	obscurest	*obscureth*	surfy
	poorest	*procureth*	turfy
ÛR'el	*procurest*	*secureth*	
squirrel	purest	*assureth*	**ÛR'fit**
Burrell	*reassurest*	*ensureth*	surfeit
	securest	*insureth*	
ÛR'ens	surest	*mooreth*	**ÛR'for**
concurrence	*tourest*	*reassureth*	therefore
deterrence	*unmoorest*	*toureth*	(cf. wherefore)
incurrence		*unmooreth*	
intercurrence	**ÛR'est**		**ÛR'fum**
occurrence	*bestirrest*	**ÛR'eth**	perfume
recurrence	*blurrest*	*bestirreth*	
transference	*concurrest*	*blurreth*	**ÛR'gat**
	conferrest	*concurreth*	expurgate
ÛR'ent, ÛR'ant	*deferrest*	*conferreth*	objurgate
concurrent	*demurrest*	*deferreth*	virgate
currant	*errest*	*erreth*	
current	*incurrest*	*demurreth*	**ÛR'g'l**
decurrent	*inferrest*	*incurreth*	burgle
deterrent	*interrest*	*inferreth*	gurgle
intercurrent	*preferrest*	*interreth*	
recurrent	*purrest*	*occurreth*	**ÛR'glar**
susurrant	*referrest*	*preferreth*	burglar
undercurrent	*spurrest*	*purreth*	gurgler

āle,   câre,   ădd,   ärm,   åsk;   mē,   hĕre,   ĕnd;   īce,   ĭll;

ŪR'go

a tergo
ergo
Virgo

ŪR'gur

burgher
jerguer

ŪR'gus

demiurgus
Mergus
thaumaturgus

ŪR'i

de jure
Drury
ewry
fury
houri
Jewry
jury
Missouri

ŪR'i

burry
curry
firry
flurry
furry
hurry
hurry-scurry
lurry
Murray
scurry
Surrey
slurry
whirry
worry

ŪR'id

lurid

ŪR'id

curried
flurried
hurried
scurried
worried

ŪR'ij

moorage
murage

ŪR'ij

courage
demurrage
discourage
encourage

ŪR'ik

hydrosulphuric
hydrotelluric
purpuric
sulphuric
telluric

ŪR'ik

myrrhic

ŪR'im

purim
urim

ŪR'in

burin
daturin
neurin
neurine

ŪR'ing

abjuring
adjuring
alluring

assuring
conjuring
curing
during
enduring
ensuring
everduring
immuring
insuring
inuring
juring
luring
manuring
maturing
mooring
non-juring
obscuring
procuring
reassuring
securing
touring
unmooring

ŪR'ing

astirring
bestirring
blurring
concurring
conferring
deferring
demurring
erring
incurring
inferring
interring
non-concurring
occurring
preferring
purring
recurring
referring

shirring
slurring
spurring
stirring
transferring
unerring
whirring
(cf. herring)

ŪR'ish

amateurish
boorish
Moorish
poorish

ŪR'ish

burrish
currish
flourish
nourish

ŪR'ist

caricaturist
jurist
purist
tourist

ŪR'iz

curries
flurries
hurries
scurries
worries

ŪR'izm

purism
tourism

ŪR'jens

convergence
deturgence

divergence
emergence
resurgence
submergence

ÛR'jent

abstergent
assurgent
convergent
detergent
divergent
emergent
insurgent
resurgent
splurgent
turgent
urgent
vergent

ÛR'jest

convergest
dirgest
divergest
emergest
mergest
purgest
scourgest
splurgest
submergest
surgest
urgest

ÛR'jeth

convergeth
dirgeth
divergeth
emergeth
mergeth
purgeth
scourgeth
splurgeth

submergeth
surgeth
urgeth

ÛR'jez

asperges
Boanerges
converges
dirges
diverges
emerges
merges
purges
scourges
serges
submerges
surges
urges
verges

ÛR'ji

aciurgy
clergy
dirgie
dramaturgy
metallurgy
periergy
surgy
thaumaturgy

ÛR'jid

turgid

ÛR'jik

chirurgic
demiurgic
dramaturgic
energic
liturgic
metallurgic

thaumaturgic
theurgic

ÛR'jin

virgin

ÛR'jing

converging
dirging
diverging
emerging
immerging
merging
purging
scourging
splurging
submerging
surging
urging
verging

ÛR'jist

dramaturgist
metallurgist
thaumaturgist

ÛR'jun

burgeon
Spurgeon
sturgeon
surgeon

ÛR'jūr

perjure
(cf. verdure)

ÛR'jŭr

converger
dirger
diverger
emerger

merger
purger
scourger
submerger
urger
verger

ÛR'jus

verjuice

ÛR'kal

Lupercal
novercal
(cf. circle)

ÛR'kest

clerkest, etc.

ÛR'keth

clerketh, etc.

ÛR'ki

jerky
lurky
mirky
murky
perky
quirky
shirky
smirky
talk turkey
turkey

ÛR'kin

firkin
gherkin
jerkin
merkin

ÛR'kins

Firkins

āle, câre, ădd, ärm, ȧsk; mē, hĕre, ĕnd; īce, ĭll;

Perkins
gherkins, etc.

ŬR′king

aworking
clerking
hard-working
jerking
lurking
perking
shirking
smirking
working

ŬR′kish

quirkish
Turkish

ŬR′kit

circuit

ŬR′k′l

circle
encircle
Merkle
semicircle
turkle

ŬR′klet

circlet

ŬR′kli

circly
clerkly

ŬR′kling

circling

ŬRK′man

Turkman
workman

ŬRK′som

irksome
mirksome

ŬR′kur

burker
jerker
jerquer
lurker
shirker
smirker
wonder-worker
worker

ŬR′kus

bifurcous
circus
Quercus
(cf. work-
house)

ŬR′kwoiz

turquoise

ŬRLD′li

worldly

ŬRLD′ling

worldling

ŬR′lest

curlest
furlest
hurlest
swirlest
twirlest
unfurlest
whirlest

ŬR′leth

curleth

furleth
hurleth
purleth
swirleth
twirleth
unfurleth
whirleth

ŬRL′hood

girlhood

ŬR′li

demurely
maturely
obscurely
poorly
purely
securely

ŬR′li

burly
churly
curly
early
girlie
girly
hurly-burly
knurly
pearly
Shirley
surly
swirly
whirly

ŬR′lin

merlin
pearlin

ŬR′ling

curling
furling
herling

hurling
pearling
purling
Sperling
sterling
Stirling
swirling
twirling
uncurling
unfurling
upcurling
upwhirling

ŬR′lish

churlish
girlish
pearlish

ŬR′loin

purloin
sirloin

ŬR′lu

curlew
purlieu

ŬR′lur

burler
curler
furler
hurler
pearler
purler
skirler
twirler
whirler

ŬR′ma

Burma
derma
Irma
syrma

ÛR′mad
mermaid

ÛR′mal
dermal
diathermal
epidermal
geothermal
hydrothermal
hypodermal
isogeothermal
isothermal
pachydermal
synthermal
taxidermal
thermal

ÛR′man
cousin-german
firman
German
merman
(cf. sermon)

ÛR′mans
affirmance
confirmance
disaffirmance

ÛR′ment
abjurement
allurement
conjurement
immurement
obscurement
procurement

ÛR′ment,
  ÛR′mant
affirmant

averment
deferment
determent
disinterment
ferment
interment
preferment
referment

ÛR′mest
confirmest
firmest
infirmest
squirmest
termest
wormest

ÛR′meth
confirmeth, etc.

ÛR′mez
Hermes
kermes

ÛR′mi
germy
taxidermy
wormy

ÛR′mik
adiathermic
dermic
diathermic
endermic
epidermic
geothermic
hydrodermic
hypodermic
isogeothermic
pachydermic
sclerodermic

taxidermic
thermic

ÛR′min
determine
ermine
vermin

ÛR′mind
determined
ermined
undetermined

ÛR′ming
affirming
confirming
squirming
worming

ÛR′mis
dermis
epidermis

ÛR′mish
skirmish

ÛR′mīt
termite

ÛR′mĭt
hermit
permit

ÛRM′li
firmly
termly

ÛR′moil
turmoil

ÛR′mur
affirmer

bemurmur
confirmer
firmer
infirmer
murmur
squirmer
termer
termoɪ
wormer

ÛR′na
Myrna
Verna

ÛR′nal
cavernal
coeternal
colonel
diurnal
diuternal
eternal
external
fraternal
hesternal
hibernal
hodiernal
infernal
internal
journal
kernel
lucernal
maternal
nocturnal
paraphernal
paternal
semi-diurnal
sempiternal
sternal
supernal
urnal
vernal

ŬR′nant,
  ŬR′nent

alternant
secernent
vernant

ŬR′nard

Bernard

ŬR′nas

furnace

ŬR′nat

alternate
cothurnate
subalternate
ternate

ŬR′ned

learned
(see ŬRN +
  ed)

ŬR′nes

demureness
immatureness
impureness
insecureness
matureness
obscureness
poorness
pureness
secureness
sureness

ŬR′nes

Furness
(cf. furnace)

ŬR′nest

adjournest

burnest
churnest
concernest
discernest
earnest
Ernest
learnest
over-earnest
overturnest
returnest
sojournest
spurnest
sternest
turnest
yearnest

ŬR′neth

adjourneth
burneth
churneth
concerneth
discerneth
learneth
overturneth
returneth
sojourneth
spurneth
turneth
yearneth

ŬR′ni

attorney
Berney
Birney
burny-burny
ferny
Gurney
journey
Turney
tourney

ŬR′ning

adjourning
booklearning
burning
churning
concerning
discerning
earning
heart-burning
learning
overburning
overturning
returning
sojourning
spurning
table-turning
turning
undiscerning
unlearning
upturning
urning
yearning

ŬR′nish

burnish
furnish

ŬR′nisht

burnished
furnished
unburnished
unfurnished

ŬRN′ment

adjournment
attornment
concernment
discernment
secernment
sojournment

ŬRN′nes

sternness

ŬR′no

inferno
Sterno

ŬR′num

laburnum

ŬR′nur

adjourner
burner
discerner
earner
learner
overturner
returner
sojourner
spurner
sterner
turner
yearner

ŬR′nus

cothurnus

ŬR′o

bureau
chiaroscuro
maduro

ŬR′o

borough
burrow
furrow
thorough

ŬR′od

burrowed
furrowed
unfurrowed

ŪR'or
furor
juror
(cf. ŪR'ur)

ŪR'pent
serpent

ŪR'pest
chirpest, etc.

ŪR'peth
chirpeth
turpeth
usurpeth

ŪR'ping
burping
chirping
usurping

ŪR'p'l
empurple
purple

ŪR'pos
purpose

ŪR'pur
burper
chirper
usurper

ŪR'sa
ursa
vice versa

ŪR'sal
controversal
rehearsal
reversal

tercel
transversal
universal
ursal
versal

ŪR'sant
aversant
recursant
versant

ŪR'sed
accursed
(see ŪRS+ed)

ŪR'sest
accursest
becursest
coercest
conversest
cursest
disbursest
dispersest
immersest
interspersest
nursest
rehearsest
reimbursest
reversest
traversest

ŪR'set
tercet

ŪR'seth
accurseth
becurseth
coerceth
converseth
curseth
disburseth

disperseth
immerseth
intersperseth
nurseth
rehearseth
reimburseth
reverseth
traverseth

ŪR'sez
accurses
amerces
becurses
coerces
converses
curses
disburses
disperses
hearses
immerses
intersperses
nurses
purses
rehearses
reimburses
reverses
submerses
traverses
verses

ŪR'shal
commercial
controversial
tertial
uncommercial

ŪR'ship
worship

ŪR'shum
nasturtium

ŪR'shun
abstersion
animadversion
apertion
aspersion
assertion
aversion
circumversion
coercion
concertion
contraversion
controversion
conversion
demersion
desertion
disconcertion
discursion
dispersion
diversion
emersion
eversion
excursion
exertion
extersion
immersion
incursion
insertion
inspersion
intersertion
interspersion
introversion
inversion
mersion
nasturtion
obversion
perversion
recursion
retroversion
reversion
self-assertion
submersion

subversion
tertian
version
(cf. ÛR'si-an)

ÛR'si
Circe
controversy
gramercy
mercy
Mersey
Percy
pursy
Searcy

ÛR'sing
accursing
becursing
coercing
conversing
cursing
disbursing
dispersing
immersing
nursing
rehearsing
reimbursing
reversing
transversing
traversing
versing

ÛR'siv
abstersive
animadversive
aspersive
aversive
coercive
conversive
cursive
decursive

detersive
discursive
dispersive
eversive
excursive
incursive
perversive
precursive
subversive

ÛRS'ment
amercement
disbursement
imbursement
reimburse-
    ment

ÛRS'nes
adverseness
averseness
perverseness
terseness

ÛR'son
Gerson
McPherson
person

ÛR'sted
bursted
thirsted
worsted

ÛR'stest
burstest, etc.

ÛR'steth
bursteth, etc.

ÛR'sti
thirsty

ÛR'sting
bursting
thirsting
worsting

ÛR'stur
burster
thirster

ÛR'sur
accurser
amercer
ante-cursor
bursar
coercer
commercer
converser
curser
cursor
disburser
disperser
hearser
immerser
mercer
nurser
perverser
precursor
purser
rehearser
reimburser
reverser
traverser
verser
worser

ÛR'sus
excursus
thyrsus
ursus
versus

ÛR'ta
Alberta
Elberta

ÛR'tan
certain
curtain
encurtain
incertain
uncertain

ÛR'ted
adverted
asserted
averted
blurted
concerted
converted
deserted
disconcerted
diverted
exerted
flirted
inserted
interserted
inverted
perverted
preconcerted
reverted
spurted
squirted
subverted
undiverted
unperverted

ÛR'ten
thirteen

ÛR'tens
advertence
inadvertence
misadvertence

ŬR'test	**ŬR'tha**	flirty	**ŬR'tis**
advertest	Bertha	Gertie	Curtis
assertest	Hertha	thirty	
avertest			**ŬR't'l**
blurtest	**ŬR'THen**	**ŬR'ting**	fertile
concertest	burthen	adverting	hurtle
controvertest	disburthen	asserting	kirtle
convertest	unburthen	averting	myrtle
curtest		blurting	spurtle
disconcertest	**ŬR'then**	concerting	turtle
divertest	earthen	controverting	whortle
exertest		converting	
hurtest	**ŬR'THur**	deserting	**ŬRT'les**
insertest	further	disconcerting	shirtless
invertest		diverting	skirtless
pertest	**ŬR'THest**	exerting	
pervertest	furthest	flirting	**ŬRT'li**
revertest		hurting	alertly
skirtest	**ŬRth'ful**	inserting	curtly
spurtest	mirthful	interserting	expertly
subvertest	worthful	interverting	inertly
		inverting	inexpertly
ŬR'teth	**ŬRth'les**	perverting	pertly
averteth	birthless	preconcerting	
asserteth	mirthless	retroverting	**ŬRT'nes**
averteth	worthless	reverting	alertness
blurteth		self-asserting	curtness
concerteth	**ŬR'THi**	shirting	expertness
controverteth	noteworthy	skirting	inertness
converteth	sea-worthy	spurting	inexpertness
disconcerteth	trust-worthy	squirting	pertness
diverteth	worthy	subverting	
exerteth	unworthy		**ŬR'ton**
hurteth		**ŬR'tiv**	Berton
inserteth	**ŬR'thi**	assertive	(cf. ŬR'tan)
inverteth	earthy	divertive	
perverteth		exertive	**ŬR'trud**
reverteth	**ŬR'ti**	furtive	Gertrude
skirteth	cherty	revertive	
spurteth	dirty	self-assertive	**ŬRT'si**
subverteth			curtsey

āle, câre, ădd, ärm, ȧsk; mē, hẹre, ĕnd; īce, ĭll;

ÛR′tu
virtue

ÛR′tŭr
nurture
(cf. ÛR′chur)

ÛR′tŭr
adverter
animadverter
asserter
averter
converter
curter
disconcerter
diverter
exerter
hurter
inserter
inverter
perter
perverter
preconcerter
spurter
squirter
subverter

ÛR′up
stirrup
(cf. ĬR′up)

ÛR′ur
abjurer
adjurer
allurer
assurer
conjurer
curer
demurer
endurer
ensurer

immurer
impurer
insurer
inurer
juror
lurer
manurer
maturer
moorer
nonjuror
obscurer
poorer
procurer
purer
reassurer
securer
surer
tourer
unmoorer
(cf. ÛR′or)

ÛR′ur
averrer
bestirrer
blurrer
concurrer
conferrer
deferrer
demurrer
incurrer
inferrer
interrer
preferrer
spurrer
stirrer
transferrer

ÛR′us
anurous
Arcturus
dolichurus

Eurus
urus

ÛR′us
susurrous
wurrus

ÛR′uz
Burroughs
Burrows
(cf. ÛR′o + s)

ÛR′va
Minerva

ÛR′val
acerval
curval

**ÛR′vans,
ÛR′vens**
fervence
inobservance
observance
unobservance

**ÛR′vant,
ÛR′vent**
conservant
curvant
fervent
inobservant
observant
recurvant
servant
unobservant

ÛR′vat
acervate
curvate
enervate

incurvate
recurvate
trinervate

ÛR′ven
nervine

ÛR′vest
conservest
curvest
deservest
observest
preservest
reservest
servest
swervest
unnervest

ÛR′veth
conserveth
curveth
deserveth
observeth
preserveth
reserveth
serveth
swerveth
unnerveth

ÛR′vi
nervy
scurvy
topsy-turvy

ÛR′vid
fervid
perfervid
topsy-turvied

ÛR′vĭl
servile

ÛR'vĭl

chervil

servile

ÛR'vĭm

cervine

nervine

ÛR'vĭng

conserving

curving

deserving

Irving

nerving

observing

preserving

reserving

serving

swerving

time-serving

undeserving

unnerving

unobserving

unswerving

ÛR'vĭs

lip-service

merchant-serv-
ice

Purvis

sea-service

service

unservice

ÛRV'les

nerveless

ÛR'vur

conserver

deserver

fervor

game-preserver

life-preserver

nerver

observer

preserver

reserver

server

swerver

time-server

unnerver

ÛR'vus

nervous

recurvous

ÛR'wĭn

Erwin

Irwin

Merwin

ÛRZ'da

Thursday

ÛR'zha

Persia

ÛR'zhun

animadver-
sion

aspersion

aversion

conversion

demersion

discursion

dispersion

diversion

excursion

incursion

introversion

inversion

perversion

reversion

subversion

version

ÛR'zi

furzy

jersey

kersey

Ū'sa

Arethusa

Coosa

Medusa

Sousa

Susa

Tallapoosa

Tuscaloosa

ŪS'al

hypotenusal

ŪS'chun

adustion

combustion

fustian

ŪS'ed

deuced

(see ŪS+ed)

ŪS'en

loosen

unloosen

ŪS'ens

translucence

ŪS'ent

abducent

adducent

conducent

interlucent

lucent

producent

reducent

relucent

traducent

tralucent

translucent

unlucent

ŪS'est

abstrusest

adducest

conducest

deducest

inducest

introducest

loosest

producest

profusest

reducest

reproducest

seducest

sprucest

traducest

unloosest

ŪS'est

fussest, etc.

ŪS'et

gusset

russet

ŪS'eth

adduceth

conduceth

deduceth

educeth

induceth

introduceth

āle,   câre,   ădd,   ärm,   åsk;   mē,   hẽre,   ĕnd;   īce,   ĭll;

looseth
produceth
reduceth
reproduceth
seduceth
spruceth
traduceth
unlooseth

ŪS'eth
fusseth, etc.

ŪS'ez
abuses
adduces
burnooses
cabooses
conduces
deduces
Druses
excuses
induces
introduces
juices
looses
nooses
produces
reduces
reproduces
seduces
sluices
spruces
traduces
truces
unlooses
uses

ŪS'ez
buses
busses
cusses

discusses
fusses
Gus's
musses
trusses

ŪS'ful
juiceful
useful

ŪSH'a
Jerusha

ŪSH'a
Prussia
Russia

ŪSH'al
crucial
fiducial

ŪSH'an
Prussian
Russian

ŪSH'est
blushest
brushest
crushest
flushest
gushest
hushest
rushest

ŪSH'eth
blusheth
brusheth
crusheth
flusheth
gusheth
husheth
rusheth

ŪSH'ez
blushes
brushes
crushes
flushes
gushes
hushes
lushes
mushes
onrushes
plushes
rushes
thrushes
tushes
uprushes

ŪSH'i
blushy
brushy
gushy
lushy
rushy
slushy

ŪSH'ing
douching
ruching

ŪSH'ing
blushing
brushing
crushing
flushing
gushing
hushing
lushing
rushing
unblushing

Ū'shun
ablution

absolution
allocution
attribution
circumlocution
circumvolution
collocution
comminution
constitution
contribution
convolution
destitution
devolution
dilution
diminution
dissolution
distribution
electrocution
elocution
evolution
execution
imminution
insecution
institution
interlocution
involution
irresolution
Lilliputian
locution
obvolution
persecution
pollution
prosecution
prostitution
redargution
resolution
restitution
retribution
revolution
solution
substitution

ōld, ôr, ŏdd, oil, fŏŏt, out; ūse, ûrn, ŭp; THis, thin

ventrilocution
volution

ŬSH'un
concussion
discussion
incussion
percussion
Prussian
recussion
repercussion
Russian
succussion

ŬSH'ur
blusher
brusher
crusher
flusher
gusher
husher
plusher
rusher
usher

ŪSH'us
Lucius

ŬSH'us
luscious

ŬS'i
goosy
juicy
Lucy
sluicy

ŬS'i
fussy
hussy
mussy

ŬS'id
lucid
mucid
pellucid
translucid

ŬS'ij
abusage
usage

ŬS'il
protrusile

ŬS'ing
adducing
conducing
deducing
educing
inducing
introducing
loosing
producing
reducing
reproducing
seducing
sprucing
traducing
unloosing

ŬS'ing
bussing
cussing
discussing
fussing
mussing
trussing

ŪS'iv
abusive
allusive
collusive

conclusive
conducive
confusive
contusive
deducive
delusive
diffusive
effusive
elusive
exclusive
illusive
inclusive
inconclusive
infusive
inobtrusive
intrusive
obtrusive
perfusive
reclusive
seclusive
seducive
transfusive

ŬS'iv
concussive
discussive
percussive
repercussive
succussive

ŬS'kan
Della-Cruscan
dusken
Etruscan
molluscan
Tuscan

ŬS'kat
coruscate
infuscate
obfuscate

conclusive
ŬS'kest
duskest, etc.

ŬS'ket
busket
musket

ŬS'keth
dusketh, etc.

ŬSki
dusky
husky
musky
tusky

ŬS'kin
buskin
Ruskin

ŬS'king
dusking
husking
tusking

ŬS'kul
crepuscule
majuscule
minuscule
opuscule

ŬS'kur
husker
tusker

ŬS'l
bustle
corpuscle
hustle
justle
muscle

āle, câre, ădd, ärm, ăsk; mē, hẹre, ĕnd; īce, ĭll;

mussel
opuscle
rustle
tussle

ŬS'les
juiceless
useless

ŬS'lest
bustlest, etc.

ŬS'leth
bustleth, etc.

ŬS'ling
bustling
hustling
muscling
rustling
tussling

ŬS'lur
bustler
hustler
rustler
tussler

ŬS"lz
Brussels
bustles, etc.

ŪS'ment
conducement
deducement
inducement
reducement
seducement
superinduce-
  ment
traducement

ŬS'nes
abstruseness
diffuseness
looseness
obtuseness
profuseness
recluseness
spruceness

Ū'so
Crusoe
trousseau
whoso

Ū'som
gruesome
twosome

ŬS'ta
Augusta

ŬS'tas
Eustace

ŬS'tat
incrustate

ŬS'ted
adjusted
bedusted
betrusted
busted
combusted
crusted
disgusted
distrusted
dusted
encrusted
entrusted
fusted
lusted

mistrusted
rusted
trusted

ŬS'test
adjustest
disgustest
distrustest
dustest
encrustest
entrustest
justest
lustest
mistrustest
robustest
rustest
thrustest
trustest

ŬS'teth
adjusteth
disgusteth
distrusteth
dusteth
encrusteth
entrusteth
lusteth
mistrusteth
thrusteth
trusteth

ŬST'ful
distrustful
lustful
mistrustful
overtrustful
trustful
untrustful

ŬS'ti
crusty

dusty
fustie
fusty
gusty
lusty
musty
rusty
trusty

ŬS'tik
fustic
rustic

ŬS'tin
Dustin
Justin

ŬS'ting
adjusting
bedusting
betrusting
busting
coadjusting
crusting
disgusting
distrusting
dusting
encrusting
entrusting
lusting
mistrusting
overtrusting
rusting
self-adjusting
thrusting
trusting
unmistrusting

ŬS'tingz
dustings
hustings
thrustings

ŬS'tis
Custis
justice

ŬS'tiv
adjustive
combustive

ŬST'li
augustly
justly
robustly

ŬST'ment
adjustment
encrustment
maladjustment

ŬST'nes
augustness
justness
robustness

ŬS'to
gusto

ŬS'tom
custom
(cf. Rustum)

ŬS'tral
lacustral
lustral
palustral

ŬS'trat
frustrate
illustrate

ŬS'trin
lacustrine
palustrine

ŬS'trum
flustrum
lustrum

ŬS'trus
blustrous
lustrous

ŬS'tur
booster
brewster
Fewster
jouster
rooster
Worcester

ŬS'tur
adjuster
bluster
buster
coadjuster
cluster
Custer
distruster
duster
filibuster
fluster
juster
knuckle-duster
lack-lustre
luster
lustre
muster
robuster
thruster
trust-buster
truster

ŬS'turd
blustered
bustard

clustered
custard
flustered
lustered
mustard
mustered

ŬS'tus
Augustus
Justus

ŬS'ur
abstruser
adducer
conducer
deducer
inducer
introducer
looser
producer
reducer
reproducer
seducer
sprucer
traducer

ŬS'ur
cusser
discusser
fusser
musser
trusser

ŪT'al
brutal
footle
tootle
(cf. ŪT'il)

ŪT'at
circumnutate

immutate
scutate

ŪT'ed
allocuted
bebooted
booted
bruited
comminuted
commuted
computed
confuted
constituted
convoluted
deputed
diluted
disputed
elocuted
electrocuted
executed
fluted
fruited
hooted
immuted
imputed
instituted
involuted
looted
mooted
persecuted
polluted
prosecuted
prostituted
recruited
refuted
reputed
rooted
saluted
self-constituted
substituted
suited

tooted	*substitutest*	**ŪTH'est**	**Ŭth'ur**
transmuted	*suitest*	smoothest	Luther
unbooted	*transmutest*	soothest	uncouther
unconfuted	*uprootest*		
undisputed		**Ŭth'ful**	**Ŭth'ur**
unpersecuted	**ŬT'est**	ruthfu	another
unpolluted	*buttest*	toothful	brother
unrooted	*ruttest*, etc.	truthful	Charter
unsuited		untruthful	brother
uprooted	**ŬT'eth**	youthful	foremother
voluted	*commuteth*		foster-brother
(cf. bootied,	*confuteth*	**ŪTH'ing**	foster-mother
putid)	*constituteth*	smoothing	half-brother
	deputeth	soothing	mother
ŬT'ed	*diluteth*		other
butted	*disputeth*	**Ŭth'ing**	smother
rutted, etc.	*executeth*	toothing	t'other
	hooteth		
ŪT'est	*imputeth*	**Ŭth'ing**	**ŬTH'urn**
acutest	*instituteth*	*doth*-ing	Sothern
astutest	*looteth*	nothing	southern
commutest	*overshooteth*		
confutest	*persecuteth*	**Ŭth'les**	**ŪT'i**
constitutest	*polluteth*	ruthless	agouti
cutest	*prosecuteth*	toothless	booty
deputest	*recruiteth*	truthless	beauty
dilutest	*refuteth*		cootie
disputest	*rooteth*	**ŪTH'nes**	cutie
executest	*saluteth*	smoothness	Djibouti
hootest	*shooteth*		duty
imputest	*suiteth*	**Ŭth'nes**	fluty
institutest	*transmuteth*	uncouthness	freebooty
lootest	*unbooteth*		fruity
minutest	*uprooteth*	**Ŭth'som**	Jibuti
mutest		toothsome	looty
persecutest	**ŬT'eth**	youthsome	rooty
recruitest	*butteth*		snooty
refutest	*rutteth*, etc.	**ŪTH'ur**	sooty
resolutest		smoother	tutti-frutti
salutest	**ŪT'ful**	soother	
shootest	fruitful		

ŬT'i
butty
gutty
jutty
nutty
putty
rutty
smutty
tutty

ŬT'ij
fruitage
mutage
scutage

ŬT'ik
diazeutic
emphyteutic
hermeneutic
maieutic
pharmaceutic
propædeutic
scorbutic
therapeutic
toreutic

ŬT'il
futile
inutile
rutile
sutile
(cf. ŬT'al)

ŬT'ing
booting
comminuting
commuting
computing
confuting
constituting
darned tooting

deputing
diluting
disputing
executing
fluting
fruiting
high-faluting
hooting
imputing
instituting
looting
mooting
offshooting
outshooting
overshooting
permuting
persecuting
polluting
prosecuting
prostituting
reconstituting
recruiting
refuting
rooting
saluting
scooting
shooting
substituting
suiting
tooting
transmuting
unbooting
unrooting
uprooting

ŬT'ing
abutting
butting
crosscutting
cutting
glass-cutting

glutting
gutting
jutting
nutting
putting
rebutting
rutting
shutting
strutting

ŬT'ish
brutish
sootish

ŬT'ish
ruttish
sluttish

ŬT'ist
flutist
hermeneutist
lutist
pharmaceutist
therapeutist

ŬT'iv
coadjutive
constitutive
indutive
persecutive
resolutive

ŬT'izm
brutism
mutism

ŬT'l
abuttal
cuttle
guttle
rebuttal

ruttle
scuttle
shuttle
subtle
suttle
Tuttle

ŬT'las
cutlass

ŬT'les
bootless
fruitless

ŬT'lest
scuttlest, etc.

ŬT'let
cutlet

ŬT'leth
scuttleth, etc.

ŬT'li
absolutely
posilutely

ŬT'ling
footling
tootling

ŬT'ling
gutling
scuttling
sutling

ŬT'lur
butler
cutler
scuttler
subtler
sutler

ŪT'ment

confutement
imbrutement
recruitment

ŪT'nes

absoluteness
acuteness
astuteness
cuteness
hirsuteness
minuteness
muteness

Ū'to

Pluto

Ū'ton

Brewton
Newton
Teuton

ŬT'on

bachelor-
  button
button
Dutton
glutton
Hutton
mutton
Sutton

ŪT'or

suitor
tutor, etc.
(see ŪT'ur)

ŪT'ral

neutral

ŬT'res

buttress

ŪT'rid

putrid

ŪT'riks

persecutrix
tutrix

ŪT'ron

neutron

ŪT'si

tootsie-wootsie

ŪT'ūr

future
puture
suture

ŪT'ūr

accoutre
acuter
astuter
booter
chuter
coadjutor
commuter
computer
confuter
constitutor
cuter
deputer
diluter
disputer
executor
fluter
fouter
freebooter
hooter
imputer
institutor
looter

luter
minuter
mooter
muter
neuter
parachuter
pea-shooter
permuter
persecutor
pewter
polluter
prosecutor
prostitutor
recruiter
refuter
restitutor
ringtailed
  tooter
rooter
saluter
sharp-shooter
shooter
substitutor
suitor
tooter
transmuter
tutor
uprooter

ŬT'ur

abutter
bread-and-
  butter
butter
clutter
cutter
flutter
glutter
gutter
mutter
nutter

pilot-cutter
putter
rebutter
scutter
shutter
splutter
sputter
strutter
stutter
utter
wood-cutter

ŬT'urd

unuttered
fluttered, etc.

Ū'ur

bedewer
bestrewer
bluer
brewer
canoer
chewer
cooer
derring-doer
doer
enduer
eschewer
evildoer
ewer
fewer
gluer
hallooer
hewer
imbuer
interviewer
mewer
misconstruer
misdoer
newer
outdoer

ōld, ôr, ŏdd, oil, fŏŏt, out; ūse, ûrn, ŭp; THis, thin

overdoer
pursuer
renewer
reviewer
ruer
sewer
screwer
shampooer
shoer
skewer
stewer
subduer
tattooer
truer
undoer
unscrewer
viewer
well-doer
wooer
wrong-doer

Ū'urd
leeward
sewered
skewered
steward

ŪV'al
approval
disapproval
disproval
removal
reproval

ŬV'ed
beloved

ŬL'el
scovel
shovel

ŬV'en
hooven
proven

ŬV'en
coven
oven
sloven

ŪV'est
approvest
disapprovest
disprovest
improvest
movest
provest
removest
reprovest

ŬV'eth
approveth
disapproveth
disproveth
improveth
moveth
proveth
removeth
reproveth

ŪV'i
movie

ŪV'i
covey
dovey
lovey

ŬV'ing
approving
disapproving
disproving
grooving

improving
moving
proving
removing
reproving
unmoving

ŬV'ing
gloving
loving
self-loving
shoving
ungloving
unloving

ŬV'les
gloveless
loveless

ŬV'ment
approvement
improvement
movement

ŬV'ur
approver
disapprover
disprover
groover
Hoover
improver
maneuver
mover
prover
remover
reprover
Vancouver
(cf. Louvre)

ŬV'ur
cover
discover

glover
lover
plover
recover
rediscover
shover
table-cover
uncover

ŬV'urn
govern

Ū'ya
alleluia

Ū'yans
buoyance

Ū'yant
buoyant

ŪZ'a
lallapalooza

ŪZ'al
musal
refusal
(cf. fusil)

ŪZ'an
Susan

ŬZ'ard
buzzard

ŬZ'band
husband

ŪZ'di
Tuesday

ŪZ'est
abusest

accusest
amusest
boozest
bruisest
choosest
confusest
cruisest
diffusest
excusest
fusest
infusest
losest
musest
oozest
perusest
refusest
snoozest
suffusest
transfusest
usest

ŬZ'est

buzzest, etc.

ŬZ'eth

abuseth
accuseth
amuseth
boozeth
bruiseth
chooseth
confuseth
cruiseth
diffuseth
excuseth
fuseth
infuseth
loseth
museth
oozeth

peruseth
refuseth
snoozeth
suffuseth
transfuseth
useth

ŬZ'eth

buzzeth, etc.

ŪZ'ez

abuses
accuses
amuses
bemuses
bruises
chooses
circumfuses
confuses
contuses
cruises
diffuses
disabuses
disuses
druses
excuses
fuses
infuses
interfuses
loses
misuses
muses
nooses
oozes
peruses
refuses
snoozes
suffuses
transfuses
uses

ŬZ'ez

buzzes
fuzzes

Ū'zhun

abstrusion
abusion
affusion
allusion
circumfusion
collusion
conclusion
confusion
contusion
delusion
detrusion
diffusion
dissillusion
effusion
elusion
exclusion
extrusion
fusion
illusion
inclusion
infusion
interclusion
interfusion
intrusion
Malthusian
obtrusion
occlusion
perfusion
pertusion
preclusion
profusion
prolusion
protrusion
reclusion
refusion
retrusion

seclusion
self-delusion
suffusion
transfusion
trusion
(cf. ŪZ'i-an)

ŪZ'ï

boozy
fluzie
oozy
woozy

ŬZ'ï

fuzzy
hussy

ŪZ'ik

music

ŬZ'in

cousin
cozen
dozen

ŪZ'ing

abusing
accusing
amusing
boozing
bruising
choosing
confusing
contusing
cruising
diffusing
disusing
excusing
fusing
infusing
interfusing

ōld, ôr, ŏdd, oil, fŏŏt, out; ūse, ûrn, ŭp; THis, thin

losing
musing
oozing
perusing
refusing
self-accusing
snoozing
suffusing
transfusing
using

ŬZ'ing

buzzing
fuzzing

ŬZ'inz

cousins
cozens
couzens
dozens

ŬZ'iv

amusive
unamusive

ŬZ"l, ŬZ'al

bamboozle

foozle
gumfoozle
perusal
refusal

ŬZ"l

bemuzzle
fuzzle
guzzle
muzzle
nuzzle
puzzle
unmuzzle

ŬZ'lest

bemuzzlest, etc.

ŬZ'leth

bemuzzleth, etc.

ŬZ'lin

muslin

ŬZ'ling

bemuzzling
guzzling
muzzling

nuzzling
puzzling

ŬZ'lur

bamboozler
foozler

ŬZ'lur

guzzler
muzzler
puzzler

ŬZ'm

izzum-wuzzum

ŬZ'man

newsman
trewsman

ŬZ'ment

amusement

ŬZ'om

bosom

Ŭz'rel

newsreel

ŬZ'ur

abuser
accuser
amuser
boozer
bruiser
chooser
confuser
cruiser
diffuser
excuser
fuser
infuser
interfuser
lallapaloozer
loser
muser
non-user
oozer
peruser
refuser
snoozer
suffuser
transfuser
user

āle, câre, ădd, ärm, åsk; mē, hĕre, ĕnd; īce, ĭll;

WORDS ACCENTED ON THE THIRD SYLLABLE FROM THE END: ANTEPENULTS; TRIPLE RHYMES

A

For a discussion of words included under the accented vowels following, see the beginning of A rhymes in Section I.

(Note on Archaic Verb-forms among Triple Rhymes.—The archaic verb forms ending in-*est* and -*eth* have not as a rule been listed among the triple rhymes, to avoid needlessly expanding the book. When desired, they can be found by locating the present participles of triple-rhymed verbs, the -*ing* form: such forms as *laboring, bracketing, fracturing, dallying, hampering, clamoring, meandering,* and the rest. These can be turned without difficulty into the desired archaic forms: as, *laborest, laboreth; bracketest, bracketeth;* and so with all of them.)

Ā'a-b'l
conveyable
defrayable
impayable
payable
portrayable
repayable
unpayable
unprayable
unswayable

ĂB'a-sis
anabasis
catabasis
metabasis

ĂB'el-ur
gabeler
labeller

ĂB'i-a
Arabia
labia
Suabia

ĂB'i-an
Arabian
Fabian
Sabian
Sorabian
Suabian

ĂB'id-nes
rabidness
tabidness

ĂB'i-est
flabbiest
shabbiest

ĂB'i-ez
rabies
scabies

ĂB'i-fi
dissyllabify
labefy
syllabify
tabefy

ĂB'i-kal
Arabical
monosyllabical
polysyllabical

ĂB'i-li
flabbily
shabbily

ĂB'i-nes
flabbiness
scabbiness
shabbiness
slabbiness

ĂB'i-net
cabinet
tabinet

ĂB'i-tud
habitude
tabitude

ĂB'i-ur
flabbier
gabbier
shabbier

ĂB'la-tiv
ablative
bablative

ĂB''l-ment
babblement
brabblement
dabblement
gabblement
rabblement

ĂB''l-nes
sableness
stableness
unstableness

ĂB'o-la
Metabola
parabola

ĂB'ri-el
Gabriel

ĂB'u-lar
confabular
pabular
tabular
tintinnabular

ĂB'u-lat
confabulate
tabulate

ĂB'u-list
fabulist
vocabulist

ĂB'u-lum
acetabulum
pabulum
tintinnabulum

ĂB'u-lus
fabulous
pabulous
sabulous
tintinnabulous

ĀB'ur-ing
belaboring
laboring
neighboring
unlaboring

ĀB'ur-ur
laborer
taborer

ĂCH'a-b'l
attachable
catchable
detachable
immatchable
matchable
scratchable
unmatchable

ĀD'a-b'l,
  ĀD'i-b'l
evadible
persuadable
shadable
tradable
wadable

ĀD'ed-nes
bejadedness
degradedness
fadedness
jadedness
persuadedness
shadedness

ĂD'e-us
Amadeus

ĂD'e-us
Thaddeus

ĂD'i-an
Acadian
Arcadian
Barbadian
Canadian
nomadian
Orcadian
Palladian

ĂD'i-ant
irradiant
radiant

ĂD'i-ent
gradient

ĂD'i-tiv
additive
traditive

ĂD'i-um
palladium
radium
stadium
vanadium

ĂD'o-ing
foreshadowing
overshadowing
shadowing

ĂF'a-nus
diaphanous

ĂF'i-kal
autobiographi-
  cal

autographical
bibliographical
biographical
calligraphical
cartographical
cosmographical
diagraphical
ethnographical
geographical
glossographical
graphical
lexicographical
lexigraphical
orthographical
palæonto-
  graphical
photographical
physiograph-
  ical
phytographical
pterylograph-
  ical
seraphical
topographical
typographical

ĂF'ti-li
craftily
draughtily

ĂG'ed-li
jaggedly
raggedly

ĂG'ed-nes
craggedness
jaggedness
raggedness

ĂG'i-nes
bagginess

āle, câre, ădd, ärm, åsk; mē, hĕre, ĕnd; īce, ĭll;

cragginess
knagginess
scragginess
shagginess

ĂG′on-ist

agonist
antagonist
protagonist

ĂG′on-iz

agonize
antagonize

ĂG′on-izm

agonism
antagonism

ĂG′ran-si

flagrancy
fragrancy
vagrancy

ĂG′ur-i

faggery
jaggery
raggery
waggery
zigzaggery

ĂG′ur-ing

staggering
swaggering

ĂG′ur-ur

staggerer
swaggerer

Ā′ik-al

algebraical
archaical
Hebraical

laical
paradisaical
pharisaical

Ā′it-i

gaiety
laity

ĂJ′a-b′l

assuageable
gaugeable

ĂJ′i-an

Brobdignagian
magian
pelagian
(cf. contagion)

ĂJ′i-kal

magical
tragical

ĂJ′il-nes

agileness
fragileness

ĂJ′in-al

imaginal
paginal
vaginal

ĂJ′in-us

cartilaginous
farraginous
lumbaginous
mucilaginous
oleaginous
voraginous

ĂJ′us-nes

advantageous-
  ness

courageous-
  ness
disadvan-
  tageousness
outrageous-
  ness
rampageous-
  ness
umbrageous-
  ness

ĀK′a-b′l

breakable
impacable
implacable
mistakable
pacable
placable
undertakable
unshakable

ĂK′et-ed

bracketed
jacketed
racketed

ĂK′et-ing

bracketing
jacketing
racketing

ĂK′i-an

batrachian
eustachian
Noachian

ĀK′i-nes

flakiness
quakiness
shakiness
snakiness

ĂK′ish-nes

brackishness
knackishnes
slackishness

ĂK′ri-ti

acrity
alacrity

ĂK′ron-izm

anachronism
metachronism

ĂK′sa-b′l

relaxable
taxable

ĂK′shun-al

factional
fractional
pactional

ĂK′shus-nes

factiousness
fractiousness

**ĂK′ta-b′l,
ĂK′ti-b′l**

attractable
compactible
contractible
detractible
distractible
extractible
infractible
intactable
intractable
refractable
retractable
tactable
tractable

ōld, ôr, ŏdd, oil, fŏŏt, out; ⁿse, ûrn. ŭp; THis, thin

ĂK'ted-nes	refractory	ĂK'ur-i	Ā'li-a
abstractednĕss	satisfactory	hackery	Adalia
contractedness	tractory	hijackery	Attalia
distractedness		knick-knackery	Australia
protractedness	ĂK'tu-al	quackery	Centralia
	actual	Thackeray	echolalia
ĂK'ti-kal	factual	Zachary	Eulalia
didactical	tactual		Fidelia
practical		ĂK'ur-izm	regalia
	ĂK'tur-ing	fakirism	Rosalia
ĂK'ti-lus	fracturing	Quakerism	Sedalia
didactylous	manufacturing	Shakerism	Thalia
hexadactylous			(cf. azalea, and
leptodactylous	ĂK'u-lar	ĂK'we-us	ĀL'ya)
pachydacty-	oracular	aqueous	
lous	piacular	subaqueous	ĂL'i-bur
pterodacty-	spectacular	terraqueous	caliber
lous	supernacular		Excalibur
	tabernacular	ĀL'a-b'l	
ĂK'tiv-nēs	tentacular	assailable	ĂL'id-nes
abstractive-	vernacular	available	impallidness
ness		bailable	invalidness
activeness	ĂK'u-lat	exhalable	pallidness
attractiveness	bimaculate	mailable	validness
contractive-	ejaculate	retailable	
ness	immaculate	sailable	ĂL'i-fi
detractiveness	jaculate	saleable	alkaify
distractiveness	maculate	unassailable	calefy
protractiveness		unavailable	salify
putrefactive-	ĂK'u-lus	unsailable	
ness	abaculus		ĂL'i-ing
refractiveness	miraculous	ĀL'e-a	dallying
	oraculous	azalea	rallying
ĂK'to-ri	piaculous	(cf. regalia)	sallying
detractory	vernaculous		tallying
dissatisfactory		ĀL'ē-at, ĂL'i-at	
factory	ĂK'ur-i	malleate	ĀL'i-nes
lactary	bakery	palliate	dailiness
manufactory	fakery		scaliness
olfactory	fakiry	ĀL'en-tin	
phylactery	rakery	Ballantine	ĀL'i-sis
		Valentine	analysis

āle,   câre,   ădd,   ārm,   åsk;   mē,   hēre,   ĕnd;   īce,   ĭll;

catalysis
dialysis
paralysis

ĂL′ĭ-son
Alison
Callison

ĂL′ĭ-tĭ
abnormality
accidentality
actuality
alamodality
animality
artificiality
banality
bestiality
Biblicality
brutality
carnality
causality
centrality
circumstan-
    tiality
classicality
comicality
confidentiality
congeniality
conjecturality
conjugality
connubiality
constitution-
    ality
consubstan-
    tiality
conventionality
conviviality
cordiality
corporality
corporeality
criminality

curiality
dextrality
duality
egality
elementality
ephemerality
essentiality
ethereality
eventuality
externality
exterritorial-
    ity
fantasticality
fatality
feminality
feudality
finality
finicality
formality
frugality
fundamen-
    tality
generality
geniality
graduality
gutturality
horozontality
hospitality
ideality
illegality
immateriality
immorality
immortality
impartiality
imperiality
impersonality
inconsequen-
    tialty
individuality
ineffectuality
informality

inimicality
instrumen-
    tality
integrality
intellectuality
intentionality
intrinsicality
irrationality
joviality
laicality
laterality
legality
liberality
lineality
literality
locality
logicality
magistrality
materiality
mentality
meridionality
mesnality
modality
morality
mortality
municipality
mutuality
nasality
nationality
naturality
neutrality
notionality
occidentality
officiality
orientality
originality
orthodoxality
parochiality
partiality
pedality
penality

personality
plurality
potentiality
practicality
preternatur-
    ality
principality
prodigality
proportion-
    ality
provinciality
prudentiality
punctuality
radicality
rascality
rationality
reality
reciprocality
regality
rivality
rurality
sectionality
sensuality
sentimentality
septentrion-
    ality
seriality
sesquiped-
    ality
severality
sexuality
signality
sociality
sodality
speciality
spectrality
spirality
spirituality
substantiality
superficiality
supernaturality

ōld, ôr, ŏdd, oil, fŏŏt, out; ūse, ûrn, ŭp; THis, thin

technicality	ĂL'o-gi	sallowness	ĂM'a-ri
temporality	analogy	shallowness	gramarye
theatricality	crustalogy		mammary
tonality	genealogy	ĂL'o-ur	
totality	genethlialogy	callower	ĂM'a-tist
traditionality	mammalogy	hallower	dramatist
transcenden-	mineralogy	sallower	epigrammatist
tality	paralogy	shallower	grammatist
triality	petralogy	tallower	hierogram-
triviality	*pyroballogy*		matist
universality	tetralogy	ĂL'ur-i	lipogrammatist
unusuality		nailery	melodramatist
vegetality	ĂL'o-gist	raillery	
venality	analogist	ĂL'ur-i	ĂM'a-tiv
veniality	decalogist		amative
verbality	dialogist	gallery	exclamative
verticality	genealogist	*raillery*	
visuality	mammalogist	salary	ĂM'a-tiz
vitality	mineralogist	ĂL'yen-izm,	anagramma-
vocality	penalogist	ĂL'yan-izm	tize
whimsicality		alienism	diagramma-
	ĂL'o-giz	bacchanalian-	tize
ĂL'i-um	analogize	ism	dramatize
pallium	dialogize	episcopalian-	epigramma-
thallium	genealogize	ism	tize
	paralogize	saturnalianism	
ĂL'i-ur		sesquipeda-	ĂM'bu-lat
dallier	ĂL'o-gizm	lianism	ambulate
rallier	analogism	universalian-	deambulate
sallier	dialogism	ism	funambulate
tallier	paralogism		perambulate
		ĂM'a-b'l	somnambu-
ĂL'ji-a	ĂL'o-ish	blamable	late
neuralgia	sallowish	claimable	
nostalgia	shallowish	framable	ĂM'bu-list
	tallowish	irreclaimable	funambulist
ĂL'o-est		namable	noctambulist
callowest	ĂL'o-nes	reclaimable	somnambulist
hallowest	callowness	tamable	
sallowest	fallownes	unblamable	ĂM'bu-lizm
shallowest		untamable	funambulism

āle, câre, ădd, ärm, åsk; mē, hęre, ĕnd; īce, ĭll;

noctambulism
somnambulism

ĂM'et-er
diameter
dynameter
hexameter
octameter
parameter
pentameter
peirameter
pluviameter
tetrameter
viameter
voltameter

ĂM'ful-nes
blamefulness
shamefulness

Ā'mi-a
lamia
Mesoptomania

ĂM'i-kal
amical
balsamical
dynamical

ĂM'in-a
lamina
stamina

ĂM'i-nat
contaminate
laminate

ĂM'is-tri
palmistry
psalmistry

ĂM'i-ti
amity
calamity

ĂM'les-nes
aimlessness
blamelessness
damelessness
famelessness
namelessness
shamelessness
tamelessness

ĂM'on-it
Ammonite
Mammonite

ĂM'on-izm
Mammonism
Shamanism

ĂM'or-us
amorous
clamorous
glamorous

ĂM'pi-on
campion
champion
tampion

ĂM'pur-ing
hampering
pampering
scampering
tampering

ĂM'pur-ur
hamperer
pamperer
scamperer
tamperer

ĂM'ul-us
famulus
hamulus
ramulous

ĂM'ur-ing
clamoring
hammering
stammering
yammering

ĂM'ur-on
Decameron
Heptameron

ĂM'ur-ur
clamorer
hammerer
stammerer

ĂN'a-b'l
ascertainable
attainable
chainable
constrainable
containable
detainable
distrainable
drainable
explainable
gainable
maintainable
obtainable
ordainable
overstrainable
restrainable
retainable
sprainable
strainable
sustainable

trainable
unattainable

ĂN'a-b'l
insanable
sanable
tannable
(cf. cannibal)

ĂN'ar-i
chicanery
lanary
planary

ĂN'a-ri
granary
panary
(see ĂN'ur-i)

ĂN'ches-tur
Granchester
Manchester

AND'a-b'l
commandable
countermand-
  able
demandable
reprimandable
sandable
understandable

ĂN'di-fi
candify
dandify

ĂN'di-nes
dandiness
handiness
sandiness

ÄN'dri-an
Alexandrian
meandrian
Menandrian

ÄN'dur-ing
meandering
pandering
philandering
slandering

ÄN'dur-ing
wandering
(see ŎN-dur-
ing)

ÄN'dur-son
Anderson
Sanderson

ÄN'dur-ur
meanderer
panderer
philanderer
slanderer

ÄN'dur-ur
launderer
wanderer
(see ŎN'dur-
ur)

ÄN'dur-us
panderous
slanderous

ÄN'el-ing
channelling
panelling

ÄN'e-us
antecedaneous

araneous
circumforane-
    ous
coëtaneous
contemporane-
    ous
cutaneous
dissentaneous
extemporane-
    ous
exterraneous
extraneous
instantaneous
mediterra-
    neous
membraneous
miscellaneous
momentaneous
porcelaneous
simultaneous
spontaneous
subcutaneous
subterraneous
succedaneous
temporaneous
terraneous

ÄN'ful'i
banefully
disdainfully
painfully

ÄN'ful-nes
disdainfulness
gainfulness
painfulness

ÄNGK'ur-ing,
ÄNGK'or-ing
anchoring
cankering

encankering
hankering

ÄNGKur-us
cankerous
cantankerous

ÄNG"lsom
anglesome
tanglesome
wranglesome

ÄNG'u-lar
angular
octangular
pentangular
quadrangular
rectangular
slangular
triangular

Ä-ni-a
Albania
Anglo-mania
Aquitania
bibliomania
decalcomania
demonomania
dipsomania
eleuthero-
    mania
erotomania
Gallomania
kleptomania
Lithuania
logomania
Lusitania
mania
Mauretania
megalomania
metromania

miscellanea
monomania
nymphomania
Pennsylvania
pyromania
Rumania
succedanea
Tasmania
Titania
Transylvania
Tripolitania
Ukrainia
Urania

Ä'ni-ak
bibliomaniac
dipsomaniac
eleutheroman-
    iac
kleptomaniac
maniac
megalomaniac
monomaniac
nymphomaniac

Ä'ni-al
cranial
domanial
subterraneal

Ä-ni-an
Albanian
Alcmanian
Aquitanian
circumforanean
cyanean
extemporanean
Iranian
Lithuanian
Mauretanian
Mediterranean

āle, câre, ădd, ärm, ȧsk; mē, hẹre, ĕnd; īce, ĭll;

Pennsylvani-	ĂN'i-mus	Ā'ni-um	ĂN'siv-nes
an	animus	cranium	advanciveness
Rumanian	magnanimous	geranium	expansiveness
Sandemanian	multanimous	pericranium	
subterranean	pusillanimous	succedaneum	ĂN'som-est
Tasmanian	unanimous	titanium	handsomest
Transylvanian		uranium	*ransomest*
Tripolitanian	ĂN'i-shing		
Turanian	banishing	ĂN'jen-si	ĂN'som-ur
Ukrainian	planishing	plangency	handsomer
Uranian	vanishing	tangency	ransomer
volcanian			
	ĂN'ish-ment	ĂN'ji-b'l	ĂNT'a-b'l
ĂN'i-bal	banishment	frangible	grantable
cannibal	evanishment	infrangible	plantable
Hannibal	vanishment	intangible	
(cf. sanable)		refrangible	ĂN'tur-ing
	ĂN'is-tur	tangible	bantering
ĂN'i-el	banister		cantering
Daniel	canister	ĂN'i-kin	
Nathaniel	ganister	manikin	ĂNT'ur-ur
(cf. spaniel)		pannikin	banterer
	ĂN'i-ti		canterer
ĂN'i-gan	aldermanity	ĂN'o-graf	
Brannigan	Christianity	galvanograph	ĂN'thro-pi
Flannigan	gigmanity	pianograph	apanthropy
Mullanigan	humanity		aphilanthropy
	immanity	ĂN'o-skop	lycanthropy
ĂN'i-kal	inanity	diaphanoscope	misanthropy
botanical	inhumanity	galvanoscope	philanthropy
Brahmanical	inorganity		physianthropy
charlatanical	insanity	ĂN'shi-an	psilanthropy
galvanical	inurbanity	Byzantian	theanthropy
mechanical	mundanity	(cf. ĂN'shun)	theophilan-
panicle	paganity		thropy
tyrannical	profanity	ĂN'shi-at	zoanthropy
	sanity	circumstantiate	
ĂN'i-fi	subterranity	substantiate	ĂN'thro-pist
humanify	urbanity	transubstanti-	misanthropist
insanify	vanity	ate	philanthropist
sanify	volcanity		

psilanthropist
theophilan-
   thropist

ĂN'thro-pizm
psilanthropism
theanthropism
theophilanthro-
   pism

ĂN'ti-sid
giganticide
infanticide

ĂN'tik-nes
franticness
giganticness
romanticness

ĂN'u-al
annual
manual

ĂN'u-la
cannula
granula

ĂN'u-lar
annular
cannular
penannular

ĂN'u-lat
annulate
campanulate
granulate

ĂN'ur-et
banneret
lanneret

ĂN'ur-i
cannery

charlatanery
granary
panary
stannary
tannery

ĂP'a-b'l
capable
drapable
escapable
incapable
inescapable
papable
shapeable

ĂP'id-li
rapidly
sapidly
vapidly

ĂP'id-nes
rapidness
sapidness
vapidness

ĂP'i-est
happiest
sappiest
snappiest

ĂP'i-li
happily
snappily

ĂP'i-nes
happiness
sappiness
snappiness

ĂP'i-ur
happier

sappier
snappier

ĂP'o-lis
Annapolis
Indianapolis
Minneapolis

ĂP'ur-i
apery
drapery
grapery
napery
papery
vapory

ĂP'ur-ing
capering
papering
tapering
vaporing

ĂP'ur-ur
caperer
paperer
vaporer

ĂR'a-b'l
airable
bearable
dareable
declarable
pairable
repairable
swearable
tearable
unbearable
unwearable
wearable

ĂR'a-b'l
arable
parable

ĂR'a-dis
imparadise
paradise

ĂR'as-ing
embarrassing
harassing

ĂR'as-ment
embarrassment
harassment

ĂR'a-tiv
comparative
declarative
narrative
preparative
reparative

ĂR'bur-ing
barbering
harboring

ĂR'di-an
guardian
pericardian

ĂR'di-nes
fool-hardiness
hardiness
tardiness

Â're-a
area
(see Â'ri-a)

ĂR'ful-i
carefully
prayerfully
uncarefully

ÅR'ful-nes
carefulness
prayerfulness
sparefulness
uncarefulness
warefulness

A'ri-a
adversaria
area
Bulgaria
caballeria
Calceolaria
Cineraria
dataria
digitaria
Hilaria
malaria
wistaria
(cf. pariah)

ÅR'i-al
actuarial
areal
calendarial
commissarial
diarial
glossarial
malarial
nectarial
notarial
ovarial
puparial
secretarial
vicarial

ÅR'i-an
abecedarian
Adessenarian
agrarian
alphabetarian

altitudinarian
anecdotarian
antiquarian
antisabbatarian
antitrinitarian
apiarian
Apollinarian
aquarian
Arian
Aryan
atrabilarian
attitudinarian
barbarian
Bavarian
Briarean
Bulgarian
Cæsarian
centenarian
diarian
dietarian
disciplinarian
doctrinarian
equalitarian
estuarian
experimenta-
    rian
futilitarian
grammarian
humanitarian
Hungarian
Icarian
Janizarian
lapidarian
latitudinarian
libertarian
librarian
limitarian
lunarian
Megarian
millenarian
miscellanarian

necessarian
necessitarian
nectarian
nonagenarian
octagenarian
ovarian
Parian
parliamenta-
    rian
platitudinarian
plenitudinarian
predestinarian
proletarian
riparian
sabbatarian
sacramentarian
sanitarian
sectarian
sententiarian
septuagenarian
sexagenarian
societarian
stipendarian
sublapsarian
supralapsarian
Tartarean
tractarian
trinitarian
ubiquarian
ubiquitarian
unitarian
utilitarian
valetudinarian
vegetarian
veterinarian
vulgarian

ÅR'i-ant
contrariant
omniparient
variant

ÅR'i-at
variate
vicariate

ÅR'i-at
commissariat
lariat
proletariat
prothonotariat
secretariat

ÅR'i-est
chariest
variest
wariest

ÅR'i-et, ÅR'i-ot
Harriet
Iscariot
Marryatt
Marriott

A'ri-ez
Aries
caries

ÅR'i-fi
clarify
saccharify
scarify

ÅR'i-form
peariform
scalariform

ÅR'i-gan
Garrigan
Harrigan

ÅR'i-ing
carrying
harrying

marrying
tarrying

ĂR'i-nes
airiness
arbitrariness
chariness
contrariness
glariness
hairiness
salutariness
sanguinariness
sedentariness
solitariness
temporariness
tumultuariness
ubiquitariness
voluntariness
wariness

ĂR'i-nes
starriness
tarriness

ĂR'ing-li
blaringly
daringly
flaringly
glaringly
sparingly
tearingly

ĂR'ing-ton
Barrington
Carrington
Farrington
Harrington

ĂR'i-o
impresario
(cf. Lothario)

ĂR'i-on
clarion
Marion
(cf. Marian)

ĂR'i-son
garrison
Harrison

ĂR'i-ti
debonairity
rarity

ĂR'i-ti
angularity
barbarity
charity
circularity
clarity
disparity
dissimilarity
exemplarity
familiarity
fissiparity
gemmiparity
globularity
hilarity
imparity
insularity
irregularity
jocularity
molecularity
muscularity
omniparity
parity
particularity
peculiarity
perpendicu-
    larity
piacularity
polarity

popularity
pupilarity
rectangularity
rectilinearity
regularity
secularity
similarity
singularity
solidarity
titularity
triangularity
uncharity
vascularity
viviparity
vulgarity

ĂR'i-tud
amaritude
claritude

ĂR'i-um
aquarium
aqua-vivarium
barium
columbarium
glaciarium
honorarium
sacrarium
sanitarium
tepidarium
termitarium
vivarium

ĂR'i-ur
charier
warier

ĂR'i-ur
barrier
carrier

farrier
harrier
marrier
tarrier

ĂR'i-us
arbitrarious
arenarious
Aquarius
atrabilarious
calcareous
contrarious
denarius
frumentarious
gregarious
hilarious
horarious
malarious
multifarious
nectareous
nefarious
omnifarious
precarious
quadragena-
    rious
Sagittarius
tartareous
temerarious
testudinarious
vagarious
valetudinarious
various
vicarious
viparious

ĂR'ki-kal
archical
hierarchical
hylarchical
monarchical
tetrarchical

āle. câre, ădd, ärm, ăsk; mē, hęre, ĕnd; īce, ĭll;

ÄR'la-tan
charlatan
tarlatan

ÄR'ming-li
alarmingly
charmingly
farmingly
harmingly

ÄR'nish-ing
garnishing
tarnishing
varnishing

ÄR'nish-ur
garnisher
tarnisher
varnisher

ÄR'o-est
harrowest
narrowest

ÄR'o-i
arrowy
marrowy
sparrowy
yarrowy

ÄR'o-ing
harrowing
narrowing

A'ron-it
Aaronite
Maronite

ÄR'o-ur
harrower
narrower

ÄR'sen-i
coparceny
larceny

ÄR'sen-ur
coparcener
larcener
parcener

ÄR'shal-izm
martialism
partialism

ÄR'ted-nes
departedness
false-
  heartedness
frank-
  heartedness
free-
  heartedness
hard-
  heartedness
kind-
  heartedness
light-
  heartedness
open-
  heartedness
soft-
  heartedness
tender-
  heartedness
true-
  heartedness
warm-
  heartedness

ÄR'ti-k'l
article
particle

ÄR'ti-zan
artizan
bartizan
partisan

ÄRT'les-li
artlessly
heartlessly

ÄRT'les-nes
artlessness
heartlessness

ÄRT'ur-ing
bartering
chartering
martyring

ÄRT'ur-ur
barterer
charterer

ÄS'a-b'l
chasable
effaceable
erasible
evasible
ineffaceable
retraceable
traceable

ÄS'en-si
adjacency
complacency
interjacency

ÄS'ful-nes
disgracefulness

gracefulness
ungracefulness

A'shi-a
acacia
Asia
Aspasia
(cf. Ā'zhi-a,
  Ā'zi-a, Ā'sha,
  Ā'zha. So in
  all similar
  cases)

ÄSH'i-a
cassia
Parnassia
quassia

Ā'shi-al
basial
(cf. spatial)

A'shi-an
Alsatian
Asian
Athanasian
Australasian
Galatian
Haytian
Hieracian
Horatian
Latian
Pancratian
Thracian
(cf. Ā'shun,
  Ā'zhun)

ÄSH'i-an
Circassian
Parnassian
(cf. ÄSH'un)

Ā'shi-at
emaciate
expatiate
glaciate
ingratiate
insatiate
satiate

Ā'shi-ent
calefacient
delirefacient
facient
liquefacient
parturifacient
rubefacient
sensifacient
sorbefacient
stupefacient
tumefacient
(cf. Ā'shent)

ĂSH'i-nes
ashiness
flashiness
trashiness

Ā'shun-al
associational
congregational
conservational
conversational
creational
denominational
derivational
dissertational
educational
emigrational
gradational
gyrational
ideational
imitational

inspirational
observational
probational
relational
representational
respirational
rotational
sensational
stational
terminational

ĂSH'un-al
international
irrational
national
rational

ĂSH'un-at
compassionate
dispassionate
impassionate
incompassion-
  ate
passionate

ĂSH'un-ing
compassioning
fashioning
passioning

Ā'shun-ist
annexationist
annihilationist
annotationist
causationist
conversationist
convocationist
cremationist
degenerationist
educationist
emancipationist

emigrationist
imitationist
inflationist
innovationist
inspirationist
repudiationist
restorationist
transmutation-
  ist

Ā'shun-les
conversation-
  less
educationless
emigrationless
foundationless
immigration-
  less
imitationless
inspirationless
temptationless

Ā'shun-ur
foundationer
oblationer
probationer
reprobationer
restorationer
stationer

ĂSH'ur-i
fashery
haberdashery
sashery

Ā'shus-nes
audaciousness
capaciousness
contumacious-
  ness

disputatious-
  ness
edaciousness
efficaciousness
fallaciousness
fugaciousness
graciousness
incapacious-
  ness
ineffacious-
  ness
loquaciousness
mendaciousness
ostentatious-
  ness
perspicacious-
  ness
pertinacious-
  ness
pugnaciousness
rapaciousness
sagaciousness
salaciousness
sequaciousness
spaciousness
tenaciousness
ungraciousness
veraciousness
vexatiousness
vivaciousness
voraciousness

ĂS'i-b'l
impassible
irascible
passable
passible
renascible
surpassable

ĂS'i-nat
abbacinate

assassinate
deracinate
exacinate
fascinate

ĂS'i-nes
laciness
raciness

ĂS'i-nes
brassiness
classiness
glassiness
grassiness
massiness
sassiness

ĂS'i-ti
audacity
bellacity
bibacity
capacity
contumacity
dicacity
edacity
feracity
fugacity
incapacity
loquacity
mendacity
minacity
mordacity
opacity
perspicacity
pertinacity
pervicacity
procacity
pugnacity
rapacity
sagacity
salacity

saponacity
sequacity
tenacity
veracity
vivacity
voracity

ĂS'iv-li
impassively
massively
passively

Ā'siv'nes
dissuasiveness
evasiveness
persuasiveness
pervasiveness
suasiveness

ĂS'iv-nes
impassiveness
massiveness
passiveness

ĂSP'ing-li
gaspingly
raspingly

ĂS'tar-di
bastardy
dastardy

ĂST'ful-i
tastefully
wastefully
distastefully

ĂS'ti-kal
ecclesiastical
elastical
encomiastical

enthusiastical
fantastical
gymnastical

ĂS'ti-li
hastily
pastily
tastily

ĂS'ti-sizm
ecclesiasticism
fantasticism
monasticism
scholasticism

ĂS'tri-an
alabastrian
Lancastrian
Zoroastrian

ĂS'tro-fe
catastrophe
epanastrophe

ĂS'tur-ship
mastership
pastorship

ĂS'tur-i
dicastery
mastery
plastery
self-mastery

ĂS'tur-ing
beplastering
mastering
overmastering
plastering

ĂS'ur-at
emacerate

lacerate
macerate

ĀS'ur-i
bracery
embracery
tracery

ĀT'a-b'l
abatable
beratable
collatable
creatable
debatable
dilatable
gratable
hatable
matable
ratable
regulatable
statable
translatable
untranslatable

ĀT'a-b'l
combatable
(see ĀT'i-b'l)

ĀT'e-lit
patellite
satellite

Ā'ten-si
latency
patency

ĀT'ful-i
fatefully
gratefully
hatefully

ĀT'ful-nes
fatefulness

gratefulness
hatefulness

Ā'thi-an
Carpathian
Sabbathian

Ăth'e-sis
diathesis
parathesis

Ăth'i-kal
anthropopath-
 ical
chrestomath-
 ical

ĂTH'ur-ing
blathering
foregathering
gathering
lathering
upgathering
wool-gathering

ĂTH'ur-ur
foregatherer
gatherer
latherer
tax-gatherer
toll-gatherer
upgatherer

ĂT'i-b'l
combatable
come-atable
compatible
impatible
incompatible
patible

ĂT'i-fi
beatify
gratify
ratify
stratify

ĂT'ik-a
Attica
dalmatica
hepatica
sciatica

ĂT'ik-al
abbatical
acroamatical
aerostatical
anathematical
anidiomatical
apophthegmat-
 ical
apostatical
aristocratical
asthmatical
autocratical
automatical
axiomatical
bureaucratical
climatical
democratical
diplomatical
dogmatical
dramatical
ecstatical
emblematical
emphatical
enigmatical
epigrammat-
 ical
fanatical
grammatical
hebdomatical

idiomatical
leviratical
mathematical
phantasmatical
piratical
pragmatical
primatical
sabbatical
schismatical
separatical
Socratical
spasmatical
statical
vatical

ĂT'in-at
gelatinate
Palatinate

ĂT'i-nes
slatiness
weightiness

ĂT'i-nes
chattiness
fattiness
nattiness

ĂT'in-iz
gelatinize
Latinize
platinize

ĂT'i-nus
gelatinous
platinous

ĂT'i-siz
emblematicize
fanaticize
grammaticize

ĂT'i-sizm
Asiaticism

fanaticism
grammaticism

ĂT'i-tud
attitude
beatitude
gratitude
ingratitude
latitude
platitude

Ā'tiv-nes
alliterativeness
imitativeness
nativeness
penetrative-
 ness

ĂT"l-ment
battlement
embattlement
prattlement
tattlement

ĂT'om-i
anatomy
atomy

ĂT'om-ist
anatomist
atomist

ĂT'om-iz
anatomize
atomize

ĂT'om-izm
anatomism
atomism

ĂT'om-us
diatomous
paratomous

ĀT′or-i
obsecratory
ratiocinatory
recapitulatory

ĂT′ri-kal
idolatrical
theatrical

ĂT′ri-sid
fratricide
matricide
patricide

Ā′tron-al
matronal
patronal

Ā′tron-ij
matronage
patronage

Ā′tron-iz
matronize
patronize

ĂT′u-lat
congratulate
gratulate
spatulate

ĂT′ūr-al
natural
preternatural
supernatural

ĂT′ŭr-al
bilateral
collateral
equilateral
lateral

quadrilateral
unilateral

ĂT′ur-an
cateran
Lateran

ĂT′ur-at
maturate
saturate
supersaturate

ĂT′ur-i
battery
flattery
shattery
slattery
tattery

ĂT′ur-ing
battering
beflattering
bepattering
bescattering
bespattering
blattering
chattering
clattering
flattering
pattering
scattering
shattering
smattering
spattering
splattering

ĂT′ur-ur
batterer
blatterer
chatterer
clatterer

flatterer
patterer
scatterer
shatterer
smatterer
splatterer

Ā′ur-i
aëry
faërie

ĀV′an-ez
Havanese
Javanese

ĂV′el-ing
gravelling
ravelling
travelling
unravelling

ĂV′el-ur
raveller
traveller
unraveller

ĂV′en-dur
chavender
lavender

Ā′vi-a
Batavia
Belgravia
Jugo-slavia
Moravia
Octavia
Pavia
Scandinavia

Ā′vi-an
avian

Batavian
Belgravian
Moravian
Scandinavian
Shavian

ĂV′ij-ing
ravaging
scavaging

ĂV′ij-ur
ravager
savager
scavager

ĂV′ish-ing
enravishing
lavishing
ravishing

ĂV′ish-ment
enravishment
lavishment
ravishment

ĂV′ish-nes
knavishness
slavishness

ĂV′ish-ur
lavisher
ravisher

ĂV′i-ti
cavity
concavity
depravity
gravity
pravity
suavity

ĀV′ur-i
bravery

gravery	**ĀV'ur-ur**	**A'zi-a**	Rabelaisian
savory	favorer	Aspasia	(cf. Ā'zhun)
slavery	flavorer	athanasia	
unsavory	quaverer	aphasia	**ĀZ'i-b'l**
	waverer	euthanasia	persuasible
		paronomasia	praisable
ĀV'ur-ing	**ĀV'ur-us**		raisable
favoring	flavorous	**A'zi-an**	suasible
flavoring	savorous	Asian	**ĀZ'i-nes**
quavering		Athanasian	craziness
savoring	**ĂV'ur-us**	Australasian	haziness
unwavering	cadaverous	Caucasian	laziness
wavering	papaverous	Eurasian	maziness

E

For a discussion of words included under the accented vowels following, see the beginning of E rhymes in Section I.

Ē'a-b'l	**Ē'al-ti**	impeachable	impedible
agreeable	fealty	reachable	obedible
creable	realty	teachable	pleadable
decreeable		unimpeachable	readable
disagreeable	**Ē'an-izm**	unteachable	
feeable	epicureanism		**ĔD'a-b'l**
irremeable	Laodiceanism	**ĔCH'i-nes**	dreadable
	peanism	sketchiness	(see ĔD'i-b'l)
Ē'al'ist	plebeianism	tetchiness	
idealist	Pythagorean-		**ĔD'ful-nes**
realist	ism	**ĔCH'ur-i**	heedfulness
	Sabæanism	lechery	needfulness
Ē'al-iz		treachery	unheedfulness
idealise	**ĒB'ri-us**		unneedfulness
realise	ebrious	**ĔCH'ur-us**	
	funebrious	lecherous	**Ē'di-al**
Ē'al-izm	inebrious	treacherous	bimedial
idealism	tenebrious		intermedial
realism	**ĒCH'a-b'l**	**ĒD'a-b'l**	medial
	bleachable	exceedable	pedial
			remedial

āle,   câre,   ădd,   ärm,   åsk;   mē,   hĕre,   ĕnd,   īce,   ĭll;

Ē′di-an
comedian
encyclopedian
median
tragedian

Ē′di-at
immediate
intermediate
mediate

ĔD′i-b'l
credible
dreadable
edible
incredible

Ē′di-ens
disobedience
expedience
inexpedience
obedience

Ē′di-ent
disobedient
expedient
inexpedient
ingredient
obedient

ĔD′i-est
beadiest
greediest
neediest
reediest
seediest
speediest
weediest

ĔD′i-est
headiest

readiest
steadiest
unsteadiest

ĔD′i-kal
medical
pedicle

ĔD′i-kant
medicant
predicant

ĔD′i-kat
dedicate
medicate
predicate

ĔD′i-li
greedily
needily
speedily

ĔD′i-li
headily
readily
steadily
unsteadily

ĔD′i-ment
impediment
pediment
sediment

ĔD′i-nes
greediness
neediness
seediness
speediness
weediness

ĔD′i-nes
headiness

readiness
steadiness
threadiness
unreadiness
unsteadiness

ĔD′i-nus
mucedinous
putredinous
rubedinous

ĔD′i-ted
accredited
credited
discredited
edited
miscredited
unaccredited

ĔD′i-ting
accrediting
crediting
discrediting
editing
miscrediting

ĔD′i-tiv
redditive
sedative

ĔD′i-tor
creditor
editor

Ē′di-um
medium
tedium

ĔD′i-ur
beadier
greedier

needier
reedier
seedier
speedier
weedier

ĔD′i-ur
headier
readier
steadier
unsteadier

Ē′di-us
intermedious
tedious

ĔD′les-li
heedlessly
needlessly

ĔD′les-nes
heedlessness
needlessness

ĔD′u-lus
credulous
incredulous
sedulous

ĔD′ur-al
federal
hederal

ĔD′ur-ship
leadership
readership

ĒF′i-nes
beefiness
leafiness

õld, ôr, ŏdd, oil, fŏŏt, out; ūse, ûrn, ŭp; THis, thin

ĔF′i-sens
beneficence
maleficence

ĔF′i-sent
beneficent
maleficent

ĔF′ur-ens
cross-reference
deference
preference
reference

ĔF′ur-ent
deferent
efferent

ĔG′a-b'l
beggable
legable

Ē′gal-izm
legalism
regalism

Ē′gal-nes
illegalness
legalness
regalness

ĔG′i-nes
dregginess
legginess

ĔG′nan-si
pregnancy
regnancy

ĔG′ur-i
beggary

eggery
(cf. Gregory)

Ē′gur-li
eagerly
meagrely
overeagerly

Ē′gur-nes
eagerness
meagreness
overeagerness

Ē′i-ti
aseity
contempora-
  neity
corporeity
deity
diathermaneity
extraneity
femineity
gaseity
hæcceity
hermaphro-
  deity
heterogeneity
homogeneity
incorporeity
instantaneity
multeity
omneity
personeity
plebeity
seity
simultaneity
spontaneity
terreity
velleity

Ē′ji-an
collegian

Fuegian
Norwegian
(cf. ĒJ′un)

ĔJ′i-b'l
allegeable
illegible
legible

Ē′jus-nes
egregiousness
sacrilegious-
  ness

ĔK′a-b'l
speakable
unspeakable

ĔK′a-b'l
impeccable
insecable
peccable

ĔK′i-li
cheekily
creakily
leakily
sleekily
sneakily
squeakily

ĔK′i-nes
cheekiness
creakiness
leakiness
sneakiness
squeakiness

ĔK′ish-nes
cliquishness
freakishness
sneakishness

ĔK′on-ing
beckoning
dead-reckoning
reckoning

ĔK′re-ment
decrement
recrement

ĔK′shun-al
affectional
complexional
correctional
inflectional
insurrectional
interjectional
intersectional
protectional
sectional

ĔK′shun-ist
insurrectionist
perfectionist
protectionist
resurrectionist

ĔK′shun-iz
resurrectionize
sectionize

ĔK′si-b'l
flexible
inflexible
nexible
reflexible

ĔK′si-ti
complexity
convexity
intercom-
  plexity

āle,   câre,   ădd,   ärm,   åsk;   mē,   hẽre,   ĕnd;   īce,   ĭll;

perplexity
reflexity

ĔK′siv-nes
perplexiveness
reflexiveness

ĔK′ta-b'l
respectable
(see ĔK′ti-b'l)

ĔK′tar-i
nectary
(see ĔK′to-ri)

ĔK′ted-nes
abjectedness
affectedness
dejectedness
disaffectedness
infectedness
suspectedness
unsuspected-
　ness

ĔK′ti-b'l
affectible
collectible
correctible
defectible
delectable
detectible
dissectible
effectible
erectable
expectable
indefectible
indelectable
objectable
prefectible
reflectible

rejectable
respectable
suspectable

ĔK′ti-fi
objectify
rectify

ĔK′ti-kal
apoplectical
dialectical

ĔK′ti-tud
rectitude
senectitude

ĔK′tiv-li
collectively
defectively
effectively, etc.

ĔK′tiv-nes
collectiveness
defectiveness
effectiveness
ineffectiveness
objectiveness
prospectiveness
protectiveness
reflectiveness
subjectiveness

ĔK′to-ral
electoral
pectoral
protectoral
rectoral
sectoral

ĔK′to-rat
directorate

electorate
expectorate
protectorate
rectorate

ĔK′to-ri
correctory
directory
nectary
rectory
refectory
sectary

ĔK′tu-al
effectual
ineffectual
intellectual
lectual

ĔK′tur-al
architectural
conjectural

ĔK′tur-ur
conjecturer
lecturer

ĔK′u-lar
molecular
secular
specular

ĔK′u-lat
peculate
speculate

ĔK′u-tiv
consecutive
executive
subsecutive

ĒL′a-b'l
concealable
congealable
healable
inconcealable
repealable
revealable

ĒL′a-tiv
compellative
correlative
relative

ĒL′e-gat
delegate
relegate

ĒL′fish-nes
elfishness
selfishness

Ē′li-a
Amelia
Aurelia
Bedelia
Cecelia
Celia
Cordelia
Cornelia
Fidelia
Lelia
Ophelia
(also ĒL′ya)

Ē′li-an
Aristotelian
carnelian
Delian
Hegelian
Ismaelian
Machiavelian

ōld, ôr, ŏdd, oil, fŏŏt, out; ūse, ûrn, ŭp; THis, thin

Mephisto-
  phelian
Mingrelian
(also ĔL'yan)

ĔL'i-an
Boswellian
Cromwellian
evangelian
selion
(also ĔL'yan,
  ĔL'yun,
  which see)

**ĔL'i-b'l,
ĔL'a-b'l**
compellable
delible
expellable
fellable
gelable
indelible
ingelable
spellable
tellable

ĔL'i-kal
angelical
bellical
evangelical
helical
pellicle

Ē'li-on
anthelion
aphelion
chameleon

ĔL'ish-ing
embellishing
relishing

ĔL'ish-ment
embellishment
relishment

Ē'li-us
Aurelius
Cornelius
(also ĔL'yus)

ĔL'o-est
bellowest
mellowest
yellowest

ĔL'o-ing
bellowing
mellowing
yellowing

ĔL'on-i
felony
melony

ĔL'o-ur
bellower
mellower
yellower

ĔL'thi-est
healthiest
stealthiest
wealthiest

ĔL'thi-li
healthily
stealthily
wealthily

ĔL'thi-ur
healthier
stealthier
wealthier

ĔL'tur-i
sheltery
smeltery

ĔL'tur-ing
sheltering
weltering

ĔL'tur-ur
shelterer
welterer

ĔL'u-lar
cellular
intercellular
stellular
unicellular

ĔL'ur-i
celery
stellary

ĔL'us-li
jealously
overzealously
zealously

ĒM'a-b'l
esteemable
redeemable

Ē'ma-tist
schematist
thematist

ĔM'a-tist
emblematist
theorematist

ĔM'bur-ing
Decembering

dismembering
membering
Novembering
remembering
unremembering

Ē'mi-a
Bohemia
Euphemia

Ē'mi-al
academial
endemial
gremial
vindemial

Ē'mi-an
academian
Bohemian

ĔM'i-kal
academical
alchemical
chemical
electro-chem-
  ical
endemical
epidemical
polemical

ĔM'i-li
beamily
creamily
dreamily
steamily

ĔM'i-nal
feminal
geminal
seminal

ĔM'i-nat
effeminate

āle,   câre,   ădd,   ärm,   åsk;   mē,   hẹre,   ĕnd;   īce,   ĭll;

geminate
ingeminate

ĔM'i-nes

creaminess
dreaminess
steaminess

Ē'mi-on
anthemion
procemion

ĔM'i-ur
beamier
creamier
dreamier
premier

ĔM'ni-ti
indemnity
solemnity

ĔM'on-e
Agapemone
anemone
(cf. Gethsem-
   ane)

ĔM'or-al
femoral
nemoral
(cf. ephemeral)

ĔM'o-ri
Emery
Emory
memory

ĔM'por-ur,
   ĔM'pur-ur
emperor
temperer

ĔM'u-lent
temulent
tremulent

ĔM'u-lus
emulous
tremulous

Ĕm'ur-ald
emerald
ephemeralled

ĔM'ur-i
creamery
dreamery

ĔM'ur-i
gemmery
(cf. ĔM'o-ri)

ĔM'ur-ist
ephemerist
euhemerist

Ē'na-b'l
amenable
convenable

ĔN'a-ri
centenary
denary
decennary
hennery

ĔN'a-tor
senator
progenitor

ĔND'i-b'l
accendible

amendable
commendable
comprehendible
defendable
dependable
descendable
endable
extendible
invendible
lendable
mendable
recommendable
rendible
unascendable
vendible

ĔN'den-si
ascendancy
attendancy
dependency
equipendency
impendency
independency
intendancy
interdepend-
   ency
resplendency
superintend-
   ency
tendency
transcendency
transplendency

ĔN'di-us
compendious
incendious

ĔND'les-li
endlessly
friendlessly

ĔND'les-nes
endlessness
friendlessness

ĔN'dur-est
engenderest
renderest
slenderest
surrenderest
tenderest

ĔN'dur-ing
engendering
gendering
rendering
surrendering
tendering

ĔN'dur-li
slenderly
tenderly

ĔN'dur-nes
slenderness
tenderness

ĔN'dur-ur
engenderer
renderer
slenderer
surrendered
tenderer

ĔN'dus-li
(not ĔN'jus-li)
stupendously
tremendously

ĔN'e-sis
abiogenesis
biogenesis

ōld, ôr, ŏdd, oil, fŏŏt, out; ūse, ûrn, ŭp; THis, thin

ectogenesis	**ĔN'i-al**	**ĔN'i-form**	ingenious
eugenesis	biennial	antenniform	nitrogeneous
genesis	centennial	penniform	pergameneous
heterogenesis	decennial		primigenious
homogenesis	duodecennial	**ĔN'i-kal**	selenious
ontogenesis	millennial	arsenical	
organogenesis	novennial	cathechumen-	**ĔN'i-zon**
palingenesis	octennial	ical	benison
pangenesis	perennial	ecumenical	denizen
paragenesis	quadrennial	scenical	endenizen
parenesis	quinquennial	sirenical	venison
partheno-	septennial		
genesis	triennial	**ĔN'i-ti**	**ĔN'sa-b'l**
phylogenesis	vicennial	amenity	condensable
phytogenesis		lenity	(see ĔN'si-b'l)
polygenesis	**Ē'ni-an**	obscenity	
psychogenesis	Armenian	serenity	**ĔN'sa-ri**
xenogenesis	Athenian	terrenity	dispensary
	Cyrenian		(see ĔN'so-ri)
ĔN'et-ing	Estremenian	**ĔN'i-tiv**	
jenneting	Fenian	genitive	**ĔN'sa-tiv**
renneting	Hellenian	lenitive	compensative
	Madrilenian	primogenitive	condensative
Ē'ni-a	Ruthenian	splenitive	defensative
Armenia			dispensative
Eugenia	**Ē'ni-ens**	**ĔN'i-tud**	insensitive
gardenia	convenience	lenitude	intensitive
neurosthenia	inconvenience	plenitude	pensative
Parthenia	lenience	serenitude	sensitive
Xenia	(cf. ĔN'yens)		
		Ē'ni-um	**ĔN'sha-ri**
Ē'ni-al	**Ē'ni-ent**	proscenium	penitentiary
congenial	advenient	selenium	residentiary
demesnial	convenient	xenium	
genial	inconvenient		**ĔN'shi-at**
menial	intervenient	**Ē'ni-us**	essentiate
primigenial	introvenient	arsenious	licentiate
uncongenial	lenient	extrageneous	potentiate
venial	supervenient	genius	
(cf. ĔN'yal)	(cf. ĔN'yent)	heterogeneous	**ĔN'shi-ent**
		homogeneous	assentient

āle, câre, ădd, ärm, åsk; mē, hĕre, ĕnd; īce, ĭll;

consentient
dissentient
insentient
presentient
sentient

ĚN'shun-al
ascensional
conventional
descensional
extensional
intentional
preventional

ĚN'shun-ist
ascentionist
extensionist
recensionist

ĚN'shus-nes
conscientious-
  ness
contentiousness
licentiousness
pretentious-
  ness

ĚN'si-b'l
comprehensible
condensable
defensible
deprehensible
dispensable
distensible
extensible
incomprehen-
  sible
incondensable
indefensible
indispensable
insensible

ostensible
reprehensible
sensible
subsensible
suspensible
tensible

ĚN'si-kal
forensical
nonsensical

ĚN'si-ti
condensity
density
immensity
intensity
propensity
tensity

ĚN'siv-nes
comprehensive-
  ness
expensiveness
extensiveness
inoffensive-
  ness
intensiveness
offensiveness
pensiveness

ĚNS'les-li
defencelessly
senselessly

ĚNS'les-nes
defencelessness
senselessness

ĚN'so-ri
defensory
dispensary

incensory
ostensory
prehensory
reprehensory
sensory
suspensory

ĚN'ta-b'l
fermentable
frequentable
inventible
presentable
preventable
rentable
representable

ĚN'ta-k'l
pentacle
tentacle

ĚN'tal-i
accidentally
experimentally
fundamentally
incidentally
instrumentally
sentimentally
transcendent-
  ally

ĚN'tal-ist
experimentalist
fundamentalist
instrumentalist
Orientalist
sentimentalist
transcendenta-
  list

ĚN'tal-iz
experimental-
  ize

Orientalize
sentimentalize

ĚN'tal-izm
accidentalism
elementalism
Orientalism
sentimentalism
transcendental-
  ism

ĚN'tal-nes
accidentalness
fundamental-
  ness
gentleness
incidentalness
instrumental-
  ness
sentimental-
  ness
ungentleness

ĚN'ta-ri
accidentary
alimentary
complementary
complimentary
dentary
elementary
filamentary
instrumentary
integumentary
parliamentary
pigmentary
placentary
rudimentary
sacramentary
sedimentary
tegumentary
tenementary

ōld, ôr, ŏdd, oil, fŏŏt, out; ūse, ûrn, ŭp; THis, thin

testamentary
unparliamen-
   tary

ĔN'ta-tiv
argumentative
augmentative
commentative
complimenta-
   tive
alimentative
experimenta-
   tive
fermentative
frequentative
misrepresenta-
   tive
presentative
pretentative
preventative
representative
tentative

ĔN'ti-kal
authentical
conventical
conventicle
denticle
identical

ĔN'ti-kul
denticule
lenticule

ĔN'ti-ment
presentiment
sentiment

ĔN'ti-nal
dentinal
sentinel

ĔN'ti-ti
entity
identity
nonentity

ĔN'tiv-nes
alimentiveness
attentiveness
inattentiveness
inventiveness
retentiveness

ĔN'tu-al
accentual
adventual
conventual
eventual

ĔN'tu-at
accentuate
eventuate

ĔN'tus-li
momentously
portentously

ĔN'tus-nes
momentous-
   ness
portentousness

ĔN'u-ant
attenuant
genuant

ĔN'u-at
attenuate
extenuate
tenuate

ĔN'ur-at
degenerate

generate
ingenerate
intenerate
progenerate
regenerate
venerate

ĔN'ur-i
deanery
greenery
machinery
plenary
scenery

ĔN'ū-ri
penury

ĔN'ŭr-i
denary
decennary
hennery
senary
venery

ĔN'u-us
disingenuous
ingenuous
strenuous
tenuous

ĔN'yen-si
conveniency
inconveniency
leniency

ĔP'i-li
creepily
sleepily

ĔP'i-nes
creepiness

sleepiness
steepiness
weepiness

ĔP'ta-b'l
acceptable
deceptible
imperceptible
insusceptible
perceptible
receptible
susceptible

ĔP'ti-kal
antiseptical
protreptical
receptacle
sceptical

ĔP'tiv-nes
deceptiveness
receptiveness
susceptiveness

ĔP'ur-us
leperous
obstreperous
perstreperous
streperous

ĔR'an-si
aberrancy
errancy
inerrancy

ĔR'a-pi
balneotherapy
hydrotherapy
kinesitherapy
phototherapy
radiotherapy

āle, câre, ădd, ärm, åsk; mē, hẹre, ĕnd; īce, ĭll;

ĔR'ful-i
cheerfully
fearfully
tearfully

ĔR'ful-nes
cheerfulness
fearfulness
tearfulness

ĔR'i-a, Ē'ri-a
Algeria
diphtheria
Egeria
eleutheria
Etheria
hesperia
hysteria
icteria
Liberia
Nigeria
Valkyria

ĔR'i-al, Ē'ri-al
aerial
arterial
cereal
ethereal
ferial
funereal
immaterial
imperial
magisterial
managerial
manerial
material
ministerial
monasterial
presbyterial
rhinocerial
serial

siderial
vizierial

ĔR'i-an
Abderian
aerian
Algerian
Celtiberian
Cimmerian
Hanoverian
Hesperian
Iberian
Keplerian
Luciferian
phalansterian
Pierian
Presbyterian
Shakespearean
Shakesperian
Siberian
Spenserian
Valerian
Valkyrian
Wertherian
(cf. ĔR'i-on
    and ĬR'i-an)

ĔR'i-dez
Anterides
Hesperides
Pierides

ĔR'i-est
beeriest
bleariest
cheeriest
dreariest
eeriest
weariest

ĔR'i-est
buriest

ferriest, etc.
merriest

ĔR'i-ez
congeries
series

ĔR'-ing
berrying
burying
ferrying
wherrying

ĔR'i-kal
alexiterical
atmospherical
chimerical
clerical
climacterical
esoterical
exoterical
heliospherical
helispherical
hysterical
numerical
phylacterical
rhinocerical
spherical
sphericle

ĔR'i-li
cheerily
drearily
eerily
wearily

ĔR'i-li
merrily
verily

ĔR'i-man
ferryman

Merriman
wherryman

ĔR'i-ment
merriment
(cf. ŬR'i-ment)

ĔR'i-nes
beeriness
bleariness
cheeriness
dreariness
eeriness
weariness

ĔR'i-on
allerion
criterion
Hyperion
(cf. ĔR'i-an)

ĔR'i-or
anterior
exterior
inferior
interior
posterior
superior
ulterior
(cf. ĔR'i-ur)

ĔR'ish-ing
cherishing
perishing
unperishing

ĔR'i-ted
disherited
disinherited
emerited
ferreted

inherited
merited
(cf. turreted)

ĔR'i-ti

ambidexterity
asperity
austerity
celerity
dexterity
indexterity
insincerity
legerity
posterity
procerity
prosperity
severity
sincerity
temerity
verity

ĔR'it-ing

ferreting
inheriting
meriting

Ē'ri-um

acroterium
apodyterium
dinotherium
megatherium
palæotherium
titanotherium

ĘR'i-ur

beerier
blearier
bleerier
cheerier
drearier
eerier

wearier
(cf. ĘR'i-or)

ĔR'i-ur

burier
merrier
terrier

Ē'ri-us, ĘR'i-us

cereous
cereus
deleterious
ethereous
imperious
mysterious
serious
sidereous

ĘR'les-nes

cheerlessness
fearlessness
peerlessness

ĔR'o-gat

interrogate
(cf. ŬR'o-gat)

ĘR'yal-ist

immaterialist
imperialist
materialist

ĘR'yal-izm

immaterialism
imperialism
materialism

ĔS'a-b'l

creasable
releasable

ĔS'a-ri

confessary

intercessory
pessary
professory
successary

Ē'sen-si

decency
indecency
recency

ĔS'en-si

acescency
acquiescency
adolescency
alkalescency
convalescency
defervescency
delitescency
effervescency
efflorescency
erubescency
excrescency
incalescency
incandescency
liquescency
pubescency
quiescency
recrudescency
rejuvenescency
turgescency

Ē'sent-li

decently
indecently
recently

Ē'shi-an

Capetian
Epictetian
Grecian
Venetian

geodesian
gynæcian
Megalesian
Melanesian
Peloponnesian
Silesian
(cf. ĒSH'an,
ĒSH'un)

ĒSH'i-ens

nescience
prescience

ĒSH'i-nes

fleshiness
meshiness

ĔSH'li-nes

fleshliness
freshliness
unfleshliness

ĔSH'un-al

accessional
confessional
congressional
digressional
discretional
expressional
intercessional
possessional
processional
professional
progressional
recessional
retrocessional
sessional
successional
transgressional

ĔSH'un-ist

impressionist

progressionist
secessionist
successionist

ĔSH′un-ur
possessioner
processioner
secessioner

Ē′shus-nes
facetiousness
speciousness

ĔS′ĭ-b′l
accessible
compressible
concessible
concrescible
effervescible
expressible
fermentescible
impressible
imputrescible
inaccessible
incessable
incompressible
ineffervescible
inexpressible
insuppressible
irrepressible
marcescible
putrescible
redressible
repressible
suppressible
transgressible
vitrescible

ĔS′ĭ-mal
centesimal
decimal

infinitesimal
millesimal
nonagesimal
quadragesimal
septuagesimal
sexagesimal

ĔS′ĭ-ti
obesity

ĔS′ĭ-ti
necessity
obesity

ĔS′iv-nes
aggressiveness
depressiveness
excessiveness
expressiveness
impressiveness
inexpressive-
   ness
oppressiveness
progressiveness

ĔS′ti-al
agrestial
bestial
celestial
supercelestial

ĔS′ti-b′l
comestible
congestible
contestable
detestable
digestible
divestible
incontestable
indigestible

intestable
testable

ĔS′tin-al
destinal
intestinal

ĔS′tin-at
destinate
festinate
predestinate

ĔS′ti-nes
reastiness
yeastiness

ĔS′ti-nes
restiness
testiness

ĔS′tiv-nes
festiveness
restiveness
suggestiveness

ĔST′li-nes
beastliness
priestliness

ĔS′tri-al
pedestrial
superterrestrial
terrestrial
trimestrial

ĔS′tri-an
campestrian
equestrian
palestrian
pedestrian
sylvestrian

ĔS′tri-us
pedestrious
terestrious

ĔS′tu-ral
gestural
vestural

ĔS′tur-ing
festering
pestering
westering

ĔS′tu-us
incestuous
tempestuous

ĔT′a-b′l
cheatable
eatable
entreatable
escheatable
uneatable

ĔT′a-b′l
forgetable
getable
regretable
setable
unforgetable

ĔT′al-en
acetylene

ĔT′a-lin
metalline
petaline

ĔT′al-izm
bimetallism

ōld, ôr, ŏdd, oil, fŏŏt, out; ūse, ûrn, ŭp; THis, thin

monometallism
petalism

ĔT'ful-i
forgetfully
fretfully
regretfully

ĔT'ful-nes
forgetfulness
fretfulness
regretfulness

Ĕth'les-li
breathlessly
deathlessly

Ĕth'les-nes
breathlessness
deathlessness

ĔTH'ur-i
feathery
heathery
leathery
weathery

ĔTH'ur-ing
feathering
leathering
tethering
weathering

ĔT'i-kal
æsthetical
aloetical
alphabetical
anchoretical
antipathetical
antithetical
apathetical

apologetical
arithmetical
catechetical
cosmetical
dietetical
emporetical
energetical
epithetical
exegetical
heretical
hermetical
homiletical
hypothetical
noetical
planetical
poetical
theoretical

ĔT'i-kul
poeticule
reticule

ĔT'i-nes
meatiness
peatiness
sleetiness

ĔT'i-nes
jettiness
pettiness
sweatiness

ĔT'in-u
detinue
retinue

ĔT'ish-li
coquettishly
pettishly

ĔT'ish'nes
coquettishness
pettishness

ĔT'i-sizm
æstheticism
asceticism
athleticism
peripateticism

ĔT'o-ri
completory
depletory
repletory
secretory

ĔT'ri-kal
alkalimetrical
asymmetrical
barometrical
craniometrical
diametrical
geometrical
gnomiometrical
graphometrical
horometrical
isoperimetrical
metrical
obstetrical
perimetrical
planimetrical
pluviometrical
stichometrical
symmetrical
trigonometrical

ĔT'ri-ment
detriment
retriment

ĔT'ur-ing
bettering
fettering
lettering

ĔV'a-b'l
achievable
believable
cleavable
conceivable
deceivable
grievable
imperceivable
inconceivable
irretrievable
perceivable
receivable
relievable
retrievable
unbelievable
undeceivable

ĔV'el-est
bevellest
dishevellest
levellest
revellest

ĔV'el-ing
bedevilling
bevelling
dishevelling
levelling
revelling

ĔV'el-izm
devilism
levelism

ĔV'el-ur
beveller
bedeviller
disheveller
leveller
reveller

āle, câre, ădd, ärm, ȧsk; mē, hẽre, ĕnd; īce, ĭll;

Ē'vi-at
abbreviate
alleviate
deviate

ĔV'il-ment
bedevilment
devilment
revelment

ĔV'il-ry
devilry
revelry

Ē'vish-li
peevishly
thievishly

Ē'vish-nes
peevishness
thievishness

ĔV'i-ti
brevity
levity
longevity

Ē'vi-us
devious
previous

ĔV'ol-ens
benevolence
malevolence

ĔV'ol-ent
benevolent
malevolent

ĔV'ol-us
benevolous
malevolous

ĔV'ol-ut
evolute
revolute

ĔV'ur-est
cleverest
endeavourest
Everest
severest

ĔV'ur-mor
evermore
nevermore

ĔV'ur-ur
cleverer
endeavorer
severer

Ē'za-b'l
appeasable
cohesible
defeasible
feasible
freezable
inappeasable
indefeasible
infeasible
seizable
squeezable
unappeasable

ĔZ'an-tri
peasantry
pheasantry
pleasantry

Ē'zhi-a, Ē'zi-a
amnesia
anæsthesia
ecclesia
esthesia
magnesia
parrhesia
Rhodesia
Silesia
Zambesia

Ē'zi-an
artesian
cartesian
ecclesian
Ephesian
etesian
magnesian
Milesian
Polynesian
trapezian
(cf. ĒZH'yan)

ĔZ'i-dent
president
resident

ĔZ'i-li
breezily
easily
greasily
uneasily
wheezily

ĔZ'i-nes
breezines
cheesiness
easiness
greasiness
queasiness
sleaziness
uneasiness
wheeziness

ĔZ'ing-li
appeasingly
freezingly
pleasingly
teasingly
wheezingly

Ē'zon-ing
reasoning
seasoning
unreasoning

ĔZ'ur-ing
measuring
pleasuring
treasuring

ĔZ'ur-ur
measurer
pleasurer
treasurer

ōld, ôr, ŏdd, oil, fŏŏt, out; ūse, ûrn, ŭp; THis, thin

I

For a discussion of words included under the accented vowels following, see the beginning of I rhymes in Section I.

Ĭ'a-b'l
acidifiable
appliable
classifiable
compliable
deniable
diversifiable
electrifiable
exemplifiable
falsifiable
fortifiable
friable
impliable
justifiable
liable
liquefiable
magnifiable
modifiable
pacifiable
petrifiable
pliable
qualifiable
rarefiable
rectifiable
reliable
saponifiable
satisfiable
solidifiable
triable
undeniable
verifiable
viable
vitrifiable

Ĭ'a-bli
deniably

justifiably
reliably
undeniably, etc.

Ĭ'a-dez
hamadryades
Hyades
Pleiades

Ĭ'a-kal
bibliomaniacal
cardiacal
demoniacal
elegiacal
encyclopediacal
heliacal
hypochondria-
    cal
maniacal
monomaniacal
paradisiacal
prosodiacal
simoniacal
zodiacal

Ĭ'an-si, Ĭ'en-si
cliency
compliancy
pliancy
riancy

Ĭ'ant-li
compliantly
defiantly
pliantly
reliantly

Ĭ'ar-i
friary
(see Ĭ'ur-i)

Ĭ'ar-ist
diarist
Piarist

Ĭ'ar-ki
diarchy
triarchy

Ĭ'a-sis
elephantiasis
hypochondria-
    sis

Ĭ'a-sizm
demoniacism
hypochondriac-
    ism

Ĭ'a-tur
psychiater
(cf. archiater)

ĬB'a-b'l
bribable
describable
indescribable
inscribable
scribable
subscribable
undescribable

ĬB'i-a
amphibia

Libya
tibia

ĬB'i-al
amphibial
stibial
tibial

ĬB'i-an
amphibian
Libyan

ĬB'i-tiv
exhibitive
prohibitive

ĬB'i-us
amphibious
bathybius
stibious

ĬB'u-lar
fibular
infundibular
mandibular
vestibular

ĬCH'i-nes
itchiness
pitchiness

ĬCH'ur-i
bewitchery
michery
stitchery
witchery

āle,   câre,   ădd,   ärm,   ȧsk;   mē,   hḙre,   ĕnd;   īce,   ĭll;

ĬD'a-b'l

decidable
dividable
ridable
bestridable, etc.

ĬD'en-nes

forbiddenness
hiddenness

ĬD'e-us

hideous
(see ĬD'i-us)

ĬD'i-al

noctidial
presidial

ĬD'i-an

antemeridian
Gideon
Lydian
meridian
Midian
nullifidian
Numidian
obsidian
ophidian
Ovidian
postmeridian
quotidian
rachidian

ĬD'i-at

dimidiate
insidate

ĬD'i-fi

acidify
lapidify
solidify

ĬD'i-kal

druidical
juridical
pyramidical
veridical

ĬD'i-nus

libidinous
(cf. pingue-
dinous)

ĬD'i-ti

acidity
acridity
aridity
avidity
cupidity
frigidity
insipidity
insolidity
intrepidity
invalidity
gelidity
gravidity
hispidity
humidity
hybridity
limpidity
liquidity
lividity
lucidity
marcidity
morbidity
pallidity
pavidity
pellucidity
putidity
putridity
quiddity
rabidity

rancidity
rapidity
rigidity
sapidity
solidity
squalidity
stolidity
stupidity
timidity
torpidity
torridity
trepidity
tumidity
turbidity
turgidity
validity
vapidity
viridity
viscidity
vividity

**ĬD'i-om,
ĬD'i-um**

idiom
iridium
peridium

ĬD'i-us

avidious
fastidious
hideous
insidious
invidious
lapideous
ophidious
parricidious
perfidious
Phidias
splendidious
stillicidious

ĬD'u-al

individual
residual

ĬD'u-at

assiduate
individuate

ĬD'u-lat

acidulate
stridulate

ĬD'u-lus

acidulous
stridulous

ĬD'u-us

assiduous
deciduous
prociduous
residuous
succiduous
viduous

Ī'en-si

cliency
(see Ī'an-si)

Ī'et-al

dietal
hyetal
parietal
varietal

Ī'et-ed

dieted
disquieted
quieted
rioted

Ī'et-est

dietest

quietest	Ī′et-izm	ĬF′lu-us	aluminiferous
riotest	pietism	dulcifluous	ammonitiferous
	quietism	fellifluous	antenniferous
Ī′et-i	varietism	ignifluous	argentiferous
anxiety		mellifluous	armiferous
contrariety	**Ī′et-ur, Ī′et-or**	sanguifluous	astriferous
dubiety	dieter		auriferous
ebriety	proprietor	**ĬF′on-i**	balaniferous
filiety	quieter	antiphony	balsamiferous
impiety	rioter	oxyphony	bulbiferous
impropriety		polyphony	calcariferous
inebriety	**ĬF′i-kal**		calciferous
insobriety	beatifical	**ĬF′ra-gus**	carboniferous
luxuriety	dolorifical	*fedrifragous*	cheliferous
mediety	*lanifical*	ossifragous	cirriferous
nimiety	pontifical	saxifragous	conchiferous
notoriety	specifical		coniferous
nullibiety		**ĬF′ta-b′l**	coralliferous
omniety	**ĬF′i-kant**	liftable	cruciferous
piety	insignificant	shiftable	diamantiferous
propriety	mundificant		diamondiferous
satiety	sacrificant	**ĬF′ti-li**	doloriferous
sobriety	significant	shiftily	*ensiferous*
society		thriftily	fatiferous
ubiety	**ĬF′i-kat**		ferriferous
variety	certificate	**ĬF′ti-nes**	filiferous
	pontificate	shiftiness	flammiferous
Ī′et-ing	significate	thriftiness	floriferous
dieting			fluctiferous
disquieting	**ĬF′i-sens**	**ĬFT′les-nes**	foliferous
quieting	magnificence	shiftlessness	foraminiferous
rioting	munificence	thriftlessness	fossiliferous
			frondiferous
Ī′et-ist	**ĬF′i-sent**	**ĬF′u-gal**	frugiferous
anxietist	magnificent	centrifugal	fumiferous
dietist	*mirificent*	febrifugal	furciferous
pietist	munificent	vermifugal	gemmiferous
proprietist			geodiferous
quietist	**ĬF′i-sur**	**ĬF′ur-us**	glandiferous
varietiest	artificer	acidiferous	glandiferous
	opificer	aliferous	glanduliferous

graniferous
granuliferous
guttiferous
gypsiferous
hederiferous
herbiferous
igniferous
lactiferous
lamelliferous
laminiferous
lanciferous
laniferous
laticiferous
lauriferous
lethiferous
ligniferous
lignitiferous
luciferous
lucriferous
luminiferous
magnetiferous
maliferous
mammaliferous
mammiferous
margaritiferous
melliferous
membrani-
    ferous
metalliferous
monstriferous
mortiferous
multiferous
nectariferous
nickeliferous
nimbiferous
nitriferous
noctiferous
nubiferous
nuciferous
odoriferous
oleiferous

omniferous
oolitiferous
ossiferous
ostriferous
ozoniferous
palmiferous
pestiferous
pistilliferous
platiniferous
plumbiferous
polypiferous
proliferous
pruniferous
pulmoniferous
quartiziferous
racemiferous
resiniferous
roriferous
sacchariferous
sacciferous
saliferous
saliniferous
salutiferous
sanguiferous
scopiferous
scutiferous
sebiferous
sensiferous
setiferous
siliciferous
somniferous
soniferous
soporiferous
spiciferous
spiniferous
spumiferous
stameniferous
stanniferous
stelliferous
stoloniferous
succiferous

sudoriferous
tentaculiferous
tergiferous
thuriferous
tuberiferous
umbelliferous
umbraculifer-
    ous
umbriferous
vaporiferous
vasculiferous
vociferous
zinciferous

ĬG'am-i
bigamy
digamy
polygamy
trigamy

ĬG'am-ist
bigamist
polygamist
trigamist

ĬG'am-us
bigamous
digamous
polygamous
trigamous

ĬG'ma-tist
enigmatist
stigmatist

ĬG'ma-tiz
enigmatize
paradigmatize
stigmatize

ĬG'nan-si
indignancy
malignancy

ĬG'ne-us
igneous
ligneous

ĬG'ni-fi
dignify
ignify
lignify
malignify
signify
undignify

ĬG'ni-ti
benignity
dignity
indignity
malignity

ĬG'or-us
rigorous
vigorous

ĬG'ra-fi
calligraphy
epigraphy
lexigraphy
pasigraphy
poligraphy
pseudepigrahy
stratigraphy
tachygraphy

ĬG'u-lat
figulate
ligulate

ĬG'ur-i
piggery
Whiggery
wiggery

ĬG′u-us

ambiguous
contiguous
exiguous
irriguous

ĬJ′en-us

alkaligenous
coralligenous
epigenous
fuliginous
gelatigenous
ignigenous
indigenous
marigenous
melligenous
montigenous
nubigenous
omnigenous
oxygenous
polygenous
pruriginous
sanguigenous
terrigenous
uliginous
unigenous
vertiginous
vortiginous

ĬJ′i-an

Cantabrigian
Phrygian
Stygian

ĬJ′id-li

frigidly
rigidly

ĬJ′id-nes

frigidness
rigidness

ĬJ′i-ti

digity
fidgety

ĬJ′ur-at

belligerate
frigerate
refrigerate

ĬJ′ur-ent

belligerent
refrigerant

ĬJ′ur-us

aligerous
armigerous
belligerous
cirrigerous
coralligerous
cornigerous
crucigerous
dentigerous
immorigerous
lanigerous
linigerous
morigerous
navigerous
ovigerous
palpigerous
pedigerous
pennigerous
piligerous
plumigerous
proligerous
setigerous
spinigerous

ĬJ′us-nes

litigiousness
prodigiousness
religiousness

ĬK′a-ment

medicament
predicament

ĬK′a-tiv

abdicative
desiccative
exsiccative
fricative
indicative
predicative
siccative

ĬK′en-ing

quickening
sickening
thickening

ĬK′et-i

pernicketty
rickety
thicketty

ĬK′et-ing

cricketing
picketing
ticketing

ĬK′et-ur

cricketer
picketer

ĬK′i-li

stickily
trickily

ĬK′i-nes

stickiness
trickiness

ĬK′li-nes

prickliness
sickliness

ĬK′o-list

agricolist
ignicolist
plebicolist

ĬK′o-lus

agricolous
sepicolous
terricolous

ĬK′o-mus

auricomous
flavicomous

ĬK′sa-b'l

fixable
mixable

ĬK′shun-al

contradictional
fictional
frictional
jurisdictional

ĬK′si-ti

fixity
prolixity
siccity

ĬK′tiv-li

restrictively
vindictively

ĬK′tiv-nes

restrictiveness
vindictiveness

ĬK′to-ri

benedictory
contradictory
interdictory

āle, câre, ădd, ärm, ȧsk; mē, hĕre, ĕnd; īce, ĭll;

valedictory
victory

ĬK′u-la
Canicula
fidicula
zeticula

ĬK′u-lar
acicular
adminicular
articular
auricular
calycular
canicular
clavicular
cubicular
cuticular
fascicular
follicular
funicular
lenticular
navicular
orbicular
ovicular
particular
pellicular
perpendicular
quinquarticular
radicular
reticular
spicular
subcuticular
vehicular
ventricular
vermicular
versicular
vesicular

ĬK′u-lat
articulate

canaliculate
denticulate
fasciculate
funiculate
geniculate
gesticulate
matriculate
monticulate
paniculate
particulate
reticulate
spiculate
vehiculate
vermiculate
vesiculate

ĬK′u-lum
curriculum
geniculum

ĬK′u-lus
dendiculus
denticulus
fasciculus
folliculous
meticulous
ridiculous
urbiculous
ventriculous
vermiculous
vesiculous

ĬK′wi-ti
antiquity
iniquity
obliquity
ubiquity

ĬK′wi-tus
iniquitous
ubiquitous

ĬL′a-b'l
distillable
fillable
refillable
syllable
tillable
unrefillable

Ĭ′lan-dur
highlander
islander

ĬL′a-ri
Hilary
(see ĬL′ur-i)

ĬL′et-ed
billeted
filleted
unfilleted

ĬL′et-ing
billeting
filleting

ĬL′ful-i
guilefully
wilefully

ĬL′ful-i
skilfully
wilfully
unskilfully

ĬL′ful-nes
guilefulness
wilefulness

ĬL′ful-nes
skilfulness

wilfulness
unskilfulness

ĬL′i-a
memorabilia
notabilia
sedilia

ĬL′i-ad
chiliad
Iliad
(cf. Gilead)

ĬL′i-an
Brazilian
Castilian
Cecilian
crocodilian
Kurilian
lacertilian
Lilian
Maximilian
perfectibilian
reptilian
Virgilian
(cf. ĬL′yun)

ĬL′i-ar
atrabiliar
auxiliar
conciliar
domiciliar
(see ĬL′yar)

ĬL′i-at
affiliate
conciliate
domiciliate
filiate
humiliate

ĬL'ĭ-ens
consilience
dissilience
resilience
transilience
(cf. brilliance)

ĬL'ĭ-ent
dissilient
resilient
transilient
(cf. brilliant)

ĬL'ĭ-est
chilliest
hilliest
silliest
stilliest

ĬL'ĭ-fi
fossilify
nobilify
stabilify
vilify

ĬL'ĭ-form
filiform
plumiliform

ĬL'ĭ-gan
Gilligan
McMilligan

ĬL'ĭj-ur
pillager
villager

ĬL'ĭ-ka
basilica
silica

ĬL'ĭ-kal
basilical

filical
silicle
umbilical

ĬL'ĭ-nes
chilliness
hilliness
silliness

ĬL'ing-li
killingly
thrillingly
trillingly
willingly

ĬL'ĭ-o
pulvillio
punctilio

ĬL'ĭ-tat
abilitate
debilitate
facilitate
habilitate
impossibilitate
militate
nobilitate
rehabilitate
stabilitate

ĬL'ĭ-ti
ability
absorbability
accendibility
acceptability
accessibility
accountability
acquirability
adaptability
addibility
admirability

admissibility
adoptability
adorability
advisability
affability
affectibility
agility
agreeability
alienability
alterability
amenability
amiability
amicability
amissibility
anility
appetibility
applicability
assimilability
associability
attainability
attemptability
attractability
audibility
availability
capability
changeability
civility
cognoscibility
cohesibility
combustibility
communicabil-
ity
commutability
compatibility
comprehensibil-
ity
compressibility
computability
conceivability
condensability
conducibility

conductability
conformability
confusability
contemptibility
contractibility
contractility
convertibility
corrigibility
corrodibility
corrosibility
credibility
creditability
crocodility
culpability
curability
damnability
debility
deceptibility
deducibility
defectibility
demisability
demonstrabil-
ity
deplorability
descendibility
desirability
despicability
destructibility
determinability
detestability
diffusibility
digestibility
dilatability
disability
dissolubility
dissolvability
distensibility
divisibility
docibility
docility
ductility

durability
edibility
educability
eligibility
equability
exchangeability
excitability
exhaustibility
expansibility
extensibility
facility
fallibility
feasibility
fermentability
fertility
fictility
flexibility
fluctuability
fluxibility
formidability
fossility
fragility
frangibility
friability
fusibility
futility
generability
gentility
gracility
gullibility
habitability
hostility
humility
ignobility
illability
imbecility
imitability
immeability
immeasura-
  bility
immiscibility

immovability
immutability
impalpability
impartibility
impassibility
impeccability
impenetrability
impercepti-
  bility
imperdibility
impermeability
imperturba-
  bility
imperviability
implacability
impossibility
impregnability
imprescripti-
  bility
impressibility
impressiona-
  bility
improbability
imputability
inability
inaccessibility
incivility
incogitability
incognoscibility
incombusti-
  bility
incommensura-
  bility
incommunica-
  bility
incommuta-
  bility
incompatibility
incomprehensi-
  bility

incompressi-
  bility
inconceiva-
  bility
incondensa-
  bility
incontroverti-
  bility
inconvertibility
incorrigibility
incorruptibility
incredibility
incurability
indefatigability
indefeasibility
indefectibility
indelibility
indemonstra-
  bility
indestructi-
  bility
indigestibility
indiscernibility
indiscerpti-
  bility
indispensability
indisputability
indissolubility
indivisibility
indocibility
indocility
inductility
ineffability
ineffervesci-
  bility
ineligibility
inevitability
inexhaustibility
inexorability
inexplicability
infallibility

infeasibility
infertility
inflammability
inflexibility
infrangibility
infusibility
inhability
inhabitability
inheritability
inimitability
innumbera-
  bility
insanability
insatiability
insensibility
inseparability
insociability
insolubility
instability
insuperability
insurmounta-
  bility
insusceptibility
intangibility
intelligibility
interchange-
  ability
intractability
inutility
invendibility
invincibility
inviolability
invisibility
invulnerability
irascibility
irreconcilability
irreductibility
irremovability
irreparability
irresistibility
irresponsibility

ōld, ôr, ŏdd, oil, fŏŏt, out; ūse, ûrn, ŭp; THis, thin

irritability
juvenility
lability
laminability
laudability
legibility
liability
malleability
manageability
memorability
mensurability
miscibility
mobility
modifiability
modificability
motility
movability
mutability
navigability
negotiability
neurility
nihility
nobility
notability
opposability
organizability
ostensibility
palpability
partibility
passibility
peccability
penetrability
pensility
perceptibility
perdurability
perfectibility
permissibility
persuasibility
perturbability
placability
plausibility

pliability
ponderability
portability
possibility
practicability
precipitability
preferability
prescriptibility
preventability
probability
producibility
puerility
quotability
ratability
readability
receivability
receptibility
redeemability
reductibility
reflexibility
refragability
refrangibility
refutability
reliability
remissibility
removability
remunerability
renewability
reparability
repealability
resistibility
resolvability
respectability
responsibility
reversibility
revocability
risibility
saleability
salvability
sanability
satiability

scurrility
senility
sensibility
separability
servility
sociability
solubility
solvability
sportability
squeezability
stability
sterility
suability
subtility
suitability
susceptibility
suspensibility
tactility
tamability
tangibility
taxability
temptability
tenability
tensibility
tensility
tolerability
torsibility
tortility
tractability
tractility
tranquillity
transferability
transmissibility
transmutability
transportability
unaccount-
  ability
unbelievability
unutterability
utility
vaporability

variability
vegetability
vendibility
venerability
verisimility
vernility
versability
versatility
viability
vibratility
vindicability
virility
visibility
volatility
volubility
vulnerability
writability

ĬL′ĭ-us

atrabilious
bilious
punctilious
supercilious
(cf. as ĬL′yus)

ĬL′kĭ-est

milkiest
silkiest

ĬL′kĭ-ur

milkier
silkier

Ī′lo-bat

stylobate
trilobate

ĬL′o-ĭ

billowy
pillowy
willowy

āle, câre, ădd, ärm, ȧsk; mē, hĕre, ĕnd; īce, ĭll;

ĬL'o-ing
billowing
pillowing

ĬL'o-ji
antilogy
brachylogy
dilogy
fossilogy
palilogy
trilogy

ĬL'o-jiz
epilogize
syllogize

ĬL'o-jizm
epilogism
episyllogism
syllogism

ĬL'o-ri
pillory
(see ĬL'ur-i)

ĬL'o-kwens
blandiloquence
breviloquence
grandiloquence
magniloquence
somniloquence
stultiloquence

ĬL'o-kwent
flexiloquent
grandiloquent
magniloquent
melliloquent
pauciloquent
sanctiloquent
stultiloquent

suaviloquent
veriloquent

ĬL'o-kwi
dentiloquy
gastriloquy
pauciloquy
pectoriloquy
soliloquy
somniloquy
stultiloquy
suaviloquy
ventriloquy

ĬL'o-kwist
dentiloquist
gastriloquist
somniloquist
ventriloquist

ĬL'o-kwiz
soliloquize
ventriloquize

ĬL'o-kwizm
gastriloquism
pectoriloquism
somniloquism
ventriloquism

ĬL'o-kwus
grandiloquous
magniloquous
pectoriloquous
somniloquous
ventriloquous

ĬL'ur-i
artillery
capillary
cilery

codicillary
distillery
Hilary
phyllary
pillory
Sillery

ĬL'yan-si
brilliancy
resiliency
transiliency

ĬL'yar-i
atrabiliary
auxiliary

ĬM'a-nus
longimanous
pedimanous

ĬM'a-tur
climature
limature

ĬM'bri-kat
fimbricate
imbricate

Ĭ'mer-i
primary
rhymery

ĬM'et-ri
alkalimetry
asymmetry
bathymetry
calorimetry
isoperimetry
longimetry
planimetry
polarimetry

saccharimetry
symmetry

ĬM'et-ur
alkalimetēr
altimeter
calorimeter
dasymeter
dimeter
focimeter
gravimeter
limiter
lucimeter
pelvimeter
perimeter
planimeter
polarimeter
pulsimeter
rhysimeter
saccharimeter
salimeter
scimiter
tasimeter
trimeter
velocimeter
zymosimeter
(cf. scimitar)

ĬM'ĭ-an,
  ĬM'ĭ-on
Endymion
simian
Simeon

ĬM'ĭ-kal
alchymical
homonymical
inimical
metonymical
mimical

ĬM'i-nal
criminal
regiminal
subliminal
viminal

ĬM'i-nat
accriminate
criminate
discriminate
eliminate
incriminate
indiscriminate
recriminate

ĬM'i-nes
griminess
sliminess

ĬM'i-ni
Bimini
jiminy
nimini-pimini
postliminy

ĬM'i-nus
criminous
moliminous

ĬM'i-ti
anonymity
dimity
equanimity
magnanimity
parvanimity
proximity
pseudonymity
pusillanimity
sanctanimity
sublimity
unanimity

ĬM'pur-ing
simpering
whimpering

ĬM'pur-ur
simperer
whimperer

ĬM'u-lat
assimulate
dissimulate
simulate
stimulate

ĬM'u-lus
limulus
stimulus

ĬM'ur-us
dimerous
polymerous

ĬN'a-b'l
assignable
combinable
declinable
definable
designable
finable
inclinable
indeclinable
indefinable
signable

ĬN'ar-i
binary
(see ĬN'ur-i)

ĬN'a-tiv
combinative
finative

ĬN'di-kat
indicate
syndicate
vindicate

ĬN'dur-i
bindery
grindery

ĬN'dur-i
cindery
tindery

ĬN'e-al, ĬN'i-al
consanguineal
finial
gramineal
interlineal
lineal
pectineal
pineal
stamineal

ĬN'e-ma
cinema
kinema

ĬN'e-us
cartilagineous
consanguine-
  ous
flamineous
fulmineous
gramineous
ignominious
sanguineous
stamineous
stramineous
testudineous
vimineous

ĬNG'gur-ing
fingering
lingering
malingering

ĬNG'gur-ur
fingerer
lingerer
malingerer

ĬNG'i-nes
ringiness
springiness
stringiness

ĬNGK'a-b'l
drinkable
shrinkable
thinkable
undrinkable
unshrinkable
unsinkable
unthinkable

ĬNGK'i-nes
inkiness
kinkiness
pinkiness
slinkiness

ĬNGK'wi-ti
longinquity
propinquity

ĬN'i-al
finial
(see ĬN'e-al)

ĬN'i-a
Abyssinia
Lavinia

āle,   câre,   ădd,   ärm,   ăsk;   mē,   hĕre,   ĕnd;   īce,   ĭll;

Sardinia
Virginia
zinnia

ĬN'i-an
Abyssinian
anthropopha-
  ginian
Arminian
Augustinian
Carolinian
Carthaginian
czarinian
Darwinian
Delphinian
Eleusinian
Hercynian
Justinian
Palestinean
Sardinian
serpentinian
Socinian
viraginian
Virginian
(cf. ĬN'yon)

ĬN'i-at, ĬN'e-at
delineate
laciniate
lineate
miniate

ĬN'i-est
briniest
shiniest
spiniest
tiniest

ĬN'i-form
actiniform

aluminiform
laciniform

ĬN'i-kin
finikin
minikin

ĬN'i-k'l
adminicle
binnacle
binocle
Brahminical
clinical
cynical
dominical
finical
flaminical
pinnacle
Sinical
synclinical

ĬN'i-ment
liniment
miniment

ĬN'ish-ing
diminishing
finishing

ĬN'is-tral
ministral
sinistral

ĬN'is-tur
administer
minister
sinister

ĬN'i-ti
affinity
alkalinity
asininity

consanguinity
divinity
felinity
femininity
infinity
Latinity
masculinity
patavinity
peregrinity
salinity
sanguinity
satinity
trinity
vicinity
viraginity
virginity

ĬN'i-tiv
combinative
finitive
infinitive

ĬN'i-ur
brinier
shinier
spinier
tinier

ĬN'jen-si
astringency
contingency
refringency
stringency

ĬN'ji-an
Carlovingian
Merovingian
Thuringian

ĬN'ji-li
dingily
stingily

consanguinity
dinginess
stinginess

ĬN'lan-dur
Finlander
inlander

ĬN'o-lin
crinoline
quinoline

ĬN'thi-an
absinthian
Corinthian
hyacinthian
labyrinthian

ĬN'tur-est
interest
splinterest
winterest

ĬN'tur-i
printery
splintery
wintery

ĬN'ur-i
alpinery
binary
finary
finery
pinery
quinary
refinery
swinery
vinery

ĬN'u-at
continuate

insinuate
sinuate

ĬN'u-us
continuous
sinuous

Ĭ'ol-a
variola
viola

Ī'o-let
triolet
violet

Ī'o-list
sciolist
violist

Ī'o-lus
gladiolus
sciolous
variolous

Ī'o-pe
Calliope
myopy
presbyopy

Ī'o-tur
rioter
(see Ī'et-ur)

Ī'o-sen
Miocene
Pliocene
post-Pliocene

ĬP'ar-us
biparous
criniparous

deiparous
fissiparous
floriparous
foliiparous
frondiparous
fructiparous
gemelliparous
gemmiparous
larviparous
multiparous
omniparous
opiparous
oviparous
ovoviviparous
polyparous
polypiparous
sebiparous
sudoriparous
tomiparous
uniparous
vermiparous
viviparous

ĬP'a-thi
antipathy
kinesipathy
somnipathy

ĬP'a-thist
antipathist
somnipathist

ĬP'ed-al
equipedal
solipedal
(cf. ĒD'al)

ĬP'li-kat
sesquiplicate
triplicate

ĬP'o-li
Gallipoli
Tripoli

ĬP'o-tens
armipotence
ignipotence
omnipotence
plenipotence

ĬP'o-tent
armipotent
bellipotent
ignipotent
multipotent
omnipotent
plenipotent

ĬP'ti-kal
apocalyptical
cryptical
elliptical

ĬP'tur-us
dipterous
peripterous
tripterous

ĬP'u-lat
astipulate
manipulate
stipulate

ĬP'ur-i
frippery
slippery

ĬR'a-b'l
acquirable
desirable
expirable

perspirable
requirable
respirable
transpirable
untirable

ĪR'as-i
piracy
retiracy

ĬR'as-i
conspiracy
deliracy

ĪR'ful-nes
direfulness
irefulness

ĬR'i-an
Assyrian
Styrian
Syrian
Tyrian
(cf. ĒR'i-an)

ĬR'i-kal
empirical
lyrical
miracle
panegyrical
satirical

ĬR'i-sizm
empiricism
lyricism

ĬR'i-us
delirious
Sirius
(cf. ĒR'i-us)

āle, câre, ădd, ärm, åsk; mē, hĕre, ĕnd; īce, ĭll;

ĬR'on-i
gyronny
irony

ĬS'en-ing
christening
glistening
listening
unlistening

ĬS'en-si
reminiscency
reviviscency

ĬS'en-ur
christener
listener

ĬSH'al-i
judicially
officially
prejudicially
superficially

ĬSH'al-izm
judicialism
officialism

ĬSH'en-si
alliciency
beneficiency
deficiency
efficiency
inefficiency
insitiency
insufficiency
proficiency
self-sufficiency
sufficiency

ĬSH'i-a
Alicia

Delicia
Felicia

ĬSH'i-at
initiate
maleficiate
novitiate
officiate
patriciate
propitiate
vitiate

ĬSH'i-ens
omniscience
(cf. ĬSH'ens)

ĬSH'i-ent
omniscient
(cf. ĬSH'ent)

ĬSH'on-al
additional
commissional
conditional
definitional
dispositional
disquisitional
inquisitional
intuitional
positional
prepositional
propositional
repetitional
suppositional
traditional
transitional
transpositional
volitional

ĬSH'on-ist
abolitionist
coalitionist

exhibitionist
expeditionist
oppositionist
prohibitionist
requisitionist
traditionist

ĬSH'on-ur
admonitioner
coalitioner
commissioner
exhibitioner
missioner
practitioner
traditioner

ĬSH'us-nes
adventitious-
  ness
auspiciousness
avariciousness
capriciousness
deliciousness
expeditiousness
fictitiousness
flagitiousness
inauspicious-
  ness
judiciousness
maliciousness
meretricious-
  ness
perniciousness
propitiousness
seditiousness
superstitious-
  ness
supposititious-
  ness
suspiciousness
viciousness

ĬS'i-b'l
admissible
amissible
dismissible
immiscible
incommiscible
irremissable
miscible
omissible
permiscible
permissible
remissible
scissible
transmissible

ĬS'i-est
iciest
spiciest

Ĭ'si-k'l
bicycle
icicle
tricycle

ĬS'i-li
icily
spicily

ĬS'i-mo
bravissimo
fortissimo
generalissimo
pianissimo
prestissimo

ĬS'i-nal
fidicinal
medicinal
officinal
vaticinal
vicinal

ōld, ôr, ŏdd, oil, fŏŏt, out; ūse, ûrn, ŭp; THis, thin

ĬS'ĭ-nes
iciness
spiciness

ĬS'ĭ-ti
accomplicity
achromaticity
authenticity
benedicite
caloricity
canonicity
catholicity
causticity
centricity
clericity
complicity
conicity
domesticity
duplicity
eccentricity
elasticity
electricity
electrotonicity
ellipticity
endemicity
evangelicity
felicity
historicity
hygroscopicity
immundicity
impudicity
inelasticity
infelicity
lubricity
mendicity
multiplicity
pepticity
periodicity
plasticity
publicity
pudicity

rubricity
rusticity
simplicity
spasticity
sphericity
spheroidicity
stoicity
stypticity
tonicity
triplicity
unicity
verticity
volcanicity
vulcanicity

ĬS'ĭt-nes
explicitness
illicitness
implicitness
licitness

ĬS'ĭ-tud
solicitude
spissitude
vicissitude

Ī'sĭ-us
Dionysius
(cf. Lycias)

ĬS'ĭv-li
decisively
derisively
incisively
indecisively

ĬS'ĭv-nes
decisiveness
derisiveness
incisiveness
indecisivenes

ĬS'kĭ-est
friskiest
riskiest

ĬS'on-us
fluctisonous
unisonous

ĬS'or-i, ĬS'ur-i
decisory
derisory
incisory
spicery

ĬS'or-i
admissory
dismissory
emissory
remisory
rescissory

ĬS'ten-si
consistency
distancy
existency
inconsistency
persistency
pre-existency
subsistency

ĬS'tĭ-kal
agonistical
alchemistical
anarchistical
anomalistical
antagonistical
antarchistical
aoristical
apathistical
aphoristical
artistical

atheistical
cabalistical
Calvanistical
casuistical
cathechistical
characteristical
chemistical
deistical
dialogistical
egostical
egotistical
eucharistical
eulogistical
euphemistical
hemistichal
linguistical
methodistical
mystical
paragraphisti-
  cal
pietistical
puristical
sophistical
statistical
theistical
theosophistical

ĬS'tĭ-kat
dephlogisticate
sophisticate

ĬST'les-nes
listlessness
resistlessness

ĬS'to-ri
consistory
history
mystery

ĪT'a-b'l
citable

excitable
ignitible
incitable
indictable
lightable
requitable
unitable
writable

ĬT′a-b′l
admittable
fittable
irremittable
knittable
quittable
transmittible

ĬT′an-i
dittany
kitteny
litany

ĬT′a-tiv
excitative
incitative
writative

ĬT′ful-i
delightfully
frightfully
rightfully
spitefully

Ĭth′e-sis
antithesis
epithesis

ĬTH′som-li
blithesomely
lithesomely

ĬTH′som-nes
blithesomeness
lithesomeness

ĬTH′ur-ward
hitherward
thitherward
whitherward

ĬT′i-gant
litigant
mitigant

ĬT′i-gat
litigate
mitigate

ĬT′i-kal
Abrahamitical
acritical
analytical
anchoritical
cosmopolitical
critical
diacritical
electrolytical
hermitical
hypercritical
hypocritical
Jesuitical
Levitical
political
pulpitical
soritical
thersitical

ĬT′i-li
grittily
prettily
wittily

ĬT′i-nes
almightiness
flightiness
mightiness

ĬT′i-nes
flittiness
grittiness
prettiness
wittiness

ĬT′i-sizm
Britticism
witticism

ĬT′li-nes
knightliness
spriteliness
unsightliness

ĬT″l-nes
brittleness
littleness

ĬT′u-al
habitual
obitual
ritual

ĬT′u-at
habituate
situate

ĬT′u-lar
capitular
titular

ĬT′ur-at
illiterate
iterate
literate

obliterate
reiterate
transliterate

ĬT′ur-est
bitterest
embitterest
fritterest
glitterest

ĬT′ur-ing
bittering
embittering
frittering
glittering
tittering
twittering

Ĭ′ur-i
briery
fiery
friary
(cf. diary)

ĬV′a-b′l
contrivable
deprivable
derivable
revivable

ĬV′a-b′l
forgivable
givable
livable
unforgivable

ĬV′a-lent
equivalent
multivalent
omnivalent
quinquivalent

trivalent
univalent

ĬV′an-si

connivancy
survivancy

ĬV′a-tiv

derivative
privative

ĬV′el-ur,
  ĬV′il-ur

civiller
driveller
sniveller

ĬV′i-a

Bolivia
Livia
Olivia
trivia

ĬV′i-al

convivial
lixivial
oblivial
quadrivial
trivial

ĬV′i-an

Bolivian
Vivian
(cf. Vivien)

ĬV′id-nes

lividness
vividness

ĬV′i-ti

absorptivity

acclivity
activity
captivity
causativity
cogitativity
collectivity
conductivity
declivity
festivity
impassivity
incogitativity
instinctivity
motivity
nativity
negativity
objectivity
passivity
perceptivity
positivity
privity
proclivity
productivity
receptivity
relativity
sensitivity
subjectivity

ĬV′i-us

bivious
lascivious
lixivious
multivious
oblivious

ĬV′o-kal

equivocal
univocal

ĬV′o-li

Rivoli
Tivoli

ĬV′o-ri, ĬV′ar-i

ivory
vivary

ĬV′or-us

carnivorous
equivorous
frugivorous
fucivorous
graminivorous
granivorous
herbivorous
insectivorous
omnivorous
ossivorous
panivorous
phytivorous
piscivorous
sanguinivorous
vermivorous

ĬV′ur-i

delivery
gaol-delivery
jail-delivery
livery
rivery
shivery

ĬV′ur-ing

delivering
quivering
shivering

ĬV′ur-ur

deliverer
quiverer
shiverer

ĬZ′a-b'l

advisable

analysable
crystallizable
demisable
despisable
devisable
electrolysable
excisable
exercisable
magnetizable
organizable
oxidizable
prizable
realizable
recognizable
sizable
vaporizable

ĬZ′a-b'l

acquisible
divisible
indivisible
invisible
risible
visible

ĬZH′on-al

divisional
provisional
revisional
transitional
visional

ĬZ′i-an

Elysian
Frisian
Paradisean
Parisian
precisian
(cf. ĬZH′un)

ĬZ′i-est   physical   inquisitor   **ĪZ′or-i**
busiest   psychophysical   requisitor   advisory
dizziest   visitor   irrisory
                   ĬZ′i-li   provisory
ĬZ′i-kal   busily   **ĬZ′i-ur**   revisory
metaphysical   dizzily   busier   supervisory
paradisical   **ĬZ′i-tor**   dizzier
phthisical   acquisitor   frizzier

O

For a discussion of words included under the accented vowels
following, see the beginning of O rhymes in Section I.

Ō′bi-a   snobbery   **ŎD′i-fi**   **ŌD′i-um**
hydrophobia,   stockjobbery   codify   odium
  etc.   modify   rhodium
phobia   **ŎB′ur-ing**   sodium
Zenobia   clobbering   **ŎD′i-kal**
                    slobbering   codical   **ŌD′i-us**
ŎB′i-net   episcodical   commodious
bobbinet   **ŎD′i-al**   methodical   incommodious
robinet   allodial   monodical   melodious
                    custodial   nodical   odious
ŎB′u-lar   episodial   periodical
globular   palinodial   prosodical   **ŌD′ri-nes**
lobular   prosodial   rhapsodical   bawdriness
                    threnodial   spasmodical   tawdriness
ŎB′ur-i   synodical   **ŎD′u-lar**
daubery   **ŌD′i-an**   modular
(cf. straw-   custodian   **ŎD′i-nes**   nodular
  berry)   Herodian   bawdiness
                    prosodian   gaudiness   **ŎD′ur-ik**
ŎB′ur-i   Rhodian   Roderick
bobbery   (cf. ŌD′i-on)   Theoderic
jobbery   **ŎD′i-ti**
robbery   **ŎD′el-ur**   commodity   **ŎD′ur-ing**
slobbery   modeller   incommodity   doddering
                    (cf. ŎD′lur)   oddity   foddering

ōld, ôr, ŏdd, oil, fŏŏt, out; ūse, ûrn, ŭp; THis, thin

ŎF′a-gan

saprophagan
sarcophagan
theophagan
zoophagan

ŎF′a-gī

androphagi
anthropophagi
cardophagi
heterophagi
hippophagi
lithophagi
Lotophagi
sarcophagi

ŎF′a-gĭ

anthropophagy
chthonophagy
hippiphagy
ichthyophagy
pantophagy
phytophagy
theophagy
xerophagy

ŎF′a-gist

galactophagist
geophagist
hippophagist
ichthyophagist
pantophagist

ŎF′a-gus

androphagous
batrachopha-
  gous
esophagus
galactophagous
geophagous
hippophagous

hylophagous
lithophagous
necrophagous
ophiophagous
pantophagous
phytophagous
saprophagous
sarcophagus
theophagous
xylophagous
zoophagous

ŎF′i-kal

philosophical
theosophical
trophical

ŎF′i-list

bibliophilist
Russophilist
zoophilist

ŎF′i-lizm

bibliophilism
necrophilism
Russophilism

ŎF′il-us

acidophilus
anemophilous
Theophilus
xylophilous

ŎF′o-ni

cacophony
homophony
laryngophony
microphony
orthophony
photophony
Satanophany

tautophony
theophany

ŎF′on-us

cacophonous
homophonous
hydrophanous
hygrophanous
megalophonous
monophanous
pyrophanous

ŎF′or-us

actinophorous
adenophorous
electrophorus
galactophorous
isophorus
mastigo-
  phorous
phyllophorous
pyrophorous
zoophorous

Ŏ′ful-i

awfully
lawfully
unlawfully

Ŏ′ful-nes

awfulness
lawfulness
unlawfulness

ŎF′ur-ing

coffering
offering
peace-offering
proffering

ŎG′am-i

cœnogamy

deuterogamy
endogamy
exogamy
misogamy
monogamy

ŎG′am-ist

deuterogamist
misogamist
monogamist
neogamist

ŎG′am-us

endogamus
exogamous
heterogamous
monogamous
phænogamous
phanerog-
  amous

ŎG′a-tiv

derogative
interrogative
prerogative

Ŏ′gi-ism

bogeyism
fogeyism

ŎG′no-mi

craniognomy
pathognomy
physiognomy

ŎG′ra-fi

anthography
anthropog-
  raphy
autobiography
autography

āle, câre, ădd, ärm, åsk; mē, hẹre, ĕnd; īce, ĭll;

balneography
bibliography
biography
cacography
calcography
chartography
chirography
chorography
Christianog-
  raphy
chromatog-
  raphy
chromophotog-
  raphy
chromotypog-
  raphy
chromoxylog-
  raphy
climatography
cosmography
cryptography
crystalography
dactyliography
demography
dendrography
epistolography
ethnography
galvanography
geography
glossography
glyphography
glyptography
gypsography
hagiography
haliography
heliography
heliotypog-
  raphy
hematography
heresiography
heterography

hierography
histography
historiography
horography
horologi-
  ography
hyalography
hydrography
hyetography
hymnography
ichnography
ichthyography
iconography
ideography
isography
lexicography
lichenography
lithography
logography
mechanog-
  raphy
metallography
microcosmog-
  raphy
monography
neography
neurography
nomography
nosography
numismatog-
  raphy
odontography
ophiography
oreography
organography
orography
orthography
osteography
palæography
palæontog-
  raphy

paneiconog-
  raphy
pantography
perspectog-
  raphy
petrography
phantasma-
  tography
pharmacog-
  raphy
phonography
photography
phycography
physiography
phytography
plastography
pneumography
pornography
potamography
psalmography
pseudography
psychography
pterylography
rhyparography
scenography
sciography
seismography
selenography
semeiography
siderography
sphenography
steganography
stelography
stenography
stereography
steoreotypog-
  raphy
stratography
stylography
symbolæog-
  raphy

tacheography
thermography
topography
toreumatog-
  raphy
typography
uranography
xylography
xylopyrography
zincograyhy
zoography

ŎG′ra-fist

chirographist
lichenographist
mechano-
  graphist
metallo-
  graphist
monographist
museographist
organogra-
  phist
orthographist
palæographist
phonographist
photographist
psalmographist
selenographist
siderographist
sphenographist
steganogra-
  phist
stenographist
topographist
uranographist
zoographist

ŎG′ra-fur

autobiographer
bibliographer

biographer
calcographer
cartographer
chartographer
chorographer
chronographer
cosmographer
cryptographer
crystallogra-
  pher
ethnographer
geographer
glossographer
glyphographer
glyptographer
haliographer
heresiographer
hierographer
historiographer
horologiogra-
  pher
hydrographer
hymnographer
iambographer
lexicographer
lichenographer
lithographer
logographer
mimographer
monographer
mythographer
nomographer
orthographer
osteographer
palæographer
petrographer
phonographer
photographer
psalmographer
selenographer
sphenographer

stenographer
topographer
typographer
xylographer
zincographer
zoographer

OI′a-b′l
employable
enjoyable

OI′al-i
loyally
royally

OI′al-ist
loyalist
royalist

OI′al-izm
loyalism
royalism

OI′al-ti
loyalty
royalty
viceroyalty

Ō′i-kal
egoical
heroical
stoical

OIN′ted-li
disjointedly
pointedly

OIS′tur-ing
cloistering
roistering

ŎJ′en-i
abiogeny
anthropogeny
biogeny
embryogeny
ethnogeny
geogeny
heterogeny
histogeny
homogeny
hymenogeny
misogyny
monogeny
odontogeny
ontogeny
osteogeny
pathogeny
philogyny
photogeny
phylogeny
progeny
protogyny
zoogeny

ŎJ′en-ist
abiogenist
biogenist
heterogenist
misogynist
monogenist
philogynist

ŎJ′en-us
endogenous
exogenous
hydrogenous
hypogynous
lithogenous
nitrogenous
pyrogenous
thermogenous

Ō′ji-an
archæologian
astrologian
gambogian
geologian
mythologian
neologian
philologian
theologian

ŎJ′i-kal
aërological
amphibiological
amphibological
analogical
anthological
anthropological
archæological
astrological
bibliological
biological
bryological
chronological
climatological
conchological
cosmological
craniological
demagogical
demonological
deontological
dialogical
doxological
Egpytological
etiological
etymological
genealogical
geological
glossological
glottological
homological
hydrological

āle,   câre,   ădd,   ärm,   åsk;   mē,   hęre,   ĕnd;   īce,   ĭll;

ichnological	tautological	**ŏK'en-li**	pantisocracy
ideological	technicological	brokenly	pedantocracy
illogical	technological	outspokenly	plantocracy
lithological	teleological		plousiocracy
logical	teratological	**ŏK'i-li**	plutocracy
mazological	terminological	chalkily	shopocracy
metalogical	theological	gawkily	slavocracy
meteorological	toxicological	pawkily	snobocracy
mythological	tropological		stratocracy
necrological	universological	**ŏK'i-nes**	theocracy
neological	zoological	chalkiness	theocrasy
neurological	zoophytological	gawkiness	timocracy
nosological	zymological	pawkiness	
odontological		squawkiness	**ŏK'ra-tizm**
organological	**ŏJ'on-i**	talkiness	democratism
ornithological	autogony		Socratism
orological	cosmogony	**ŏK'i-nes**	
osteological	geogony	cockiness	**ŏK'ro-mi**
palæontolog-	pathogony	rockiness	heliochromy
ical	physiogony	stockiness	metallochromy
pantological	theogony		monochromy
paralogical	zoogony	**ŏK'ra-si**	stereochromy
penological		aristocracy	
perissological	**ŏJ'o-nist**	arithmocracy	**ŏK'ron-us**
petrological	cosmogonist	autocracy	isochronous
philological	theogonist	cottonocracy	tautochronous
phraseological		democracy	
phrenological	**ŏK'a-liz**	demonocracy	**ŏK'si-kal**
physiological	focalize	despotocracy	orthodoxical
phytological	localize	gerontocracy	paradoxical
pneumatologi-	vocalize	gynæcocracy	toxical
cal		hagiocracy	
pomological	**ŏK'al-izm**	hierocracy	**ŏK'tor-ship**
psychological	localism	hypocrisy	doctorship
selenological	vocalism	idiocrasy	proctorship
semeiological		logocracy	
Sinological	**ŏK'a-tiv**	mobocracy	**ŏK'u-lar**
sociological	locative	monocracy	binocular
spectrological	invocative	neocracy	jocular
symbological	provocative	nomocracy	locular
synagogical	vocative	ochlocracy	monocular

ōld, ôr. ŏdd, oil, fŏŏt, out; ūse, ûrn, ŭp; THis, thin

ocular
vocular

ŎK'ur-i
crockery
mockery
rockery

ŎL'a-b'l
consolable
controllable
rollable
tollable

ŎL'a-b'l
enthrallable
recallable

ŎL'a-ri
bolary
cajolery
polary
solary
volary

ŎL'ar-iz
polarize
solarize

ŎL'a-tri
anthropolatry
astrolatry
bibliolatry
cosmolatry
demonolatry
geolatry
gyneolatry
heliolatry
hierolatry
ichthyolatry
idiolatry

idolatry
litholatry
lordolatry
Mariolatry
necrolatry
ophiolatry
physiolatry
pyrolatry
symbolatry
thaumatolatry
topolatry
zoolatry

ŎL'a-trus
idolatrous
symbolatrous

ŎL'a-tur
bibliolater
heliolater
iconolater
idolater
Mariolater
pyrolater

ŎL'e-um
linoleum
petroleum
(cf. ŎL'i-um)

ŎL'ful-nes
dolefulness
soulfulness

Ō'li-a
Aetolia
magnolia
melancholia
Mongolia

Ō'li-an
Æolian

capitolian
Creolean
melancholian
metabolian
Mongolian
Pactolian
(cf. Napoleon)

ŎL'i-at
foliate
infoliate
spoliate

ŎL'id-li
solidly
squalidly
stolidly

ŎL'id-nes
solidness
squalidness
stolidness

Ō'li-est
holiest
lowliest

ŎL'i-fi
idolify
mollify
qualify

ŎL'i-fid
mollified
qualified
unqualified

ŎL'i-kal
apostolical
bibliopolical
catholical

diabolical
hyperbolical
parabolical
symbolical

ŎL'ik-som
frolicsome
rollicksome

Ō'li-nes
holiness
lowliness
shoaliness
unholiness

Ō'li-o
folio
olio
portfolio
Sapolio

ŎL'ish-ing
abolishing
demolishing
polishing

ŎL'ish-ur
abolisher
demolisher
polisher

ŎL'i-ti
equality
frivolity
inequality
interpolity
isopolity
jollity
polity
quality

ŌL'i-um
scholium
trifolium

Ō'li-ur
Grolier
holier
lowlier
olier
unholier

ŌL'i-vur
Oliver
Taliaferro
Tolliver

ŌL'o-gus
heterologous
homologous
isologous
tautologous

ŌL'o-ing
following
holloing
hollowing
swallowing
wallowing

ŌL'o-ji
actinology
adenochirapsol-
   ogy
aerology
æsthematology
æsthesiology
agmatology
agriology
alethiology
amphibiology
amphibology

angelology
anthology
anthropology
aphnology
apology
arachnology
archæology
aretology
aristology
arteriology
asthenology
astrology
astrometeorol-
   ogy
astro-theology
atomology
balneology
barology
battology
bibliology
biology
botanology
bromatology
brontology
bryology
bugology
cacology
campanology
cephalology
Christology
chromatology
chronology
climatology
conchology
conchyliology
cosmology
craniology
cryptology
dactyliology
dactylology
demonology

dendrology
deontology
dermatology
desmology
dialectology
dicæology
dittology
dosology
doxology
ecclesiology
eccrinology
Egyptology
electro-biology
electrology
electro-physi-
   ology
embryology
emetology
emmenology
endemiology
enteradenology
enterology
entomology
entozoology
epidemiology
epistemology
eschatology
ethnology
ethology
etiology
etymology
filicology
fossilology
fungology
galvanology
gastrology
genesiology
geology
gigantology
glossology
glottology

gnomology
gnomonology
gynæcology
gypsology
hagiology
heterology
hierology
histology
historiology
homology
horology
hydrology
hyetology
hygiology
hygrology
hylology
hymenology
hymnology
hypnology
hysterology
ichnolithnology
ichnology
ichorology
ichthyology
iconology
ideology
insectology
kinology
laryngology
leptology
lexicology
lichenology
lithology
liturgiology
macrology
malacology
mantology
martyrology
mastology
mazology
membranology

ōld, ôr, ŏdd, oil, fŏŏt, out; ūse, ûrn, ŭp; THis, thin

menology
meteorology
methodology
metrology
miasmology
microgeology
micrology
misology
monadology
monology
morphology
muscology
mycology
myology
mythology
necrology
neology
nephrology
neurology
neurypnology
nomology
noölogy
nosology
numismatology
oceanology
odontology
ology
oneirology
onology
onomatology
ontology
oology
ophiology
ophthalmology
orchidology
organology
orismology
*ornithichnol-
  ogy*
ornithology
orology

osmonosolgy
osteology
otology
ovology
palæoëthnology
palæology
palæontology
palæophy-
  tology
palæozoology
palætiology
pantheology
pantology
paradoxology
parasitology
parisology
paromology
parthenology
pathology
patronomatol-
  ogy
penology
periodology
perissology
petrology
pharmacology
pharology
pharyngology
phenomenol-
  ogy
philology
phlebology
phonology
photology
phraseolgy
phrenology
phycology
physiology
phytolithology
phytology

phytopathol-
  ogy
phyto-
  physiology
pneumatology
pneumology
pomology
ponerology
posology
potamology
protophytology
psilology
psychology
psychonosol-
  ogy
pteridology
punnology
pyretology
pyritology
pyrology
quinology
runology
sarcology
seismology
selenology
sematology
semeiology
sinology
sitology
skeletology
sociology
somatology
soteriology
spasmology
speciology
spectrology
spermatology
spermology
splanchnology
splenology
statistology

stoichiology
stromatology
symbology
symptomatol-
  ogy
synchronology
syndesmology
systematology
tautology
taxology
technology
teleology
teratology
terminology
termonology
testaceology
thanatology
theology
thereology
thermology
therology
threpsology
tidology
topology
toreumatology
toxicology
tropology
typology
universology
uranology
urology
uronology
vulcanology
zoology
zoophytology
zymology

ŎL'o-jist
aërologist
agriologist
anthropologist

āle,   câre,   ădd,   ärm,   ȧsk: mē,   hẹre,   ĕnd;   īce,   ĭll;

apologist
archæologist
Assyriologist
battologist
biologist
campanologist
chronologist
conchologist
cosmologist
craniologist
crustaceologist
demonologist
dendrologist
deontologist
dermatologist
ecclesiologist
Egyptologist
electro-
  biologist
embryologist
entomologist
ethnologist
ethologist
etymologist
galvanologist
geologist
glossologist
glottologist
gypsologist
hagiologist
hierologist
histologist
horologist
hydrologist
hymnologist
hypnologist
ichthyologist
ideologist
lexicologist
lithologist
mantologist

martyrologist
mazologist
meteorologist
monologist
morphologist
mycologist
myologist
mythologist
necrologist
neologist
neurologist
noölogist
nosologist
numismatolo-
  gist
oneirologist
onomatologist
ontologist
oologist
ophiologist
orchidologist
ornithologist
orologist
osteologist
palæoethnolo-
  gist
palæologist
palæontologist
palætiologist
pantheologist
pantologist
pathologist
petrologist
pharmacologist
philologist
phonologist
photologist
phraseologist
phrenologist
physiologist

phytolitholo-
  gist
phytologist
phytopatholo-
  gist
pneumatologist
pomologist
pseudologist
psychologist
pteridologist
pyrologist
quinologist
runologist
saintologist
sarcologist
seismologist
sinologist
sociologist
symbologist
tautologist
technologist
teleologist
teratologist
theologist
thereologist
therologist
toxicologist
universologist
vulcanologist
zoologist
zymologist, etc.

ŎL'o-jiz

apologize
astrologize
battologize
doxologize
entomologize
etymologize
geologize
mythologize

neologize
philologize
sociologize
tautologize
theologize
zoologize, etc.

ŎL'o-jur

acknowledger
astrologer
botanologer
etymologer
geologer
horologer
mythologer
osteologer
philologer
phonologer
phrenologer
physiologer
sockdolager
theologer

ŎL'o-ur

follower
hollower
swallower
wallower

ŎL'ti-est

faultiest
saltiest

ŎL'ti-nes

faultiness
maltiness
saltiness

ŎL'tur-ing

altering
faltering

paltering
unaltering
unfaltering

ŌL'tur-ur
alterer
falterer
palterer

ŌL'u-b'l
insoluble
soluble
voluble

ŌL'u-tiv
solutive
supervolutive
(cf. evolutive,
  revolutive)

ŌL'va-b'l
absolvable
dissolvable
indissolvable
insolvable
resolvable
solvable

ŌL'ven-si
insolvency
revolvency
solvency

ŎM'ak-i
alectryomachy
gigantomachy
iconomachy
logomachy
monomachy
psychomachy

sciomachy
theomachy

ŎM'ath-i
chrestomathy
philomathy

Ō'ma-tizm
achromatism
chromatism
diplomatism

ŎM'en-a
antilegomena
paralipomena
phenomena
prolegomena

ŎM'en-on
phenomenon
prolegomenon

ŎM'e-tri
barometry
biometry
chronometry
craniometry
eudiometry
galvanometry
gasometry
geometry
goniometry
helicometry
horometry
hydrometry
hygrometry
hypsometry
Mahometry
micrometry
odometry
orthometry

ozonometry
pathometry
photometry
planometry
pneumometry
polygonometry
pyrometry
rheometry
saccharometry
seismometry
stereometry
stichometry
stoichiometry
trigonometry

ŎM'e-tur
absorptiometer
actinometer
altometer
astrometer
audiometer
barometer
bathometer
cephalometer
chartometer
chromatometer
chronometer
clinometer
craniometer
declinometer
dendrometer
drosometer
dynamometer
echometer
electrometer
endosmometer
eudiometer
galvanometer
geometer
geothermo-
  meter

goniometer
graphometer
heliometer
horometer
hydrometer
hygrometer
hypsometer
lactometer
logometer
macrometer
magnetometer
micrometer
micronometer
monometer
nauropometer
odometer
oleometer
ombrometer
optometer
ozonometer
pantometer
pedometer
phonometer
photometer
piezometer
planometer
platometer
pluviometer
pneumatometer
pulsometer
pyrometer
radiometer
refractometer
rheometer
saccharometer
salinometer
seismometer
sonometer
spectrometer
speedometer
spherometer

---

stereometer
stethometer
stratometer
tachometer
tannometer
thermometer
tribometer
trochometer
udometer
vinometer
volumenometer
zymometer

ŏM'ik-al
anatomical
agronomical
astronomical
atomical
comical
coxcombical
domical
economical
iconomachal
tragi-comical
zootomical

ŏM'in-al
abdominal
cognominal
nominal
prenominal
surnominal

ŏM'in-ans
dominance
predominance
prominence

ŏM'in-ant
dominant
predominant

prominent
subdominant
superdominant

ŏM'i-nat
abominate
agnominate
comminate
denominate
dominate
nominate
ominate
predominate
prenominate

ŏM'in-i
Chickahomini
dominie
hominy
(cf. Romany)

ŏM'in-us
abdominous
dominus
ominous
prolegomenous

ŏM'ur-us
glomerous
isomerous

ŏN'a-b'l
loanable
tonable
unatonable

ŏN'dur-ing
pondering
squandering
unwandering
wandering

ŏN'dur-ur
ponderer
squanderer
wanderer

ŏN'el-i
Connolly
Donnelly

Ō'ni-a
Adonia
ammonia
Ansonia
Antonia
aphonia
begonia
bryonia
Donia
Fredonia
Ionia
Laconia
Latonia
Patagonia
pneumonia
Slavonia
Sonia
Sophronia
valonia

Ō'ni-ak
demoniac
simoniac

Ō'ni-al
baronial
ceremonial
colonial
demonial
intercolonial
matrimonial
monial

oxygonial
patrimonial
sanctimonial
testimonial

Ō'ni-an
Aberdonian
Amazonian
Ammonian
Aonian
Ausonion
Babylonian
Baconian
bezonian
Caledonian
Cameronian
Catonian
Chelonian
Chthonian
Ciceronian
colophonian
Cottonian
Daltonian
demonian
Devonian
Draconian
Etonian
Favonian
Gorgonean
Grandisonian
halcyonian
Heliconian
Ionian
Johnsonian
Laconian
Lapponian
Livonian
Macedonian
Miltonian
Myrmidonian
Neronian

Newtonian
Oxonian
Patagonian
Plutonian
Pyrrhonian
Sardonian
Serbonian
Simonian
Slavonian
Thessalonian

ŎN′i-est
brawnies
tawniest

ŎN′i-fi
personify
saponify
(cf. ozonify)

ŎN′i-ka
harmonica
veronica

ŎN′i-kal
acronycal
antichronical
antiphonical
architectonical
Babylonical
canonical
chronicle
conical
diaphonical
euphonical
geoponical
harmonical
iconical
ironical
Sorbonical
synchronical

tautophonical
thrasonical
tonical
uncanonical

ŎN′i-kon
chronicon
harmonicon

ŎN′i-mi
homonymy
metonymy
paronymy
polyonymy
synonymy
(cf. ŎN′o-mi)

ŎN′i-mus
anonymous
autonomous
eponymous
heteronymous
homonymous
paronymous
polyonymous
pseudnymous
synonymous

ŎN′ish-ing
admonishing
astonishing
monishing

ŎN′ish-ment
admonishment
astonishment
premonishment

ŎN′i-sizm
histrionicism

laconicism
Teutonicism

Ō′ni-um
harmonium
pandemonium
pelargonium
stramonium
zirconium

Ō′ni-us
acrimonious
alimonious
Antonius
ceremonious
erroneous
euphonious
felonious
harmonious
inharmonious
matrimonious
parsimonious
querimonious
sanctimonious
simonious
symphonious
Trebonius
ultroneous

ŎN′o-graf
chronograph
monograph
(cf. phono-
graph)

ŎN′o-mi
agronomy
astronomy
autonomy
dactylonomy
Deuteronomy

economy
gastronomy
heteronomy
isonomy
morphonomy
taxonomy

ŎN′o-mist
agronomist
autonomist
economist
eponymist
gastronomist
synonymist

ŎN′o-miz
astronomize
economize
gastronomize

ŎN′o-mur
astronomer
gastronomer

OŌD′i-nes
woodiness
(cf. ŪD′i-nes)

OŌK′ur-i
bookery
cookery
rookery

Ō′o-lit
oolite
zoolite

OŌM′an-li
womanly
(cf. Ū′man-li)

āle, câre, ădd, ärm, ăsk; mē, hẹre, ĕnd; īce. ĭll;

ŎP′ath-i
allopathy
enantiopathy
heteropathy
homœopathy
hydropathy
ideopathy
isopathy
neuropathy
psychopathy
somnopathy
theopathy

ŎP′ath-ist
allopathist
homœopathist
hydropathist
hylopathist
osteopathist
somnopathist

Ō′pi-a
Ethiopia
myopia
presbyopia
Utopia

Ō′pi-an,
   Ō′pe-an
Aesopian
Esopian
Ethiopian
Fallopian
Utopian

ŎP′i-kal
allotropical
metoposcopical
microscopical
misanthropical
sub-tropical

topical
tropical

ŎP′i-nes
dopiness
ropiness
slopiness
soapiness

ŎP′i-nes
choppiness
sloppiness
soppiness

ŎP′ish-nes
dopishness
mopishness
popishness

ŎP′o-lis
acropolis
cosmopolis
Heliopolis
metropolis
necropolis

ŎP′o-list
bibliopolist
monopolist
pharmacopolist

ŎP′o-lit
cosmopolite
metropolite

ŎP′si-kal
dropsical
mopsical
Popsicle

ŎP′ti-kal
autoptical
optical

ŎP′tur-us
lepidopterous
macropterous
orthopterous

ŎP′u-lat
copulate
populate

ŎP′ur-i
dopery
popery
ropery

ŎP′ur-i
coppery
foppery

ŌR′a-b'l
adorable
deplorable
explorable
restorable

ŌR′a-tiv
explorative
restorative

ŌR′di-al
cordial
exordial
primordial

ŌR′di-nat
co-ordinate
foreordinate
insubordinate
ordinate
subordinate

ŌR′di-on,
   ŌR′di-an
accordion
Gordian

ŌR′dur-ing
bordering
ordering

ŌR′e-at
aureate
baccalaureate
laureate
poet-laureate

ŌR′e-ol
aureole
laureole

ŌR′gon-iz,
   ŌR′gan-iz
gorgonize
organize

Ō′ri-a
aporia
Astoria
Castoria
dysphoria
euphoria
Gloria
Honoria
infusoria
littoria
Peoria
phantasma-
   goria
Pretoria
scoria
victoria

Ō′ri-al
accessorial
accusatorial
adaptorial
admonitorial

---

amatorial
ambassadorial
ancestorial
arboreal
armorial
accessorial
auditorial
authorial
boreal
censorial
commentatorial
compromis-
   sorial
compurgatorial
consistorial
corporeal
cursorial
dedicatorial
dictatorial
directorial
disquisitorial
editorial
electorial
emporial
equatoreal
escritorial
executorial
expurgatorial
exterritorial
extraterritorial
factorial
fossorial
gladiatorial
grallatorial
gressorial
gubernatorial
historial
immemorial
imperatorial
improvisatorial
incorporeal

infusorial
inquisitorial
insessorial
intercessorial
inventorial
legislatorial
manorial
marmoreal
mediatorial
memorial
mentorial
monitorial
motorial
oratorial
phantasma-
   gorial
pictorial
piscatorial
preceptorial
prefatorial
proctorial
procuratorial
professorial
proprietorial
protectorial
purgatorial
raptorial
rasorial
rectorial
reportorial
risorial
sartorial
scansorial
sectorial
seigniorial
senatorial
sensorial
spectatorial
speculatorial
sponsorial
suctorial

territorial
textorial
tinctorial
tonsorial
tutorial
uxorial
victorial
visitatorial

Ō′ri-an

amatorian
Bosphorian
censorian
consistorian
dictatorian
Dorian
gladiatorian
Gregorian
Hectorean
historian
hyperborean
marmorean
mid-Victorian
Nestorian
oratorian
prætorian
purgatorian
salutatorian
senatorian
stentorian
valedictorian
Victorian

Ō′ri-at

excoriate
professoriate

ŏR′id-li

floridly
horridly
torridly

Ō′ri-fi

glorify
scorify

ŏR′i-fi

historify
horrify
torrefy

ŏR′i-kal

allegorical
categorical
coracle
historical
metaphorical
oracle
oratorical
pictorical
rhetorical
tautegorical

ŏR′i-nes

desultoriness
dilatoriness
goriness
hoariness
peremptoriness

Ō′ri-ol

gloriole
gloryhole
oriole

ŏR′i-ti

anteriority
authority
deteriority
exteriority
inferiority
interiority
juniority

āle, câre, ădd, ärm, ăsk; mē, hẹre, ĕnd; īce, ĭll;

majority

meliority

minority

posteriority

priority

seniority

sorority

superiority

Ō'ri-um

aspersorium

auditorium

ciborium

corium

crematorium

digitorium

emporium

fumatorium

haustorium

inclinatorium

moratorium

prætorium

prospectorium

sanatorium

scriptorium

sensorium

sudatorium

suspensorium

thorium

triforium

Ō'ri-us

amatorious

arboreous

censorious

circulatorious

desultorious

expiatorious

expurgatorious

glorious

hippicanorious

inglorious

inquisitorious

laborious

lusorious

meritorious

notorious

oratorious

purgatorious

raptorious

saltatorious

scorious

senatorious

stentorious

stertorious

suctorious

uproarious

ustorious

uxorious

vainglorious

victorious

ŎR'ma-tiv

afformative

dormitive

formative

informative

reformative

transformative

ŎR'mi-ti

abnormity

conformity

deformity

enormity

inconformity

multiformity

noncomformity

uniformity

ŎR'o-ing

borrowing

sorrowing

ŎR'o-ur

borrower

sorrower

ŎRS'a-b'l,

ŎRS'i-b'l

divorceable

enforceable

forcible

ŎR'ti-fī

fortify

mortify

ŎRT'i-kal

cortical

vortical

ŎRT'i-nes

swartiness

wartiness

ŎRT'li-nes

courtliness

portliness

uncourtliness

ŎR'tu-nat

fortunate

importunate

Ō'rus-li

decorously

porously

sonorously

ŎR'yus-li

gloriously

ingloriously

laboriously

meritoriously

notoriously

stentoriously

uproariously

uxoriously

vaingloriously

victoriously

ŎS'for-us

Bosphorus

phosphorus

Ō'shi-an

Bœotian

Nicotian

(cf. Ō'shun)

Ō'shun-al

devotional

emotional

notional

Ō'shus-nes

atrociousness

ferociousness

precociousness

ŎS'i-nat

patrocinate

ratiocinate

ŎS'i-nes

drossiness

glossiness

mossiness

ŎS'i-ti

paucity

raucity

ŎS'i-ti

actuosity

anfractuosity
angulosity
animosity
anonymosity
aquosity
atrocity
caliginosity
callosity
carnosity
curiosity
docity
dubiosity
ebriosity
fabulosity
ferocity
foliosity
fuliginosity
fumosity
fungosity
furiosity
gemmosity
generosity
gibbosity
glandulosity
glebosity
globosity
glutinosity
grandiosity
gulosity
gummosity
hideosity
impecuniosity
impetuosity
ingeniosity
inunctuosity
libidinosity
litigiosity
lugubriosity
luminosity
monstrosity
muscosity

musculosity
nebulosity
negotiosity
nervosity
nodosity
oleosity
otiosity
pilosity
plumosity
pomposity
ponderosity
porosity
preciosity
precocity
pretiosity
reciprocity
religiosity
ridiculosity
rimosity
rugosity
sabulosity
saporosity
scirrhosity
scrupulosity
sensuosity
serosity
sinuosity
speciosity
spicosity
spinosity
tenebrosity
torosity
tortuosity
tuberosity
tumulosity
unctuosity
varicosity
velocity
verbosity
viciosity
villosity

vinosity
virtuosity
viscosity
vitiosity
vociferosity

Ō′siv-nes

corrosiveness
explosiveness

ŏS′ko-pi

cranioscopy
geloscopy
geoscopy
hieroscopy
horoscopy
meteoroscopy
metoposcopy
omoplatoscopy
oneiroscopy
organoscopy
ornithoscopy
retinoscopy
stereoscopy
stethoscopy
uranoscopy

ŏS′ko-pist

metoposcopist
microscopist
oneiroscopist
ornithoscopist
stereoscopist
stethoscopist

ŏS′of-i

gymnosophy
philosophy
psilosophy
theosophy

ŏS′o-fist

chirosophist
deipnosophist
gymnosophist
philosophist
theosophist

ŏS′o-fiz

philosophize
theosophize

ŏS′o-fur

philosopher
psilosopher
theosopher

Ō′ta-b'l

floatable
notable
potable
quotable
votable

Ō′tal-izm

sacerdotalism
teetotalism

ŏT′an-i

botany
botonee
cottony
monotony

Ō′ta-ri

notary
rotary
votary

Ō′ta-tiv

connotative

āle, câre, ădd, ärm, åsk; mē, hĕre, ĕnd; īce, ĭll;

denotative
rotative

ŎT′ed-li
bloatedly
devotedly
notedly

ŎT′i-est
haughtiest
naughtiest

ŎT′i-kal
anecdotical
bigotical
despotical
erotical
exotical
zealotical

ŎT′i-li
haughtily
naughtily

ŎT′i-nes
haughtiness
naughtiness

ŎT′i-nes
dottiness
knottiness
spottiness

ŎT′i-ur
haughtier
naughtier

ŎT′om-i
apotome
bottomy
bronchotomy

dermotomy
dichotomy
encephalotomy
ichthyotomy
phlebotomy
phytotomy
scotomy
stereotomy
tracheotomy
zootomy

ŎT′o-mist
ichthyotomist
phlebotomist
phytotomist
zootomist

ŎT′ur-i
cautery
watery

ŎT′ur-i
lottery
pottery
tottery
trottery

ŎT′ur-ing
slaughtering
watering

ŎT′ur-ur
slaughterer
waterer

OU′a-b'l
allowable
avowable
endowable

OUD′ed-nes
cloudedness

crowdedness
overcrowded-
ness
uncloudedness

OUD′i-izm
dowdyism
rowdyism

OUD′i-nes
cloudiness
dowdiness
rowdiness

OUL′ur-i
owlery
prowlery

OUND′a-b'l
compoundable
soundable
unsoundable

OUND′ed-nes
astoundedness
confounded-
ness
dumfounded-
ness
unboundedness
ungrounded-
ness

OUND′les-li
boundlessly
groundlessly
soundlessly

OUND′les-nes
boundlessness

groundlessness
soundlessness

OUNT′a-b'l
countable
discountable
insurmountable
mountable
surmountable
unaccountable

OUT′i-nes
doughtiness
droughtiness
goutiness

OU′ur-i
bowery
dowery
flowery
glowery
lowery
showery
towery
(cf. OUR′i)

OU′ur-ing
cowering
dowering
empowering
flowering
glowering
lowering
overpowering
overtowering
showering
towering
(cf. OUR′ing)

OUZ′i-nes
drowsiness
frowziness

ōld, ôr, ŏdd, oil, fŏŏt, out; ūse, ûrn, ŭp; THis, thin

ŎV′el-ing
grovelling
hovelling

Ō′vi-al
jovial
synovial

Ō′vi-an
Cracovian
Jovian

Ō′zhi-a, Ō′zi-a
ambrosia
symposia
(cf. Theodosia)

Ō′zhi-al, Ō′zi-al
ambrosial
roseal

O′zhi-an,
  Ō′zi-an
ambrosian
(cf. Ō′zhun)

Ō′zi-est
coziest
nosiest
prosiest
rosiest

Ō′zi-li
cozily
nosily
prosily
rosily

Ō′zi-nes
coziness
doziness
nosiness
prosiness
rosiness

Ō′zi-ur
cozier

crosier
Dozier
hosier
nosier
osier
prosier
rosier

Ō′zur-i
composery
dozery
rosary
(not hosiery)

U

For a discussion of words included under the accented vowels
following, see the beginning of U rhymes in Section I.

Ū′a-b'l
doable
pursuable
renewable
reviewable
suable
subduable

Ū′bi-an
Danubian
Nubian
rubian

Ū′bi-kal
cubical
cherubical

Ū′bi-lat
enubilate

jubilate
nubilate
obnubilate
volubilate

ŬB′i-nes
chubbiness
grubbiness
scrubbiness
shrubbiness
stubbiness

Ū′bi-us
dubious
rubious

Ū′bri-kat
lubricate
rubricate

Ū′bri-us
insalubrious
lugubrious
salubrious

Ū′bur-us
protuberous
suberous
tuberous

ŬD′a-b'l
alludable
deludable
includable
protrudable

ŬD′en-si
concludency

pudency
recrudency

ŬD′i-b'l
eludible
includible

ŬD′i-li
bloodily
muddily
ruddily

Ū′di-nal
aptitudinal
attitudinal
consuetudinal
longitudinal
testudinal

āle,   câre,   ădd,   ärm,   åsk;   mē,   hĕre,   ĕnd;   īce,   ĭll;

ŪD'i-nes
moodiness
(cf. ŌOD'i-nes)

ŬD'i-nes
bloodiness
muddiness
ruddiness

Ū'di-niz
attitudinize
platitudinize

Ū'di-nus
fortitudinous
latitudinous
multitudinous
paludinous
platitudinous
solicitudinous
vicissitudinous

Ū'di-ti
crudity
nudity
rudity

Ū'di-us
preludious
studious

ŬD'ur-i
duddery
shuddery
studdery

Ū'el-ing
bejewelling
duelling
fueling
gruelling

Ū'el-ur
crueller
dueller
fueller
jeweller

ŬF'i-nes
fluffiness
huffiness
puffiness
stuffiness

ŬG'ur-i
pugaree
snuggery
thuggery

Ū'i-nes
dewiness
glueyness

Ū'in-us
pruinous
ruinous

Ū'ish-nes
Jewishness
shrewishness

Ū'i-ti
acuity
ambiguity
annuity
assiduity
circuity
conspicuity
contiguity
continuity
discontinuity
exiguity
fatuity

gratuity
ingenuity
innocuity
perpetuity
perspicuity
promiscuity
strenuity
suety
superfluity
tenuity
vacuity

Ū'i-tus
circuitous
fatuitous
fortuitous
gratuitous
pituitous

ŪJ'i-nus
æruginous
ferruginous
lanuginous
salsuginous

ŬK'i-li
luckily
pluckily

ŬK'shun-al
constructional
fluxional
inductional
instructional

ŬK'shun-ist
constructionist
destructionist
fluxionist

ŬK'ti-b'l
conductible

destructible
indestructible
instructible

ŬK'tiv-li
constructively
destructively
instructively
productively

ŬK'tiv-nes
constructive-
   ness
destructiveness
instructiveness
productiveness

ŬK'to-ri
conductory
introductory
reproductory

Ū'ku-lent
luculent
muculent
(cf. succulent)

ŬK'ur-ing
puckering
succoring

Ū'le-an
cerulean
herculean
Julian

ŪL'ish-nes
foolishness
mulishness

Ū'li-ti
credulity

garrulity
incredulity
sedulity

ŬL'ki-nes
bulkiness
sulkiness

ŬL'mi-nant
culminant
fulminant

ŬL'mi-nat
culminate
fulminate

ŬL'siv-li
convulsively
impulsively
repulsively

ŬL'siv-nes
compulsiveness
convulsiveness
impulsiveness
repulsiveness
revulsiveness

ŬL'tur-i
adultery
consultary

ŬL'tur-ism
agriculturism,
  etc.
vulturism

ŬL'ur-i
gullery
medullary
scullery

ŬL'vur-in
culverin
pulverin

ŪM'a-b'l
assumable
consumable
presumable
resumable

Ū'man-li
humanly
(cf. womanly)

ŬM'bur-i
slumbery
umbery

ŬM'bur-ing
cumbering
encumbering
lumbering
numbering
outnumbering
slumbering
unslumbering

ŬM'bur-ur
cumberer
encumberer
lumberer
numberer
slumberer

Ū'mi-nant
illuminant
luminant
ruminant

Ū'mi-nat
acuminate

catechumenate
ferruminate
illuminate
luminate
ruminate

ŪM'i-nes
gloominess
roominess
spuminess

ŬM'ing-li
becomingly
benumbingly
hummingly
numbingly
unbecomingly

Ū'mi-nus
aluminous
bituminous
fluminous
leguminous
luminous
voluminous

ŬM'pish-nes
dumpishness
frumpishness
grumpishness
lumpishness
mumpishness

ŬMP'shus-li
bumptiously
scrumptiously

ŬMP'tu-us
presumptuous
sumptuous

Ū'mu-lat
accumulate
tumulate

Ū'mu-lus
cumulus
tumulous

Ū'mur-al
humeral
numeral

ŪM'ur-i
perfumery
plumery
rumory
(cf. roomery)

ŬM'ur-i
flummery
mummery
nummary
plumbery
summary
summery

Ū'mur-us
humerus
humorous
numerous
rumorous

ŪN'a-b'l
expugnable
tunable

Ū'na-ri
lunary
(cf. Ū'nur-i)

ŬN'di-ti
fecundity

āle, câre, ădd, ärm, åsk; mē, hēre, ĕnd; īce, ĭll;

jocundity
jucundity
moribundity
profundity
rotundity
rubicundity

ŬN'dur-ing
blundering
plundering
sundering
thundering
wondering

ŬN'dur-song
undersong
wonder-song

ŬN'dur-ur
blunderer
plunderer
sunderer
thunderer
wonderer

ŬN'dur-us
blunderous
thunderous
wonderous

ŬN'dur-world
under-world
wonder-world

ŬNG'gur-ing
hungering
mongering

ŬNGK'shun-al
conjunctional
functional

ŬNGK'u-lar
avuncular
carbuncular
caruncular
peduncular
uncular

Ū'ni-kat
communicate
excommunicate
tunicate

Ū'ni-form
cuniform
luniform
uniform

ŬN'i-li
funnily
sunnily

Ū'ni-ti
community
immunity
importunity
impunity
inopportunity
intercommu-
   nity
jejunity
opportunity
triunity
unity

Ū'ni-tiv
punitive
unitive

ŬNT'ed-li
affrontedly

stuntedly
unwontedly
wontedly

ŬN'ur-i
buffoonery
cocoonery
pantaloonery
poltroonery

ŬN'ur-i
gunnery
nunnery

Ū'pur-at
recuperate
vituperate

Ū'ra-b'l
assurable
curable
durable
endurable
incurable
insurable
procurable
securable

ŬR'a-b'l
conferrable
demurrable
inferable
referable
transferable

Ū'ral-ist
ruralist
(cf. pluralist)

Ū'ral-ism
ruralism
(cf. pluralism)

Ū'ra-tiv
curative
depurative
indurative
maturative

ŬR'bal-ist
herbalist
verbalist

ŬR'bal-izm
herbalism
verbalism

ŬRB'i-al
adverbial
proverbial
suburbial

ŬR'bu-lent
herbulent
turbulent

ŬR'di-li
sturdily
wordily

ŬRD'ur-ur
murderer
verderer

ŬR'en-si
concurrency
currency
recurrency

ŬR'et-ed
turreted
(cf. ĔR'i-ted)

ŬR'flu-us
subterfluous
superfluous

Ū'ri-a
Lemuria
Manchuria

Ū'ri-al
augurial
figurial
mercurial
purpureal
seigneurial

ŨR'ĭ-an
Ū'ri-an
centurian
Etrurian
Missourian
scripturian
Silurian

Ū'ri-ans
luxuriance

Ū'ri-ant
luxuriant

Ū'ri-at
infuriate
luxuriate
muriate
parturiate

Ū'ri-ens
prurience

Ū'ri-ent
esurient
parturient
prurient
scripturient

ŨR'ĭ-est
furriest

hurriest
worriest

Ū'ri-fi
purify
thurify

ŨR'i-ing
currying
flurrying
hurrying
scurrying
worrying

ŨR'i-ment
worriment
(cf. ĔR'i-ment)

ŨR'ish-ing
flourishing
nourishing

Ū'ri-ti
demurity
immaturity
impurity
insecurity
maturity
obscurity
prematurity
purity
security

ŨR'i-ur
currier
flurrier
furrier
hurrier
scurrier
worrier

Ū'ri-us
curious

furious
incurious
injurious
luxurious
penurious
perjurious
spurious
strangurious
sulphureous
usurious

ŨR'jen-si
assurgency
convergency
detergency
divergency
emergency
insurgency
urgency
vergency

ŨR'ji-kal
chirurgical
clergical
demiurgical
energical
liturgical
surgical
thaumaturgical
theurgical

ŨR'jur-i
chirurgery
perjury
purgery
surgery

ŨR'ku-lar
circular
furcular
tubercular

ŨR'ku-lat
circulate
tuberculate

ŨR'ku-lus
surculus
surculous
tuberculous

ŨR'li-est
burliest
churliest
curliest
earliest
pearliest
surliest

ŨR'li-nes
burliness
curliness
earliness
pearliness
surliness

ŨR'lish-li
churlishly
girlishly

ŨR'lish-nes
churlishness
girlishness

ŨR'mi-nal
germinal
terminal

ŨR'mi-nant
determinant
germinant
terminant

ŨR'mi-nat
determinate

āle,   câre,   ădd,   ärm,   åsk;   mē,   hẹre,   ĕnd;   īce,   ĭll;

exterminate
germinate
indeterminate
interminate
terminate

ŬR'mi-nus
coterminous
terminus
verminous

ŬR'na-b'l
burnable
discernible
indiscernible
learnable
overturnable
returnable

ŬR'nal-ist
eternalist
journalist

ŬR'nal-iz
eternalize
externalize
journalize

ŬR'nal-izm
externalism
infernalism
journalism

ŬR'ni-an
Avernian
Falernian
Hibernian
Saturnian

ŬR'nish-ing
burnishing
furnishing

ŬR'nish-ur
burnisher
furnisher

ŬR'ni-ti
alternity
diuternity
eternity
fraternity
maternity
modernity
paternity
sempiternity
taciturnity

ŬR'nur-i
fernery
turnery

ŬR'o-gat
surrogate
(cf. ĔR'o-gat)

ŬR'pen-tin
serpentine
turpentine

ŬR'sa-ri
anniversary
aspersory
bursary
controversary
cursory
nursery
percursory

ŬR'shi-al
controversial
(cf. ŬR'shal)

ŬR'shi-an
Cistercian

lacertian
Persian
(also as
ŬR'shan,
ŬR'zhan)

ŬR'si-b'l,
ŬR'sa-b'l
amerceable
conversable
conversible
coercible
immersible
incoercible
irreversible
reimbursable
reversible

ŬR'si-form
diversiform
ursiform
versiform

ŬR'siv-nes
coerciveness
detersiveness
discursiveness
excursiveness

ŬRth'les-nes
mirthlessness
worthlessness

ŬR'ti-tud
certitude
incertitude
inertitude

ŬR'van-si
conservancy
fervency

ŬR'va-tiv
conservative
curvative
enervative
observative
preservative
reservative

ŬR'zhun-ist
excursionist
immersionist
versionist

Ū'se-an, Ū'si-an
caducean
Confucian
Rosicrucian

Ū'sed'li
deucedly
lucidly
mucidly
pellucidly

Ū'sen-si
lucency
tralucency
translucency

Ū'shi-al
crucial
fiducial

Ū'shun-al
circumlocu-
    tional
constitutional
elocutional
evolutional
institutional
substitutional

Ŭ'shun-ist
circumlocution-
　ist
constitutionist
elocutionist
evolutionist
resolutionist
revolutionist

Ŭ'shun-ur
ablutioner
executioner
resolutioner
revolutioner

Ŭ'si-b'l
adducible
conducible
crucible
deducible
educible
inducible
irreducible
producible
reducible
seducible
traducible

Ŭ'siv-nes
abusiveness
allusiveness
conclusiveness
conduciveness
delusiveness
diffusiveness
effusiveness
exclusiveness
illusiveness
inconclusive-
　ness
inobtrusiveness

intrusiveness
obtrusiveness

Ŭs'ki-li
duskily
huskily
muskily

Ŭs'ku-lar
bimuscular
corpuscular
crepuscular
muscular

Ŭs'ku-lus
corpusculous
crepusculous
musculous

Ŭ'so-ri
collusory
conclusory
delusory
elusory
exclusory
extrusory
illusory
lusory
prelusory
reclusory

Ŭst'ful-i
distrustfully
lustfully
mistrustfully
trustfully

Ŭst'i-b'l
adjustible
combustible
dustible

incombustible
(cf. bustable,
　etc.)

Ŭs'ti-est
crustiest
dustiest
fustiest
gustiest
lustiest
mustiest
rustiest
trustiest

Ŭs'ti-li
crustily
dustily
fustily
gustily
lustily
mustily
rustily
thrustily

Ŭs'ti-nes
crustiness
dustiness
fustiness
gustiness
lustiness
mustiness
rustiness
trustiness

Ŭs'tri-us
illustrious
industrious

Ŭs'tur-ing
blustering
clustering

flustering
mustering

Ŭ'ta-b'l
commutable
computable
confutable
disputable
executable
immutable
imputable
incommutable
inscrutable
mootable
mutable
permutable
refutable
scrutable
suitable
transmutable

Ŭ'ta-tiv
commutative
confutative
disputative
imputative
putative
sputative
sternutative

Ŭ'te-us
beauteous
duteous
luteous

Ŭth'ful-i
ruthfully
truthfully
youthfully

Ŭth'ful-nes
truthfulness
youthfulness

Ŭth'les-li
ruthlessly
truthlessly
youthlessly

ŬTH'ur-hood
brotherhood
motherhood

ŬTH'ur-i
brothery
mothery
smothery

ŬTH'ur-ing
brothering
mothering
smothering

ŬTH'ur-li
brotherly
motherly
southerly
unbrotherly
unmotherly

ŬTH'ur-lik
brotherlike
motherlike

Ū'ti-fi
beautify
brutify

Ū'ti-ful
beautiful
dutiful

Ū'ti-k'l, Ū'ti-kal
cuticle
latreutical
pharmaceutical
scorbutical
therapeutical

Ū'ti-ner
mutineer
scrutineer

Ū'ti-ni
mutiny
scrutiny

Ū'ti-nus
glutinous
mutinous
velutinous
scrutinous

ŬT'lur-i
cutlery
sutlery

ŬT'on-i
buttony
gluttony
muttony

Ū'tur-i
freebootery
fruitery
pewtery
rootery

ŬT'ur-ing
buttering
fluttering
guttering
muttering
spluttering
sputtering
stuttering
uttering

ŬT'ur-ur
butterer
flutterer
mutterer
splutterer
sputterer
stutterer
utterer

ŪV'a-b'l
approvable
immovable
improvable
irremovable
movable
provable
removable
reprovable

Ū'vi-al
alluvial
antediluvial
diluvial
effluvial
exuvial

fluvial
postdiluvial
pluvial

Ū'vi-an
antediluvian
diluvian
Peruvian
postdiluvian
Vesuvian

Ū'vi-us
Jupiter Pluvius
Vesuvius

Ū'za-b'l
amusable
confusable
diffusible
excusable
fusible
inexcusable
infusible
losable
transfusible
usable

Ū'zi-an
Carthusian
(cf. Ū'zhun)

ŬZ'i-nes
fuzziness
muzziness
wuzziness

6